ISBN: 978-1-964079-66-0

Disclaimer: The contents of this book are intended solely for informational and educational purposes. While every effort has been made to ensure the accuracy and completeness of the information provided, neither the authors, publishers, nor any other party associated with the creation of this book can guarantee the correctness, reliability, or applicability of the content within.

No Professional Advice

The information contained in this book does not constitute professional advice, nor is it intended to replace such advice. Readers should consult a qualified professional for advice tailored to their specific needs and circumstances. The authors and publishers disclaim any liability arising directly or indirectly from the use or application of the information contained in this book.

Trademark Acknowledgements

ISACA®, CISM®, and all related trademarks, service marks, and logos are the property of ISACA. This publication is not affiliated with, endorsed by, or approved by ISACA. All references to ISACA, CISM, or other trademarks are for informational purposes only and do not imply endorsement or sponsorship.

Copyright

Limitation of Liability

To the fullest extent permitted by law, the authors and publishers of this book disclaim all warranties, express or implied, including but not limited to implied warranties of merchantability and fitness for a particular purpose. The authors and publishers shall not be liable for any direct, indirect, incidental, consequential, or punitive damages arising out of the use of, or inability to use, this book or any content therein.

Accuracy and Completeness

While efforts have been made to ensure that the information in this book is accurate and up-to-date, the dynamic nature of the information security field means that changes may occur over time. The authors and publishers do not warrant that the information provided will remain accurate, complete, or current, and they undertake no obligation to update any content in light of new information or future developments.

Third-Party Links and References

This book may contain references or links to third-party websites, resources, or services. These links are provided for the reader's convenience and do not constitute an endorsement or approval by the authors or publishers. The authors and publishers are not responsible for the content or practices of any third-party sites and recommend that readers exercise caution and perform their own due diligence when accessing external resources.

Table of Contents

Introduction:

The High-Stakes World of Information Security Management

Picture this: It's a typical Monday morning, and you, as the Chief Information Security Manager (CISM) of a major financial institution, are sipping your coffee, reviewing the latest security reports. Suddenly, an alert flash across your screen—a potential data breach is in progress. Your heart races, but you spring into action. This is what you've trained for.

As you dive into the details, you see that a sophisticated phishing attack has infiltrated your company's network. The attackers are trying to exfiltrate sensitive customer information, which could spell disaster in terms of financial loss and reputational damage. With a clear head, you assemble your incident response team, quickly sharing critical information and delegating tasks.

Your team employs advanced intrusion detection systems (IDS) and real-time monitoring tools to trace the source of the breach. You instruct your network engineers to isolate affected systems, preventing the attackers from accessing further data. Simultaneously, you communicate with the legal and PR teams to prepare a response strategy, keeping stakeholders informed while managing potential fallout.

Thanks to your swift actions and strategic planning, the breach is contained. Forensic analysis reveals the attack's entry point, and you oversee the implementation of additional security measures to prevent future incidents. By the end of the day, not only have you protected millions of dollars in assets, but you've also safeguarded the trust your customers place in your company.

The sense of accomplishment is profound. You've just experienced one of the many high-stakes challenges that come with being a CISM. Your role is pivotal in ensuring the confidentiality, integrity, and availability of critical information assets.

Now, imagine yourself in this role. As a knowledgeable and strategic CISM, you are on the front lines in the fight against cybercrime. Every day, you make decisions that protect your organization from threats that could cripple its operations. The CISM certification is your badge of honor, validating your expertise and opening doors to exciting career opportunities in information security management.

The path to becoming a CISM is rigorous, but it's this very rigor that ensures you have the skills and knowledge needed to excel in the field. By earning your CISM certification, you not only demonstrate your proficiency in managing and mitigating risks but also your commitment to the highest standards of information security.

This journey will challenge you, but the rewards are immense. You'll be equipped to make a tangible difference, safeguarding vital information and contributing to the security and success of your organization. As you embark on this path, remember that every piece of knowledge and every skill you acquire brings you one step closer to becoming a trusted leader in information security management.

Information Security Governance

Establishing and maintaining an information security governance framework aligns security strategies with business goals. This involves creating policies, procedures, and controls that ensure the organization's information security posture supports its mission and objectives.

Developing an Information Security Strategy

Begin by understanding your organization's mission. Align security objectives with business goals. For example, if protecting customer data is a priority, focus on robust data protection measures and compliance with laws like GDPR and CCPA. This alignment ensures that security initiatives support the broader business strategy.

Implementing Governance Frameworks

Frameworks like COBIT 2019 and ISO/IEC 27001 are essential. COBIT 2019 helps align IT and business goals, offering a governance model that integrates with corporate governance. ISO/IEC 27001 provides a systematic approach to managing sensitive company information, ensuring it remains secure. These frameworks offer structured guidance for effective information security governance.

Creating and Enforcing Policies

Policies form the foundation of your security program. Develop clear, enforceable policies such as Acceptable Use Policies (AUP) that dictate proper use of company resources. Data Protection Policies ensure confidentiality and integrity of data. Incident Response Policies outline procedures for handling security breaches. Each policy should be concise, clear, and easily understood by all employees.

Measuring and Reporting Governance Metrics

Metrics are vital for evaluating the effectiveness of your security program. Key Performance Indicators (KPIs) like the number of security incidents, compliance rates, and audit findings provide insights into how well security measures are working. Regularly report these metrics to senior management and the board to ensure transparency and accountability. Dashboards can help visualize these metrics, making it easier to track progress and make informed decisions.

By implementing a strong governance framework and aligning it with business objectives, you ensure that information security is an integral part of your organization's strategy. This proactive approach not only mitigates risks but also builds a culture of security awareness and responsibility.

Information Risk Management

Managing information risks involves identifying, analyzing, and mitigating risks to ensure the organization's resilience and business continuity. Think of it as detective work, where you uncover potential threats and vulnerabilities to safeguard valuable assets.

Identifying Risks

Start by identifying your organization's assets, threats, and vulnerabilities. Techniques like asset inventories and threat modeling help you understand where risks lie. For example, a financial institution might identify risks related to cyber-attacks on transaction systems. This initial step is crucial for effective risk management.

Analyzing and Evaluating Risks

Risk analysis involves assessing the impact and likelihood of identified risks. Use qualitative methods like high, medium, and low ratings, or quantitative methods such as Annual Loss Expectancy (ALE) to understand financial implications. This analysis helps prioritize risks and allocate resources effectively.

Developing Risk Treatment Plans

Choose from four risk treatment strategies: mitigate, transfer, accept, or avoid. Implementing controls like multifactor authentication (MFA) can significantly reduce the risk of unauthorized access. Transferring risk might involve purchasing cyber insurance. Accepting risk requires a thorough cost-benefit analysis to justify the decision. Avoiding risk might mean altering business practices to eliminate certain exposures.

Continuous Monitoring of Risks

Continuous risk monitoring is essential. Use tools like Security Information and Event Management (SIEM) systems for real-time insights into your security posture. Regular audits and assessments ensure your risk management program remains effective and adapts to new threats. This proactive approach helps maintain a strong defense against emerging risks.

By systematically identifying, analyzing, and managing risks, you protect your organization's assets and ensure its resilience against threats. This structured approach not only mitigates risks but also supports the organization's strategic objectives.

Information Security Governance

Developing an Information Security Strategy

Creating an effective information security strategy involves aligning security goals with business objectives. For instance, if the company aims to maintain customer trust, prioritizing data protection is essential. This involves implementing robust data security measures and ensuring compliance with regulations like GDPR (General Data Protection Regulation) and CCPA (California Consumer Privacy Act).

Implementing Governance Frameworks

Governance frameworks provide the foundation for building a solid security structure. COBIT 2019 and ISO/IEC 27001 are widely recognized frameworks. COBIT 2019 focuses on aligning IT goals with business strategies and integrating IT governance with corporate governance. ISO/IEC 27001 offers a systematic approach to managing sensitive company information, ensuring its security through a risk management process. These frameworks guide the establishment of effective governance structures, policies, and procedures.

Creating and Enforcing Policies

Policies are the backbone of your security program. They need to be clear, enforceable, and understood by all employees. Essential policies include:

- **Acceptable Use Policy (AUP):** Dictates the proper use of company resources.
- **Data Protection Policy:** Ensures data confidentiality and integrity.
- **Incident Response Policy:** Outlines procedures for handling security incidents.

Each policy should be regularly reviewed and updated to adapt to new threats and changes in the business environment.

Measuring and Reporting Governance Metrics

Using metrics is crucial for evaluating the effectiveness of your security program. Key Performance Indicators (KPIs) provide insights into how well your security measures are working. Examples of useful KPIs include the number of security incidents, compliance rates, and audit findings. Regular reporting to senior management and the board ensures transparency and accountability. Dashboards can help visualize these metrics, making it easier to track progress and make informed decisions.

Information Risk Management

Identifying Risks

Risk identification is the first step in the risk management process. It involves understanding your organization's assets, threats, and vulnerabilities. Techniques like asset inventories and threat modeling help identify where risks lie. For instance, a financial institution might identify cyber-attacks on transaction systems as a significant risk.

Analyzing and Evaluating Risks

Once risks are identified, they need to be analyzed and evaluated. This involves assessing the impact and likelihood of each risk. Methods like qualitative risk assessment (using high, medium, and low ratings) and quantitative risk assessment (such as Annual Loss Expectancy – ALE) provide a clear picture of the risk landscape. This analysis helps prioritize risks and allocate resources effectively.

Developing Risk Treatment Plans

Developing a risk treatment plan involves choosing from four main strategies: mitigate, transfer, accept, or avoid. Implementing controls like multifactor authentication (MFA) can significantly reduce the risk of unauthorized access. Transferring risk might involve purchasing cyber insurance, while accepting risk requires a thorough cost-benefit analysis. Avoiding risk might mean altering business practices to eliminate certain exposures.

Continuous Monitoring of Risks

Continuous monitoring is crucial for adapting to new threats and vulnerabilities. Tools like Security Information and Event Management (SIEM) systems provide real-time insights into your security posture. Regular audits and assessments ensure your risk management program remains effective and up-to-date. This proactive approach helps maintain a strong defense against emerging risks.

Information Security Program Development and Management

Creating a Security Program Framework

Use frameworks like the NIST Cybersecurity Framework and ISO/IEC 27001 to guide your security program. These frameworks emphasize risk management, continuous monitoring, and incident response, providing a solid foundation for your security initiatives.

Managing Security Resources

Effective resource management ensures the necessary personnel, technology, and budget are allocated to security initiatives. This might involve investing in advanced security tools, hiring skilled professionals, and ensuring ongoing training for employees. Adequate resources are crucial for maintaining a robust security posture.

Implementing Security Awareness and Training

Security awareness training is essential for building a security-conscious culture. Employees should be educated on topics like phishing, password management, and data protection. Simulated phishing exercises help employees recognize and avoid common threats, reducing the risk of successful attacks.

Evaluating Security Program Metrics

Use metrics to evaluate the effectiveness of your security program. Metrics like the security incident rate, compliance rates, and the effectiveness of controls provide insights into the program's performance. Regular evaluations help you adapt to changing threats and ensure your security program aligns with business objectives.

Information Security Incident Management

Developing Incident Response Plans

An effective incident response plan defines roles, communication protocols, and steps for containment, eradication, and recovery. Regular testing of the plan with tabletop exercises ensures preparedness. Everyone involved should know their role and be ready to act quickly during an incident.

Detecting and Analyzing Incidents

Use tools like intrusion detection systems (IDS) and Security Information and Event Management (SIEM) systems to detect incidents. Analyze incidents using root cause analysis and forensic techniques to understand the scope and impact. This analysis helps you respond effectively and prevent future incidents.

Responding and Recovering from Incidents

Responding promptly to incidents minimizes damage and restores normal operations. Recovery involves restoring affected systems and data. A well-documented response plan ensures quick, coordinated actions during an incident, maintaining business continuity.

Conducting Post-Incident Activities

Post-incident reviews are essential for learning from incidents and improving future responses. Update security policies, enhance controls, and provide additional training to employees based on lessons learned. This continuous improvement process ensures your organization is better prepared for future incidents.

Practice Questions and Quizzes

Interactive practice questions and quizzes reinforce learning and provide a realistic exam experience. Full-length practice exams simulate the actual test environment, helping you assess readiness and identify areas for improvement.

Test-Taking Strategies

Effective test-taking strategies include managing your time well, understanding question formats, and using techniques for handling difficult questions. Practice exams and quizzes build your confidence and improve your performance on the actual exam.

Additional Resources

Recommended books, articles, online resources, and communities provide further learning opportunities. A glossary of key terms and acronyms helps familiarize you with essential vocabulary.

By following these principles and utilizing the provided resources, you can effectively prepare for the CISM exam, ensuring you have the knowledge and skills needed to succeed in the field.

About the CISM Certification

The Certified Information Security Manager (CISM) certification, offered by ISACA, is one of the most esteemed credentials in the field of information security management. This certification is designed for professionals who design, manage, and assess an enterprise's information security program. The CISM credential signifies a strong commitment to information security management and showcases an individual's expertise in aligning information security with business goals.

Significance of the CISM Certification

In the rapidly evolving world of information security, the CISM certification is a benchmark for excellence. It validates a professional's ability to manage and oversee information security practices, and it is recognized globally as a symbol of knowledge and competency. Organizations around the world seek out CISMs for their ability to implement and manage effective security practices, ensuring the protection of critical information assets.

Core Domains of the CISM Certification

The CISM exam covers four key domains that encompass the essential areas of information security management:

1. **Information Security Governance**
2. **Information Risk Management**
3. **Information Security Program Development and Management**
4. **Information Security Incident Management**

These domains represent the critical skills and knowledge required to effectively manage an information security program.

Information Security Governance

This domain focuses on establishing and maintaining an information security governance framework. It involves aligning the security strategy with business goals, developing policies, and integrating security into corporate governance. Effective governance ensures that security practices support the organization's objectives and comply with regulations.

Information Risk Management

Risk management is the cornerstone of any security program. This domain covers the identification, analysis, and mitigation of risks. It involves developing risk treatment plans and continuously monitoring the risk landscape. Understanding how to manage risks ensures that the organization can protect its assets and maintain business continuity.

Information Security Program Development and Management

Developing and managing a security program involves creating a structured approach to security that includes policies, procedures, and controls. This domain covers the implementation of security frameworks, resource management, and security awareness training. A well-managed security program is crucial for maintaining a strong security posture.

Information Security Incident Management

Incident management focuses on preparing for, detecting, and responding to security incidents. This domain involves developing incident response plans, analyzing incidents, and conducting post-incident reviews. Effective incident management minimizes damage and ensures quick recovery from security breaches.

Path to Certification

To achieve the CISM certification, candidates must pass the CISM exam and demonstrate a minimum of five years of work experience in information security management. However, certain educational qualifications and certifications can substitute for up to two years of experience. Candidates must also adhere to ISACA's Code of Professional Ethics and commit to ongoing professional development through continuing education.

Benefits of CISM Certification

Earning the CISM certification provides numerous benefits:

- **Career Advancement:** CISMs are in high demand, and the certification opens doors to higher-level positions and increased responsibilities.
- **Industry Recognition:** The CISM credential is globally recognized, enhancing your credibility and reputation in the information security field.
- **Knowledge and Skills:** The certification process ensures you have the knowledge and skills to effectively manage information security programs.
- **Networking Opportunities:** Being part of the ISACA community connects you with a global network of information security professionals.

Conclusion

The CISM certification is a valuable asset for any information security professional. It demonstrates a deep understanding of information security management and aligns your expertise with the needs of businesses. By achieving this certification, you position yourself as a leader in the field, capable of protecting and managing an organization's most critical information assets.

Benefits of Obtaining the CISM Certification

Obtaining the Certified Information Security Manager (CISM) certification offers numerous advantages for professionals in the field of information security. This credential, provided by ISACA, is highly respected worldwide and signifies expertise in information security management. Here are some of the key benefits of earning the CISM certification:

1. Enhanced Career Opportunities

Earning the CISM certification significantly boosts your career prospects. Employers highly value this credential, and it can open doors to senior-level positions such as Chief Information Security Officer (CISO), Information Security Manager, and IT Risk Manager. The certification sets you apart from non-certified peers, showcasing your ability to manage and lead information security programs effectively.

2. Industry Recognition

The CISM certification is globally recognized and respected across various industries. It validates your skills and knowledge in information security management, making you a credible and trusted professional. Organizations worldwide recognize the CISM as a mark of excellence and often require or prefer it for key security roles.

3. Higher Earning Potential

Certified professionals generally earn higher salaries compared to their non-certified counterparts. According to various industry salary surveys, CISMs often command premium salaries due to their specialized knowledge and skills in managing information security programs. The investment in obtaining the certification pays off with better job opportunities and increased earning potential.

4. Holistic Understanding of Information Security Management

The CISM certification covers all critical aspects of information security management, including governance, risk management, program development, and incident management. This comprehensive knowledge base ensures you understand the broader picture of information security and can develop strategies that align with organizational goals.

5. Improved Skills and Knowledge

Preparing for the CISM exam deepens your understanding of key information security concepts and best practices. The certification process ensures you are well-versed in identifying, analyzing, and managing security risks. You also gain expertise in developing and implementing effective security policies, ensuring your organization's information assets are well-protected.

6. Networking Opportunities

Becoming a CISM certified professional connects you with a global network of information security experts. ISACA offers numerous networking opportunities through conferences, seminars, and local chapter meetings. These connections can be invaluable for career growth, knowledge sharing, and staying updated with the latest industry trends and threats.

7. Commitment to Professional Development

Maintaining your CISM certification requires ongoing professional education, ensuring you stay current with the latest developments in information security. This commitment to continuous learning enhances your skills and keeps you updated on emerging threats and technologies, making you a valuable asset to your organization.

8. Organizational Benefits

Organizations employing CISMs benefit from having professionals who can align security strategies with business objectives. CISMs are skilled in managing and mitigating risks, developing robust security programs, and responding effectively to incidents. This expertise helps organizations protect their assets, maintain regulatory compliance, and build customer trust.

9. Greater Job Satisfaction

With the CISM certification, you gain the confidence and recognition that comes with being a highly skilled information security professional. This confidence can lead to greater job satisfaction as you play a crucial role in protecting your organization's information assets and contributing to its overall success.

10. Access to Exclusive Resources

ISACA provides its members, including CISMs, with access to a wealth of resources such as research papers, whitepapers, industry reports, and webinars. These resources help you stay informed about the latest trends, tools, and best practices in information security management.

11. Leadership and Influence

CISMs are often seen as leaders within their organizations. The certification equips you with the skills to influence senior management and drive security initiatives that align with business goals. Your ability to communicate the importance of security measures and their impact on business success is enhanced, making you a key player in strategic decision-making.

Earning the CISM certification is a strategic move for any information security professional. It not only validates your expertise and dedication but also enhances your career prospects, earning potential, and professional growth. With the CISM credential, you become part of a prestigious community of information security leaders, ready to tackle the evolving challenges of the digital world.

Detailed Breakdown of the CISM Domains

The CISM certification exam is divided into four critical domains, each focusing on a distinct aspect of information security management. Understanding these domains and mastering their content is essential for passing the CISM exam and becoming an effective information security manager.

1. Information Security Governance (24%)

Overview

Information Security Governance involves establishing and maintaining a framework to ensure that the security strategies align with business objectives and comply with regulations.

Key Concepts

- **Aligning Security with Business Goals:** Ensuring that security initiatives support the organization's overall objectives.
- **Frameworks and Standards:** Utilizing frameworks such as COBIT 2019 and ISO/IEC 27001 to create structured governance.

- **Policy Development:** Crafting clear and enforceable security policies.
- **Metrics and Reporting:** Developing key performance indicators (KPIs) and reporting mechanisms to measure and communicate the effectiveness of the security program.

Example Scenario

A multinational corporation needs to ensure its information security policies are consistent across all regions. By implementing a governance framework like COBIT 2019, the organization can align its security measures with global business strategies, ensuring compliance and effective risk management.

2. Information Risk Management (30%)

Overview

This domain focuses on identifying, assessing, and mitigating risks to ensure the protection of information assets and continuity of business operations.

Key Concepts

- **Risk Identification:** Using tools like asset inventories and threat modeling to identify potential risks.
- **Risk Assessment:** Evaluating the impact and likelihood of risks using methods such as qualitative analysis and Annual Loss Expectancy (ALE).
- **Risk Mitigation:** Developing and implementing risk treatment plans to reduce, transfer, accept, or avoid risks.
- **Continuous Monitoring:** Using tools like SIEM systems to monitor the risk landscape continuously.

Example Scenario

An e-commerce company faces the risk of data breaches due to increasing cyber-attacks. By conducting a thorough risk assessment, the company identifies its most vulnerable points and implements MFA and other controls to mitigate these risks, ensuring customer data remains secure.

3. Information Security Program Development and Management (27%)

Overview

Developing and managing a security program involves creating comprehensive policies, procedures, and controls to protect information assets.

Key Concepts

- **Security Frameworks:** Utilizing frameworks like the NIST Cybersecurity Framework to guide program development.
- **Resource Management:** Allocating appropriate personnel, technology, and budget for security initiatives.
- **Security Awareness:** Implementing training programs to educate employees about security best practices.
- **Program Evaluation:** Using metrics to assess the effectiveness of the security program and making necessary adjustments.

Example Scenario

A tech startup aims to build a robust security program from the ground up. By adopting the NIST Cybersecurity Framework, the startup develops comprehensive policies and procedures, ensuring that security measures grow in tandem with the business.

4. Information Security Incident Management (19%)

Overview

Incident management involves preparing for, detecting, and responding to security incidents to minimize damage and ensure quick recovery.

Key Concepts

- **Incident Response Planning:** Developing plans that define roles, communication protocols, and steps for responding to incidents.
- **Incident Detection:** Using IDS and SIEM systems to identify security breaches.
- **Incident Analysis:** Conducting root cause analysis to understand the impact and prevent future occurrences.
- **Post-Incident Review:** Learning from incidents to improve response plans and security measures.

Example Scenario

A healthcare provider experiences a ransomware attack. The incident response team quickly isolates the affected systems, communicates with stakeholders, and restores data from backups. Post-incident, they update their response plan and enhance their security controls to prevent similar attacks in the future.

Tips for Effective CISM Exam Preparation

1. Create a Study Plan

Develop a detailed study schedule that covers all four domains. Allocate specific times for each topic and stick to the plan to ensure thorough preparation.

2. Use Multiple Resources

Leverage a variety of study materials, including ISACA's official study guide, review books, online courses, and practice exams. Each resource offers unique insights and reinforces your understanding of key concepts.

3. Practice with Exam Questions

Regularly practice with sample questions and full-length practice exams. This helps you become familiar with the exam format and identify areas that need further study.

4. Join Study Groups

Participate in study groups or online forums where you can discuss concepts, share resources, and get support from peers who are also preparing for the CISM exam.

5. Focus on Weak Areas

Identify your weak areas and spend extra time reinforcing those topics. Use additional resources and seek help from knowledgeable peers or mentors if needed.

6. Stay Updated

Information security is a dynamic field. Stay informed about the latest developments, trends, and best practices by reading industry blogs, attending webinars, and participating in professional events.

Test-Taking Strategies

1. Time Management

During the exam, manage your time efficiently. Allocate an average of 1.6 minutes per question and move on if you get stuck. Return to difficult questions if you have time left.

2. Understand the Question Format

CISM exam questions often test your practical knowledge and ability to apply concepts. Read each question carefully, understand what is being asked, and consider all options before selecting the best answer.

3. Use Elimination Techniques

If unsure about an answer, use the process of elimination to narrow down your choices. Remove the clearly incorrect options to increase your chances of selecting the correct answer.

4. Stay Calm and Focused

Maintain a calm and focused mindset during the exam. Stress and anxiety can affect your performance, so practice relaxation techniques and stay confident in your preparation.

Conclusion

The CISM certification is a valuable credential that validates your expertise in information security management. By thoroughly understanding the four domains, using effective study strategies, and mastering test-taking techniques, you can successfully pass the CISM exam and advance your career in information security. Embrace the journey, invest in your learning, and become a leader in the fight against cyber threats.

Overview of the Exam Structure and Scoring

The CISM (Certified Information Security Manager) certification exam, offered by ISACA, is a rigorous assessment designed to evaluate a candidate's expertise in information security management. Understanding the exam structure and scoring methodology is crucial for effective preparation and successful certification.

Exam Structure

The CISM exam consists of 150 multiple-choice questions, which must be completed within a four-hour time frame. The questions are designed to test your knowledge and application of information security management principles across four domains:

1. **Information Security Governance (24%)**
2. **Information Risk Management (30%)**
3. **Information Security Program Development and Management (27%)**
4. **Information Security Incident Management (19%)**

Each question is intended to assess your practical experience and ability to apply information security management concepts in real-world scenarios.

Question Types

The exam questions are scenario-based and require you to apply your knowledge to specific situations. These questions may involve:

- Identifying the most appropriate course of action given a particular security challenge.
- Choosing the best risk mitigation strategy for a described scenario.
- Selecting the correct process or procedure to address a security incident.

Scoring Methodology

The CISM exam is scored on a scaled basis, with scores ranging from 200 to 800. To pass the exam, you must achieve a minimum score of 450. Here's a breakdown of how the scoring works:

- **Scaled Scores:** ISACA uses a scaled scoring system to ensure consistency across different versions of the exam. This means your raw score (the number of questions answered correctly) is converted into a scaled score.
- **Passing Score:** A scaled score of 450 represents the minimum threshold for demonstrating sufficient knowledge and competence in information security management.

Domain Weighting

Each of the four domains carries a specific weight in the overall exam score:

1. **Information Security Governance (24%):** This domain assesses your ability to develop and maintain an information security governance framework and supporting processes.
2. **Information Risk Management (30%):** This domain evaluates your skills in identifying, assessing, and managing information security risks.
3. **Information Security Program Development and Management (27%):** This domain tests your knowledge of creating and managing an information security program that supports the organization's goals.
4. **Information Security Incident Management (19%):** This domain focuses on your ability to prepare for and respond to information security incidents.

Preparation Tips

Understanding the exam structure and scoring is essential, but effective preparation is key to passing the CISM exam. Here are some tips to help you get ready:

1. **Create a Study Plan:** Allocate time to study each domain based on its weight in the exam. Prioritize areas where you feel less confident.
2. **Use Multiple Resources:** Study using ISACA's official guide, practice exams, review books, and online courses.

3. **Practice Time Management:** Simulate exam conditions by taking practice tests within the four-hour time limit to improve your time management skills.
4. **Join Study Groups:** Engage with peers to discuss concepts and share study tips.
5. **Focus on Real-World Applications:** Since the exam questions are scenario-based, focus on understanding how to apply concepts in practical situations.

By thoroughly understanding the exam structure, focusing your study efforts on the weighted domains, and practicing with realistic scenarios, you can effectively prepare for the CISM exam and achieve certification.

Overview of the Exam Structure and Scoring

The CISM (Certified Information Security Manager) certification exam, offered by ISACA, is a rigorous assessment designed to evaluate a candidate's expertise in information security management. Understanding the exam structure and scoring methodology is crucial for effective preparation and successful certification.

Exam Structure

The CISM exam consists of 150 multiple-choice questions, which must be completed within a four-hour time frame. The questions are designed to test your knowledge and application of information security management principles across four domains:

1. **Information Security Governance (24%)**
2. **Information Risk Management (30%)**
3. **Information Security Program Development and Management (27%)**
4. **Information Security Incident Management (19%)**

Each question is intended to assess your practical experience and ability to apply information security management concepts in real-world scenarios.

Question Types

The exam questions are scenario-based and require you to apply your knowledge to specific situations. These questions may involve:

- Identifying the most appropriate course of action given a particular security challenge.
- Choosing the best risk mitigation strategy for a described scenario.
- Selecting the correct process or procedure to address a security incident.

Scoring Methodology

The CISM exam is scored on a scaled basis, with scores ranging from 200 to 800. To pass the exam, you must achieve a minimum score of 450. Here's a breakdown of how the scoring works:

- **Scaled Scores:** ISACA uses a scaled scoring system to ensure consistency across different versions of the exam. This means your raw score (the number of questions answered correctly) is converted into a scaled score.
- **Passing Score:** A scaled score of 450 represents the minimum threshold for demonstrating sufficient knowledge and competence in information security management.

Domain Weighting

Each of the four domains carries a specific weight in the overall exam score:

1. **Information Security Governance (24%):** This domain assesses your ability to develop and maintain an information security governance framework and supporting processes.
2. **Information Risk Management (30%):** This domain evaluates your skills in identifying, assessing, and managing information security risks.
3. **Information Security Program Development and Management (27%):** This domain tests your knowledge of creating and managing an information security program that supports the organization's goals.
4. **Information Security Incident Management (19%):** This domain focuses on your ability to prepare for and respond to information security incidents.

Preparation Tips

Understanding the exam structure and scoring is essential, but effective preparation is key to passing the CISM exam. Here are some tips to help you get ready:

1. **Create a Study Plan:** Allocate time to study each domain based on its weight in the exam. Prioritize areas where you feel less confident.
2. **Use Multiple Resources:** Study using ISACA's official guide, practice exams, review books, and online courses.
3. **Practice Time Management:** Simulate exam conditions by taking practice tests within the four-hour time limit to improve your time management skills.
4. **Join Study Groups:** Engage with peers to discuss concepts and share study tips.
5. **Focus on Real-World Applications:** Since the exam questions are scenario-based, focus on understanding how to apply concepts in practical situations.

By thoroughly understanding the exam structure, focusing your study efforts on the weighted domains, and practicing with realistic scenarios, you can effectively prepare for the CISM exam and achieve certification.

Study Strategies and Tips for Success

Preparing for the CISM (Certified Information Security Manager) exam requires a strategic approach to ensure comprehensive understanding and retention of the material. Here are some effective study strategies and tips to help you succeed:

1. Develop a Study Plan

Creating a detailed study plan is the first step in your preparation journey. Break down the four domains into manageable sections and allocate specific time slots for each topic. Ensure that your study plan covers all the domains, with extra time dedicated to areas where you feel less confident.

2. Use Multiple Study Resources

Diversify your study materials to gain different perspectives on the subject matter. Utilize ISACA's official study guide, review books, online courses, and practice exams. Each resource can provide unique insights and help reinforce your understanding of key concepts.

3. Practice with Exam Questions

Familiarize yourself with the exam format by practicing with sample questions and full-length practice exams. This not only helps you understand the types of questions that will be asked but also improves your time management skills. Aim to complete practice exams within the four-hour time limit to simulate actual exam conditions.

4. Join Study Groups

Engage with study groups or online forums where you can discuss concepts, share resources, and gain support from peers. Collaborative learning can help you gain new insights and clarify any doubts you may have. Additionally, teaching others can reinforce your own understanding of the material.

5. Focus on Real-World Applications

The CISM exam is heavily scenario-based, requiring you to apply your knowledge to real-world situations. Focus on understanding how theoretical concepts are implemented in practice. Use case studies and examples to see how information security principles are applied in various scenarios.

6. Master the Key Domains

Concentrate on mastering the four key domains of the CISM exam:

- **Information Security Governance:** Understand how to establish and maintain an information security governance framework. Focus on aligning security strategies with business goals and developing effective policies and procedures.
- **Information Risk Management:** Learn to identify, assess, and manage information security risks. Familiarize yourself with risk assessment methodologies and risk treatment strategies.

- **Information Security Program Development and Management:** Gain insights into creating and managing an information security program that supports organizational objectives. Understand resource management, security awareness training, and the evaluation of security program effectiveness.
- **Information Security Incident Management:** Develop skills in preparing for and responding to information security incidents. Focus on incident response planning, detection and analysis of incidents, and conducting post-incident reviews.

7. Create Summary Notes and Flashcards

Summarize key points and create flashcards for important concepts and definitions. These tools are great for quick revisions and reinforcing your memory. Reviewing summary notes regularly can help keep the material fresh in your mind.

8. Stay Updated with Industry Trends

Information security is a dynamic field with constantly evolving threats and technologies. Stay updated with the latest trends, best practices, and regulatory changes by reading industry blogs, attending webinars, and participating in professional events. This not only helps you with the exam but also keeps your knowledge relevant in the real world.

9. Focus on Weak Areas

Identify your weak areas early in your preparation and devote extra time to reinforcing those topics. Use additional resources and seek help from knowledgeable peers or mentors if needed. Don't hesitate to revisit difficult concepts until you feel confident.

10. Manage Your Stress and Health

Maintaining a healthy study-life balance is crucial. Ensure you get enough sleep, eat healthily, and exercise regularly. Stress management techniques such as meditation, deep breathing exercises, or short breaks during study sessions can help keep your mind fresh and focused.

11. Develop Effective Test-Taking Strategies

On exam day, effective test-taking strategies can make a significant difference:

- **Read Questions Carefully:** Take your time to understand what each question is asking before selecting an answer.
- **Eliminate Wrong Answers:** Narrow down your choices by eliminating clearly incorrect options.
- **Manage Your Time:** Allocate time to each question and move on if you get stuck. You can always return to difficult questions later.
- **Stay Calm and Focused:** Keep a positive mindset and stay focused on the task at hand. Confidence in your preparation will help you perform better.

By following these study strategies and tips, you can enhance your preparation and increase your chances of passing the CISM exam. Remember, consistent effort and a strategic approach are key to achieving certification and advancing your career in information security management.

Part I: Information Security Governance:

Information Security Governance

Definition

Information security governance is the framework and set of responsibilities and practices exercised by the board and executive management to provide strategic direction, ensure objectives are achieved, manage risks appropriately, and verify that the organization's resources are used responsibly in the context of information security. It involves establishing and maintaining an information security management system that aligns with business goals and ensures the confidentiality, integrity, and availability of information assets.

Importance in Protecting Information Assets

Effective information security governance is crucial for several reasons:

1. **Alignment with Business Goals:** It ensures that information security strategies are in sync with the organization's overall objectives, thus supporting business continuity and growth.
2. **Risk Management:** It helps in identifying, assessing, and managing information security risks, protecting the organization from potential threats and vulnerabilities.
3. **Regulatory Compliance:** It ensures compliance with relevant laws, regulations, and standards, thereby avoiding legal penalties and protecting the organization's reputation.
4. **Resource Optimization:** It ensures that information security investments are appropriate and effective, optimizing the use of resources.
5. **Accountability:** It establishes clear roles and responsibilities, ensuring accountability at all levels of the organization.

Key Principles of Effective Information Security Governance

1. **Strategic Alignment:**
    - Aligning information security strategies with business goals to support organizational objectives.
    - Integrating security considerations into the overall corporate governance framework.
2. **Risk Management:**
    - Identifying and assessing information security risks.
    - Developing and implementing risk mitigation strategies to manage identified risks.
    - Continuously monitoring and reviewing risks.
3. **Resource Management:**
    - Allocating appropriate resources (financial, technological, and human) to information security efforts.
    - Ensuring efficient use of resources to achieve security objectives.
4. **Performance Measurement:**
    - Establishing metrics to evaluate the effectiveness of information security programs.
    - Regularly reporting on security performance to senior management and the board.
    - Using performance data to drive continuous improvement.
5. **Value Delivery:**
    - Ensuring that information security investments deliver value by protecting critical information assets and supporting business objectives.
    - Balancing security investments with other business priorities.
6. **Integration:**
    - Integrating information security governance into the organization's overall governance framework.
    - Ensuring that security policies and procedures are well-defined, communicated, and enforced across the organization.

Objectives of Effective Information Security Governance

1. **Protect Information Assets:**
    - Ensuring the confidentiality, integrity, and availability of information assets.
    - Implementing appropriate security controls to protect sensitive data from unauthorized access, disclosure, alteration, and destruction.
2. **Support Business Objectives:**
    - Aligning security initiatives with business goals to support strategic objectives and ensure business continuity.
    - Facilitating secure business operations and enabling innovation.
3. **Ensure Regulatory Compliance:**
    - Complying with relevant laws, regulations, and industry standards (e.g., GDPR, HIPAA, PCI DSS).
    - Avoiding legal penalties and protecting the organization's reputation.
4. **Foster a Security-Conscious Culture:**

    - Promoting awareness and understanding of information security risks and responsibilities among employees.
    - Encouraging a proactive approach to information security throughout the organization.
5. **Optimize Security Investments:**
    - Ensuring that information security investments are effective and provide value to the organization.
    - Balancing security spending with other business priorities to achieve optimal resource allocation.
6. **Ensure Accountability:**
    - Defining clear roles and responsibilities for information security at all levels of the organization.
    - Establishing accountability for security performance and compliance with policies and procedures.

Effective information security governance is the cornerstone of a robust security program. By aligning security strategies with business goals, managing risks, ensuring compliance, and fostering a security-conscious culture, organizations can protect their information assets and support their overall objectives.

Essential Components of an Information Security Governance Framework

A comprehensive information security governance framework comprises several essential components. These elements work in concert to ensure that information security practices align with organizational goals, manage risks effectively, comply with regulations, and measure performance accurately. Here's a detailed look at each component and how they integrate to form an effective governance structure.

1. Leadership and Oversight

Role and Importance:

- Leadership and oversight are the cornerstone of any governance framework. This involves the active participation of the board of directors and executive management in setting the strategic direction for information security.
- Leadership provides the vision and mandates necessary to integrate information security into the organizational culture and business processes.

Key Activities:

- Establishing an information security governance committee to oversee the development and implementation of the information security strategy.
- Defining roles and responsibilities for information security across the organization.
- Ensuring top management's commitment to information security initiatives through regular briefings and involvement in key decision-making processes.

2. Risk Management

Role and Importance:

- Risk management identifies, assesses, and mitigates risks to protect the organization's information assets. It ensures that security measures are proportional to the level of risk faced by the organization.
- A robust risk management process is essential for prioritizing security efforts and allocating resources effectively.

Key Activities:

- Conducting risk assessments to identify potential threats and vulnerabilities.
- Developing risk treatment plans to address identified risks through mitigation, transfer, acceptance, or avoidance.
- Continuously monitoring and reviewing risks to adapt to changing threat landscapes and business environments.

3. Compliance

Role and Importance:

- Compliance ensures that the organization adheres to relevant laws, regulations, and industry standards. This helps in avoiding legal penalties and maintaining the organization's reputation.
- Compliance frameworks also guide the development of internal policies and procedures that align with external requirements.

Key Activities:

- Identifying applicable regulatory requirements (e.g., GDPR, HIPAA, PCI DSS) and ensuring they are integrated into the information security program.
- Conducting regular audits and assessments to verify compliance.
- Implementing corrective actions to address any identified compliance gaps.

4. Performance Measurement

Role and Importance:

- Performance measurement involves tracking and evaluating the effectiveness of information security initiatives. It provides insights into how well security measures are working and identifies areas for improvement.
- Metrics and key performance indicators (KPIs) enable organizations to make data-driven decisions about their security posture.

Key Activities:

- Developing and implementing metrics to measure the effectiveness of security controls (e.g., incident response times, number of security incidents, compliance rates).
- Regularly reporting performance metrics to senior management and the board.
- Using performance data to drive continuous improvement in the security program.

Integration of Components for Effective Governance

Strategic Alignment:

- Leadership and oversight ensure that information security initiatives are aligned with business objectives. This alignment is crucial for integrating security into the broader organizational strategy.

Holistic Risk Management:

- The risk management process identifies and prioritizes risks, guiding the allocation of resources and the implementation of appropriate security controls. Leadership ensures these efforts are consistent with the organization's risk appetite and tolerance.

Ensuring Compliance:

- Compliance activities ensure that the organization's policies and procedures meet regulatory requirements. Performance measurement tracks compliance rates and identifies areas for improvement, ensuring that the organization remains compliant over time.

Continuous Improvement:

- Performance measurement provides the data needed to assess the effectiveness of security controls and initiatives. This data informs risk management and compliance activities, creating a feedback loop that drives continuous improvement.

Resource Optimization:

- Leadership and oversight allocate resources based on the prioritized risks identified through the risk management process. Performance measurement ensures that these resources are used effectively and provide value to the organization.

By integrating these components, an information security governance framework ensures a comprehensive and effective governance structure. Leadership and oversight provide the strategic direction, risk management prioritizes and addresses risks, compliance ensures adherence to legal and regulatory requirements, and performance measurement tracks effectiveness and drives continuous improvement. Together, these elements create a robust and resilient information security posture that aligns with organizational goals and adapts to evolving threats.

Aligning Information Security with Business Objectives

Aligning information security with business objectives involves integrating security strategies into the core business processes to ensure that the organization's goals are supported and protected. This alignment helps in making information security an enabler of business growth rather than just a set of controls and compliance measures. Here are strategies to ensure that information security initiatives support and enable the organization's overall goals and priorities:

1. Understand the Business Context

Know the Business Goals:

- Gain a deep understanding of the organization's mission, vision, and strategic goals. This includes knowing what drives the business, its key products or services, target markets, and competitive landscape.

Engage with Business Leaders:

- Regularly communicate with business leaders to understand their objectives and priorities. This helps in aligning security initiatives with business needs and demonstrating the value of security to business success.

2. Risk Management Aligned with Business Impact

Identify and Prioritize Risks:

- Conduct thorough risk assessments to identify potential threats to business-critical processes and assets. Focus on risks that have the highest potential impact on business objectives.

Business Impact Analysis (BIA):

- Perform a BIA to understand the consequences of security incidents on business operations. This helps in prioritizing security measures that protect the most critical business functions.

3. Develop a Business-Aligned Security Strategy

Integrate Security into Business Processes:

- Ensure that security is considered in all business processes and decision-making. This includes integrating security requirements into project management, procurement, and product development processes.

Strategic Security Initiatives:

- Develop security initiatives that directly support business goals. For example, if the business goal is to expand into new markets, ensure that security measures are in place to protect customer data and comply with local regulations in those markets.

4. Foster a Security-Conscious Culture

Awareness and Training Programs:

- Implement security awareness and training programs that are tailored to different roles within the organization. Ensure that employees understand how their actions impact information security and the overall business.

Leadership Support:

- Secure support from top management to champion security initiatives. Leadership buy-in is crucial for fostering a culture where security is seen as a shared responsibility.

5. Metrics and Reporting

Define Relevant Metrics:

- Develop metrics that measure the effectiveness of security initiatives in supporting business goals. Metrics should be relevant to business leaders and demonstrate how security contributes to achieving business objectives.

Regular Reporting:

- Regularly report security metrics to senior management and the board. Use dashboards and scorecards to present data in a business-friendly manner, highlighting the impact of security on business performance.

6. Continuous Improvement and Adaptation

Feedback Loop:

- Establish a feedback loop to continuously assess and improve security initiatives. Use performance data, incident reports, and business changes to refine security strategies and ensure they remain aligned with business goals.

Stay Agile:

- Be prepared to adapt security strategies to changing business needs and emerging threats. An agile approach ensures that security remains relevant and effective in a dynamic business environment.

7. Collaboration and Integration

Cross-Functional Teams:

- Form cross-functional teams that include representatives from security, IT, and various business units. This collaboration ensures that security considerations are integrated into business decisions from the outset.

Integrated Solutions:

- Implement integrated security solutions that work seamlessly with business systems and processes. This minimizes disruption and ensures that security measures are user-friendly and effective.

Example Scenario

Consider a healthcare organization aiming to enhance patient care through digital transformation. Aligning information security with this goal involves implementing robust data protection measures to secure electronic health records (EHRs), ensuring compliance with regulations like HIPAA, and enabling secure remote access for healthcare professionals. By integrating these security measures into the digital transformation strategy, the organization can achieve its goal of improving patient care while safeguarding sensitive patient information.

Conclusion

Aligning information security with business objectives ensures that security initiatives are not seen as obstacles but as enablers of business success. By understanding the business context, managing risks in line with business impact, developing business-aligned security strategies, fostering a security-conscious culture, and continuously improving security measures, organizations can protect their information assets while supporting and achieving their overall goals. This holistic approach ensures that information security contributes to the resilience, growth, and success of the organization.

The Critical Role of the Information Security Manager in Governance

The Information Security Manager plays a pivotal role in establishing and maintaining an effective information security governance framework. This role involves strategic planning, risk management, policy development, and ensuring compliance with regulations. The Information Security Manager is essential in aligning security initiatives with business objectives and fostering a culture of security within the organization.

Key Responsibilities

1. **Developing and Implementing Security Policies and Procedures**
   - Crafting clear, comprehensive policies that define acceptable use, data protection, incident response, and more.

- Ensuring these policies are communicated, understood, and adhered to across the organization.

2. **Risk Management**
   - Conducting risk assessments to identify potential threats and vulnerabilities.
   - Developing and implementing risk treatment plans to mitigate identified risks.
   - Continuously monitoring the risk landscape and adjusting strategies as needed.
3. **Strategic Planning and Alignment**
   - Aligning information security strategies with the organization's business goals.
   - Integrating security considerations into the business planning process.
   - Ensuring that security initiatives support overall business objectives.
4. **Compliance and Regulatory Adherence**
   - Ensuring the organization complies with relevant laws, regulations, and industry standards (e.g., GDPR, HIPAA, PCI DSS).
   - Conducting regular audits and assessments to verify compliance.
   - Implementing corrective actions to address compliance gaps.
5. **Incident Management**
   - Developing and maintaining an incident response plan.
   - Leading the incident response team during security incidents.
   - Conducting post-incident reviews to improve response strategies and prevent future incidents.
6. **Resource Management**
   - Allocating and managing resources (personnel, technology, budget) to ensure effective information security.
   - Advocating for necessary investments in security tools and training.
7. **Performance Measurement and Reporting**
   - Establishing metrics to measure the effectiveness of security initiatives.
   - Regularly reporting security performance to senior management and the board.
   - Using performance data to drive continuous improvement.

Key Skills and Competencies

1. **Technical Knowledge**
   - Deep understanding of information security principles, technologies, and practices.
   - Familiarity with security frameworks such as ISO/IEC 27001, NIST, and COBIT.
   - Knowledge of current and emerging threats and vulnerabilities.
2. **Risk Management**
   - Ability to identify, assess, and prioritize information security risks.
   - Proficiency in developing and implementing risk treatment plans.
   - Experience with risk assessment methodologies.
3. **Strategic Thinking**
   - Capability to align security strategies with business goals.
   - Understanding of how security can enable business growth and continuity.
   - Ability to see the big picture and anticipate future security needs.
4. **Leadership and Communication**
   - Strong leadership skills to guide the security team and influence organizational culture.
   - Excellent communication skills to convey complex security concepts to non-technical stakeholders.
   - Ability to advocate for security initiatives and secure necessary resources.
5. **Compliance and Regulatory Knowledge**
   - Familiarity with relevant laws, regulations, and industry standards.
   - Experience in conducting compliance audits and assessments.
   - Ability to implement policies and procedures that ensure regulatory adherence.
6. **Incident Response**
   - Expertise in developing and executing incident response plans.
   - Ability to lead the incident response team effectively during security incidents.
   - Skill in conducting post-incident reviews and implementing improvements.

7. **Project Management**
    - Strong project management skills to oversee security projects from inception to completion.
    - Ability to manage multiple projects simultaneously and meet deadlines.
    - Experience in resource allocation and budget management.
8. **Analytical Skills**
    - Proficiency in analyzing security data and metrics to assess performance.
    - Ability to identify trends and make data-driven decisions.
    - Skill in conducting forensic analysis and root cause investigation.

Example Scenario

Consider a large financial institution where the Information Security Manager is tasked with enhancing the organization's security posture. This involves conducting a comprehensive risk assessment, updating security policies to comply with new regulations, and implementing advanced threat detection tools. The manager must communicate these changes to senior leadership, secure funding for new initiatives, and lead the response to any security incidents. Through strategic planning and effective leadership, the Information Security Manager ensures that the organization's information assets are protected, and that security initiatives support the institution's business goals.

Conclusion

The Information Security Manager is integral to establishing and maintaining an effective information security governance framework. This role requires a blend of technical expertise, strategic thinking, leadership, and communication skills. By fulfilling these responsibilities, the Information Security Manager ensures that the organization's information assets are secure, regulatory requirements are met, and security initiatives are aligned with business objectives. This comprehensive approach not only protects the organization but also enables it to achieve its strategic goals.

Differentiating Between Information Security Policies, Procedures, and Standards

In an information security program, policies, procedures, and standards play distinct but interrelated roles in establishing a comprehensive security framework. Understanding the differences and interrelationships among these components is crucial for effective implementation and governance.

1. Information Security Policies

Definition: Policies are high-level, formal statements that outline an organization's guiding principles, rules, and objectives regarding information security. They establish the foundation for the information security program and set the direction for security efforts across the organization.

Purpose:

- To define the organization's commitment to information security.
- To set clear expectations for behavior and responsibilities.
- To provide a framework for decision-making and enforcement of security measures.

Example:

- **Acceptable Use Policy (AUP):** This policy outlines the acceptable and unacceptable use of organizational resources such as email, internet, and information systems. It aims to protect the organization's assets and ensure their proper use.
    - **Purpose:** To prevent misuse of organizational resources and ensure that employees understand their responsibilities.

2. Information Security Procedures

Definition: Procedures are detailed, step-by-step instructions on how to implement policies and execute specific tasks or processes. They provide the operational framework needed to achieve the objectives outlined in policies.

Purpose:

- To provide clear, actionable instructions for carrying out security-related tasks.
- To ensure consistency and repeatability in security operations.

- To facilitate compliance with policies and standards.

Example:

- **Incident Response Procedure:** This procedure outlines the steps to be taken in the event of a security incident, including identification, containment, eradication, recovery, and post-incident review.
    - **Purpose:** To ensure a systematic and effective response to security incidents, minimizing impact and aiding in quick recovery.

3. Information Security Standards

Definition: Standards are specific, mandatory requirements that provide detailed guidance on the implementation of policies and procedures. They establish the criteria for how security measures should be applied consistently across the organization.

Purpose:

- To ensure uniformity and consistency in the application of security controls.
- To provide measurable and enforceable criteria for security practices.
- To support compliance with internal policies and external regulations.

Example:

- **Password Standard:** This standard specifies the requirements for creating and managing passwords, such as minimum length, complexity, expiration, and storage.
    - **Purpose:** To enforce strong password practices across the organization, reducing the risk of unauthorized access.

Interrelationships Within an Information Security Program

Hierarchy and Flow:

1. **Policies:** At the top of the hierarchy, policies set the high-level goals and expectations for information security. They are broad and enduring, providing the overarching direction for the security program.
2. **Standards:** Standards provide the specific, mandatory requirements that operationalize the policies. They translate policy directives into actionable and measurable criteria.
3. **Procedures:** Procedures offer the detailed, step-by-step instructions for meeting the standards and implementing the policies. They ensure that tasks are performed consistently and effectively.

Example of Interrelationship: Consider an organization's approach to data protection:

- **Data Protection Policy:** The policy mandates the protection of sensitive data to ensure confidentiality, integrity, and availability.
- **Encryption Standard:** This standard requires all sensitive data to be encrypted using AES-256 encryption both at rest and in transit.
- **Data Encryption Procedure:** The procedure provides detailed steps for implementing AES-256 encryption on various systems and ensuring that encryption keys are managed securely.

Purpose and Implementation:

- **Policies** provide the "what" and "why" of security practices, guiding overall strategy and behavior.
- **Standards** specify the "what" in detail, establishing clear, consistent, and enforceable requirements.
- **Procedures** explain the "how," offering detailed instructions to ensure that standards are met and policies are implemented effectively.

Conclusion

Information security policies, procedures, and standards are essential components of a robust security program. Policies set the high-level direction and expectations, standards provide specific and enforceable requirements, and procedures offer detailed instructions for implementation. Together, they ensure a comprehensive and coherent approach to information security, aligning with organizational goals and enabling effective risk management. Understanding and correctly implementing these components are crucial for maintaining a strong security posture and achieving compliance with regulatory and industry requirements.

Policy Development Life Cycle

The policy development life cycle ensures that information security policies are created, maintained, and retired in a structured manner. Here are the typical stages and key activities involved in the policy development life cycle:

1. Initiation

Key Activities:

- **Identify the Need:** Determine the need for a new policy or the revision of an existing one based on risk assessments, regulatory requirements, or organizational changes.
- **Define Objectives:** Clearly define the objectives and scope of the policy. Understand what the policy aims to achieve and which areas it will cover.
- **Form a Policy Development Team:** Assemble a team with representatives from relevant departments, including IT, legal, HR, and management, to ensure a comprehensive approach.

Considerations:

- Ensure alignment with organizational goals and compliance requirements.
- Engage stakeholders early to gather input and build support.

2. Development

Key Activities:

- **Conduct Research:** Review relevant laws, regulations, industry standards, and best practices. Analyze existing policies for gaps and improvements.
- **Draft the Policy:** Develop a draft policy that includes the purpose, scope, responsibilities, procedures, and compliance requirements. Use clear and concise language.
- **Review and Revise:** Circulate the draft policy among key stakeholders for feedback. Revise the policy based on the feedback received.

Considerations:

- Ensure the policy is clear, enforceable, and aligned with organizational culture.
- Consider the implications of the policy on different departments and operations.

3. Approval

Key Activities:

- **Present to Management:** Submit the draft policy to senior management or the policy approval committee for review.
- **Revise if Necessary:** Make any required revisions based on management feedback.
- **Obtain Formal Approval:** Secure formal approval from the appropriate authority within the organization (e.g., board of directors, executive management).

Considerations:

- Ensure all necessary approvals are obtained to legitimize the policy.
- Communicate the importance and benefits of the policy to gain support.

4. Implementation

Key Activities:

- **Communicate the Policy:** Announce the new or revised policy to all relevant stakeholders. Use multiple channels such as emails, meetings, and training sessions.
- **Train Employees:** Conduct training sessions to ensure employees understand the policy and their responsibilities.
- **Distribute Documentation:** Provide access to the policy documents through the organization's intranet or document management system.

Considerations:

- Ensure clear communication and training to promote understanding and compliance.

- Use effective change management strategies to address resistance.

5. Maintenance

Key Activities:

- **Monitor Compliance:** Regularly monitor adherence to the policy through audits, assessments, and feedback mechanisms.
- **Review and Update:** Periodically review the policy to ensure it remains relevant and effective. Update the policy as needed to reflect changes in laws, regulations, or organizational objectives.

Considerations:

- Establish a schedule for regular policy reviews (e.g., annually or biennially).
- Solicit feedback from employees to identify areas for improvement.

6. Retirement

Key Activities:

- **Evaluate Necessity:** Determine if the policy is no longer needed due to changes in business processes, technology, or regulatory requirements.
- **Plan for Retirement:** Develop a plan for retiring the policy, including communication and transition strategies.
- **Archive Documentation:** Archive the retired policy and related documentation for historical reference and compliance purposes.

Considerations:

- Ensure that retiring the policy does not create gaps in the information security framework.
- Communicate the retirement of the policy clearly and provide guidance on any new or revised policies that replace it.

Summary of Key Activities and Considerations

- **Initiation:** Identify the need, define objectives, form a team. Ensure alignment with goals and engage stakeholders early.
- **Development:** Conduct research, draft the policy, review and revise. Ensure clarity, enforceability, and alignment with culture.
- **Approval:** Present to management, revise if needed, obtain approval. Communicate importance and benefits to gain support.
- **Implementation:** Communicate the policy, train employees, distribute documentation. Ensure understanding and compliance.
- **Maintenance:** Monitor compliance, review and update. Schedule regular reviews and solicit feedback.
- **Retirement:** Evaluate necessity, plan for retirement, archive documentation. Ensure no gaps in the security framework and communicate changes clearly.

The policy development life cycle is a systematic approach that ensures information security policies are effectively created, maintained, and retired. Each stage involves specific activities and considerations to align policies with organizational goals, comply with regulations, and ensure effective implementation and management.

Essential Elements of a Comprehensive Information Security Policy

A comprehensive information security policy should include several key elements to ensure it is effective, enforceable, and aligned with organizational goals. Here are the essential elements and examples of how they are addressed in real-world policies:

1. Purpose

Definition: The purpose section explains why the policy exists and what it aims to achieve.
Example:

- **Purpose Statement:** "The purpose of this policy is to establish the principles and procedures to ensure the confidentiality, integrity, and availability of the organization's information assets."

2. Scope

Definition: The scope defines the boundaries of the policy, including who and what it applies to.
Example:

- **Scope Statement:** "This policy applies to all employees, contractors, consultants, temporary staff, and other workers at [Organization Name], including all personnel affiliated with third parties. It covers all information assets owned, leased, or otherwise managed by the organization."

3. Objectives

Definition: Objectives outline the specific goals the policy aims to achieve in support of the organization's information security strategy.
Example:

- **Objectives Statement:** "The objectives of this policy are to protect the organization's information assets from unauthorized access, use, disclosure, disruption, modification, or destruction; to comply with legal and regulatory requirements; and to support the organization's business objectives."

4. Roles and Responsibilities

Definition: This section assigns specific information security responsibilities to various roles within the organization.
Example:

- **Roles and Responsibilities:**
  - **Chief Information Security Officer (CISO):** "Responsible for developing, implementing, and maintaining the information security program, and ensuring compliance with this policy."
  - **IT Department:** "Responsible for implementing technical controls to protect information assets and responding to security incidents."
  - **Employees:** "Responsible for adhering to the information security policy and reporting any security incidents or vulnerabilities."

5. Policy Statements

Definition: Policy statements are the core directives that outline the specific rules and requirements for information security.
Example:

- **Access Control:** "Access to information systems and data is granted on a need-to-know basis and must be authorized by the appropriate manager. Multi-factor authentication (MFA) is required for all remote access."
- **Data Protection:** "Sensitive data must be encrypted both at rest and in transit using industry-standard encryption methods. Regular backups must be performed, and backup data must be stored securely."

6. Compliance Requirements

Definition: This section outlines the legal, regulatory, and industry standards the organization must comply with.
Example:

- **Compliance Statement:** "This policy ensures compliance with relevant regulations and standards, including but not limited to GDPR, HIPAA, PCI DSS, and ISO/IEC 27001. Regular audits will be conducted to ensure ongoing compliance."

7. Incident Response

Definition: This section describes the procedures for responding to information security incidents.
Example:

- **Incident Response Procedure:** "All employees must report suspected security incidents to the IT Department immediately. The incident response team will follow the defined incident response plan, which includes identification, containment, eradication, recovery, and post-incident review."

8. Training and Awareness

Definition: Outlines the organization's approach to training and raising awareness about information security.
Example:

- **Training Statement:** "All employees must complete mandatory information security training upon hire and annually thereafter. Additional training will be provided for specific roles as needed."

9. Enforcement and Sanctions

Definition: Details the consequences of non-compliance with the policy.
Example:

- **Enforcement Statement:** "Failure to comply with this policy may result in disciplinary action, up to and including termination of employment. Contractors and third parties may face contract termination or legal action."

10. Review and Updates

Definition: Describes the process for regularly reviewing and updating the policy to ensure its relevance and effectiveness.
Example:

- **Review Statement:** "This policy will be reviewed annually or whenever significant changes occur in the organization's information security environment. Updates will be approved by senior management and communicated to all employees."

Real-World Examples

Example 1: Financial Institution Data Protection Policy

- **Purpose:** To protect customer data and ensure regulatory compliance.
- **Scope:** Applies to all employees and contractors handling customer data.
- **Objectives:** Safeguard customer information, ensure compliance with financial regulations, and maintain customer trust.
- **Roles and Responsibilities:** The CISO oversees the policy; IT staff implement encryption; employees follow data handling procedures.
- **Policy Statements:** All customer data must be encrypted using AES-256; data access is restricted to authorized personnel.
- **Compliance Requirements:** Complies with GLBA, PCI DSS, and SOX.
- **Incident Response:** Report data breaches to the CISO immediately; follow the incident response plan.
- **Training and Awareness:** Mandatory annual data protection training for all employees.
- **Enforcement and Sanctions:** Non-compliance may result in disciplinary action, including termination.
- **Review and Updates:** Reviewed annually by the compliance team.

Example 2: Healthcare Organization Access Control Policy

- **Purpose:** To protect patient information and comply with healthcare regulations.
- **Scope:** Applies to all employees and third-party service providers accessing patient data.
- **Objectives:** Ensure patient confidentiality, integrity, and availability; comply with HIPAA.
- **Roles and Responsibilities:** The IT Director manages access control systems; department heads authorize access; employees use unique IDs.
- **Policy Statements:** Access to patient records is granted based on job role; MFA is required for system access.
- **Compliance Requirements:** HIPAA, HITECH Act.
- **Incident Response:** Report unauthorized access to the IT Director; follow the incident response procedure.
- **Training and Awareness:** Annual HIPAA compliance training for all staff.
- **Enforcement and Sanctions:** Violations may lead to disciplinary action, up to termination.
- **Review and Updates:** Policy reviewed biannually or after significant changes in regulations.

Conclusion

Including these essential elements in an information security policy ensures it is comprehensive, enforceable, and aligned with organizational goals. Real-world examples demonstrate how these elements can be effectively addressed to create robust security policies that protect information assets, ensure compliance, and support business objectives.

Challenges and Best Practices in Implementing and Enforcing Information Security Policies

Implementing and enforcing information security policies across an organization can be challenging due to a variety of factors, including resistance to change, lack of awareness, and varying levels of technical expertise among employees. Here are some common challenges and best practices to address them:

Challenges

1. Resistance to Change

- Employees may resist new policies, especially if they perceive them as hindering their productivity or adding complexity to their tasks.

2. Lack of Awareness and Understanding

- Employees may not understand the importance of information security policies or how to comply with them.

3. Inconsistent Enforcement

- Policies may not be enforced uniformly across different departments or locations, leading to gaps in security.

4. Varying Levels of Technical Expertise

- Employees with different levels of technical skills may find it challenging to understand and adhere to technical security measures.

5. Keeping Policies Up-to-Date

- Rapid technological advancements and evolving threats require regular updates to policies, which can be difficult to manage.

6. Cultural and Organizational Differences

- Global organizations may face challenges in implementing policies consistently across different cultures and regulatory environments.

Best Practices for Implementation and Enforcement

1. Leadership Support and Engagement

- **Top-Down Approach:** Ensure that senior management supports and actively promotes information security policies. Their endorsement can significantly influence the organization's culture and employees' attitudes toward compliance.
- **Executive Sponsorship:** Having a dedicated executive sponsor for the information security program can help in securing necessary resources and overcoming resistance.

2. Clear and Concise Policies

- **Simplicity:** Draft policies in clear and simple language to ensure they are easily understood by all employees. Avoid technical jargon where possible.
- **Relevance:** Tailor policies to be relevant to different departments and roles. Generic policies may not address specific needs and risks.

3. Effective Communication

- **Multi-Channel Communication:** Use various communication channels such as emails, intranet, meetings, and newsletters to disseminate policies.
- **Regular Updates:** Keep employees informed about any changes or updates to policies through regular communication.
- **Interactive Sessions:** Conduct Q&A sessions, workshops, and seminars to explain the policies and their importance.

4. Comprehensive Training and Awareness Programs

- **Mandatory Training:** Implement mandatory training programs for all employees upon joining the organization and at regular intervals thereafter.
- **Role-Based Training:** Provide specialized training for different roles based on their specific responsibilities and access levels.
- **Simulations and Drills:** Conduct phishing simulations, security drills, and tabletop exercises to reinforce training and prepare employees for real-world scenarios.

5. Consistent Enforcement

- **Uniform Application:** Ensure that policies are enforced consistently across all departments and locations. This helps in maintaining a uniform security posture.
- **Audits and Monitoring:** Regularly audit compliance with policies and monitor for any deviations. Use automated tools where possible to streamline this process.
- **Clear Consequences:** Establish and communicate clear consequences for non-compliance. Consistent enforcement of penalties can deter policy violations.

6. Regular Review and Updates

- **Scheduled Reviews:** Establish a schedule for regular review and updating of policies to ensure they remain relevant and effective.
- **Feedback Mechanism:** Implement a feedback mechanism for employees to provide input on policies. This can help identify gaps and areas for improvement.
- **Adaptation to Changes:** Stay informed about changes in technology, threats, and regulations, and update policies accordingly.

7. Building a Security-Conscious Culture

- **Cultural Integration:** Integrate security into the organizational culture by embedding it in daily operations and decision-making processes.
- **Recognition and Rewards:** Recognize and reward employees who adhere to and promote information security policies. This can motivate others to follow suit.
- **Security Champions:** Identify and train security champions within departments who can advocate for and support the enforcement of security policies.

8. Use of Technology

- **Automated Enforcement:** Utilize technological solutions such as endpoint protection, access control systems, and data loss prevention (DLP) tools to enforce policies automatically.
- **Monitoring and Reporting Tools:** Implement monitoring tools to track compliance and generate reports. This provides visibility into the effectiveness of policy enforcement.

Example Scenario: Implementing a Data Protection Policy

Challenges:

- Resistance from employees due to perceived inconvenience of new data handling procedures.
- Lack of understanding of data protection requirements among non-technical staff.
- Inconsistent enforcement across different departments.

Best Practices Applied:

1. **Leadership Support:** Senior management sends a company-wide memo emphasizing the importance of the new data protection policy.
2. **Clear Policy:** The policy is written in simple language, explaining the rationale behind data protection measures.
3. **Effective Communication:** The policy is communicated through emails, a dedicated intranet page, and during departmental meetings.

4. **Training:** Mandatory training sessions are conducted, with additional role-based training for departments handling sensitive data.
5. **Consistent Enforcement:** Regular audits are conducted to ensure compliance, and any violations are addressed promptly.
6. **Regular Updates:** The policy is reviewed every six months and updated as needed, with changes communicated to all employees.
7. **Building Culture:** Employees who demonstrate exemplary data protection practices are recognized in the company newsletter.
8. **Technology:** DLP tools are implemented to monitor and prevent unauthorized data transfers.

Conclusion

Implementing and enforcing information security policies requires a multifaceted approach that addresses resistance, ensures understanding, and maintains consistent application. By securing leadership support, communicating effectively, providing comprehensive training, and leveraging technology, the Information Security Manager can ensure that policies are effectively implemented and adhered to by all stakeholders. Building a security-conscious culture and regularly updating policies to reflect changing conditions are also crucial for maintaining a robust security posture.

Policy Exception Management

Concept

Policy exception management refers to the process of handling requests for deviations from established information security policies. It allows for flexibility in specific situations where adhering strictly to a policy might not be feasible or where an alternative approach may be more appropriate. The primary goal of policy exception management is to maintain the overall integrity of the organization's information security posture while accommodating legitimate business needs.

Importance

Policy exceptions are crucial for several reasons:

1. **Flexibility:** They provide necessary flexibility in unique or unforeseen circumstances, ensuring that security measures do not hinder business operations.
2. **Risk Management:** Properly managed exceptions allow for a controlled approach to handling risks that arise from deviations from standard policies.
3. **Compliance and Accountability:** Documenting exceptions ensures compliance with regulatory requirements and demonstrates due diligence in managing security risks.
4. **Transparency:** Maintaining a formal process for policy exceptions ensures transparency and accountability within the organization.

Key Considerations in Policy Exception Management

1. Risk Assessment

Before granting a policy exception, it is essential to assess the risks associated with the deviation. This involves evaluating the potential impact on the organization's security posture and identifying any additional risks that may arise.

- **Impact Analysis:** Determine how the exception could affect the confidentiality, integrity, and availability of information assets.
- **Threat and Vulnerability Assessment:** Identify potential threats and vulnerabilities that could exploit the exception.
- **Mitigation Measures:** Consider additional controls or measures that can mitigate the identified risks.

2. Business Justification

Each exception request should be accompanied by a clear business justification explaining why the deviation from the policy is necessary. This includes:

- **Business Need:** A detailed explanation of the business requirement or operational necessity driving the exception request.
- **Benefits:** An outline of the expected benefits of granting the exception, such as improved efficiency, cost savings, or enhanced functionality.

3. Approval Process

A formal approval process is critical to ensure that exceptions are granted only after thorough consideration and authorization by appropriate stakeholders.

- **Review Committee:** Establish a committee or designate specific roles responsible for reviewing and approving exception requests. This typically includes representatives from information security, IT, legal, and business units.
- **Approval Criteria:** Define clear criteria and guidelines for approving exceptions, including acceptable risk levels and required mitigation measures.
- **Documentation:** Ensure all decisions are well-documented, including the rationale for approval or denial, and any conditions attached to the exception.

4. Documentation and Record-Keeping

Maintaining comprehensive records of all policy exceptions is vital for accountability and compliance purposes.

- **Exception Log:** Maintain an exception log or database to track all requests, decisions, and associated documentation.
- **Audit Trail:** Ensure an audit trail is in place to facilitate periodic reviews and audits of the exception management process.
- **Expiration and Review Dates:** Document the duration of the exception and establish review dates to reassess the necessity and impact of the exception over time.

5. Monitoring and Review

Ongoing monitoring and periodic reviews of granted exceptions ensure that they remain justified and that associated risks are managed effectively.

- **Regular Monitoring:** Continuously monitor the implementation and impact of granted exceptions to ensure they do not introduce unacceptable risks.
- **Periodic Review:** Conduct regular reviews to reassess the necessity of the exception and its compliance with current security requirements and business needs.
- **Revocation:** Be prepared to revoke exceptions if they are no longer justified or if the associated risks become unacceptable.

Example Scenario: Policy Exception Management Process

Scenario:

A software development team requests an exception to the organization's strict password policy, which mandates complex passwords and frequent changes. The team argues that the policy hampers their efficiency during rapid development cycles and proposes using passphrases instead.

Process:

1. **Risk Assessment:**
   - **Impact Analysis:** Determine how using passphrases instead of complex passwords affects security.
   - **Threat and Vulnerability Assessment:** Assess the potential threats and vulnerabilities associated with passphrases.
   - **Mitigation Measures:** Consider additional controls, such as multi-factor authentication (MFA), to mitigate risks.
2. **Business Justification:**

    - **Business Need:** The team explains that the current policy slows down development and increases the likelihood of password-related errors.
    - **Benefits:** Using passphrases can improve efficiency and reduce the cognitive load on developers.
3. **Approval Process:**
    - **Review Committee:** The exception request is reviewed by representatives from information security, IT, and the development team.
    - **Approval Criteria:** The committee evaluates the request based on defined criteria, including risk levels and mitigation measures.
    - **Documentation:** The decision to approve the exception is documented, along with the rationale and any conditions, such as mandatory use of MFA.
4. **Documentation and Record-Keeping:**
    - **Exception Log:** The exception is logged in the exception database, including all relevant details and the expiration date.
    - **Audit Trail:** An audit trail is created to ensure transparency and facilitate future reviews.
5. **Monitoring and Review:**
    - **Regular Monitoring:** The information security team monitors the use of passphrases and the effectiveness of MFA.
    - **Periodic Review:** The exception is reviewed quarterly to ensure it remains justified and does not introduce unacceptable risks.
    - **Revocation:** The exception is subject to revocation if the risks become unacceptable or if the business need changes.

Conclusion

Policy exception management is essential for maintaining a flexible yet secure information security posture. By conducting thorough risk assessments, requiring clear business justifications, following a formal approval process, maintaining comprehensive documentation, and monitoring granted exceptions, organizations can effectively manage deviations from standard policies. This approach ensures that exceptions are justified, risks are mitigated, and the integrity of the information security program is upheld.

Relationship Between Information Security Governance and Key Organizational Functions

Information security governance is intricately linked with other key organizational functions, such as IT governance, corporate governance, and risk management. Understanding and managing these relationships are crucial for a holistic approach to organizational security and risk management. Here's an exploration of these relationships and strategies for fostering collaboration and alignment.

1. Information Security Governance and IT Governance

Relationship:

- **Integration of Objectives:** Information security governance focuses on protecting information assets, while IT governance ensures that IT supports and extends the organization's strategies and objectives. Both governance structures aim to align their respective objectives to achieve overall business goals.
- **Shared Responsibilities:** Both functions share responsibilities such as policy development, resource management, and compliance. Effective IT governance incorporates security considerations into IT projects, infrastructure, and operations.

Collaboration Strategies:

- **Joint Committees:** Establish joint committees or working groups that include representatives from both information security and IT to ensure ongoing collaboration and alignment.
- **Integrated Frameworks:** Use integrated frameworks like COBIT 2019, which provides a comprehensive approach that aligns IT goals with business strategies and incorporates security measures.
- **Unified Reporting:** Develop unified reporting mechanisms that track both IT and security metrics, providing a holistic view of how IT initiatives impact security and vice versa.

2. Information Security Governance and Corporate Governance

Relationship:

- **Strategic Alignment:** Corporate governance sets the overall direction and control for the organization. Information security governance ensures that the organization's information security strategy aligns with the broader corporate governance objectives.
- **Board Oversight:** The board of directors, as part of corporate governance, has oversight responsibilities for ensuring that information security risks are managed effectively.

Collaboration Strategies:

- **Board Engagement:** Regularly engage with the board to communicate information security risks, strategies, and performance. Ensure that security is a standing agenda item in board meetings.
- **Policy Integration:** Align information security policies with corporate governance policies to ensure consistency and support from top management.
- **Risk Reporting:** Develop clear and concise risk reports that can be easily understood by non-technical board members, highlighting the business impact of security issues and the effectiveness of mitigation strategies.

3. Information Security Governance and Risk Management

Relationship:

- **Holistic Risk Management:** Risk management involves identifying, assessing, and mitigating risks across the organization. Information security governance focuses specifically on managing risks to information assets.
- **Integrated Risk Frameworks:** Both functions use risk assessment methodologies and frameworks to identify and address risks. Effective risk management integrates security risks into the overall risk management framework.

Collaboration Strategies:

- **Unified Risk Assessments:** Conduct joint risk assessments that include both information security risks and other organizational risks. This ensures a comprehensive understanding of the risk landscape.
- **Common Risk Frameworks:** Use common risk frameworks such as ISO/IEC 27005 (information security risk management) alongside broader risk management frameworks like ISO 31000.
- **Cross-Functional Teams:** Establish cross-functional risk management teams that include members from information security, IT, compliance, finance, and other relevant departments to ensure comprehensive risk identification and mitigation.

Fostering Collaboration and Alignment

1. Establish Clear Communication Channels

- **Regular Meetings:** Schedule regular meetings between information security, IT, corporate governance, and risk management teams to discuss ongoing projects, risks, and strategies.
- **Shared Platforms:** Use shared communication platforms and tools to facilitate information sharing and collaboration across departments.

2. Develop Unified Policies and Procedures

- **Integrated Policies:** Develop policies and procedures that consider the requirements and objectives of all related functions. This ensures consistency and supports integrated governance and risk management practices.
- **Standardized Documentation:** Use standardized templates and documentation practices to ensure that all relevant information is captured and easily accessible across functions.

3. Promote a Collaborative Culture

- **Joint Training Programs:** Conduct joint training programs and workshops to build a common understanding of governance, risk, and security principles. This fosters a culture of collaboration and mutual respect.
- **Recognition Programs:** Recognize and reward collaborative efforts and successful cross-functional initiatives that enhance the organization's security posture.

4. Align Metrics and Reporting

- **Unified Metrics:** Develop metrics that reflect the performance and effectiveness of both information security and related governance functions. Unified metrics provide a holistic view of the organization's security and risk posture.
- **Integrated Dashboards:** Create integrated dashboards that present data from information security, IT governance, corporate governance, and risk management. This helps in identifying trends and making informed decisions.

5. Engage in Strategic Planning

- **Joint Strategic Planning:** Include representatives from information security, IT, corporate governance, and risk management in the strategic planning process. This ensures that security considerations are embedded in the organization's long-term plans.
- **Scenario Planning:** Conduct scenario planning exercises that consider the impact of various risks and security threats on the organization's strategic objectives. This helps in aligning risk mitigation strategies with business goals.

Conclusion

Information security governance must work in tandem with IT governance, corporate governance, and risk management to ensure a cohesive and effective approach to managing the organization's security and risk posture. By establishing clear communication channels, developing unified policies, promoting a collaborative culture, aligning metrics and reporting, and engaging in strategic planning, the Information Security Manager can foster collaboration and alignment across these areas. This integrated approach enhances the organization's resilience, supports its strategic objectives, and ensures a robust security posture.

Role of Industry Standards, Frameworks, and Best Practices in Information Security Governance

Industry standards, frameworks, and best practices play a pivotal role in shaping an organization's information security governance approach. They provide structured methodologies, guidelines, and benchmarks that organizations can use to develop, implement, and manage their information security programs. Adopting these standards and frameworks ensures that security measures are effective, consistent, and aligned with industry expectations and regulatory requirements.

Key Industry Standards and Frameworks

1. ISO/IEC 27001

Overview: ISO/IEC 27001 is an international standard for information security management systems (ISMS). It provides a systematic approach to managing sensitive company information, ensuring its confidentiality, integrity, and availability.

Key Principles:

- **Risk Management:** Emphasizes the identification, assessment, and treatment of information security risks.
- **Continuous Improvement:** Advocates for the continual improvement of the ISMS through regular reviews and updates.
- **Documentation and Controls:** Requires comprehensive documentation of the ISMS and implementation of a broad set of controls (detailed in ISO/IEC 27002).

Benefits:

- **Global Recognition:** Provides a globally recognized framework for managing information security.
- **Compliance:** Helps organizations comply with regulatory requirements and industry standards.
- **Risk Mitigation:** Enhances the ability to identify and mitigate information security risks systematically.
- **Customer Confidence:** Demonstrates a commitment to information security, enhancing customer trust and confidence.

2. NIST Cybersecurity Framework (CSF)

Overview: The NIST Cybersecurity Framework is a voluntary framework developed by the National Institute of Standards and Technology (NIST) for improving critical infrastructure cybersecurity. It provides a comprehensive guide for organizations to manage and reduce cybersecurity risks.

Key Principles:

- **Core Functions:** The framework is built around five core functions: Identify, Protect, Detect, Respond, and Recover.
- **Framework Tiers:** Defines four tiers (Partial, Risk Informed, Repeatable, Adaptive) to represent the organization's cybersecurity maturity.
- **Framework Profiles:** Allows organizations to create profiles that align their cybersecurity activities with business requirements and risk tolerance.

Benefits:

- **Flexibility:** Provides a flexible approach that can be tailored to different organizations and industries.
- **Alignment with Business Objectives:** Helps align cybersecurity practices with business goals and risk management strategies.
- **Risk Management:** Enhances risk management capabilities through a structured and comprehensive approach.
- **Stakeholder Communication:** Facilitates communication of cybersecurity activities and outcomes with stakeholders.

Examples of Widely Recognized Standards and Their Key Principles

1. COBIT 2019

Overview: COBIT (Control Objectives for Information and Related Technologies) 2019 is a framework developed by ISACA for governing and managing enterprise IT. It provides a comprehensive framework that aligns IT goals with business objectives.

Key Principles:

- **Governance and Management Objectives:** Defines governance and management objectives to help achieve enterprise IT goals.
- **Performance Management:** Emphasizes the measurement and monitoring of IT performance.
- **Continuous Improvement:** Advocates for continuous improvement of IT governance and management practices.

Benefits:

- **Alignment:** Aligns IT initiatives with business strategies and objectives.
- **Performance Measurement:** Provides tools for measuring and improving IT performance.
- **Compliance and Risk Management:** Enhances compliance and risk management capabilities.

2. CIS Controls

Overview: The Center for Internet Security (CIS) Controls are a set of best practices for securing IT systems and data. They are designed to help organizations prioritize their cybersecurity efforts.

Key Principles:

- **Prioritization:** Focuses on implementing high-impact security controls first.
- **Simplification:** Provides a simplified approach to cybersecurity, making it accessible to organizations of all sizes.
- **Actionable Guidelines:** Offers clear and actionable guidelines for implementing security controls.

Benefits:

- **Effectiveness:** Helps organizations implement effective security measures that address the most critical risks.
- **Accessibility:** Makes cybersecurity best practices accessible to a wide range of organizations.
- **Risk Reduction:** Enhances the ability to reduce cybersecurity risks systematically.

Benefits of Adopting Industry Standards and Frameworks

1. **Consistency and Best Practices:**
    - Adopting industry standards and frameworks ensures consistency in implementing security measures. They provide a set of best practices that have been validated by industry experts and organizations.
2. **Compliance:**
    - Standards and frameworks help organizations comply with regulatory requirements and industry expectations. This is crucial for avoiding legal penalties and maintaining a positive reputation.
3. **Risk Management:**
    - These frameworks provide structured methodologies for identifying, assessing, and managing risks. This systematic approach enhances an organization's ability to protect its information assets.
4. **Continuous Improvement:**
    - Most standards and frameworks emphasize the importance of continuous improvement. Regular reviews and updates ensure that security measures remain effective and relevant in the face of evolving threats.
5. **Enhanced Credibility:**
    - Certification and compliance with recognized standards enhance an organization's credibility. It demonstrates a commitment to information security and can improve relationships with customers, partners, and regulators.

How the Information Security Manager Can Foster Collaboration and Alignment

1. **Cross-Functional Teams:**
    - Establish cross-functional teams that include representatives from IT, risk management, compliance, and business units. This ensures that different perspectives are considered and fosters a collaborative approach to security governance.
2. **Integrated Risk Management:**
    - Integrate information security risk management with the organization's overall risk management framework. This ensures that security risks are considered alongside other business risks and that mitigation strategies are aligned.
3. **Unified Reporting:**
    - Develop unified reporting mechanisms that provide a holistic view of the organization's security posture. This includes aligning metrics and performance indicators across different functions.
4. **Regular Communication:**
    - Facilitate regular communication and information sharing between information security, IT governance, corporate governance, and risk management teams. This can be achieved through regular meetings, joint projects, and shared documentation.
5. **Shared Objectives:**
    - Align information security objectives with broader business objectives. Ensure that security initiatives support the organization's strategic goals and that all stakeholders understand the importance of security in achieving these goals.
6. **Training and Awareness:**
    - Conduct joint training sessions and awareness programs to build a common understanding of security principles and practices. This helps in fostering a culture of security across the organization.

Conclusion

Industry standards, frameworks, and best practices are essential for shaping an effective information security governance approach. They provide structured methodologies and guidelines that help organizations manage risks, ensure compliance, and achieve consistency in their security efforts. By adopting widely recognized standards like ISO/IEC 27001, NIST CSF, COBIT 2019, and CIS Controls, organizations can enhance their security posture, improve risk management, and foster a culture of continuous improvement. The Information Security Manager plays a crucial role in fostering collaboration and alignment across different organizational functions to ensure a holistic and effective approach to information security governance.

Importance of Regularly Reviewing and Updating Information Security Policies, Procedures, and Standards

Regular reviews and updates of information security policies, procedures, and standards are crucial to maintaining their relevance and effectiveness in an ever-evolving threat landscape. This proactive approach ensures that the organization's security measures remain aligned with current risks, regulatory requirements, and business objectives.

1. Adapting to Evolving Threats

- **Cybersecurity Landscape:** The threat landscape is continuously changing, with new vulnerabilities and attack vectors emerging regularly. Policies, procedures, and standards must be updated to address these evolving threats effectively.
- **Example:** An increase in ransomware attacks may necessitate updates to incident response procedures and data backup policies to ensure rapid recovery and mitigation.

2. Compliance with Regulatory Changes

- **Regulatory Environment:** Laws and regulations governing information security are frequently updated to address new challenges and technological advancements. Organizations must ensure their policies comply with the latest legal and regulatory requirements.
- **Example:** Changes in data protection regulations, such as GDPR or CCPA updates, require immediate review and modification of data handling and privacy policies.

3. Alignment with Business Objectives

- **Business Strategy:** As organizations grow and evolve, their business objectives and strategies change. Security policies must be aligned with these changes to support new business initiatives and processes.
- **Example:** Expanding into new markets may introduce different regulatory requirements and business risks, necessitating updates to existing security policies.

4. Technological Advancements

- **Technology Evolution:** Advances in technology can introduce new security challenges or solutions. Policies and procedures must be updated to incorporate new technologies and address associated risks.
- **Example:** The adoption of cloud services or Internet of Things (IoT) devices requires updates to access control policies and data protection standards.

5. Lessons Learned from Incidents

- **Incident Response:** Analyzing security incidents and breaches provides valuable insights into policy weaknesses and areas for improvement. Updating policies based on these lessons helps prevent recurrence.
- **Example:** A data breach investigation may reveal gaps in user access controls, leading to updates in authentication and authorization procedures.

Triggers for Initiating Updates

1. Regulatory and Legal Changes

- Changes in data protection laws, industry standards, or regulatory requirements often necessitate immediate updates to ensure compliance.

2. Security Incidents and Breaches

- Post-incident reviews frequently uncover policy gaps or procedural weaknesses that must be addressed to prevent future incidents.

3. Technological Changes

- The adoption of new technologies, software updates, or infrastructure changes can require modifications to security policies and procedures.

4. Business Changes

- Organizational changes such as mergers, acquisitions, expansions, or shifts in business strategy can trigger the need for policy updates.

5. Regular Review Cycles

- Scheduled periodic reviews (e.g., annually or biannually) are essential for ensuring that all policies, procedures, and standards remain current and effective.

Best Practices for Managing Updates

1. Establish a Regular Review Process

- **Scheduled Reviews:** Implement a regular review cycle for all security policies, procedures, and standards. This ensures that updates are timely and consistent.
- **Review Committee:** Form a committee responsible for reviewing and approving updates, including representatives from key departments such as IT, legal, HR, and business units.

2. Monitor Regulatory and Industry Changes

- **Stay Informed:** Regularly monitor changes in relevant laws, regulations, and industry standards. Subscribe to regulatory updates, participate in industry forums, and engage with legal advisors to stay current.
- **Compliance Checks:** Conduct periodic compliance checks to ensure that all policies align with current regulatory requirements.

3. Conduct Post-Incident Reviews

- **Root Cause Analysis:** After any security incident, conduct a thorough root cause analysis to identify policy or procedural gaps.
- **Update Recommendations:** Develop and implement recommendations for policy and procedural updates based on the findings of the incident review.

4. Engage Stakeholders

- **Collaboration:** Engage stakeholders from across the organization in the review and update process to ensure policies are comprehensive and practical.
- **Feedback Mechanism:** Establish a mechanism for employees to provide feedback on policies and suggest improvements. This helps identify practical challenges and areas for enhancement.

5. Communicate Changes Effectively

- **Clear Communication:** Communicate updates clearly and promptly to all employees. Use multiple channels such as emails, intranet announcements, and meetings to ensure widespread awareness.
- **Training and Awareness:** Provide training sessions to ensure employees understand the updates and their implications. Tailor training to different roles and responsibilities.

6. Document Changes

- **Version Control:** Maintain detailed records of all policy changes, including the rationale, approval dates, and version history.
- **Accessibility:** Ensure that the latest versions of all policies, procedures, and standards are easily accessible to all employees.

7. Continuous Improvement

- **Iterative Process:** Treat policy development and maintenance as an iterative process. Continuously seek ways to improve and refine security measures based on feedback, new information, and emerging best practices.
- **Benchmarking:** Regularly benchmark against industry best practices and standards to identify areas for improvement and ensure that the organization's policies remain cutting-edge.

Conclusion

Regularly reviewing and updating information security policies, procedures, and standards are essential for maintaining their relevance and effectiveness in a dynamic threat landscape. By establishing a structured review process, staying informed about regulatory changes, conducting post-incident reviews, engaging stakeholders, communicating changes effectively, and continuously seeking improvement, organizations can ensure that their security measures remain robust and aligned with business objectives. This proactive approach not only enhances security posture but also supports regulatory compliance and fosters a culture of continuous improvement.

Information Security Governance Metrics

Now would be a great time to talk about the concept of information security governance metrics, an essential aspect of any robust governance program. Information security governance metrics are quantifiable measures used to assess the effectiveness of an organization's information security policies, processes, and controls. These metrics enable organizations to gauge their security posture, ensure compliance with regulations, and communicate the state of security to stakeholders effectively.

The Role of Information Security Governance Metrics

In addition to providing a snapshot of the current security environment, these metrics play several critical roles:

1. **Performance Measurement:** Metrics help in assessing how well security policies and controls are functioning. This involves evaluating the implementation of security measures and their effectiveness in mitigating risks.
2. **Regulatory Compliance:** They aid in demonstrating compliance with various regulations and standards such as GDPR, HIPAA, and ISO/IEC 27001, ensuring that the organization meets its legal and regulatory obligations.
3. **Risk Management:** By identifying vulnerabilities and potential threats, metrics help in prioritizing risk management activities. They offer insights into areas requiring immediate attention and resources.
4. **Resource Allocation:** Metrics guide the allocation of resources by highlighting the most critical areas needing investment, whether it's in technology, personnel, or training.
5. **Communication:** They provide a clear and concise way to communicate the status of the information security program to executives, board members, and other stakeholders, facilitating informed decision-making.

Commonly Used Information Security Governance Metrics

Let's get into some of the commonly used metrics in information security governance:

1. **Incident Response Time:** Measures the time taken to respond to security incidents. It includes detection, reporting, and resolution times.
   - **Collection:** Incident logs, helpdesk tickets, and automated monitoring systems.
   - **Analysis:** Calculate average response times and identify trends or outliers.
   - **Reporting:** Regular reports to senior management, highlighting improvements or areas needing attention.
2. **Number of Security Incidents:** Tracks the total number of security incidents over a specific period.
   - **Collection:** Incident reports, security software logs, and audit trails.
   - **Analysis:** Trend analysis to identify patterns, seasonal spikes, or specific vulnerabilities.
   - **Reporting:** Monthly or quarterly summaries to management with incident types and resolutions.
3. **User Compliance Rates:** Assesses the percentage of users complying with security policies and procedures, such as password policies or mandatory training completion.
   - **Collection:** User activity logs, training completion records, and compliance audits.
   - **Analysis:** Compare compliance rates across departments and over time.
   - **Reporting:** Dashboards and reports for department heads and compliance officers.
4. **Patch Management:** Evaluates the timeliness and effectiveness of applying security patches and updates.
   - **Collection:** System update logs, patch deployment records, and vulnerability scans.
   - **Analysis:** Measure the time between patch release and deployment, and the success rate of patch application.
   - **Reporting:** Regular updates to IT management with status on critical and non-critical patches.
5. **Security Awareness Training Effectiveness:** Gauges the effectiveness of security training programs through pre- and post-training assessments or simulated phishing tests.
   - **Collection:** Training attendance records, quiz scores, and phishing test results.
   - **Analysis:** Compare pre- and post-training knowledge levels and the incidence of successful phishing attempts.
   - **Reporting:** Detailed analysis to HR and IT security teams, with recommendations for improvement.

Collecting, Analyzing, and Reporting Metrics

Collection: Data collection involves gathering information from various sources such as security tools (e.g., firewalls, intrusion detection systems), user activity logs, compliance reports, and incident response records. Automated tools and software can streamline this process, ensuring accuracy and consistency.

Analysis: Once collected, data must be analyzed to extract meaningful insights. This could involve statistical analysis, trend analysis, and benchmarking against industry standards. The goal is to interpret the raw data to understand underlying patterns and issues.

Reporting: Effective reporting translates analytical insights into understandable and actionable information for stakeholders. This includes creating visual dashboards, summary reports, and detailed analysis documents. Reports should be tailored to the audience; for example, executive summaries for senior management and detailed technical reports for IT staff.

Example of a Reporting Structure

Executive Summary: A high-level overview of key metrics, trends, and overall security posture, aimed at senior management and board members.

Detailed Analysis: In-depth examination of specific metrics, including incident details, compliance rates, and training effectiveness, targeted at IT and security professionals.

Dashboards: Visual representations of metrics for real-time monitoring and quick assessment, useful for operational managers and IT staff.

By leveraging these metrics, organizations can maintain a vigilant and proactive stance on information security, ensuring they are well-prepared to tackle any challenges that come their way.

Role of Training and Awareness in Supporting Effective Information Security Governance

Training and awareness are critical components of an effective information security governance framework. They ensure that all stakeholders understand their roles and responsibilities in protecting the organization's information assets. By fostering a security-conscious culture and providing the necessary knowledge and skills, training and awareness programs help mitigate risks, prevent incidents, and support compliance with policies and regulations.

1. Importance of Training and Awareness

Enhancing Knowledge and Skills:

- Training programs equip employees with the necessary knowledge and skills to recognize and respond to security threats, follow security policies, and use security tools effectively.

Promoting Compliance:

- Awareness initiatives ensure that all employees are aware of regulatory requirements, organizational policies, and best practices, thereby promoting compliance and reducing the risk of legal and regulatory penalties.

Fostering a Security Culture:

- Regular training and awareness activities help build a security-conscious culture where employees take an active role in protecting information assets and understand the importance of security in their daily activities.

Supporting Incident Response:

- Well-informed employees are better prepared to respond appropriately to security incidents, reducing the potential impact on the organization.

Strategies for Designing and Delivering Training to Different Stakeholder Groups

1. Executives

Objective:

- Ensure that executives understand the strategic importance of information security, their role in governance, and the business implications of security risks.

Strategies:

- **Customized Content:** Tailor training content to focus on strategic aspects of information security, such as risk management, compliance, and the impact on business objectives.
- **Executive Briefings:** Conduct high-level briefings and workshops that highlight the latest threats, regulatory changes, and the organization's security posture.
- **Case Studies:** Use real-world case studies to illustrate the consequences of security breaches and the importance of proactive security governance.
- **Metrics and Dashboards:** Provide dashboards and key performance indicators (KPIs) that demonstrate the effectiveness of security initiatives and support data-driven decision-making.

2. Managers

Objective:

- Equip managers with the knowledge to implement and enforce security policies within their teams, understand their role in incident response, and manage security-related risks.

Strategies:

- **Role-Based Training:** Develop role-specific training modules that address the unique security responsibilities of managers, such as policy enforcement, risk assessment, and incident management.
- **Interactive Workshops:** Conduct interactive workshops and scenario-based exercises that allow managers to practice handling security incidents and making informed decisions.
- **Policy Implementation Guides:** Provide practical guides and checklists to help managers implement security policies and procedures within their departments.
- **Regular Updates:** Ensure managers receive regular updates on new security policies, emerging threats, and best practices.

3. Employees

Objective:

- Raise awareness among employees about security policies, common threats, and best practices to ensure they can recognize and respond to security incidents.

Strategies:

- **Onboarding Training:** Incorporate information security training into the onboarding process for new employees to ensure they understand the organization's security expectations from day one.
- **E-Learning Modules:** Develop engaging e-learning modules that cover essential topics such as phishing, password management, and data protection. These modules should include quizzes and interactive elements to reinforce learning.
- **Regular Awareness Campaigns:** Launch regular awareness campaigns using emails, posters, and newsletters to remind employees of key security practices and updates.
- **Phishing Simulations:** Conduct periodic phishing simulations to test employees' ability to recognize phishing attempts and reinforce the importance of vigilance.

Best Practices for Effective Training and Awareness Programs

1. Tailored Content

- Ensure that training content is tailored to the specific needs, roles, and responsibilities of different stakeholder groups. This helps make the training relevant and engaging.

2. Interactive and Engaging Formats

- Use interactive formats such as simulations, role-playing, and gamification to make training sessions engaging and memorable. Encourage participation and provide opportunities for hands-on practice.

3. Regular and Ongoing Training

- Information security training should not be a one-time event. Implement regular training sessions and refreshers to keep employees updated on the latest threats, policies, and best practices.

4. Measurement and Feedback

- Measure the effectiveness of training programs through assessments, surveys, and feedback. Use this data to identify areas for improvement and adjust training content accordingly.

5. Leadership Involvement

- Encourage active involvement and support from leadership to demonstrate the importance of information security. Leadership endorsement can significantly enhance the credibility and impact of training programs.

6. Real-World Relevance

- Use real-world examples and scenarios to illustrate the relevance of security policies and practices. This helps employees understand the practical implications of security measures.

7. Accessible Resources

- Provide easy access to training materials, policy documents, and additional resources through the organization's intranet or learning management system (LMS). Ensure employees know where to find help and support.

Example Training Programs

Executive Training Program

- **Content:** Strategic importance of information security, risk management, compliance, and the impact on business objectives.
- **Format:** High-level briefings, workshops, case studies, and performance dashboards.
- **Frequency:** Quarterly briefings with periodic workshops.

Manager Training Program

- **Content:** Policy implementation, risk assessment, incident response, and enforcement responsibilities.
- **Format:** Role-specific modules, interactive workshops, scenario-based exercises, and practical guides.
- **Frequency:** Initial training with semi-annual refreshers and updates.

Employee Training Program

- **Content:** Basic security principles, common threats (e.g., phishing, social engineering), policy awareness, and best practices.
- **Format:** Onboarding sessions, e-learning modules, regular awareness campaigns, and phishing simulations.
- **Frequency:** Initial training during onboarding with monthly refreshers and annual comprehensive sessions.

Conclusion

Training and awareness are fundamental to effective information security governance. By designing and delivering targeted training programs to different stakeholder groups—executives, managers, and employees—organizations can ensure that everyone understands their roles and responsibilities in protecting information assets. Tailored content, engaging formats, regular updates, and active leadership involvement are key strategies for building a security-conscious culture and maintaining a robust information security posture.

Governance, Risk, and Compliance (GRC) in Information Security

Now, let's look into the concept of Governance, Risk, and Compliance (GRC), a framework crucial for the holistic management of an organization's information security. GRC encompasses three interconnected components that work together to ensure an organization's activities align with its objectives, manage risks effectively, and comply with relevant laws and regulations.

Understanding GRC and Its Components

Governance: This involves the frameworks, policies, and processes established by an organization to ensure it operates within its defined goals and strategies. Effective governance ensures that all business units and activities align with the overall mission and objectives of the organization.

Risk Management: This is the process of identifying, assessing, and mitigating risks that could potentially impact the organization. In the context of information security, it involves protecting data and systems from threats like cyber attacks, data breaches, and other vulnerabilities.

Compliance: This ensures that the organization adheres to legal, regulatory, and internal policies and standards. Compliance is crucial in maintaining the organization's reputation and avoiding legal penalties.

Relevance of GRC to Information Security

GRC is particularly relevant to information security for several reasons:

1. **Holistic View:** GRC provides a comprehensive perspective on how information security fits into the broader business context, ensuring that security measures support the overall business strategy.
2. **Enhanced Decision-Making:** By integrating governance, risk, and compliance, organizations can make more informed decisions that balance security needs with business priorities.
3. **Regulatory Adherence:** A structured GRC framework helps ensure that security practices meet all regulatory and legal requirements, avoiding fines and other legal repercussions.
4. **Risk Mitigation:** Through risk management, GRC helps identify and address potential security threats before they can cause significant damage.

Benefits of an Integrated GRC Approach

An integrated GRC approach can significantly enhance an organization's ability to align its information security efforts with overall business objectives and risk management priorities. Here's how:

Alignment with Business Objectives: An integrated GRC framework ensures that information security initiatives support and enhance the organization's strategic goals. For example, if a company's objective is to expand its digital presence, a GRC approach ensures that security measures are implemented to protect new digital assets and maintain customer trust.

Risk Management Priorities: GRC helps prioritize risks by evaluating their potential impact on business operations. By understanding the most critical risks, organizations can allocate resources efficiently to mitigate them. For instance, if a risk assessment identifies a significant vulnerability in a customer-facing application, the organization can prioritize its remediation to prevent data breaches.

Streamlined Processes: An integrated GRC approach breaks down silos between departments, fostering better communication and collaboration. This leads to more streamlined and efficient processes, as security policies and procedures are consistently applied across the organization. For example, a unified incident response plan ensures that all teams know their roles and responsibilities in the event of a security breach.

Continuous Monitoring and Improvement: GRC emphasizes continuous monitoring and improvement of security practices. Regular audits, risk assessments, and compliance checks help identify areas for enhancement and ensure that security measures evolve with changing threats and regulatory landscapes. For instance, frequent reviews of security controls ensure they remain effective against emerging cyber threats.

Implementing an Integrated GRC Approach

Establish a GRC Framework: Start by defining the governance structure, risk management processes, and compliance requirements. This involves setting up policies, standards, and procedures that align with industry best practices and regulatory requirements.

Engage Stakeholders: Engage key stakeholders from various departments, including IT, legal, finance, and operations, to ensure a comprehensive approach to GRC. Their input is crucial for identifying risks and ensuring compliance across the organization.

Utilize Technology Solutions: Leverage GRC tools and software to automate processes, facilitate real-time monitoring, and enhance reporting capabilities. These tools can help manage documentation, track compliance status, and generate insights into risk management activities.

Conduct Training and Awareness Programs: Educate employees about the importance of GRC and their roles in maintaining information security. Regular training sessions and awareness programs help foster a security-conscious culture within the organization.

Monitor and Review: Continuously monitor GRC activities and review their effectiveness. Conduct regular audits and assessments to identify gaps and implement corrective actions. This ensures that the GRC framework remains robust and responsive to new challenges.

Real-World Example

Consider a financial institution implementing an integrated GRC approach. By aligning its information security efforts with business goals, the institution can protect sensitive customer data, comply with financial regulations, and manage risks effectively. Regular risk assessments identify potential threats, while compliance checks ensure adherence to standards like PCI DSS. This comprehensive approach not only enhances security but also builds customer trust and supports business growth.

By embracing an integrated GRC approach, organizations can create a resilient and secure environment that supports their strategic objectives, mitigates risks, and ensures compliance with regulatory requirements. This holistic approach not only strengthens information security but also enhances overall organizational performance.

Importance of Ensuring Compliance in Information Security Governance

Ensuring compliance with legal, regulatory, and contractual requirements is a fundamental aspect of information security governance. Compliance not only helps in safeguarding sensitive information but also protects the organization from legal, financial, and reputational risks. Here's why it's crucial and the potential consequences of non-compliance:

Importance of Compliance

1. Legal and Regulatory Compliance

Protection of Sensitive Data:

- Compliance with laws and regulations ensures that sensitive information, such as personal data, financial records, and health information, is protected from unauthorized access, disclosure, and misuse.

Examples:

- **GDPR (General Data Protection Regulation):** Mandates stringent data protection measures for organizations handling personal data of EU citizens.
- **HIPAA (Health Insurance Portability and Accountability Act):** Sets standards for the protection of health information in the healthcare industry.

2. Contractual Obligations

Adhering to Agreements:

- Organizations often enter into contracts with clients, vendors, and partners that include specific information security requirements. Fulfilling these contractual obligations is essential for maintaining business relationships and trust.

Examples:

- **Service Level Agreements (SLAs):** May include provisions for data security, incident response, and compliance with industry standards.
- **Vendor Contracts:** Often specify security measures and audit rights to ensure the protection of shared information.

3. Risk Management

Mitigating Risks:

- Compliance frameworks help organizations identify, assess, and manage risks. By following established guidelines and standards, organizations can reduce vulnerabilities and enhance their security posture.

Examples:

- **ISO/IEC 27001:** Provides a systematic approach to managing sensitive information and reducing information security risks.
- **NIST Cybersecurity Framework:** Helps organizations manage and reduce cybersecurity risks through a structured approach.

4. Enhancing Trust and Reputation

Building Credibility:

- Demonstrating compliance with recognized standards and regulations enhances an organization's credibility and trustworthiness. Clients, partners, and stakeholders are more likely to do business with organizations that prioritize information security.

Examples:

- **Third-Party Audits and Certifications:** Obtaining certifications like ISO/IEC 27001 or SOC 2 can serve as proof of an organization's commitment to information security.

Potential Consequences of Non-Compliance

1. Legal Penalties

Fines and Sanctions:

- Non-compliance with laws and regulations can result in substantial fines and sanctions. Regulatory bodies enforce compliance through financial penalties to incentivize adherence to legal requirements.

Examples:

- **GDPR:** Non-compliance can lead to fines of up to €20 million or 4% of the company's global annual revenue, whichever is higher.
- **HIPAA:** Violations can result in fines ranging from $100 to $50,000 per violation, with a maximum annual penalty of $1.5 million.

2. Financial Losses

Direct and Indirect Costs:

- Beyond legal penalties, non-compliance can lead to significant financial losses due to data breaches, incident response, legal fees, and loss of business.

Examples:

- **Data Breach Costs:** Expenses related to breach notification, investigation, remediation, and potential lawsuits.
- **Business Interruption:** Financial losses due to downtime and disruption of operations.

3. Reputational Damage

Loss of Trust:

- Non-compliance and resulting security incidents can severely damage an organization's reputation. Loss of trust among customers, partners, and stakeholders can have long-term business impacts.

Examples:

- **Customer Attrition:** Customers may leave for competitors perceived as more secure.
- **Negative Publicity:** Media coverage of security breaches can tarnish an organization's public image.

4. Operational Disruptions

Business Continuity:

- Regulatory violations and security incidents can disrupt business operations, impacting productivity and service delivery.

Examples:

- **Regulatory Investigations:** Investigations and audits by regulatory bodies can consume significant resources and time.
- **Operational Downtime:** Cyber-attacks and breaches can lead to operational disruptions, affecting service availability.

5. Legal Actions

Litigation and Settlements:

- Non-compliance can result in legal actions from affected parties, leading to costly settlements and prolonged litigation.

Examples:

- **Class-Action Lawsuits:** Customers or employees affected by data breaches may file class-action lawsuits seeking damages.
- **Contractual Disputes:** Non-compliance with contractual security requirements can lead to legal disputes and compensation claims.

Strategies for Ensuring Compliance

1. Establish a Compliance Framework

Adopt Recognized Standards:

- Implement compliance frameworks such as ISO/IEC 27001, NIST CSF, and PCI DSS to establish a structured approach to managing information security and ensuring compliance.

2. Conduct Regular Audits and Assessments

Internal and External Audits:

- Perform regular internal audits and engage external auditors to assess compliance with regulatory requirements, industry standards, and contractual obligations.

3. Implement Robust Policies and Procedures

Policy Development:

- Develop and enforce comprehensive information security policies and procedures that align with legal, regulatory, and contractual requirements.

4. Training and Awareness Programs

Educate Employees:

- Conduct regular training and awareness programs to ensure employees understand their roles and responsibilities in maintaining compliance and protecting information assets.

5. Monitor Regulatory Changes

Stay Informed:

- Keep abreast of changes in laws, regulations, and industry standards. Establish a process for updating policies and procedures in response to regulatory changes.

6. Engage Legal and Compliance Experts

Seek Expertise:

- Engage legal and compliance experts to provide guidance on regulatory requirements and help navigate complex compliance landscapes.

Conclusion

Ensuring compliance with legal, regulatory, and contractual requirements is integral to effective information security governance. Compliance helps protect sensitive information, mitigate risks, and maintain trust with clients and stakeholders. Non-compliance can result in severe legal, financial, and reputational consequences. By adopting recognized standards, conducting regular audits, implementing robust policies, and fostering a culture of awareness, organizations can achieve and maintain compliance, supporting their overall security and business objectives.

Major Information Security-Related Laws and Regulations

Now, let's get into the key provisions and implications of major information security-related laws and regulations. Understanding these laws is crucial for designing and implementing a robust information security program that ensures compliance and mitigates risks. We'll explore the General Data Protection Regulation (GDPR), the Health Insurance Portability and Accountability Act (HIPAA), and the Sarbanes-Oxley Act (SOX).

General Data Protection Regulation (GDPR)

Key Provisions:

1. **Data Protection Principles:** GDPR mandates that personal data must be processed lawfully, fairly, and transparently. It should be collected for specified, legitimate purposes and only as much as necessary for those purposes.

2. **Data Subject Rights:** Individuals have the right to access their data, correct inaccuracies, erase data (right to be forgotten), and restrict processing. They also have the right to data portability and to object to processing.
3. **Consent:** Organizations must obtain explicit consent from individuals to process their personal data unless another legal basis applies.
4. **Data Protection Officer (DPO):** Organizations must appoint a DPO if they process large amounts of personal data or handle special categories of data.
5. **Breach Notification:** Organizations must report data breaches to the relevant supervisory authority within 72 hours of becoming aware of the breach.

Implications for Information Security:

- **Data Inventory:** Organizations must maintain an accurate inventory of personal data and ensure they have legal grounds for processing it.
- **Security Measures:** Implement technical and organizational measures to protect personal data, such as encryption, access controls, and regular security assessments.
- **Incident Response:** Develop a robust incident response plan to detect, respond to, and report data breaches promptly.
- **Privacy by Design:** Incorporate data protection into the design of systems and processes from the outset.

Health Insurance Portability and Accountability Act (HIPAA)

Key Provisions:

1. **Privacy Rule:** Sets standards for the protection of individuals' medical records and other personal health information (PHI). It grants patients rights over their health information, including rights to examine and obtain a copy of their health records.
2. **Security Rule:** Establishes standards for protecting electronic PHI (ePHI) with administrative, physical, and technical safeguards.
3. **Breach Notification Rule:** Requires covered entities to notify affected individuals, the Secretary of Health and Human Services (HHS), and, in some cases, the media, of a breach of unsecured PHI.

Implications for Information Security:

- **Access Controls:** Implement strict access controls to ensure that only authorized personnel can access PHI.
- **Training and Awareness:** Conduct regular training programs for employees to ensure they understand HIPAA requirements and how to handle PHI securely.
- **Risk Management:** Perform regular risk assessments to identify vulnerabilities and implement measures to mitigate risks to ePHI.
- **Audit Controls:** Implement mechanisms to record and examine access and other activity in information systems containing ePHI.

Sarbanes-Oxley Act (SOX)

Key Provisions:

1. **Section 302:** Requires senior executives to certify the accuracy of financial reports and establish and maintain internal controls for financial reporting.
2. **Section 404:** Mandates management and external auditors to report on the adequacy of the company's internal control over financial reporting.
3. **Section 802:** Introduces criminal penalties for altering, destroying, or falsifying records and mandates the retention of relevant records for a specified period.

Implications for Information Security:

- **Internal Controls:** Design and implement robust internal controls to ensure the accuracy and integrity of financial data.

- **Data Retention:** Establish policies and systems for the retention and protection of records, ensuring they cannot be altered or destroyed.
- **Auditing and Monitoring:** Implement audit trails and monitoring systems to detect and prevent unauthorized access or manipulation of financial data.
- **Certification and Reporting:** Ensure senior executives are involved in the oversight of internal controls and can certify their effectiveness.

Impact on Information Security Programs

Design Considerations:

1. **Compliance Frameworks:** Develop a comprehensive compliance framework that integrates the requirements of GDPR, HIPAA, SOX, and other relevant regulations. This framework should guide the design of policies, procedures, and controls.
2. **Risk-Based Approach:** Adopt a risk-based approach to prioritize security measures based on the potential impact and likelihood of risks identified through regular assessments.
3. **Cross-Functional Collaboration:** Foster collaboration between IT, legal, compliance, and other departments to ensure a cohesive approach to information security and compliance.

Implementation Strategies:

1. **Policies and Procedures:** Develop detailed policies and procedures that address the specific requirements of each regulation, such as data protection policies for GDPR, access control policies for HIPAA, and internal control policies for SOX.
2. **Technology Solutions:** Leverage technology solutions such as data encryption, access management systems, and audit logging tools to meet regulatory requirements and enhance security.
3. **Training and Awareness:** Conduct ongoing training and awareness programs to ensure all employees understand their responsibilities under each regulation and how to comply with organizational policies.
4. **Monitoring and Reporting:** Establish continuous monitoring mechanisms to detect compliance violations and security incidents. Regularly report on compliance status and security posture to senior management and regulatory authorities as required.

By integrating these laws and regulations into the design and implementation of an information security program, organizations can not only achieve compliance but also enhance their overall security posture, protect sensitive data, and maintain trust with customers and stakeholders.

Role of the Information Security Manager in Managing Contractual Requirements

The Information Security Manager plays a critical role in identifying, analyzing, and addressing contractual requirements related to information security. This involves ensuring that security obligations are clearly defined, consistently applied, and effectively managed throughout the lifecycle of contracts with clients, vendors, and partners.

Identifying Contractual Requirements

1. Review Contractual Documents

- **Initial Review:** At the outset of contract negotiations, the Information Security Manager must review all relevant contractual documents to identify security-related requirements.
- **Key Documents:** This includes master service agreements (MSAs), service level agreements (SLAs), non-disclosure agreements (NDAs), and any specific security clauses included in these documents.

2. Collaborate with Legal and Procurement Teams

- **Legal Collaboration:** Work closely with the legal team to ensure that all security requirements are appropriately captured in contracts and that they comply with legal and regulatory standards.
- **Procurement Involvement:** Engage with the procurement team to ensure that security considerations are factored into vendor selection and contract management processes.

3. Understand Business Requirements

- **Business Needs:** Understand the specific business requirements and how they translate into security obligations. This includes knowing what data will be shared, processed, or stored and the associated risks.

- **Risk Assessment:** Conduct a risk assessment to determine the level of security required based on the sensitivity and criticality of the information involved.

Analyzing Contractual Requirements

1. Identify Security Obligations

- **Detailed Analysis:** Identify specific security obligations outlined in contracts, such as data protection measures, access controls, incident response protocols, and compliance with industry standards (e.g., PCI DSS, ISO/IEC 27001).
- **Regulatory Compliance:** Ensure that the contractual requirements align with applicable regulatory and legal obligations, such as GDPR, HIPAA, or CCPA.

2. Evaluate the Impact

- **Impact Assessment:** Assess the impact of these requirements on the organization's existing security policies, procedures, and controls. Determine if current measures are sufficient or if additional controls are needed.
- **Resource Allocation:** Identify the resources (personnel, technology, budget) required to meet these contractual obligations.

3. Develop Security Clauses

- **Standard Clauses:** Develop and maintain standard security clauses that can be included in contracts to ensure consistency and comprehensiveness. These clauses should address key areas such as data protection, breach notification, and compliance.
- **Custom Requirements:** Tailor security clauses to meet specific client or vendor requirements as needed. This might include specifying encryption standards, audit rights, or particular security certifications.

Addressing Contractual Requirements

1. Implement Necessary Controls

- **Policy Updates:** Update information security policies and procedures to reflect the contractual requirements. Ensure that these policies are communicated to relevant stakeholders.
- **Technical Controls:** Implement technical controls such as encryption, access controls, and monitoring tools to comply with contractual security obligations.

2. Training and Awareness

- **Employee Training:** Conduct training sessions for employees to ensure they understand and comply with the security requirements outlined in contracts. This includes specific training for those involved in managing and handling contractual data.
- **Vendor Training:** Ensure that vendors and partners are aware of and comply with the security requirements. Provide them with necessary resources and training as needed.

3. Monitoring and Auditing

- **Continuous Monitoring:** Implement continuous monitoring mechanisms to ensure ongoing compliance with contractual security requirements. This includes regular audits, vulnerability assessments, and compliance checks.
- **Performance Metrics:** Develop and track key performance indicators (KPIs) to measure compliance and identify areas for improvement.

4. Incident Response

- **Incident Management Plan:** Ensure that an incident management plan is in place that aligns with contractual requirements. This plan should outline how to respond to security incidents, including notification procedures and timelines.
- **Breach Notification:** Establish protocols for breach notification to comply with contractual obligations and regulatory requirements. Ensure that all parties are aware of these protocols.

Common Types of Contractual Requirements

1. Service Level Agreements (SLAs)

- **Security Clauses:** SLAs often include specific security requirements such as data protection measures, access controls, and incident response times.
- **Management:** Regularly review SLAs to ensure compliance. Use performance metrics to monitor adherence to SLA requirements and address any breaches promptly.

2. Non-Disclosure Agreements (NDAs)

- **Confidentiality Obligations:** NDAs require parties to protect confidential information and prevent unauthorized disclosure.
- **Management:** Ensure that employees and vendors understand their confidentiality obligations. Implement access controls and monitoring to prevent unauthorized access to confidential information.

3. Data Processing Agreements (DPAs)

- **Data Protection Requirements:** DPAs specify how personal data should be processed, including data protection measures and compliance with data protection regulations.
- **Management:** Ensure compliance with DPA requirements by implementing appropriate data protection controls and conducting regular audits.

4. Vendor Contracts

- **Security Obligations:** Vendor contracts often include security requirements such as compliance with industry standards, audit rights, and breach notification obligations.
- **Management:** Regularly assess vendors' compliance with contractual security requirements. Conduct security assessments and audits as stipulated in the contracts.

Best Practices for Effective Management

1. Standardization

- **Standard Templates:** Use standard contract templates that include comprehensive security clauses to ensure consistency across all contracts.
- **Best Practices:** Incorporate industry best practices and guidelines into contractual clauses to ensure robust security measures.

2. Clear Communication

- **Stakeholder Engagement:** Ensure clear communication of security requirements to all relevant stakeholders, including employees, vendors, and partners.
- **Regular Updates:** Provide regular updates and reminders about contractual obligations and any changes to security requirements.

3. Regular Audits and Assessments

- **Compliance Audits:** Conduct regular audits to verify compliance with contractual security requirements. Address any non-compliance issues promptly.
- **Risk Assessments:** Perform periodic risk assessments to identify and mitigate any new risks associated with contractual obligations.

4. Continuous Improvement

- **Feedback Mechanism:** Establish a feedback mechanism to gather input from stakeholders on the effectiveness of security measures and contractual clauses.
- **Policy Review:** Regularly review and update security policies and procedures to reflect changes in contractual requirements and emerging threats.

Conclusion

The Information Security Manager plays a vital role in managing contractual requirements related to information security. By identifying, analyzing, and addressing these requirements, the Information Security Manager ensures that the organization meets its security obligations, mitigates risks, and maintains trust with clients, vendors, and partners. Through effective collaboration, continuous monitoring, and regular training, organizations can achieve compliance with contractual requirements and enhance their overall security posture.

Effective Compliance Monitoring and Reporting Program

Now, let's explore the key components and best practices for establishing an effective compliance monitoring and reporting program. A robust program not only ensures adherence to laws and regulations but also supports the overall governance, risk management, and compliance (GRC) framework of an organization.

Key Components of a Compliance Monitoring and Reporting Program

1. Governance Structure:

- **Compliance Policies and Procedures:** Develop clear policies and procedures that outline compliance requirements and how they should be met.
- **Compliance Committee:** Establish a committee responsible for overseeing the compliance program, including representatives from key departments such as legal, IT, and operations.
- **Compliance Officer:** Designate a compliance officer or team to manage the program and serve as a point of contact for compliance issues.

2. Risk Assessment:

- **Identify Compliance Risks:** Conduct regular risk assessments to identify potential compliance risks related to laws, regulations, and internal policies.
- **Prioritize Risks:** Evaluate and prioritize risks based on their potential impact and likelihood, focusing on areas that pose the greatest threat to the organization.

3. Monitoring and Auditing:

- **Continuous Monitoring:** Implement continuous monitoring processes to detect compliance violations and risks in real-time.
- **Internal Audits:** Conduct regular internal audits to assess compliance with policies, procedures, and regulatory requirements. These audits should be systematic and comprehensive.

4. Training and Awareness:

- **Employee Training:** Provide ongoing training for employees to ensure they understand compliance requirements and their roles in maintaining compliance.
- **Awareness Programs:** Develop awareness programs to keep compliance top-of-mind and to communicate updates on regulations and policies.

5. Reporting and Communication:

- **Regular Reporting:** Establish regular reporting mechanisms to communicate compliance status to senior management, the board of directors, and other stakeholders.
- **Transparency:** Ensure transparency in reporting, providing clear and concise information on compliance activities, findings, and corrective actions.

Best Practices for Compliance Monitoring and Reporting

1. Use of Technology:

- **Automated Tools:** Utilize automated compliance management tools to streamline monitoring and reporting processes. These tools can track compliance activities, generate reports, and alert relevant personnel to potential issues.
- **Data Analytics:** Leverage data analytics to identify patterns and trends in compliance data, helping to predict and prevent potential compliance issues.

2. Regular Reviews and Updates:

- **Policy Reviews:** Regularly review and update compliance policies and procedures to reflect changes in laws, regulations, and business operations.
- **Audit Follow-Up:** Follow up on audit findings to ensure corrective actions are implemented and effective.

3. Stakeholder Engagement:

- **Involve Key Stakeholders:** Engage key stakeholders in the development and implementation of the compliance program to ensure buy-in and accountability.
- **Clear Communication:** Communicate compliance expectations clearly and consistently across the organization.

4. Documentation:

- **Maintain Records:** Keep detailed records of compliance activities, including training sessions, risk assessments, audits, and corrective actions. This documentation is crucial for demonstrating compliance during external audits and inspections.

Tools, Techniques, and Metrics

1. Tools:

- **Compliance Management Software:** Tools like GRC platforms (e.g., MetricStream, RSA Archer) and specialized compliance software (e.g., NAVEX Global, ComplySci) can automate compliance tracking, reporting, and risk management.
- **Audit Management Tools:** Software like ACL and AuditBoard can streamline internal audit processes, from planning to reporting.
- **Data Analytics Tools:** Tools such as Tableau, Power BI, and Splunk can analyze compliance data and generate actionable insights.

2. Techniques:

- **Risk-Based Monitoring:** Focus monitoring efforts on high-risk areas identified through risk assessments. This ensures resources are allocated effectively.
- **Key Risk Indicators (KRIs):** Develop KRIs to monitor potential compliance risks and trigger proactive responses.
- **Self-Assessments:** Encourage departments to conduct regular self-assessments to identify and address compliance gaps.

3. Metrics:

- **Compliance Rate:** The percentage of compliance with specific regulations or policies, indicating overall adherence levels.
- **Incident Response Time:** The average time taken to respond to and resolve compliance incidents, reflecting the efficiency of the compliance program.
- **Audit Findings:** The number and severity of findings from internal and external audits, providing insight into areas needing improvement.
- **Training Completion Rates:** The percentage of employees who have completed required compliance training, ensuring staff are knowledgeable about compliance requirements.
- **Breach and Incident Metrics:** The number of compliance breaches or incidents reported, highlighting trends and areas for improvement.

Example of a Reporting Structure

Executive Summary:

- High-level overview of compliance status, key metrics, and major findings.
- Key compliance risks and actions taken to mitigate them.
- Summary of training completion rates and major audit findings.

Detailed Analysis:

- In-depth analysis of compliance activities, including risk assessments, monitoring results, and audit outcomes.
- Detailed breakdown of compliance incidents and responses.
- Metrics on policy adherence and areas of non-compliance.

Dashboards:

- Visual representations of key metrics and trends, providing real-time insights.
- Interactive dashboards for different stakeholders, such as compliance officers, senior management, and department heads.

By implementing these components, best practices, tools, techniques, and metrics, organizations can establish an effective compliance monitoring and reporting program. This not only ensures adherence to regulations but also enhances overall governance, risk management, and security posture.

Risk-Based Compliance in Information Security Governance

Concept of Risk-Based Compliance

Risk-based compliance is an approach to managing regulatory and legal requirements by prioritizing compliance efforts based on the level of risk associated with specific requirements and information assets. Rather than treating all compliance obligations as equally critical, risk-based compliance focuses on identifying and addressing the most significant risks to the organization's information security and overall business objectives.

This approach integrates risk management principles into compliance processes, ensuring that resources are allocated efficiently to mitigate the highest risks while maintaining regulatory and legal adherence. By doing so, organizations can balance their compliance efforts with their risk management strategies, optimizing both.

Relevance to Information Security Governance

1. Aligning Compliance with Risk Management:

- **Integration:** Risk-based compliance aligns compliance activities with the organization's risk management framework. It ensures that compliance efforts support broader risk management goals and strategies.
- **Effectiveness:** This alignment increases the effectiveness of both compliance and risk management initiatives, as resources are directed towards mitigating the most critical risks.

2. Resource Optimization:

- **Efficiency:** By focusing on high-risk areas, organizations can allocate their resources more efficiently. This prevents the wastage of resources on low-risk areas while ensuring that high-risk areas receive the necessary attention and controls.
- **Cost Management:** Risk-based compliance helps in managing compliance costs by prioritizing investments in areas that pose the highest risk to the organization.

3. Enhanced Decision-Making:

- **Informed Choices:** Incorporating risk assessments into compliance efforts enables better decision-making. Organizations can make informed choices about where to implement controls and how to address compliance gaps.
- **Proactive Management:** This approach allows organizations to proactively manage compliance issues before they become significant problems, reducing the likelihood of regulatory penalties and reputational damage.

Prioritizing Compliance Efforts Based on Risk

To prioritize compliance efforts based on the level of risk, organizations can follow a structured process that involves identifying and assessing risks, categorizing information assets, and implementing appropriate controls. Here's how organizations can achieve this:

1. Identify and Assess Risks:

Risk Assessment:

- Conduct comprehensive risk assessments to identify potential threats and vulnerabilities. Evaluate the likelihood and impact of these risks on the organization's information assets.
- Use frameworks like ISO/IEC 27005 or NIST SP 800-30 for structured risk assessment methodologies.

Risk Categorization:

- Categorize risks based on their severity (e.g., high, medium, low). High-severity risks are those that could have significant impacts on the organization, such as regulatory fines, data breaches, or operational disruptions.

2. Categorize Information Assets:

Asset Inventory:

- Create and maintain an inventory of all information assets, including data, systems, applications, and processes. Each asset should be classified based on its criticality and sensitivity.
- Examples of asset categories include personal data, financial records, intellectual property, and critical infrastructure.

Risk Mapping:

- Map identified risks to the relevant information assets. This helps in understanding which assets are most at risk and require prioritized compliance efforts.

3. Prioritize Compliance Efforts:

High-Risk Areas:

- Focus compliance efforts on high-risk areas first. Implement robust controls and monitoring mechanisms for assets and processes that pose the highest risk to the organization.
- Examples: Strengthening data protection measures for sensitive personal data, enhancing access controls for critical financial systems, and ensuring robust incident response plans for business-critical applications.

Compliance Roadmap:

- Develop a compliance roadmap that outlines the prioritized actions to be taken. This roadmap should include timelines, resource allocation, and specific compliance goals for each high-risk area.
- Examples: Immediate implementation of encryption for high-risk data, regular audits for high-risk processes, and mandatory training for employees handling sensitive information.

4. Implement and Monitor Controls:

Control Implementation:

- Implement controls based on the prioritized compliance roadmap. Ensure that these controls are designed to mitigate the identified risks effectively.
- Examples: Deploying multi-factor authentication (MFA) for critical systems, conducting regular vulnerability assessments, and implementing data loss prevention (DLP) tools for sensitive data.

Continuous Monitoring:

- Establish continuous monitoring mechanisms to track the effectiveness of implemented controls. Use tools such as Security Information and Event Management (SIEM) systems, automated compliance checkers, and regular audits.
- Examples: Monitoring access logs for unauthorized access attempts, using SIEM to detect and respond to security incidents in real-time, and conducting quarterly compliance reviews.

Example Scenario: Prioritizing Compliance Efforts

Scenario: A financial services company needs to comply with several regulations, including GDPR for data protection and PCI DSS for payment card security. The company handles large volumes of personal and financial data, making compliance a complex task.

Process:

1. Identify and Assess Risks:

- Conduct risk assessments to identify threats such as data breaches, unauthorized access, and payment fraud.
- Assess the impact and likelihood of these risks. For example, a data breach involving customer financial information could result in significant financial and reputational damage.

2. Categorize Information Assets:

- Inventory and classify information assets, such as customer databases, payment processing systems, and internal financial records.
- Map identified risks to these assets. Customer databases and payment processing systems are categorized as high-risk due to the sensitive nature of the data they contain.

3. Prioritize Compliance Efforts:

- Prioritize compliance efforts on GDPR and PCI DSS requirements for high-risk assets.

- Develop a compliance roadmap with immediate actions such as encrypting customer data, implementing MFA for access to payment systems, and conducting regular security audits.

4. Implement and Monitor Controls:

- Implement necessary controls such as encryption, MFA, and regular audits.
- Use SIEM systems to continuously monitor compliance with GDPR and PCI DSS requirements. Regularly review and update controls based on monitoring results and changes in the threat landscape.

Conclusion

Risk-based compliance is essential for effective information security governance. By prioritizing compliance efforts based on the level of risk associated with specific requirements and assets, organizations can ensure that their resources are used efficiently and that high-risk areas receive the necessary attention. This approach not only helps in achieving compliance with legal, regulatory, and contractual obligations but also enhances the overall security posture of the organization. Through structured risk assessments, asset categorization, and continuous monitoring, organizations can proactively manage compliance and mitigate potential risks.

Maintaining Accurate and Up-to-Date Compliance Documentation

Now, let's discuss the importance of maintaining accurate and up-to-date documentation of an organization's compliance activities. Proper documentation is a cornerstone of a robust compliance program, providing a clear record of policies, procedures, and audit trails that demonstrate an organization's commitment to regulatory adherence and effective governance.

Importance of Compliance Documentation

1. Evidence of Compliance:

- Documentation serves as tangible proof that an organization adheres to laws, regulations, and internal policies. This is crucial during audits, inspections, and investigations by regulatory bodies.

2. Risk Management:

- Detailed records help identify potential compliance risks and facilitate proactive risk management. They provide insights into areas that require improvement and help prioritize compliance efforts.

3. Accountability and Transparency:

- Maintaining comprehensive documentation ensures transparency in compliance activities, promoting accountability among employees and management. It clarifies roles and responsibilities, ensuring everyone understands their compliance obligations.

4. Continuous Improvement:

- Documentation allows organizations to track compliance activities over time, assess their effectiveness, and implement necessary changes. This continuous feedback loop supports the ongoing improvement of the compliance program.

5. Legal Protection:

- In the event of legal disputes or regulatory scrutiny, accurate documentation can serve as a defense, demonstrating that the organization took reasonable steps to comply with relevant regulations.

Best Practices for Creating, Managing, and Retaining Compliance Documentation

1. Establish a Documentation Framework:

- **Define Clear Policies and Procedures:** Develop comprehensive policies and procedures that outline compliance requirements and the processes for meeting them. Ensure these documents are clear, accessible, and regularly updated.
- **Standardize Documentation Practices:** Use standardized templates and formats for all compliance documents to ensure consistency and ease of use.

2. Regular Updates and Reviews:

- **Periodic Reviews:** Regularly review and update compliance documentation to reflect changes in laws, regulations, and business practices. Establish a schedule for routine reviews and revisions.

- **Version Control:** Implement version control to track changes and maintain a history of document revisions. This helps in understanding the evolution of compliance practices and ensuring the use of the most current documents.

3. Centralized Document Management:

- **Document Repository:** Use a centralized document management system (DMS) to store and organize all compliance documentation. This system should be secure, easily accessible, and support search functionality.
- **Access Controls:** Implement access controls to ensure that only authorized personnel can view or edit compliance documents. This helps maintain the integrity and confidentiality of sensitive information.

4. Comprehensive Audit Trails:

- **Logging Changes:** Maintain detailed audit trails that log all changes to compliance documents, including who made the changes and when. This ensures accountability and provides a clear record of document history.
- **Tracking Compliance Activities:** Keep records of all compliance-related activities, such as risk assessments, training sessions, and audit findings. Ensure these records are detailed and easily traceable.

5. Employee Training and Awareness:

- **Regular Training:** Conduct regular training sessions to ensure employees understand the importance of compliance documentation and their roles in maintaining it. Training should cover how to create, manage, and use compliance documents effectively.
- **Awareness Programs:** Develop awareness programs to keep employees informed about updates to compliance policies and procedures. Use newsletters, emails, and meetings to disseminate this information.

6. Retention Policies:

- **Retention Schedules:** Establish and enforce retention schedules for compliance documents, specifying how long each type of document should be kept based on legal, regulatory, and business requirements.
- **Secure Disposal:** Implement secure disposal methods for outdated or no longer needed documents to prevent unauthorized access or data breaches.

Example of Effective Compliance Documentation Practices

Creating Policies and Procedures:

- Draft clear, detailed policies and procedures outlining compliance requirements for various regulations (e.g., GDPR, HIPAA). Ensure these documents are reviewed by legal and compliance experts before implementation.
- Example: A data protection policy detailing how personal data should be collected, stored, processed, and disposed of, including roles and responsibilities.

Managing Documents:

- Use a document management system like SharePoint or a specialized GRC tool to store and organize all compliance-related documents.
- Example: Implementing access controls in the DMS so that only compliance officers and department heads can edit compliance policies, while other employees have read-only access.

Maintaining Audit Trails:

- Ensure the DMS has audit trail capabilities to log all changes made to compliance documents.
- Example: An audit trail showing the history of a particular policy, including all edits and the individuals who made them, providing a clear record of policy evolution.

Training and Awareness:

- Conduct monthly training sessions on compliance topics relevant to the organization, ensuring all employees understand how to adhere to and document compliance requirements.
- Example: A training session on how to document compliance activities in daily operations, such as logging incident reports and maintaining records of data access requests.

By following these best practices, organizations can ensure their compliance documentation is accurate, up-to-date, and effectively supports their compliance program. This not only helps in demonstrating compliance but also enhances overall organizational governance and risk management.

Real-World Compliance Failures and Their Consequences

Understanding the ramifications of compliance failures through real-world examples can offer valuable insights for shaping an effective compliance strategy. Here are notable cases of compliance failures, their consequences, and lessons that can be learned from them.

Examples of Compliance Failures

1. Equifax Data Breach (2017)

Incident:

- Equifax, one of the largest credit reporting agencies, suffered a massive data breach that exposed the personal information of approximately 147 million people, including Social Security numbers, birth dates, addresses, and in some cases, driver's license numbers.

Consequences:

- **Financial Penalties:** Equifax agreed to a global settlement with the Federal Trade Commission (FTC), the Consumer Financial Protection Bureau (CFPB), and 50 U.S. states and territories. The settlement included up to $425 million in compensation for affected consumers.
- **Reputational Damage:** Equifax faced severe reputational damage, losing the trust of consumers and business partners. The breach highlighted significant flaws in their security practices and response mechanisms.
- **Operational Impact:** The company had to invest heavily in security upgrades and customer compensation efforts, diverting resources from other strategic initiatives.

Lessons Learned:

- **Patch Management:** Regular and prompt patch management is critical. The breach occurred due to a vulnerability in the Apache Struts web application framework that had not been patched, despite available fixes.
- **Incident Response:** A robust and well-practiced incident response plan is essential. Equifax's delayed detection and poor handling of the breach exacerbated the situation.
- **Transparency:** Timely and transparent communication with stakeholders is crucial during a security incident to maintain trust and manage the impact.

2. Target Data Breach (2013)

Incident:

- Target experienced a data breach during the holiday shopping season, compromising the credit and debit card information of approximately 40 million customers and the personal information of up to 70 million customers.

Consequences:

- **Financial Penalties:** Target agreed to pay $18.5 million in a multistate settlement and incurred costs exceeding $200 million related to the breach, including legal fees, settlements, and technology upgrades.
- **Reputational Damage:** The breach significantly damaged Target's reputation, resulting in a loss of customer trust and a temporary decline in sales.
- **Leadership Changes:** The breach led to the resignation of Target's CEO and CIO, highlighting the serious leadership accountability in such incidents.

Lessons Learned:

- **Third-Party Risk Management:** The breach was initiated through a third-party HVAC vendor. Organizations must ensure that third-party vendors adhere to robust security standards.
- **Network Segmentation:** Implementing proper network segmentation can limit the spread of breaches and protect critical assets.
- **Proactive Monitoring:** Continuous monitoring and threat detection are crucial for identifying and mitigating breaches in their early stages.

3. British Airways Data Breach (2018)

Incident:

- British Airways suffered a data breach that affected approximately 500,000 customers. Hackers were able to divert users from the British Airways website to a fraudulent site, stealing personal and financial details.

Consequences:

- **Financial Penalties:** The Information Commissioner's Office (ICO) in the UK fined British Airways £20 million (reduced from an initial £183 million proposal) for failing to protect customers' personal and financial information.
- **Reputational Damage:** The breach damaged British Airways' reputation, leading to a loss of customer trust and potential long-term impacts on customer loyalty.

Lessons Learned:

- **Website Security:** Ensuring the security of the website and online platforms is crucial. Implementing robust security measures and regular security assessments can prevent similar attacks.
- **Encryption:** Encrypting sensitive data can protect customer information even if it is intercepted during a breach.
- **Regulatory Compliance:** Adhering to regulations like GDPR is essential. The fine imposed by the ICO underscores the importance of regulatory compliance and robust data protection measures.

Informing Compliance Strategy

1. Regular Risk Assessments:

- Conduct frequent risk assessments to identify vulnerabilities and ensure that controls are in place to mitigate risks. This proactive approach can prevent breaches by addressing potential issues before they are exploited.

2. Patch Management:

- Implement a rigorous patch management process to ensure that all systems and applications are updated with the latest security patches. This helps protect against known vulnerabilities.

3. Third-Party Risk Management:

- Evaluate and monitor the security practices of third-party vendors. Ensure that they comply with your organization's security standards and have appropriate controls in place to protect shared information.

4. Incident Response Planning:

- Develop and regularly update an incident response plan. Conduct regular drills and simulations to ensure that the response team is prepared to handle real incidents effectively.

5. Continuous Monitoring:

- Implement continuous monitoring and threat detection systems to identify and respond to suspicious activities promptly. This includes using advanced security information and event management (SIEM) systems.

6. Data Encryption:

- Encrypt sensitive data both at rest and in transit to protect it from unauthorized access. Encryption adds an additional layer of security, making it difficult for attackers to use the data even if they gain access.

7. Employee Training and Awareness:

- Conduct regular training and awareness programs for employees to ensure they understand the importance of security practices and how to recognize and report potential threats.

8. Regulatory Compliance:

- Stay informed about regulatory changes and ensure that your compliance program is updated accordingly. Regular audits and assessments can help maintain compliance with relevant laws and standards.

Conclusion

Real-world examples of compliance failures, such as those experienced by Equifax, Target, and British Airways, highlight the severe consequences of inadequate security practices and the importance of a robust compliance strategy. Organizations can learn from these cases by implementing regular risk assessments, ensuring effective patch management, managing third-party risks, developing robust incident response plans, continuous monitoring, encrypting data, training employees, and maintaining regulatory compliance. By adopting these best practices, organizations can enhance their information security governance, protect their information assets, and avoid the significant financial, reputational, and operational impacts of compliance failures.

Internal and External Audits in Compliance

Now, let's look into the role of internal and external audits in assessing and validating an organization's compliance with legal, regulatory, and contractual requirements. Audits are essential tools for ensuring that an organization's compliance efforts are effective and aligned with applicable standards. Understanding the nuances between internal and external audits helps organizations prepare adequately and respond effectively to audit findings.

Role of Internal Audits

1. Assessment and Improvement:

- Internal audits are conducted by the organization's own audit department or internal auditors. They assess the effectiveness of internal controls, risk management processes, and compliance with policies and procedures.
- The primary goal is to identify areas for improvement and ensure that the organization's compliance program is operating effectively.

2. Proactive Risk Management:

- Internal audits help identify potential compliance issues before they become significant problems. This proactive approach enables organizations to address vulnerabilities and mitigate risks in a timely manner.
- Regular internal audits foster a culture of continuous improvement and accountability within the organization.

3. Preparation for External Audits:

- Internal audits prepare the organization for external audits by ensuring that all compliance requirements are being met and that documentation is up-to-date and accurate.
- They provide a trial run for identifying and rectifying issues that could be flagged during an external audit.

Role of External Audits

1. Independent Validation:

- External audits are conducted by independent third-party auditors. They provide an objective assessment of the organization's compliance with legal, regulatory, and contractual requirements.
- These audits validate the effectiveness of the internal controls and compliance programs from an external perspective, ensuring impartiality.

2. Regulatory and Legal Compliance:

- External audits often focus on compliance with specific regulations and standards, such as GDPR, HIPAA, and SOX. They are essential for demonstrating compliance to regulators, investors, and other stakeholders.
- Successful external audits can enhance the organization's credibility and reputation.

3. Certification and Accreditation:

- Many external audits are required for obtaining certifications or accreditations, such as ISO/IEC 27001 for information security management systems. These certifications can be critical for business operations and competitive advantage.

Key Differences Between Internal and External Audits

1. Purpose and Scope:

- **Internal Audits:** Focus on internal controls, risk management, and operational efficiency. They are broader in scope and can be tailored to the organization's specific needs.
- **External Audits:** Focus on compliance with external standards and regulations. They are narrower in scope but have a specific focus on legal and regulatory requirements.

2. Independence:

- **Internal Audits:** Conducted by internal staff who, although independent within the organization, are still part of the entity being audited.
- **External Audits:** Conducted by independent third parties, providing an unbiased assessment.

3. Frequency and Timing:

- **Internal Audits:** Conducted regularly throughout the year based on an internal audit schedule.
- **External Audits:** Conducted annually or at specific intervals, often dictated by regulatory or contractual requirements.

4. Reporting and Follow-Up:

- **Internal Audits:** Reports are typically used for internal improvements and are shared with management and the audit committee.
- **External Audits:** Reports are often required to be submitted to regulatory bodies, shareholders, or other external stakeholders.

Preparing for and Responding to Audit Findings

Preparation for Audits:

1. Documentation:

- Ensure that all compliance documentation, including policies, procedures, and records, is up-to-date and readily accessible.
- Maintain detailed records of all compliance activities, including training sessions, risk assessments, and incident reports.

2. Internal Controls:

- Review and test internal controls to ensure they are functioning as intended. Address any weaknesses identified during internal audits.
- Implement a robust internal audit program to regularly assess compliance and readiness for external audits.

3. Employee Training:

- Conduct regular training sessions to ensure employees understand compliance requirements and their roles in the audit process.
- Prepare staff for potential interactions with external auditors, including interview techniques and information provision.

Responding to Audit Findings:

1. Action Plans:

- Develop and implement action plans to address any findings or recommendations from the audit. Assign responsibilities and set deadlines for corrective actions.
- Ensure that action plans are realistic, achievable, and aligned with the organization's resources and capabilities.

2. Continuous Monitoring:

- Establish continuous monitoring mechanisms to track the progress of corrective actions and ensure that issues are addressed promptly.
- Use technology solutions to automate monitoring and reporting processes where possible.

3. Communication:

- Communicate audit findings and action plans to all relevant stakeholders, including senior management, the board of directors, and regulatory bodies as required.
- Maintain transparency in addressing audit findings to build trust and demonstrate the organization's commitment to compliance.

4. Follow-Up Audits:

- Conduct follow-up audits to verify that corrective actions have been implemented effectively and that compliance gaps have been closed.
- Document the results of follow-up audits and incorporate them into ongoing compliance and risk management efforts.

By understanding the roles of internal and external audits, organizations can better prepare for these assessments and respond effectively to audit findings. This ensures a strong compliance posture, reduces risks, and enhances overall organizational governance and accountability.

Importance of Employee Training and Awareness in Promoting a Culture of Compliance

Employee training and awareness are critical components in promoting a culture of compliance within an organization. A well-informed workforce is better equipped to adhere to regulatory requirements, follow company policies, and respond effectively to potential security threats. Here's why training and awareness are essential:

1. Enhancing Knowledge and Skills:

- **Awareness of Policies:** Employees need to be aware of the organization's compliance policies and procedures to follow them correctly.
- **Skill Development:** Training provides employees with the necessary skills to handle compliance-related tasks, recognize potential risks, and respond appropriately.

2. Reducing Risk:

- **Preventing Violations:** Well-informed employees are less likely to engage in activities that violate compliance policies, reducing the risk of regulatory penalties.
- **Mitigating Threats:** Awareness programs help employees recognize and report potential security threats, thereby mitigating risks.

3. Promoting Accountability:

- **Individual Responsibility:** Training fosters a sense of personal responsibility for compliance, ensuring that all employees understand their role in maintaining the organization's compliance posture.
- **Organizational Culture:** A culture of compliance is built when all employees, from executives to front-line workers, are committed to following regulations and policies.

4. Enhancing Incident Response:

- **Timely Response:** Trained employees can respond more quickly and effectively to incidents, minimizing the impact of security breaches or compliance violations.
- **Improved Reporting:** Awareness programs encourage employees to report incidents promptly, ensuring that issues are addressed swiftly.

Strategies for Designing and Delivering Compliance-Related Training

To effectively design and deliver compliance-related training, it is essential to tailor the content and delivery methods to different stakeholder groups: executives, managers, and employees. Here are some strategies for each group:

1. Executives

Objective:

- Ensure that executives understand the strategic importance of compliance, their role in governance, and the business implications of non-compliance.

Strategies:

- **Customized Content:** Develop training that focuses on the strategic aspects of compliance, including risk management, regulatory requirements, and the impact on business objectives.
- **Executive Workshops:** Conduct high-level workshops and briefings that highlight the latest compliance trends, regulatory changes, and the organization's compliance posture.
- **Case Studies:** Use real-world case studies to illustrate the consequences of compliance failures and the importance of proactive governance.
- **Performance Metrics:** Provide dashboards and key performance indicators (KPIs) that demonstrate the effectiveness of compliance initiatives and support data-driven decision-making.

2. Managers

Objective:

- Equip managers with the knowledge to implement and enforce compliance policies within their teams, understand their role in incident response, and manage compliance-related risks.

Strategies:

- **Role-Specific Training:** Develop role-specific training modules that address the unique compliance responsibilities of managers, such as policy enforcement, risk assessment, and incident management.
- **Interactive Workshops:** Conduct interactive workshops and scenario-based exercises that allow managers to practice handling compliance issues and making informed decisions.
- **Practical Guides:** Provide practical guides and checklists to help managers implement compliance policies and procedures within their departments.
- **Regular Updates:** Ensure managers receive regular updates on new compliance policies, emerging risks, and best practices.

3. Employees

Objective:

- Raise awareness among employees about compliance policies, common threats, and best practices to ensure they can recognize and respond to compliance-related issues.

Strategies:

- **Onboarding Training:** Incorporate compliance training into the onboarding process for new employees to ensure they understand the organization's compliance expectations from day one.
- **E-Learning Modules:** Develop engaging e-learning modules that cover essential topics such as data protection, anti-bribery, and harassment prevention. These modules should include quizzes and interactive elements to reinforce learning.
- **Regular Awareness Campaigns:** Launch regular awareness campaigns using emails, posters, and newsletters to remind employees of key compliance practices and updates.
- **Simulations and Drills:** Conduct periodic simulations and drills to test employees' ability to recognize and respond to compliance-related issues, such as phishing attacks or data breaches.

Best Practices for Effective Compliance Training and Awareness Programs

1. Tailored Content:

- Ensure that training content is tailored to the specific needs, roles, and responsibilities of different stakeholder groups. This helps make the training relevant and engaging.

2. Interactive and Engaging Formats:

- Use interactive formats such as simulations, role-playing, and gamification to make training sessions engaging and memorable. Encourage participation and provide opportunities for hands-on practice.

3. Regular and Ongoing Training:

- Compliance training should not be a one-time event. Implement regular training sessions and refreshers to keep employees updated on the latest regulations, policies, and best practices.

4. Measurement and Feedback:

- Measure the effectiveness of training programs through assessments, surveys, and feedback. Use this data to identify areas for improvement and adjust training content accordingly.

5. Leadership Involvement:

- Encourage active involvement and support from leadership to demonstrate the importance of compliance. Leadership endorsement can significantly enhance the credibility and impact of training programs.

6. Real-World Relevance:

- Use real-world examples and scenarios to illustrate the relevance of compliance policies and practices. This helps employees understand the practical implications of compliance measures.

7. Accessible Resources:

- Provide easy access to training materials, policy documents, and additional resources through the organization's intranet or learning management system (LMS). Ensure employees know where to find help and support.

Example Compliance Training Programs

Executive Training Program:

- **Content:** Strategic importance of compliance, risk management, regulatory requirements, and the impact on business objectives.
- **Format:** High-level briefings, workshops, case studies, and performance dashboards.
- **Frequency:** Quarterly briefings with periodic workshops.

Manager Training Program:

- **Content:** Policy implementation, risk assessment, incident response, and enforcement responsibilities.
- **Format:** Role-specific modules, interactive workshops, scenario-based exercises, and practical guides.
- **Frequency:** Initial training with semi-annual refreshers and updates.

Employee Training Program:

- **Content:** Basic compliance principles, common threats (e.g., phishing, social engineering), policy awareness, and best practices.
- **Format:** Onboarding sessions, e-learning modules, regular awareness campaigns, and simulations.
- **Frequency:** Initial training during onboarding with monthly refreshers and annual comprehensive sessions.

Conclusion

Employee training and awareness are vital to promoting a culture of compliance within an organization. By designing and delivering targeted training programs to different stakeholder groups—executives, managers, and employees—organizations can ensure that everyone understands their roles and responsibilities in maintaining compliance. Tailored content, engaging formats, regular updates, and active leadership involvement are key strategies for building a compliance-conscious culture and maintaining a robust compliance posture.

Integration of Compliance with Information Security Governance Functions

Now, let's look into the relationship between compliance and other key information security governance functions such as risk management and incident response. Ensuring that these functions are integrated and aligned is essential for maintaining a robust and cohesive information security program.

Relationship Between Compliance, Risk Management, and Incident Response

1. Compliance and Risk Management:

- **Interdependence:** Compliance and risk management are closely interrelated. Compliance involves adhering to laws, regulations, and standards, many of which are designed to mitigate risks. Conversely, effective risk management practices help ensure compliance by identifying and addressing potential regulatory and legal risks.
- **Risk-Based Compliance:** A risk-based approach to compliance prioritizes resources and efforts towards the highest risk areas, ensuring that the most critical compliance issues are addressed first. This approach helps organizations manage their risk exposure while meeting regulatory requirements.

2. Compliance and Incident Response:

- **Regulatory Requirements:** Many regulations mandate specific incident response procedures, including the reporting of security breaches within a specified timeframe. Compliance efforts must therefore include the development and maintenance of an incident response plan that meets these regulatory requirements.
- **Documentation and Reporting:** Effective incident response involves documenting incidents thoroughly and reporting them to relevant authorities as required by compliance standards. This ensures that the organization can demonstrate its adherence to regulatory requirements during an incident.

3. Risk Management and Incident Response:

- **Proactive vs. Reactive:** Risk management is a proactive function, identifying and mitigating potential risks before they materialize. Incident response, on the other hand, is reactive, dealing with risks that have already materialized. Both functions must work together to ensure a comprehensive security strategy.

- **Feedback Loop:** Incident response activities provide valuable data and insights that inform risk management practices. Analyzing incidents helps identify vulnerabilities and threats, which can then be addressed through risk management measures.

Ensuring Integration and Alignment

1. Unified Governance Framework:

- **Holistic Approach:** Develop a unified governance framework that incorporates compliance, risk management, and incident response. This framework should outline how each function interacts with and supports the others.
- **Integrated Policies and Procedures:** Ensure that policies and procedures for compliance, risk management, and incident response are aligned and integrated. For example, risk management policies should include compliance considerations, and incident response procedures should address regulatory reporting requirements.

2. Cross-Functional Collaboration:

- **Interdepartmental Teams:** Establish cross-functional teams that include representatives from compliance, risk management, IT, legal, and other relevant departments. These teams can work together to develop and implement integrated strategies.
- **Regular Meetings:** Hold regular meetings between compliance, risk management, and incident response teams to discuss ongoing activities, share insights, and coordinate efforts. This promotes a collaborative approach and ensures that all functions are aligned.

3. Centralized Documentation and Reporting:

- **Unified Reporting System:** Implement a centralized system for documenting and reporting compliance activities, risk assessments, and incident responses. This ensures consistency and provides a single source of truth for all related information.
- **Shared Metrics and Dashboards:** Develop shared metrics and dashboards that provide a holistic view of compliance, risk management, and incident response activities. This facilitates monitoring and decision-making at the organizational level.

4. Training and Awareness:

- **Integrated Training Programs:** Develop training programs that cover compliance, risk management, and incident response together. This helps employees understand how these functions are interconnected and their roles in each.
- **Ongoing Awareness:** Promote ongoing awareness of the importance of integrated governance through newsletters, workshops, and other communication channels. Highlight examples of how effective integration improves overall security and compliance.

5. Continuous Improvement:

- **Feedback Mechanisms:** Establish feedback mechanisms to continuously improve the integration of compliance, risk management, and incident response. For example, conduct post-incident reviews to assess how well compliance and risk management processes supported the incident response.
- **Regular Audits and Assessments:** Conduct regular internal audits and assessments that evaluate the effectiveness of the integrated governance framework. Use the findings to make necessary adjustments and improvements.

Practical Example

Scenario: Implementing an Integrated Security Governance Framework in a Healthcare Organization

Unified Governance Framework:

- The healthcare organization develops a comprehensive governance framework that aligns compliance (e.g., HIPAA), risk management, and incident response. Policies and procedures are created to ensure that patient data protection measures meet regulatory standards and mitigate identified risks.

Cross-Functional Collaboration:

- A cross-functional team is formed, including representatives from compliance, IT security, risk management, and patient services. This team meets monthly to discuss emerging threats, compliance updates, and recent incidents.

Centralized Documentation and Reporting:

- The organization uses a centralized compliance management system that tracks all compliance activities, risk assessments, and incident reports. This system allows for seamless reporting and ensures that all relevant data is easily accessible for audits and reviews.

Training and Awareness:

- Regular training sessions are conducted, covering HIPAA compliance, risk management practices, and incident response procedures. Employees across the organization understand their roles in maintaining compliance and managing risks.

Continuous Improvement:

- After a data breach incident, a post-incident review is conducted. The review highlights gaps in the incident response plan and provides recommendations for improving both the response process and compliance measures. These findings are used to update the governance framework and enhance overall security practices.

By following these practices, organizations can ensure that their compliance efforts are not isolated but are effectively integrated and aligned with risk management and incident response functions. This integrated approach not only enhances overall information security but also ensures a cohesive and efficient response to emerging threats and regulatory changes.

Case Study: Successful Implementation of a Comprehensive Information Security Governance Framework at TechCorp Inc.

Organization Overview: TechCorp Inc. is a global technology company specializing in software development and IT services. With over 10,000 employees and operations in multiple countries, TechCorp handles vast amounts of sensitive data, including intellectual property, customer information, and financial records.

Key Components of the Information Security Governance Framework

1. Leadership and Oversight

Executive Support:

- TechCorp's executive leadership, including the CEO and Board of Directors, provided strong support for the information security program. A dedicated Chief Information Security Officer (CISO) was appointed to lead the initiative.

Governance Committee:

- An Information Security Governance Committee was established, comprising senior executives, IT leaders, legal advisors, and representatives from key business units. This committee was responsible for overseeing the development and implementation of the security strategy.

2. Risk Management

Risk Assessment Framework:

- TechCorp adopted the ISO/IEC 27005 risk management framework to identify, assess, and prioritize risks. Regular risk assessments were conducted to evaluate potential threats and vulnerabilities.

Risk Treatment Plans:

- Based on the assessments, risk treatment plans were developed to mitigate identified risks. These plans included technical controls, policy updates, and employee training programs.

3. Policies and Procedures

Comprehensive Policy Suite:

- TechCorp developed a comprehensive suite of information security policies, including Data Protection, Access Control, Incident Response, and Acceptable Use Policies. These policies were aligned with industry standards such as ISO/IEC 27001 and NIST CSF.

Standard Operating Procedures (SOPs):

- Detailed SOPs were created to provide step-by-step instructions for implementing security policies. These procedures covered areas such as data encryption, secure software development, and incident reporting.

4. Compliance and Legal

Regulatory Compliance:

- TechCorp ensured compliance with relevant regulations, including GDPR, HIPAA, and SOX. Regular audits and assessments were conducted to verify compliance and identify areas for improvement.

Contractual Obligations:

- Security requirements were integrated into contracts with vendors and partners. Non-disclosure agreements (NDAs) and service level agreements (SLAs) included specific security clauses to protect sensitive information.

5. Training and Awareness

Employee Training Programs:

- Comprehensive training programs were implemented for all employees. These programs included onboarding training, regular refresher courses, and specialized training for high-risk roles.

Awareness Campaigns:

- Ongoing awareness campaigns were launched to keep security top-of-mind. This included monthly newsletters, security bulletins, and simulated phishing exercises.

6. Monitoring and Incident Management

Continuous Monitoring:

- TechCorp deployed advanced monitoring tools such as Security Information and Event Management (SIEM) systems to continuously monitor network activity and detect potential security incidents.

Incident Response Team:

- A dedicated Incident Response Team (IRT) was established to manage security incidents. The IRT followed a predefined incident response plan, which included steps for identification, containment, eradication, and recovery.

Challenges Faced

1. Cultural Resistance:

- Initially, there was resistance from employees who perceived security measures as cumbersome and disruptive to their workflow.

2. Resource Allocation:

- Securing adequate resources and budget for the implementation of the security framework was challenging, particularly in convincing stakeholders of the long-term benefits.

3. Maintaining Compliance:

- Keeping up with evolving regulatory requirements and ensuring continuous compliance across multiple jurisdictions was complex and resource-intensive.

Benefits Realized

1. Enhanced Security Posture:

- TechCorp significantly improved its security posture, reducing the risk of data breaches and other security incidents. The implementation of robust security controls and continuous monitoring helped in early detection and mitigation of threats.

2. Regulatory Compliance:

- The company achieved compliance with key regulations, avoiding potential fines and legal penalties. Regular audits and assessments ensured ongoing compliance and readiness for regulatory changes.

3. Increased Employee Awareness:

- Employee awareness and engagement in security practices improved markedly. The training and awareness programs fostered a culture of security, making employees active participants in protecting the organization's assets.

4. Business Continuity:

- The implementation of a comprehensive incident response plan ensured that TechCorp could quickly and effectively respond to security incidents, minimizing downtime and operational disruption.

Lessons Learned

1. Executive Support is Crucial:

- Strong support from executive leadership is essential for the success of an information security governance program. It helps in securing necessary resources and driving cultural change across the organization.

2. Continuous Improvement:

- Information security is an ongoing process. Regular risk assessments, audits, and updates to policies and procedures are necessary to adapt to evolving threats and regulatory requirements.

3. Employee Engagement:

- Engaging employees at all levels through training and awareness programs is vital. When employees understand the importance of security and their role in maintaining it, they are more likely to comply with policies and report suspicious activities.

4. Integrated Approach:

- An integrated approach that aligns security with business objectives and incorporates risk management, compliance, and incident response ensures a holistic and effective security strategy.

5. Vendor and Partner Management:

- Ensuring that vendors and partners comply with the organization's security requirements is critical. This can be achieved through thorough contract management and regular security assessments of third parties.

Applying Lessons to Other Organizations

1. Secure Executive Buy-In:

- Gain the support of executive leadership by clearly articulating the business benefits of a robust security governance framework. Present case studies and potential risk scenarios to highlight the importance of investment in security.

2. Establish Clear Governance Structures:

- Create a governance committee that includes representatives from various departments to oversee the development and implementation of security strategies. Ensure that this committee has the authority to enforce policies and allocate resources.

3. Focus on Risk Management:

- Implement a structured risk management framework to identify, assess, and prioritize risks. Regularly update risk assessments and treatment plans to address new threats and vulnerabilities.

4. Develop Comprehensive Policies:

- Create a suite of comprehensive security policies and standard operating procedures. Ensure that these documents are regularly reviewed and updated to reflect changes in the threat landscape and regulatory requirements.

5. Prioritize Training and Awareness:

- Invest in regular training and awareness programs for all employees. Use interactive and engaging formats to keep training relevant and memorable. Regularly test employee awareness through simulated exercises.

6. Implement Advanced Monitoring and Incident Response:

- Deploy advanced monitoring tools to continuously track network activity and detect potential threats. Develop a robust incident response plan and regularly test it through drills and simulations.

By applying these lessons, other organizations can build a resilient information security governance framework that not only protects their information assets but also supports their business objectives and compliance requirements.

Real-World Examples of Information Security Governance Across Industries

Now, let's explore several real-world examples and scenarios illustrating the application of information security governance principles and best practices across different industries and organizational contexts. These examples will help readers better understand and relate to the concepts by seeing how they are implemented in practice.

Example 1: Financial Services Industry

Scenario: Implementing Strong Data Protection Measures

Context: A large financial institution must comply with regulations such as the Gramm-Leach-Bliley Act (GLBA) and the Sarbanes-Oxley Act (SOX). These regulations require stringent measures to protect customer financial information and ensure the integrity of financial reporting.

Governance Principles and Best Practices:

- **Risk Management:** The institution conducts regular risk assessments to identify potential threats to customer data and financial reporting systems. These assessments focus on external threats such as cyber-attacks and internal risks such as employee negligence.
- **Compliance Monitoring:** Automated tools are used to monitor compliance with GLBA and SOX requirements. This includes monitoring access to sensitive data, ensuring encryption standards are met, and verifying that internal controls are in place.
- **Incident Response:** A robust incident response plan is developed, including detailed procedures for reporting breaches to regulatory bodies and affected customers. Regular drills and simulations are conducted to ensure preparedness.
- **Employee Training:** Ongoing training programs are implemented to educate employees on data protection practices and regulatory requirements. This includes phishing awareness training and secure handling of customer information.

Impact: By applying these governance principles, the financial institution enhances its security posture, reduces the risk of data breaches, and ensures compliance with regulatory requirements. This not only protects customer data but also maintains the institution's reputation and trust.

Example 2: Healthcare Industry

Scenario: Ensuring HIPAA Compliance

Context: A mid-sized healthcare provider must comply with the Health Insurance Portability and Accountability Act (HIPAA) to protect patient health information (PHI). Failure to comply can result in significant fines and loss of patient trust.

Governance Principles and Best Practices:

- **Governance Framework:** The healthcare provider establishes a governance framework that includes HIPAA-specific policies and procedures. This framework outlines roles and responsibilities for protecting PHI.
- **Risk-Based Approach:** Regular risk assessments are conducted to identify vulnerabilities in the handling and storage of PHI. This includes evaluating electronic health record (EHR) systems and physical security measures.
- **Audit and Monitoring:** Continuous monitoring systems are implemented to track access to PHI and detect unauthorized access. Regular internal audits are conducted to ensure compliance with HIPAA requirements.
- **Incident Response:** A detailed incident response plan is developed, specifying actions to be taken in the event of a data breach. This includes notifying affected patients and reporting the breach to the Department of Health and Human Services (HHS) within the required timeframe.
- **Training and Awareness:** Comprehensive training programs are provided to all staff members, covering HIPAA regulations, privacy practices, and the importance of safeguarding PHI. This includes specialized training for employees with access to sensitive patient information.

Impact: The healthcare provider's application of these governance principles ensures the protection of patient data, compliance with HIPAA, and the avoidance of costly penalties. This fosters patient trust and demonstrates the provider's commitment to safeguarding sensitive health information.

Example 3: Retail Industry

Scenario: Securing Payment Card Information

Context: A large retail chain must comply with the Payment Card Industry Data Security Standard (PCI DSS) to protect customers' payment card information. This includes ensuring secure transactions and safeguarding stored cardholder data.

Governance Principles and Best Practices:

- **Compliance Framework:** The retail chain establishes a compliance framework that aligns with PCI DSS requirements. This includes policies for data encryption, secure network architecture, and access controls.
- **Risk Assessment:** Regular risk assessments are conducted to identify and mitigate risks related to payment card data. This includes evaluating point-of-sale (POS) systems, payment gateways, and data storage practices.
- **Security Controls:** Robust security controls are implemented, such as encryption of payment card data, tokenization, and regular vulnerability scanning of payment systems. Multi-factor authentication (MFA) is enforced for accessing sensitive systems.
- **Incident Response:** A comprehensive incident response plan is developed, detailing procedures for addressing payment card data breaches. This includes steps for containing the breach, notifying affected customers, and coordinating with payment card companies and law enforcement.
- **Training and Awareness:** Employees are trained on PCI DSS requirements and secure handling of payment card information. This includes awareness of social engineering attacks and secure processing of transactions.

Impact: By adhering to these governance principles, the retail chain ensures the security of payment card information, maintains PCI DSS compliance, and minimizes the risk of data breaches. This not only protects customers but also avoids financial penalties and damage to the brand's reputation.

Example 4: Technology Industry

Scenario: Protecting Intellectual Property (IP)

Context: A technology company must protect its intellectual property, including software code, proprietary algorithms, and product designs. This is crucial for maintaining competitive advantage and complying with IP laws.

Governance Principles and Best Practices:

- **IP Protection Policy:** The company develops a comprehensive policy for protecting intellectual property. This includes guidelines for classifying, handling, and storing IP-related information.
- **Access Controls:** Strict access controls are implemented to ensure that only authorized personnel can access sensitive IP. This includes role-based access controls (RBAC) and encryption of IP data.
- **Risk Management:** Regular risk assessments are conducted to identify threats to IP, such as insider threats, cyber-attacks, and industrial espionage. Mitigation strategies are developed to address these risks.
- **Incident Response:** An incident response plan is created to address IP theft or breaches. This includes procedures for investigating incidents, containing the impact, and notifying relevant authorities.
- **Employee Training:** Training programs are conducted to educate employees on the importance of protecting IP and following security protocols. This includes training on identifying and reporting suspicious activities.

Impact: The technology company's implementation of these governance principles ensures the protection of its intellectual property, compliance with IP laws, and maintenance of its competitive edge. This also fosters innovation and secures valuable assets.

Learning from Real-World Examples

These real-world examples help readers understand and relate to information security governance concepts by illustrating practical applications across different industries. They demonstrate how governance principles and best practices can be tailored to meet specific regulatory requirements and organizational contexts. By studying these examples, readers can gain insights into:

- **Tailoring Governance to Industry Needs:** Understanding how governance practices vary across industries helps readers appreciate the importance of customizing approaches to fit specific regulatory and business environments.
- **Practical Application:** Seeing real-world scenarios provides concrete illustrations of how theoretical concepts are put into practice, making the principles more tangible and easier to grasp.
- **Comprehensive Approach:** Examples highlight the interconnected nature of compliance, risk management, and incident response, emphasizing the need for an integrated and holistic approach to information security governance.
- **Lessons Learned:** Analyzing the successes and challenges faced by organizations in different sectors offers valuable lessons and best practices that readers can apply in their own contexts.

By connecting theory to practice, these examples make information security governance more relatable and actionable for readers, enhancing their understanding and ability to implement effective governance strategies.

Practice Questions and Quizzes for Information Security Governance

To test readers' knowledge and understanding of key information security governance topics, it is important to create a variety of question types that address different aspects of the material. Below are practice questions and quizzes covering topics such as risk management, policy development, and compliance. Additionally, strategies for creating effective and engaging assessment materials are provided.

Practice Questions

Risk Management

Question 1: What is the primary goal of risk management in information security governance?
A) To eliminate all risks
B) To identify, assess, and mitigate risks to acceptable levels
C) To transfer all risks to third parties
D) To comply with all regulatory requirements
Answer: B

Question 2: Which of the following is a commonly used risk assessment framework?
A) COBIT
B) ISO/IEC 27005
C) ITIL
D) NIST CSF
Answer: B

Question 3: Match the following risk treatment options with their descriptions:

1. Avoidance
2. Mitigation
3. Transfer
4. Acceptance

A) Implementing measures to reduce the risk
B) Choosing to accept the risk without taking action
C) Avoiding activities that introduce risk
D) Sharing the risk with a third party (e.g., through insurance)
Answers: 1-C, 2-A, 3-D, 4-B

Policy Development

Question 4: What is the main purpose of an information security policy?
A) To provide detailed technical procedures for IT staff
B) To outline the organization's guiding principles and rules for information security
C) To describe the organization's products and services
D) To list the penalties for security violations
Answer: B

Question 5: Which of the following should be included in an information security policy?

A) Scope and objectives
B) Roles and responsibilities
C) Compliance requirements
D) All of the above
Answer: D
Question 6: True or False: Information security policies should be written in highly technical language to ensure precision.
Answer: False
Compliance
Question 7: Which regulation primarily focuses on protecting the personal data of EU citizens?
A) HIPAA
B) GDPR
C) SOX
D) PCI DSS
Answer: B
Question 8: What are the potential consequences of non-compliance with information security regulations?
A) Financial penalties
B) Reputational damage
C) Legal action
D) All of the above
Answer: D
Question 9: Which document typically outlines the security requirements between an organization and its vendors?
A) Service Level Agreement (SLA)
B) Non-Disclosure Agreement (NDA)
C) Data Processing Agreement (DPA)
D) All of the above
Answer: D
Quizzes
Quiz 1: Risk Management

1. **Multiple Choice:** What is the purpose of a Business Impact Analysis (BIA) in risk management?

A) To identify and evaluate potential risks
B) To assess the financial impact of security incidents
C) To prioritize business processes based on their criticality
D) To develop risk mitigation strategies
Answer: C

2. **True or False:** Risk assessments should only be conducted annually.

Answer: False

3. **Short Answer:** Describe the steps involved in a typical risk assessment process.

Answer: The steps typically include identifying assets, identifying threats and vulnerabilities, assessing the likelihood and impact of risks, prioritizing risks, and developing mitigation strategies.
Quiz 2: Policy Development

1. **Multiple Choice:** What is the first step in developing an information security policy?

A) Drafting the policy document
B) Identifying the need for the policy
C) Obtaining executive approval
D) Implementing the policy
Answer: B

2. **True or False:** Policies should be reviewed and updated only when a security incident occurs.

Answer: False

3. **Fill in the Blanks:** Information security policies should be ________, ensuring they are easily understood by all employees and ________ to address specific organizational needs.

Answer: clear; tailored

Quiz 3: Compliance

1. **Multiple Choice:** Which of the following frameworks is specifically designed to guide organizations in protecting payment card information?

A) ISO/IEC 27001
B) HIPAA
C) PCI DSS
D) COBIT

Answer: C

2. **True or False:** Compliance with GDPR only applies to organizations based in the EU.

Answer: False

3. **Short Answer:** List three key actions an organization can take to ensure compliance with data protection regulations.

Answer: Actions include conducting regular data protection impact assessments, implementing strong access controls, and providing ongoing training and awareness programs for employees.

Strategies for Creating Effective and Engaging Assessment Materials

1. Diverse Question Types:

- Use a variety of question types such as multiple-choice, true/false, short answer, fill-in-the-blank, and matching questions. This approach keeps assessments engaging and tests different levels of understanding.

2. Real-World Scenarios:

- Incorporate real-world scenarios and case studies into the questions. This helps learners apply theoretical knowledge to practical situations and enhances critical thinking skills.

3. Interactive Elements:

- Use interactive elements such as drag-and-drop activities, simulations, and gamified quizzes. These elements make assessments more engaging and can improve retention of information.

4. Immediate Feedback:

- Provide immediate feedback on answers. This helps learners understand their mistakes and reinforces correct information, promoting better learning outcomes.

5. Incremental Difficulty:

- Design questions with varying levels of difficulty, starting with basic concepts and progressing to more complex topics. This ensures that assessments are challenging yet achievable for all learners.

6. Clear Instructions:

- Provide clear and concise instructions for each question or activity. Ambiguous instructions can confuse learners and skew assessment results.

7. Regular Assessments:

- Implement regular assessments throughout the training program. Frequent quizzes and practice questions help reinforce learning and identify areas where learners may need additional support.

8. Real-Time Analytics:

- Use learning management systems (LMS) to track and analyze assessment results in real-time. This allows instructors to identify trends, address common misconceptions, and tailor future training sessions accordingly.

By employing these strategies, organizations can create effective and engaging assessment materials that reinforce learning, identify areas for improvement, and ensure that all stakeholders have a strong understanding of key information security governance concepts.

Future of Information Security Governance: Emerging Trends, Technologies, and Challenges

Now, let's explore the future of information security governance, focusing on the emerging trends, technologies, and challenges that organizations need to be aware of. We'll also discuss how Information Security Managers can stay informed and adapt their governance approaches to meet evolving needs.

Emerging Trends in Information Security Governance

1. **Increased Focus on Privacy Regulations:**
   - **Trend:** Privacy regulations like the GDPR and CCPA have set high standards for data protection, and more regions are adopting similar laws.
   - **Implication:** Organizations need to stay updated on global privacy laws and integrate compliance with these regulations into their governance frameworks.
2. **Zero Trust Architecture:**
   - **Trend:** Zero Trust security models, which assume that threats could be inside or outside the network, are becoming more prevalent.
   - **Implication:** Implementing Zero Trust principles requires continuous verification of user identities, strict access controls, and comprehensive monitoring of network activity.
3. **AI and Machine Learning in Security:**
   - **Trend:** Artificial intelligence (AI) and machine learning (ML) are increasingly used to detect and respond to threats in real-time.
   - **Implication:** Leveraging AI and ML can enhance threat detection, but it also requires careful management to ensure these technologies are used ethically and effectively.
4. **Cloud Security and Multi-Cloud Environments:**
   - **Trend:** The shift to cloud computing and multi-cloud environments is accelerating, posing new security challenges.
   - **Implication:** Organizations need to adopt cloud-specific security strategies and ensure that their governance policies cover data protection across different cloud platforms.
5. **Regulatory Technology (RegTech):**
   - **Trend:** The use of RegTech solutions to automate compliance processes and enhance regulatory monitoring is growing.
   - **Implication:** Adopting RegTech can streamline compliance efforts, reduce costs, and improve accuracy in regulatory reporting.

Emerging Technologies

1. **Blockchain Technology:**
   - **Application:** Blockchain can enhance data integrity and security through its decentralized and immutable ledger.
   - **Implication:** Organizations can use blockchain for secure transactions, identity management, and supply chain security, requiring updates to governance policies to incorporate these technologies.
2. **Quantum Computing:**
   - **Application:** Quantum computing promises significant advancements in processing power, but it also poses risks to current encryption methods.
   - **Implication:** Information Security Managers must stay informed about quantum-resistant cryptographic algorithms and prepare for future transitions.
3. **Internet of Things (IoT) Security:**
   - **Application:** The proliferation of IoT devices introduces new vulnerabilities and expands the attack surface.
   - **Implication:** Governance frameworks need to include IoT-specific security measures, such as device authentication, encryption, and regular firmware updates.

Key Challenges

1. **Evolving Threat Landscape:**
   - **Challenge:** Cyber threats are becoming more sophisticated, with advanced persistent threats (APTs) and ransomware attacks on the rise.
   - **Implication:** Organizations must continuously update their threat intelligence and incident response capabilities to stay ahead of emerging threats.
2. **Skills Gap:**

- **Challenge:** There is a shortage of skilled cybersecurity professionals, making it difficult to implement and maintain robust security governance.
- **Implication:** Investing in employee training, certification programs, and fostering a culture of security awareness are essential to bridging the skills gap.

3. Compliance Complexity:

- **Challenge:** Managing compliance with multiple overlapping regulations across different jurisdictions can be complex and resource-intensive.
- **Implication:** Organizations need integrated compliance management systems and dedicated teams to navigate the regulatory landscape effectively.

Adapting Governance Approaches

1. Continuous Learning and Professional Development:

- **Stay Informed:** Information Security Managers should pursue ongoing education through certifications (e.g., CISSP, CISM), attending industry conferences, and participating in professional networks.
- **Engage with Thought Leaders:** Following cybersecurity experts and thought leaders on social media and subscribing to relevant publications can provide valuable insights into emerging trends and best practices.

2. Adopting Agile Security Practices:

- **Agile Methodologies:** Implementing agile methodologies in security operations allows for more flexible and responsive governance practices. This includes iterative development, frequent reviews, and rapid adaptation to new threats.
- **DevSecOps:** Integrating security into the DevOps pipeline (DevSecOps) ensures that security is considered at every stage of the development process, leading to more secure applications and infrastructure.

3. Leveraging Advanced Technologies:

- **AI and Automation:** Utilize AI and automation to enhance threat detection, streamline compliance tasks, and improve incident response times. This allows for more efficient use of resources and reduces the burden on security teams.
- **Blockchain and IoT Security:** Stay abreast of developments in blockchain and IoT security, and incorporate these technologies into governance frameworks where applicable.

4. Enhancing Collaboration and Communication:

- **Cross-Functional Teams:** Foster collaboration between IT, legal, compliance, and business units to ensure a holistic approach to security governance. This can be achieved through regular cross-functional meetings and integrated project teams.
- **Stakeholder Engagement:** Engage with stakeholders at all levels to communicate the importance of information security and compliance. Providing clear, concise reports and updates helps build a culture of security awareness and accountability.

5. Implementing a Risk-Based Approach:

- **Prioritize Risks:** Focus on high-impact risks and allocate resources accordingly. Regular risk assessments and continuous monitoring help identify and address the most pressing threats.
- **Adaptive Risk Management:** Implement adaptive risk management strategies that can evolve with the changing threat landscape. This includes leveraging real-time data and threat intelligence to make informed decisions.

Real-World Example: A Financial Services Firm Adapting to Emerging Trends

Scenario: A global financial services firm is facing increasing regulatory scrutiny, sophisticated cyber threats, and a rapid shift to cloud services.

Actions Taken:

1. **Zero Trust Implementation:** The firm adopts a Zero Trust security model, requiring continuous verification of user identities and strict access controls.
2. **AI-Powered Threat Detection:** The firm implements AI-driven threat detection systems to identify and respond to cyber threats in real-time.

3. **Cloud Security Strategy:** A comprehensive cloud security strategy is developed, including encryption, access controls, and continuous monitoring across all cloud platforms.
4. **RegTech Adoption:** The firm uses RegTech solutions to automate compliance processes, reducing the time and effort required to meet regulatory requirements.
5. **Employee Training:** Continuous training programs are provided to employees, focusing on new regulations, security best practices, and emerging threats.

Outcome: By staying informed about emerging trends and technologies and adapting their governance approaches, the financial services firm enhances its security posture, ensures compliance, and effectively manages risks in a dynamic environment.

Conclusion

As the landscape of information security continues to evolve, it is crucial for Information Security Managers to stay informed and adaptable. By understanding emerging trends and technologies, adopting agile and risk-based approaches, and fostering a culture of continuous learning and collaboration, organizations can maintain robust information security governance and effectively protect their assets and stakeholders.

The Future of Information Security Governance

As technology evolves and cyber threats become more sophisticated, information security governance must also adapt to meet new challenges and leverage emerging trends and technologies. Here's a look at the future of information security governance, key trends, and how Information Security Managers can stay informed and adapt their approaches.

Emerging Trends in Information Security Governance

1. Increased Focus on Data Privacy and Protection

Trend:

- With regulations like GDPR, CCPA, and upcoming privacy laws in various jurisdictions, organizations must prioritize data privacy and protection more than ever.

Implications:

- Organizations need to implement stringent data protection measures, conduct regular privacy impact assessments, and ensure compliance with evolving data privacy regulations.

2. Integration of Artificial Intelligence and Machine Learning

Trend:

- AI and ML are increasingly being used to enhance threat detection, response capabilities, and overall security posture.

Implications:

- Leveraging AI/ML can help organizations identify and respond to threats more quickly and accurately. However, it also introduces new risks, such as adversarial attacks on AI systems, which must be managed.

3. Adoption of Zero Trust Architecture

Trend:

- Zero Trust Architecture (ZTA) is gaining traction as organizations move away from traditional perimeter-based security models.

Implications:

- Implementing ZTA requires organizations to continuously verify user identities, enforce least privilege access, and monitor all network traffic. This shift can improve security but requires significant changes to existing infrastructure and processes.

4. Emphasis on Cyber Resilience

Trend:

- Cyber resilience focuses on the ability to prepare for, respond to, and recover from cyber incidents.

Implications:

- Organizations need to develop comprehensive incident response plans, conduct regular drills, and invest in technologies that enhance their resilience, such as automated backup and recovery solutions.

5. Increased Regulatory Scrutiny and Compliance Requirements
Trend:

- Governments and regulatory bodies are introducing more stringent cybersecurity regulations and compliance requirements.

Implications:

- Organizations must stay abreast of regulatory changes and ensure their governance frameworks are flexible enough to adapt to new requirements. This includes regular audits, compliance checks, and continuous improvement of security practices.

6. Rise of Quantum Computing
Trend:

- Quantum computing poses both opportunities and threats to cybersecurity. While it promises advanced computational capabilities, it also threatens current cryptographic algorithms.

Implications:

- Organizations must begin exploring quantum-resistant cryptographic methods and understand the potential impact of quantum computing on their security posture.

7. Increased Use of Cloud Services and IoT
Trend:

- The widespread adoption of cloud services and Internet of Things (IoT) devices introduces new security challenges.

Implications:

- Organizations need to implement robust cloud security practices, ensure secure configuration of IoT devices, and continuously monitor for vulnerabilities in these environments.

Challenges in Information Security Governance

1. Evolving Threat Landscape
Challenge:

- Cyber threats are becoming more sophisticated, diverse, and persistent, making it challenging to keep up with new attack vectors and techniques.

Solution:

- Organizations must invest in advanced threat intelligence, continuous monitoring, and adaptive security measures to stay ahead of threats.

2. Skills Shortage
Challenge:

- The cybersecurity skills gap continues to widen, with a shortage of qualified professionals to address growing security needs.

Solution:

- Investing in training and development programs, leveraging automation, and outsourcing certain security functions can help mitigate the impact of the skills shortage.

3. Balancing Security and Business Objectives
Challenge:

- Ensuring robust security measures without hindering business operations or innovation can be difficult.

Solution:

- Adopt a risk-based approach to security governance that aligns with business objectives, and involve stakeholders in security decision-making to balance security and business needs.

Staying Informed and Adapting Governance Approaches

1. Continuous Learning and Professional Development
Action:

- Information Security Managers should engage in continuous learning through certifications, professional development courses, and industry conferences.

Examples:

- Certifications like CISSP, CISM, and CEH.
- Conferences such as RSA Conference, Black Hat, and DEF CON.

2. Engaging with Industry Communities and Networks
Action:

- Participate in industry groups, forums, and networks to stay updated on the latest trends and best practices.

Examples:

- Joining professional organizations like ISACA, (ISC)², and SANS Institute.
- Participating in online forums and discussion groups on platforms like LinkedIn and Reddit.

3. Leveraging Threat Intelligence and Research
Action:

- Use threat intelligence platforms and subscribe to cybersecurity research publications to stay informed about emerging threats and vulnerabilities.

Examples:

- Platforms like ThreatConnect, Recorded Future, and Anomali.
- Publications such as Verizon's Data Breach Investigations Report (DBIR) and Gartner's cybersecurity reports.

4. Adopting Agile and Flexible Governance Frameworks
Action:

- Implement agile and flexible governance frameworks that can quickly adapt to changing regulatory requirements and threat landscapes.

Examples:

- Utilizing frameworks like NIST Cybersecurity Framework and ISO/IEC 27001, which allow for continuous improvement and adaptability.

5. Collaboration with Regulatory Bodies and Industry Peers
Action:

- Collaborate with regulatory bodies and industry peers to share knowledge, resources, and best practices.

Examples:

- Participating in information sharing and analysis centers (ISACs) and industry consortia.

Conclusion

The future of information security governance is shaped by emerging trends, technologies, and challenges. Information Security Managers must stay informed and adapt their governance approaches to address these changes effectively. By engaging in continuous learning, leveraging threat intelligence, adopting agile frameworks, and collaborating with industry peers, organizations can enhance their security posture and remain resilient in the face of evolving threats. This proactive approach ensures that security governance remains robust, relevant, and aligned with organizational goals and regulatory requirements.

Comprehensive Glossary of Information Security Governance Terms

Here is a glossary of key terms, concepts, and acronyms related to information security governance. This glossary can serve as a valuable reference tool for readers, helping them navigate the complex landscape of information security governance by providing clear and concise definitions and examples.

A

Access Control: Mechanisms that restrict access to information systems and data to authorized users only.
Example: Using multi-factor authentication (MFA) to ensure only authorized personnel can access sensitive data.
Audit Trail: A record of all activities and transactions in an information system, used for monitoring and reviewing purposes.
Example: Logs that track user login attempts, file accesses, and changes to system settings.

B

Breach Notification: A legal requirement to inform affected individuals and authorities when a data breach occurs.
Example: Under GDPR, organizations must notify the relevant data protection authority within 72 hours of becoming aware of a data breach.

C

Compliance: Adherence to laws, regulations, guidelines, and specifications relevant to the organization's industry.
Example: Ensuring compliance with the Health Insurance Portability and Accountability Act (HIPAA) for healthcare organizations.

Continuous Monitoring: The ongoing observation and analysis of security controls and systems to detect vulnerabilities and incidents in real-time.
Example: Using security information and event management (SIEM) systems to continuously monitor network traffic for suspicious activities.

D

Data Encryption: The process of converting plaintext data into a coded format to prevent unauthorized access.
Example: Encrypting emails and files to ensure that only the intended recipients can read them.

Data Protection Officer (DPO): A role required by GDPR for organizations that process large amounts of personal data, responsible for overseeing data protection strategy and compliance.
Example: A DPO ensures that a company complies with GDPR by conducting data protection impact assessments and training staff on data privacy.

E

Encryption: The process of encoding information to prevent unauthorized access.
Example: Using AES (Advanced Encryption Standard) to secure sensitive data stored on servers.

External Audit: An independent review conducted by a third-party auditor to assess an organization's compliance with laws and regulations.
Example: An external auditor reviews a company's financial statements and internal controls to ensure compliance with the Sarbanes-Oxley Act (SOX).

F

Firewall: A network security device that monitors and filters incoming and outgoing network traffic based on predetermined security rules.
Example: A firewall blocks unauthorized access to a company's internal network while allowing legitimate traffic.

G

Governance, Risk, and Compliance (GRC): An integrated approach to managing an organization's overall governance, risk management, and compliance with regulations.
Example: A GRC platform helps organizations manage policies, assess risks, and ensure compliance with regulatory requirements.

General Data Protection Regulation (GDPR): A regulation that mandates data protection and privacy for individuals within the European Union (EU).
Example: GDPR requires organizations to obtain explicit consent before collecting and processing personal data from EU citizens.

H

Health Insurance Portability and Accountability Act (HIPAA): A US law that establishes standards for protecting sensitive patient health information.
Example: Healthcare providers must implement physical, administrative, and technical safeguards to protect patient data.

Honeypot: A security mechanism that creates a decoy system to attract cyber attackers and study their activities.
Example: Deploying a honeypot to detect and analyze attempts to exploit vulnerabilities in a simulated environment.

I

Incident Response: The process of detecting, investigating, and responding to security incidents to mitigate their impact.
Example: Activating an incident response plan after detecting a data breach to contain the damage and notify affected parties.

Internal Audit: An internal review conducted by an organization's own audit team to evaluate the effectiveness of its risk management, control, and governance processes.
Example: Internal auditors assess the organization's compliance with internal policies and regulatory requirements.

J

Jurisdiction: The legal authority or power that a particular court or regulatory body has over a specific geographic area or type of case.
Example: GDPR applies to organizations that process personal data of individuals within the EU, regardless of the organization's location.

K

Key Risk Indicator (KRI): A metric used to signal the potential for future risk exposure within an organization.
Example: The number of failed login attempts could be a KRI indicating an increased risk of a potential security breach.

L

Least Privilege: A security principle that ensures users are granted the minimum levels of access necessary to perform their job functions.
Example: An employee only has access to the files and systems required for their specific role, reducing the risk of unauthorized access.

Log Management: The process of collecting, storing, and analyzing log data from various systems and applications to detect and investigate security incidents.
Example: Using a log management solution to aggregate and analyze logs from firewalls, servers, and applications.

M

Multi-Factor Authentication (MFA): A security process that requires two or more verification factors to access a system.
Example: Combining a password with a fingerprint scan to log into a secure system.

N

Network Segmentation: The practice of dividing a network into smaller segments to enhance security and limit the spread of potential breaches.
Example: Separating the corporate network from the guest Wi-Fi network to prevent unauthorized access to sensitive data.

O

Open Web Application Security Project (OWASP): A nonprofit organization focused on improving the security of software and applications.
Example: OWASP provides a list of the top 10 most critical web application security risks and best practices for mitigating them.

P

Penetration Testing (Pen Test): A simulated cyber attack on a system to identify vulnerabilities that could be exploited by attackers.
Example: Conducting regular pen tests to identify and address security weaknesses before they can be exploited.

Privacy Impact Assessment (PIA): A process to evaluate the impact of a project or initiative on the privacy of individuals.
Example: Conducting a PIA before implementing a new data collection system to ensure compliance with privacy regulations.

Q

Qualitative Risk Assessment: An assessment that evaluates risks based on subjective criteria, such as expert opinions and scenarios.
Example: Using interviews and workshops to identify and prioritize potential security risks.

Quantitative Risk Assessment: An assessment that evaluates risks based on numerical data and statistical methods.
Example: Calculating the potential financial impact of a data breach based on historical data and probability models.

R

Regulatory Technology (RegTech): Technology solutions designed to help organizations comply with regulatory requirements efficiently.
Example: Using RegTech tools to automate compliance reporting and monitoring for financial regulations.

Risk Appetite: The amount of risk an organization is willing to accept in pursuit of its objectives.
Example: A company with a low risk appetite may implement stringent security controls to minimize potential risks.

S

Security Information and Event Management (SIEM): A technology that provides real-time analysis of security alerts generated by applications and network hardware.
Example: A SIEM system aggregates logs from various sources to detect and respond to security incidents.

Social Engineering: Manipulating individuals into divulging confidential information or performing actions that compromise security.
Example: Phishing emails that trick recipients into clicking malicious links or providing sensitive information.

T

Threat Intelligence: Information about current and emerging threats that helps organizations protect against cyber attacks.
Example: Subscribing to threat intelligence feeds to stay informed about the latest malware and attack vectors.

Tokenization: The process of replacing sensitive data with unique identification symbols that retain essential information without compromising security.
Example: Using tokenization to protect credit card information during transactions.

U

User Behavior Analytics (UBA): Monitoring and analyzing user behavior to detect potential security threats.
Example: UBA tools identify unusual login patterns that may indicate compromised accounts.

V

Vulnerability Assessment: The process of identifying, classifying, and prioritizing security vulnerabilities in systems and applications.
Example: Running regular vulnerability scans to detect and address weaknesses in the network.

W

Whitelisting: Allowing only pre-approved applications or processes to run on a system to enhance security.
Example: Implementing application whitelisting to prevent unauthorized software from executing on corporate devices.

X

XSS (Cross-Site Scripting): A type of security vulnerability that allows attackers to inject malicious scripts into web pages viewed by other users.
Example: Ensuring input validation and output encoding to prevent XSS attacks on web applications.

Y

YARA (Yet Another Recursive Acronym): A tool used to identify and classify malware based on patterns and signatures.
Example: Using YARA rules to detect and analyze new malware strains in a security operations center (SOC).

Z

Zero-Day Vulnerability: A security flaw that is unknown to the software vendor and has no patch available, posing a significant risk.
Example: Deploying advanced threat detection systems to identify and mitigate zero-day vulnerabilities before they can be exploited.

Conclusion

This glossary serves as a valuable reference tool by providing clear and concise definitions of key terms, concepts, and acronyms in information security governance. It helps readers understand complex topics, facilitates better communication among stakeholders, and supports the implementation of effective security governance practices. By having a comprehensive glossary at their disposal, information security professionals can navigate the intricate landscape of information security governance with greater confidence and clarity.

Part II: Information Risk Management:

Comparison of Risk Identification Techniques: STRIDE, DREAD, and OCTAVE

Risk identification techniques are crucial for understanding potential threats and vulnerabilities in information security. Different techniques offer various approaches to identifying and assessing risks, each with its own strengths and weaknesses. Here's a comparison of STRIDE, DREAD, and OCTAVE, along with their appropriate use cases.

STRIDE

Overview: STRIDE is a threat modeling technique developed by Microsoft to identify and categorize threats against an application or system. It stands for Spoofing, Tampering, Repudiation, Information Disclosure, Denial of Service, and Elevation of Privilege.

Strengths:

- **Comprehensive Coverage:** STRIDE provides a comprehensive framework for identifying different types of threats, covering a wide range of security issues.
- **Simplicity:** It offers a straightforward and structured approach, making it easy to understand and apply.
- **Focus on Application Security:** STRIDE is particularly useful for identifying threats in software and application development, helping to secure the development lifecycle.

Weaknesses:

- **High-Level Analysis:** While comprehensive, STRIDE can be somewhat high-level and may miss nuanced or specific threats in complex systems.
- **Resource Intensive:** Applying STRIDE thoroughly can be resource-intensive, requiring detailed analysis and expertise.

Use Cases:

- **Application Development:** Ideal for use during the software development lifecycle to identify potential security threats in applications.
- **System Design:** Useful in the early stages of system design to identify and mitigate security risks.

DREAD

Overview: DREAD is a risk assessment model used to quantify, compare, and prioritize the severity of different threats. It stands for Damage, Reproducibility, Exploitability, Affected Users, and Discoverability.

Strengths:

- **Quantitative Assessment:** DREAD provides a numerical scoring system that helps prioritize threats based on their potential impact.
- **Comparative Analysis:** It allows for easy comparison between different threats, aiding in decision-making and resource allocation.
- **Focus on Severity:** Emphasizes the severity and exploitability of threats, helping prioritize those that pose the greatest risk.

Weaknesses:

- **Subjectivity:** The scoring system can be subjective, as different assessors may have varying opinions on the severity of each factor.
- **Limited Scope:** DREAD focuses more on the impact and likelihood of threats rather than identifying a comprehensive range of threats.

Use Cases:

- **Threat Prioritization:** Ideal for environments where prioritizing and comparing threats is critical to managing resources effectively.
- **Post-Identification Analysis:** Useful after initial threat identification to assess and prioritize threats based on their potential impact.

OCTAVE

Overview: OCTAVE (Operationally Critical Threat, Asset, and Vulnerability Evaluation) is a risk assessment methodology designed to help organizations identify, prioritize, and manage information security risks. It focuses on organizational risk management rather than specific technical vulnerabilities.

Strengths:

- **Holistic Approach:** OCTAVE takes a broad, organizational view of risk management, considering both technical and non-technical aspects.
- **Self-Directed:** It empowers organizations to conduct their own assessments without relying heavily on external consultants.
- **Strategic Focus:** Emphasizes strategic planning and integrating risk management into organizational processes.

Weaknesses:

- **Complexity:** OCTAVE can be complex and time-consuming, requiring significant effort and resources to implement effectively.
- **Less Technical:** It may not provide the detailed technical analysis needed for specific threat identification in IT environments.

Use Cases:

- **Organizational Risk Management:** Best suited for organizations looking to integrate risk management into their overall strategy and processes.
- **Comprehensive Risk Assessment:** Ideal for large organizations needing a thorough assessment that considers both technical and operational risks.

Comparison Summary

1. Scope and Focus:

- **STRIDE:** Focuses on identifying a wide range of specific threats in application security, making it highly suitable for developers and system designers.
- **DREAD:** Provides a method to quantify and prioritize threats based on their potential impact, useful for threat prioritization and resource allocation.
- **OCTAVE:** Takes a holistic approach to organizational risk management, considering both technical and operational risks.

2. Strengths and Weaknesses:

- **STRIDE:**
  - **Strengths:** Comprehensive coverage of threats, straightforward application.
  - **Weaknesses:** Can be high-level and resource-intensive.
- **DREAD:**
  - **Strengths:** Quantitative, comparative, focuses on severity.
  - **Weaknesses:** Subjective scoring, limited scope.
- **OCTAVE:**
  - **Strengths:** Holistic, strategic, self-directed.
  - **Weaknesses:** Complex, less technical detail.

3. Appropriate Use Cases:

- **STRIDE:** Best for application and system design stages to identify potential security threats.
- **DREAD:** Suitable for environments needing to prioritize and compare threats based on their impact.
- **OCTAVE:** Ideal for organizations seeking comprehensive risk management integrated into their strategic planning.

Conclusion

Choosing the appropriate risk identification technique depends on the specific needs and context of the organization. STRIDE is excellent for detailed threat identification in software development, DREAD is valuable for prioritizing threats based on their potential impact, and OCTAVE is suitable for comprehensive organizational risk management. By understanding the strengths and weaknesses of each method, Information Security Managers can select and apply the most effective techniques to enhance their information security governance and risk management practices.

Quantitative vs. Qualitative Risk Assessment Methodologies

Understanding the differences between quantitative and qualitative risk assessment methodologies is essential for effective risk management. Each approach has its strengths and is suitable for different scenarios. Combining both methods can lead to a comprehensive risk assessment strategy, leveraging the benefits of each.

Quantitative Risk Assessment

Definition: Quantitative risk assessment involves using numerical data and statistical methods to evaluate risks. It focuses on measuring the likelihood and impact of risks in financial terms, providing precise, data-driven insights.

Key Steps:

1. **Identify Risks:** List potential risks that could affect the organization.
2. **Gather Data:** Collect historical data, industry benchmarks, and statistical information related to each risk.
3. **Analyze Risks:** Use mathematical models and statistical techniques to determine the probability and potential impact of each risk.
4. **Calculate Expected Losses:** Estimate the potential financial loss for each risk, typically using formulas such as Expected Value (EV) = Probability x Impact.
5. **Prioritize Risks:** Rank risks based on their financial impact and likelihood to focus on the most significant threats.
6. **Develop Mitigation Strategies:** Plan and implement measures to reduce the likelihood and impact of the highest-priority risks.

Considerations:

- Requires accurate and comprehensive data.
- Can be resource-intensive due to the need for detailed data analysis.
- Provides precise and objective results that are useful for financial planning and decision-making.

Example of Use: A financial services company might use quantitative risk assessment to evaluate the risk of market fluctuations on their investment portfolio. By analyzing historical market data, they can predict potential losses and develop strategies to mitigate these risks.

Qualitative Risk Assessment

Definition: Qualitative risk assessment relies on subjective criteria, such as expert opinions and scenarios, to evaluate risks. It uses descriptive terms and ratings (e.g., high, medium, low) to assess the likelihood and impact of risks.

Key Steps:

1. **Identify Risks:** List potential risks that could affect the organization.
2. **Gather Input:** Conduct interviews, workshops, and brainstorming sessions with stakeholders and experts to gather insights.
3. **Assess Risks:** Use techniques such as risk matrices and scenario analysis to evaluate the likelihood and impact of each risk qualitatively.
4. **Prioritize Risks:** Categorize risks based on their qualitative ratings and focus on those deemed most critical.
5. **Develop Mitigation Strategies:** Plan and implement measures to address the highest-priority risks based on qualitative insights.

Considerations:

- Easier and quicker to implement compared to quantitative methods.
- Relies heavily on the expertise and judgment of participants.
- Provides a broad overview that can guide initial risk management efforts.

Example of Use: A healthcare organization might use qualitative risk assessment to evaluate the risk of patient data breaches. By conducting workshops with IT staff and healthcare providers, they can identify high-risk areas and develop strategies to enhance data security.

Combining Quantitative and Qualitative Approaches

Combining both methodologies can create a more comprehensive risk assessment strategy, leveraging the strengths of each approach.

Steps to Combine Approaches:

1. **Initial Qualitative Assessment:** Start with a qualitative assessment to quickly identify and prioritize risks based on expert opinions and stakeholder input.
2. **Quantitative Analysis of Key Risks:** For the highest-priority risks identified in the qualitative assessment, conduct a detailed quantitative analysis to obtain precise, data-driven insights.
3. **Integrated Reporting:** Combine the results of both assessments into an integrated risk report, providing a holistic view of the organization's risk landscape.
4. **Balanced Mitigation Strategies:** Develop risk mitigation strategies that address both the subjective insights from the qualitative assessment and the objective data from the quantitative analysis.

Example of Use: A large manufacturing company might use qualitative methods to identify risks related to supply chain disruptions and then apply quantitative techniques to analyze the financial impact of the most critical risks. This combined approach allows them to develop well-rounded strategies to ensure supply chain resilience.

Key Considerations for Conducting Risk Assessments

For Quantitative Assessments:

- **Data Quality:** Ensure accurate, comprehensive, and relevant data is used.
- **Statistical Expertise:** Employ individuals with strong statistical and analytical skills.
- **Tool Selection:** Use appropriate tools and software for data analysis.

For Qualitative Assessments:

- **Stakeholder Involvement:** Engage a diverse group of stakeholders to gather a wide range of insights.
- **Structured Approach:** Use structured techniques such as risk matrices and Delphi method to ensure consistency.
- **Documentation:** Keep detailed records of discussions and decisions to support transparency and accountability.

General Considerations:

- **Objective Alignment:** Align the assessment approach with the organization's overall objectives and risk management strategy.
- **Continuous Monitoring:** Regularly review and update risk assessments to reflect changes in the risk landscape.
- **Integration:** Ensure risk assessment findings are integrated into broader governance, risk management, and compliance frameworks.

Conclusion

By understanding and applying both quantitative and qualitative risk assessment methodologies, organizations can create a robust and comprehensive risk management strategy. This approach not only identifies and prioritizes risks effectively but also supports informed decision-making and enhances overall organizational resilience.

Purpose and Key Components of a Business Impact Analysis (BIA) in Information Security Risk Management

Purpose: A Business Impact Analysis (BIA) is a systematic process used to identify and evaluate the potential effects of disruptions to business operations. In the context of information security risk management, a BIA helps organizations understand the criticality of their assets, processes, and dependencies, and prioritize their efforts to protect and recover these elements in the event of a disruption. The primary goal is to minimize the impact on business operations and ensure continuity.

Key Components:

1. **Identification of Critical Assets and Processes:**
    - Determine the assets (data, systems, applications) and business processes that are essential to the organization's operations.
2. **Impact Assessment:**
    - Evaluate the potential consequences of disruptions, including financial loss, reputational damage, legal and regulatory impacts, and operational setbacks.
3. **Dependencies:**

- Identify internal and external dependencies, such as personnel, technology, suppliers, and partners, that are crucial for the functioning of critical assets and processes.

4. **Recovery Objectives:**
    - Establish Recovery Time Objectives (RTOs) and Recovery Point Objectives (RPOs) for critical assets and processes to guide recovery efforts.
5. **Mitigation Strategies:**
    - Develop strategies and plans to mitigate the identified risks and ensure timely recovery of critical operations.

How a BIA Helps Organizations

1. **Identification of Critical Assets and Processes:**
    - A BIA identifies the most important assets and processes that need to be protected and recovered first during a disruption.
2. **Prioritization:**
    - By assessing the impact of disruptions, organizations can prioritize their resources and efforts to protect the most critical components.
3. **Understanding Dependencies:**
    - It helps in understanding the interdependencies among different processes and assets, enabling better planning and coordination.
4. **Consequences of Disruptions:**
    - A BIA outlines the potential consequences of disruptions, helping stakeholders understand the importance of investing in robust security measures and recovery plans.

Step-by-Step Guide for Conducting a BIA

Step 1: Define the Scope and Objectives

- Determine the scope of the BIA, including which parts of the organization and which assets, processes, and dependencies will be analyzed.
- Establish clear objectives for the BIA, such as identifying critical assets, assessing potential impacts, and setting recovery priorities.

Step 2: Gather Information

- **Interviews and Surveys:** Conduct interviews and distribute surveys to gather information from key stakeholders, including process owners, IT staff, and business managers.
- **Documentation Review:** Review existing documentation, such as process flowcharts, IT architecture diagrams, and previous incident reports.

Step 3: Identify Critical Assets and Processes

- **Asset Inventory:** Create a comprehensive inventory of all assets, including hardware, software, data, and human resources.
- **Process Mapping:** Map out business processes to understand their flow and interdependencies.

Step 4: Assess Impact

- **Impact Criteria:** Define impact criteria such as financial loss, operational disruption, legal implications, and reputational damage.
- **Impact Assessment:** Evaluate the potential impact of disruptions on each critical asset and process based on the defined criteria.

Step 5: Identify Dependencies

- **Internal Dependencies:** Identify internal dependencies, such as key personnel, internal systems, and support functions.
- **External Dependencies:** Identify external dependencies, such as third-party vendors, service providers, and supply chain partners.

Step 6: Establish Recovery Objectives

- **Recovery Time Objectives (RTOs):** Determine the maximum acceptable downtime for each critical asset and process.
- **Recovery Point Objectives (RPOs):** Determine the maximum acceptable data loss for each critical asset and process.

Step 7: Develop Mitigation Strategies

- **Risk Mitigation:** Identify and implement measures to mitigate the identified risks, such as backup solutions, redundant systems, and alternative suppliers.
- **Recovery Planning:** Develop detailed recovery plans for each critical asset and process, including specific actions to be taken during a disruption.

Step 8: Review and Validate

- **Stakeholder Review:** Review the BIA findings and recommendations with key stakeholders to ensure accuracy and completeness.
- **Validation:** Validate the BIA through simulations, tabletop exercises, or real-world incident analysis to test the effectiveness of the recovery plans.

Step 9: Document and Report

- **BIA Report:** Compile the findings, impact assessments, recovery objectives, and mitigation strategies into a comprehensive BIA report.
- **Executive Summary:** Provide an executive summary highlighting the key findings, priorities, and recommendations for senior management.

Interpreting BIA Results

1. **Prioritization of Assets and Processes:**
    - Use the BIA results to prioritize assets and processes based on their criticality and the potential impact of disruptions.
2. **Allocation of Resources:**
    - Allocate resources (personnel, budget, technology) to protect and recover the most critical assets and processes.
3. **Risk Mitigation Planning:**
    - Develop and implement risk mitigation plans to address identified vulnerabilities and dependencies.
4. **Recovery Planning:**
    - Establish and regularly update recovery plans to ensure they align with the organization's current operational environment and risk landscape.
5. **Continuous Improvement:**
    - Use the BIA results to continuously improve the organization's information security governance and risk management practices.

Conclusion

A Business Impact Analysis (BIA) is a vital tool in information security risk management, helping organizations identify and prioritize critical assets, processes, and dependencies. By following a structured approach to conducting a BIA and interpreting its results, organizations can develop effective mitigation and recovery strategies to minimize the impact of disruptions and ensure business continuity. This proactive approach not only enhances the organization's resilience but also supports informed decision-making and resource allocation in the face of potential threats and vulnerabilities.

Risk Register: Definition and Role

The concept of a risk register is fundamental in risk management, serving as a dynamic tool for documenting, tracking, and communicating identified risks across an organization. A risk register provides a structured approach to capturing and managing information about risks, facilitating effective decision-making and strategic planning.

Role of a Risk Register

1. Documentation:

- The risk register acts as a centralized repository for all identified risks, ensuring that no risk is overlooked and all relevant information is documented comprehensively.

2. Tracking:

- It enables continuous monitoring of risks, tracking their status, and documenting any changes in their nature, likelihood, impact, or mitigation efforts.

3. Communication:

- The risk register facilitates clear and consistent communication about risks among stakeholders, including senior management, risk owners, and regulatory bodies. This ensures that everyone is aware of the current risk landscape and the actions being taken to manage it.

Essential Elements of a Risk Register

1. Risk Description:

- **Definition:** A clear and concise description of the risk, detailing what might happen and how it could affect the organization.
- **Example:** "Data breach due to phishing attack leading to unauthorized access to customer data."

2. Likelihood:

- **Definition:** An assessment of the probability that the risk will occur, often categorized as low, medium, or high.
- **Example:** "Medium" likelihood of a data breach occurring due to the current frequency of phishing attacks.

3. Impact:

- **Definition:** An assessment of the potential consequences if the risk materializes, usually categorized as low, medium, or high.
- **Example:** "High" impact if a data breach occurs, resulting in financial losses, regulatory fines, and reputational damage.

4. Risk Owner:

- **Definition:** The individual or team responsible for managing and monitoring the risk, ensuring that appropriate actions are taken.
- **Example:** Chief Information Security Officer (CISO) or IT security team.

5. Mitigation Plans:

- **Definition:** Detailed strategies and actions to reduce the likelihood or impact of the risk.
- **Example:** Implementing multi-factor authentication, conducting regular security awareness training, and deploying advanced email filtering systems.

6. Status:

- **Definition:** Current state of the risk, indicating whether it is open, closed, or being monitored.
- **Example:** "Open" status for an ongoing risk that is actively being managed.

7. Target Resolution Date:

- **Definition:** The expected date by which the risk mitigation measures should be implemented and the risk should be reduced or resolved.
- **Example:** "December 31, 2024."

8. Risk Score:

- **Definition:** A numerical value or rating calculated by combining the likelihood and impact assessments, often using a predefined scoring system.
- **Example:** A risk score of 15 on a scale of 1-25, where higher scores represent higher risks.

Best Practices for Creating, Maintaining, and Updating a Risk Register

1. Initial Creation:

a. Comprehensive Identification:

- Conduct thorough risk identification processes, such as brainstorming sessions, SWOT analysis, and consultations with various departments to capture a wide range of potential risks.

b. Standardized Format:

- Use a standardized template for the risk register to ensure consistency and ease of use. This template should include all essential elements, such as risk description, likelihood, impact, owner, and mitigation plans.

2. Maintenance and Updates:

a. Regular Reviews:

- Schedule regular reviews of the risk register, such as quarterly or bi-annually, to assess the status of identified risks, update their likelihood and impact, and evaluate the effectiveness of mitigation measures.

b. Dynamic Updates:

- Update the risk register dynamically as new risks emerge, existing risks change, or mitigation plans are implemented. Ensure that changes are documented promptly and communicated to relevant stakeholders.

c. Stakeholder Involvement:

- Involve key stakeholders in the review and update process to ensure comprehensive risk management. This includes risk owners, senior management, and representatives from affected departments.

3. Communication and Reporting:

a. Transparent Communication:

- Communicate the contents and updates of the risk register transparently across the organization. Use dashboards, reports, and meetings to ensure all relevant parties are informed about the current risk landscape.

b. Regular Reporting:

- Generate regular reports based on the risk register for senior management and the board of directors, highlighting key risks, their status, and the actions being taken to manage them.

4. Integration with Risk Management Framework:

a. Align with Organizational Objectives:

- Ensure that the risk register is integrated with the broader risk management framework and aligned with the organization's objectives and strategic goals.

b. Use Technology:

- Leverage risk management software and tools to automate the maintenance and updating of the risk register. These tools can provide real-time updates, analytics, and visualization features to enhance risk management.

Conclusion

A well-maintained risk register is an invaluable tool for documenting, tracking, and communicating risks within an organization. By following best practices for creating, maintaining, and updating the risk register, organizations can ensure a proactive approach to risk management, enhance decision-making, and support strategic planning. This comprehensive approach to managing risks fosters a culture of transparency, accountability, and continuous improvement.

Importance of Risk Prioritization

Risk prioritization is crucial for focusing an organization's risk management efforts and resources on the most significant threats. By identifying which risks pose the greatest potential impact, organizations can allocate their limited resources more effectively, ensuring that the most critical vulnerabilities are addressed first. This strategic approach enhances overall security posture, compliance, and operational resilience.

Common Risk Prioritization Techniques

1. Risk Ranking Matrices

Overview:

- Risk ranking matrices provide a systematic way to evaluate and compare risks based on predefined criteria, typically considering both the likelihood of occurrence and the potential impact.

Structure:

- **Likelihood:** The probability that a risk event will occur (e.g., rare, unlikely, possible, likely, almost certain).
- **Impact:** The potential consequences or severity of the risk event (e.g., negligible, minor, moderate, major, catastrophic).

Example:

- Risks are plotted in a matrix format, with likelihood on one axis and impact on the other. Each risk is assigned a score based on its position in the matrix, allowing easy comparison and prioritization.

Visualization:

- Risks in the upper right corner (high likelihood, high impact) are prioritized for immediate attention.
- Example Matrix:

lua

Copy code

```
  Impact
------------------------------
|  |  |  | H | H | H |
|  |  | M | M | H | H |
|  | L | M | M | H | H |
| L | L | M | M | M | H |
| L | L | L | L | M | M |
------------------------------
 Likelihood
```

2. Heat Maps

Overview:

- Heat maps visually represent the level of risk across an organization using color coding to indicate severity.

Structure:

- Similar to risk ranking matrices, heat maps plot risks on a grid with axes for likelihood and impact.
- Colors (e.g., green, yellow, red) are used to indicate risk levels, with red representing high risk and green representing low risk.

Example:

- A heat map provides a quick visual overview of risk distribution, highlighting areas of greatest concern.
- Example Heat Map:

mathematica

Copy code

```
  Impact
------------------------------
|  |  |  |Red |Red |Red |
|  |  |Yellow|Yellow|Red |
|  |Green|Yellow|Yellow|Red |
|Green|Green|Yellow|Yellow|Yellow|
|Green|Green|Green|Green|Yellow|
------------------------------
 Likelihood
```

3. Risk Registers

Overview:

- A risk register is a detailed log that captures information about identified risks, their assessment, and mitigation strategies.

Structure:

- Columns typically include risk ID, description, likelihood, impact, risk score, mitigation actions, and responsible parties.

Example:

- A risk register provides a comprehensive view of all risks and their management status.

- Example Risk Register:

mathematica
Copy code

Risk ID	Description	Likelihood	Impact	Risk Score	Mitigation Action	Owner
R1	Data Breach	High	Major	15	Implement MFA	IT Security
R2	Phishing Attack	Medium	Moderate	9	Conduct Employee Training	HR

Factors to Consider When Prioritizing Risks

1. Organization's Risk Appetite

Definition:

- Risk appetite refers to the amount and type of risk an organization is willing to accept to achieve its objectives.

Considerations:

- Align risk prioritization with the organization's strategic goals and risk tolerance levels.
- Different departments may have varying risk appetites, which should be considered when prioritizing risks.

2. Industry Benchmarks

Definition:

- Industry benchmarks provide a standard or point of reference against which risks can be measured.

Considerations:

- Compare the organization's risk profile with industry standards to identify common threats and best practices for mitigation.
- Use industry-specific risk data to inform prioritization decisions.

3. Regulatory Requirements

Definition:

- Regulatory requirements mandate certain risk management practices to ensure compliance with laws and regulations.

Considerations:

- Ensure that prioritized risks include those with regulatory implications to avoid legal penalties and reputational damage.
- Regularly review and update risk management practices to remain compliant with evolving regulations.

4. Business Impact

Definition:

- The potential impact of a risk event on business operations, finances, reputation, and legal standing.

Considerations:

- Prioritize risks that could have significant negative impacts on critical business functions and assets.
- Evaluate both direct and indirect impacts of risks on the organization.

5. Historical Data and Trends

Definition:

- Historical data and trends provide insights into past incidents and their impacts.

Considerations:

- Use historical data to identify patterns and trends in risk occurrence and impact.
- Prioritize risks that have a history of recurrence or have previously caused significant damage.

Example of Using Risk Prioritization Techniques

Scenario: A financial services company is conducting a risk assessment to identify and prioritize information security risks.

Step-by-Step Process:

1. **Identify Risks:**
    - The company identifies several risks, including data breaches, phishing attacks, insider threats, and system failures.

2. **Assess Risks:**
    - Each risk is assessed for likelihood and impact using qualitative and quantitative methods.
3. **Create a Risk Ranking Matrix:**
    - Risks are plotted on a risk ranking matrix:

```
lua
Copy code
 Impact
 ------------------------------
 |  |  |  | H | H | H |
 |  |  | M | M | H | H |
 |  | L | M | M | H | H |
 | L | L | M | M | M | H |
 | L | L | L | L | M | M |
 ------------------------------
 Likelihood
```

    - Data breaches and phishing attacks are placed in the high-risk quadrant (high likelihood, high impact).
4. **Develop a Heat Map:**
    - A heat map is created to visualize the risks:

```
mathematica
Copy code
 Impact
 ------------------------------
 |  |  |  |Red |Red |Red |
 |  |  |Yellow|Yellow|Red |
 |  |Green|Yellow|Yellow|Red |
 |Green|Green|Yellow|Yellow|Yellow|
 |Green|Green|Green|Green|Yellow|
 ------------------------------
 Likelihood
```

5. **Review Risk Register:**
    - The risk register is updated to include details about each risk, mitigation actions, and responsible parties.
6. **Prioritize Risks Based on Factors:**
    - The company considers its risk appetite, industry benchmarks, regulatory requirements, and historical data.
    - Data breaches and phishing attacks are prioritized for immediate attention due to their high potential impact and regulatory implications.

Conclusion

Risk prioritization is essential for effective risk management, allowing organizations to focus their efforts and resources on the most critical threats. Techniques such as risk ranking matrices, heat maps, and risk registers provide structured approaches to evaluating and visualizing risks. When prioritizing risks, organizations should consider factors such as risk appetite, industry benchmarks, regulatory requirements, business impact, and historical data. By systematically prioritizing risks, organizations can enhance their security posture, ensure compliance, and protect their critical assets and processes.

Comparing Popular Risk Management Frameworks: NIST RMF vs. ISO 27005

Information security risk management is a critical component of an organization's overall risk management strategy. Two popular frameworks that organizations often use are the NIST Risk Management Framework (RMF) and ISO 27005. Both provide structured approaches to identifying, assessing, and managing risks, but they have different origins, structures, and applications. Let's compare and contrast these frameworks, discuss their key components, benefits, and limitations, and provide examples of their real-world application.

NIST Risk Management Framework (RMF)

Overview: The NIST RMF, developed by the National Institute of Standards and Technology, is primarily used by U.S. federal agencies but is also applicable to other organizations seeking a comprehensive risk management approach.

Key Components:

1. **Categorize Information Systems:** Determine the impact level (low, moderate, high) based on the potential impact of a security breach.
2. **Select Security Controls:** Choose appropriate security controls from the NIST Special Publication 800-53 based on the system's impact level.
3. **Implement Security Controls:** Put the selected controls into place and document how they are implemented.
4. **Assess Security Controls:** Evaluate the effectiveness of the controls to ensure they are working as intended.
5. **Authorize Information System:** Senior management formally authorizes the system to operate, based on the risk assessment.
6. **Monitor Security Controls:** Continuously monitor the controls to ensure they remain effective and make necessary adjustments.

Benefits:

- **Comprehensive and Detailed:** Provides a detailed and structured approach to risk management.
- **Alignment with Federal Standards:** Aligns with U.S. federal information security requirements, making it essential for government agencies.
- **Continuous Monitoring:** Emphasizes ongoing monitoring and improvement of security controls.

Limitations:

- **Complexity:** Can be complex and resource-intensive to implement, especially for smaller organizations.
- **Specific to U.S. Standards:** Primarily tailored for U.S. federal agencies, which may limit its applicability in international contexts.

Real-World Example: A federal agency implementing the NIST RMF would start by categorizing their information systems based on FIPS 199 standards, selecting and tailoring controls from NIST SP 800-53, and conducting continuous monitoring as part of their ongoing security operations.

ISO 27005

Overview: ISO 27005 is part of the ISO/IEC 27000 family of standards and provides guidelines for information security risk management. It supports the implementation of an Information Security Management System (ISMS) based on ISO/IEC 27001.

Key Components:

1. **Context Establishment:** Define the context of the risk management process, including scope, boundaries, and objectives.
2. **Risk Assessment:** Identify, analyze, and evaluate risks.
    - **Risk Identification:** Determine potential threats and vulnerabilities.
    - **Risk Analysis:** Assess the likelihood and impact of identified risks.
    - **Risk Evaluation:** Compare risks against risk criteria to prioritize them.
3. **Risk Treatment:** Select and implement measures to mitigate identified risks.
4. **Risk Acceptance:** Determine whether the residual risk is acceptable.
5. **Risk Communication and Consultation:** Communicate and consult with stakeholders throughout the risk management process.
6. **Risk Monitoring and Review:** Continuously monitor and review risks and the effectiveness of risk treatment measures.

Benefits:

- **International Standard:** Recognized and applicable globally, supporting international business and compliance.

- **Integration with ISO/IEC 27001:** Complements ISO/IEC 27001, facilitating a holistic approach to information security management.
- **Flexibility:** Offers a flexible approach that can be tailored to different organizational contexts and needs.

Limitations:

- **Less Prescriptive:** Provides general guidelines rather than specific controls, requiring more interpretation and customization by the organization.
- **Implementation Variability:** The effectiveness can vary depending on how well the guidelines are interpreted and applied.

Real-World Example: A multinational corporation implementing ISO 27005 would start by establishing the context of their risk management process, conducting a thorough risk assessment to identify and evaluate risks, and then implementing and monitoring risk treatment measures as part of their ISMS aligned with ISO/IEC 27001.

Comparison and Alignment with Other Standards

NIST RMF:

- **Alignment:** Strongly aligns with other NIST standards, such as NIST SP 800-53 for security controls and FIPS 199 for system categorization.
- **Best Practices:** Emphasizes federal best practices and regulatory requirements, making it ideal for U.S. government and affiliated organizations.
- **Process Steps:**
    1. Categorize Information Systems
    2. Select Security Controls
    3. Implement Security Controls
    4. Assess Security Controls
    5. Authorize Information System
    6. Monitor Security Controls

ISO 27005:

- **Alignment:** Complements ISO/IEC 27001, facilitating a holistic approach to information security management through its risk management guidelines.
- **Best Practices:** Provides a flexible framework that can be adapted to various industries and international contexts.
- **Process Steps:**
    1. Context Establishment
    2. Risk Assessment
        - Risk Identification
        - Risk Analysis
        - Risk Evaluation
    3. Risk Treatment
    4. Risk Acceptance
    5. Risk Communication and Consultation
    6. Risk Monitoring and Review

Combining NIST RMF and ISO 27005

Organizations can benefit from combining both frameworks to leverage their respective strengths. For example, a company might use the detailed control selection and continuous monitoring process from NIST RMF, while adopting the broader, internationally recognized risk management principles of ISO 27005.

Steps to Combine:

1. **Initial Context Establishment (ISO 27005):** Define the scope and context of risk management.
2. **Categorize Information Systems (NIST RMF):** Determine impact levels using NIST standards.
3. **Risk Assessment (ISO 27005):** Identify, analyze, and evaluate risks.
4. **Select and Implement Security Controls (NIST RMF):** Choose appropriate controls from NIST SP 800-53.

5. **Risk Treatment and Acceptance (ISO 27005):** Implement measures and decide on risk acceptance.
6. **Continuous Monitoring (NIST RMF):** Monitor security controls and adjust as necessary.
7. **Communication and Consultation (ISO 27005):** Engage stakeholders and ensure transparency throughout the process.

Conclusion

Both NIST RMF and ISO 27005 offer robust frameworks for managing information security risks, each with its unique strengths and ideal contexts for application. By understanding their key components, benefits, and limitations, and how they align with other standards, organizations can select or combine these frameworks to create a comprehensive and effective risk management strategy that meets their specific needs.

Four Main Risk Treatment Options

Risk treatment involves selecting and implementing measures to manage risk effectively. The four main risk treatment options are Avoid, Transfer, Mitigate, and Accept. Each option has its own set of considerations and is suitable for different types and levels of risk.

1. Avoid

Definition: Avoiding risk involves changing plans or processes to eliminate the risk entirely.

Examples:

- **Example 1:** A company planning to launch a new online service decides not to proceed with the project due to the high risk of cyber-attacks and potential data breaches.
- **Example 2:** A manufacturer discontinues a product line that uses hazardous materials to avoid the risk of regulatory non-compliance and environmental liabilities.

Considerations:

- **Feasibility:** Is it practical to avoid the risk without significantly impacting business objectives?
- **Opportunity Cost:** What are the potential benefits or opportunities lost by avoiding the risk?
- **Strategic Fit:** Does avoiding the risk align with the organization's long-term strategy and goals?

Trade-offs:

- **Cost Savings vs. Lost Opportunities:** While avoiding risk can save costs associated with mitigation, it may also result in lost opportunities or competitive advantages.
- **Operational Impact:** Changes to plans or processes to avoid risk can disrupt normal operations.

2. Transfer

Definition: Transferring risk involves shifting the risk to a third party, typically through insurance, outsourcing, or contractual agreements.

Examples:

- **Example 1:** A company purchases cybersecurity insurance to cover potential losses from data breaches.
- **Example 2:** A business outsources its IT operations to a third-party provider with strong security measures, transferring the risk of IT system failures.

Considerations:

- **Cost:** What are the costs of transferring the risk (e.g., insurance premiums, outsourcing fees)?
- **Reliability of Third Party:** Can the third party effectively manage the risk? What is their track record and expertise?
- **Legal and Contractual Issues:** What are the legal implications and contractual obligations involved in transferring the risk?

Trade-offs:

- **Cost vs. Risk Reduction:** Transferring risk often involves significant costs, which must be weighed against the potential reduction in risk.
- **Dependence on Third Parties:** Transferring risk can lead to reliance on third parties, which may introduce new risks.

3. Mitigate

Definition: Mitigating risk involves implementing measures to reduce the likelihood or impact of the risk.

Examples:

- **Example 1:** A company implements multi-factor authentication (MFA) to reduce the risk of unauthorized access to its systems.
- **Example 2:** An organization conducts regular security awareness training for employees to mitigate the risk of phishing attacks.

Considerations:

- **Effectiveness:** How effective are the mitigation measures in reducing the risk?
- **Cost:** What are the costs associated with implementing and maintaining the mitigation measures?
- **Residual Risk:** What level of risk remains after mitigation, and is it acceptable?

Trade-offs:

- **Implementation Cost vs. Risk Reduction:** Mitigation measures can be costly and require ongoing investment, which must be balanced against the potential risk reduction.
- **Complexity:** Some mitigation measures can add complexity to operations and may require significant changes to processes or systems.

4. Accept

Definition: Accepting risk involves acknowledging the risk and deciding to live with it without taking additional measures to address it.

Examples:

- **Example 1:** A startup company accepts the risk of launching a new product with limited market research, acknowledging the potential for failure but also the possibility of high rewards.
- **Example 2:** An organization decides to accept the risk of occasional power outages in a region with generally reliable electricity supply, deeming the likelihood and impact to be low.

Considerations:

- **Risk Appetite:** Does accepting the risk align with the organization's risk appetite and tolerance?
- **Impact:** What are the potential consequences of accepting the risk, and are they manageable?
- **Monitoring:** What mechanisms are in place to monitor the risk and reassess it over time?

Trade-offs:

- **No Immediate Cost:** Accepting risk often involves no immediate cost, but potential future impacts must be considered.
- **Preparedness:** Accepting risk requires robust monitoring and preparedness to respond to potential incidents.

Key Considerations and Trade-offs in Selecting a Risk Treatment Strategy

1. Cost:

- **Initial Investment:** The cost of implementing risk treatment measures can vary significantly. Organizations must consider both the upfront investment and ongoing maintenance costs.
- **Long-Term Savings:** While some treatments may be costly initially, they can result in long-term savings by preventing costly incidents.

2. Feasibility:

- **Practicality:** Some risk treatments may be impractical due to technical, operational, or resource constraints.
- **Organizational Fit:** The selected treatment must align with the organization's capabilities and strategic objectives.

3. Residual Risk:

- **Risk Remaining:** All treatments leave some level of residual risk. Organizations must assess whether the residual risk is acceptable within their risk tolerance.
- **Continuous Monitoring:** Ongoing monitoring is necessary to ensure residual risks remain within acceptable levels and to identify any changes.

4. Impact on Operations:

- **Operational Disruption:** Implementing certain risk treatments can disrupt normal operations and require changes to processes.
- **Efficiency:** Some treatments can improve operational efficiency (e.g., automated controls), while others may add complexity.

Combining and Adjusting Risk Treatment Options

1. Dynamic Risk Management:

- **Continuous Review:** Regularly review and update risk assessments and treatment strategies to adapt to new threats and changes in the business environment.
- **Scenario Analysis:** Use scenario analysis to anticipate potential changes and their impact on risk treatment effectiveness.

2. Layered Approach:

- **Defense in Depth:** Combine multiple risk treatments for robust protection. For example, use mitigation (e.g., firewalls) alongside transfer (e.g., cybersecurity insurance) to address the same risk.
- **Redundancy:** Implement redundant measures to ensure that if one treatment fails, others are in place to provide protection.

3. Flexibility:

- **Adaptive Strategies:** Be prepared to adjust risk treatment strategies based on changes in risk levels, organizational priorities, and external factors.
- **Feedback Loops:** Establish feedback loops to gather information on the effectiveness of risk treatments and make adjustments as necessary.

Example: Implementing a Dynamic Risk Management Approach

Scenario: A financial services company faces multiple risks, including cyber-attacks, regulatory non-compliance, and operational disruptions.

Step-by-Step Process:

1. **Risk Identification:**
    - Identify risks through risk assessments, including potential cyber-attacks, regulatory changes, and operational failures.
2. **Risk Treatment Selection:**
    - **Cyber-Attacks:**
        - Mitigate: Implement firewalls, intrusion detection systems, and regular security audits.
        - Transfer: Purchase cybersecurity insurance.
    - **Regulatory Non-Compliance:**
        - Mitigate: Conduct regular compliance audits and employee training.
        - Accept: Accept minor non-compliance risks with low impact.
    - **Operational Disruptions:**
        - Mitigate: Develop a business continuity plan and conduct regular disaster recovery drills.
        - Avoid: Discontinue high-risk operations in unstable regions.
3. **Implementation:**
    - Allocate resources to implement selected risk treatments.
    - Monitor the effectiveness of mitigation measures and the performance of third parties involved in risk transfer.
4. **Continuous Review:**
    - Regularly review the risk environment and adjust treatments as needed.
    - Use scenario analysis to anticipate future risks and prepare adaptive strategies.
5. **Feedback and Adjustment:**
    - Gather feedback from incidents and near-misses to improve risk treatments.
    - Adjust strategies based on changes in risk appetite, regulatory requirements, and business objectives.

Conclusion

Selecting the appropriate risk treatment strategy involves evaluating the nature and level of each risk, considering factors such as cost, feasibility, and residual risk. By understanding the strengths and weaknesses of Avoid, Transfer, Mitigate, and Accept, organizations can make informed decisions to protect their critical assets and ensure business continuity. A dynamic risk management approach that combines multiple treatments and adapts to changing conditions enhances resilience and helps maintain a robust security posture.

Implementing Risk Mitigation Controls

Implementing risk mitigation controls is a crucial step in the risk management process. These controls are designed to reduce the likelihood or impact of identified risks, ensuring the protection of information assets and maintaining the integrity, confidentiality, and availability of information. The process involves selecting appropriate controls, implementing them effectively, and regularly testing their effectiveness.

Types of Controls

Controls can be categorized into three main types based on their purpose: preventive, detective, and corrective. These controls can be further divided into technical, administrative, and physical controls.

1. Preventive Controls:

- **Purpose:** Aim to prevent security incidents from occurring by eliminating vulnerabilities or blocking threats.
- **Examples:**
  - **Technical:** Firewalls, antivirus software, encryption, access control lists (ACLs).
  - **Administrative:** Security policies, user training, background checks.
  - **Physical:** Locks, security guards, biometric access controls.

2. Detective Controls:

- **Purpose:** Identify and detect security incidents that have occurred, enabling timely response.
- **Examples:**
  - **Technical:** Intrusion detection systems (IDS), security information and event management (SIEM) systems, audit logs.
  - **Administrative:** Security audits, monitoring and review processes, anomaly detection.
  - **Physical:** Security cameras, motion detectors, alarm systems.

3. Corrective Controls:

- **Purpose:** Respond to and mitigate the impact of security incidents, restoring systems to normal operations.
- **Examples:**
  - **Technical:** Patch management, backup and recovery solutions, incident response plans.
  - **Administrative:** Incident response procedures, disciplinary actions, root cause analysis.
  - **Physical:** Repairs to physical infrastructure, replacement of faulty equipment.

Common Technical, Administrative, and Physical Controls

1. Technical Controls:

- **Firewalls:** Block unauthorized access to networks.
- **Antivirus Software:** Detect and remove malicious software.
- **Encryption:** Protect data in transit and at rest.
- **Multi-Factor Authentication (MFA):** Require multiple forms of verification for access.

2. Administrative Controls:

- **Security Policies:** Define the organization's security posture and guidelines.
- **User Training:** Educate employees about security best practices and threat awareness.
- **Access Management:** Implement role-based access control (RBAC) to limit access based on job roles.
- **Vendor Management:** Ensure third-party compliance with security standards.

3. Physical Controls:

- **Locks and Security Gates:** Restrict physical access to sensitive areas.
- **Security Guards:** Monitor and control access to facilities.

- **Surveillance Cameras:** Monitor and record activities in critical areas.
- **Environmental Controls:** Use of fire suppression systems, temperature and humidity controls to protect hardware.

Best Practices for Selecting, Implementing, and Testing Controls

1. Risk Assessment and Prioritization:

- **Assess Risk Level:** Evaluate the likelihood and impact of identified risks to prioritize which controls to implement first.
- **Asset Value:** Consider the value of the assets being protected to ensure that controls are cost-effective and appropriate.
- **Organizational Constraints:** Factor in budget, resources, and regulatory requirements when selecting controls.

2. Selecting Controls:

- **Layered Security (Defense in Depth):** Implement multiple layers of controls to protect against different types of threats.
- **Alignment with Standards:** Choose controls that align with recognized security standards (e.g., NIST, ISO 27001).
- **Customizability:** Ensure controls can be tailored to the organization's specific needs and environment.

3. Implementing Controls:

- **Clear Implementation Plan:** Develop a detailed plan that outlines the steps for deploying each control, including timelines and responsible parties.
- **Training and Awareness:** Train employees on new controls and procedures to ensure they understand their roles and responsibilities.
- **Integration:** Ensure new controls integrate smoothly with existing systems and processes to avoid disruptions.

4. Testing Controls:

- **Regular Testing:** Conduct regular tests to verify that controls are functioning as intended (e.g., penetration testing, vulnerability scans).
- **Simulation Exercises:** Perform incident response drills and tabletop exercises to evaluate the effectiveness of detective and corrective controls.
- **Review and Update:** Continuously review and update controls based on test results, changes in the threat landscape, and feedback from stakeholders.

Real-World Example: Implementing Controls in a Healthcare Organization

Scenario: A healthcare organization needs to protect patient data to comply with HIPAA regulations and prevent data breaches.

1. Preventive Controls:

- **Technical:** Implement encryption for all patient data, both in transit and at rest. Use MFA for accessing electronic health records (EHR).
- **Administrative:** Develop and enforce a comprehensive security policy that includes guidelines for data handling and access control. Conduct regular training sessions on HIPAA compliance.
- **Physical:** Use biometric access controls to restrict entry to data centers and areas where sensitive patient data is stored.

2. Detective Controls:

- **Technical:** Deploy an IDS to monitor network traffic for suspicious activity. Use SIEM systems to aggregate and analyze log data from various sources.
- **Administrative:** Conduct regular security audits and reviews to ensure compliance with policies and identify potential weaknesses.
- **Physical:** Install surveillance cameras to monitor entry points and sensitive areas within the facility.

3. Corrective Controls:

- **Technical:** Implement a robust backup and recovery solution to restore data in case of a breach. Regularly apply patches and updates to systems and software.
- **Administrative:** Develop an incident response plan that outlines steps for addressing data breaches, including communication with affected patients and regulatory bodies.
- **Physical:** Have procedures in place for repairing physical security measures, such as broken locks or malfunctioning biometric scanners.

Testing and Continuous Improvement:

- Conduct regular penetration tests and vulnerability scans to identify and address security gaps.
- Perform incident response drills to ensure readiness for potential data breaches.
- Continuously review and update security policies and controls based on test results and changes in the regulatory environment.

By following these best practices and implementing a comprehensive set of controls, organizations can effectively mitigate risks and protect their information assets. Regular testing and continuous improvement ensure that controls remain effective and adaptive to evolving threats and organizational needs.

Importance of Continuous Risk Monitoring and Review

Continuous risk monitoring and review are essential components of an effective risk management process. This ongoing approach ensures that risk mitigation controls remain effective, new or evolving risks are promptly identified, and risk assessments and treatment plans are regularly updated to reflect the current threat landscape. Continuous monitoring helps organizations maintain a proactive stance in managing risks, improving resilience, and supporting strategic objectives.

Key Activities and Techniques for Continuous Risk Monitoring

1. Monitoring the Effectiveness of Risk Mitigation Controls

Regular Audits and Assessments:

- Conduct regular internal and external audits to evaluate the effectiveness of risk mitigation controls.
- Use frameworks like ISO/IEC 27001, NIST, and COBIT to guide audit processes.

Control Testing:

- Perform periodic testing of security controls, such as penetration testing, vulnerability assessments, and red teaming exercises.
- Assess both technical controls (e.g., firewalls, intrusion detection systems) and administrative controls (e.g., policies, procedures).

Automated Monitoring:

- Implement automated tools and systems, such as Security Information and Event Management (SIEM) solutions, to continuously monitor network activity and detect anomalies.
- Use endpoint detection and response (EDR) tools to monitor endpoints for signs of compromise.

User Activity Monitoring:

- Track user activities, especially those with elevated privileges, to identify unusual or unauthorized actions.
- Implement user behavior analytics (UBA) to detect deviations from normal behavior patterns.

2. Identifying New or Changing Risks

Threat Intelligence:

- Subscribe to threat intelligence feeds and participate in information-sharing communities (e.g., ISACs) to stay informed about emerging threats and vulnerabilities.
- Use threat intelligence platforms to aggregate and analyze threat data.

Environmental Scanning:

- Regularly scan the internal and external environment for changes that could introduce new risks, such as changes in business operations, regulatory updates, and technological advancements.
- Conduct scenario analysis and stress testing to anticipate the impact of potential changes.

Incident Analysis:

- Analyze security incidents and near-misses to identify root causes and trends.
- Use findings from incident analysis to update risk assessments and improve mitigation strategies.

Risk Assessments:

- Conduct regular risk assessments to identify and evaluate new risks.
- Update risk registers and treatment plans based on the latest assessment results.

3. Updating Risk Assessments and Treatment Plans

Periodic Reviews:

- Schedule regular reviews of risk assessments and treatment plans (e.g., quarterly, semi-annually) to ensure they remain current and relevant.
- Include key stakeholders in review processes to gather diverse perspectives and insights.

Dynamic Adjustment:

- Adjust risk treatment strategies dynamically based on monitoring results, new risk information, and changing business priorities.
- Implement an agile approach to risk management that allows for rapid adaptation to new risks.

Continuous Improvement:

- Use feedback from monitoring and review activities to drive continuous improvement in risk management practices.
- Document lessons learned and integrate them into updated policies, procedures, and training programs.

Role of Metrics, Key Risk Indicators (KRIs), and Reporting

1. Metrics

Definition:

- Metrics are quantitative measures used to evaluate and track the performance of risk management activities and controls.

Examples:

- Number of detected vulnerabilities.
- Average time to detect and respond to incidents.
- Percentage of employees completing security awareness training.

Importance:

- Metrics provide objective data to assess the effectiveness of risk management efforts.
- They help identify areas for improvement and support data-driven decision-making.

2. Key Risk Indicators (KRIs)

Definition:

- KRIs are metrics that signal potential changes in the risk profile of an organization. They provide early warnings of increasing risk levels.

Examples:

- Number of phishing attempts detected.
- Frequency of unauthorized access attempts.
- Rate of data transfer anomalies.

Importance:

- KRIs help organizations anticipate and respond to emerging risks before they materialize into significant issues.
- They support proactive risk management by highlighting areas that require attention.

3. Reporting

Definition:

- Reporting involves communicating risk status, trends, and management efforts to stakeholders through structured reports and presentations.

Examples:

- Risk dashboards.

- Quarterly risk management reports.
- Incident and breach reports.

Importance:

- Effective reporting keeps stakeholders informed about the organization's risk posture and management efforts.
- It fosters transparency and accountability, enabling informed decision-making and strategic planning.

Steps for Effective Risk Monitoring and Reporting

1. Define Clear Objectives and Metrics:

- Establish clear objectives for risk monitoring and define relevant metrics and KRIs.
- Align metrics with organizational goals and regulatory requirements.

2. Implement Monitoring Tools and Processes:

- Deploy tools and technologies to automate monitoring and data collection.
- Establish processes for regular audits, control testing, and user activity monitoring.

3. Analyze and Interpret Data:

- Regularly analyze collected data to identify trends, anomalies, and potential risks.
- Use data analytics and visualization tools to support interpretation and decision-making.

4. Communicate Findings:

- Develop comprehensive reports and dashboards to communicate findings to stakeholders.
- Use visual aids (e.g., charts, graphs) to enhance clarity and impact.

5. Engage Stakeholders:

- Involve key stakeholders in the monitoring and review processes.
- Schedule regular meetings to discuss risk status, review reports, and make informed decisions.

6. Update Risk Management Plans:

- Use insights from monitoring and reporting to update risk assessments and treatment plans.
- Implement changes dynamically to address new or evolving risks.

7. Foster a Culture of Continuous Improvement:

- Encourage a culture of continuous improvement by regularly reviewing and refining risk management practices.
- Provide training and awareness programs to keep employees informed and engaged in risk management efforts.

Example: Implementing Continuous Risk Monitoring and Review

Scenario: A multinational financial services company seeks to enhance its risk management process through continuous monitoring and review.

Step-by-Step Process:

1. **Define Objectives and Metrics:**
    - Objective: Improve the effectiveness of risk mitigation controls and identify emerging risks.
    - Metrics: Number of vulnerabilities detected, average incident response time, employee training completion rate.
    - KRIs: Frequency of unauthorized access attempts, rate of phishing emails detected.
2. **Implement Monitoring Tools:**
    - Deploy a SIEM system for continuous network monitoring.
    - Use EDR tools to monitor endpoints.
    - Implement UBA to detect anomalies in user behavior.
3. **Analyze Data:**
    - Regularly review SIEM and EDR alerts to identify potential threats.
    - Analyze incident reports to determine root causes and trends.
4. **Communicate Findings:**
    - Develop a quarterly risk management report for senior management.

    - Create a risk dashboard to visualize key metrics and KRIs.
5. **Engage Stakeholders:**
    - Schedule monthly risk review meetings with the risk management committee.
    - Present findings and discuss necessary actions.
6. **Update Plans:**
    - Adjust risk treatment plans based on new insights.
    - Implement additional controls for emerging risks identified through KRIs.
7. **Continuous Improvement:**
    - Conduct post-incident reviews and integrate lessons learned into training programs.
    - Regularly update monitoring tools and processes to stay current with evolving threats.

Conclusion

Continuous risk monitoring and review are vital for maintaining an effective risk management process. By regularly assessing the effectiveness of risk mitigation controls, identifying new risks, and updating risk management plans, organizations can proactively manage their risk profile. Using metrics, KRIs, and effective reporting ensures that stakeholders are informed and engaged in the risk management process. This dynamic approach enables organizations to adapt to changing threats and maintain a robust security posture.

Case Study: Successful Implementation of a Comprehensive Information Security Risk Management Program

Organization: MedHealth, a mid-sized healthcare provider

Objective: To implement a comprehensive information security risk management program to protect patient data, ensure compliance with HIPAA regulations, and enhance overall cybersecurity posture.

Stage 1: Risk Identification

Challenges:

- Diverse sources of data, including electronic health records (HER), medical devices, and administrative systems.
- Rapid digital transformation increasing the attack surface.
- Existing ad-hoc security measures without a formalized risk management approach.

Decisions:

- Establish a cross-functional risk management team comprising IT, legal, compliance, and healthcare professionals.
- Conduct a thorough risk identification process using tools such as SWOT analysis, brainstorming sessions, and consultations with departmental heads.

Outcomes:

- Identified critical risks, including data breaches, ransomware attacks, insider threats, and compliance violations.
- Created a comprehensive list of potential threats and vulnerabilities associated with patient data and IT infrastructure.

Stage 2: Risk Assessment

Challenges:

- Assessing the likelihood and impact of identified risks accurately.
- Limited historical data on security incidents specific to the healthcare sector.

Decisions:

- Adopt both qualitative and quantitative risk assessment methods.
- Use expert judgment and industry benchmarks to assess risks qualitatively.
- Implement quantitative methods to calculate potential financial impacts where data was available.

Outcomes:

- Developed a risk matrix categorizing risks based on their likelihood and impact (low, medium, high).

- Prioritized risks, with data breaches and ransomware attacks identified as high-priority risks requiring immediate attention.

Stage 3: Risk Treatment

Challenges:

- Balancing the need for robust security measures with the need for seamless healthcare operations.
- Budget constraints limiting the ability to implement all desired security controls simultaneously.

Decisions:

- Develop a risk treatment plan focusing on high-priority risks first.
- Select a mix of preventive, detective, and corrective controls.
- Align risk treatment strategies with HIPAA compliance requirements.

Outcomes:

- **Preventive Controls:**
    - Implemented multi-factor authentication (MFA) for accessing HER systems.
    - Deployed endpoint protection solutions on all workstations and servers.
    - Encrypted all patient data, both in transit and at rest.
- **Detective Controls:**
    - Installed intrusion detection systems (IDS) and security information and event management (SIEM) systems to monitor network traffic and detect suspicious activities.
    - Conducted regular security audits and vulnerability assessments.
- **Corrective Controls:**
    - Developed an incident response plan detailing steps for addressing data breaches and other security incidents.
    - Implemented a robust backup and disaster recovery plan to ensure data availability and integrity in case of an attack.

Stage 4: Risk Monitoring

Challenges:

- Ensuring continuous monitoring and timely updates to the risk management program.
- Keeping up with evolving cyber threats and regulatory changes.

Decisions:

- Establish a continuous monitoring program using SIEM for real-time alerts and analysis.
- Conduct periodic reviews and updates of the risk management program.
- Engage in threat intelligence sharing with other healthcare providers and industry bodies.

Outcomes:

- Regularly updated risk assessments and treatment plans based on new threats and vulnerabilities.
- Improved ability to detect and respond to security incidents quickly.
- Ensured ongoing compliance with HIPAA and other relevant regulations.

Benefits Realized

1. Reduced Incident Frequency and Impact:

- Significant reduction in the number of successful phishing attacks and data breaches.
- Improved incident response times, minimizing the impact of security incidents on operations and patient care.

2. Improved Compliance:

- Achieved full compliance with HIPAA regulations, avoiding potential fines and legal actions.
- Demonstrated a proactive approach to regulatory bodies and auditors, strengthening compliance posture.

3. Enhanced Stakeholder Confidence:

- Increased trust among patients, knowing their sensitive health information is well-protected.

- Improved confidence among employees, who are now better educated and aware of security practices.
- Enhanced reputation among industry peers and partners as a leader in healthcare information security.

Summary

MedHealth's successful implementation of a comprehensive information security risk management program illustrates the importance of a structured approach to identifying, assessing, treating, and monitoring risks. By prioritizing high-impact risks and implementing a balanced mix of controls, MedHealth was able to significantly enhance its cybersecurity posture, ensure regulatory compliance, and build stronger relationships with stakeholders. This case study underscores the value of continuous improvement and adaptation in the face of evolving cyber threats and regulatory requirements.

Real-World Scenarios Illustrating Common Information Security Risks

Scenario 1: Financial Services - Data Breach

Context: A large financial services firm experienced a data breach that exposed sensitive customer information, including account numbers, social security numbers, and transaction histories.

Key Risk Factors:

- **High Value Targets:** Financial institutions are prime targets for cybercriminals due to the sensitive financial data they hold.
- **Sophisticated Attacks:** Cybercriminals often use advanced techniques, such as phishing and malware, to breach financial systems.
- **Regulatory Pressure:** Financial institutions are subject to stringent regulatory requirements for data protection (e.g., GDPR, PCI DSS).

Assessment Findings:

- **Weak Authentication:** The breach was traced back to weak authentication mechanisms, allowing attackers to gain access through compromised employee credentials.
- **Insufficient Monitoring:** The firm lacked adequate monitoring and detection capabilities, leading to delayed breach detection and response.
- **Poor Incident Response:** The incident response plan was outdated and not effectively communicated to employees.

Recommended Treatment Options:

- **Mitigate:** Implement multi-factor authentication (MFA) to strengthen access controls.
- **Mitigate:** Deploy advanced monitoring tools, such as Security Information and Event Management (SIEM) systems, to detect and respond to threats in real-time.
- **Mitigate:** Update and test the incident response plan regularly, ensuring all employees are aware of their roles and responsibilities during an incident.
- **Transfer:** Purchase cyber insurance to mitigate the financial impact of future breaches.

Lessons Learned:

- **Proactive Measures:** Implementing strong authentication and continuous monitoring are critical in preventing data breaches.
- **Regular Training:** Conduct regular training and simulations to ensure employees are prepared for security incidents.
- **Timely Detection:** Early detection and rapid response can significantly reduce the impact of a breach.

Broader Implications:

- Financial institutions must prioritize cybersecurity due to the high value of the data they handle and the severe consequences of breaches.
- Continuous investment in advanced security technologies and practices is essential to stay ahead of evolving threats.

Scenario 2: Healthcare – Ransomware Attack

Context: A regional hospital network suffered a ransomware attack that encrypted patient records and disrupted critical medical services.

Key Risk Factors:

- **Critical Services:** Healthcare organizations provide essential services, making them attractive targets for ransomware attacks.
- **Sensitive Data:** Patient records contain sensitive information that can be exploited for financial gain.
- **Legacy Systems:** Many healthcare organizations use outdated systems with known vulnerabilities.

Assessment Findings:

- **Vulnerable Systems:** The attack exploited unpatched vulnerabilities in the hospital's legacy systems.
- **Lack of Backups:** The hospital did not have a comprehensive backup strategy, resulting in the loss of critical data.
- **Inadequate Awareness:** Employees were not sufficiently trained to recognize and respond to phishing emails, the initial vector of the attack.

Recommended Treatment Options:

- **Mitigate:** Patch and update all systems regularly to protect against known vulnerabilities.
- **Mitigate:** Implement a robust backup strategy, including regular backups and secure offsite storage.
- **Mitigate:** Conduct regular training and awareness programs to educate employees about phishing and other social engineering attacks.
- **Accept:** Given the high probability of attacks, develop and test a detailed incident response plan tailored to ransomware scenarios.

Lessons Learned:

- **Patch Management:** Keeping systems up to date is essential in preventing ransomware attacks.
- **Data Backup:** Regular and secure backups are crucial for recovery from ransomware attacks.
- **Employee Awareness:** Continuous training can help employees recognize and avoid phishing attacks.

Broader Implications:

- Healthcare organizations must invest in modernizing their IT infrastructure to reduce vulnerabilities.
- Developing and testing incident response plans for ransomware is critical for minimizing downtime and data loss.

Scenario 3: Retail - Point of Sale (POS) System Compromise

Context: A national retail chain discovered that its POS systems were compromised, leading to the theft of customers' credit card information.

Key Risk Factors:

- **High Transaction Volume:** Retail environments process numerous transactions, making them lucrative targets for attackers seeking financial data.
- **Distributed Locations:** Retail chains have numerous locations, increasing the attack surface and complexity of security management.
- **Outsourced Systems:** POS systems are often managed by third-party vendors, introducing additional risk.

Assessment Findings:

- **Third-Party Risk:** The compromise was linked to vulnerabilities in the third-party POS software.
- **Lack of Encryption:** Customer credit card information was not encrypted during transmission.
- **Insufficient Segmentation:** The network was not properly segmented, allowing the attacker to move laterally and access sensitive data.

Recommended Treatment Options:

- **Mitigate:** Encrypt credit card information both at rest and in transit to protect sensitive data.
- **Mitigate:** Segment the network to isolate POS systems from other parts of the network, reducing the attack surface.

- **Transfer:** Ensure third-party vendors comply with the organization's security policies and conduct regular security assessments.
- **Mitigate:** Implement continuous monitoring and threat detection solutions to identify and respond to suspicious activities promptly.

Lessons Learned:

- **Vendor Management:** Regularly assess and monitor the security practices of third-party vendors.
- **Data Encryption:** Encrypting sensitive data is critical to protecting it from unauthorized access.
- **Network Segmentation:** Proper network segmentation can limit the impact of a breach by containing the attacker's movement.

Broader Implications:

- Retailers must prioritize securing POS systems and ensure robust vendor management practices.
- Implementing encryption and network segmentation can significantly enhance security and protect customer data.

Scenario 4: Manufacturing – Industrial Control System (ICS) Attack

Context: A manufacturing company experienced a cyber attack targeting its industrial control systems (ICS), disrupting production and causing significant financial losses.

Key Risk Factors:

- **Critical Infrastructure:** ICS are crucial for manufacturing operations, making them attractive targets for cyber attacks.
- **Legacy Technology:** Many ICS run on outdated software and hardware, increasing vulnerability.
- **Complexity:** The complexity of ICS environments makes it challenging to secure them effectively.

Assessment Findings:

- **Vulnerable Systems:** The attack exploited outdated and unpatched ICS software.
- **Lack of Monitoring:** There was insufficient monitoring of ICS networks, leading to delayed detection of the attack.
- **Inadequate Segmentation:** The IT and ICS networks were not adequately segmented, allowing the attacker to move between them.

Recommended Treatment Options:

- **Mitigate:** Update and patch ICS software and hardware regularly to address vulnerabilities.
- **Mitigate:** Implement dedicated monitoring solutions for ICS networks to detect anomalies and potential threats.
- **Mitigate:** Segment IT and ICS networks to prevent lateral movement by attackers.
- **Mitigate:** Conduct regular security assessments and penetration testing to identify and address vulnerabilities in ICS environments.

Lessons Learned:

- **Patch Management:** Regular updates and patching are essential for securing ICS.
- **Dedicated Monitoring:** Specialized monitoring tools are necessary to detect threats in ICS environments.
- **Network Segmentation:** Segmentation can prevent the spread of attacks between IT and ICS networks.

Broader Implications:

- Manufacturers must invest in modernizing ICS security and implementing best practices for critical infrastructure protection.
- Continuous monitoring and regular security assessments are crucial for maintaining the security of ICS environments.

Conclusion

These real-world scenarios highlight the diverse and significant information security risks faced by different industries. By understanding the key risk factors, assessment findings, and recommended treatment options, organizations can develop more effective risk management strategies. Continuous monitoring, regular updates, employee training, and robust incident response plans are essential components of a proactive and resilient information security posture. By learning from these scenarios, organizations can better anticipate and mitigate potential risks, ensuring the security and continuity of their operations.

Practice Questions and Exercises for Information Risk Management

These practice questions and exercises will challenge you to apply your knowledge of information risk management concepts and techniques to realistic situations. The questions cover a range of topics and difficulty levels to ensure a comprehensive understanding of the subject.

Multiple-Choice Questions

1. Which of the following is NOT a step in the NIST Risk Management Framework (RMF)? A. Categorize Information Systems
B. Implement Security Controls
C. Conduct a Privacy Impact Assessment
D. Authorize Information System
Answer: C. Conduct a Privacy Impact Assessment
Explanation: While conducting a Privacy Impact Assessment is important for protecting personal data, it is not explicitly listed as a step in the NIST RMF. The RMF steps are: Categorize, Select, Implement, Assess, Authorize, and Monitor security controls.

2. In ISO 27005, which activity is performed first in the risk management process? A. Risk Treatment
B. Risk Assessment
C. Context Establishment
D. Risk Monitoring
Answer: C. Context Establishment
Explanation: The first step in ISO 27005 is Context Establishment, which involves defining the scope, boundaries, and objectives of the risk management process.

3. Which type of control is designed to identify and detect security incidents that have occurred? A. Preventive
B. Detective
C. Corrective
D. Deterrent
Answer: B. Detective
Explanation: Detective controls are used to identify and detect security incidents, enabling timely responses. Examples include intrusion detection systems and audit logs.

Short-Answer Questions

4. Explain the difference between quantitative and qualitative risk assessment methodologies.
Answer: Quantitative risk assessment uses numerical data and statistical methods to measure the likelihood and impact of risks in financial terms, providing precise, data-driven insights. Qualitative risk assessment relies on subjective criteria, such as expert opinions and scenarios, to evaluate risks using descriptive terms and ratings (e.g., high, medium, low). Quantitative assessments are often more precise but require detailed data, whereas qualitative assessments are quicker and more flexible but less precise.

5. Describe three types of controls (preventive, detective, corrective) and provide an example of each.
Answer:

- **Preventive Controls:** Aim to prevent security incidents from occurring. Example: Firewalls that block unauthorized access to the network.
- **Detective Controls:** Identify and detect security incidents that have occurred. Example: Intrusion detection systems (IDS) that monitor network traffic for suspicious activity.
- **Corrective Controls:** Respond to and mitigate the impact of security incidents. Example: Patch management systems that apply updates to fix vulnerabilities in software.

Case Study-Based Questions

6. Case Study: A financial services company is implementing a new risk management program. They need to protect sensitive customer data, ensure compliance with regulations such as GDPR and SOX, and mitigate the risk of cyber attacks.

a. Identify and describe the steps the company should take to establish this program using the NIST RMF.

Answer:

1. **Categorize Information Systems:** Determine the impact levels of information systems based on FIPS 199 standards.
2. **Select Security Controls:** Choose appropriate security controls from NIST SP 800-53 based on the system's impact level.
3. **Implement Security Controls:** Deploy the selected controls and document how they are implemented.
4. **Assess Security Controls:** Evaluate the effectiveness of the controls to ensure they function as intended.
5. **Authorize Information System:** Senior management formally authorizes the system to operate based on the risk assessment.
6. **Monitor Security Controls:** Continuously monitor the controls to ensure they remain effective and make necessary adjustments.

b. Explain how the company can use both qualitative and quantitative risk assessments to prioritize risks.

Answer: The company can begin with a qualitative assessment to quickly identify and categorize risks based on expert judgment and stakeholder input, using descriptive terms (e.g., high, medium, low). For high-priority risks identified qualitatively, they can then conduct a quantitative assessment to measure the likelihood and financial impact using numerical data and statistical methods. This combined approach ensures a comprehensive understanding of risks and effective prioritization.

c. Recommend a mix of technical, administrative, and physical controls to mitigate identified risks and provide examples of each.

Answer:

- **Technical Controls:** Implement encryption for customer data, deploy multi-factor authentication (MFA), and use intrusion detection systems (IDS).
- **Administrative Controls:** Develop and enforce security policies, conduct regular security awareness training for employees, and perform background checks on employees with access to sensitive data.
- **Physical Controls:** Secure data centers with biometric access controls, install surveillance cameras, and employ security guards to monitor facilities.

References and Explanations

Reference 1: NIST Special Publication 800-37, "Risk Management Framework for Information Systems and Organizations"

Explanation: This document provides guidelines for applying the Risk Management Framework to federal information systems and is a key reference for understanding the NIST RMF steps and processes.

Reference 2: ISO/IEC 27005:2018, "Information security risk management"

Explanation: This standard outlines guidelines for information security risk management, supporting the implementation of an ISMS based on ISO/IEC 27001. It explains the risk management process, including context establishment, risk assessment, risk treatment, and monitoring.

Reference 3: NIST Special Publication 800-53, "Security and Privacy Controls for Information Systems and Organizations"

Explanation: This document provides a catalog of security and privacy controls for federal information systems and organizations, detailing the implementation of various types of controls, including preventive, detective, and corrective.

By working through these practice questions and exercises, you can reinforce your understanding of information risk management concepts and techniques, applying them to realistic situations and enhancing your preparedness for real-world challenges.

Role of Risk Management in Supporting Information Security Governance and Compliance

Risk management is integral to an organization's information security governance and compliance efforts. It involves identifying, assessing, prioritizing, and mitigating risks to ensure the protection of information assets and compliance with legal, regulatory, and contractual requirements. Effective risk management supports the development and implementation of security policies, procedures, and controls, aligning them with the organization's strategic objectives.

How Risk Management Supports Information Security Governance

1. Comprehensive Risk Identification and Assessment:

- **Purpose:** Identifies potential threats and vulnerabilities that could impact the organization's information assets.
- **Outcome:** Provides a clear understanding of the risk landscape, enabling the organization to prioritize its security efforts.

2. Informed Decision-Making:

- **Purpose:** Provides a basis for making informed decisions about resource allocation and risk mitigation strategies.
- **Outcome:** Ensures that limited resources are directed towards the most critical risks, enhancing overall security posture.

3. Policy Development and Implementation:

- **Purpose:** Guides the creation of robust security policies, procedures, and controls based on identified risks.
- **Outcome:** Ensures that policies and controls are tailored to address specific threats and vulnerabilities, thereby improving their effectiveness.

4. Compliance and Regulatory Alignment:

- **Purpose:** Helps the organization understand and meet legal, regulatory, and contractual requirements related to information security.
- **Outcome:** Reduces the risk of non-compliance penalties and enhances the organization's reputation and credibility.

Risk Assessment Results and Treatment Decisions Informing Security Policies, Procedures, and Controls

1. Risk Assessment Results:

- **Identification of Critical Assets:** Determines which information assets are most critical to the organization's operations and require the highest level of protection.
- **Vulnerability Analysis:** Identifies weaknesses in existing systems, processes, and controls that could be exploited by threats.
- **Impact Analysis:** Evaluates the potential consequences of different risks, helping prioritize them based on their severity.

2. Treatment Decisions:

- **Avoidance:** Identifying risks that can be eliminated by discontinuing high-risk activities.
    - **Example:** Discontinuing the use of legacy systems that are no longer supported and pose significant security risks.
- **Transfer:** Shifting risks to third parties, such as through insurance or outsourcing.
    - **Example:** Purchasing cybersecurity insurance to cover potential financial losses from data breaches.
- **Mitigation:** Implementing measures to reduce the likelihood or impact of risks.
    - **Example:** Deploying multi-factor authentication (MFA) to enhance access control security.
- **Acceptance:** Acknowledging and accepting the risk when it falls within the organization's risk tolerance.
    - **Example:** Accepting the risk of minor software vulnerabilities that are unlikely to be exploited and have minimal impact.

3. Development and Implementation of Policies and Controls:

- **Access Control Policies:** Based on risk assessments, develop policies that define who has access to what information and under what conditions.
    - **Example:** Implementing role-based access control (RBAC) to ensure that employees can only access data necessary for their job functions.
- **Incident Response Procedures:** Create procedures for responding to security incidents, informed by potential impact and likelihood of identified risks.
    - **Example:** Establishing a detailed incident response plan that outlines steps for detecting, containing, and recovering from data breaches.
- **Security Controls:** Implement technical and administrative controls to mitigate identified risks.
    - **Example:** Installing firewalls, intrusion detection systems, and regular patch management processes to protect against cyber threats.

Aligning Risk Management Activities with Other Governance Processes

1. Strategic Planning:

- **Integration:** Align risk management with strategic planning to ensure that security initiatives support the organization's long-term goals.
- **Example:** Including cybersecurity goals in the organization's strategic plan, such as achieving compliance with specific standards (e.g., ISO 27001) within a set timeframe.

2. Budgeting:

- **Allocation:** Use risk assessment results to justify budget allocations for security initiatives and technologies.
- **Example:** Allocating funds for upgrading outdated security infrastructure based on the high risk of potential breaches identified in the risk assessment.

3. Performance Measurement:

- **Metrics:** Develop metrics and Key Risk Indicators (KRIs) to measure the effectiveness of risk management activities and their impact on overall performance.
- **Example:** Tracking the number of detected and mitigated vulnerabilities over time to assess the effectiveness of patch management processes.

Examples of Risk Management Supporting Governance Processes

1. Example: Strategic Planning

- **Scenario:** An organization plans to expand its digital services.
- **Risk Management Alignment:** Risk assessments identify potential security threats associated with new digital services, such as increased exposure to cyber-attacks.
- **Integration:** Incorporate cybersecurity objectives into the strategic plan, such as enhancing digital service security through advanced threat detection systems and employee training programs.

2. Example: Budgeting

- **Scenario:** An organization needs to allocate its annual IT budget.
- **Risk Management Alignment:** Risk assessments reveal critical vulnerabilities in the current IT infrastructure.
- **Allocation:** Budgeting decisions prioritize funding for security upgrades, such as implementing advanced encryption technologies and upgrading firewall protections.

3. Example: Performance Measurement

- **Scenario:** An organization wants to measure the effectiveness of its risk management program.
- **Risk Management Alignment:** Develop KRIs based on risk assessment findings, such as the frequency of security incidents and the average time to detect and respond to threats.
- **Measurement:** Regularly monitor these KRIs to evaluate and improve the performance of the risk management program.

Conclusion

Risk management plays a vital role in supporting an organization's information security governance and compliance efforts. By identifying, assessing, and prioritizing risks, organizations can make informed decisions about resource allocation and policy development. Aligning risk management activities with strategic planning, budgeting, and performance measurement ensures that security initiatives support overall business objectives and enhance resilience. Continuous monitoring, regular updates, and proactive risk treatment are essential for maintaining a robust security posture and achieving compliance in an ever-evolving threat landscape.

Exploring the Relationship Between Information Security Risk Management and Related Disciplines

Information security risk management is closely related to several other disciplines, including business continuity management, incident response, and vendor risk management. These disciplines intersect and complement each other in creating a holistic and resilient information security posture. Understanding how they integrate helps organizations develop comprehensive strategies to protect their information assets and ensure operational resilience.

1. Business Continuity Management (BCM)

Relationship and Intersection:

- **Risk Identification and Assessment:** Both disciplines involve identifying and assessing risks that could disrupt business operations. While information security risk management focuses on cybersecurity threats, BCM covers a broader range of risks, including natural disasters, power outages, and pandemics.
- **Mitigation and Controls:** Information security risk management contributes to BCM by implementing controls that protect critical information assets, ensuring that data is available and secure during disruptions.
- **Resilience Planning:** Information security measures, such as data encryption, backup, and disaster recovery plans, are integral components of a business continuity plan.

Example Application:

- **Scenario:** A financial institution implements a business continuity plan to ensure that critical operations can continue during a cyberattack.
- **Actions:** The institution conducts a risk assessment to identify key information assets and potential cyber threats. It then implements controls such as off-site backups, redundant systems, and network segmentation. These measures ensure that, in the event of an attack, the institution can quickly restore operations and minimize downtime.

2. Incident Response (IR)

Relationship and Intersection:

- **Preparation and Planning:** Information security risk management involves identifying potential threats and vulnerabilities, which informs the development of an incident response plan.
- **Detection and Analysis:** Effective risk management includes implementing controls to detect security incidents, such as intrusion detection systems (IDS) and security information and event management (SIEM) systems. These tools are critical for incident detection and analysis.
- **Response and Recovery:** Incident response plans outline the steps to take when a security incident occurs, including containment, eradication, and recovery. Risk management ensures that the appropriate controls and resources are in place to execute these steps effectively.

Example Application:

- **Scenario:** A healthcare organization faces a ransomware attack, encrypting patient data and disrupting services.
- **Actions:** The organization's incident response team, informed by prior risk assessments, quickly identifies the ransomware variant and isolates affected systems. They use predefined playbooks and communication plans to coordinate the response, restore data from backups, and notify stakeholders. Post-incident, the team reviews the event to update the risk management and incident response strategies.

3. Vendor Risk Management (VRM)

Relationship and Intersection:

- **Third-Party Risk Assessment:** Information security risk management includes assessing the risks associated with third-party vendors. This involves evaluating vendors' security practices, compliance with regulations, and potential impact on the organization's security posture.
- **Contractual Controls:** Organizations use risk management principles to define security requirements and controls in vendor contracts. These controls help ensure vendors meet the organization's security standards.
- **Continuous Monitoring:** Ongoing risk monitoring is essential for both disciplines. Information security risk management ensures that vendors are regularly assessed for compliance and security performance.

Example Application:

- **Scenario:** A retail company uses a third-party payment processor for handling customer transactions.
- **Actions:** The company conducts a thorough risk assessment of the payment processor, reviewing their security policies, compliance certifications (e.g., PCI DSS), and incident history. It incorporates security requirements into the contract, such as regular security audits and data encryption standards. The company also implements continuous monitoring to ensure ongoing compliance and address any emerging risks.

Integrating Risk Management with Related Disciplines

Holistic Approach:

- **Unified Risk Management Framework:** Develop a comprehensive risk management framework that integrates information security, business continuity, incident response, and vendor risk management. This framework should ensure that all aspects of risk are considered and managed cohesively.
- **Collaboration and Communication:** Foster collaboration between teams responsible for information security, business continuity, incident response, and vendor management. Regular communication ensures that risk information is shared and that strategies are aligned.
- **Training and Awareness:** Provide cross-disciplinary training to ensure that all team members understand the interconnected nature of these disciplines and their roles in maintaining security and resilience.

Example of a Holistic Approach:

- **Scenario:** A multinational corporation aims to strengthen its overall security posture by integrating its risk management practices.
- **Actions:** The corporation establishes a unified risk management framework that includes representatives from information security, business continuity, incident response, and vendor management. They conduct joint risk assessments, share threat intelligence, and coordinate response plans. Regular tabletop exercises and training sessions ensure that all teams are prepared to respond to incidents and disruptions cohesively.

Conclusion

The relationship between information security risk management and related disciplines such as business continuity management, incident response, and vendor risk management is essential for creating a holistic and resilient security posture. By integrating these disciplines, organizations can better prepare for, respond to, and recover from a wide range of risks and threats. This comprehensive approach enhances overall security, ensures compliance, and builds confidence among stakeholders.

Emerging Trends and Challenges in Information Security Risk Management

1. Increasing Complexity and Interconnectedness of Digital Ecosystems

Trend:

- Digital ecosystems are becoming increasingly complex and interconnected, incorporating a vast array of devices, platforms, and services, including cloud computing, IoT, and mobile technologies.

Challenges:

- **Integration Risks:** Integrating diverse systems and technologies can create new vulnerabilities and potential points of failure.
- **Visibility and Control:** Maintaining visibility and control over a distributed and interconnected environment is difficult, complicating risk management and incident response.

- **Supply Chain Security:** The interconnected nature of digital ecosystems means that security weaknesses in one part of the supply chain can impact the entire ecosystem.

2. Evolving Threat Landscape

Trend:

- The threat landscape is continuously evolving, with cybercriminals using increasingly sophisticated techniques, such as ransomware, advanced persistent threats (APTs), and zero-day exploits.

Challenges:

- **Adaptive Threats:** Attackers are constantly adapting their tactics to bypass existing security measures, requiring organizations to stay ahead with advanced defense mechanisms.
- **Volume of Attacks:** The sheer volume of cyber-attacks can overwhelm security teams, making it difficult to prioritize and respond effectively.
- **Nation-State Actors:** The involvement of nation-state actors adds a layer of complexity, as these adversaries often have significant resources and capabilities.

3. Growing Regulatory and Public Scrutiny

Trend:

- Regulatory bodies and the public are increasingly scrutinizing organizations' security practices, demanding higher standards of data protection and privacy.

Challenges:

- **Regulatory Compliance:** Organizations must navigate a complex landscape of regulations, such as GDPR, CCPA, HIPAA, and others, each with its own requirements and penalties for non-compliance.
- **Reputational Risk:** Public awareness and concern about data privacy mean that security breaches can lead to significant reputational damage and loss of customer trust.
- **Legal Liabilities:** Non-compliance with regulations can result in severe legal penalties, including fines and sanctions.

Key Skills and Competencies for Information Security Professionals

To effectively navigate these challenges and drive risk-informed decision-making, information security professionals need to develop a broad range of skills and competencies:

1. Technical Proficiency

Key Skills:

- **Cybersecurity Fundamentals:** Understanding core concepts such as encryption, firewalls, intrusion detection/prevention systems, and secure coding practices.
- **Advanced Threat Detection:** Proficiency with advanced threat detection tools and techniques, including SIEM, EDR, and threat intelligence platforms.
- **Cloud Security:** Knowledge of securing cloud environments, including AWS, Azure, and Google Cloud, and familiarity with cloud-specific security challenges.

Competencies:

- **Incident Response:** Ability to effectively respond to security incidents, including detecting, containing, eradicating, and recovering from attacks.
- **Vulnerability Management:** Expertise in identifying, assessing, and mitigating vulnerabilities in IT systems and applications.
- **Forensics and Investigation:** Skills in conducting digital forensics and investigations to analyze and understand security incidents.

2. Risk Management and Compliance

Key Skills:

- **Risk Assessment:** Proficiency in conducting risk assessments to identify, evaluate, and prioritize risks based on their potential impact.
- **Regulatory Knowledge:** Understanding of relevant regulations and standards, such as GDPR, HIPAA, PCI DSS, and ISO/IEC 27001, and how to achieve and maintain compliance.
- **Policy Development:** Ability to develop, implement, and enforce security policies, procedures, and controls.

- **Competencies:**
- **Audit and Compliance:** Experience in conducting security audits and assessments to ensure compliance with regulatory and organizational standards.
- **Third-Party Risk Management:** Skills in assessing and managing risks associated with third-party vendors and partners.
- **Business Continuity Planning:** Expertise in developing and testing business continuity and disaster recovery plans.

3. Strategic and Analytical Thinking

Key Skills:

- **Strategic Planning:** Ability to align security initiatives with organizational goals and develop long-term security strategies.
- **Data Analysis:** Proficiency in analyzing security data to identify trends, patterns, and potential threats.
- **Scenario Analysis:** Skills in conducting scenario analysis and simulations to anticipate and prepare for potential security incidents.

Competencies:

- **Decision-Making:** Strong decision-making skills to prioritize security initiatives and allocate resources effectively.
- **Critical Thinking:** Ability to critically assess security risks and develop innovative solutions to complex problems.
- **Risk Communication:** Expertise in communicating risk to non-technical stakeholders, including executives and board members, to drive informed decision-making.

4. Leadership and Collaboration

Key Skills:

- **Team Leadership:** Ability to lead and manage security teams, including setting goals, providing guidance, and fostering a collaborative environment.
- **Cross-Functional Collaboration:** Skills in working with other departments, such as IT, legal, and finance, to integrate security into all aspects of the organization.
- **Training and Awareness:** Proficiency in developing and delivering security training and awareness programs to educate employees about security best practices.

Competencies:

- **Influence and Advocacy:** Ability to advocate for security initiatives and influence decision-making at the executive level.
- **Change Management:** Skills in managing organizational change to implement new security policies and practices effectively.
- **Crisis Management:** Expertise in managing security crises, including coordinating response efforts and communicating with stakeholders.

Conclusion

Emerging trends and challenges in information security risk management require professionals to develop a diverse set of skills and competencies. Technical proficiency, risk management and compliance knowledge, strategic and analytical thinking, and leadership and collaboration abilities are all essential for navigating the complexities of modern digital ecosystems, evolving threats, and regulatory scrutiny. By fostering these skills, information security professionals can drive effective risk management and support their organizations in achieving robust security and compliance.

Presenting Risk Assessment Results and Recommendations to Stakeholders

Presenting risk assessment results effectively is crucial for gaining stakeholder buy-in and ensuring that the necessary actions are taken to mitigate identified risks. Key components of effective presentations include clear communication, compelling language, and the use of visual aids. Here's a comprehensive guide on how to present risk assessment results and recommendations effectively.

Key Components of Effective Risk Assessment Presentations

1. **Executive Summary:**
   - Provide a brief overview of the key findings, risks identified, and recommended actions. This section should give stakeholders a quick snapshot of the most critical information.
2. **Introduction:**
   - Explain the purpose of the risk assessment, the methodology used, and the scope of the assessment. This sets the context and helps stakeholders understand the basis for the findings.
3. **Detailed Findings:**
   - Present the identified risks in a structured manner, categorizing them by their likelihood and impact.
   - Use clear, concise language to describe each risk, its potential consequences, and the assets it affects.
4. **Visual Aids:**
   - Use graphs, charts, and heatmaps to illustrate the risks. Visual aids help convey the significance and urgency of the risks more effectively than text alone.
   - Examples include risk matrices, bar charts showing the number of risks per category, and heatmaps highlighting high-risk areas.
5. **Recommendations:**
   - Provide actionable recommendations for mitigating each identified risk. Prioritize these recommendations based on their potential impact and feasibility.
   - Include short-term and long-term actions, and specify the resources required for implementation.
6. **Conclusion:**
   - Summarize the key points and reinforce the importance of taking action. Highlight the benefits of addressing the risks and the potential consequences of inaction.

Best Practices for Effective Communication

1. **Clear and Concise Language:**
   - Avoid technical jargon and use plain language that is easily understandable by all stakeholders, including non-technical audiences.
   - Be direct and to the point, focusing on the most critical information.
2. **Compelling Language:**
   - Use persuasive language to emphasize the significance of the risks and the urgency of taking action.
   - Highlight the potential impacts on business operations, compliance, reputation, and financial performance.
3. **Visual Aids:**
   - **Graphs and Charts:** Use bar graphs, pie charts, and line charts to show the distribution and trends of risks. Ensure these visuals are clearly labeled and easy to interpret.
   - **Heatmaps:** Create heatmaps to visually represent the severity and likelihood of risks, making it easy to identify high-risk areas.
   - **Tables:** Use tables to provide detailed information on each risk, including descriptions, impacts, and mitigation strategies.

Step-by-Step Guide for Creating Effective Risk Assessment Reports and Presentations

1. **Preparation:**
   - Identify your audience and tailor the presentation to their needs and level of understanding.
   - Gather all necessary data and ensure it is accurate and up-to-date.
   - Outline the structure of your report and presentation.
2. **Executive Summary:**
   - Write a concise executive summary that highlights the main findings and recommendations.
   - Keep this section to one page or less.
3. **Introduction:**

- Explain the purpose, methodology, and scope of the risk assessment.
- Provide background information that sets the context for the findings.

4. **Detailed Findings:**
   - Categorize risks by their likelihood and impact.
   - Use clear descriptions and avoid overly technical language.
   - Support your findings with data and evidence.
5. **Visual Aids:**
   - Create graphs, charts, and heatmaps to illustrate key points.
   - Ensure visual aids are simple, clear, and add value to the presentation.
6. **Recommendations:**
   - Provide specific, actionable recommendations for each identified risk.
   - Prioritize recommendations based on their potential impact and feasibility.
   - Include both short-term and long-term actions.
7. **Conclusion:**
   - Summarize the key points and reinforce the importance of taking action.
   - Highlight the benefits of mitigating risks and the potential consequences of inaction.
8. **Anticipate Questions and Concerns:**
   - Prepare for common questions and concerns stakeholders might have.
   - Provide clear, concise answers and be ready to explain the rationale behind your findings and recommendations.

Tips for Anticipating and Addressing Common Questions and Concerns

1. **Be Prepared:**
   - Anticipate questions about the methodology, data sources, and assumptions used in the risk assessment.
   - Be ready to explain how risks were identified, categorized, and prioritized.
2. **Provide Evidence:**
   - Support your findings with data and evidence. Have backup documentation and detailed analysis available if needed.
3. **Explain the Impact:**
   - Be prepared to discuss the potential impacts of identified risks on different areas of the business, such as operations, compliance, and reputation.
4. **Justify Recommendations:**
   - Clearly explain the rationale behind your recommendations. Discuss the benefits of each proposed action and how it will mitigate the identified risks.
5. **Address Resource Concerns:**
   - Be ready to discuss the resources required for implementing the recommended actions, including time, budget, and personnel.
   - Provide a cost-benefit analysis to justify the investment in risk mitigation.

Example of a Risk Assessment Report Outline

1. **Executive Summary:**
   - Key Findings
   - Major Risks
   - Top Recommendations
2. **Introduction:**
   - Purpose
   - Methodology
   - Scope
3. **Risk Identification and Assessment:**
   - Overview of Identified Risks
   - Risk Categorization (Likelihood and Impact)

    - Visual Aids (Risk Matrix, Heatmaps)
4. **Detailed Risk Descriptions:**
    - Risk 1: Description, Impact, Likelihood, Affected Assets
    - Risk 2: Description, Impact, Likelihood, Affected Assets
    - (Repeat for each identified risk)
5. **Recommendations:**
    - Risk 1: Recommended Mitigations, Priority, Resources Required
    - Risk 2: Recommended Mitigations, Priority, Resources Required
    - (Repeat for each identified risk)
6. **Conclusion:**
    - Summary of Key Points
    - Urgency of Action
    - Benefits of Mitigation
7. **Appendices:**
    - Detailed Data and Analysis
    - Methodology Details
    - Glossary of Terms

By following these guidelines and best practices, you can create effective risk assessment reports and presentations that clearly communicate the significance and urgency of identified risks, persuade stakeholders to take action, and support informed decision-making.

Concept of Risk Appetite

Definition: Risk appetite is the amount and type of risk an organization is willing to accept in pursuit of its strategic objectives. It reflects the organization's tolerance for uncertainty and potential adverse outcomes and serves as a guiding principle for decision-making and prioritization in risk management.

Role in Guiding Risk Management Decisions and Priorities:

- **Alignment with Strategy:** Ensures that risk-taking is consistent with the organization's strategic goals and objectives.
- **Resource Allocation:** Helps prioritize resource allocation by focusing efforts on risks that are within the acceptable range and need management.
- **Decision-Making Framework:** Provides a clear framework for decision-making, ensuring that risk considerations are integrated into business planning and operations.
- **Stakeholder Assurance:** Demonstrates to stakeholders, including investors, regulators, and customers, that the organization has a structured approach to managing risk.

Importance of Establishing and Communicating Risk Appetite Statements

1. Strategic Alignment:

- Risk appetite statements ensure that the organization's approach to risk management aligns with its strategic objectives. This alignment helps in achieving business goals while managing risks appropriately.

2. Organizational Values and Culture:

- A well-defined risk appetite reflects the organization's values and culture, indicating how much risk it is willing to take in various areas. This sets the tone for risk-taking behavior across the organization.

3. Clarity and Consistency:

- Clearly articulated risk appetite statements provide consistency in risk-related decisions, ensuring that all employees and departments understand the boundaries within which they should operate.

4. Enhanced Decision-Making:

- Risk appetite statements provide a basis for evaluating potential opportunities and threats, enabling better-informed decisions that consider both risk and reward.

5. Stakeholder Communication:

- Communicating risk appetite to stakeholders enhances transparency and trust, showing that the organization has a proactive and responsible approach to managing risk.

Defining and Measuring Risk Appetite

Risk appetite can be defined and measured using both quantitative and qualitative criteria. Below are examples of how organizations can approach this:

Quantitative Criteria:

1. Financial Thresholds:

- **Example:** An organization might set a risk appetite statement indicating that it is willing to accept up to a 5% variance in its annual revenue due to market risks.
- **Measurement:** This can be measured by monitoring financial performance metrics, such as revenue variance, profit margins, and return on investment (ROI).

2. Regulatory Requirements:

- **Example:** A financial institution might define its risk appetite to ensure compliance with regulatory capital requirements, stating that it will maintain a minimum capital adequacy ratio of 12%.
- **Measurement:** Compliance can be measured through regular audits and financial reporting, ensuring that capital levels meet or exceed regulatory standards.

3. Operational Limits:

- **Example:** A manufacturing company may set a risk appetite statement limiting production downtime to less than 2% annually due to equipment failures.
- **Measurement:** This can be monitored by tracking equipment uptime, mean time between failures (MTBF), and maintenance costs.

Qualitative Criteria:

1. Stakeholder Expectations:

- **Example:** An organization might articulate that it aims to maintain a high level of customer satisfaction, accepting no more than a 1% drop in customer satisfaction scores annually due to service disruptions.
- **Measurement:** This can be gauged through customer satisfaction surveys, Net Promoter Scores (NPS), and feedback mechanisms.

2. Reputational Impact:

- **Example:** A company might define its risk appetite in terms of reputational risk, stating that it will avoid any actions that could lead to negative media coverage or a significant loss of public trust.
- **Measurement:** This can be measured through media monitoring, public perception surveys, and analysis of social media sentiment.

3. Compliance and Legal Risks:

- **Example:** An organization may state that it has zero tolerance for legal and compliance risks, ensuring that all operations strictly adhere to relevant laws and regulations.
- **Measurement:** This can be assessed through regular compliance audits, legal reviews, and incident tracking.

Examples of Risk Appetite Statements

1. Financial Sector:

- **Credit Risk:** "We will maintain a loan default rate of less than 2% by implementing stringent credit evaluation processes."
- **Market Risk:** "We accept a maximum potential loss of 3% of our trading portfolio value in a single trading day."

2. Healthcare Sector:

- **Patient Safety:** "We have zero tolerance for risks that could lead to patient harm. All procedures and treatments must adhere to the highest safety standards."
- **Regulatory Compliance:** "We will ensure full compliance with HIPAA regulations, accepting no incidents of non-compliance."

3. Technology Sector:

- **Data Security:** "We accept a maximum of one security breach per year, provided it does not result in significant data loss or regulatory penalties."

- **Innovation Risk:** "We are willing to invest up to 10% of our annual budget in high-risk, high-reward research and development projects."

Implementing Risk Appetite in Practice

1. Integrating with Risk Management Frameworks:

- Embed risk appetite statements into the organization's overall risk management framework, ensuring they inform risk assessments, treatment plans, and monitoring activities.

2. Regular Review and Adjustment:

- Continuously review and adjust risk appetite statements to reflect changes in the organization's strategy, external environment, and risk landscape.

3. Communication and Training:

- Clearly communicate risk appetite statements across the organization and provide training to ensure that all employees understand and adhere to them.

4. Monitoring and Reporting:

- Establish robust monitoring and reporting mechanisms to track adherence to risk appetite statements and take corrective actions when necessary.

Conclusion

Risk appetite plays a critical role in guiding an organization's risk management decisions and priorities. By establishing and communicating clear risk appetite statements that align with strategic objectives, values, and culture, organizations can ensure consistent and informed decision-making. Defining and measuring risk appetite using both quantitative and qualitative criteria enables organizations to manage risks effectively, aligning risk-taking behaviors with their overall goals and stakeholder expectations. Regular review and adjustment, along with effective communication and training, are essential for maintaining an appropriate risk appetite that supports long-term success and resilience.

Obtaining Buy-In and Support for Risk Management Initiatives

Gaining buy-in and support for risk management initiatives from key stakeholders is crucial for the success of these programs. Senior executives, board members, and business unit leaders must recognize the value of risk management not just as a necessary expense but as a strategic enabler of business value and innovation. Here are the challenges and strategies for securing stakeholder support, along with examples of building a compelling business case for risk management investments.

Challenges

1. **Perception as a Cost Center:**
    - Risk management is often seen as an overhead expense that does not directly contribute to revenue generation.
2. **Lack of Understanding:**
    - Stakeholders may not fully understand the technical aspects of risk management and its importance to the organization's overall strategy.
3. **Competing Priorities:**
    - Senior executives and business unit leaders may prioritize short-term gains over long-term risk management investments.
4. **Quantifying ROI:**
    - Demonstrating the return on investment (ROI) for risk management initiatives can be challenging since the benefits are often preventive and intangible.

Strategies for Obtaining Buy-In

1. Framing Risk Management as a Business Enabler:

- **Link to Business Objectives:**

    - Highlight how risk management aligns with and supports the organization's strategic goals and objectives. Show how effective risk management can protect and enhance revenue, reputation, and operational efficiency.
- **Innovation and Competitive Advantage:**
    - Emphasize how proactive risk management can foster innovation by creating a secure environment for new initiatives. Demonstrate that managing risks effectively can lead to a competitive advantage, enabling the organization to take calculated risks in pursuit of growth and innovation.

2. Building a Compelling Business Case:

- **Use Metrics and KPIs:**
    - Develop and present metrics that clearly demonstrate the impact of risk management initiatives. Use Key Performance Indicators (KPIs) such as reduction in incident frequency, cost savings from preventing breaches, and improved compliance rates.
- **Financial Impact Analysis:**
    - Conduct a detailed financial impact analysis to show potential cost savings and avoided losses due to effective risk management. Compare the costs of risk management investments with the potential financial impact of unmitigated risks.

3. Communicating Effectively:

- **Tailored Communication:**
    - Tailor your message to the audience. For senior executives, focus on strategic alignment and financial benefits. For business unit leaders, emphasize how risk management can support their specific operational goals.
- **Use Real-World Examples:**
    - Provide case studies and real-world examples of how similar organizations benefited from risk management investments. Use these examples to illustrate the tangible and intangible benefits.

4. Demonstrating Alignment with Organizational Priorities:

- **Risk Appetite and Tolerance:**
    - Align risk management initiatives with the organization's risk appetite and tolerance levels. Show how your proposals help maintain these levels while supporting business objectives.
- **Regulatory Compliance:**
    - Highlight the importance of risk management in ensuring regulatory compliance, avoiding fines, and protecting the organization's reputation.

Examples of Building a Compelling Business Case

1. Example 1: Financial Services Firm

- **Scenario:**
    - A financial services firm needs to invest in advanced threat detection systems to prevent cyber attacks.
- **Business Case:**
    - **Link to Business Objectives:** Emphasize how protecting customer data and ensuring the availability of financial services are critical to maintaining customer trust and loyalty.
    - **Metrics:** Show historical data on the frequency and cost of cyber incidents, and project the potential reduction in incidents and associated costs with the new system.
    - **Financial Impact Analysis:** Demonstrate the ROI by comparing the cost of the threat detection system to the potential losses from a major data breach (e.g., regulatory fines, loss of customers, remediation costs).

2. Example 2: Healthcare Provider

- **Scenario:**
    - A healthcare provider needs to implement a comprehensive risk management program to comply with HIPAA and protect patient data.

- **Business Case:**
    - **Link to Business Objectives:** Highlight the importance of patient trust and the legal requirement to protect patient data. Explain how risk management supports the organization's mission of providing high-quality healthcare.
    - **Metrics:** Use compliance audit results to show current gaps and the risk of non-compliance fines. Present statistics on data breaches in the healthcare industry and their impact.
    - **Financial Impact Analysis:** Compare the cost of the risk management program to the potential fines, legal costs, and reputational damage from a data breach.

Metrics for Demonstrating ROI

1. Incident Reduction:

- Measure the decrease in the number of security incidents after implementing risk management initiatives.

2. Cost Savings:

- Calculate cost savings from avoided incidents, including direct costs (e.g., fines, legal fees) and indirect costs (e.g., reputational damage, customer churn).

3. Compliance Improvements:

- Track improvements in compliance audit scores and the reduction in compliance violations.

4. Operational Efficiency:

- Measure improvements in operational efficiency, such as reduced downtime and faster incident response times.

Anticipating and Addressing Common Questions and Concerns

1. Cost Justification:

- **Question:** "Why should we invest in this now?"
- **Response:** Present data showing the rising trend of cyber threats and the increasing costs of incidents. Highlight how early investment in risk management can prevent much larger future losses.

2. Impact on Business Operations:

- **Question:** "Will this disrupt our operations?"
- **Response:** Explain the implementation plan, including how it minimizes disruption. Provide examples of how similar initiatives were successfully implemented with minimal impact.

3. Measuring Success:

- **Question:** "How will we know if it's working?"
- **Response:** Present the KPIs and metrics that will be used to measure the success of the initiative. Set clear, achievable targets for these metrics.

Conclusion

Securing stakeholder buy-in for risk management initiatives requires demonstrating how these initiatives support business objectives, enhance innovation, and provide a compelling ROI. By framing risk management as a strategic enabler and using clear, data-driven communication, you can build a strong case that resonates with senior executives, board members, and business unit leaders. Through effective presentation of the benefits and addressing potential concerns, you can ensure that your organization prioritizes and invests in robust risk management practices.

Roles and Responsibilities in Establishing and Maintaining Effective Risk Ownership and Accountability

1. Executive Management

Roles and Responsibilities:

- **Setting the Tone:** Executive management sets the overall risk culture and appetite for the organization. They define strategic objectives and ensure alignment with risk management practices.
- **Policy Development:** Approve and support the development of risk management policies, frameworks, and guidelines.
- **Resource Allocation:** Ensure that adequate resources (personnel, budget, tools) are allocated to risk management activities.
- **Oversight:** Provide oversight to ensure effective implementation and continuous improvement of risk management practices.

2. Risk Management Team

Roles and Responsibilities:

- **Framework Development:** Develop and maintain the risk management framework, policies, and procedures.
- **Risk Assessment:** Conduct regular risk assessments to identify and evaluate risks.
- **Guidance and Support:** Provide guidance and support to risk owners across the organization.
- **Monitoring and Reporting:** Monitor risk exposure and effectiveness of risk treatment plans, and report to executive management and the board.

3. Risk Owners

Roles and Responsibilities:

- **Risk Identification:** Identify risks within their area of responsibility.
- **Risk Assessment:** Assess the likelihood and impact of identified risks.
- **Risk Mitigation:** Develop and implement risk mitigation strategies and controls.
- **Monitoring:** Continuously monitor risk exposure and the effectiveness of controls.
- **Reporting:** Report on risk status, incidents, and mitigation progress to the risk management team and executive management.

4. Business Units/Departments

Roles and Responsibilities:

- **Implementation:** Implement risk management policies and procedures within their operations.
- **Risk Ownership:** Take ownership of risks related to their specific functions.
- **Collaboration:** Collaborate with the risk management team and other departments to manage cross-functional risks.
- **Training:** Ensure that team members are trained and aware of their risk management responsibilities.

5. Internal Audit

Roles and Responsibilities:

- **Independent Assurance:** Provide independent assurance on the effectiveness of the risk management framework and controls.
- **Audit Activities:** Conduct audits to ensure compliance with risk management policies and procedures.
- **Reporting:** Report findings and recommendations to executive management and the audit committee.

Importance of Defining and Assigning Risk Owners

1. Clear Accountability:

- Assigning risk owners ensures that specific individuals or teams are accountable for managing identified risks. This clarity helps prevent risks from being overlooked or inadequately addressed.

2. Effective Risk Management:

- Risk owners are responsible for developing and implementing risk mitigation strategies, ensuring that risks are managed proactively and effectively.

3. Escalation and Reporting:

- Clear risk ownership establishes escalation channels, ensuring that significant risks or incidents are promptly reported to the appropriate levels of management for timely decision-making.

Establishing Escalation and Reporting Channels

1. Escalation Channels:

- Define clear escalation paths for reporting risks that exceed predefined thresholds or when risk mitigation measures fail.
- Ensure that escalation procedures are well-documented and communicated across the organization.

2. Reporting Channels:

- Establish regular reporting mechanisms for risk owners to update the risk management team and executive management on risk status, incidents, and mitigation progress.
- Use risk management software or dashboards to facilitate real-time reporting and monitoring.

Creating a Risk Ownership Matrix

Purpose:

- A risk ownership matrix maps identified risks to specific individuals, teams, or departments, ensuring clear accountability and facilitating effective risk management.

Components:

- **Risk ID:** Unique identifier for each risk.
- **Risk Description:** Brief description of the risk.
- **Risk Owner:** Individual or team responsible for managing the risk.
- **Risk Category:** Category or type of risk (e.g., financial, operational, strategic).
- **Risk Assessment:** Assessment of the risk's likelihood and impact.
- **Mitigation Actions:** Description of risk mitigation strategies and controls.
- **Reporting Frequency:** Frequency of reporting on the risk status (e.g., monthly, quarterly).

Example of a Risk Ownership Matrix

Risk ID	Risk Description	Risk Owner	Risk Category	Risk Assessment	Mitigation Actions	Reporting Frequency
R1	Data Breach	IT Security Team	Cybersecurity	High Likelihood, High Impact	Implement MFA, conduct regular audits	Monthly
R2	Supply Chain Disruption	Procurement Dept	Operational	Medium Likelihood, High Impact	Diversify suppliers, create backup plans	Quarterly
R3	Regulatory Non-Compliance	Compliance Officer	Compliance	Low Likelihood, High Impact	Regular compliance audits, staff training	Monthly
R4	Financial Fraud	Finance Dept	Financial	Medium Likelihood, Medium Impact	Strengthen internal controls, conduct forensic audits	Monthly

Using the Risk Ownership Matrix

1. Driving Risk-Informed Performance Management:

- **Performance Metrics:** Incorporate risk management responsibilities into performance metrics for risk owners. Evaluate their effectiveness in managing assigned risks.
- **Accountability:** Use the matrix to hold risk owners accountable for implementing mitigation actions and achieving risk management objectives.

2. Enhancing Decision-Making:

- **Prioritization:** Use the matrix to prioritize risks based on their assessment and potential impact. Focus resources on high-priority risks.
- **Resource Allocation:** Allocate resources (budget, personnel, tools) based on the risk assessment and the effectiveness of mitigation actions.

3. Facilitating Communication:

- **Regular Updates:** Ensure that risk owners provide regular updates on risk status and mitigation progress. Use these updates for informed decision-making.
- **Cross-Functional Collaboration:** Promote collaboration among different departments to address cross-functional risks and share best practices.

Conclusion

Establishing and maintaining effective risk ownership and accountability is critical for successful risk management. Clearly defining and assigning risk owners ensures that specific individuals or teams are accountable for managing identified risks. Establishing escalation and reporting channels facilitates timely communication and decision-making. A risk ownership matrix provides a structured approach to mapping risks to responsible parties, driving risk-informed performance management, and enhancing decision-making. By fostering a culture of accountability and proactive risk management, organizations can better navigate the complexities of the risk landscape and achieve their strategic objectives.

Case Study: Successful Implementation of a Risk-Based Approach to Information Security Management at TechHealth

Organization: TechHealth, a mid-sized healthcare technology provider
Objective: To implement a risk-based approach to information security management to protect sensitive patient data, ensure compliance with healthcare regulations, and enhance overall cybersecurity posture.

Key Drivers

1. **Regulatory Compliance:**
    - Need to comply with HIPAA and other healthcare regulations.
    - Increasing scrutiny from regulatory bodies regarding data protection and privacy.
2. **Protection of Sensitive Data:**
    - High volume of sensitive patient data requiring robust security measures.
    - Growing threat landscape with increased frequency of cyberattacks targeting healthcare providers.
3. **Operational Continuity:**
    - Ensuring that critical healthcare services and operations remain uninterrupted and secure.
    - Mitigating risks that could lead to operational downtime or data breaches.

Initial Risk Assessment and Prioritization

Challenges:

- Diverse sources and types of data across multiple systems.
- Limited initial understanding of the organization's risk exposure.
- Need for a structured approach to identify and prioritize risks effectively.

Approach:

- **Risk Assessment Framework:** Adopted the NIST Risk Management Framework (RMF) to guide the risk assessment process.
- **Comprehensive Assessment:** Conducted a thorough risk assessment involving asset identification, threat modeling, and vulnerability analysis.
- **Stakeholder Engagement:** Involved key stakeholders from IT, compliance, legal, and operations to ensure a comprehensive understanding of risks.

Tools and Techniques:

- **Automated Risk Assessment Tools:** Utilized tools like RiskWatch and FAIR (Factor Analysis of Information Risk) to identify and assess risks quantitatively and qualitatively.
- **Workshops and Interviews:** Conducted workshops and interviews with key stakeholders to gather insights and validate findings.
- **Risk Matrix:** Developed a risk matrix to categorize and prioritize risks based on their likelihood and impact.

Outcomes:

- **Risk Inventory:** Created a detailed inventory of identified risks, categorized by their likelihood and impact.
- **Prioritization:** Prioritized risks based on their potential impact on patient data, regulatory compliance, and operational continuity.

Risk Treatment and Mitigation

Challenges:

- Balancing the implementation of security measures with maintaining efficient healthcare operations.
- Ensuring that risk mitigation strategies were cost-effective and aligned with regulatory requirements.

Approach:

- **Control Selection:** Selected appropriate controls from NIST SP 800-53 based on the prioritized risks.
- **Balanced Strategy:** Developed a balanced risk treatment plan combining preventive, detective, and corrective controls.

Tools and Techniques:

- **Technical Controls:** Implemented advanced technical controls such as:
    - **Encryption:** Ensured all patient data was encrypted both in transit and at rest.
    - **Multi-Factor Authentication (MFA):** Required MFA for accessing critical systems and data.
    - **Intrusion Detection Systems (IDS):** Deployed IDS to monitor network traffic and detect anomalies.
- **Administrative Controls:** Strengthened administrative controls including:

    - **Security Policies and Procedures:** Developed and enforced comprehensive security policies and procedures.
    - **Training and Awareness Programs:** Conducted regular training and awareness programs for all employees on data protection and cybersecurity best practices.
- **Physical Controls:** Enhanced physical security measures such as:
    - **Access Control Systems:** Implemented biometric access controls for data centers.
    - **Surveillance:** Installed surveillance cameras to monitor critical areas.

Outcomes:

- **Reduced Risk Exposure:** Significant reduction in the likelihood and impact of identified risks.
- **Enhanced Compliance:** Achieved full compliance with HIPAA and other relevant healthcare regulations.
- **Improved Security Posture:** Strengthened overall cybersecurity posture, protecting sensitive patient data and ensuring operational continuity.

Ongoing Monitoring and Optimization

Challenges:

- Keeping up with the evolving threat landscape and emerging risks.
- Ensuring continuous improvement and optimization of security measures.

Approach:

- **Continuous Monitoring:** Established a continuous monitoring program to detect and respond to security incidents in real-time.
- **Regular Audits and Assessments:** Conducted regular internal audits and risk assessments to identify new risks and evaluate the effectiveness of existing controls.
- **Feedback Loop:** Created a feedback loop to incorporate lessons learned from incidents and audits into the risk management process.

Tools and Techniques:

- **Security Information and Event Management (SIEM) Systems:** Utilized SIEM systems like Splunk and IBM QRadar to aggregate and analyze security event data in real-time.
- **Incident Response Plans:** Developed and regularly updated incident response plans to ensure swift and effective responses to security incidents.
- **Metrics and Reporting:** Established key metrics and reporting mechanisms to track the performance of risk management initiatives and communicate with stakeholders.

Outcomes:

- **Proactive Risk Management:** Enhanced ability to proactively identify and mitigate emerging risks.
- **Improved Incident Response:** Faster detection and response to security incidents, minimizing their impact.
- **Stakeholder Confidence:** Increased confidence among stakeholders, including patients, regulatory bodies, and employees, in the organization's commitment to security and compliance.

Lessons Learned and Best Practices

1. Comprehensive Stakeholder Engagement:

- Involving key stakeholders from the outset ensures a thorough understanding of risks and fosters a culture of security awareness and collaboration.

2. Balanced Approach to Risk Mitigation:

- Combining preventive, detective, and corrective controls provides a robust defense against a wide range of threats.

3. Continuous Monitoring and Improvement:

- Regular audits, assessments, and continuous monitoring are critical for adapting to the evolving threat landscape and maintaining an effective security posture.

4. Effective Communication and Reporting:

- Clear, concise, and regular communication with stakeholders is essential for maintaining support and demonstrating the value of risk management initiatives.

5. Leveraging Technology:

- Utilizing advanced tools and technologies, such as SIEM systems and automated risk assessment tools, enhances the efficiency and effectiveness of risk management efforts.

Conclusion

TechHealth's successful implementation of a risk-based approach to information security management demonstrates the importance of a structured, comprehensive, and proactive approach to managing information security risks. By leveraging established frameworks like NIST RMF, engaging stakeholders, and continuously monitoring and optimizing their security measures, TechHealth significantly enhanced its security posture, ensured compliance, and protected sensitive patient data. These best practices and lessons learned can be applied to other organizational contexts to achieve similar success in information security risk management.

Real-World Examples of Risk Management Across Different Industries

Example 1: Financial Services - Insider Threat

Industry: Financial Services

Scenario: A mid-sized bank detected suspicious activities within its IT systems. An internal audit revealed that a disgruntled employee had been accessing and attempting to steal sensitive customer data.

Key Risk Factors:

- **Insider Access:** Employees with access to sensitive information.
- **Lack of Monitoring:** Inadequate monitoring of user activities.
- **Weak Access Controls:** Insufficient role-based access controls (RBAC).

Assessment Findings:

- **Risk Identification:** The risk of insider threats was high due to broad access permissions and lack of monitoring.
- **Vulnerability:** Lack of real-time monitoring tools to detect unusual access patterns.
- **Impact:** Potential financial loss, legal consequences, and reputational damage.

Treatment Options:

- **Mitigate:** Implement RBAC to ensure that employees only have access to data necessary for their roles.
- **Mitigate:** Deploy user behavior analytics (UBA) to monitor and detect unusual activities.
- **Mitigate:** Conduct regular training and awareness programs to educate employees on data protection and ethical behavior.
- **Transfer:** Purchase cyber insurance to cover potential financial losses from insider threats.

Broader Implications:

- Enhancing monitoring and access controls can significantly reduce the risk of insider threats.
- Regular training helps build a security-conscious culture, mitigating the risk of insider attacks.
- Investing in advanced security tools, such as UBA, can provide early detection and response to insider threats.

Common Pitfalls:

- Over-reliance on perimeter defenses without addressing internal threats.
- Inadequate monitoring and auditing of user activities.
- Failing to update access controls regularly to reflect changes in roles and responsibilities.

Emerging Trends:

- Increasing use of AI and machine learning in detecting insider threats through behavior analysis.
- Enhanced focus on employee behavior and ethics training to prevent insider incidents.

Innovative Approaches:

- Implementing deception technologies to detect and investigate insider threats by creating honeypots and decoy systems.

Example 2: Healthcare - Ransomware Attack

Industry: Healthcare

Scenario: A regional hospital network experienced a ransomware attack that encrypted patient records and disrupted medical services. The attackers demanded a substantial ransom for the decryption key.

Key Risk Factors:

- **Critical Data:** High-value targets due to sensitive patient information.
- **Legacy Systems:** Use of outdated and vulnerable systems.
- **Emergency Services:** Disruption of critical medical services.

Assessment Findings:

- **Risk Identification:** High risk of ransomware attacks due to inadequate security measures.
- **Vulnerability:** Lack of regular updates and patches for legacy systems.
- **Impact:** Severe operational disruption, patient safety risks, and financial losses.

Treatment Options:

- **Mitigate:** Implement regular patch management to keep systems updated and secure.
- **Mitigate:** Deploy advanced endpoint protection solutions to detect and prevent ransomware.
- **Mitigate:** Establish a robust data backup and recovery strategy to ensure quick restoration of encrypted data.
- **Mitigate:** Conduct regular security awareness training for staff to recognize and avoid phishing emails.
- **Accept:** Accept the residual risk of potential downtime during recovery and ensure comprehensive incident response planning.

Broader Implications:

- Regular updates and patches are critical for protecting against ransomware and other cyber threats.
- A robust backup strategy can mitigate the impact of ransomware by enabling quick data recovery.
- Continuous staff training is essential to prevent phishing attacks, which are common vectors for ransomware.

Common Pitfalls:

- Neglecting to update and patch systems regularly.
- Inadequate backup strategies that do not ensure quick data restoration.
- Lack of employee training on recognizing phishing attempts.

Emerging Trends:

- Increased adoption of cloud-based backup solutions to ensure data availability and redundancy.
- Use of AI-driven threat detection systems to identify and block ransomware in real-time.

Innovative Approaches:

- Implementing zero-trust architectures to limit the spread of ransomware by restricting lateral movement within networks.

Example 3: Retail - Data Breach

Industry: Retail

Scenario: A large retail chain suffered a data breach, exposing millions of customers' credit card information. The breach was traced back to vulnerabilities in the point-of-sale (POS) system.

Key Risk Factors:

- **High Transaction Volume:** High volume of transactions makes retail chains attractive targets.
- **Outdated Systems:** Use of outdated POS systems with known vulnerabilities.
- **Customer Data:** Handling of sensitive financial information.

Assessment Findings:

- **Risk Identification:** High risk of data breaches due to outdated POS systems and lack of encryption.
- **Vulnerability:** Insufficient security measures in place to protect POS systems.
- **Impact:** Significant financial losses, regulatory penalties, and reputational damage.

Treatment Options:

- **Mitigate:** Upgrade POS systems to the latest versions with enhanced security features.
- **Mitigate:** Encrypt customer data both in transit and at rest to protect against unauthorized access.
- **Mitigate:** Conduct regular security assessments and penetration testing to identify and address vulnerabilities.

- **Transfer:** Purchase cyber liability insurance to cover potential financial losses and legal fees associated with data breaches.
- **Mitigate:** Implement a continuous monitoring system to detect and respond to suspicious activities in real-time.

Broader Implications:

- Upgrading systems and implementing encryption are crucial steps in protecting customer data.
- Regular security assessments can identify and mitigate vulnerabilities before they are exploited.
- Continuous monitoring helps in early detection and response to data breaches.

Common Pitfalls:

- Failing to regularly update and secure POS systems.
- Lack of encryption for sensitive customer data.
- Inadequate monitoring and response capabilities.

Emerging Trends:

- Growing use of end-to-end encryption in retail transactions.
- Adoption of tokenization to protect credit card information during transactions.

Innovative Approaches:

- Utilizing blockchain technology to enhance transaction security and data integrity in retail operations.

Example 4: Manufacturing - Supply Chain Disruption

Industry: Manufacturing

Scenario: A global manufacturing company faced a significant disruption in its supply chain due to a cyber attack on one of its major suppliers. The attack halted production and caused delays in product delivery.

Key Risk Factors:

- **Supply Chain Dependencies:** Reliance on third-party suppliers for critical components.
- **Global Operations:** Complexity of managing a global supply chain.
- **Lack of Visibility:** Limited visibility into the cybersecurity posture of suppliers.

Assessment Findings:

- **Risk Identification:** High risk of supply chain disruptions due to reliance on external suppliers with varying security practices.
- **Vulnerability:** Lack of comprehensive third-party risk management processes.
- **Impact:** Operational disruptions, delayed deliveries, and financial losses.

Treatment Options:

- **Mitigate:** Develop and implement a robust third-party risk management program to assess and monitor the security practices of suppliers.
- **Mitigate:** Diversify the supply chain to reduce reliance on a single supplier.
- **Mitigate:** Establish contingency plans and alternate sourcing strategies to mitigate the impact of supply chain disruptions.
- **Transfer:** Obtain business interruption insurance to cover financial losses from supply chain disruptions.

Broader Implications:

- Comprehensive third-party risk management is essential for mitigating supply chain risks.
- Diversifying the supply chain can reduce the impact of disruptions.
- Contingency planning and alternate sourcing strategies enhance supply chain resilience.

Common Pitfalls:

- Over-reliance on a single supplier without assessing their cybersecurity posture.
- Lack of visibility and monitoring of third-party risks.
- Inadequate contingency planning for supply chain disruptions.

Emerging Trends:

- Increased focus on supply chain cybersecurity as part of overall risk management strategies.
- Adoption of technologies like blockchain for enhanced supply chain transparency and security.

Innovative Approaches:

- Implementing predictive analytics to anticipate and mitigate supply chain risks proactively.

Conclusion

These real-world scenarios illustrate the application of risk management principles across different industries and business contexts. By understanding key risk factors, conducting thorough assessments, and implementing effective treatment options, organizations can enhance their information security posture and achieve their business objectives. Common pitfalls, such as neglecting system updates and lacking comprehensive third-party risk management, highlight areas for improvement. Emerging trends and innovative approaches, such as AI-driven threat detection and blockchain technology, offer new ways to address evolving risks and enhance resilience. Through continuous improvement and proactive risk management, organizations can navigate the complexities of the modern threat landscape.

Practice Questions and Exercises for Information Security Risk Management

These practice questions and exercises are designed to assess and reinforce your understanding of information security risk management concepts and techniques. The questions cover a range of topics and difficulty levels, from basic risk identification and assessment to advanced risk communication and reporting. Detailed explanations and references are provided to enhance learning and direct you to additional resources for further study.

Multiple-Choice Questions

1. What is the primary purpose of a risk assessment in information security? A. To eliminate all security risks
B. To identify and evaluate risks to determine their impact on the organization
C. To implement security controls without assessing risks
D. To comply with regulatory requirements without further action
Answer: B. To identify and evaluate risks to determine their impact on the organization
Explanation: The primary purpose of a risk assessment is to identify potential risks and evaluate their likelihood and impact on the organization, which helps in prioritizing risk mitigation efforts. (Reference: NIST SP 800-30)

2. Which of the following is NOT a preventive control? A. Firewalls
B. Antivirus software
C. Intrusion detection systems (IDS)
D. Security training programs
Answer: C. Intrusion detection systems (IDS)
Explanation: IDS are detective controls designed to identify and alert on potential security incidents, whereas firewalls, antivirus software, and security training programs are preventive controls aimed at stopping incidents before they occur. (Reference: NIST SP 800-53)

3. In the context of ISO 27005, what is the first step in the risk management process? A. Risk assessment
B. Risk treatment
C. Context establishment
D. Risk monitoring
Answer: C. Context establishment
Explanation: The first step in ISO 27005 is context establishment, which involves defining the scope, boundaries, and objectives of the risk management process. (Reference: ISO/IEC 27005)

Short-Answer Questions

4. Describe the difference between qualitative and quantitative risk assessment methodologies.
Answer:
Qualitative risk assessment uses subjective criteria, such as expert judgment and descriptive terms (e.g., high, medium, low), to evaluate risks. Quantitative risk assessment uses numerical data and statistical methods to measure the likelihood and impact of risks in financial terms, providing precise, data-driven insights. (Reference: NIST SP 800-30)

5. What are the key components of a risk register? Provide a brief description of each component.
Answer:

- **Risk Description:** A clear and concise description of the risk.
- **Likelihood:** The probability of the risk occurring.
- **Impact:** The potential consequences if the risk materializes.

- **Risk Owner:** The individual or team responsible for managing the risk.
- **Mitigation Plans:** Strategies and actions to reduce the likelihood or impact of the risk.
- **Status:** The current state of the risk (e.g., open, closed, being monitored).
- **Target Resolution Date:** The expected date by which the risk should be mitigated or resolved. (Reference: NIST SP 800-37)

Case Study-Based Questions

6. Case Study: A retail company is implementing a risk management program to protect customer data and ensure compliance with PCI DSS.

a. Identify and describe the steps the company should take to establish this program using the NIST Risk Management Framework (RMF).

Answer:

1. **Categorize Information Systems:** Determine the impact levels of information systems based on the sensitivity of customer data.
2. **Select Security Controls:** Choose appropriate security controls from NIST SP 800-53 based on the system's impact level.
3. **Implement Security Controls:** Deploy the selected controls and document how they are implemented.
4. **Assess Security Controls:** Evaluate the effectiveness of the controls to ensure they function as intended.
5. **Authorize Information System:** Senior management formally authorizes the system to operate based on the risk assessment.
6. **Monitor Security Controls:** Continuously monitor the controls to ensure they remain effective and make necessary adjustments. (Reference: NIST SP 800-37)

b. Explain how the company can use both qualitative and quantitative risk assessments to prioritize risks.

Answer:

The company can start with a qualitative assessment to quickly identify and categorize risks based on expert judgment and stakeholder input, using descriptive terms like high, medium, and low. For high-priority risks identified qualitatively, the company can then conduct a quantitative assessment to measure the likelihood and financial impact using numerical data and statistical methods. This combined approach ensures a comprehensive understanding of risks and effective prioritization. (Reference: NIST SP 800-30)

c. Recommend a mix of technical, administrative, and physical controls to mitigate identified risks and provide examples of each.

Answer:

- **Technical Controls:** Implement encryption for customer data, deploy multi-factor authentication (MFA), and use intrusion detection systems (IDS).
- **Administrative Controls:** Develop and enforce security policies, conduct regular security awareness training for employees, and perform background checks on employees with access to sensitive data.
- **Physical Controls:** Secure data centers with biometric access controls, install surveillance cameras, and employ security guards to monitor facilities. (Reference: NIST SP 800-53)

Detailed Explanations and References

1. Risk Assessment Purpose:

NIST SP 800-30: Risk assessment is critical for identifying and evaluating risks to understand their impact on the organization and prioritize mitigation efforts.

2. Preventive vs. Detective Controls:

NIST SP 800-53: Differentiate between preventive controls (firewalls, antivirus software, training) and detective controls (IDS).

3. ISO 27005 Context Establishment:

ISO/IEC 27005: Establishing the context is the foundational step in the risk management process, defining scope and objectives.

4. Qualitative vs. Quantitative Risk Assessment:

NIST SP 800-30: Qualitative assessments use subjective measures, while quantitative assessments use numerical data for risk evaluation.

5. Risk Register Components:
NIST SP 800-37: A risk register includes descriptions, likelihood, impact, ownership, mitigation plans, status, and target resolution dates to manage risks effectively.
6. NIST RMF Implementation:
NIST SP 800-37: Follow the RMF steps to establish a comprehensive risk management program, ensuring continuous monitoring and authorization of security controls.
By practicing these questions and reviewing the detailed explanations, you can reinforce your understanding of information security risk management concepts and techniques, preparing you to apply them effectively in real-world scenarios.
Role of Risk Management Metrics and Key Risk Indicators (KRIs)
Risk management metrics and KRIs are essential tools for measuring and communicating the effectiveness of an organization's risk management program. They provide quantifiable data that helps organizations track their risk exposure, evaluate the effectiveness of controls, and make informed decisions. KRIs, in particular, serve as early warning signals that alert organizations to potential risk events, allowing for proactive risk management.
Commonly Used Metrics and KRIs
1. Risk Assessment Coverage
Definition:

- Measures the extent to which risk assessments have been conducted across the organization's processes, systems, and assets.

Example:

- Percentage of business units that have completed a formal risk assessment in the past year.

Calculation:

- (Number of business units with completed risk assessments / Total number of business units) * 100

Interpretation:

- High coverage indicates comprehensive risk assessment practices, while low coverage may suggest gaps in risk identification.

2. Control Effectiveness
Definition:

- Evaluates the effectiveness of risk controls in mitigating identified risks.

Example:

- Percentage of key controls that have been tested and found effective in the past year.

Calculation:

- (Number of effective controls / Total number of key controls tested) * 100

Interpretation:

- High effectiveness suggests robust control mechanisms, while low effectiveness indicates areas needing improvement.

3. Incident Frequency and Impact
Definition:

- Tracks the number of security incidents and their impact on the organization.

Example:

- Number of data breaches per quarter and the associated financial losses.

Calculation:

- Frequency: Count of incidents within a specific period.
- Impact: Sum of financial losses or other impact measures (e.g., downtime, reputational damage) per incident.

Interpretation:

- Increasing incident frequency or impact indicates rising risk levels or ineffective controls, prompting further investigation.

4. Risk Mitigation Progress
Definition:

- Measures progress in implementing risk mitigation strategies and actions.

Example:

- Percentage of risk mitigation actions completed on schedule.

Calculation:

- (Number of completed mitigation actions / Total number of planned mitigation actions) * 100

Interpretation:

- High completion rates suggest proactive risk management, while low rates may indicate delays or resource constraints.

Selecting, Calculating, and Interpreting Metrics and KRIs

1. Align with Organizational Objectives:

- Select metrics and KRIs that align with the organization's strategic goals and risk management objectives.

2. Relevance to Risk Profile:

- Choose measures that are relevant to the specific risks and threats the organization faces.

3. Consistency and Comparability:

- Ensure metrics and KRIs are consistent over time and comparable across different parts of the organization.

4. Data Availability and Quality:

- Use reliable data sources and ensure the accuracy and timeliness of the data collected.

5. Actionability:

- Select metrics and KRIs that provide actionable insights and can drive decision-making.

Examples of Metrics and KRIs Selection and Calculation

1. Risk Assessment Coverage:

Selection:

- Relevant to organizations aiming to ensure comprehensive risk identification.

Calculation:

- Calculate the percentage of business units with completed risk assessments.
    - Example: If 20 out of 25 business units have completed risk assessments, the coverage is (20/25) * 100 = 80%.

Interpretation:

- Aim for high coverage (e.g., >90%) to ensure all areas are assessed for risk.

2. Control Effectiveness:

Selection:

- Critical for organizations focusing on the effectiveness of their risk controls.

Calculation:

- Calculate the percentage of effective controls.
    - Example: If 15 out of 20 key controls are effective, the control effectiveness is (15/20) * 100 = 75%.

Interpretation:

- High effectiveness (e.g., >85%) indicates strong control mechanisms, while lower effectiveness signals areas for improvement.

3. Incident Frequency and Impact:

Selection:

- Important for organizations monitoring the occurrence and consequences of security incidents.

Calculation:

- Calculate the number of incidents and their financial impact.
    - Example: If there are 10 data breaches in a quarter with total losses of $500,000, the average impact per breach is $500,000 / 10 = $50,000.

Interpretation:

- Monitor trends over time to identify increasing or decreasing risk levels.

4. Risk Mitigation Progress:

Selection:

- Relevant to organizations tracking the implementation of risk mitigation strategies.

Calculation:

- Calculate the percentage of completed mitigation actions.
  - Example: If 18 out of 25 mitigation actions are completed on schedule, the progress is (18/25) * 100 = 72%.

Interpretation:

- Aim for high completion rates (e.g., >80%) to ensure timely risk mitigation.

Using Metrics and KRIs to Drive Continuous Improvement and Demonstrate Value

1. Continuous Improvement:

Regular Review and Analysis:

- Continuously review and analyze metrics and KRIs to identify trends, gaps, and areas for improvement.

Root Cause Analysis:

- Conduct root cause analysis for recurring issues or ineffective controls to address underlying problems.

Adjust Strategies:

- Use insights from metrics and KRIs to adjust risk management strategies and actions.

Benchmarking:

- Compare metrics and KRIs against industry benchmarks to identify best practices and areas for enhancement.

2. Demonstrating Value to Stakeholders:

Transparent Reporting:

- Provide clear and transparent reports on risk management performance to stakeholders, including executives, board members, and regulators.

Highlighting Achievements:

- Showcase achievements, such as improved control effectiveness or reduced incident frequency, to demonstrate the effectiveness of risk management efforts.

Actionable Insights:

- Present actionable insights and recommendations based on metrics and KRIs to support informed decision-making.

Alignment with Objectives:

- Ensure that reported metrics and KRIs align with organizational goals and demonstrate how risk management contributes to achieving these objectives.

Conclusion

Risk management metrics and KRIs are vital tools for measuring and communicating the effectiveness of an organization's risk management program. By selecting relevant metrics and KRIs, calculating them accurately, and interpreting their results, organizations can gain valuable insights into their risk exposure and control effectiveness. Using these measures to drive continuous improvement and demonstrate value to stakeholders ensures that risk management efforts are aligned with strategic objectives and contribute to the overall success and resilience of the organization.

Risk Aggregation: Concept and Importance

Concept of Risk Aggregation

Risk aggregation involves the process of combining individual risk assessments to understand and manage the cumulative impact of multiple risks across an organization. This holistic approach ensures that decision-makers can see the big picture of their risk landscape, rather than just isolated incidents. By aggregating risks, organizations can identify systemic vulnerabilities, prioritize risk treatment efforts, and inform strategic decision-making.

Importance of Risk Aggregation

1. **Holistic View of Risk:** Aggregating risk data from different sources provides a comprehensive overview of the organization's risk profile, helping to identify patterns and interdependencies that may not be apparent when risks are assessed in isolation.
2. **Identification of Systemic Risks:** By looking at the aggregated data, organizations can identify systemic risks that affect multiple areas or processes, enabling more effective risk management.

3. **Prioritization of Risk Treatment:** Aggregated risk data helps prioritize risk treatment efforts by highlighting the most significant risks, allowing resources to be allocated more efficiently.
4. **Strategic Decision-Making:** Provides senior management with critical information to make informed strategic decisions, balancing risk and opportunity to achieve organizational objectives.

Challenges in Risk Aggregation

1. **Data Silos:** Risk data often resides in different departments, business units, and systems, making it difficult to consolidate.
2. **Inconsistent Metrics:** Different units may use varying metrics and assessment methods, complicating the aggregation process.
3. **Volume and Complexity of Data:** Managing large volumes of complex data from diverse sources requires robust data management and analytical capabilities.
4. **Lack of Standardization:** Without standardized risk assessment frameworks, aggregating risks across the organization can be challenging.
5. **Third-Party Risks:** Aggregating risk data from third-party vendors adds another layer of complexity due to varying risk management practices and data availability.

Techniques for Aggregating Risk Data

1. **Standardized Risk Assessment Frameworks:**
    - Adopt standardized frameworks such as NIST RMF or ISO 27005 to ensure consistent risk assessment across the organization.
    - **Example:** Use a common risk matrix with standardized impact and likelihood scales to evaluate risks in all business units.
2. **Centralized Risk Management Systems:**
    - Implement centralized risk management systems or platforms that can collect, consolidate, and analyze risk data from different sources.
    - **Example:** Use a GRC (Governance, Risk, and Compliance) tool like RSA Archer or MetricStream to aggregate and analyze risk data across the organization.
3. **Automated Data Collection:**
    - Utilize automated tools and technologies to collect risk data from various IT systems, business processes, and third-party vendors.
    - **Example:** Integrate SIEM (Security Information and Event Management) systems to collect and aggregate security-related risk data.
4. **Data Normalization:**
    - Normalize data to ensure consistency in metrics and terminology across different sources.
    - **Example:** Convert all risk assessments to a standardized scale (e.g., 1-5 for likelihood and impact) for easier aggregation and comparison.
5. **Regular Reporting and Dashboards:**
    - Develop regular risk reports and dashboards to visualize aggregated risk data and trends.
    - **Example:** Create dashboards that display risk heatmaps, top risks, and risk trends over time, accessible to senior management and risk owners.

Examples of Risk Aggregation in Practice

1. Identifying Systemic Risks:

- **Scenario:** A financial institution aggregates risk data from various business units, including retail banking, investment banking, and IT.
- **Outcome:** The aggregated data reveals that cyber threats pose a systemic risk across all units, highlighting the need for a comprehensive cybersecurity strategy.

2. Prioritizing Risk Treatment Efforts:

- **Scenario:** A manufacturing company aggregates risk data from different plants and processes.
- **Outcome:** The data shows that supply chain disruptions and equipment failures are the top risks across the organization. The company prioritizes investments in supply chain resilience and predictive maintenance technologies.

3. Informing Strategic Decision-Making:

- **Scenario:** A healthcare provider aggregates risk data from clinical operations, patient data management, and third-party service providers.
- **Outcome:** The aggregated data indicates high risks associated with data breaches and regulatory compliance. The organization decides to invest in advanced data encryption and enhanced compliance training programs.

Best Practices for Risk Aggregation

1. **Adopt a Unified Framework:**
   - Use a unified risk management framework to ensure consistency in risk assessment across all units.
   - **Reference:** NIST RMF and ISO 27005.
2. **Leverage Technology:**
   - Utilize risk management software and automated tools to facilitate data collection, aggregation, and analysis.
   - **Reference:** GRC tools like RSA Archer, MetricStream, and SIEM systems.
3. **Standardize Metrics:**
   - Develop and enforce standardized risk metrics and assessment criteria across the organization.
   - **Reference:** Common risk matrix with standardized impact and likelihood scales.
4. **Foster Collaboration:**
   - Encourage collaboration and communication between risk owners, business units, and senior management to ensure comprehensive risk aggregation.
   - **Reference:** Regular cross-functional risk assessment workshops and meetings.
5. **Continuous Monitoring:**
   - Implement continuous monitoring and regular updates to the risk aggregation process to adapt to changing risk landscapes.
   - **Reference:** Continuous monitoring programs as outlined in NIST SP 800-137.

Conclusion

Risk aggregation is essential for understanding and managing the cumulative impact of multiple risks across an organization. By addressing challenges and using effective techniques for aggregating risk data, organizations can identify systemic risks, prioritize risk treatment efforts, and make informed strategic decisions. Implementing standardized frameworks, leveraging technology, and fostering collaboration are key to successful risk aggregation, ultimately enhancing the organization's overall risk management capabilities and resilience.

Relationship Between Information Security Risk Management and Other ERM Functions

Information security risk management (ISRM) is a critical component of Enterprise Risk Management (ERM), which encompasses the full spectrum of risks that an organization faces, including financial, operational, and reputational risks. Aligning and integrating these different risk management perspectives is essential for creating a holistic and resilient risk management framework.

Importance of Aligning and Integrating Different Risk Management Perspectives

1. Comprehensive Risk View:

- Integrating ISRM with other ERM functions provides a comprehensive view of the organization's risk landscape. This helps in identifying interdependencies and cumulative impacts of different risks.

2. Resource Optimization:

- A unified risk management approach allows for better allocation of resources, ensuring that risk mitigation efforts are prioritized based on overall business impact rather than siloed perspectives.

3. Consistent Risk Appetite and Tolerance:

- Aligning different risk management functions ensures that the organization maintains a consistent risk appetite and tolerance across various domains, fostering better decision-making and risk-taking behaviors.

4. Improved Decision-Making:

- Holistic risk management enables informed decision-making by providing insights into how different risks interact and affect the organization's objectives and performance.

5. Enhanced Resilience:

- By considering the interconnected nature of risks, organizations can develop more robust and resilient strategies to withstand adverse events.

Examples of Information Security Risks Impacting Other Risk Domains

1. Financial Risk:

- **Example:** A data breach in a financial institution can lead to significant financial losses due to fines, legal costs, and compensation to affected customers.
- **Impact:** Compromised financial stability and increased financial risk due to loss of assets and revenue.

2. Operational Risk:

- **Example:** A ransomware attack on a manufacturing company's IT infrastructure can halt production lines, causing operational disruptions and delays.
- **Impact:** Reduced operational efficiency, increased production costs, and potential loss of business.

3. Reputational Risk:

- **Example:** A publicized security breach at an e-commerce company can damage its reputation and erode customer trust.
- **Impact:** Loss of customer confidence, decreased sales, and long-term brand damage.

Applying ERM Principles and Practices to Enhance ISRM

1. Risk Identification and Assessment:

- **ERM Principle:** Conduct comprehensive risk assessments that include all types of risks (financial, operational, reputational, and information security).
- **Application to ISRM:** Integrate information security risk assessments with enterprise-wide risk assessments to identify interdependencies and cumulative impacts.

2. Risk Mitigation and Control:

- **ERM Principle:** Develop and implement risk mitigation strategies that address multiple risk domains.
- **Application to ISRM:** Design security controls that not only protect information assets but also support financial, operational, and reputational risk management. For example, implementing robust access controls can prevent both data breaches (information security) and fraud (financial risk).

3. Risk Monitoring and Reporting:

- **ERM Principle:** Establish continuous monitoring and reporting mechanisms to track risk exposure and the effectiveness of mitigation measures.
- **Application to ISRM:** Use integrated dashboards and reporting tools to provide a unified view of information security risks and their impact on other risk domains. Regularly report on key risk indicators (KRIs) to senior management and the board.

4. Risk Communication and Culture:

- **ERM Principle:** Foster a risk-aware culture across the organization, ensuring that all employees understand their role in managing risks.
- **Application to ISRM:** Conduct regular training and awareness programs that emphasize the importance of information security in the context of broader enterprise risk management. Encourage collaboration between IT, finance, operations, and other departments to enhance collective risk management efforts.

5. Incident Response and Business Continuity:

- **ERM Principle:** Develop comprehensive incident response and business continuity plans that address various risk scenarios.
- **Application to ISRM:** Ensure that information security incident response plans are integrated with business continuity plans to minimize operational disruptions and financial losses. For example, a business continuity plan for a cyber-attack should include measures to maintain critical business functions and communication strategies to manage reputational risks.

Example: Integrating Information Security with Financial Risk Management

Scenario: A global retail company experiences a significant data breach, exposing customer payment information and leading to financial penalties and loss of revenue.

Integration Approach:

- **Risk Assessment:** Conduct a joint risk assessment involving the information security and finance teams to identify vulnerabilities and potential financial impacts.
- **Mitigation Strategy:** Implement security measures such as encryption, tokenization, and enhanced access controls to protect payment information. Additionally, secure cyber insurance to mitigate financial losses.
- **Monitoring and Reporting:** Develop a dashboard that tracks security incidents, financial impacts, and mitigation effectiveness. Report findings to senior management and the board.
- **Incident Response:** Create an integrated incident response plan that includes steps for immediate financial impact assessment, customer notification, and public relations management.

Outcome: By integrating information security with financial risk management, the company can better protect sensitive data, reduce financial losses, and maintain customer trust.

Example: Integrating Information Security with Operational Risk Management

Scenario: A manufacturing company's production line is halted due to a cyber-attack on its industrial control systems (ICS), leading to operational disruptions and increased production costs.

Integration Approach:

- **Risk Assessment:** Perform a combined risk assessment with the IT and operations teams to identify vulnerabilities in the ICS and potential operational impacts.
- **Mitigation Strategy:** Implement network segmentation, advanced threat detection, and regular patch management to protect ICS. Develop alternative production plans to mitigate operational disruptions.
- **Monitoring and Reporting:** Establish continuous monitoring of ICS networks and integrate findings with operational performance metrics. Report incidents and mitigation progress to senior management.
- **Incident Response:** Develop an integrated incident response plan that includes steps for ICS recovery, operational continuity, and communication with stakeholders.

Outcome: Integrating information security with operational risk management ensures that the company can quickly respond to cyber-attacks, minimize operational disruptions, and maintain production efficiency.

Conclusion

Aligning and integrating information security risk management with other ERM functions is essential for creating a holistic and resilient risk management framework. By considering the interconnected nature of risks, organizations can better allocate resources, make informed decisions, and enhance their overall risk posture. Integrating risk management practices across financial, operational, and reputational domains enables organizations to proactively address risks, improve resilience, and achieve their strategic objectives. Through continuous improvement and a unified approach to risk management, organizations can navigate the complexities of the modern threat landscape and maintain long-term success.

Ethical Considerations and Professional Responsibilities in Information Security Risk Management

Information security risk managers play a critical role in safeguarding an organization's assets while balancing the interests of various stakeholders, including customers, employees, shareholders, and regulators. This responsibility entails navigating ethical considerations and maintaining high standards of professionalism.

Balancing Stakeholder Interests

1. Customers:

- **Expectation:** Customers expect their personal data to be protected and used responsibly.
- **Responsibility:** Ensure robust data protection measures and transparent communication about data usage and security practices.

2. Employees:

- **Expectation:** Employees expect a secure work environment that protects their personal information and job security.
- **Responsibility:** Implement internal security measures and provide training to promote a security-aware culture.

3. Shareholders:

- **Expectation:** Shareholders expect the organization to manage risks effectively to safeguard their investment and ensure financial stability.
- **Responsibility:** Make decisions that balance risk mitigation with cost-effectiveness and align with the organization's strategic goals.

4. Regulators:

- **Expectation:** Regulators expect compliance with legal and regulatory requirements.
- **Responsibility:** Ensure that risk management practices meet or exceed regulatory standards and promptly report any compliance issues.

Importance of Maintaining Objectivity, Transparency, and Accountability

1. Objectivity:

- **Definition:** Making unbiased decisions based on factual evidence and thorough analysis.
- **Practice:** Use objective criteria and standardized processes for risk assessments to avoid personal biases.

2. Transparency:

- **Definition:** Openly sharing information about risk management practices, decisions, and incidents with stakeholders.
- **Practice:** Communicate clearly about the risks, mitigation measures, and the rationale behind decisions. Provide regular updates and reports to stakeholders.

3. Accountability:

- **Definition:** Taking responsibility for the outcomes of risk management decisions and actions.
- **Practice:** Establish clear roles and responsibilities within the risk management framework. Hold individuals and teams accountable for their part in managing risks and responding to incidents.

Considering Broader Societal and Environmental Impacts

1. Societal Impact:

- **Data Privacy:** Safeguarding personal data to prevent misuse and protect individuals' privacy rights.
- **Digital Inclusion:** Ensuring that security measures do not exclude or disadvantage certain groups.

2. Environmental Impact:

- **Sustainable Practices:** Considering the environmental footprint of data centers and IT infrastructure. Implementing energy-efficient practices and supporting green initiatives.

Navigating Common Ethical Dilemmas and Conflicts

1. Conflict of Interest:

- **Scenario:** A risk manager may face pressure to downplay risks to secure funding or maintain a positive public image.
- **Guidance:** Always prioritize factual and evidence-based assessments. Disclose potential conflicts of interest and seek impartial input or oversight.

2. Data Privacy vs. Security Measures:

- **Scenario:** Implementing intrusive security measures that may infringe on individual privacy rights.
- **Guidance:** Balance security needs with privacy rights. Implement privacy-by-design principles and seek to minimize data collection and intrusion.

3. Cost vs. Security:

- **Scenario:** Balancing the cost of implementing security measures with the need to protect assets.
- **Guidance:** Conduct cost-benefit analyses to make informed decisions. Prioritize risks based on their potential impact and likelihood, and seek cost-effective solutions that do not compromise security.

4. Reporting and Disclosure:

- **Scenario:** Deciding whether to disclose a security breach to customers and the public.

- **Guidance:** Follow regulatory requirements and ethical standards for breach notification. Be transparent and timely in communicating breaches to affected parties.

Example Scenarios and Ethical Navigation

Scenario 1: Pressure to Downplay Risks

- **Situation:** A senior executive pressures the risk manager to downplay a significant cybersecurity risk to avoid alarming shareholders.
- **Action:** The risk manager should present an unbiased risk assessment, highlighting the potential impacts and likelihood. They should advocate for transparency and communicate the need for appropriate mitigation measures to protect shareholder interests in the long term.

Scenario 2: Intrusive Employee Monitoring

- **Situation:** Implementing extensive employee monitoring to detect insider threats raises privacy concerns.
- **Action:** The risk manager should implement monitoring practices that are proportionate to the risk and ensure they comply with privacy laws. Employees should be informed about monitoring practices, and their privacy should be respected wherever possible.

Scenario 3: Environmental Considerations

- **Situation:** A data center expansion project faces criticism for its potential environmental impact.
- **Action:** The risk manager should advocate for sustainable practices, such as energy-efficient infrastructure, renewable energy sources, and carbon offset initiatives. They should consider the long-term environmental impact and work towards minimizing it.

Guidance on Navigating Ethical Dilemmas

1. Establish Clear Ethical Guidelines:

- Develop and communicate a code of ethics for risk management that outlines expected behaviors and decision-making principles.

2. Promote a Speak-Up Culture:

- Encourage employees to report unethical behavior or conflicts of interest without fear of retaliation. Provide clear channels for reporting and addressing concerns.

3. Regular Training and Awareness:

- Conduct regular training on ethical considerations and professional responsibilities in risk management. Ensure that all employees understand the importance of ethics in their daily activities.

4. Seek External Perspectives:

- Engage with external auditors, legal advisors, and ethics committees to review and provide input on challenging decisions and practices.

5. Document Decisions and Rationale:

- Maintain thorough documentation of risk assessments, decisions, and the rationale behind them. This transparency aids accountability and allows for review and learning from past decisions.

Conclusion

Information security risk managers have a duty to balance the interests of various stakeholders while upholding ethical standards and professional responsibilities. Maintaining objectivity, transparency, and accountability in risk assessment and decision-making is critical to fostering trust and ensuring effective risk management. By considering broader societal and environmental impacts, risk managers can contribute to sustainable and responsible business practices. Navigating ethical dilemmas requires a clear framework, ongoing training, and a culture that values integrity and ethical behavior. Through these practices, information security risk managers can effectively protect their organizations and uphold the highest standards of professionalism.

Part III: Information Security Program Development and Management:

Critical First Steps in Developing an Information Security Program

Developing an information security program involves several foundational steps to ensure it is comprehensive, aligned with business goals, and effective in managing risks. Here's a detailed look at these critical first steps:

1. Define the Program's Scope

Objective:

- Establish the boundaries and coverage of the information security program, ensuring all relevant areas are included.

Steps:

- **Identify Assets:** Catalog all information assets, including data, systems, hardware, software, and network infrastructure.
- **Determine Coverage:** Specify which business units, departments, and locations will be included in the program.
- **Classify Data:** Categorize data based on sensitivity and criticality, such as public, internal, confidential, and restricted.

Example:

- A retail company defines the scope of its information security program to include all customer data, payment processing systems, employee records, and point-of-sale (POS) systems across all stores and online operations.

2. Establish Program Objectives

Objective:

- Define clear, measurable goals for the information security program that align with the organization's strategic objectives.

Steps:

- **Security Goals:** Set specific goals such as protecting customer data, ensuring regulatory compliance, preventing data breaches, and maintaining business continuity.
- **Performance Metrics:** Establish metrics to measure the success of the program, such as incident response time, number of detected threats, and compliance audit results.

Example:

- An objective might be to reduce the number of data breaches by 50% within the first year of implementation.

3. Align with Business Goals and Risk Appetite

Objective:

- Ensure the information security program supports the organization's overall business strategy and aligns with its risk tolerance levels.

Steps:

- **Business Objectives:** Understand the organization's strategic goals, such as expanding into new markets, improving customer trust, and enhancing operational efficiency.
- **Risk Appetite:** Define the organization's risk appetite by determining the level of risk it is willing to accept in different areas, such as financial loss, reputational damage, and operational disruption.

Example:

- A financial services firm aligns its information security program with its goal of maintaining customer trust by implementing stringent data protection measures and aligning with its low risk appetite for data breaches.

Using Frameworks to Guide Program Development

1. ISO/IEC 27000 Series

Overview:

- The ISO/IEC 27000 series provides a comprehensive framework for managing information security, including best practices for establishing, implementing, maintaining, and continually improving an information security management system (ISMS).

Key Components:

- **ISO/IEC 27001:** Specifies requirements for establishing, implementing, maintaining, and continually improving an ISMS.
- **ISO/IEC 27002:** Provides guidelines for organizational information security standards and information security management practices.

Application:

- **Gap Analysis:** Conduct a gap analysis to compare current security practices with ISO/IEC 27001 requirements.
- **Risk Assessment:** Use ISO/IEC 27005 to perform detailed risk assessments and develop a risk treatment plan.
- **ISMS Implementation:** Implement an ISMS based on ISO/IEC 27001, ensuring all identified controls are in place and effective.

Example:

- An organization uses ISO/IEC 27001 to establish an ISMS, ensuring that all security measures are documented, implemented, and regularly reviewed for effectiveness.

2. NIST Cybersecurity Framework (CSF)

Overview:

- The NIST Cybersecurity Framework provides a policy framework of computer security guidance for how private sector organizations can assess and improve their ability to prevent, detect, and respond to cyber-attacks.

Key Components:

- **Core Functions:** Identify, Protect, Detect, Respond, Recover.
- **Implementation Tiers:** Describe the degree to which an organization's cybersecurity risk management practices exhibit the characteristics defined in the Framework.
- **Profiles:** Represent the alignment of standards, guidelines, and practices to the Framework Core in a particular implementation scenario.

Application:

- **Framework Core:** Use the core functions to structure the information security program around identifying, protecting, detecting, responding, and recovering from security incidents.
- **Implementation Tiers:** Assess the current maturity level of the organization's cybersecurity practices and set goals for improvement.
- **Framework Profiles:** Develop a profile that outlines the current state of cybersecurity practices and a target state to guide improvements.

Example:

- A healthcare organization uses the NIST CSF to develop a comprehensive cybersecurity program, ensuring that all aspects of security, from identification to recovery, are covered.

3. COBIT (Control Objectives for Information and Related Technologies)

Overview:

- COBIT provides a framework for developing, implementing, monitoring, and improving IT governance and management practices.

Key Components:

- **Processes:** 40 governance and management objectives organized into five domains: Evaluate, Direct and Monitor (EDM); Align, Plan, and Organize (APO); Build, Acquire, and Implement (BAI); Deliver, Service, and Support (DSS); and Monitor, Evaluate, and Assess (MEA).
- **Management Guidelines:** Provide a structured approach for integrating IT governance with business goals.

Application:

- **Governance Framework:** Use COBIT to establish a governance framework that aligns IT and business strategies.
- **Process Improvement:** Identify and implement key processes to manage IT and security risks effectively.
- **Performance Measurement:** Develop performance metrics to evaluate the effectiveness of IT governance and management practices.

Example:

- A large enterprise uses COBIT to integrate IT governance with its overall business strategy, ensuring that information security practices support business goals and objectives.

Conclusion

Developing an effective information security program begins with defining its scope, establishing clear objectives, and aligning with the organization's business goals and risk appetite. Utilizing frameworks such as ISO/IEC 27000, NIST CSF, and COBIT provides structured guidance and best practices to ensure comprehensive coverage and effective implementation. By following these steps and leveraging established frameworks, organizations can build a robust information security program that not only protects their assets but also supports their strategic objectives and fosters a resilient security posture.

Essential Components of a Comprehensive Information Security Program

A comprehensive information security program is designed to protect an organization's information assets and ensure the confidentiality, integrity, and availability of data. The essential components of such a program include policies, procedures, standards, guidelines, and controls. Each component plays a crucial role in supporting the program's objectives and maintaining a strong security posture.

1. Policies

Definition: Policies are high-level statements that define the organization's approach to information security. They establish the framework for the information security program and set the overall direction.

Examples:

- **Information Security Policy:** Outlines the organization's commitment to information security, key principles, and high-level responsibilities.
- **Data Protection Policy:** Specifies how sensitive data should be handled, including access controls, encryption requirements, and data classification.

Role: Policies provide the foundation for the security program by setting the tone from the top and defining the organization's security goals and objectives.

2. Procedures

Definition: Procedures are detailed, step-by-step instructions on how to implement policies. They provide the specific actions required to achieve the objectives outlined in the policies.

Examples:

- **Incident Response Procedure:** Details the steps to be taken when a security incident is detected, including identification, containment, eradication, and recovery.
- **User Access Management Procedure:** Describes the process for granting, reviewing, and revoking user access to information systems.

Role: Procedures translate policies into actionable steps, ensuring that security measures are implemented consistently and effectively across the organization.

3. Standards

Definition: Standards provide specific, mandatory requirements for implementing policies and procedures. They ensure uniformity and consistency in the application of security controls.
Examples:

- **Password Standards:** Define the minimum requirements for password complexity, length, and expiration.
- **Encryption Standards:** Specify the types of encryption algorithms and key lengths to be used for protecting sensitive data.

Role: Standards ensure that security controls are applied consistently and meet a predefined level of effectiveness.

4. Guidelines

Definition: Guidelines are recommended practices that provide additional context and suggestions for implementing policies, procedures, and standards. They offer flexibility and support best practices.
Examples:

- **Email Security Guidelines:** Recommend best practices for using email securely, such as avoiding phishing attacks and using encrypted communication.
- **Remote Work Guidelines:** Provide suggestions for securing remote work environments, including VPN usage and secure Wi-Fi practices.

Role: Guidelines offer advice and best practices to help users implement security measures effectively, especially in situations where flexibility is needed.

5. Controls

Definition: Controls are specific measures implemented to mitigate risks and protect information assets. They can be technical, administrative, or physical in nature.
Examples:

- **Technical Controls:** Firewalls, intrusion detection systems (IDS), and encryption.
- **Administrative Controls:** Security training programs, background checks, and access reviews.
- **Physical Controls:** Locks, security guards, and surveillance cameras.

Role: Controls are the tangible mechanisms that enforce security policies, procedures, and standards, directly protecting the organization's information assets.

Interrelationships and Roles in Supporting Program Objectives

Policies to Controls:

- Policies set the strategic direction and goals for information security.
- Procedures provide detailed instructions on how to implement these policies.
- Standards ensure that procedures are followed consistently and meet specific requirements.
- Guidelines offer best practices and additional recommendations.
- Controls are the practical implementations that enforce policies and procedures, mitigating risks.

Importance of Regular Review and Update

1. **Evolving Threat Landscape:**
    - The threat landscape is constantly changing with new vulnerabilities and attack vectors emerging. Regular updates ensure that security measures remain effective against the latest threats.
2. **Regulatory Requirements:**
    - Compliance requirements can change due to new regulations or updates to existing ones. Keeping security components updated ensures continued compliance and avoids potential fines and legal issues.
3. **Organizational Changes:**
    - Organizational changes such as mergers, acquisitions, or shifts in business strategy can introduce new risks. Regular reviews help adapt the security program to address these changes.
4. **Technological Advancements:**

- Advances in technology can both introduce new risks and provide new tools for enhancing security. Updating security components ensures that the organization leverages the latest technologies and addresses associated risks.

Best Practices for Regular Review and Update:

- **Scheduled Reviews:** Establish a regular schedule for reviewing and updating policies, procedures, standards, guidelines, and controls (e.g., annually or bi-annually).
- **Risk Assessments:** Conduct regular risk assessments to identify new risks and determine if current controls are adequate.
- **Stakeholder Involvement:** Involve key stakeholders from different departments to ensure comprehensive updates and buy-in.
- **Monitoring and Feedback:** Continuously monitor the effectiveness of security measures and gather feedback from users to inform updates.
- **Change Management:** Implement a formal change management process to manage updates systematically and ensure that changes are communicated effectively.

Conclusion

A comprehensive information security program integrates policies, procedures, standards, guidelines, and controls to protect an organization's information assets. These components must be regularly reviewed and updated to keep pace with evolving threats, regulatory changes, and organizational needs. By maintaining a dynamic and adaptive security program, organizations can ensure robust protection of their information assets and support their overall business objectives.

Concept of Information Security Program Governance

Information security program governance is the framework that provides oversight, direction, and accountability for the activities and outcomes of an information security program. It ensures that the program aligns with the organization's strategic objectives, effectively manages risks, and complies with relevant regulations and standards.

Role of Information Security Program Governance

1. Oversight:

- **Purpose:** Ensure that the information security program is effectively managing risks and achieving its objectives.
- **Activities:** Regularly review the program's performance, approve significant initiatives, and evaluate the effectiveness of security measures.

2. Direction:

- **Purpose:** Provide strategic guidance and set priorities for the information security program.
- **Activities:** Define the program's scope, objectives, and alignment with business goals. Develop and communicate security policies and standards.

3. Accountability:

- **Purpose:** Ensure that individuals and teams are responsible for implementing and maintaining security controls.
- **Activities:** Establish clear roles and responsibilities, monitor compliance, and hold stakeholders accountable for their actions.

Key Functions and Responsibilities of a Program Governance Body

1. Setting Strategic Priorities:

- **Function:** Define the strategic direction for the information security program, ensuring it supports the organization's overall business objectives.
- **Responsibilities:** Identify key security initiatives, develop long-term plans, and allocate resources to high-priority areas.

Example:

- A governance body may prioritize initiatives such as implementing multi-factor authentication (MFA) and migrating critical systems to the cloud to enhance security and operational efficiency.

2. Allocating Resources:

- **Function:** Ensure that the information security program has the necessary resources (budget, personnel, technology) to achieve its goals.
- **Responsibilities:** Approve budgets, allocate funds to specific projects, and ensure that the security team is adequately staffed.

Example:

- Allocating funds to upgrade legacy systems, invest in advanced threat detection tools, and provide ongoing training for security personnel.

3. Monitoring Performance:

- **Function:** Regularly assess the performance of the information security program against defined metrics and objectives.
- **Responsibilities:** Review performance reports, conduct audits, and evaluate the effectiveness of security controls and initiatives.

Example:

- Monitoring metrics such as the number of security incidents, average incident response time, and compliance audit results to ensure the program is meeting its goals.

4. Ensuring Compliance:

- **Function:** Ensure that the organization complies with relevant laws, regulations, and industry standards.
- **Responsibilities:** Develop and enforce policies and procedures, conduct regular compliance assessments, and address any identified gaps.

Example:

- Ensuring compliance with regulations such as GDPR, HIPAA, or PCI DSS by regularly reviewing and updating security policies and conducting compliance audits.

Establishing an Effective Governance Structure

1. Define Governance Roles and Responsibilities:

Executive Management:

- **Role:** Provide strategic oversight and support for the information security program.
- **Responsibilities:** Approve the program's strategic direction, allocate resources, and ensure alignment with business objectives.

Business Units:

- **Role:** Integrate security practices into daily operations and support the implementation of security initiatives.
- **Responsibilities:** Identify specific security needs, participate in risk assessments, and implement security controls.

IT Department:

- **Role:** Implement and manage technical security controls and infrastructure.
- **Responsibilities:** Deploy and maintain security technologies, monitor systems for threats, and respond to security incidents.

Legal and Compliance:

- **Role:** Ensure that the information security program complies with legal and regulatory requirements.
- **Responsibilities:** Develop and enforce security policies, conduct compliance audits, and manage legal risks related to security.

2. Establish a Governance Body:

Security Steering Committee:

- **Composition:** Include representatives from executive management, business units, IT, legal, and compliance.
- **Responsibilities:** Provide strategic guidance, approve major security initiatives, review program performance, and ensure alignment with business goals.

Example Structure:

- **Chairperson:** Chief Information Security Officer (CISO)
- **Members:**
    - Chief Information Officer (CIO)
    - Chief Financial Officer (CFO)
    - Head of Legal/Compliance
    - Business Unit Leaders
    - IT Security Manager

3. Develop Governance Policies and Procedures:

Risk Management Policy:

- **Purpose:** Outline the process for identifying, assessing, and mitigating risks.
- **Content:** Include risk assessment methodologies, risk tolerance levels, and procedures for reporting and addressing risks.

Example:

- A policy that requires annual risk assessments for all critical systems and outlines the process for reporting and mitigating identified risks.

Security Policy:

- **Purpose:** Define the organization's security objectives, standards, and guidelines.
- **Content:** Cover areas such as access control, data protection, incident response, and compliance requirements.

Example:

- A comprehensive security policy that mandates the use of strong passwords, regular security training for employees, and encryption of sensitive data.

4. Implement Monitoring and Reporting Mechanisms:

Performance Metrics:

- **Purpose:** Measure the effectiveness of the information security program.
- **Examples:** Incident response time, number of detected threats, compliance audit results, and user training completion rates.

Reporting Tools:

- **Purpose:** Provide visibility into the program's performance and ensure accountability.
- **Examples:** Dashboards, regular performance reports, and automated alerts for significant security incidents.

5. Foster a Culture of Security:

Training and Awareness Programs:

- **Purpose:** Educate employees about their security responsibilities and promote a security-conscious culture.
- **Content:** Regular training sessions, phishing simulations, and awareness campaigns.

Example:

- Implementing quarterly security training sessions for all employees and conducting regular phishing simulations to test and improve their awareness.

Conclusion

Information security program governance is crucial for providing oversight, direction, and accountability for an organization's security activities and outcomes. By setting strategic priorities, allocating resources, monitoring performance, and ensuring compliance, a well-structured governance body can significantly enhance the effectiveness of the information security program. Establishing an effective governance structure that includes representatives from key stakeholder groups, defining clear roles and responsibilities, and fostering a culture of security are essential steps in building a robust and resilient information security framework.

Comparison of Different Types of Security Controls

Security controls are essential for protecting an organization's information assets. They can be broadly categorized into administrative, technical, and physical controls. Each type of control has its own strengths, limitations, and use cases. Implementing a layered, defense-in-depth approach that combines multiple types of controls is crucial for creating a robust and resilient security posture.

1. Administrative Controls

Definition: Administrative controls are policies, procedures, and guidelines that govern how an organization manages its information security.

Examples:

- **Policies:** Information Security Policy, Data Protection Policy, Access Control Policy.
- **Procedures:** Incident Response Procedure, User Access Management Procedure, Backup and Recovery Procedure.
- **Guidelines:** Email Security Guidelines, Password Creation Guidelines, Remote Work Guidelines.

Strengths:

- **Foundation:** Provides the framework and direction for the entire security program.
- **Standardization:** Ensures consistent implementation of security practices across the organization.
- **Awareness:** Enhances security awareness and culture among employees through training and clear guidelines.

Limitations:

- **Dependence on Enforcement:** Effectiveness depends on how well policies and procedures are enforced and followed.
- **Non-Technical Nature:** Cannot directly prevent or detect security incidents; relies on human compliance.

Use Cases:

- **Regulatory Compliance:** Ensuring compliance with laws and regulations such as GDPR, HIPAA, and SOX.
- **Organizational Governance:** Establishing security governance and defining roles and responsibilities.

2. Technical Controls

Definition: Technical controls involve the use of software and hardware to protect information assets.

Examples:

- **Software:** Antivirus software, firewalls, intrusion detection systems (IDS), encryption.
- **Hardware:** Secure access points, hardware firewalls, biometric authentication devices.

Strengths:

- **Automation:** Can automatically detect and respond to security incidents, reducing human error.
- **Scalability:** Can be scaled to protect large and complex IT environments.
- **Effectiveness:** Provides direct protection against a wide range of cyber threats.

Limitations:

- **Cost:** Can be expensive to implement and maintain.
- **Complexity:** Requires specialized knowledge and skills to configure and manage effectively.
- **Dependence on Technology:** May become obsolete as technology evolves and new threats emerge.

Use Cases:

- **Network Security:** Protecting networks from unauthorized access and cyber attacks using firewalls and IDS.
- **Data Protection:** Ensuring data confidentiality and integrity through encryption and access controls.

3. Physical Controls

Definition: Physical controls involve barriers and mechanisms to prevent unauthorized physical access to information assets.

Examples:

- **Barriers:** Fences, walls, locked doors.
- **Access Controls:** Security guards, surveillance cameras, biometric access systems.

Strengths:

- **Deterrence:** Acts as a visible deterrent to potential intruders.
- **Immediate Protection:** Provides direct and immediate protection against physical threats.
- **Visibility:** Enhances monitoring and control of physical access to sensitive areas.

Limitations:

- **Cost:** Can be expensive to implement and maintain.
- **Limited Scope:** Only effective against physical threats, not cyber threats.
- **Vulnerabilities:** Can be bypassed if not properly monitored and maintained.

Use Cases:

- **Facility Security:** Protecting data centers, server rooms, and offices from unauthorized physical access.
- **Surveillance:** Monitoring sensitive areas to detect and respond to physical security incidents.

Importance of a Layered, Defense-in-Depth Approach

Definition: A defense-in-depth approach involves implementing multiple layers of security controls across different categories (administrative, technical, and physical) to protect information assets.

Benefits:

- **Redundancy:** Provides multiple layers of protection, ensuring that if one control fails, others are in place to mitigate the risk.
- **Comprehensive Coverage:** Addresses a wide range of threats, including physical, technical, and administrative risks.
- **Enhanced Security Posture:** Increases the overall security resilience of the organization by combining the strengths of different types of controls.

Examples of Defense-in-Depth Approach:

- **Access Control:** Implementing a combination of policies (administrative control), biometric authentication (physical control), and multi-factor authentication (technical control) to secure access to sensitive information.
- **Incident Response:** Developing an incident response policy (administrative control), deploying IDS and SIEM systems (technical controls) to detect incidents, and securing the physical location of the incident response team (physical control).
- **Data Protection:** Enforcing a data protection policy (administrative control), using encryption (technical control) to protect data, and securing data storage locations with locks and surveillance cameras (physical control).

Conclusion

Understanding and effectively implementing different types of security controls—administrative, technical, and physical—are essential for a robust information security program. Each type of control has its own strengths and limitations, making it important to use a layered, defense-in-depth approach. This approach ensures comprehensive protection by addressing a wide range of threats and vulnerabilities, ultimately enhancing the organization's overall security posture. Regularly reviewing and updating these controls is critical to adapt to the evolving threat landscape and maintain effective protection of information assets.

Selecting and Prioritizing Security Controls

The process for selecting and prioritizing security controls involves several steps, taking into account risk assessment results, business impact, regulatory requirements, and resource constraints. Effective selection and prioritization ensure that security efforts are focused on the most critical areas, providing the greatest return on investment and enhancing the overall security posture.

1. Conduct Risk Assessment

Objective:

- Identify and evaluate the potential risks to the organization's information assets.

Steps:

- **Identify Assets:** Catalog all information assets and their value to the organization.
- **Identify Threats and Vulnerabilities:** Determine potential threats and vulnerabilities affecting these assets.
- **Evaluate Risks:** Assess the likelihood and impact of identified risks.

Example:

- A financial institution identifies customer data, transaction systems, and financial records as critical assets. Threats include cyber-attacks, data breaches, and insider threats.

2. Determine Business Impact

Objective:

- Understand the potential impact of risks on business operations and objectives.

Steps:

- **Impact Analysis:** Assess how each identified risk could affect business processes, financial performance, legal compliance, and reputation.
- **Prioritize Risks:** Rank risks based on their potential impact and likelihood.

Example:

- A data breach at the financial institution could result in significant financial losses, regulatory fines, and reputational damage, making it a high-priority risk.

3. Identify Regulatory Requirements

Objective:

- Ensure compliance with relevant laws, regulations, and industry standards.

Steps:

- **Identify Requirements:** Determine applicable regulations (e.g., GDPR, HIPAA, PCI DSS) and their specific requirements.
- **Map Requirements to Risks:** Link regulatory requirements to identified risks to ensure compliance.

Example:

- The financial institution must comply with PCI DSS for handling payment card data and GDPR for protecting customer personal information.

4. Evaluate Resource Constraints

Objective:

- Assess the availability of resources (budget, personnel, technology) to implement security controls.

Steps:

- **Resource Inventory:** Determine available resources for implementing and maintaining controls.
- **Feasibility Analysis:** Evaluate the feasibility of implementing different controls based on available resources.

Example:

- The financial institution has a limited budget for security but must prioritize high-impact controls.

5. Use Tools and Techniques

A. Control Frameworks:

Objective:

- Provide a structured approach to identifying and implementing security controls.

Steps:

- **Select Framework:** Choose a control framework such as NIST SP 800-53, ISO/IEC 27001, or CIS Controls.
- **Map Controls to Risks:** Align controls from the selected framework with identified risks.

Example:

- The financial institution uses NIST SP 800-53 to identify controls such as access control (AC-1) and audit logging (AU-2).

B. Gap Analysis:

Objective:

- Identify gaps between current security posture and desired state.

Steps:

- **Current State Assessment:** Assess the current state of security controls.
- **Desired State Definition:** Define the desired state based on best practices and regulatory requirements.
- **Gap Identification:** Identify gaps and areas for improvement.

Example:

- The gap analysis reveals that the financial institution lacks multi-factor authentication (MFA) and comprehensive data encryption.

C. Cost-Benefit Analysis:

Objective:

- Evaluate the costs and benefits of implementing specific security controls.

Steps:

- **Cost Estimation:** Estimate the implementation and maintenance costs for each control.
- **Benefit Estimation:** Assess the potential benefits in terms of risk reduction and compliance.
- **Analysis:** Compare costs and benefits to prioritize controls.

Example:

- Implementing MFA is estimated to cost $50,000 but can significantly reduce the risk of unauthorized access, making it a high-priority control.

6. Create a Prioritized Control Implementation Plan

Objective:

- Develop a plan that prioritizes the implementation of security controls based on risk, impact, regulatory requirements, and resource constraints.

Steps:

- **Rank Controls:** Prioritize controls based on risk assessment, business impact, and cost-benefit analysis.
- **Develop Timeline:** Create a timeline for implementing controls, considering resource availability and operational impact.
- **Assign Responsibilities:** Assign responsibilities for implementing and monitoring each control.

Example:

- **High-Priority Controls:** Implement MFA, data encryption, and access controls within the first six months.
- **Medium-Priority Controls:** Enhance audit logging and incident response capabilities in the next six to twelve months.
- **Low-Priority Controls:** Conduct additional training and awareness programs within twelve to eighteen months.

Sample Implementation Plan:

Control	Priority	Implementation Timeline	Responsible Team	Estimated Cost
Multi-Factor Authentication (MFA)	High	0-6 months	IT Security Team	$50,000
Data Encryption	High	0-6 months	IT Security Team	$75,000

Control	Priority	Implementation Timeline	Responsible Team	Estimated Cost
Access Control (AC-1)	High	0-6 months	IT Security Team	$30,000
Audit Logging (AU-2)	Medium	6-12 months	Compliance Team	$20,000
Incident Response Enhancement	Medium	6-12 months	Incident Response Team	$40,000
Security Awareness Training	Low	12-18 months	HR & IT Security Team	$10,000

Conclusion

Selecting and prioritizing security controls involves a comprehensive process that includes risk assessment, business impact analysis, consideration of regulatory requirements, and evaluation of resource constraints. Utilizing tools and techniques such as control frameworks, gap analysis, and cost-benefit analysis helps identify and justify the most appropriate controls for a given context. By creating a prioritized control implementation plan, organizations can balance risk mitigation, operational efficiency, and user productivity, ensuring a robust and effective information security

Implementing and Testing Security Controls in Complex IT Environments

Challenges

1. **Complexity:**
    - Diverse technologies and systems often create integration challenges.
    - Dependencies between different systems can lead to cascading failures.
2. **Distribution:**
    - Geographically dispersed environments complicate centralized management.
    - Inconsistent implementation across different locations can weaken security posture.
3. **Rapid Change:**
    - Continuous deployment of new technologies and updates can outpace security measures.
    - Keeping documentation and training up-to-date with frequent changes is challenging.

Best Practices for Implementation

1. **Standardization and Automation:**
    - Use standardized templates and automated deployment tools to ensure consistent implementation of controls across all environments.
    - Example: Using Infrastructure as Code (IaC) tools like Terraform or Ansible to automate the deployment of security controls.
2. **Centralized Management:**
    - Implement centralized management tools to monitor and enforce security policies across distributed environments.
    - Example: Using a centralized SIEM system like Splunk or IBM QRadar for real-time monitoring and incident response.
3. **Continuous Monitoring:**
    - Establish continuous monitoring and logging to detect and respond to security incidents promptly.
    - Example: Implementing continuous integration and continuous deployment (CI/CD) pipelines with integrated security testing.
4. **Training and Awareness:**
    - Provide regular training and updates to ensure that all staff are aware of security policies and procedures.
    - Example: Regular security awareness training sessions and phishing simulation exercises.

Project Management Methodologies

1. **Agile Methodology:**
    - **Flexibility:** Allows for iterative development and rapid response to changes.

- **Collaboration:** Emphasizes teamwork and continuous feedback, enhancing security control implementation.
- **Example:** Implementing security controls in short sprints, with regular reviews and adjustments based on feedback and emerging threats.

2. **Waterfall Methodology:**
    - **Structured Approach:** Follows a sequential process, providing clear stages and deliverables.
    - **Predictability:** Well-suited for projects with well-defined requirements and minimal changes.
    - **Example:** Using a Waterfall approach for implementing large-scale security infrastructure projects, where requirements are clear and changes are infrequent.

Comprehensive Testing Strategy

1. **Vulnerability Scanning:**
    - **Purpose:** Identify known vulnerabilities in systems and applications.
    - **Tools:** Use automated tools like Nessus, Qualys, or OpenVAS.
    - **Frequency:** Conduct regular scans (e.g., weekly or monthly) and after significant changes.
    - **Example:** Schedule automated vulnerability scans to identify and remediate vulnerabilities in real-time.
2. **Penetration Testing:**
    - **Purpose:** Simulate real-world attacks to identify and exploit vulnerabilities.
    - **Scope:** Define the scope and rules of engagement, including target systems and testing boundaries.
    - **Frequency:** Conduct at least annually or after major changes to the environment.
    - **Tools:** Use tools like Metasploit, Burp Suite, and manual testing techniques.
    - **Example:** Engage a third-party penetration testing firm to conduct an annual comprehensive assessment of critical systems.
3. **Social Engineering Exercises:**
    - **Purpose:** Assess the effectiveness of administrative and human controls against social engineering attacks.
    - **Types:** Phishing simulations, pretexting, baiting, and tailgating.
    - **Frequency:** Conduct regular exercises (e.g., quarterly) to keep staff vigilant.
    - **Example:** Launch phishing simulations to evaluate and improve employees' ability to recognize and respond to phishing attempts.

Developing and Executing a Testing Strategy

1. **Define Objectives and Scope:**
    - Identify the key objectives of the testing strategy, such as identifying vulnerabilities, validating controls, and improving security posture.
    - Define the scope, including systems, networks, applications, and physical locations to be tested.
2. **Select Appropriate Tools and Techniques:**
    - Choose the right mix of tools and techniques for vulnerability scanning, penetration testing, and social engineering exercises.
    - Ensure the tools are regularly updated and align with industry best practices.
3. **Schedule and Plan Tests:**
    - Develop a testing schedule that includes regular scans, annual penetration tests, and frequent social engineering exercises.
    - Coordinate with relevant stakeholders to minimize disruptions and ensure awareness.
4. **Execute Tests:**
    - Conduct tests as planned, ensuring thorough documentation of findings and observations.
    - Maintain clear communication with all involved parties to address any immediate issues identified during testing.
5. **Analyze Results and Remediate:**
    - Analyze test results to identify vulnerabilities and areas for improvement.

    - Prioritize remediation efforts based on the risk and potential impact of identified issues.
    - Example: After a penetration test, prioritize fixing critical vulnerabilities that could lead to data breaches.
6. **Review and Improve:**
    - Regularly review the testing strategy to incorporate lessons learned, new tools, and techniques.
    - Update the testing schedule and methodologies to adapt to evolving threats and organizational changes.

Importance of Defense-in-Depth

Implementing a layered, defense-in-depth approach is critical in complex IT environments. By combining multiple types of controls—administrative, technical, and physical—organizations can:

- **Enhance Security Posture:** Multiple layers of defense make it harder for attackers to penetrate.
- **Increase Resilience:** If one control fails, others can compensate, reducing overall risk.
- **Ensure Comprehensive Coverage:** Addresses a wide range of threats, including cyber-attacks, insider threats, and physical breaches.

Example: Defense-in-Depth in Practice

Scenario: A multinational corporation with a distributed IT environment.

1. **Administrative Controls:**
    - Implement global security policies and procedures.
    - Conduct regular security training and awareness programs for all employees.
2. **Technical Controls:**
    - Deploy firewalls and IDS/IPS across all network segments.
    - Use endpoint protection software and encryption for all devices and data.
    - Implement access controls and multi-factor authentication (MFA) for all critical systems.
3. **Physical Controls:**
    - Secure data centers with biometric access controls and surveillance cameras.
    - Implement physical security policies for all office locations, including visitor management systems.

By adopting these practices and integrating them into a comprehensive security program, organizations can effectively manage and mitigate risks in complex, distributed, and rapidly changing IT environments. This layered approach ensures that security measures are robust, resilient, and capable of adapting to new challenges.

Importance of Ongoing Monitoring and Evaluation of Security Control Performance

Ongoing monitoring and evaluation of security control performance are crucial to ensure that security controls remain effective, relevant, and capable of adapting to evolving threats. Continuous monitoring helps identify control weaknesses, verify compliance with policies, and drive timely corrective actions. This proactive approach is essential for maintaining a robust security posture and ensuring that controls continue to protect the organization's assets effectively.

Key Metrics and Key Performance Indicators (KPIs) for Measuring Control Effectiveness

1. Number of Incidents Prevented or Detected

Metric:

- Tracks the number of security incidents that were either prevented by controls or detected promptly.

KPI:

- **Incident Detection Rate:** Number of detected incidents compared to the total number of incidents.
- **Incident Prevention Rate:** Number of prevented incidents compared to attempted incidents.

Example:

- An increase in the detection rate of phishing attempts indicates improved email filtering controls.

2. Time to Respond and Recover from Incidents

Metric:

- Measures the time taken to respond to and recover from security incidents.

KPI:

- **Mean Time to Detect (MTTD):** Average time taken to detect an incident.
- **Mean Time to Respond (MTTR):** Average time taken to respond to an incident.
- **Mean Time to Recover (MTTR):** Average time taken to recover from an incident.

Example:

- A reduction in the MTTR for ransomware attacks from 12 hours to 4 hours shows enhanced incident response capabilities.

3. Level of User Awareness and Compliance

Metric:

- Assesses the effectiveness of security awareness programs and user compliance with security policies.

KPI:

- **Training Completion Rate:** Percentage of employees who have completed security training.
- **Policy Compliance Rate:** Percentage of users adhering to security policies.
- **Phishing Simulation Success Rate:** Percentage of employees who successfully identify phishing attempts during simulations.

Example:

- An increase in the phishing simulation success rate from 70% to 90% indicates improved user awareness and training effectiveness.

Establishing a Continuous Monitoring Program

1. Automated Tools

Objective:

- Utilize automated tools to provide real-time monitoring and analysis of security controls and incidents.

Tools:

- **Security Information and Event Management (SIEM):** Aggregates and analyzes security data from various sources to detect anomalies and incidents.
- **Intrusion Detection Systems (IDS) and Intrusion Prevention Systems (IPS):** Monitor network traffic for suspicious activity and take preventive actions.
- **Endpoint Detection and Response (EDR):** Monitors and responds to threats on endpoints.

Example:

- Implementing a SIEM solution that provides real-time alerts and dashboards for monitoring security events across the organization.

2. Manual Assessments

Objective:

- Conduct regular manual assessments to verify the effectiveness of security controls and identify areas for improvement.

Activities:

- **Penetration Testing:** Simulate attacks to identify vulnerabilities and test the effectiveness of security controls.
- **Vulnerability Assessments:** Regularly scan systems and applications for known vulnerabilities.
- **Compliance Audits:** Verify adherence to security policies, procedures, and regulatory requirements.

Example:

- Conducting quarterly penetration tests to identify and remediate security weaknesses before they can be exploited.

3. Feedback Loops

Objective:

- Establish feedback mechanisms to continuously improve security controls based on monitoring and assessment results.

Activities:

- **Incident Reviews:** Conduct post-incident reviews to analyze the root causes and effectiveness of the response. Use findings to improve controls.
- **User Feedback:** Collect feedback from employees on the usability and effectiveness of security controls and training programs.
- **Regular Reporting:** Provide regular reports to stakeholders, highlighting control performance, identified weaknesses, and corrective actions taken.

Example:

- Implementing a monthly review process where incident response teams analyze recent incidents, identify lessons learned, and recommend improvements to controls and processes.

Continuous Monitoring Program Example

1. Automated Tools:

Implementation:

- Deploy a SIEM system that integrates with IDS/IPS, EDR, and other security tools to provide comprehensive monitoring and real-time alerts.

Usage:

- Monitor logs from firewalls, servers, applications, and endpoints to detect suspicious activity.
- Configure automated alerts for predefined thresholds, such as multiple failed login attempts or unusual data transfers.

2. Manual Assessments:

Schedule:

- **Penetration Testing:** Quarterly
- **Vulnerability Scans:** Monthly
- **Compliance Audits:** Annually

Process:

- Use a combination of internal and external resources to conduct assessments.
- Document findings, prioritize vulnerabilities based on risk, and track remediation efforts.

3. Feedback Loops:

Incident Reviews:

- Conduct reviews within 24 hours of incident resolution.
- Include cross-functional teams to provide diverse perspectives and identify comprehensive solutions.

User Feedback:

- Conduct semi-annual surveys to gather user insights on security controls and training effectiveness.
- Incorporate feedback into training updates and control improvements.

Regular Reporting:

- Produce monthly performance reports for management, highlighting key metrics, KPIs, and action plans.
- Use visual aids (e.g., dashboards, charts) to clearly communicate trends and progress.

Example: Implementing Continuous Monitoring for a Financial Institution

Scenario: A financial institution aims to enhance its continuous monitoring program to improve control effectiveness and regulatory compliance.

Automated Tools:

- Implement a SIEM system to monitor and analyze security events in real-time.
- Deploy EDR solutions to detect and respond to endpoint threats.

Manual Assessments:

- Schedule quarterly penetration tests to evaluate the security of critical systems and applications.
- Conduct monthly vulnerability scans to identify and remediate security weaknesses.
- Perform annual compliance audits to ensure adherence to PCI DSS and GDPR requirements.

Feedback Loops:

- Establish a monthly incident review process to analyze recent incidents, identify root causes, and recommend control improvements.
- Collect user feedback through semi-annual surveys and integrate findings into training programs and control updates.
- Provide regular performance reports to senior management, highlighting key metrics, trends, and areas for improvement.

Metrics and KPIs:

- Incident Detection Rate: Aim for a detection rate of 95% for phishing attempts.
- Mean Time to Respond (MTTR): Reduce MTTR for ransomware incidents from 12 hours to 4 hours within six months.
- Training Completion Rate: Achieve a 100% completion rate for mandatory security training by year-end.
- Policy Compliance Rate: Maintain a compliance rate of 95% for access control policies.

Example Monitoring Dashboard:

Metric	Current Value	Target Value	Status
Incident Detection Rate	92%	95%	🚧
Mean Time to Respond (MTTR)	6 hours	4 hours	✔
Training Completion Rate	85%	100%	🚧
Policy Compliance Rate	97%	95%	✔

Conclusion

Ongoing monitoring and evaluation of security control performance are essential for ensuring their continued effectiveness and relevance. Using key metrics and KPIs such as incident detection rates, response times, and user compliance levels, organizations can measure control effectiveness and identify areas for improvement. Establishing a continuous monitoring program that leverages automated tools, manual assessments, and feedback loops enables proactive identification of control weaknesses and drives corrective actions. By implementing these practices, organizations can maintain a robust security posture and effectively protect their assets against evolving threats.

Managing Information Security Projects: Unique Challenges and Considerations

Information security projects come with unique challenges that set them apart from other IT or business projects. These challenges necessitate tailored project management methodologies to ensure the projects' success and alignment with security goals.

Unique Challenges in Information Security Projects

1. **Confidentiality Requirements:**
    - **Challenge:** Information security projects often involve sensitive data that must be protected throughout the project lifecycle.
    - **Consideration:** Implement strict access controls and confidentiality agreements for project team members.
2. **Unintended Consequences:**
    - **Challenge:** Security implementations can inadvertently impact system functionality or performance.
    - **Consideration:** Thoroughly test all changes in a controlled environment before deployment.
3. **Rapidly Evolving Threat Landscape:**
    - **Challenge:** New threats and vulnerabilities emerge continuously, requiring adaptable and up-to-date security measures.
    - **Consideration:** Incorporate continuous monitoring and regular updates into the project plan.
4. **Regulatory Compliance:**

- **Challenge:** Projects must comply with various regulations (e.g., GDPR, HIPAA, PCI DSS) which can vary by region and industry.
    - **Consideration:** Ensure all project activities are aligned with relevant legal and regulatory requirements.
5. **Complex Dependencies:**
    - **Challenge:** Security projects often depend on other IT systems and processes, making coordination critical.
    - **Consideration:** Identify and manage dependencies meticulously to avoid disruptions.
6. **Stakeholder Involvement:**
    - **Challenge:** Diverse stakeholders with varying levels of understanding and interest in information security.
    - **Consideration:** Engage stakeholders effectively to ensure their support and alignment with project objectives.

Importance of Tailored Project Management Methodologies

Using project management methodologies tailored to the specific needs and constraints of information security initiatives is crucial for addressing these unique challenges effectively.

1. Agile Methodology:

- **Flexibility:** Agile's iterative approach allows for rapid adjustments in response to new threats or requirements.
- **Continuous Feedback:** Frequent reviews and stakeholder feedback ensure the project remains aligned with security goals.
- **Example:** Implementing security controls in sprints, allowing for continuous improvement based on the latest threat intelligence.

2. Waterfall Methodology:

- **Structured Approach:** Suitable for projects with well-defined requirements and regulatory constraints.
- **Clear Phases:** Each phase is completed before the next begins, providing a clear roadmap and ensuring thorough planning.
- **Example:** Large-scale compliance projects, where each regulatory requirement must be meticulously addressed in sequence.

Project Management Best Practices

1. Defining Clear Goals and Success Criteria:

- **Practice:** Establish specific, measurable, achievable, relevant, and time-bound (SMART) goals for the project.
- **Example:** For a data encryption project, the goal might be "Encrypt all sensitive data in transit and at rest by Q3 2024, ensuring compliance with GDPR and HIPAA standards."

2. Identifying and Managing Risks and Dependencies:

- **Practice:** Conduct a thorough risk assessment at the project outset to identify potential risks and dependencies.
- **Example:** Use a risk register to document identified risks (e.g., potential impact on system performance), assess their likelihood and impact, and develop mitigation strategies.

3. Engaging Stakeholders Throughout the Project Lifecycle:

- **Practice:** Identify all relevant stakeholders and establish regular communication channels.
- **Example:** Hold bi-weekly progress meetings with stakeholders, including IT, legal, compliance, and business unit leaders, to ensure alignment and address concerns promptly.

Examples of Applying Project Management Best Practices

1. Encryption Implementation Project:

- **Goals:** Encrypt all sensitive data in transit and at rest by the end of Q3 2024.
- **Success Criteria:** Compliance with GDPR and HIPAA, no data breaches, minimal impact on system performance.

- **Risks and Dependencies:** Dependency on IT infrastructure readiness; risk of performance degradation.
- **Mitigation Strategies:** Conduct performance testing in a staging environment, implement in phases, and monitor system performance continuously.
- **Stakeholder Engagement:** Regular updates to compliance officers, IT teams, and business unit leaders to ensure alignment and address potential issues.

2. Incident Response Plan Development:

- **Goals:** Develop a comprehensive incident response plan by Q2 2024.
- **Success Criteria:** Plan tested and validated through simulations, aligns with industry best practices, and includes roles and responsibilities.
- **Risks and Dependencies:** Dependency on input from various departments; risk of plan being outdated due to rapidly evolving threats.
- **Mitigation Strategies:** Schedule regular plan reviews and updates, incorporate feedback from simulations.
- **Stakeholder Engagement:** Involve representatives from all key departments (IT, legal, HR, communications) in the development and review process.

Conclusion

Managing information security projects requires addressing unique challenges related to confidentiality, evolving threats, compliance, and complex dependencies. Tailored project management methodologies, such as Agile or Waterfall, can help navigate these challenges effectively. By defining clear goals and success criteria, identifying and managing risks and dependencies, and engaging stakeholders throughout the project lifecycle, organizations can ensure successful implementation and sustainment of security initiatives. These best practices not only enhance project outcomes but also strengthen the organization's overall security posture.

Key Aspects of Budgeting and Resource Allocation for an Information Security Program

1. Prioritizing Investments

Risk Exposure:

- **Risk Assessment:** Conduct regular risk assessments to identify and evaluate threats, vulnerabilities, and potential impacts.
- **Prioritization:** Prioritize investments based on the level of risk exposure, focusing on high-impact and high-likelihood risks first.

Business Value:

- **Alignment with Business Goals:** Ensure that security investments align with the organization's strategic objectives and business goals.
- **Cost-Benefit Analysis:** Evaluate the potential return on investment (ROI) of security measures, considering both tangible (e.g., financial savings) and intangible (e.g., reputational protection) benefits.

Regulatory Compliance:

- **Legal Requirements:** Identify and prioritize investments needed to comply with relevant regulations and standards (e.g., GDPR, HIPAA, PCI DSS).
- **Audit and Compliance Costs:** Allocate resources for regular compliance audits and any necessary remediation actions.

2. Types of Costs Associated with an Information Security Program

Personnel Costs:

- **Salaries and Benefits:** Costs for full-time security staff, including salaries, benefits, and bonuses.
- **Contractors and Consultants:** Fees for external experts and consultants hired for specific projects or expertise.

Technology Costs:

- **Hardware:** Investment in security hardware such as firewalls, intrusion detection systems (IDS), and encryption devices.

- **Software:** Licensing and subscription fees for security software, including antivirus, SIEM, and endpoint protection solutions.
- **Infrastructure:** Costs associated with securing IT infrastructure, including network segmentation and cloud security.

Training Costs:

- **Employee Training:** Expenses for regular security awareness training programs for all employees.
- **Specialized Training:** Advanced training for security staff, including certifications (e.g., CISSP, CISM) and specialized courses.

Consulting Costs:

- **Risk Assessments and Audits:** Fees for third-party risk assessments, penetration testing, and compliance audits.
- **Strategy Development:** Costs for consulting services to develop and refine security strategies and policies.

3. Developing and Justifying a Comprehensive Budget

Assess Current Needs and Gaps:

- **Current State Analysis:** Review the current security posture, identify gaps, and determine immediate needs.
- **Benchmarking:** Compare the organization's security spending and practices with industry standards and peers.

Prioritize Investments:

- **Critical Needs:** Focus on addressing high-priority risks and compliance requirements first.
- **Strategic Initiatives:** Allocate resources for long-term strategic initiatives that enhance overall security posture.

Justify Budget Requests:

- **Risk Reduction:** Demonstrate how proposed investments will reduce risk exposure and potential losses.
- **Regulatory Compliance:** Highlight the necessity of investments to meet legal and regulatory requirements.
- **Business Impact:** Provide a cost-benefit analysis showing the business value of the investments, including potential ROI and improved operational efficiency.

Align with Financial Management Practices:

- **Integrate with Budget Cycles:** Align the security budget with the organization's overall budgeting cycle and financial planning processes.
- **Phased Approach:** Propose a phased investment plan to spread costs over multiple periods and manage financial impact.
- **Stakeholder Engagement:** Engage key stakeholders (e.g., CFO, CIO) early in the budgeting process to gain support and ensure alignment with organizational priorities.

4. Importance of Regularly Reviewing and Adjusting the Budget

Changing Threat Landscape:

- **Threat Intelligence:** Stay informed about emerging threats and trends through threat intelligence and industry reports.
- **Adaptive Budgeting:** Adjust the budget to address new threats and vulnerabilities promptly.

Organizational Priorities:

- **Business Changes:** Consider changes in business priorities, such as new product launches, market expansions, or mergers and acquisitions.
- **Resource Reallocation:** Reallocate resources to support new strategic initiatives or address evolving business needs.

Program Performance:

- **Performance Metrics:** Use key performance indicators (KPIs) to monitor the effectiveness of security investments and controls.

- **Continuous Improvement:** Regularly review program performance and make adjustments to improve efficiency and effectiveness.

Example of a Comprehensive Information Security Budget

Cost Category	Item	Cost Estimate	Justification
Personnel Costs	Salaries for security staff	$500,000	Essential for maintaining and managing security operations
	Consultants for risk assessment	$150,000	Expertise for comprehensive risk evaluations
Technology Costs	SIEM software	$200,000	Critical for real-time threat detection and response
	Firewalls and IDS	$100,000	Necessary for network security and threat prevention
Training Costs	Employee awareness training	$50,000	Ensures all employees are aware of security policies and threats
	Advanced training for security team	$75,000	Keeps security staff up-to-date with the latest threats and techniques
Consulting Costs	Compliance audits	$60,000	Ensures adherence to regulatory requirements
	Penetration testing	$40,000	Identifies vulnerabilities to be addressed
Total		**$1,175,000**	

Conclusion

Budgeting and resource allocation are critical for the success of an information security program. Prioritizing investments based on risk exposure, business value, and regulatory compliance ensures that resources are effectively utilized. Understanding the different types of costs—personnel, technology, training, and consulting—helps in developing a comprehensive budget that aligns with the organization's financial management practices. Regularly reviewing and adjusting the budget based on changes in the threat landscape, organizational priorities, and program performance is essential for maintaining an effective and adaptive security posture. Through strategic budgeting and resource allocation, organizations can effectively manage their information security risks and support their overall business objectives.

Vendor Risk Management: Ensuring Security and Resilience in the Supply Chain

Concept of Vendor Risk Management

Vendor risk management (VRM) involves assessing, monitoring, and mitigating the risks associated with third-party vendors that provide products or services to an organization. Ensuring the security and resilience of an organization's supply chain and third-party ecosystem is critical because vulnerabilities in these external entities can directly impact the organization's operations, data security, and overall risk posture.

Importance of Vendor Risk Management

1. **Security and Compliance:**
    - Ensures that vendors comply with the organization's security policies and regulatory requirements.
    - Protects sensitive data and intellectual property shared with vendors.
2. **Operational Continuity:**
    - Reduces the risk of disruptions in the supply chain caused by vendor issues.
    - Ensures that critical services provided by vendors remain reliable and secure.
3. **Reputation Management:**
    - Protects the organization's reputation by ensuring that vendors adhere to high standards of ethical and secure business practices.

- Mitigates the risk of publicized breaches or compliance failures involving third parties.

Key Steps in the Vendor Risk Management Process

1. Vendor Selection:

- **Identify Needs:** Determine the specific products or services required.
- **Research Vendors:** Compile a list of potential vendors and gather information about their capabilities and reputation.
- **Preliminary Screening:** Conduct initial assessments based on predefined criteria such as financial stability, security practices, and compliance history.

2. Due Diligence:

- **Security Assessment:** Evaluate the vendor's security posture through questionnaires, audits, and review of security certifications (e.g., ISO 27001, SOC 2).
- **Compliance Check:** Verify that the vendor complies with relevant regulatory requirements and industry standards.
- **Risk Analysis:** Assess the potential risks associated with engaging the vendor, including operational, financial, and reputational risks.

3. Contracting:

- **Security Requirements:** Include specific security requirements and expectations in the contract.
- **Service Level Agreements (SLAs):** Define clear performance metrics and responsibilities.
- **Compliance Clauses:** Ensure the contract includes clauses for regulatory compliance, data protection, and audit rights.

4. Onboarding:

- **Integration:** Integrate the vendor into the organization's systems and processes securely.
- **Training:** Provide necessary training to the vendor on the organization's security policies and procedures.
- **Access Controls:** Implement strict access controls to limit the vendor's access to sensitive information and systems.

5. Monitoring:

- **Continuous Monitoring:** Regularly monitor the vendor's performance and security practices.
- **Audits and Assessments:** Conduct periodic audits and assessments to ensure ongoing compliance and security.
- **Incident Management:** Establish protocols for incident reporting and response involving the vendor.

6. Termination:

- **Exit Plan:** Develop a clear exit plan to manage the termination of the vendor relationship.
- **Data Protection:** Ensure the secure return or destruction of data shared with the vendor.
- **Transition Management:** Plan for the transition of services to another vendor or back in-house to minimize disruption.

Examples of Vendor Risks and Mitigation Strategies

1. Cloud Service Providers (CSPs):

- **Risks:**
  - Data breaches due to insufficient security controls.
  - Service outages affecting business continuity.
  - Compliance failures impacting regulatory standing.
- **Mitigation Strategies:**
  - **Contractual Provisions:** Include clauses for data protection, incident response, and compliance with standards like GDPR or CCPA.
  - **Technical Controls:** Implement encryption, multi-factor authentication, and regular security assessments.

- **Ongoing Oversight:** Monitor the CSP's security practices and performance through continuous audits and reviews.

2. Software Developers:

- **Risks:**
  - Introduction of vulnerabilities through insecure code.
  - Intellectual property theft or misuse.
  - Failure to comply with licensing agreements.
- **Mitigation Strategies:**
  - **Contractual Provisions:** Require secure coding practices, code reviews, and intellectual property protection clauses.
  - **Technical Controls:** Conduct regular code reviews and vulnerability scans.
  - **Ongoing Oversight:** Implement continuous integration and continuous deployment (CI/CD) pipelines with integrated security checks.

3. Managed Security Service Providers (MSSPs):

- **Risks:**
  - Misconfiguration of security tools leading to gaps in protection.
  - Delayed response to security incidents.
  - Potential conflicts of interest if the MSSP serves competitors.
- **Mitigation Strategies:**
  - **Contractual Provisions:** Define clear SLAs for incident response times and conflict of interest clauses.
  - **Technical Controls:** Implement robust monitoring and reporting mechanisms.
  - **Ongoing Oversight:** Regularly review the MSSP's performance and conduct joint incident response exercises.

Best Practices for Vendor Risk Management

1. **Standardized Processes:**
   - Develop standardized processes for vendor selection, due diligence, contracting, onboarding, monitoring, and termination.
   - Example: Create a vendor risk management checklist to ensure all critical aspects are covered consistently.
2. **Risk-Based Approach:**
   - Prioritize vendors based on the level of risk they pose to the organization.
   - Example: Apply more rigorous assessments and monitoring for vendors handling sensitive data or critical services.
3. **Regular Reviews and Updates:**
   - Continuously review and update vendor risk management policies and procedures to adapt to changing threats and regulatory requirements.
   - Example: Conduct an annual review of all vendor contracts and risk assessments.
4. **Cross-Functional Collaboration:**
   - Involve stakeholders from different departments, including legal, compliance, IT, and procurement, in the vendor risk management process.
   - Example: Establish a cross-functional vendor risk management committee to oversee and coordinate efforts.
5. **Technology Solutions:**
   - Utilize technology solutions such as vendor risk management platforms to streamline and automate the process.
   - Example: Use platforms like RSA Archer or MetricStream to manage vendor risk assessments, documentation, and monitoring.

Conclusion

Vendor risk management is critical for ensuring the security and resilience of an organization's supply chain and third-party ecosystem. By following a structured process—vendor selection, due diligence, contracting, onboarding, monitoring, and termination—organizations can effectively manage risks associated with their vendors. Implementing a combination of contractual provisions, technical controls, and ongoing oversight helps mitigate these risks and safeguard the organization's information assets. Regular reviews, a risk-based approach, cross-functional collaboration, and leveraging technology solutions further enhance the effectiveness of vendor risk management efforts.

Critical Role of Staffing and Competency Development in Information Security

Building and sustaining a high-performing information security program depends significantly on having a skilled and knowledgeable team. Effective staffing and competency development ensure that the security program can adapt to evolving threats, maintain robust defenses, and support the organization's strategic objectives.

Key Roles and Responsibilities in an Information Security Organization

1. Chief Information Security Officer (CISO):

Role and Responsibilities:

- **Strategic Leadership:** Develop and implement the overall information security strategy.
- **Policy Development:** Establish security policies, standards, and procedures.
- **Risk Management:** Identify and manage security risks, aligning them with business goals.
- **Incident Response:** Oversee the response to significant security incidents.
- **Stakeholder Communication:** Communicate with executive management, the board, and other stakeholders about security matters.

2. Security Architect:

Role and Responsibilities:

- **Design Security Infrastructure:** Create and maintain the security architecture.
- **Technology Evaluation:** Assess and select security technologies and solutions.
- **Standards and Protocols:** Develop and enforce security standards and protocols.
- **Integration:** Ensure that security measures are integrated into IT systems and processes.

3. Security Analyst:

Role and Responsibilities:

- **Threat Monitoring:** Continuously monitor systems for security threats.
- **Incident Analysis:** Analyze security incidents to determine causes and impacts.
- **Vulnerability Management:** Identify and mitigate vulnerabilities in systems and applications.
- **Reporting:** Generate reports on security events and trends.

4. Incident Responder:

Role and Responsibilities:

- **Incident Detection:** Identify and respond to security incidents promptly.
- **Forensic Analysis:** Conduct forensic analysis to understand the nature and scope of incidents.
- **Remediation:** Implement measures to contain and remediate incidents.
- **Documentation:** Document incidents and responses for future reference and learning.

Attracting, Developing, and Retaining Talent

Attracting Talent:

1. Competitive Compensation:

- Offer competitive salaries and benefits to attract top talent.

- Provide performance-based incentives and bonuses.

2. Employer Branding:

- Build a strong employer brand that highlights the organization's commitment to cybersecurity.
- Showcase career growth opportunities and a positive work culture.

3. Recruitment Channels:

- Use diverse recruitment channels, including job boards, social media, and industry conferences.
- Partner with universities and training institutions to tap into emerging talent.

Developing Talent:

1. Certification Programs:

- Encourage and support employees in obtaining industry-recognized certifications (e.g., CISSP, CISM, CEH).
- Provide funding and time off for certification preparation and exams.

2. On-the-Job Training:

- Offer hands-on training opportunities through real-world projects and scenarios.
- Use job rotation and cross-training to broaden employees' skill sets and perspectives.

3. Mentoring and Coaching:

- Establish mentoring programs where experienced professionals guide and support junior staff.
- Provide regular coaching sessions to address specific skill gaps and career aspirations.

4. Continuous Learning:

- Encourage participation in workshops, webinars, and conferences.
- Provide access to online learning platforms and resources.

Retaining Talent:

1. Career Development Plans:

- Develop personalized career development plans that align with individual goals and organizational needs.
- Offer clear pathways for career progression and promotion.

2. Recognition and Rewards:

- Recognize and reward outstanding performance and contributions.
- Implement employee recognition programs and award ceremonies.

3. Work-Life Balance:

- Promote a healthy work-life balance with flexible work arrangements.
- Offer wellness programs and support for mental health.

Competency Development Approaches

1. Certification Programs:

Purpose:

- Validate expertise and knowledge in specific areas of information security.

Examples:

- CISSP (Certified Information Systems Security Professional)
- CISM (Certified Information Security Manager)
- CEH (Certified Ethical Hacker)

2. On-the-Job Training:

Purpose:

- Develop practical skills through real-world experience and problem-solving.

Examples:

- Hands-on projects, such as implementing a new security solution or responding to a simulated attack.
- Job rotation programs that expose employees to different aspects of security operations.

3. Mentoring and Coaching:

Purpose:

- Provide personalized guidance and support for professional growth.

Examples:

- Pairing junior analysts with experienced mentors who provide ongoing advice and feedback.
- Regular coaching sessions to discuss career goals, challenges, and development opportunities.

Creating a Comprehensive Learning and Development Plan

1. Assess Current Skills and Gaps:

Steps:

- Conduct a skills assessment to identify current competencies and gaps.
- Use surveys, self-assessments, and performance reviews to gather data.

2. Define Learning Objectives:

Steps:

- Align learning objectives with the organization's security goals and individual career aspirations.
- Set specific, measurable, achievable, relevant, and time-bound (SMART) goals.

3. Develop a Training Plan:

Steps:

- Identify relevant training programs, certifications, and learning resources.
- Create a schedule that includes a mix of formal training, on-the-job learning, and mentoring.

Example Training Plan:

Training Activity	Frequency	Responsible Party	Resources Needed
Certification Preparation	Annually	Employee/HR	Course fees, study materials
On-the-Job Training	Ongoing	Team Leads	Project assignments, supervision
Mentoring Sessions	Monthly	Mentors/Mentees	Meeting space, feedback forms
Security Workshops/Webinars	Quarterly	Security Team	Registration fees, online access

4. Implement and Monitor:

Steps:

- Launch the training plan and track participation and progress.
- Use performance metrics to evaluate the effectiveness of training programs.

5. Review and Adjust:

Steps:

- Regularly review the learning and development plan to ensure it remains relevant and effective.
- Gather feedback from employees and adjust the plan based on their needs and the evolving threat landscape.

Conclusion

Staffing and competency development are crucial for building and sustaining a high-performing information security program. By defining clear roles and responsibilities, attracting top talent, and investing in continuous learning and development, organizations can ensure their security teams are equipped to handle evolving threats and support the organization's strategic objectives. Implementing a comprehensive learning and development plan that includes certification programs, on-the-job training, and mentoring helps align individual career aspirations with the program's goals, fostering a motivated and capable security workforce.

Case Study: Successful Development and Management of an Information Security Program at HealthGuard

Organization: HealthGuard, a mid-sized healthcare provider

Objective: Develop and manage an information security program that aligns with HealthGuard's business objectives and risk appetite, ensuring the protection of sensitive patient data, compliance with healthcare regulations, and operational resilience.

Initial Planning and Design

Key Challenges:

- **Regulatory Compliance:** Ensuring compliance with HIPAA and other healthcare regulations.
- **Data Sensitivity:** Protecting highly sensitive patient data.
- **Resource Constraints:** Limited budget and personnel for security initiatives.

Success Factors:

- **Executive Support:** Obtained strong support from senior leadership, including the CEO and Board of Directors.
- **Stakeholder Engagement:** Engaged key stakeholders from IT, legal, compliance, and clinical departments early in the planning process.
- **Risk Assessment:** Conducted a comprehensive risk assessment to identify and prioritize security risks.

Tools and Techniques:

- **Risk Assessment Tools:** Utilized tools like FAIR (Factor Analysis of Information Risk) to quantify risks.
- **Frameworks:** Adopted the NIST Cybersecurity Framework to guide the program's structure and development.

Implementation

Key Challenges:

- **Integration:** Integrating new security controls with existing systems and workflows.
- **User Resistance:** Overcoming resistance to changes in security practices among staff.
- **Technical Complexity:** Addressing the technical complexity of deploying advanced security measures.

Success Factors:

- **Clear Roadmap:** Developed a detailed implementation roadmap with phased milestones.
- **Training and Awareness:** Conducted comprehensive training and awareness programs for all staff.
- **Pilot Testing:** Implemented a pilot phase to test new controls and processes in a controlled environment before full-scale deployment.

Tools and Techniques:

- **Project Management:** Used Agile methodology for flexibility and continuous improvement.
- **Security Controls:** Deployed multi-factor authentication (MFA), endpoint protection, and data encryption solutions.
- **Training Programs:** Leveraged online training platforms to deliver security awareness training.

Operation

Key Challenges:

- **Continuous Monitoring:** Ensuring continuous monitoring and real-time threat detection.
- **Incident Response:** Developing and maintaining an effective incident response plan.
- **Resource Allocation:** Allocating sufficient resources for ongoing security operations.

Success Factors:

- **SIEM Systems:** Implemented a Security Information and Event Management (SIEM) system for real-time monitoring and alerting.
- **Incident Response Team:** Established a dedicated incident response team with clear roles and responsibilities.
- **Periodic Reviews:** Conducted regular reviews and updates of security policies and procedures.

Tools and Techniques:

- **SIEM Tools:** Deployed Splunk for log management and real-time threat analysis.
- **Incident Response Playbooks:** Developed detailed incident response playbooks for various types of security incidents.

- **Regular Audits:** Conducted regular internal and external audits to ensure compliance and identify areas for improvement.

Continuous Improvement

Key Challenges:

- **Evolving Threat Landscape:** Keeping pace with the rapidly evolving threat landscape.
- **Metric Tracking:** Developing meaningful metrics to measure security program effectiveness.
- **Stakeholder Communication:** Communicating the value and performance of the security program to stakeholders.

Success Factors:

- **Threat Intelligence:** Subscribed to threat intelligence feeds to stay informed about emerging threats.
- **Metrics and KPIs:** Developed a comprehensive set of Key Performance Indicators (KPIs) to track program performance.
- **Feedback Mechanisms:** Established mechanisms for collecting feedback from stakeholders and incorporating it into program improvements.

Tools and Techniques:

- **Threat Intelligence Platforms:** Used platforms like Recorded Future to gather and analyze threat intelligence.
- **Dashboard Reporting:** Implemented dashboard reporting using tools like Power BI to visualize KPIs and metrics.
- **Surveys and Workshops:** Conducted regular surveys and workshops with stakeholders to gather feedback and identify improvement opportunities.

Measuring and Communicating Program Performance

Metrics Used:

- **Incident Metrics:** Number of incidents detected, response times, and resolution rates.
- **Compliance Metrics:** Compliance audit results, number of compliance violations, and remediation efforts.
- **User Awareness Metrics:** Training completion rates, phishing simulation results, and user-reported incidents.
- **System Metrics:** Number of vulnerabilities identified and remediated, system uptime, and performance impact of security measures.

Communication Strategies:

- **Regular Reporting:** Provided monthly and quarterly security reports to senior leadership and the Board of Directors.
- **Executive Dashboards:** Developed executive dashboards to present key metrics and trends visually.
- **Stakeholder Meetings:** Held regular meetings with key stakeholders to discuss security program performance and areas for improvement.
- **Annual Security Review:** Conducted an annual security review meeting to present the program's achievements, challenges, and future plans.

Outcomes and Benefits

Improved Security Posture:

- Significant reduction in security incidents and faster response times.
- Enhanced protection of sensitive patient data, leading to fewer data breaches.

Compliance and Trust:

- Achieved full compliance with HIPAA and other relevant regulations.
- Increased trust and confidence among patients, partners, and regulators.

Operational Resilience:

- Improved operational resilience with minimal disruption from security incidents.
- Better preparedness for handling emerging threats and vulnerabilities.

Stakeholder Engagement:

- Stronger engagement and support from senior leadership and key stakeholders.
- Improved security awareness and practices across the organization.

Lessons Learned and Best Practices

1. Executive Support is Crucial:

- Gaining strong support from senior leadership is essential for the success of the security program.

2. Continuous Improvement:

- Security programs must continuously evolve to keep pace with changing threats and organizational needs.

3. Clear Communication:

- Regular and clear communication with stakeholders helps maintain support and alignment with business objectives.

4. Training and Awareness:

- Comprehensive training and awareness programs are critical for fostering a security-conscious culture.

5. Metrics and Monitoring:

- Developing meaningful metrics and continuous monitoring helps track performance and identify areas for improvement.

Conclusion

HealthGuard's successful development and management of its information security program demonstrate the importance of aligning security initiatives with business objectives and risk appetite. By addressing key challenges at each stage of the program lifecycle and leveraging specific tools, techniques, and metrics, HealthGuard significantly improved its security posture, ensured compliance, and enhanced stakeholder confidence. The lessons learned and best practices from this case study can be applied to other organizations seeking to develop and manage effective information security programs.

Real-World Examples and Scenarios in Information Security Program Development and Management

Example 1: Pitfall – Overlooking the Importance of User Training

Scenario: A global retail company experienced a significant data breach when an employee inadvertently clicked on a phishing email, allowing attackers to access sensitive customer data.

Key Lessons Learned:

1. **User Training is Critical:** Employees are often the weakest link in security. Comprehensive training can significantly reduce the risk of phishing attacks and other social engineering tactics.
2. **Continuous Education:** Security training should be ongoing, with regular updates to reflect new threats and techniques.

Guidance:

- **Implement Regular Training Programs:** Develop and conduct regular security awareness training sessions for all employees.
- **Simulate Phishing Attacks:** Conduct simulated phishing campaigns to test and improve employees' ability to recognize and avoid phishing attempts.
- **Update Training Materials:** Regularly update training materials to include the latest threat intelligence and emerging attack vectors.

Example 2: Best Practice - Adopting a Zero Trust Security Model

Scenario: A financial services firm adopted a Zero Trust security model, which assumes that threats could come from inside or outside the network. They implemented strict access controls, continuous monitoring, and verification for all users and devices.

Key Lessons Learned:

1. **Enhanced Security Posture:** Zero Trust significantly reduces the attack surface and improves the organization's ability to detect and respond to threats.

2. **Access Control is Crucial:** Implementing stringent access controls and verifying every access request strengthens overall security.

Guidance:

- **Implement Multi-Factor Authentication (MFA):** Require MFA for all users to ensure that even if credentials are compromised, unauthorized access is prevented.
- **Continuous Monitoring:** Use advanced monitoring tools to continuously assess and verify all network activities and access requests.
- **Micro-Segmentation:** Segment the network to limit lateral movement by attackers and protect critical assets.

Example 3: Emerging Trend – Integrating AI and Machine Learning

Scenario: A healthcare organization integrated AI and machine learning into its cybersecurity strategy to enhance threat detection and response capabilities. They deployed AI-driven tools to analyze network traffic and user behavior, identifying anomalies that indicate potential threats.

Key Lessons Learned:

1. **Proactive Threat Detection:** AI and machine learning can identify threats faster and more accurately than traditional methods.
2. **Efficiency and Scalability:** AI-driven solutions can scale with the organization and adapt to evolving threats without constant manual intervention.

Guidance:

- **Adopt AI-Based Security Tools:** Invest in AI and machine learning tools for threat detection, user behavior analytics, and automated response.
- **Train AI Models:** Continuously train AI models with updated threat intelligence and data to improve their accuracy and effectiveness.
- **Integrate with Existing Systems:** Ensure AI tools integrate seamlessly with existing security infrastructure for a cohesive defense strategy.

Example 4: Pitfall - Inadequate Incident Response Planning

Scenario: A large manufacturing company suffered a ransomware attack that disrupted production for several days. The lack of a well-defined incident response plan led to a slow and ineffective response, exacerbating the impact.

Key Lessons Learned:

1. **Preparedness is Key:** A well-defined and tested incident response plan is crucial for minimizing the impact of security incidents.
2. **Speed and Coordination:** Quick, coordinated responses can significantly reduce downtime and financial losses.

Guidance:

- **Develop an Incident Response Plan:** Create a detailed incident response plan that outlines roles, responsibilities, and procedures for handling different types of incidents.
- **Regular Drills:** Conduct regular incident response drills and tabletop exercises to test and refine the plan.
- **Post-Incident Reviews:** After each incident, conduct a review to identify lessons learned and update the response plan accordingly.

Example 5: Best Practice – Aligning Security with Business Objectives

Scenario: An e-commerce company aligned its information security program with its business objectives by involving business leaders in security decision-making. This ensured that security initiatives supported business goals and did not hinder operational efficiency.

Key Lessons Learned:

1. **Business Alignment:** Security initiatives should align with and support the organization's strategic objectives.
2. **Cross-Functional Collaboration:** Involving business leaders in security decisions fosters a collaborative approach and ensures security measures are practical and effective.

Guidance:

- **Engage Business Leaders:** Regularly involve business leaders in security discussions and decision-making processes.
- **Business Impact Analysis:** Conduct business impact analyses to understand how security measures affect business operations and prioritize initiatives accordingly.
- **Communicate Effectively:** Clearly communicate the business benefits of security initiatives to gain buy-in and support from all levels of the organization.

Example 6: Emerging Trend - Emphasizing Cyber Resilience

Scenario: A multinational corporation adopted a cyber resilience strategy, focusing not only on preventing and detecting threats but also on maintaining business operations during and after a cyber incident. They invested in robust backup solutions, disaster recovery plans, and business continuity planning.

Key Lessons Learned:

1. **Beyond Prevention:** Cyber resilience encompasses prevention, detection, response, and recovery, ensuring that the organization can continue operating despite cyber threats.
2. **Holistic Approach:** A comprehensive approach to resilience includes technical measures, process improvements, and cultural changes.

Guidance:

- **Invest in Resilience:** Develop and implement robust backup and disaster recovery solutions to ensure data integrity and availability.
- **Business Continuity Planning:** Create and regularly update business continuity plans to prepare for potential disruptions.
- **Culture of Resilience:** Foster a culture that emphasizes the importance of resilience, involving all employees in resilience planning and preparation.

Conclusion

Real-world examples and scenarios highlight the importance of adaptive, risk-based, and business-aligned approaches to information security program management. Common pitfalls, such as neglecting user training and inadequate incident response planning, demonstrate the need for continuous improvement and proactive measures. Best practices, like adopting a Zero Trust model and aligning security with business objectives, ensure a comprehensive and effective security posture. Emerging trends, including AI integration and cyber resilience, show how organizations can leverage new technologies and strategies to enhance their security programs. By applying these insights, organizations of varying maturity levels can build robust and dynamic information security programs that effectively manage risks and support business goals.

Measuring and Reporting on the Effectiveness of an Information Security Program

Importance:

1. **Demonstrating Value:**
    - Showcases the impact and benefits of the security program to senior management and stakeholders.
    - Helps justify investments in security initiatives by illustrating their contribution to the organization's goals.
2. **Justifying Investments:**
    - Provides evidence of the need for ongoing or increased funding to maintain and enhance security measures.
    - Highlights cost savings from prevented incidents and improved efficiencies.
3. **Driving Continuous Improvement:**
    - Identifies areas for improvement and tracks progress over time.
    - Ensures that security efforts are aligned with evolving threats and business needs.

Challenges in Quantifying the Impact of Security Initiatives

1. **Intangible Benefits:**

    - Many security benefits, such as enhanced reputation or increased customer trust, are difficult to quantify.
2. **Evolving Threat Landscape:**
    - The dynamic nature of threats makes it challenging to measure the effectiveness of specific controls consistently.
3. **Alignment with Business Objectives:**
    - Security metrics need to be relevant to business goals, but translating technical security measures into business terms can be difficult.
4. **Data Collection and Accuracy:**
    - Collecting accurate and comprehensive data on security incidents and control effectiveness can be resource-intensive.

Establishing a Metrics Framework

Balanced Set of Indicators: A robust metrics framework should include a mix of leading and lagging indicators that provide a comprehensive view of the security program's performance.

1. **Leading Indicators:**
    - Predictive metrics that indicate the potential for future security incidents.
    - Help proactively address risks before they materialize.
    - Examples: Number of vulnerabilities detected, employee training completion rates, frequency of security audits.
2. **Lagging Indicators:**
    - Retrospective metrics that measure past performance and outcomes.
    - Help assess the impact of security incidents and the effectiveness of controls.
    - Examples: Number of security incidents, incident response times, compliance audit results.

Categories of Metrics:

1. **Risk Reduction:**
    - **Definition:** Measures the effectiveness of efforts to identify and mitigate risks.
    - **Examples:** Reduction in the number of high-severity vulnerabilities, decrease in incident frequency, risk assessment scores.
2. **Compliance:**
    - **Definition:** Tracks adherence to regulatory and policy requirements.
    - **Examples:** Compliance audit scores, number of compliance violations, percentage of systems compliant with security standards.
3. **Operational Efficiency:**
    - **Definition:** Assesses the efficiency and performance of security operations.
    - **Examples:** Incident response time, mean time to recovery (MTTR) for security incidents, cost savings from automated security processes.
4. **User Satisfaction:**
    - **Definition:** Gauges the impact of security measures on end-users and their satisfaction with security processes.
    - **Examples:** User satisfaction survey results, number of reported security issues by employees, feedback on training programs.

Steps to Establish a Metrics Framework

1. **Identify Business Objectives:**
    - Align security metrics with the organization's strategic goals and objectives.
    - Example: If the goal is to enhance customer trust, focus on metrics related to data protection and incident response.
2. **Select Relevant Metrics:**
    - Choose metrics that provide meaningful insights into the security program's effectiveness.
    - Ensure a balance between leading and lagging indicators.

    - Example: Track both the number of training sessions conducted (leading) and the number of incidents involving human error (lagging).
3. **Define Metrics Clearly:**
    - Establish clear definitions and measurement criteria for each metric.
    - Ensure metrics are specific, measurable, achievable, relevant, and time-bound (SMART).
    - Example: Define "incident response time" as the time from incident detection to resolution.
4. **Implement Data Collection Processes:**
    - Set up processes and tools for accurate data collection and reporting.
    - Automate data collection where possible to ensure consistency and reduce manual effort.
    - Example: Use SIEM systems to automatically collect and report on security event data.
5. **Regular Review and Update:**
    - Continuously review and update metrics to ensure they remain relevant and aligned with changing business objectives and threat landscapes.
    - Example: Adjust metrics annually to reflect new regulatory requirements or emerging threats.
6. **Communicate Metrics Effectively:**
    - Use dashboards and reports to present metrics in a clear and concise manner.
    - Tailor communication to different audiences, such as technical teams, senior management, and board members.
    - Example: Use visual aids like charts and graphs to illustrate trends and key findings.

Example Metrics Framework

Risk Reduction:

- **Number of High-Severity Vulnerabilities:** Track monthly to ensure vulnerabilities are being addressed.
- **Incident Frequency:** Measure the number of security incidents per quarter.

Compliance:

- **Compliance Audit Scores:** Track results of internal and external audits annually.
- **Compliance Violations:** Count the number of violations detected during audits.

Operational Efficiency:

- **Incident Response Time:** Measure the average time to respond to and resolve security incidents.
- **MTTR (Mean Time to Recovery):** Track the average time taken to recover from security incidents.

User Satisfaction:

- **Training Completion Rates:** Measure the percentage of employees completing security training programs.
- **User-Reported Issues:** Track the number of security-related issues reported by employees.

Conclusion

Measuring and reporting on the effectiveness of an information security program is crucial for demonstrating its value, justifying investments, and driving continuous improvement. By addressing challenges in quantifying impact and aligning metrics with business objectives, organizations can establish a robust metrics framework. This framework should include a balanced set of leading and lagging indicators across categories like risk reduction, compliance, operational efficiency, and user satisfaction. Effective communication of these metrics helps maintain stakeholder engagement and ensures that security efforts are aligned with the organization's strategic goals.

Defining and Selecting Key Performance Indicators (KPIs) and Metrics Using the SMART Criteria

Process for Defining and Selecting SMART KPIs and Metrics

1. Identify Key Objectives:

- **Purpose:** Understand the main goals of the information security program.
- **Example:** If the goal is to reduce security incidents, a key objective might be to improve incident detection and response times.

2. Define Specific KPIs and Metrics:

- **Specific:** Ensure each KPI or metric is clear and specific.

- **Example:** Instead of a vague goal like "improve security," specify "reduce the number of successful phishing attacks."

3. Ensure KPIs and Metrics are Measurable:

- **Measurable:** Quantify the KPI to track progress effectively.
- **Example:** "Reduce the number of successful phishing attacks by 25% within six months."

4. Ensure Achievability:

- **Achievable:** Set realistic KPIs based on available resources and capabilities.
- **Example:** If the current phishing attack rate is high, a 25% reduction might be achievable with enhanced training and email filtering.

5. Ensure Relevance:

- **Relevant:** Align KPIs with the broader objectives of the security program and organization.
- **Example:** Reducing phishing attacks directly supports the goal of minimizing security incidents.

6. Set Time-Bound Targets:

- **Time-Bound:** Specify a timeframe for achieving the KPI.
- **Example:** "Reduce the number of successful phishing attacks by 25% within six months."

Commonly Used KPIs and Metrics for Different Aspects of an Information Security Program

1. Vulnerability Management

KPI: Number of Critical Vulnerabilities Identified and Remediated

- **Metric:** Percentage of critical vulnerabilities remediated within a specified timeframe.
- **Example:** "Remediate 90% of critical vulnerabilities within 30 days of discovery."

KPI: Average Time to Remediate Vulnerabilities (Mean Time to Remediate, MTTR)

- **Metric:** Average time taken to fix identified vulnerabilities.
- **Example:** "Reduce MTTR for critical vulnerabilities to less than 15 days."

2. Incident Response

KPI: Incident Detection Time (Mean Time to Detect, MTTD)

- **Metric:** Average time taken to detect security incidents.
- **Example:** "Reduce MTTD for security incidents to less than 1 hour."

KPI: Incident Response Time (Mean Time to Respond, MTTR)

- **Metric:** Average time taken to respond to and mitigate security incidents.
- **Example:** "Reduce MTTR for security incidents to less than 4 hours."

3. Access Control

KPI: Percentage of Users with Privileged Access

- **Metric:** Percentage of users with privileged access who have undergone a recent access review.
- **Example:** "Ensure 100% of users with privileged access undergo access review quarterly."

KPI: Number of Unauthorized Access Attempts Detected

- **Metric:** Total number of unauthorized access attempts detected by security systems.
- **Example:** "Reduce the number of unauthorized access attempts by 20% over the next year."

4. Security Awareness Training

KPI: Training Completion Rate

- **Metric:** Percentage of employees who have completed mandatory security awareness training.
- **Example:** "Achieve a 95% training completion rate for mandatory security awareness training within six months."

KPI: Phishing Simulation Success Rate

- **Metric:** Percentage of employees who successfully identify and report phishing simulations.
- **Example:** "Increase the phishing simulation success rate to 90% within a year."

Establishing Baseline Measurements and Setting Realistic Targets

1. Establish Baseline Measurements:

Collect Historical Data:

- Review historical data to understand current performance levels.
- Example: Analyze the past six months of data to determine the current average time to remediate vulnerabilities.

Conduct Initial Assessments:

- Perform initial assessments or audits to gather baseline data if historical data is unavailable.
- Example: Conduct a vulnerability scan and measure the time taken to remediate identified vulnerabilities.

2. Set Realistic Targets:

Use Industry Benchmarks:

- Compare performance against industry standards and best practices.
- Example: If industry best practices suggest a 15-day MTTR for critical vulnerabilities, use this as a benchmark.

Peer Comparisons:

- Compare performance with similar organizations or industry peers.
- Example: If peer organizations achieve an average phishing simulation success rate of 85%, aim for a comparable or slightly higher target.

Internal Goals and Capabilities:

- Align targets with the organization's internal goals, resources, and capabilities.
- Example: If the organization has recently invested in a new incident response tool, set a target to improve incident response times accordingly.

3. Example of Setting Realistic Targets:

Scenario: Security Awareness Training Completion Rate

Baseline Measurement:

- Current completion rate for mandatory security awareness training is 70%.

Industry Benchmark:

- Industry best practice suggests a training completion rate of 90% or higher.

Internal Goal:

- The organization aims to improve overall security posture through better-trained employees.

Target Setting:

- Set a realistic target of achieving a 95% training completion rate within six months, considering available resources and planned training initiatives.

Example of KPI Implementation Plan

KPI	Baseline	Target	Timeframe	Action Plan
Critical Vulnerabilities Remediated	60% within 30 days	90% within 30 days	6 months	Enhance vulnerability management processes and tools, provide training to IT staff.
Incident Detection Time (MTTD)	3 hours	1 hour	6 months	Implement advanced monitoring tools, conduct regular threat hunting exercises.
Training Completion Rate	70%	95%	6 months	Launch new training modules, track completion, provide incentives for timely completion.
Phishing Simulation Success Rate	65%	90%	1 year	Conduct regular phishing simulations, follow up with targeted training for those who fail.

Conclusion

Defining and selecting KPIs and metrics using the SMART criteria ensures that they are specific, measurable, achievable, relevant, and time-bound. Commonly used KPIs and metrics for different aspects of an information security program include those related to vulnerability management, incident response, access control, and security awareness training. Establishing baseline measurements and setting realistic targets based on industry benchmarks, peer comparisons, and internal goals helps ensure that KPIs are meaningful and achievable. By following these practices, organizations can effectively measure and improve their information security performance, aligning their efforts with broader business objectives and maintaining a robust security posture.

Tools and Techniques for Collecting and Analyzing Security Program Data

Collecting and analyzing security program data is crucial for understanding the effectiveness of security measures, identifying areas for improvement, and communicating performance to stakeholders. Several tools and techniques are available to assist with these tasks, including Security Information and Event Management (SIEM) systems, Governance, Risk, and Compliance (GRC) platforms, and data analytics tools. Integrating data from multiple sources and formats to create a comprehensive view of program performance can be complex but is essential for effective security management.

Key Tools and Techniques

1. Security Information and Event Management (SIEM) Systems

Function:

- Collects, analyzes, and correlates security event data from various sources in real-time.
- Provides real-time monitoring, threat detection, and incident response capabilities.

Examples:

- **Splunk:** Offers advanced data analysis and visualization capabilities, making it easier to identify and investigate security incidents.
- **IBM QRadar:** Integrates with various data sources to provide comprehensive threat intelligence and incident response.

Techniques:

- **Log Aggregation:** Collect logs from firewalls, intrusion detection systems (IDS), and servers.
- **Correlation Rules:** Set rules to correlate events and detect patterns indicative of security incidents.
- **Alerts and Dashboards:** Configure real-time alerts and dashboards to monitor critical security metrics.

2. Governance, Risk, and Compliance (GRC) Platforms

Function:

- Manages and automates compliance, risk management, and governance processes.
- Provides a centralized platform for tracking and reporting on compliance and risk activities.

Examples:

- **RSA Archer:** Helps organizations manage risks, compliance, and policy management in one platform.
- **MetricStream:** Offers modules for risk management, compliance, audit, and policy management.

Techniques:

- **Risk Assessments:** Conduct and document risk assessments within the platform.
- **Compliance Tracking:** Monitor compliance with regulations and standards, automate reporting.
- **Policy Management:** Centralize policy creation, approval, and dissemination processes.

3. Data Analytics Tools

Function:

- Analyzes large volumes of security data to identify trends, anomalies, and insights.
- Supports advanced analytics such as machine learning and predictive analytics.

Examples:

- **Tableau:** Provides powerful data visualization and dashboarding capabilities.
- **Power BI:** Integrates with various data sources to create interactive dashboards and reports.

Techniques:

- **Data Integration:** Combine data from various sources such as SIEM systems, GRC platforms, and surveys.
- **Data Cleaning:** Ensure data quality by removing duplicates, correcting errors, and standardizing formats.
- **Advanced Analytics:** Use machine learning algorithms to identify patterns and predict future security incidents.

Integrating Data from Multiple Sources

Challenges:

- **Data Variety:** Different sources produce data in various formats (logs, alerts, survey results, assessment scores).
- **Volume:** Large volumes of data can be challenging to process and analyze.
- **Velocity:** Real-time data requires timely processing to be useful for decision-making.

Techniques for Integration:

1. **Data Normalization:**
    - Convert data from different sources into a consistent format.
    - Example: Standardize timestamp formats and severity levels across logs from different systems.
2. **Data Aggregation:**
    - Combine data from multiple sources to provide a unified view.
    - Example: Aggregate log data from firewalls, IDS, and application servers into a single repository.
3. **APIs and Connectors:**
    - Use APIs and data connectors to integrate data from various systems seamlessly.
    - Example: Use Splunk's API to pull data from various security tools and consolidate it into a single dashboard.
4. **Data Warehousing:**
    - Store integrated data in a data warehouse to facilitate complex queries and historical analysis.
    - Example: Use a cloud-based data warehouse like Amazon Redshift to store and analyze security data.

Data Visualization and Dashboarding Techniques

Importance:

- Visualizing data helps stakeholders understand complex metrics and trends.
- Dashboards provide a real-time view of key performance indicators (KPIs) and security posture.

Techniques for Effective Visualization:

1. **Interactive Dashboards:**
    - Allow users to interact with the data, drill down into details, and filter views based on specific criteria.
    - Example: Create an interactive dashboard in Power BI that allows users to filter incidents by severity, date range, and affected systems.
2. **Heatmaps:**
    - Visualize the intensity of incidents or risks across different categories or geographies.
    - Example: Use a heatmap to show the concentration of security incidents across various office locations.
3. **Trend Analysis:**
    - Use line charts to show trends over time, helping to identify patterns and anomalies.
    - Example: Display the trend of phishing attacks over the past year to identify peak periods and assess the effectiveness of awareness campaigns.
4. **Pie Charts and Bar Graphs:**
    - Show the distribution of incidents by type, source, or impact.
    - Example: Use a pie chart to illustrate the proportion of incidents caused by external attacks versus insider threats.
5. **Scorecards:**
    - Summarize key metrics and KPIs in a concise, easy-to-read format.

- Example: Use a scorecard to display monthly compliance audit scores, incident response times, and user training completion rates.

Example: Using Data Visualization to Communicate Metrics

Scenario: A healthcare organization needs to present its information security program performance to the Board of Directors.

Dashboard Components:

1. **Incident Overview:**
    - **Visualization:** Bar chart showing the number of incidents by severity (high, medium, low) over the past quarter.
    - **Insight:** Helps board members understand the frequency and severity of incidents.
2. **Compliance Status:**
    - **Visualization:** Scorecard displaying current compliance levels with HIPAA, GDPR, and internal policies.
    - **Insight:** Provides a snapshot of the organization's compliance posture.
3. **Risk Assessment Results:**
    - **Visualization:** Heatmap showing the distribution of risks across different departments and their risk levels (high, medium, low).
    - **Insight:** Highlights areas with the highest risk concentrations, informing prioritization of mitigation efforts.
4. **User Training Effectiveness:**
    - **Visualization:** Line chart showing the trend of phishing simulation success rates (lower is better) before and after training sessions.
    - **Insight:** Demonstrates the effectiveness of security awareness training programs.
5. **Response Times:**
    - **Visualization:** Gauge showing the average incident response time against the target response time.
    - **Insight:** Indicates the efficiency of the incident response team and areas for improvement.

Conclusion

Collecting and analyzing security program data using SIEM systems, GRC platforms, and data analytics tools is essential for maintaining a robust security posture. Integrating data from multiple sources and formats enables organizations to create a comprehensive view of program performance. Using data visualization and dashboarding techniques effectively communicates complex metrics to different stakeholders, ensuring clarity and informed decision-making. By following these best practices, organizations can demonstrate the value of their security programs, justify investments, and drive continuous improvement.

Key Components and Best Practices for Creating Effective Reports on Information Security Program Performance

Creating effective reports on information security program performance requires a careful balance of detailed technical data and strategic insights tailored to the audience's needs. Here are the key components and best practices for developing these reports:

Key Components

1. Executive Summary:

- **Purpose:** Provide a high-level overview of the report's content, including key findings, trends, and recommendations.
- **Content:** Summarize major incidents, risk assessments, and significant changes or improvements in the security posture.

2. Strategic Risks and Opportunities:

- **Purpose:** Highlight strategic risks that could impact the organization's objectives and identify opportunities for improving security.

- **Content:** Discuss emerging threats, compliance issues, and areas where investment can enhance security.

3. **Performance Metrics and KPIs:**
   - **Purpose:** Present quantitative data that measures the effectiveness of the security program.
   - **Content:** Include metrics such as incident detection and response times, vulnerability remediation rates, and user training completion rates.
4. **Incident Reports:**
   - **Purpose:** Provide details on significant security incidents, their impact, and the response measures taken.
   - **Content:** Include timelines, root cause analyses, and corrective actions for major incidents.
5. **Risk Assessments:**
   - **Purpose:** Evaluate the current risk landscape and the organization's exposure to various threats.
   - **Content:** Include risk heat maps, likelihood and impact assessments, and mitigation strategies.
6. **Compliance and Audit Findings:**
   - **Purpose:** Report on compliance with relevant regulations and standards, and summarize audit findings.
   - **Content:** Highlight areas of non-compliance, remedial actions, and audit results.
7. **Strategic Recommendations:**
   - **Purpose:** Provide actionable recommendations to improve the security posture.
   - **Content:** Suggest specific initiatives, investments, or policy changes based on the analysis.

Best Practices for Tailoring Reports

1. Tailoring Content to the Audience:

Senior Management and Board of Directors:

- **Focus:** Strategic risks, business impact, and high-level performance metrics.
- **Format:** Concise, with visual aids such as charts and graphs to illustrate key points.
- **Frequency:** Typically quarterly, but may vary based on organizational needs.
- **Example:** Highlight a significant decrease in incident response time and its impact on reducing potential financial losses.

Operational Teams:

- **Focus:** Detailed technical metrics, incident reports, and operational challenges.
- **Format:** Detailed, with comprehensive data tables and technical explanations.
- **Frequency:** Monthly or more frequently, depending on the team's needs.
- **Example:** Provide a detailed breakdown of vulnerability remediation efforts and upcoming security patches.

2. Using Storytelling and Data-Driven Insights:

Storytelling:

- **Engage the Audience:** Start with a compelling narrative about a recent incident or a successful security initiative.
- **Example:** Describe a phishing attack that was quickly detected and mitigated, preventing potential data loss.

Data-Driven Insights:

- **Support with Data:** Use data to back up the narrative and highlight trends or patterns.
- **Example:** Show a chart illustrating the decrease in phishing incidents following the implementation of a new email filtering system.

3. Influencing Decision-Making:

Contextualize Data:

- **Purpose:** Help the audience understand the implications of the data.
- **Example:** Explain how an increase in user training completion rates correlates with a reduction in security incidents.

Highlight ROI:

- **Purpose:** Demonstrate the value of security investments.
- **Example:** Present a cost-benefit analysis showing how a recent investment in advanced threat detection tools has reduced incident response times and associated costs.

Example Reports

Report for Senior Management and Board of Directors:

Executive Summary:

- Over the past quarter, we have seen a 20% reduction in incident response times and a 15% increase in the completion rate of security awareness training.

Strategic Risks and Opportunities:

- Emerging threats from ransomware require investment in advanced threat detection.
- Opportunity to enhance our cloud security posture as we migrate more services to the cloud.

Performance Metrics:

- Mean Time to Detect (MTTD): Reduced from 2 hours to 1.5 hours.
- User Training Completion Rate: Increased from 80% to 95%.

Incident Reports:

- Major Incident: Ransomware attack on March 15, 2023. Quick detection and response prevented data loss. Root cause analysis revealed a need for stronger email filtering.

Risk Assessments:

- High-risk areas: Cloud services and remote work infrastructure.
- Mitigation strategies: Implementing multi-factor authentication and conducting regular penetration testing.

Compliance and Audit Findings:

- PCI DSS compliance achieved with minor findings, all of which are being addressed.

Strategic Recommendations:

- Invest $200,000 in advanced threat detection tools to further reduce response times.
- Launch a new security awareness campaign targeting remote workers.

Report for Operational Teams:

Performance Metrics:

- Vulnerability Remediation Rate: 85% of critical vulnerabilities remediated within 30 days.
- Phishing Simulation Success Rate: 78% of employees correctly identified phishing attempts.

Incident Reports:

- Detailed analysis of the ransomware attack on March 15, 2023, including timeline, root cause, and remediation steps.
- Summary of minor incidents and lessons learned.

Risk Assessments:

- Technical assessment of vulnerabilities in the cloud infrastructure.
- Detailed risk heat maps and recommended actions.

Compliance and Audit Findings:

- Detailed audit report for PCI DSS compliance, including all findings and corrective actions.

Action Items:

- Immediate action required on patching identified vulnerabilities.
- Schedule training sessions for teams with low phishing simulation success rates.

Conclusion

Creating effective reports on information security program performance involves tailoring the content, format, and frequency to the specific needs of different audiences. For senior management and the board, focus on strategic risks, business impact, and high-level metrics, using storytelling and data-driven insights to influence decision-making. For operational teams, provide detailed technical metrics and incident analyses to guide daily operations and continuous improvement. By following these best practices, organizations can ensure that their information security reporting is impactful, actionable, and aligned with overall business objectives.

Continuous Improvement in Information Security Programs

Concept and Role:

Continuous improvement is a systematic, ongoing effort to enhance the performance and value of an information security program. It involves regularly evaluating and refining security processes, controls, and outcomes to adapt to evolving threats, regulatory requirements, and organizational needs. The goal is to achieve incremental improvements that collectively result in significant enhancements to the overall security posture.

Key Steps in the Continuous Improvement Process:

1. **Setting Goals:**
    - Define clear, measurable objectives for improving the information security program.
    - Align goals with the organization's strategic objectives and risk appetite.
    - Example: Reduce the average incident response time by 20% within the next year.
2. **Measuring Progress:**
    - Establish metrics and Key Performance Indicators (KPIs) to track performance against goals.
    - Use tools like SIEM systems, GRC platforms, and data analytics tools to collect and analyze data.
    - Example: Track the number of incidents detected and response times monthly.
3. **Identifying Gaps and Opportunities:**
    - Conduct regular assessments, audits, and reviews to identify weaknesses and areas for improvement.
    - Gather feedback from stakeholders and incorporate threat intelligence.
    - Example: Perform a gap analysis to compare current practices against industry standards and best practices.
4. **Implementing Changes:**
    - Develop and execute action plans to address identified gaps and opportunities.
    - Ensure changes are well-documented, communicated, and supported by appropriate training.
    - Example: Implement new endpoint protection solutions to mitigate identified malware risks.
5. **Monitoring Results:**
    - Continuously monitor the impact of implemented changes to ensure they achieve the desired outcomes.
    - Use dashboards, reports, and regular reviews to track progress and make necessary adjustments.
    - Example: Review incident response metrics quarterly to assess the effectiveness of new incident response procedures.

Frameworks for Driving Continuous Improvement:

1. Plan-Do-Check-Act (PDCA) Cycle:

- **Plan:**
    - Identify improvement opportunities and develop plans to achieve specific objectives.
    - Example: Plan a security awareness campaign to reduce phishing incidents.
- **Do:**
    - Implement the planned changes on a small scale to test their effectiveness.
    - Example: Launch a pilot security awareness training session for a specific department.
- **Check:**
    - Evaluate the results of the implementation to determine if the changes achieved the desired outcomes.
    - Example: Measure the reduction in phishing incident rates in the pilot department.
- **Act:**
    - Standardize and implement the successful changes across the organization, or adjust the plan based on feedback.

- Example: Roll out the security awareness training organization-wide if the pilot is successful.

2. Six Sigma:

- **Define:**
  - Clearly define the problem or improvement opportunity, along with the project scope and objectives.
  - Example: Define the issue of high false positive rates in intrusion detection systems (IDS).
- **Measure:**
  - Collect data to establish baseline performance and identify key metrics.
  - Example: Measure the current false positive rate in IDS alerts.
- **Analyze:**
  - Analyze the data to identify root causes and areas for improvement.
  - Example: Use root cause analysis to determine why false positives are occurring.
- **Improve:**
  - Develop and implement solutions to address the identified root causes.
  - Example: Adjust IDS rules and thresholds to reduce false positives.
- **Control:**
  - Monitor the improved process to ensure sustained performance and make further adjustments as needed.
  - Example: Continuously monitor IDS performance and adjust rules as necessary.

3. Lean:

- **Identify Value:**
  - Determine the value from the perspective of the end-user and focus on activities that contribute to this value.
  - Example: Identify secure and user-friendly access to applications as a value.
- **Map the Value Stream:**
  - Map all steps in the process and identify activities that do not add value (waste).
  - Example: Map the user access request and approval process.
- **Create Flow:**
  - Streamline processes to ensure smooth flow of activities and eliminate bottlenecks.
  - Example: Automate parts of the access request process to reduce delays.
- **Establish Pull:**
  - Ensure that improvements are implemented based on actual demand rather than forecasts.
  - Example: Implement just-in-time access provisioning based on user needs.
- **Seek Perfection:**
  - Continuously pursue perfection through iterative improvements and stakeholder feedback.
  - Example: Regularly review and refine the access management process to ensure efficiency and security.

Examples of Continuous Improvement in Practice:

1. **Phishing Simulation and Training:**
   - **Goal:** Reduce the success rate of phishing attacks by improving employee awareness.
   - **PDCA Cycle:**
     - **Plan:** Design a phishing simulation campaign.
     - **Do:** Conduct the simulation and provide targeted training to those who fall for the simulated attack.
     - **Check:** Measure the success rate of subsequent phishing simulations.
     - **Act:** Adjust training content and frequency based on results.
2. **Incident Response Process Optimization:**

- Goal: Improve the speed and effectiveness of the incident response process.
- **Six Sigma:**
  - **Define:** Identify slow incident response times as the problem.
  - **Measure:** Collect data on current response times and incident resolution rates.
  - **Analyze:** Identify bottlenecks and inefficiencies in the incident response workflow.
  - **Improve:** Implement workflow changes and automate certain response actions.
  - **Control:** Monitor the response times to ensure sustained improvement.

3. **Access Management Efficiency:**
   - **Goal:** Enhance the efficiency and security of user access management.
   - **Lean:**
     - **Identify Value:** Recognize that fast and secure access to applications is crucial.
     - **Map the Value Stream:** Analyze the access request and approval process.
     - **Create Flow:** Streamline the approval process and reduce manual steps.
     - **Establish Pull:** Implement access provisioning based on real-time requests.
     - **Seek Perfection:** Continuously refine the process through regular reviews and feedback.

Conclusion

Continuous improvement is vital for optimizing the performance and value of an information security program over time. By following structured methodologies such as PDCA, Six Sigma, and Lean, organizations can systematically identify and address weaknesses, adapt to new threats, and align security initiatives with business objectives. Establishing clear goals, measuring progress, identifying gaps, implementing changes, and monitoring results ensure that security processes and controls remain effective and efficient, ultimately leading to a robust and resilient security posture.

Case Study 1: Financial Services Firm

Overview: A large financial services firm aimed to strengthen its information security program to protect sensitive customer data and comply with stringent regulatory requirements.

Key Challenges:

- Protecting a large volume of sensitive financial data.
- Ensuring compliance with multiple regulatory frameworks (e.g., PCI DSS, GDPR).
- Integrating security measures across a complex IT infrastructure.

Strategy and Planning:

- **Risk Assessment:** Conducted a comprehensive risk assessment to identify key vulnerabilities and threats.
- **Strategic Alignment:** Aligned security objectives with business goals to ensure customer trust and regulatory compliance.
- **Resource Allocation:** Secured executive buy-in and allocated a substantial budget for security enhancements.

Implementation:

- **Tools and Techniques:**
  - **SIEM Implementation:** Deployed a Security Information and Event Management (SIEM) system to monitor and analyze security events in real time.
  - **Data Encryption:** Implemented robust encryption for data at rest and in transit.
  - **Access Controls:** Strengthened access controls using multi-factor authentication (MFA) and role-based access controls (RBAC).

Operation:

- **Monitoring:** Used the SIEM system to continuously monitor network activity and detect anomalies.
- **Incident Response:** Established an incident response team and conducted regular drills to ensure preparedness.
- **Compliance Audits:** Conducted regular internal and external audits to ensure compliance with regulatory requirements.

Optimization:

- **Continuous Improvement:** Regularly updated the SIEM system and access controls based on emerging threats and audit findings.
- **Metrics and Communication:**
  - **Key Metrics:** Incident response time, number of detected threats, compliance audit results.
  - **Reporting:** Monthly reports to executive management, highlighting key metrics and areas for improvement.

Outcomes:

- **Reduced Incidents:** Significant reduction in security incidents and data breaches.
- **Improved Compliance:** Achieved and maintained compliance with PCI DSS and GDPR.
- **Enhanced Trust:** Increased customer trust and confidence in the firm's security measures.

Case Study 2: Healthcare Organization

Overview: A regional healthcare provider sought to develop a robust information security program to safeguard patient data and meet HIPAA requirements.

Key Challenges:

- Protecting sensitive patient information.
- Ensuring compliance with HIPAA.
- Addressing security gaps in legacy systems.

Strategy and Planning:

- **Risk Assessment:** Identified critical assets and vulnerabilities through a comprehensive risk assessment.
- **Strategic Priorities:** Focused on protecting patient data, ensuring regulatory compliance, and modernizing legacy systems.
- **Budget and Resources:** Secured funding for critical security upgrades and staff training.

Implementation:

- **Tools and Techniques:**
  - **Data Loss Prevention (DLP):** Implemented DLP solutions to prevent unauthorized access and transmission of patient data.
  - **Endpoint Protection:** Deployed advanced endpoint protection solutions to safeguard devices against malware and other threats.
  - **User Training:** Launched an extensive security awareness training program for all employees.

Operation:

- **Monitoring:** Continuous monitoring of network activity and endpoint devices for suspicious activity.
- **Incident Response:** Developed a comprehensive incident response plan and conducted regular tabletop exercises.
- **Compliance Checks:** Regular HIPAA compliance checks and audits.

Optimization:

- **Continuous Improvement:** Updated security policies and procedures based on incident reviews and audit findings.
- **Metrics and Communication:**
  - **Key Metrics:** Number of data loss incidents, endpoint protection effectiveness, training completion rates.
  - **Reporting:** Quarterly reports to the board, focusing on compliance status and incident trends.

Outcomes:

- **Enhanced Security:** Improved protection of patient data and reduced incidents of unauthorized access.
- **Regulatory Compliance:** Consistently met HIPAA requirements and passed regular audits.
- **Employee Awareness:** Increased employee awareness and adherence to security policies.

Case Study 3: E-Commerce Company

Overview: An e-commerce company aimed to bolster its information security program to protect customer data and support rapid business growth.

Key Challenges:

- Protecting customer payment information.
- Scaling security measures to support rapid growth.
- Balancing security with user experience.

Strategy and Planning:

- **Risk Assessment:** Conducted a detailed risk assessment to identify critical vulnerabilities and potential threats.
- **Business Alignment:** Aligned security objectives with business goals, focusing on protecting customer data and maintaining a seamless user experience.
- **Resource Planning:** Allocated resources for technology upgrades and staff training.

Implementation:

- **Tools and Techniques:**
    - **Web Application Firewalls (WAF):** Deployed WAF to protect web applications from attacks.
    - **PCI DSS Compliance:** Implemented measures to comply with PCI DSS, including encryption and secure payment processing.
    - **User Education:** Launched a customer education campaign on secure online practices.

Operation:

- **Monitoring:** Used advanced monitoring tools to track web application traffic and detect anomalies.
- **Incident Response:** Established an incident response team with clear protocols for handling data breaches and other incidents.
- **Compliance Audits:** Conducted regular PCI DSS audits and vulnerability assessments.

Optimization:

- **Continuous Improvement:** Regularly updated security measures based on emerging threats and compliance requirements.
- **Metrics and Communication:**
    - **Key Metrics:** Web application attack attempts, PCI DSS compliance status, incident response times.
    - **Reporting:** Monthly reports to senior management, focusing on key metrics and recommendations for improvements.

Outcomes:

- **Improved Security:** Significant reduction in web application attacks and data breaches.
- **Regulatory Compliance:** Maintained PCI DSS compliance, ensuring secure payment processing.
- **Customer Trust:** Enhanced customer trust and loyalty through transparent communication and robust security measures.

Key Takeaways

1. **Risk-Based Approach:** All case studies highlight the importance of conducting comprehensive risk assessments to identify and prioritize security measures.
2. **Strategic Alignment:** Aligning security initiatives with business objectives ensures that security efforts support overall business goals.
3. **Continuous Monitoring and Improvement:** Ongoing monitoring and regular updates based on new threats and audit findings are critical for maintaining a robust security posture.
4. **Stakeholder Communication:** Effective communication with stakeholders, using tailored metrics and reports, helps secure support for security initiatives and drives continuous improvement.
5. **Training and Awareness:** Regular training for employees and educating customers on security best practices are essential for reducing human error and increasing overall security awareness.

By applying these best practices and insights, organizations can develop and manage high-performing information security programs that align with their business objectives and risk appetite, ensuring resilience in an increasingly complex and dynamic threat landscape.

Real-World Examples and Scenarios in Information Security Program Development and Management

Example 1: Data Breach Due to Insufficient Access Controls

Scenario: A mid-sized retail company experienced a significant data breach where attackers gained access to sensitive customer information, including payment details. The breach was traced back to a compromised employee account with excessive permissions.

Root Causes:

- **Insufficient Access Controls:** Employees had more access rights than necessary for their roles.
- **Lack of Monitoring:** Inadequate monitoring of access control changes and user activities.
- **Poor Incident Response:** Slow detection and response to the breach.

Impacts:

- **Customer Trust:** Loss of customer trust and damage to the company's reputation.
- **Financial Loss:** Significant financial losses due to regulatory fines and compensation costs.
- **Operational Disruption:** Disruption to business operations during the investigation and recovery phase.

Lessons Learned:

- **Implement Principle of Least Privilege:** Ensure that employees only have the access necessary for their roles.
- **Regular Access Reviews:** Conduct regular reviews of user access rights and permissions.
- **Enhanced Monitoring:** Implement continuous monitoring and alerting for suspicious activities.
- **Effective Incident Response:** Develop and regularly test an incident response plan to ensure rapid detection and mitigation of breaches.

Guidance for Different Organizational Contexts:

- **Small Organizations:** Use automated tools to manage access controls and conduct periodic access reviews.
- **Large Enterprises:** Implement a centralized identity and access management (IAM) system and conduct continuous access monitoring.

Example 2: Compliance Failures Due to Inadequate Policy Management

Scenario: A healthcare provider was fined for failing to comply with HIPAA regulations. An audit revealed that the organization's security policies were outdated and not properly enforced.

Root Causes:

- **Outdated Policies:** Security policies were not reviewed or updated regularly.
- **Lack of Awareness:** Employees were unaware of existing policies and procedures.
- **Poor Enforcement:** Inconsistent enforcement of policies across different departments.

Impacts:

- **Regulatory Fines:** Substantial fines for non-compliance with HIPAA regulations.
- **Legal Consequences:** Potential legal actions and liability issues.
- **Reputation Damage:** Damage to the organization's reputation and trustworthiness.

Lessons Learned:

- **Regular Policy Reviews:** Establish a regular review and update process for security policies.
- **Employee Training:** Conduct regular training sessions to ensure employees are aware of and understand the policies.
- **Consistent Enforcement:** Implement mechanisms to enforce policies consistently across all departments.

Guidance for Different Organizational Contexts:

- **Small Organizations:** Designate a compliance officer responsible for policy management and employee training.
- **Large Enterprises:** Use GRC platforms to automate policy management and track compliance efforts.

Example 3: Cyberattack Due to Poor Patch Management

Scenario: A financial services company suffered a ransomware attack due to an unpatched vulnerability in their core banking software.

Root Causes:

- **Delayed Patching:** Patches were not applied promptly, leaving systems vulnerable.
- **Lack of Asset Inventory:** Incomplete inventory of systems and software, leading to missed patches.
- **Ineffective Patch Management Process:** No formal process for patch testing and deployment.

Impacts:

- **Service Disruption:** Significant disruption to banking services, affecting customer transactions.
- **Data Loss:** Potential loss and compromise of sensitive financial data.
- **Financial Costs:** High costs associated with incident response, recovery, and ransom payment.

Lessons Learned:

- **Timely Patching:** Implement a robust patch management process to ensure timely application of patches.
- **Comprehensive Asset Inventory:** Maintain an up-to-date inventory of all systems and software.
- **Patch Testing and Deployment:** Establish a formal process for testing and deploying patches to minimize disruptions.

Guidance for Different Organizational Contexts:

- **Small Organizations:** Use automated patch management tools to streamline the process.
- **Large Enterprises:** Implement a dedicated patch management team and use configuration management databases (CMDB) for asset tracking.

Example 4: Insider Threat Due to Lack of Monitoring

Scenario: A manufacturing company discovered that an employee had been stealing sensitive intellectual property and selling it to competitors over several months.

Root Causes:

- **Lack of Monitoring:** Inadequate monitoring of employee activities and data access.
- **Weak Access Controls:** Insufficient restrictions on access to sensitive information.
- **Absence of Insider Threat Program:** No formal program to detect and respond to insider threats.

Impacts:

- **Intellectual Property Loss:** Loss of valuable intellectual property and competitive advantage.
- **Financial Loss:** Significant financial losses due to reduced market share and legal costs.
- **Reputation Damage:** Damage to the company's reputation and customer trust.

Lessons Learned:

- **Enhanced Monitoring:** Implement comprehensive monitoring of employee activities, especially those with access to sensitive data.
- **Strict Access Controls:** Enforce strict access controls to limit access to critical information.
- **Insider Threat Program:** Develop and implement an insider threat program to detect and respond to suspicious activities.

Guidance for Different Organizational Contexts:

- **Small Organizations:** Use data loss prevention (DLP) tools to monitor data access and transfers.
- **Large Enterprises:** Establish a dedicated insider threat team and use advanced analytics to detect anomalies.

Example 5: Failure in Communication During a Security Incident

Scenario: A global technology company faced a major security incident but struggled with communication, leading to delayed responses and confusion among employees and stakeholders.

Root Causes:

- **Poor Communication Plan:** Lack of a well-defined communication plan for security incidents.
- **Inadequate Training:** Employees were not trained on how to report and respond to incidents.
- **Disjointed Response:** Lack of coordination among different teams involved in incident response.

Impacts:

- **Delayed Response:** Slower response to the incident, exacerbating its impact.
- **Increased Damage:** Greater damage due to prolonged exposure and delayed mitigation efforts.
- **Stakeholder Confusion:** Confusion and lack of trust among customers and partners.

Lessons Learned:

- **Clear Communication Plan:** Develop a clear communication plan that outlines roles, responsibilities, and protocols for incident reporting and response.
- **Regular Training:** Conduct regular training and simulations to ensure employees are prepared for incidents.
- **Coordinated Response:** Establish a coordinated incident response team with clear lines of communication and authority.

Guidance for Different Organizational Contexts:

- **Small Organizations:** Develop a simple, clear incident response and communication plan and ensure all employees are aware of it.
- **Large Enterprises:** Use incident management tools to coordinate responses and communicate effectively across teams and locations.

Conclusion

These real-world examples illustrate common challenges, pitfalls, and best practices in information security program development and management. Key takeaways include the importance of implementing strong access controls, maintaining up-to-date policies, ensuring timely patch management, monitoring for insider threats, and having effective communication plans. Leadership, communication, and collaboration skills are essential for driving successful outcomes and building a culture of security throughout the organization. By learning from these examples, organizations of different sizes and maturity levels can better manage their security programs and mitigate risks.

Practice Questions and Quizzes

Section 1: Understanding and Applying Key Concepts

Multiple Choice Questions:

1. Which of the following is NOT a key component of an information security program? A) Risk Assessment b) Strategic Planning c) Marketing Strategy d) Incident Response

Answer: c) Marketing Strategy

Explanation: Information security programs focus on risk assessment, strategic planning, and incident response, not marketing strategies.

2. What is the primary goal of the Zero Trust security model? A) Trust all internal network traffic b) Assume all users and devices are trusted c) Verify every access request regardless of origin d) Simplify access control mechanisms

Answer: c) Verify every access request regardless of origin

Explanation: Zero Trust requires verification of all access requests, assuming that threats can come from inside or outside the network.

3. Which framework is specifically designed to help organizations comply with PCI DSS requirements? A) NIST CSF b) ISO/IEC 27001 c) CIS Controls d) COBIT

Answer: b) ISO/IEC 27001

Explanation: ISO/IEC 27001 provides a comprehensive framework for information security management, including compliance with PCI DSS.

True/False Questions:

4. True or False: A Security Information and Event Management (SIEM) system is used to aggregate and analyze security data from various sources.

Answer: True

Explanation: SIEM systems collect and analyze data from different security tools to detect and respond to threats.

5. True or False: Incident response plans should only be tested after a security incident has occurred.

Answer: False

Explanation: Incident response plans should be regularly tested through drills and tabletop exercises to ensure preparedness.

Matching Questions:

6. Match the following roles with their primary responsibilities:
    - A) CISO
    - B) Security Architect
    - C) Security Analyst
    - D) Incident Responder
    - 1. Designs security infrastructure
    - 1. Manages strategic security initiatives
    - 1. Analyzes security incidents
    - 1. Responds to security incidents

Answers: A-2, B-1, C-3, D-4
Explanation: Each role has specific responsibilities that contribute to the overall security posture of the organization.

Open-Ended Questions:

7. Explain the importance of aligning an information security program with business objectives. Provide an example of how misalignment can impact the organization.

Answer: Aligning an information security program with business objectives ensures that security measures support the organization's strategic goals. Misalignment can lead to inadequate protection of critical assets or inefficient allocation of resources. For example, if a financial institution's security program is not aligned with its goal of protecting customer data, it may face regulatory fines and lose customer trust.
Explanation: Proper alignment ensures resources are effectively used to support both security and business goals.

8. Describe the role of continuous monitoring in an information security program and list three key metrics that should be monitored regularly.

Answer: Continuous monitoring involves the ongoing assessment of security controls and systems to detect and respond to threats in real time. Key metrics include:

- Incident response time: Measures how quickly the organization responds to security incidents.
- Vulnerability remediation rate: Tracks the percentage of vulnerabilities fixed within a specific timeframe.
- User training completion rate: Indicates the percentage of employees who have completed mandatory security training.

Explanation: Continuous monitoring helps maintain a strong security posture by promptly addressing vulnerabilities and threats.

Detailed Explanations and References:

1. **Question 1 Explanation:**
    - Marketing strategies are not part of information security programs, which focus on risk assessment, strategic planning, and incident response.
2. **Question 2 Explanation:**
    - The Zero Trust model emphasizes verifying every access request, assuming threats can originate from anywhere.
3. **Question 3 Explanation:**
    - ISO/IEC 27001 is designed to provide a framework for information security management, including compliance with PCI DSS.
4. **Question 4 Explanation:**

- SIEM systems are critical for collecting and analyzing security data from various sources to detect and respond to threats.

5. **Question 5 Explanation:**
   - Incident response plans should be tested regularly to ensure the organization is prepared for potential incidents.
6. **Question 6 Explanation:**
   - Matching the roles with their responsibilities helps clarify the distinct functions each role plays within the information security team.
7. **Question 7 Explanation:**
   - Aligning the security program with business objectives ensures effective resource use and supports strategic goals. Misalignment can result in inadequate protection or wasted resources.
8. **Question 8 Explanation:**
   - Continuous monitoring and key metrics like incident response time, vulnerability remediation rate, and user training completion rate are essential for maintaining a strong security posture.

References for Further Study:

- **NIST Cybersecurity Framework (CSF):** https://www.nist.gov/cyberframework
- **ISO/IEC 27001 Information Security Management:** https://www.iso.org/isoiec-27001-information-security.html
- **Center for Internet Security (CIS) Controls:** https://www.cisecurity.org/controls/
- **PCI DSS Requirements:** https://www.pcisecuritystandards.org/

By utilizing these practice questions and quizzes, readers can reinforce their understanding of key concepts, frameworks, and techniques covered in the section, ensuring they can apply this knowledge effectively in real-world scenarios.

Benchmarking and Peer Comparison in Evaluating Information Security Programs

Role of Benchmarking and Peer Comparison

Benchmarking and peer comparison are critical for evaluating the effectiveness and maturity of an information security program. These practices involve comparing an organization's security posture, practices, and performance metrics with those of similar organizations (peers) to identify strengths, weaknesses, and areas for improvement. Benchmarking helps organizations understand how they stack up against industry standards and best practices, providing a clear picture of where they excel and where they need to improve.

Identifying Relevant Benchmarks and Peers

Factors to Consider:

1. **Industry:**
   - Choose peers from the same industry to ensure relevance in regulatory requirements, threat landscape, and security practices.
   - Example: A healthcare provider should benchmark against other healthcare organizations to consider HIPAA compliance and patient data protection.
2. **Size:**
   - Compare with organizations of similar size to ensure comparable resources, budgets, and operational complexities.
   - Example: A mid-sized financial services company should benchmark against other mid-sized financial firms.
3. **Geography:**
   - Consider geographic location to account for regional regulations, cultural factors, and local threat landscapes.
   - Example: A European company should benchmark against other European companies to consider GDPR compliance.
4. **Risk Profile:**

- Select peers with similar risk profiles to ensure relevant comparisons in terms of data sensitivity, threat exposure, and operational risk.
- Example: An organization handling sensitive customer data should compare itself with other data-intensive organizations.

Collecting and Analyzing Benchmarking Data

Steps for Effective Benchmarking:

1. **Identify Key Metrics:**
    - Define the metrics that will be used for comparison, such as incident response time, number of security incidents, compliance audit scores, and training completion rates.
2. **Select Benchmarking Partners:**
    - Identify organizations willing to share their data for benchmarking purposes. This can be done through industry groups, professional networks, or third-party benchmarking services.
3. **Data Collection:**
    - Gather data on security practices and performance from internal records, peer organizations, industry reports, and benchmarking surveys.
    - Example: Use surveys to collect information on security budgets, staffing levels, incident response capabilities, and control effectiveness.
4. **Data Analysis:**
    - Analyze the collected data to identify trends, gaps, and opportunities for improvement. Use statistical methods to ensure accurate comparisons.
    - Example: Use data analytics tools to compare incident response times across peer organizations and identify outliers.

Using Benchmarking Data for Improvement

Identifying Gaps and Opportunities:

1. **Gap Analysis:**
    - Compare the organization's metrics against benchmark data to identify areas where the organization is lagging.
    - Example: If peer organizations have lower incident response times, investigate the reasons and identify ways to improve the organization's response capabilities.
2. **Best Practices Identification:**
    - Identify best practices from peer organizations that have achieved better outcomes in specific areas.
    - Example: If peers have more effective training programs, analyze their training methods and materials to adopt similar practices.
3. **Performance Targets:**
    - Set performance targets based on benchmarking data to drive continuous improvement.
    - Example: If the industry average for patch management is 90% compliance within 30 days, set a target to achieve or exceed this benchmark.

Communicating Program Value and Justifying Investments:

1. **Stakeholder Communication:**
    - Use benchmarking data to communicate the effectiveness and maturity of the security program to stakeholders.
    - Example: Present benchmarking results in executive dashboards, highlighting areas of excellence and those needing investment.
2. **Investment Justification:**
    - Use identified gaps and best practices to justify the need for additional resources or investments.
    - Example: If benchmarking reveals a need for enhanced monitoring tools, use the data to build a business case for investing in advanced SIEM systems.
3. **Strategic Planning:**

- Integrate benchmarking insights into strategic planning and decision-making processes.
- Example: Use benchmarking data to prioritize security initiatives in the organization's annual budget and strategic roadmap.

Examples of Benchmarking in Practice

Example 1: Improving Incident Response Times

Scenario: A mid-sized financial services firm finds that its incident response times are significantly longer than its peers.

Steps Taken:

1. **Gap Analysis:** Conducted a detailed analysis to compare internal response times with industry benchmarks.
2. **Best Practices:** Identified best practices from peers with faster response times, such as automated incident response tools and dedicated incident response teams.
3. **Implementation:** Implemented automated response tools and provided additional training to the incident response team.

Outcome:

- Reduced average incident response time by 30%, aligning more closely with industry benchmarks.
- Improved overall incident handling and reduced potential impact of security incidents.

Example 2: Enhancing Compliance Posture

Scenario: A healthcare provider benchmarks its compliance audit scores against other healthcare organizations and discovers it lags behind in certain areas.

Steps Taken:

1. **Gap Analysis:** Identified specific compliance areas where scores were lower compared to peers.
2. **Best Practices:** Adopted best practices from top-performing peers, such as regular compliance training and automated compliance tracking tools.
3. **Implementation:** Conducted more frequent training sessions and invested in compliance management software.

Outcome:

- Achieved higher compliance audit scores and reduced the risk of regulatory fines.
- Enhanced overall compliance posture and gained greater confidence from regulators and stakeholders.

Conclusion

Benchmarking and peer comparison are powerful tools for evaluating the effectiveness and maturity of an information security program. By identifying relevant benchmarks and peers based on industry, size, geography, and risk profile, organizations can collect and analyze data to gain valuable insights. Using benchmarking data to identify gaps and opportunities for improvement, communicate program value, and justify investments can drive systematic and sustainable improvements in security processes, controls, and outcomes. Effective leadership, communication, and collaboration are essential in leveraging benchmarking to build a culture of continuous improvement and resilience in information security.

Security Metrics Dashboards

Concept: Security metrics dashboards are visual tools that provide a real-time, comprehensive view of an organization's security posture and the performance of its information security program. These dashboards consolidate and display critical security metrics in a clear and easily understandable format, enabling stakeholders to quickly assess the status of security controls, identify trends, and make informed decisions.

Role of Security Metrics Dashboards

- **Real-Time Monitoring:** Dashboards offer real-time insights into security metrics, allowing organizations to promptly detect and respond to threats.
- **Holistic View:** They provide a unified view of various security aspects, such as incident response, vulnerability management, and compliance.

- **Performance Tracking:** Dashboards help track the effectiveness of security measures and initiatives over time.
- **Decision Support:** They support data-driven decision-making by presenting actionable insights and highlighting areas that require attention.

Key Design Principles and Best Practices

1. **Clear and Concise Visualizations:**
    - **Simplicity:** Use simple and intuitive visualizations such as bar charts, line graphs, and pie charts to represent data.
    - **Clarity:** Ensure that each visualization clearly conveys the intended message without clutter or unnecessary details.
    - **Consistency:** Maintain a consistent design language across the dashboard to enhance readability and user experience.
2. **Alignment with Business Objectives:**
    - **Relevant Metrics:** Select metrics that align with the organization's strategic goals and security objectives.
    - **Business Context:** Provide context for each metric to help stakeholders understand its relevance to business objectives.
3. **Actionable Insights and Recommendations:**
    - **Actionable Data:** Present data in a way that enables stakeholders to take specific actions based on the insights.
    - **Recommendations:** Include recommendations and suggested actions based on the analysis of the metrics.
4. **Customizability:**
    - **User-Specific Views:** Allow customization based on the user's role and responsibilities (e.g., executive view vs. operational view).
    - **Drill-Down Capabilities:** Enable users to drill down into specific metrics for more detailed analysis.
5. **Trend Monitoring and Anomaly Detection:**
    - **Trend Analysis:** Display trends over time to help identify patterns and deviations.
    - **Anomaly Detection:** Highlight anomalies or unusual patterns that may indicate potential security issues.

Examples of Using Dashboards

1. **Monitoring Trends:**
    - **Example:** A dashboard tracks the number of detected phishing attempts over the past six months. A line graph shows a steady increase, indicating a growing threat. This trend prompts the organization to enhance email filtering and user training.
2. **Identifying Anomalies:**
    - **Example:** A dashboard monitoring login attempts detects a sudden spike in failed logins from an unfamiliar location. Anomaly detection highlights this event, triggering an immediate investigation by the security team.
3. **Supporting Data-Driven Decision-Making:**
    - **Executive Level:**
        - **Dashboard Content:** High-level metrics such as incident response times, compliance status, and overall risk score.
        - **Use Case:** The dashboard shows that incident response times have improved by 30% after implementing a new SIEM system. Executives use this data to justify further investments in advanced threat detection technologies.
    - **Operational Level:**
        - **Dashboard Content:** Detailed metrics such as the number of open vulnerabilities, patching status, and endpoint protection coverage.
        - **Use Case:** The security operations team uses the dashboard to prioritize patching efforts based on the severity and age of vulnerabilities, ensuring critical issues are addressed promptly.

Best Practices for Creating Effective Dashboards

1. Define Clear Objectives:

- **Purpose:** Identify the primary objectives of the dashboard (e.g., monitoring incident response, tracking compliance, assessing risk).
- **Audience:** Determine the target audience and tailor the dashboard to their needs and decision-making processes.

2. Select Relevant Metrics:

- **Alignment:** Ensure that selected metrics align with the defined objectives and provide meaningful insights.
- **Balance:** Include a mix of leading indicators (predictive) and lagging indicators (historical performance) to provide a comprehensive view.

3. Design Intuitive Layouts:

- **Logical Flow:** Organize the dashboard logically, grouping related metrics and using clear headings and sections.
- **Interactive Elements:** Incorporate interactive elements such as filters, drill-downs, and tooltips to enhance user engagement and exploration.

4. Regular Updates and Reviews:

- **Real-Time Data:** Ensure the dashboard is updated in real-time or at regular intervals to provide current information.
- **Review and Improve:** Regularly review the dashboard's effectiveness and make adjustments based on user feedback and evolving security needs.

Example Dashboard Metrics and Visualizations

1. Incident Response:

- **Metric:** Mean Time to Detect (MTTD)
  - **Visualization:** Line graph showing MTTD over the past 12 months.
- **Metric:** Mean Time to Respond (MTTR)
  - **Visualization:** Bar chart comparing MTTR for different types of incidents.

2. Vulnerability Management:

- **Metric:** Number of Open Vulnerabilities
  - **Visualization:** Pie chart showing the distribution of vulnerabilities by severity.
- **Metric:** Patch Compliance Rate
  - **Visualization:** Bar chart showing the percentage of systems patched on time.

3. Compliance:

- **Metric:** Compliance Status
  - **Visualization:** Gauge chart indicating overall compliance with key regulations (e.g., PCI DSS, HIPAA).
- **Metric:** Audit Findings
  - **Visualization:** Table listing recent audit findings and their remediation status.

4. User Awareness:

- **Metric:** Training Completion Rate
  - **Visualization:** Bar chart showing the percentage of employees who completed mandatory security training.
- **Metric:** Phishing Simulation Success Rate
  - **Visualization:** Line graph showing the success rate of phishing simulations over time.

Conclusion

Security metrics dashboards are powerful tools for providing a real-time, holistic view of an organization's security posture and program performance. By following key design principles and best practices—such as using clear visualizations, aligning metrics with business objectives, and offering actionable insights—organizations can create effective dashboards that support trend monitoring, anomaly detection, and data-driven decision-making. Tailoring dashboards to different audience needs ensures that all stakeholders, from executives to operational teams, can quickly access the information they need to protect the organization effectively.

Aligning Information Security Program Metrics with Business Functions

Importance of Alignment

Aligning information security program metrics and reporting with other business functions such as IT, finance, risk management, and compliance is crucial for several reasons:

1. **Holistic Risk Management:**
    - Ensures that security risks are considered within the broader context of enterprise risk management.
    - Facilitates comprehensive risk assessments that include IT, financial, operational, and compliance risks.
2. **Resource Allocation:**
    - Helps prioritize security investments based on their impact on overall business objectives.
    - Aligns budget allocations with strategic priorities, ensuring that critical security needs are funded appropriately.
3. **Unified Communication:**
    - Establishes a common language for discussing security issues across different departments.
    - Enhances understanding and collaboration among stakeholders with varying expertise.
4. **Performance Management:**
    - Integrates security metrics into the broader performance management framework.
    - Provides a complete view of organizational health, linking security performance to business outcomes.

Establishing a Common Language and Framework

To achieve alignment, it is essential to establish a common language and framework for measuring and communicating security performance:

1. **Standardize Terminology:**
    - Define key terms and metrics consistently across departments.
    - Example: Use standardized definitions for terms like "incident," "vulnerability," and "compliance."
2. **Develop Unified Metrics:**
    - Create metrics that are meaningful to multiple stakeholders.
    - Example: Develop a "cost of data breaches" metric that combines IT security incidents with financial impact assessments.
3. **Cross-Functional Collaboration:**
    - Establish cross-functional teams to develop and review metrics.
    - Example: Include representatives from IT, finance, risk management, and compliance in the security metrics development process.
4. **Use Established Frameworks:**
    - Leverage widely recognized frameworks to ensure consistency and reliability.
    - Example: Use the NIST Cybersecurity Framework or ISO 27001 as a basis for developing security metrics.

Integrating Security Metrics into Broader Business Processes

1. Balanced Scorecards:

Purpose:

- Provides a holistic view of organizational performance by balancing financial and non-financial metrics.

Integration:

- **Security Metrics:** Include security-related KPIs such as the number of security incidents, compliance audit scores, and time to patch critical vulnerabilities.
- **Example:** A balanced scorecard for an organization might include a security metric under the "Internal Processes" perspective, tracking the percentage of systems compliant with security standards.

2. Risk Registers:

Purpose:

- Documents identified risks, their impact, likelihood, and mitigation measures.

Integration:

- **Security Risks:** Include information security risks such as data breaches, ransomware attacks, and insider threats.
- **Example:** A risk register might list "Phishing Attacks" as a risk, with metrics such as the number of phishing attempts detected and the success rate of employee training programs in preventing successful attacks.

3. Annual Reports:

Purpose:

- Communicates organizational performance and strategic priorities to stakeholders.

Integration:

- **Security Reporting:** Include a section on information security performance, highlighting major achievements, incident statistics, and future plans.
- **Example:** An annual report might feature a summary of security initiatives, such as the implementation of a new SIEM system, along with metrics showing reduced incident response times and improved compliance rates.

Examples of Integration

Example 1: Integrating Security Metrics into Balanced Scorecards

Scenario: A financial institution aims to integrate security metrics into its balanced scorecard to align IT security with business objectives.

Steps:

1. **Identify Relevant Metrics:** Determine security KPIs that align with the institution's strategic goals, such as reducing fraud and ensuring regulatory compliance.
2. **Incorporate into Scorecard:** Add metrics like "Number of Data Breaches," "Compliance Audit Scores," and "Incident Response Times" under relevant perspectives (e.g., Internal Processes, Learning and Growth).
3. **Regular Review:** Ensure these metrics are reviewed regularly at senior management meetings, alongside other business performance metrics.

Outcome:

- Improved visibility of security performance.
- Enhanced decision-making through a comprehensive understanding of risks and security posture.

Example 2: Using Risk Registers for Holistic Risk Management

Scenario: A healthcare provider integrates security metrics into its risk register to manage risks more effectively.

Steps:

1. **Identify Security Risks:** Include risks such as "Ransomware Attacks" and "Data Breaches" in the risk register.
2. **Define Metrics:** Develop metrics to track these risks, such as "Frequency of Ransomware Attacks" and "Number of Records Compromised."
3. **Mitigation Plans:** Document mitigation strategies and monitor their effectiveness through regular updates to the risk register.

Outcome:

- Improved risk visibility and management.
- Proactive risk mitigation efforts, leading to enhanced patient data protection.

Example 3: Reporting Security Performance in Annual Reports

Scenario: A global manufacturing company includes information security performance in its annual report to demonstrate its commitment to cybersecurity.

Steps:

1. **Highlight Key Achievements:** Summarize major security initiatives, such as the implementation of advanced threat detection systems.

2. **Present Metrics:** Include metrics like "Number of Security Incidents," "Compliance Rates," and "Average Incident Response Time."
3. **Future Plans:** Outline future security plans and investments to reassure stakeholders of ongoing commitment.

Outcome:

- Increased transparency and trust among stakeholders.
- Justified investments in security initiatives through demonstrated performance improvements.

Conclusion

Aligning information security program metrics and reporting with other business functions is essential for holistic risk management, resource allocation, and unified communication. Establishing a common language and framework for measuring and communicating security performance ensures consistency and clarity across departments. Integrating security metrics into broader business performance management processes, such as balanced scorecards, risk registers, and annual reports, provides a comprehensive view of organizational health and supports informed decision-making. Effective alignment and integration drive continuous improvement, enhance security posture, and demonstrate the value of security investments to stakeholders.

Emerging Trends and Technologies in Information Security Program Measurement and Reporting

1. Big Data Analytics

Overview: Big data analytics involves processing and analyzing large volumes of data from various sources to uncover patterns, trends, and insights. In information security, big data analytics can help organizations manage and interpret the vast amounts of data generated by security tools and systems.

Benefits:

- **Enhanced Visibility:** Aggregate data from multiple sources to get a comprehensive view of the security landscape.
- **Pattern Detection:** Identify patterns and anomalies that might indicate security threats.
- **Improved Decision-Making:** Use data-driven insights to make informed security decisions.

Example Use Case:

- **Threat Detection:** By analyzing log data from firewalls, intrusion detection systems (IDS), and endpoint protection tools, organizations can identify unusual patterns of activity that may signify a security breach.

Challenges:

- **Data Integration:** Integrating data from disparate sources can be complex.
- **Data Quality:** Ensuring the quality and consistency of data is critical for accurate analysis.

2. Machine Learning (ML)

Overview: Machine learning involves training algorithms to recognize patterns in data and make predictions or decisions without explicit programming. In security, ML can help automate the detection and response to threats.

Benefits:

- **Anomaly Detection:** ML algorithms can identify deviations from normal behavior that might indicate a security incident.
- **Automated Responses:** Automatically respond to detected threats, reducing the need for manual intervention.
- **Predictive Insights:** Predict potential security incidents based on historical data.

Example Use Case:

- **User Behavior Analytics (UBA):** ML algorithms analyze user behavior to detect unusual activities, such as unexpected access to sensitive data, which might indicate insider threats.

Challenges:

- **Training Data:** Requires large volumes of high-quality training data.
- **Model Maintenance:** ML models need regular updates to remain effective as threats evolve.

3. Artificial Intelligence (AI)

Overview: AI encompasses a broader range of technologies, including machine learning, natural language processing, and robotics, that enable machines to perform tasks typically requiring human intelligence. In security, AI can enhance threat detection, response, and reporting.

Benefits:

- **Enhanced Detection:** AI can identify complex threats that traditional methods might miss.
- **Efficient Analysis:** Analyze vast amounts of data quickly and accurately.
- **Contextual Understanding:** Provide deeper insights by understanding the context of security events.

Example Use Case:

- **Threat Intelligence:** AI systems analyze threat intelligence feeds, news sources, and social media to provide real-time insights into emerging threats and vulnerabilities.

Challenges:

- **Bias:** AI systems can inherit biases present in the training data.
- **Transparency:** The decision-making processes of AI systems can be opaque, making it challenging to understand how conclusions are reached.

Leveraging Emerging Technologies

1. Improving Efficiency:

Automated Data Collection:

- **Implementation:** Use AI and ML to automate the collection of security data from various sources, such as network logs, user activities, and endpoint devices.
- **Benefit:** Reduces the manual effort required for data aggregation and ensures more comprehensive data collection.

Real-Time Analysis:

- **Implementation:** Deploy big data analytics platforms that process and analyze data in real-time to detect threats and anomalies.
- **Benefit:** Provides immediate insights, enabling faster detection and response to security incidents.

2. Enhancing Accuracy:

Advanced Anomaly Detection:

- **Implementation:** Use ML algorithms trained on historical security data to identify unusual patterns that might indicate potential threats.
- **Benefit:** Increases the accuracy of threat detection by reducing false positives and negatives.

Predictive Analytics:

- **Implementation:** Leverage AI to predict future security incidents based on historical data and current trends.
- **Benefit:** Allows proactive measures to be taken to mitigate potential threats before they materialize.

3. Providing Value in Reporting:

Actionable Insights:

- **Implementation:** Develop dashboards that present AI-generated insights and recommendations in an easily understandable format.
- **Benefit:** Helps stakeholders quickly grasp the security posture and make informed decisions.

Trend Analysis:

- **Implementation:** Use big data analytics to identify long-term trends and patterns in security metrics.
- **Benefit:** Enables organizations to understand how their security posture is evolving and where to focus improvement efforts.

Addressing Challenges and Risks

1. Data Privacy:
Challenge: Ensuring that the collection and analysis of security data do not violate privacy regulations or internal policies.
Solution:

- **Data Anonymization:** Implement techniques to anonymize sensitive data before analysis.
- **Access Controls:** Restrict access to raw data and analytics results to authorized personnel only.

2. Bias:
Challenge: AI and ML models can inherit biases from training data, leading to inaccurate or unfair outcomes.
Solution:

- **Diverse Training Data:** Use diverse and representative training datasets to minimize biases.
- **Bias Detection:** Implement techniques to detect and mitigate bias in AI models.

3. Transparency:
Challenge: AI systems can be opaque, making it difficult to understand how decisions are made.
Solution:

- **Explainable AI:** Develop AI models that provide explanations for their decisions.
- **Transparency Reports:** Generate reports that detail the decision-making processes of AI systems.

Examples of Leveraging Emerging Technologies

1. AI-Driven Security Operations Center (SOC):

- **Implementation:** An AI-driven SOC uses AI and ML to analyze security alerts and prioritize them based on potential impact. The system can automate responses to low-level threats, freeing up analysts to focus on more complex incidents.
- **Benefit:** Increases the efficiency and effectiveness of the SOC, enabling faster detection and response to threats.

2. Predictive Vulnerability Management:

- **Implementation:** Use ML models to predict which vulnerabilities are most likely to be exploited based on historical attack data and current threat intelligence. Prioritize patching efforts accordingly.
- **Benefit:** Reduces the risk of exploitation by focusing remediation efforts on the most critical vulnerabilities.

3. AI-Powered User Behavior Analytics:

- **Implementation:** Deploy AI-powered UBA to monitor user activities and detect anomalies that may indicate insider threats or compromised accounts.
- **Benefit:** Enhances the ability to detect and respond to insider threats, improving overall security posture.

Conclusion

Emerging trends and technologies such as big data analytics, machine learning, and artificial intelligence are transforming the way organizations measure and report on their information security programs. These technologies enable more efficient data collection, real-time analysis, and predictive insights, enhancing the accuracy and value of security metrics and reporting. However, organizations must also address challenges related to data privacy, bias, and transparency to fully leverage these technologies effectively. By adopting these advanced tools and techniques, organizations can improve their security posture, support data-driven decision-making, and stay ahead of evolving threats.

Part IV: Information Security Incident Management:

Difference Between Information Security Incidents and Events

Information Security Events: An information security event is any observable occurrence in a system or network. Events are routine occurrences that can include successful or unsuccessful logins, file access, and other normal activities. Events are not necessarily indicative of a problem but are part of regular system operations.
Examples:

- A user logging into their account.
- An employee accessing a file on a shared drive.
- An automated system performing a scheduled backup.

Information Security Incidents: An information security incident is an event or series of events that indicate a possible breach of security policies, unauthorized access, or a threat to the integrity, availability, or confidentiality of information. Incidents typically require a response to mitigate potential harm.

Examples:

- A successful phishing attack that results in unauthorized access to sensitive data.
- Detection of malware on a company's network.
- A denial-of-service (DoS) attack that disrupts service availability.

Importance of Establishing Clear Criteria and Thresholds for Classifying and Escalating Incidents

1. Impact:

- **Definition:** The extent of potential damage or disruption caused by an incident.
- **Factors:** Financial loss, reputational damage, regulatory penalties, operational disruption.
- **Example:** An incident involving a data breach of customer information has a high impact due to potential legal repercussions and loss of customer trust.

2. Urgency:

- **Definition:** The time sensitivity of responding to the incident.
- **Factors:** Immediate threat to critical systems, ongoing data loss, active exploitation.
- **Example:** A ransomware attack actively encrypting files has high urgency due to the need for immediate containment and mitigation.

3. Likelihood:

- **Definition:** The probability of the incident occurring or reoccurring.
- **Factors:** Frequency of similar incidents, known vulnerabilities, threat intelligence.
- **Example:** Repeated unsuccessful login attempts from an unfamiliar IP address suggest a high likelihood of an impending brute-force attack.

Criteria for Classifying and Escalating Incidents:

- **Low Severity:** Minor incidents with limited impact and low urgency (e.g., single unsuccessful login attempt).
- **Medium Severity:** Incidents with moderate impact or potential for escalation (e.g., detection of malware on a non-critical system).
- **High Severity:** Critical incidents with high impact and urgency (e.g., confirmed data breach of sensitive information).

Escalation Protocols:

- **Low Severity:** Handled by the IT support team with regular monitoring.
- **Medium Severity:** Escalated to the information security team for further investigation and action.
- **High Severity:** Immediate notification to senior management and activation of the incident response plan.

Using Industry Standards and Frameworks

NIST Cybersecurity Framework: The NIST Cybersecurity Framework provides a structured approach for managing and improving cybersecurity risks. It includes guidelines for identifying, protecting, detecting, responding to, and recovering from cybersecurity incidents.

Key Components:

- **Identify:** Understand the organizational context and risks.
- **Protect:** Implement safeguards to ensure delivery of critical services.
- **Detect:** Develop activities to identify the occurrence of a cybersecurity event.
- **Respond:** Take action regarding a detected cybersecurity incident.

- **Recover:** Maintain plans for resilience and restoration of services.

Application:

- **Incident Classification:** Use the framework's functions and categories to classify and prioritize incidents.
- **Response Planning:** Develop response strategies aligned with NIST guidelines.

VERIS (Vocabulary for Event Recording and Incident Sharing): VERIS provides a standardized taxonomy for recording and sharing information about security incidents. It helps organizations capture consistent and comparable incident data, facilitating analysis and sharing of lessons learned.

Key Components:

- **Incident Attributes:** Describe the basic characteristics of the incident (e.g., threat actor, asset, impact).
- **Impact Classification:** Categorize the impact of the incident on confidentiality, integrity, and availability.
- **Victim Demographics:** Identify the affected entity and its attributes.

Application:

- **Consistent Recording:** Use VERIS to consistently record incident details, enhancing the ability to analyze and share data.
- **Trend Analysis:** Analyze incident data to identify trends and improve security measures.

Example Scenario

Scenario: An organization detects unusual activity on its network, including multiple failed login attempts and data exfiltration alerts from a sensitive database.

Classification:

- **Event:** The initial failed login attempts are recorded as security events.
- **Incident:** The detection of data exfiltration is classified as a security incident due to its impact and urgency.

Impact Assessment:

- **Impact:** High (potential data breach of sensitive information).
- **Urgency:** High (active data exfiltration).
- **Likelihood:** High (ongoing unauthorized access).

Response:

- **NIST Framework:** Follow the Detect and Respond functions to identify the scope of the breach and take immediate action to contain it.
- **VERIS Taxonomy:** Record the incident details using VERIS to facilitate post-incident analysis and reporting.

Actions Taken:

- **Immediate Containment:** Isolate affected systems and block suspicious IP addresses.
- **Notification:** Alert senior management and activate the incident response team.
- **Investigation:** Conduct a forensic investigation to determine the extent of the breach.
- **Remediation:** Patch vulnerabilities and strengthen access controls to prevent recurrence.

Post-Incident Analysis:

- **Review:** Analyze the incident using VERIS to identify root causes and improve detection capabilities.
- **Reporting:** Use NIST and VERIS data to create a detailed incident report for stakeholders.

Conclusion

Distinguishing between security events and incidents is crucial for effective incident management. Establishing clear criteria and thresholds for classifying and escalating incidents based on impact, urgency, and likelihood ensures timely and appropriate responses. Utilizing industry standards and frameworks like the NIST Cybersecurity Framework and the VERIS taxonomy enhances consistency, alignment with best practices, and the ability to analyze and share incident data. By adopting these practices, organizations can improve their incident response capabilities and overall security posture.

Key Components of an Incident Response Plan

An effective incident response plan (IRP) is essential for managing and mitigating the impact of security incidents. It should be comprehensive, tailored to the organization's specific needs, and integrated with broader business continuity and disaster recovery plans. Below are the key components of an incident response plan:

1. Incident Response Team Structure

Roles and Responsibilities:

- **Incident Response Manager:** Oversees the entire incident response process and coordinates efforts across the team.
- **Security Analysts:** Analyze the incident, identify the cause, and assess the impact.
- **IT Support:** Implements technical measures to contain and eradicate the threat.
- **Legal and Compliance:** Ensures that all actions comply with legal and regulatory requirements and manages communication with regulatory bodies.
- **Communications Officer:** Manages internal and external communications, including public relations.
- **Business Continuity Planner:** Coordinates with the business continuity and disaster recovery teams to maintain operations.
- **HR and Employee Relations:** Handles any internal employee-related issues, including insider threats.

2. Communication Protocols

Internal Communication:

- **Incident Notification:** Procedures for notifying the incident response team and relevant stakeholders about the incident.
- **Regular Updates:** Establish a schedule for regular updates to keep everyone informed about the status and progress of the response.

External Communication:

- **Public Relations:** Protocols for communicating with the media and the public to manage the organization's reputation.
- **Customer Notification:** Guidelines for informing affected customers, including timelines and content.
- **Regulatory Bodies:** Procedures for notifying regulatory authorities as required by law or regulation.

3. Escalation Procedures

Incident Severity Levels:

- Define levels of incident severity (e.g., low, medium, high, critical) based on the impact and urgency.

Escalation Criteria:

- Criteria for escalating incidents to higher management or specific teams, depending on severity and potential impact.
- Example: A data breach involving sensitive customer information would be escalated immediately to senior management and legal/compliance teams.

Decision-Making Authority:

- Clearly define who has the authority to make critical decisions during an incident response.

4. Recovery Strategies

Containment:

- Short-term actions to limit the damage and prevent further spread of the incident.
- Example: Isolating affected systems from the network.

Eradication:

- Identifying and eliminating the root cause of the incident.
- Example: Removing malware from infected systems.

Recovery:

- Restoring and validating system functionality to return to normal operations.
- Example: Restoring data from backups and verifying system integrity.

Post-Incident Activities:

- Conducting a thorough post-incident review to identify lessons learned and prevent future incidents.
- Example: Creating a report detailing the incident, response actions, and recommendations for improvement.

Tailoring the Plan to the Organization

Assessing Needs and Risks:

- Conduct a risk assessment to identify potential threats and vulnerabilities specific to the organization.
- Customize the plan based on the organization's size, industry, regulatory requirements, and existing capabilities.

Integration with Business Continuity and Disaster Recovery Plans:

- Ensure the incident response plan is aligned with the broader business continuity and disaster recovery plans.
- Example: Coordinating with the disaster recovery team to ensure that data recovery processes are seamless and efficient.

Templates and Best Practices:

Incident Response Plan Template Example:

1. **Introduction:**
    - Purpose and scope of the plan.
    - Objectives and goals.
2. **Incident Response Team:**
    - Team members and their roles.
    - Contact information and communication channels.
3. **Incident Identification and Classification:**
    - Methods for detecting and reporting incidents.
    - Incident severity levels and classification criteria.
4. **Incident Handling Procedures:**
    - Detailed steps for containment, eradication, and recovery.
    - Documentation requirements for each stage.
5. **Communication Plan:**
    - Internal and external communication protocols.
    - Templates for incident notifications and updates.
6. **Escalation Procedures:**
    - Criteria and process for escalating incidents.
    - Decision-making authority and approval processes.
7. **Post-Incident Review:**
    - Process for conducting post-incident analysis.
    - Reporting and documentation templates.
8. **Appendices:**
    - Contact lists, incident report forms, and additional resources.

Best Practices:

- **Regular Training:** Ensure all team members are trained on their roles and responsibilities within the incident response plan.
- **Documentation:** Maintain detailed records of all incidents, actions taken, and decisions made during the incident response process.
- **Coordination:** Foster collaboration between IT, security, legal, and business units to ensure a unified response.

Importance of Testing and Updating the Plan

Regular Testing:

- Conduct regular simulations and exercises to test the effectiveness of the incident response plan.
- Example: Tabletop exercises, red team/blue team exercises, and full-scale incident simulations.

Updating the Plan:

- Regularly review and update the plan based on lessons learned from incidents and exercises.
- Incorporate feedback from all stakeholders to continuously improve the plan.
- Ensure the plan evolves with changes in the organization's structure, technology, and threat landscape.

Conclusion

An effective incident response plan is crucial for managing and mitigating security incidents. Key components include a well-defined team structure, clear communication protocols, detailed escalation procedures, and robust recovery strategies. Tailoring the plan to the organization's specific needs and ensuring alignment with broader business continuity and disaster recovery plans are essential. Regular testing and updates through simulations and exercises ensure the plan remains effective and responsive to evolving threats and organizational changes. Implementing these best practices fosters a resilient security posture and enhances the organization's ability to respond to incidents efficiently and effectively.

Phases of the Incident Response Process

Incident response is a structured approach to handling security incidents with the goal of managing and mitigating their impact. The process is divided into several phases, each with specific activities, tools, and skills required.

1. Preparation

Key Activities:

- Develop and document an incident response plan (IRP).
- Establish an incident response team (IRT) with defined roles and responsibilities.
- Conduct regular training and simulation exercises (e.g., tabletop exercises).
- Implement security tools and technologies (e.g., firewalls, IDS/IPS, SIEM systems).

Tools:

- Incident response tools (e.g., SIEM, EDR solutions).
- Communication tools for coordinating with the team (e.g., secure messaging platforms).
- Documentation templates for incident reporting and tracking.

Skills:

- Knowledge of security policies and procedures.
- Technical expertise in detecting and responding to security incidents.
- Communication and coordination skills.

Example:

- An organization conducts regular tabletop exercises to simulate various incident scenarios, ensuring the IRT is prepared to respond effectively.

2. Detection

Key Activities:

- Monitor network and system activities using security tools (e.g., SIEM, IDS/IPS).
- Identify and investigate security alerts and anomalies.
- Correlate events from different sources to detect potential incidents.

Tools:

- SIEM systems for aggregating and analyzing security data.
- Network and host-based IDS/IPS.
- Log analysis tools.

Skills:

- Ability to analyze and interpret security alerts.
- Understanding of normal network and system behavior to identify anomalies.
- Quick decision-making skills to determine the significance of alerts.

Example:

- A security analyst notices unusual outbound traffic patterns and correlates it with multiple failed login attempts, raising an alert for potential data exfiltration.

3. Analysis

Key Activities:

- Analyze the nature and scope of the incident.
- Determine the affected systems, data, and potential impact.
- Identify the attack vector and threat actors involved.

Tools:

- Forensic analysis tools (e.g., EnCase, FTK).
- Malware analysis tools (e.g., sandbox environments).
- Network traffic analysis tools (e.g., Wireshark).

Skills:

- Forensic investigation skills to analyze compromised systems.
- Knowledge of malware behavior and attack techniques.
- Analytical skills to understand the incident's context and impact.

Example:

- The incident response team uses a forensic tool to analyze a compromised server, identifying malware used to exfiltrate data and pinpointing the initial entry point as a phishing email.

4. Containment

Key Activities:

- Implement immediate actions to contain the incident and prevent further damage.
- Isolate affected systems from the network.
- Apply temporary fixes to stop the attack's progress.

Tools:

- Network segmentation tools.
- Endpoint isolation features in EDR solutions.
- Access control mechanisms.

Skills:

- Decision-making skills to quickly determine containment strategies.
- Technical skills to isolate and secure affected systems.
- Coordination skills to manage containment actions across different teams.

Example:

- The team isolates the compromised server and blocks the malicious IP addresses identified during the analysis phase to prevent further data exfiltration.

5. Eradication

Key Activities:

- Remove the root cause of the incident (e.g., malware, unauthorized access).
- Apply patches and updates to vulnerable systems.
- Strengthen security controls to prevent recurrence.

Tools:

- Anti-malware and antivirus tools.
- Patch management systems.
- Configuration management tools.

Skills:

- Technical skills to remove malware and close vulnerabilities.
- Knowledge of system and software patching processes.
- Ability to implement and verify security controls.

Example:

- The team removes the malware from the affected server, applies security patches, and updates the firewall rules to block the attack vector.

6. Recovery

Key Activities:

- Restore affected systems and services to normal operation.
- Verify system integrity and functionality after remediation.
- Monitor for any signs of residual threats or re-infection.

Tools:

- Backup and recovery tools.
- System integrity verification tools.
- Continuous monitoring tools.

Skills:

- Knowledge of backup and recovery procedures.
- Verification skills to ensure systems are fully restored and secure.
- Monitoring skills to detect any lingering threats.

Example:

- The team restores the server from a clean backup, verifies its integrity, and monitors the network for any signs of residual threats.

7. Post-Incident Review

Key Activities:

- Conduct a thorough review of the incident and the response actions taken.
- Document lessons learned and identify areas for improvement.
- Update the incident response plan and security measures based on findings.

Tools:

- Incident documentation tools.
- Reporting templates.
- Feedback collection tools.

Skills:

- Analytical skills to evaluate the incident response effectiveness.
- Communication skills to gather feedback from team members.
- Documentation skills to record lessons learned and action items.

Example:

- The incident response team conducts a post-incident review meeting, documents the lessons learned, and updates the IRP to include new containment strategies and tools.

Importance of Documenting and Time-Stamping Actions

Documenting and time-stamping all actions taken during the incident response process is crucial for several reasons:

- **Accountability:** Ensures that all team members are accountable for their actions and decisions.

- **Legal and Compliance:** Provides a detailed record for legal and regulatory requirements.
- **Root Cause Analysis:** Facilitates thorough analysis and understanding of the incident.
- **Continuous Improvement:** Helps identify strengths and weaknesses in the response process for future improvements.

Challenges and Best Practices for Preserving Evidence and Maintaining Chain of Custody

Challenges:

- **Data Integrity:** Ensuring the integrity of evidence during collection and analysis.
- **Chain of Custody:** Maintaining a clear record of who accessed and handled the evidence.
- **Storage:** Securely storing evidence to prevent tampering or loss.

Best Practices:

- **Standard Procedures:** Establish standard operating procedures for evidence collection, handling, and storage.
- **Documentation:** Document every action taken with evidence, including who handled it, when, and why.
- **Secure Storage:** Use secure, tamper-evident storage for all collected evidence.
- **Training:** Regularly train the incident response team on proper evidence handling and chain of custody procedures.

Example:

- During a malware investigation, the incident response team follows a documented procedure to create a forensic image of the compromised system, logs all actions taken, and securely stores the image in a tamper-evident container. This ensures that the evidence can be used in legal proceedings if necessary.

Conclusion

The incident response process involves multiple phases, each requiring specific activities, tools, and skills. From preparation to post-incident review, each phase plays a critical role in managing and mitigating security incidents. Documenting and time-stamping all actions, preserving evidence, and maintaining the chain of custody are essential for ensuring accountability, legal compliance, and continuous improvement. By following these best practices, organizations can effectively respond to incidents, minimize damage, and enhance their overall security posture.

Roles and Responsibilities of the Incident Response Team

An effective incident response team (IRT) is composed of various roles, each with specific responsibilities to ensure a coordinated and efficient response to security incidents. Here are the key roles and their responsibilities:

1. Incident Response Manager

Responsibilities:

- **Leadership:** Oversee the incident response process and coordinate the activities of the IRT.
- **Decision-Making:** Make critical decisions during incidents, such as escalation, resource allocation, and communication.
- **Communication:** Act as the primary point of contact for senior management and other stakeholders.
- **Planning:** Develop and maintain the incident response plan (IRP) and ensure it aligns with organizational policies and objectives.

Skills:

- Strong leadership and decision-making skills.
- Excellent communication and organizational skills.
- In-depth understanding of security principles and incident response strategies.

Example:

- The incident response manager coordinates the team during a ransomware attack, making decisions on containment strategies, communicating with stakeholders, and overseeing the remediation process.

2. Technical Leads

Responsibilities:

- **Expertise:** Provide technical guidance and expertise in specific areas (e.g., network security, endpoint security, forensics).
- **Analysis:** Lead the technical analysis of incidents, identifying root causes and determining the impact.
- **Implementation:** Oversee the implementation of containment, eradication, and recovery measures.

Skills:

- Deep technical knowledge in their respective areas.
- Problem-solving and analytical skills.
- Ability to work under pressure and make quick, informed decisions.

Example:

- A technical lead for network security analyzes network traffic to identify the source of a DDoS attack and implements mitigation strategies.

3. Incident Response Analysts

Responsibilities:

- **Detection:** Monitor security alerts and logs to detect potential incidents.
- **Investigation:** Conduct detailed investigations to determine the scope and impact of incidents.
- **Documentation:** Document all findings, actions taken, and lessons learned.

Skills:

- Strong analytical and investigative skills.
- Proficiency in using security tools and technologies (e.g., SIEM, EDR).
- Attention to detail and excellent documentation skills.

Example:

- An incident response analyst investigates a series of phishing emails, tracing the attack back to a compromised external email account and documenting the findings.

4. Communications Specialists

Responsibilities:

- **Internal Communication:** Ensure clear and timely communication within the IRT and with other internal stakeholders.
- **External Communication:** Handle communication with external parties, such as customers, partners, and the media, during incidents.
- **Crisis Management:** Develop communication strategies to manage the organization's reputation and mitigate public relations risks.

Skills:

- Strong written and verbal communication skills.
- Ability to manage crisis communications effectively.
- Understanding of incident response processes and organizational protocols.

Example:

- A communications specialist drafts and disseminates a public statement regarding a data breach, ensuring transparency and maintaining customer trust.

Importance of Clear Lines of Authority and Decision-Making Protocols

Establishing clear lines of authority and decision-making protocols is crucial for several reasons:

- **Coordination:** Ensures that all team members understand their roles and responsibilities, leading to a more coordinated response.
- **Efficiency:** Speeds up decision-making processes by clearly defining who is authorized to make critical decisions.

- **Accountability:** Establishes accountability for actions taken during an incident, facilitating post-incident analysis and continuous improvement.

Ensuring Necessary Skills, Tools, and Resources

1. Skills:

- **Technical Expertise:** Ensure team members have the necessary technical skills through training and certification programs (e.g., CISSP, CISM, CEH).
- **Soft Skills:** Develop communication, leadership, and problem-solving skills through workshops and professional development programs.

2. Tools:

- **Security Tools:** Provide access to advanced security tools, such as SIEM, EDR, forensic analysis tools, and threat intelligence platforms.
- **Collaboration Tools:** Utilize secure communication and collaboration tools to facilitate coordination within the IRT.

3. Resources:

- **Funding:** Ensure adequate funding for incident response activities, including tool acquisition, training, and external consulting services.
- **Support:** Obtain support from senior management to prioritize incident response efforts and ensure organizational alignment.

Building and Maintaining a High-Performing Incident Response Team

1. Training:

- **Regular Training:** Conduct regular training sessions to keep the team updated on the latest threats, technologies, and best practices.
- **Certification Programs:** Encourage team members to obtain industry-recognized certifications.

Example:

- The IRT participates in quarterly training sessions on emerging threats, such as advanced persistent threats (APTs) and ransomware.

2. Exercises:

- **Tabletop Exercises:** Conduct tabletop exercises to simulate various incident scenarios and test the team's response capabilities.
- **Live Drills:** Perform live drills to practice real-time incident response and coordination.

Example:

- The organization conducts an annual live drill simulating a major data breach, involving all members of the IRT and key stakeholders.

3. Continuous Improvement:

- **Post-Incident Reviews:** Conduct thorough reviews after each incident to identify lessons learned and areas for improvement.
- **Feedback Mechanisms:** Establish mechanisms for team members to provide feedback on the incident response process.

Example:

- After a successful incident response, the team conducts a post-incident review meeting to discuss what went well, what could be improved, and updates the IRP accordingly.

Conclusion

An effective incident response team is critical for managing and mitigating the impact of security incidents. By defining clear roles and responsibilities, establishing authority and decision-making protocols, and ensuring the team has the necessary skills, tools, and resources, organizations can build and maintain a high-performing incident response team. Regular training, exercises, and continuous improvement practices are essential to keep the team prepared and capable of responding to incidents effectively. Through these efforts, organizations can enhance their resilience and protect their assets from evolving threats.

Identifying and Classifying Information Security Incidents

Process Overview

The process of identifying and classifying information security incidents involves using a combination of automated detection tools and manual methods to detect, analyze, and categorize security events. This process is critical for ensuring that incidents are promptly identified and appropriately handled to minimize damage and recovery time.

Automated Detection Tools

1. **Security Information and Event Management (SIEM) Systems:**
   - **Function:** Collects and correlates log data from various sources (e.g., network devices, servers, applications) to identify patterns indicative of security incidents.
   - **Example Tools:** Splunk, IBM QRadar, ArcSight.
   - **Capabilities:** Real-time monitoring, correlation of events, alert generation, and compliance reporting.
2. **Intrusion Detection Systems (IDS) and Intrusion Prevention Systems (IPS):**
   - **Function:** Monitors network traffic for suspicious activities and potential threats.
   - **Example Tools:** Snort, Suricata, Palo Alto Networks.
   - **Capabilities:** Signature-based detection, anomaly detection, and automated response (for IPS).
3. **Endpoint Detection and Response (EDR) Tools:**
   - **Function:** Monitors endpoint activities to detect malicious behavior.
   - **Example Tools:** CrowdStrike Falcon, Carbon Black, SentinelOne.
   - **Capabilities:** Behavioral analysis, threat hunting, and automated remediation.

Manual Detection Methods

1. **User Reports:**
   - **Function:** Employees and users report suspicious activities or security incidents to the IT or security team.
   - **Example:** A user reporting a phishing email or unusual system behavior.
2. **Threat Intelligence Feeds:**
   - **Function:** Provides real-time information about emerging threats and vulnerabilities.
   - **Example Providers:** Recorded Future, FireEye, ThreatConnect.
   - **Capabilities:** Indicators of compromise (IOCs), threat actor profiles, and attack vectors.
3. **Security Audits and Assessments:**
   - **Function:** Regularly scheduled audits and assessments to identify vulnerabilities and potential incidents.
   - **Example:** Penetration testing, vulnerability assessments, and security audits.

Challenges in Identifying Incidents

1. **Complexity of IT Environments:**
   - **Challenge:** Diverse and distributed IT environments make it difficult to get a unified view of security events.
   - **Solution:** Implement centralized monitoring tools like SIEM and ensure comprehensive log collection.
2. **High Volume of Data:**
   - **Challenge:** The sheer volume of log data and alerts can overwhelm security teams.
   - **Solution:** Use automated tools for initial tri

Challenges in Identifying Incidents (Continued)

2. **High Volume of Data:**
   - **Challenge:** The sheer volume of log data and alerts can overwhelm security teams.

- **Solution:** Use automated tools for initial triage and filtering to prioritize high-risk alerts.

3. **False Positives:**
    - **Challenge:** High rate of false positives can lead to alert fatigue and missed real incidents.
    - **Solution:** Fine-tune detection rules and use machine learning to improve accuracy.
4. **Evolving Threat Landscape:**
    - **Challenge:** Constantly changing threat landscape requires continuous adaptation of detection mechanisms.
    - **Solution:** Regularly update detection signatures and leverage threat intelligence feeds for the latest information.

Best Practices for Accurate and Efficient Incident Identification

1. **Comprehensive Data Collection:**
    - Ensure all relevant data sources are included in your monitoring setup, such as network devices, endpoints, applications, and cloud environments.
    - Example: Collect logs from firewalls, IDS/IPS, EDR solutions, and cloud services to have a complete view.
2. **Correlation and Contextualization:**
    - Use SIEM systems to correlate events from multiple sources, providing context to identify real threats more accurately.
    - Example: Correlate login attempts from an unusual location with abnormal data access patterns.
3. **Regular Tuning and Maintenance:**
    - Continuously tune detection rules and thresholds to reduce false positives and negatives.
    - Example: Adjust IDS/IPS signatures and SIEM correlation rules based on new threat intelligence.
4. **Incident Classification Framework:**
    - Develop a clear classification framework to categorize incidents based on severity, type, and impact.
    - Example: Use a classification scheme that includes categories like unauthorized access, malware infection, data breach, and service disruption.
5. **Training and Awareness:**
    - Train employees to recognize and report suspicious activities promptly.
    - Example: Conduct regular phishing simulations and security awareness training sessions.

Using Machine Learning and AI to Improve Detection

Machine learning (ML) and artificial intelligence (AI) can significantly enhance the accuracy and speed of incident detection. Here's how:

1. **Anomaly Detection:**
    - ML algorithms can learn normal behavior patterns and identify deviations that may indicate a security incident.
    - Example: An unsupervised ML model can detect unusual network traffic that doesn't match historical patterns.
2. **Behavioral Analysis:**
    - AI can analyze user and entity behavior to detect insider threats and compromised accounts.
    - Example: A behavioral analytics system flags a user downloading large amounts of sensitive data outside of normal working hours.
3. **Automated Response:**
    - AI-driven tools can automatically respond to certain types of incidents, reducing response time.
    - Example: An AI-based EDR system can isolate an infected endpoint automatically upon detecting malware.
4. **Threat Intelligence Integration:**
    - AI can process and analyze vast amounts of threat intelligence data to identify relevant threats to the organization.

- Example: An AI system ingests threat feeds and matches them against internal data to highlight potential risks.

Example Workflow Using SIEM and ML

1. **Data Ingestion:**
   - Collect logs and data from various sources using a SIEM tool.
   - Example: Splunk collects data from firewalls, IDS/IPS, endpoints, and cloud services.
2. **Preprocessing and Normalization:**
   - Normalize and preprocess the data to ensure consistency.
   - Example: Convert all timestamps to a common format and standardize IP address formats.
3. **Anomaly Detection:**
   - Use ML models to detect anomalies in the normalized data.
   - Example: An ML algorithm flags an unusual spike in outbound traffic from a normally quiet server.
4. **Correlation and Alerting:**
   - Correlate anomalies with other data to generate alerts.
   - Example: Correlate the traffic spike with a failed login attempt from an external IP address.
5. **Triage and Response:**
   - Security analysts review alerts and determine appropriate response actions.
   - Example: Analysts investigate the flagged server, confirm the presence of malware, and isolate the server from the network.

Conclusion

Effectively identifying and classifying information security incidents is crucial for maintaining a strong security posture. Combining automated tools like SIEM, IDS/IPS, and EDR with manual methods such as user reports and threat intelligence feeds provides a comprehensive detection strategy. By addressing challenges through best practices and leveraging machine learning and AI, organizations can enhance the accuracy and efficiency of their incident detection efforts. Regularly updating detection mechanisms and training employees further ensure a robust defense against evolving threats.

Concept of Incident Triage

Incident Triage: Incident triage is the process of evaluating and categorizing security incidents to prioritize response efforts based on their severity and potential impact. The goal of incident triage is to ensure that the most critical incidents receive immediate attention, while less severe incidents are managed appropriately based on available resources and their potential risk.

Role in Prioritizing Response Efforts

Prioritization:

- **Efficient Resource Allocation:** Ensures that incident response teams focus their efforts on the most severe and impactful incidents.
- **Timely Mitigation:** Helps in quickly addressing incidents that pose the highest risk to the organization, thereby minimizing potential damage.
- **Systematic Management:** Provides a structured approach to handling multiple incidents simultaneously.

Factors to Consider When Assessing Incident Severity

1. Criticality of Affected Systems and Data:

- **Business Impact:** Evaluate how critical the affected systems and data are to business operations. Systems essential to core business functions require higher prioritization.
- **Data Sensitivity:** Consider the sensitivity of the data involved, such as personal identifiable information (PII), financial records, or intellectual property.

Example:

- A compromise involving customer financial data is prioritized higher than an incident affecting non-sensitive internal documentation.

2. Extent of the Compromise:

- **Scope:** Determine the number of systems and users affected.
- **Depth:** Assess the level of access the attacker has obtained and the duration of the compromise.

Example:

- A widespread malware infection affecting multiple critical servers will be prioritized higher than a localized attack on a single workstation.

3. Potential for Further Damage or Spread:

- **Propagation Risk:** Evaluate the likelihood of the incident spreading to other systems or escalating in severity.
- **Secondary Impacts:** Consider potential cascading effects, such as the disruption of dependent services or compliance breaches.

Example:

- An active ransomware attack encrypting files poses a high risk of further damage and requires immediate containment efforts.

Examples of Incident Prioritization Matrices and Decision Trees
Incident Prioritization Matrix:

Severity Level	Criteria	Examples
Critical	- Compromise of highly sensitive data - Major disruption to business operations - High risk of spread or further damage	- Data breach involving PII - Ransomware attack on critical servers
High	- Compromise of important data - Significant impact on business operations - Moderate risk of spread or further damage	- Phishing attack with some compromised accounts - Malware infection on several user devices
Medium	- Compromise of non-sensitive data - Moderate impact on business operations - Low risk of spread or further damage	- Unauthorized access to non-critical systems - DDoS attack causing temporary disruption
Low	- Minimal impact on business operations - No sensitive data involved - No risk of spread or further damage	- Failed login attempts - Minor policy violations

Decision Tree for Incident Triage:

1. **Is the incident affecting critical systems or sensitive data?**
   - Yes: Proceed to step 2.
   - No: Classify as Low or Medium severity.
2. **Is there evidence of widespread compromise or potential for further damage?**
   - Yes: Proceed to step 3.
   - No: Classify as High severity.
3. **Is the incident actively causing business disruption or data loss?**
   - Yes: Classify as Critical severity.
   - No: Classify as High severity.

Importance of Aligning Incident Triage with Organizational Risk Appetite and Business Objectives

Alignment with Risk Appetite:

- **Risk Tolerance:** Ensure that incident prioritization aligns with the organization's defined risk tolerance levels. Incidents posing risks beyond acceptable thresholds should be prioritized higher.
- **Consistency:** Maintain consistent incident handling procedures that reflect the organization's approach to risk management.

Alignment with Business Objectives:

- **Strategic Priorities:** Prioritize incidents that threaten the organization's strategic priorities, such as customer trust, regulatory compliance, and operational continuity.
- **Resource Allocation:** Allocate resources to incident response activities that support the achievement of business objectives.

Examples of Applying Incident Triage

Example 1: Financial Institution

- **Scenario:** A phishing attack compromises several employee email accounts.
- **Assessment:**
    - **Criticality:** High (email accounts contain sensitive customer information).
    - **Extent:** Moderate (multiple accounts affected).
    - **Potential for Spread:** High (risk of further credential theft and unauthorized access).
- **Prioritization:** Classified as High severity.
- **Response:** Immediate containment of compromised accounts, forensic analysis to determine the extent, and targeted user training to prevent future incidents.

Example 2: Healthcare Organization

- **Scenario:** Malware detected on a workstation used for administrative tasks.
- **Assessment:**
    - **Criticality:** Medium (non-clinical system with limited sensitive data).
    - **Extent:** Low (single workstation).
    - **Potential for Spread:** Low (isolated system with limited network access).
- **Prioritization:** Classified as Medium severity.
- **Response:** Isolate the affected workstation, remove the malware, and review security controls on similar devices.

Example 3: E-Commerce Company

- **Scenario:** DDoS attack causing temporary website downtime.
- **Assessment:**
    - **Criticality:** High (website is critical for business operations).
    - **Extent:** High (entire website affected).
    - **Potential for Spread:** Low (no data compromise or internal system impact).
- **Prioritization:** Classified as High severity.
- **Response:** Implement DDoS mitigation strategies, communicate with customers about the issue, and investigate the source of the attack.

Conclusion

Incident triage is essential for prioritizing response efforts based on the severity and impact of incidents. By considering factors such as the criticality of affected systems and data, the extent of the compromise, and the potential for further damage, organizations can efficiently allocate resources and mitigate risks. Using incident prioritization matrices and decision trees helps ensure consistency and alignment with the organization's risk appetite and business objectives. Through effective incident triage, organizations can enhance their incident response capabilities and protect their assets and operations from evolving threats.

Tools and Techniques for Incident Investigation and Forensics

Incident investigation and forensics are critical for understanding the root cause, scope, and impact of security incidents, as well as for identifying attacker tactics, techniques, and procedures (TTPs). Effective investigation and forensics require a combination of tools and techniques, along with strict adherence to forensic procedures and chain of custody protocols to ensure the integrity and admissibility of evidence.

Key Tools and Techniques

1. Disk Imaging:

Purpose:

- Capture an exact, bit-for-bit copy of a disk or storage device to preserve evidence.

Tools:

- **FTK Imager:** Allows investigators to create forensic images and view files and folders.
- **dd (Unix/Linux):** A command-line utility to create disk images.

Procedure:

- Use a write blocker to prevent any changes to the original disk.
- Create a forensic image and verify its integrity using cryptographic hashes.

Example Use:

- Imaging a suspect's laptop to analyze for malicious files, deleted data, and traces of unauthorized access.

2. Memory Analysis:

Purpose:

- Analyze the contents of volatile memory (RAM) to identify active processes, open network connections, and in-memory artifacts.

Tools:

- **Volatility:** A powerful memory forensics framework for analyzing memory dumps.
- **Rekall:** An open-source memory forensics framework that provides detailed memory analysis capabilities.

Procedure:

- Capture a memory dump from the live system using tools like FTK Imager or DumpIt.
- Analyze the memory dump to identify suspicious processes, malware, and network connections.

Example Use:

- Identifying a malware process running in memory that does not leave traces on the disk.

3. Network Traffic Capture:

Purpose:

- Capture and analyze network traffic to detect signs of malicious activity, data exfiltration, and attacker communications.

Tools:

- **Wireshark:** A network protocol analyzer for capturing and analyzing network traffic.
- **tcpdump:** A command-line tool for capturing network packets.

Procedure:

- Deploy network sensors to capture traffic at strategic points (e.g., internet gateway, data center).
- Analyze captured traffic to identify anomalies, suspicious connections, and data transfers.

Example Use:

- Detecting data exfiltration attempts by analyzing outbound network traffic for large, unexpected data transfers.

4. Log Analysis:

Purpose:

- Analyze logs from various sources (e.g., firewalls, servers, applications) to trace attacker activities and correlate events.

Tools:

- **Splunk:** A platform for searching, monitoring, and analyzing machine-generated data.
- **ELK Stack (Elasticsearch, Logstash, Kibana):** An open-source suite for log aggregation and analysis.

Procedure:

- Aggregate logs from different sources into a centralized logging platform.
- Correlate and analyze logs to identify patterns, timelines, and indicators of compromise (IOCs).

Example Use:

- Tracing an attacker's movement within the network by analyzing server and firewall logs for unauthorized access attempts.

Importance of Forensic Procedures and Chain of Custody

Forensic Procedures:

- Following established forensic procedures ensures that evidence is collected, preserved, and analyzed correctly.
- Procedures include using write blockers, creating cryptographic hashes to verify data integrity, and documenting every step taken during the investigation.

Chain of Custody:

- Maintaining a clear chain of custody is crucial to ensure the integrity and admissibility of evidence in legal proceedings.
- Document the collection, transfer, and storage of evidence, including who handled it and when, to prevent tampering or contamination.

Examples of Forensic Analysis

1. Root Cause Analysis:

Scenario: A company experiences a data breach, and investigators need to determine how the attackers gained access.

Steps:

1. **Disk Imaging:** Create forensic images of affected servers to preserve evidence.
2. **Log Analysis:** Analyze server logs to identify the initial point of entry and attacker actions.
3. **Memory Analysis:** Examine memory dumps to uncover any in-memory malware or rootkits.

Outcome:

- Investigators find that attackers exploited an unpatched vulnerability in a web application, installed a web shell, and used it to gain administrative access to the server.

2. Scope and Impact Determination:

Scenario: An organization detects unusual outbound traffic and suspects data exfiltration.

Steps:

1. **Network Traffic Capture:** Use Wireshark to capture and analyze outbound traffic for signs of data exfiltration.
2. **Log Analysis:** Correlate network traffic data with server logs to identify the source and nature of the data being exfiltrated.
3. **Disk Imaging:** Image the affected systems to preserve evidence for further analysis.

Outcome:

- Investigators determine that attackers exfiltrated sensitive customer data over several weeks using an encrypted channel to a command-and-control server.

3. Identifying TTPs:

Scenario: A financial institution suspects it has been targeted by a sophisticated attacker using advanced persistent threats (APTs).

Steps:

1. **Log Analysis:** Aggregate and analyze logs from various systems to identify patterns and IOCs associated with APTs.
2. **Memory Analysis:** Use Volatility to analyze memory dumps for advanced malware that might evade disk-based detection.
3. **Threat Intelligence Integration:** Compare findings with threat intelligence feeds to match TTPs with known threat actor profiles.

Outcome:

- Investigators identify specific TTPs such as lateral movement using compromised administrative credentials and data exfiltration using encrypted tunnels, matching them to a known APT group.

Best Practices for Incident Investigation and Forensics

1. **Develop a Comprehensive Forensics Plan:**
    - Define procedures for evidence collection, preservation, analysis, and reporting.
    - Include clear guidelines for maintaining the chain of custody.
2. **Use Standardized Tools:**
    - Employ widely accepted forensic tools and frameworks to ensure consistency and reliability.
    - Regularly update and validate tools to handle new types of evidence and threats.
3. **Train the Incident Response Team:**
    - Provide regular training on forensic techniques and tools.
    - Conduct mock incident response exercises to ensure readiness.
4. **Document Everything:**
    - Keep detailed records of all actions taken during an investigation, including tool settings, commands used, and observations.
    - This documentation is crucial for legal proceedings and post-incident reviews.
5. **Integrate Threat Intelligence:**
    - Leverage threat intelligence to contextualize findings and enhance understanding of the attack.
    - Use IOCs from threat feeds to guide the investigation and validate findings.
6. **Regularly Review and Update Procedures:**
    - Continuously improve forensic procedures based on lessons learned from past incidents and advancements in forensic techniques.

Conclusion

Effective incident investigation and forensics are vital for understanding and mitigating security incidents. Using tools like disk imaging, memory analysis, network traffic capture, and log analysis, along with following established forensic procedures and maintaining a clear chain of custody, ensures the integrity and reliability of the investigation. By leveraging forensic analysis to determine the root cause, scope, and impact of incidents, and identifying attacker TTPs, organizations can enhance their security posture and better prepare for future threats. Regular testing, training, and updating of forensic procedures are essential to stay ahead in the dynamic field of cybersecurity.

Strategies and Approaches for Containing and Eradicating Information Security Incidents

Effective containment and eradication of information security incidents are critical to minimize damage, prevent further compromise, and restore normal operations. The strategies and approaches vary based on the nature and severity of the incident, and each has its trade-offs and considerations.

Containment Strategies

1. Isolating Affected Systems

Approach:

- **Description:** Disconnecting compromised systems from the network to prevent the spread of the incident.
- **Tools:** Network segmentation, firewall rules, VLANs, and physical disconnection.

Trade-offs and Considerations:

- **Business Impact:** May disrupt business operations if critical systems are isolated.

- **Risk Reduction:** Highly effective in stopping the spread but must be balanced against operational needs.
- **Example:** Isolating a server infected with ransomware to prevent encryption from spreading to other servers.

2. Blocking Malicious Traffic

Approach:

- **Description:** Using firewalls, IDS/IPS, and other security controls to block traffic from known malicious IP addresses or domains.
- **Tools:** Firewalls, intrusion prevention systems (IPS), and web filtering solutions.

Trade-offs and Considerations:

- **Business Impact:** Minimal impact if implemented correctly, but over-blocking can disrupt legitimate traffic.
- **Risk Reduction:** Effective for stopping external threats but requires accurate threat intelligence.
- **Example:** Blocking incoming connections from IP addresses associated with a DDoS attack.

3. Quarantine Affected Devices

Approach:

- **Description:** Moving compromised devices to a quarantine network where they can be analyzed and remediated without posing a risk to the main network.
- **Tools:** Network access control (NAC) solutions, VLANs, and endpoint detection and response (EDR) tools.

Trade-offs and Considerations:

- **Business Impact:** Ensures business continuity by isolating threats without widespread disruption.
- **Risk Reduction:** Balances containment and continued analysis but requires proper quarantine infrastructure.
- **Example:** Quarantining a laptop infected with malware to analyze the infection and prevent it from spreading.

Eradication Strategies

1. Removing Malware

Approach:

- **Description:** Using antivirus and anti-malware tools to identify and remove malicious software.
- **Tools:** Antivirus software, anti-malware tools, and EDR solutions.

Trade-offs and Considerations:

- **Business Impact:** Generally minimal if tools are effective and up-to-date, but can disrupt operations if systems need to be taken offline for scanning.
- **Risk Reduction:** Effective for known malware but may miss advanced or unknown threats.
- **Example:** Using an antivirus tool to remove a trojan from an infected workstation.

2. Deploying Security Patches and Updates

Approach:

- **Description:** Applying patches and updates to close vulnerabilities exploited by attackers.
- **Tools:** Patch management systems and software update tools.

Trade-offs and Considerations:

- **Business Impact:** Requires downtime or system restarts, which can disrupt operations.
- **Risk Reduction:** Essential for long-term remediation and prevention but must be carefully managed to avoid compatibility issues.
- **Example:** Patching a critical vulnerability in a web server software to prevent a repeat of a previously exploited attack.

3. Removing Unauthorized Access

Approach:

- **Description:** Changing passwords, revoking compromised credentials, and closing backdoors used by attackers.
- **Tools:** Identity and access management (IAM) systems, directory services, and multi-factor authentication (MFA) solutions.

Trade-offs and Considerations:

- **Business Impact:** Users may experience disruption if credentials are changed without notice.
- **Risk Reduction:** Highly effective in eliminating unauthorized access but requires coordination with affected users.
- **Example:** Resetting passwords for all compromised accounts and enabling MFA to prevent unauthorized access.

Developing and Executing a Containment and Eradication Plan

1. Assess the Incident:

- **Identify Scope:** Determine which systems, data, and users are affected.
- **Determine Severity:** Assess the potential impact on business operations and data integrity.

Example:

- An organization identifies that a phishing attack has compromised several employee email accounts, leading to potential data leakage.

2. Select Appropriate Containment Strategies:

- **Isolate Affected Systems:** Disconnect compromised email accounts and isolate affected systems.
- **Block Malicious Traffic:** Block IP addresses and domains associated with the phishing attack.

Example:

- The incident response team isolates the compromised accounts and blocks malicious IP addresses to prevent further data leakage.

3. Execute Eradication Measures:

- **Remove Malware:** Use anti-malware tools to clean affected systems.
- **Apply Patches:** Patch any vulnerabilities that were exploited in the attack.
- **Revoke Unauthorized Access:** Change passwords and enable MFA for compromised accounts.

Example:

- The team cleans the affected systems of any malware, patches vulnerabilities in email servers, and resets passwords for compromised accounts, enabling MFA.

4. Document and Time-Stamp Actions:

- **Detailed Records:** Keep detailed records of all actions taken, including timestamps, responsible individuals, and tools used.
- **Chain of Custody:** Maintain a clear chain of custody for any evidence collected to support forensic analysis and potential legal action.

Example:

- The incident response team documents all steps taken to contain and eradicate the phishing attack, including timestamps of when accounts were isolated and passwords reset.

5. Post-Incident Review:

- **Lessons Learned:** Conduct a post-incident review to identify what worked well and what needs improvement.
- **Update Policies:** Update security policies and incident response plans based on the findings.
- **Continuous Improvement:** Implement continuous improvement processes to enhance future incident responses.

Example:

- After the incident, the organization reviews the response process, updates its phishing detection measures, and enhances user training programs to prevent future attacks.

Conclusion

Effective containment and eradication of information security incidents require a combination of strategies tailored to the specific characteristics and scope of the incident. Balancing the potential impact on business operations with the need to mitigate risks is crucial. Developing and executing a well-structured containment and eradication plan, along with thorough documentation and continuous improvement, ensures a resilient and responsive incident management capability. By adopting these approaches, organizations can minimize damage, prevent further compromise, and quickly restore normal operations.

Importance of Conducting Post-Incident Reviews and Root Cause Analysis

Post-incident reviews and root cause analysis are crucial components of an effective incident response process. These activities help organizations understand what happened during an incident, why it happened, and how similar incidents can be prevented in the future. The insights gained from these reviews drive continuous improvement in security practices and resilience against future threats.

Key Benefits:

1. **Identifying Lessons Learned:**
    - Provides a detailed understanding of what worked well and what did not during the incident response.
    - Helps refine incident response plans, processes, and procedures.
2. **Preventing Recurrences:**
    - Identifies the root causes of incidents to address underlying vulnerabilities and systemic issues.
    - Leads to the implementation of corrective actions to prevent similar incidents.
3. **Enhancing Security Posture:**
    - Improves overall security practices and resilience by learning from past incidents.
    - Increases organizational awareness and readiness for future incidents.
4. **Fostering Accountability and Transparency:**
    - Encourages a culture of accountability by documenting what happened and how it was handled.
    - Builds trust with stakeholders by demonstrating a commitment to continuous improvement.

Key Steps for Conducting Effective Post-Incident Reviews

1. Involve All Relevant Stakeholders:

- Include members from IT, security, legal, compliance, business units, and any other affected areas.
- Ensure that those who were directly involved in the incident response provide their insights and feedback.

2. Analyze Timeline and Event Data:

- Reconstruct the timeline of events leading up to, during, and after the incident.
- Use logs, monitoring data, and other records to get a comprehensive view of the incident's progression.

3. Identify Key Points and Decisions:

- Examine key decisions made during the incident response and their impact on the outcome.
- Assess whether established procedures were followed and if they were effective.

4. Conduct Root Cause Analysis:

- Utilize techniques like the "5 Whys" and fishbone diagrams to dig deeper into the incident's underlying causes.
- Focus on both technical and non-technical factors that contributed to the incident.

5. Document Findings and Recommendations:

- Clearly document the findings, including what happened, why it happened, and what was done in response.
- Provide actionable recommendations for preventing future incidents and improving response efforts.

6. Implement and Monitor Improvements:

- Ensure that recommended actions are implemented and tracked for completion.
- Continuously monitor the effectiveness of these improvements and make adjustments as necessary.

Best Practices for Post-Incident Reviews

1. **Timeliness:**
    - Conduct the review as soon as possible after the incident to ensure that details are fresh and accurately recalled.

2. **Objectivity:**
    - Maintain an objective and blame-free approach to encourage honest feedback and constructive criticism.
3. **Comprehensive Documentation:**
    - Document all aspects of the review thoroughly, including the timeline, analysis, findings, and recommendations.
4. **Actionable Recommendations:**
    - Ensure that recommendations are specific, actionable, and realistic, with clear ownership and deadlines.
5. **Continuous Improvement:**
    - Regularly review and update the incident response plan based on lessons learned from post-incident reviews.

Root Cause Analysis Techniques

1. The "5 Whys":

Purpose:

- A technique to drill down into the root cause of a problem by asking "Why?" repeatedly until the underlying issue is identified.

Steps:

1. Identify the problem.
2. Ask "Why?" the problem occurred and document the answer.
3. If the answer doesn't reveal the root cause, ask "Why?" again.
4. Repeat this process five times or until the root cause is identified.

Example:

- **Problem:** The company experienced a data breach.
- **Why 1:** Why did the breach occur? Because an employee clicked on a phishing email.
- **Why 2:** Why did the employee click on the phishing email? Because they did not recognize it as a phishing attempt.
- **Why 3:** Why didn't the employee recognize it as a phishing attempt? Because they were not trained to identify phishing emails.
- **Why 4:** Why weren't they trained? Because the company does not have a regular security training program.
- **Why 5:** Why doesn't the company have a regular security training program? Because there is no policy mandating regular security awareness training.

2. Fishbone Diagrams (Ishikawa Diagrams):

Purpose:

- A visual tool used to identify, explore, and display the possible causes of a specific problem.

Steps:

1. Define the problem and write it at the head of the fishbone.
2. Draw a horizontal line (the spine) and several diagonal lines (the bones) coming off it.
3. Label each bone with a category (e.g., People, Processes, Technology, Environment).
4. For each category, brainstorm possible causes and add them as smaller bones branching off.
5. Analyze the diagram to identify the most likely root causes.

Example:

- **Problem:** Data breach due to unauthorized access.
- **Categories:**
    - **People:** Lack of training, employee negligence.
    - **Processes:** Inadequate access controls, poor incident response procedures.
    - **Technology:** Unpatched software, weak passwords.
    - **Environment:** Physical security weaknesses, inadequate monitoring.

Example of a Post-Incident Review

Scenario: A financial institution suffered a ransomware attack, leading to the encryption of critical customer data.

Steps:

1. **Stakeholder Involvement:**
    - Included IT, security, legal, compliance, business continuity, and affected business units.
2. **Timeline and Event Data Analysis:**
    - Reconstructed the timeline from initial infection to detection and response.
    - Reviewed logs, network traffic, and endpoint data.
3. **Key Points and Decisions:**
    - Assessed decisions around initial containment, communication with affected customers, and interaction with the ransomware attackers.
4. **Root Cause Analysis Using "5 Whys":**
    - **Problem:** Critical customer data was encrypted by ransomware.
    - **Why 1:** Why was the data encrypted? Because ransomware was executed on the network.
    - **Why 2:** Why was the ransomware executed? Because an employee opened a malicious email attachment.
    - **Why 3:** Why did the employee open the attachment? Because they did not recognize it as malicious.
    - **Why 4:** Why didn't they recognize it? Because of inadequate phishing training.
    - **Why 5:** Why was the phishing training inadequate? Because the training program was not regularly updated with current threats.
5. **Documentation of Findings and Recommendations:**
    - Documented the root cause as inadequate and outdated training.
    - Recommended implementing a comprehensive and regularly updated security awareness training program, enhancing email filtering, and improving endpoint security measures.
6. **Implementation and Monitoring:**
    - Assigned ownership to the HR and IT departments to implement the training program.
    - Monitored phishing simulation results and training completion rates as key metrics.

Conclusion

Conducting post-incident reviews and root cause analysis is essential for identifying lessons learned and opportunities for improvement. Effective reviews involve all relevant stakeholders, analyze detailed timeline and event data, and document actionable findings and recommendations. Techniques like the "5 Whys" and fishbone diagrams help uncover the underlying factors that contributed to incidents. Regularly testing, updating, and improving incident response plans based on these reviews drive continuous improvement and enhance organizational resilience against future incidents.

Updating Incident Response Plans and Procedures

Process Overview: The process of updating incident response plans and procedures is critical to improving an organization's ability to handle future incidents effectively. This involves conducting thorough post-incident reviews, analyzing the evolving threat landscape, prioritizing improvements, and integrating these updates into the broader security program.

1. Conducting Post-Incident Reviews

Key Activities:

- **Debriefing:** Gather the incident response team and relevant stakeholders to discuss the incident.
- **Analysis:** Analyze the incident to identify what happened, how it was detected, how it was handled, and the outcomes.
- **Documentation:** Record all findings, including the root cause, response actions, and impact on the organization.

Example:

- After a ransomware attack, the incident response team holds a debriefing session to review the timeline of events, the effectiveness of the containment and eradication measures, and the overall impact on business operations.

2. Identifying Lessons Learned

Key Activities:

- **Strengths and Weaknesses:** Identify what worked well and what did not during the incident response.
- **Improvement Areas:** Highlight areas where processes, tools, or training could be improved.
- **External Factors:** Consider any external factors or new threat vectors that influenced the incident.

Example:

- The team identifies that the incident was detected late due to inadequate monitoring and that the response was delayed by unclear communication protocols.

3. Prioritizing Improvements

Key Activities:

- **Impact Assessment:** Evaluate the potential impact of each identified improvement on the overall security posture.
- **Feasibility Analysis:** Assess the feasibility of implementing each improvement, considering factors like cost, resources, and time.
- **Prioritization:** Prioritize improvements based on their impact and feasibility.

Example:

- Improvements such as enhancing monitoring capabilities and refining communication protocols are prioritized due to their high impact and relatively low implementation cost.

4. Implementing Improvements

Key Activities:

- **Action Plans:** Develop detailed action plans for implementing the prioritized improvements.
- **Resource Allocation:** Allocate necessary resources, including budget, personnel, and tools.
- **Timeline:** Establish a timeline for implementing the improvements.

Example:

- The organization allocates budget for a new SIEM system to enhance monitoring capabilities and schedules training sessions to improve communication protocols.

5. Communicating and Integrating Updates

Key Activities:

- **Communication:** Communicate the updates to all relevant stakeholders, including the incident response team, IT staff, and management.
- **Training:** Conduct training sessions to ensure everyone understands the new procedures and tools.
- **Documentation:** Update all relevant documentation, including the incident response plan, playbooks, and standard operating procedures (SOPs).

Example:

- The incident response manager conducts a training session on the new SIEM system and updates the incident response plan to reflect the refined communication protocols.

Using Metrics and KPIs to Track Effectiveness

1. Identifying Relevant Metrics and KPIs

Metrics:

- **Mean Time to Detect (MTTD):** The average time taken to detect an incident from its initial occurrence.

- **Mean Time to Respond (MTTR):** The average time taken to respond to an incident once detected.
- **Number of Incidents:** The total number of security incidents over a given period.
- **Incident Impact:** Measure the impact of incidents, such as downtime, financial loss, or data breaches.

KPIs:

- **Detection Rate:** The percentage of incidents detected by automated systems vs. reported by users.
- **Response Effectiveness:** The percentage of incidents successfully contained and eradicated without causing further damage.
- **Training Completion Rate:** The percentage of staff who have completed incident response training.

Example:

- After implementing the new SIEM system, the organization tracks the MTTD and MTTR to measure improvements in detection and response times.

2. Setting Baselines and Targets

Baseline:

- Establish baseline metrics using historical data from previous incidents to understand current performance levels.

Targets:

- Set realistic targets for each metric and KPI based on desired improvements and industry benchmarks.

Example:

- If the baseline MTTD is 4 hours, the organization sets a target to reduce it to 2 hours within the next six months.

3. Monitoring and Reporting

Key Activities:

- **Regular Reviews:** Conduct regular reviews of the metrics and KPIs to monitor progress and identify any deviations from targets.
- **Reporting:** Provide regular reports to senior management and other stakeholders, highlighting progress, challenges, and any further actions needed.

Example:

- The incident response manager provides a monthly report to the CIO, showing a reduction in MTTD and MTTR and highlighting areas where further improvements are needed.

4. Continuous Improvement

Key Activities:

- **Feedback Loop:** Establish a feedback loop where insights from monitoring and reporting inform further updates and improvements to the incident response plan.
- **Adaptation:** Continuously adapt to new threats and changes in the organizational environment.

Example:

- Based on the feedback, the organization updates its training program to focus more on emerging threats, such as advanced persistent threats (APTs).

Conclusion

Updating incident response plans and procedures based on lessons learned from post-incident reviews and the evolving threat landscape is essential for maintaining an effective security posture. By prioritizing improvements based on their potential impact and feasibility, ensuring clear communication and integration of updates, and using metrics and KPIs to track effectiveness, organizations can enhance their incident response capabilities. Continuous monitoring, reporting, and adaptation ensure that the incident response plan remains relevant and effective in mitigating future incidents.

Types of Preventive and Corrective Actions

To effectively reduce the risk and impact of future incidents, organizations can take various preventive and corrective actions. These actions include implementing new security controls, improving detection and monitoring capabilities, and providing additional training and awareness for employees. Prioritizing these actions based on their risk reduction potential and alignment with business objectives is crucial for maximizing their effectiveness and ensuring that resources are used efficiently.

Preventive Actions

1. Implementing New Security Controls:

- **Access Controls:** Restrict access to sensitive information and systems to authorized users only.
  - Example: Implement multi-factor authentication (MFA) to enhance the security of user logins.
- **Network Security:** Protect the network infrastructure from unauthorized access and attacks.
  - Example: Deploy firewalls, IDS/IPS, and VPNs to secure network traffic.
- **Endpoint Security:** Safeguard devices from malware and other threats.
  - Example: Use advanced endpoint protection solutions, such as EDR tools.
- **Data Encryption:** Protect data at rest and in transit to prevent unauthorized access.
  - Example: Encrypt sensitive data using strong encryption algorithms and key management practices.

2. Improving Detection and Monitoring Capabilities:

- **SIEM Systems:** Centralize log collection and analysis to detect suspicious activities.
  - Example: Implement a SIEM solution like Splunk or IBM QRadar to correlate and analyze security events in real-time.
- **Network Monitoring:** Continuously monitor network traffic for anomalies.
  - Example: Use network traffic analysis tools like Wireshark to identify unusual patterns.
- **Threat Intelligence:** Integrate threat intelligence feeds to stay updated on emerging threats.
  - Example: Subscribe to threat intelligence services like Recorded Future to receive timely updates on new vulnerabilities and attack vectors.

3. Providing Additional Training and Awareness for Employees:

- **Security Awareness Training:** Educate employees on recognizing and responding to security threats.
  - Example: Conduct regular phishing simulation exercises and training sessions.
- **Role-Specific Training:** Provide specialized training for employees with specific security responsibilities.
  - Example: Train IT staff on secure coding practices and incident response procedures.
- **Policy and Procedure Education:** Ensure employees are aware of and understand security policies and procedures.
  - Example: Regularly update and distribute the organization's security policy manual.

Corrective Actions

1. Incident Response Improvements:

- **Post-Incident Reviews:** Conduct thorough post-incident reviews to identify areas for improvement.
  - Example: After a data breach, review the incident response actions and update the response plan based on lessons learned.
- **Enhanced Incident Response Tools:** Invest in tools that improve incident response capabilities.
  - Example: Deploy automated incident response tools to streamline containment and remediation processes.

2. Patch Management:

- **Regular Updates:** Ensure that all systems and applications are regularly updated with the latest security patches.
  - Example: Implement a patch management solution to automate the deployment of patches.
- **Vulnerability Management:** Continuously scan for and address vulnerabilities.

    - Example: Use vulnerability management tools like Qualys or Nessus to identify and remediate vulnerabilities.

3. Policy and Procedure Enhancements:

- **Policy Updates:** Regularly review and update security policies to address emerging threats.
    - Example: Update the data protection policy to include new regulatory requirements and best practices.
- **Procedure Improvements:** Refine procedures based on feedback and lessons learned from incidents.
    - Example: Enhance backup and recovery procedures to ensure faster restoration of services after a disruption.

Importance of Prioritizing Actions

1. Risk Reduction Potential:

- Prioritize actions that significantly reduce the likelihood or impact of security incidents.
- Example: Implementing MFA can drastically reduce the risk of unauthorized access, making it a high-priority action.

2. Alignment with Business Objectives:

- Ensure that security actions align with the organization's strategic goals and business objectives.
- Example: If maintaining customer trust is a key objective, prioritize actions that protect customer data and enhance transparency.

3. Cost-Benefit Analysis:

- Evaluate the cost and benefits of each action to ensure efficient use of resources.
- Example: Compare the cost of deploying a new SIEM system with the potential savings from preventing data breaches.

Developing and Executing a Comprehensive Prevention and Correction Plan

1. Assessment and Planning:

- **Identify Risks:** Conduct a thorough risk assessment to identify potential threats and vulnerabilities.
- **Define Objectives:** Set clear objectives for risk reduction and incident prevention.
- **Develop Action Plan:** Create a detailed action plan outlining preventive and corrective measures, responsibilities, and timelines.

2. Implementation:

- **Resource Allocation:** Allocate necessary resources (budget, personnel, tools) for implementing the plan.
- **Execution:** Implement the preventive and corrective actions as per the plan.
- **Monitoring:** Continuously monitor the implementation process to ensure it stays on track and addresses the identified risks.

3. Evaluation and Adjustment:

- **Measure Effectiveness:** Use metrics and KPIs to measure the effectiveness of the implemented actions.
- **Adjust Plan:** Adjust the plan based on the results of the evaluation and any new threats or vulnerabilities identified.
- **Continuous Improvement:** Foster a culture of continuous improvement by regularly reviewing and updating the prevention and correction plan.

Example: Comprehensive Prevention and Correction Plan

Scenario: A mid-sized e-commerce company aims to enhance its security posture after experiencing a data breach.

Assessment and Planning:

- **Risk Assessment:** Identify key risks such as unauthorized access, phishing attacks, and data breaches.
- **Objectives:** Reduce the number of security incidents by 50% in the next year and improve incident response times.
- **Action Plan:**

    - Implement MFA for all user accounts (Preventive).
    - Deploy a new SIEM system for improved detection and monitoring (Preventive).
    - Conduct quarterly security awareness training for employees (Preventive).
    - Update and enforce the data protection policy (Corrective).
    - Enhance incident response procedures based on post-incident review findings (Corrective).

Implementation:

- Allocate budget for MFA deployment and SIEM system.
- Roll out MFA and configure the SIEM system.
- Schedule and conduct security awareness training sessions.
- Update data protection policy and distribute to all employees.
- Revise incident response procedures and conduct drills.

Evaluation and Adjustment:

- Measure the number of security incidents and response times using the SIEM system.
- Gather feedback from employees on training effectiveness.
- Review incident response drills and make necessary adjustments.
- Adjust the action plan based on evaluation results and emerging threats.

Conclusion

Implementing a combination of preventive and corrective actions is essential for reducing the risk and impact of future incidents. Prioritizing these actions based on their risk reduction potential and alignment with business objectives ensures efficient and effective resource use. Developing and executing a comprehensive prevention and correction plan involves assessing risks, defining objectives, implementing actions, and continuously evaluating and adjusting the plan. By following these steps and best practices, organizations can significantly enhance their security posture and resilience against future threats.

Concept of Continuous Improvement in Incident Management

Continuous Improvement: Continuous improvement is an ongoing effort to enhance the effectiveness, efficiency, and adaptability of an organization's incident management processes. It involves regularly reviewing and refining procedures, tools, and skills to respond to incidents more effectively over time.

Role in Incident Management

Ensuring Ongoing Effectiveness:

- **Adaptation to New Threats:** Continuously updating incident response plans to address emerging threats and vulnerabilities.
- **Improvement of Response Capabilities:** Regularly refining skills, tools, and procedures to enhance the speed and quality of incident response.

Ensuring Ongoing Efficiency:

- **Resource Optimization:** Streamlining processes to make better use of resources and minimize waste.
- **Reduction of Response Times:** Implementing changes that help detect, contain, and eradicate incidents more quickly.

Key Principles and Practices of Continuous Improvement

1. Setting Measurable Goals:

Principle:

- Establish clear, quantifiable objectives to gauge progress and success.

Practice:

- Define specific, measurable, achievable, relevant, and time-bound (SMART) goals for various aspects of incident response, such as reducing mean time to detect (MTTD) or mean time to respond (MTTR).

Example:

- Set a goal to reduce MTTD from 4 hours to 2 hours within six months.

2. Collecting and Analyzing Performance Data:
Principle:

- Use data to inform decision-making and identify areas for improvement.

Practice:

- Collect data on key performance indicators (KPIs) such as incident detection rates, response times, and the number of incidents successfully resolved.

Example:

- Regularly review incident logs, response times, and post-incident reports to identify patterns and areas needing improvement.

3. Implementing Incremental Changes and Feedback Loops:
Principle:

- Make small, manageable changes based on data analysis and continuously evaluate their impact.

Practice:

- Implement changes incrementally and establish feedback loops to monitor their effectiveness and make further adjustments as needed.

Example:

- Introduce a new training module on phishing detection, collect feedback on its effectiveness, and refine the training based on employee performance in simulated phishing tests.

Applying Continuous Improvement Methodologies

Lean Methodology:
Principle:

- Focus on value creation by eliminating waste and optimizing processes.

Practice:

- Map out incident response processes to identify and eliminate steps that do not add value, thereby streamlining operations and improving efficiency.

Example:

- Use value stream mapping to identify bottlenecks in the incident detection process, such as delays in log analysis, and implement automated log analysis tools to speed up detection.

Six Sigma Methodology:
Principle:

- Use data-driven techniques to improve processes by reducing variability and defects.

Practice:

- Apply the DMAIC (Define, Measure, Analyze, Improve, Control) framework to systematically improve incident response processes.

Example:

- **Define:** Identify a recurring issue, such as delays in incident containment.
- **Measure:** Collect data on containment times for different types of incidents.
- **Analyze:** Use statistical analysis to determine the root causes of delays.
- **Improve:** Implement targeted improvements, such as enhanced training for containment procedures or better containment tools.
- **Control:** Monitor containment times post-implementation to ensure sustained improvements.

Examples of Applying Continuous Improvement

Example 1: Optimizing Incident Detection

Goal:

- Reduce MTTD from 4 hours to 2 hours.

Actions:

- Implement real-time monitoring tools to provide immediate alerts.

- Enhance threat intelligence integration to improve alert accuracy.
- Conduct regular training sessions for analysts on recognizing early signs of incidents.

Feedback Loop:

- Continuously monitor MTTD and collect feedback from analysts on the effectiveness of new tools and training.
- Make further adjustments based on performance data and feedback.

Outcome:

- Achieved a reduction in MTTD to 2 hours, improving overall incident response efficiency.

Example 2: Improving Incident Containment

Goal:

- Reduce the time to contain ransomware attacks from 1 hour to 30 minutes.

Actions:

- Deploy automated containment tools that can isolate infected systems quickly.
- Train the incident response team on using these tools effectively.
- Conduct live drills to practice rapid containment scenarios.

Feedback Loop:

- Review containment times after each incident and drill, gathering insights on what worked and what didn't.
- Adjust training and tool configurations based on these insights.

Outcome:

- Successfully reduced containment time for ransomware attacks to 30 minutes, minimizing the impact of such incidents.

Example 3: Enhancing Incident Communication

Goal:

- Improve communication efficiency during incidents to reduce confusion and delays.

Actions:

- Implement a standardized communication protocol and platform for incident response.
- Train all stakeholders on the new communication procedures.
- Conduct regular communication drills to reinforce the protocols.

Feedback Loop:

- Collect feedback after each incident and drill to identify communication gaps and areas for improvement.
- Refine the communication protocols and provide additional training as needed.

Outcome:

- Achieved clearer and more efficient communication during incidents, leading to faster and more coordinated responses.

Conclusion

Continuous improvement is essential for maintaining the effectiveness and efficiency of an organization's incident management processes. By setting measurable goals, collecting and analyzing performance data, and implementing incremental changes with feedback loops, organizations can continually refine their incident response capabilities. Applying methodologies like Lean and Six Sigma helps optimize processes, reduce waste, and improve outcomes. Through ongoing evaluation and adaptation, organizations can stay ahead of evolving threats and ensure a robust incident management framework.

Importance of Clear and Effective Incident Notification and Escalation Protocols

Establishing clear and effective incident notification and escalation protocols is crucial for ensuring timely and coordinated responses to security incidents. These protocols help ensure that all relevant stakeholders are informed and engaged quickly, enabling prompt action to mitigate the impact of the incident. Effective notification and escalation protocols also help maintain transparency, compliance, and trust among stakeholders.

Key Elements of an Incident Notification Protocol

1. Criteria for Triggering Notifications:

- **Severity Levels:** Define the severity levels (e.g., low, medium, high, critical) based on the impact and urgency of the incident.
  - Example: A data breach involving sensitive customer information might be classified as a critical incident.
- **Types of Incidents:** Specify the types of incidents that trigger notifications (e.g., data breaches, DDoS attacks, malware infections).
  - Example: Any unauthorized access to critical systems triggers an immediate notification.
- **Thresholds:** Set thresholds for each severity level to determine when notifications should be sent.
  - Example: A certain number of failed login attempts within a short period might trigger a notification.

2. Methods and Channels for Communication:

- **Notification Methods:** Use multiple methods to ensure reliable and timely delivery (e.g., email, SMS, phone calls, messaging apps).
  - Example: Send email alerts for low-severity incidents and SMS for high-severity incidents.
- **Channels:** Establish communication channels for different audiences (e.g., internal teams, external stakeholders, regulatory bodies).
  - Example: Use a dedicated incident response chat channel for internal communication.
- **Templates:** Develop templates for notifications to ensure consistent and clear communication.
  - Example: Create templates for initial incident reports, status updates, and resolution notices.

3. Roles and Responsibilities:

- **Incident Response Team:** Clearly define the roles and responsibilities of incident response team members.
  - Example: The Incident Response Manager coordinates the overall response, while security analysts investigate the incident.
- **Stakeholder Engagement:** Identify key stakeholders who need to be informed and their respective roles.
  - Example: Legal and compliance teams are notified for incidents involving regulatory implications, while the PR team handles external communications.
- **Escalation Paths:** Establish clear escalation paths for different types of incidents and severity levels.
  - Example: A critical incident is escalated to senior management and the Board of Directors.

Example Incident Notification Protocol

Criteria for Triggering Notifications:

- **Low Severity:** Minor incidents with no immediate impact (e.g., single failed login attempt).
- **Medium Severity:** Incidents with potential impact (e.g., multiple failed login attempts, minor malware detection).
- **High Severity:** Incidents with significant impact (e.g., confirmed malware infection, unauthorized access to sensitive data).
- **Critical Severity:** Incidents with severe impact (e.g., data breach, system-wide compromise).

Methods and Channels for Communication:

- **Low Severity:** Email notification to IT and security teams.
- **Medium Severity:** Email and SMS to IT, security teams, and incident response manager.
- **High Severity:** Email, SMS, and phone call to IT, security teams, incident response manager, and department heads.
- **Critical Severity:** Email, SMS, phone call, and messaging app notification to all relevant stakeholders, including senior management, legal, compliance, and PR teams.

Roles and Responsibilities:

- **Incident Response Manager:** Coordinates the response, communicates with stakeholders, and oversees the investigation.
- **Security Analysts:** Investigate the incident, gather evidence, and implement mitigation measures.
- **IT Support:** Provides technical support, helps isolate affected systems, and restores services.
- **Legal and Compliance:** Ensures regulatory requirements are met and manages communication with regulatory bodies.
- **PR Team:** Manages external communications and public relations.

Using Automation and Orchestration Tools

1. Automation Tools:

- **SIEM Systems:** Automate the detection and initial analysis of incidents, triggering notifications based on predefined criteria.
  - Example: Splunk or IBM QRadar can automatically send alerts via email or SMS when specific events are detected.
- **Incident Response Platforms:** Automate the notification and escalation processes, ensuring consistent and timely communication.
  - Example: IBM Resilient or Palo Alto Networks Cortex XSOAR can automate workflows for incident notifications and escalations.

2. Orchestration Tools:

- **Playbooks:** Develop automated playbooks to standardize and streamline response actions, including notifications and escalations.
  - Example: A playbook for a suspected data breach might automatically trigger notifications to the incident response team, legal, and senior management.
- **Integration with Communication Tools:** Integrate orchestration tools with communication platforms (e.g., Slack, Microsoft Teams) to facilitate real-time collaboration.
  - Example: An incident response platform can automatically create a dedicated Slack channel and invite relevant stakeholders when an incident is detected.

Example of Automated Notification and Escalation Workflow:

1. **Detection:** A SIEM system detects multiple failed login attempts from an unusual IP address, classifying it as a high-severity incident.
2. **Initial Notification:** The SIEM system automatically sends an email and SMS alert to the IT and security teams.
3. **Escalation:** If the issue is not resolved within a specified time frame, the incident response platform escalates the notification to the incident response manager and department heads via email, SMS, and phone call.
4. **Communication Channel Creation:** The orchestration tool creates a dedicated Microsoft Teams channel for real-time collaboration and invites all relevant stakeholders.
5. **Status Updates:** The incident response platform sends automated status updates at regular intervals until the incident is resolved.
6. **Resolution Notification:** Once the incident is resolved, the platform sends a resolution notice to all stakeholders, documenting the incident and actions taken.

Conclusion

Clear and effective incident notification and escalation protocols are essential for timely and coordinated responses to security incidents. Key elements of an effective protocol include well-defined criteria for triggering notifications, reliable methods and channels for communication, and clearly defined roles and responsibilities for all stakeholders. Automation and orchestration tools can streamline and accelerate incident notifications and escalations, ensuring consistent and timely communication. By implementing these best practices, organizations can enhance their incident response capabilities and minimize the impact of security incidents.

Communication Needs and Preferences of Stakeholders During an Information Security Incident

Effective communication during an information security incident is crucial for managing the situation and maintaining trust. Different stakeholders have varying needs and preferences for information, and it is essential to tailor communication strategies accordingly.

Internal Stakeholders

1. Executives

Needs and Preferences:

- **High-Level Overview:** Require a concise, high-level summary of the incident, including potential business impact and response actions.
- **Regular Updates:** Prefer regular updates as the situation evolves, focusing on strategic implications and decision-making needs.
- **Actionable Information:** Need clear, actionable information to make informed decisions about resources, priorities, and public statements.

Example:

- Provide a summary of the incident's impact on critical business functions and outline the steps being taken to mitigate risks and restore operations.

2. Legal Counsel

Needs and Preferences:

- **Detailed Incident Data:** Require detailed information about the incident to assess legal implications and advise on compliance with regulations.
- **Documentation:** Need thorough documentation of the incident response actions to support potential legal proceedings.
- **Confidentiality:** Prefer secure communication channels to protect sensitive information.

Example:

- Share detailed logs and timelines of the incident response activities and discuss potential legal liabilities and compliance requirements.

3. IT and Security Teams

Needs and Preferences:

- **Technical Details:** Require detailed technical information about the incident to effectively respond and mitigate threats.
- **Coordination:** Need constant communication for coordinating response efforts and sharing real-time updates.
- **Actionable Insights:** Prefer specific instructions and actionable insights to guide remediation efforts.

Example:

- Provide in-depth analysis of the malware identified, including indicators of compromise (IOCs), and coordinate containment and eradication actions.

External Stakeholders

1. Regulators

Needs and Preferences:

- **Compliance Information:** Require information on how the incident affects compliance with relevant laws and regulations.
- **Incident Impact:** Need details on the incident's impact, affected data, and the organization's response measures.
- **Timely Reporting:** Prefer prompt notification and regular updates as new information becomes available.

Example:

- Submit a detailed incident report outlining the scope of the data breach, the types of data affected, and the measures being taken to mitigate and prevent further impact.

2. Customers

Needs and Preferences:

- **Transparency:** Require transparent and honest communication about the incident and its impact on their data and services.
- **Reassurance:** Need reassurance that the organization is taking appropriate steps to protect their data and prevent future incidents.
- **Support Information:** Prefer clear instructions on steps they should take to protect themselves, such as changing passwords or monitoring accounts.

Example:

- Send a notification to affected customers explaining the breach, what data was potentially exposed, and providing guidance on steps they should take to safeguard their information.

3. Media

Needs and Preferences:

- **Public Statement:** Require a public statement that outlines the incident, its impact, and the organization's response.
- **Consistent Messaging:** Need consistent and accurate messaging to prevent misinformation and maintain public trust.
- **Updates:** Prefer timely updates as the situation develops, especially if the incident has significant public interest.

Example:

- Release a press statement summarizing the incident, its impact, and the measures being taken to address it, while ensuring all media inquiries are directed to a designated spokesperson.

Importance of Pre-Approved Communication Templates and Scripts

Consistency and Accuracy:

- Ensures all stakeholders receive the same accurate and consistent information, reducing the risk of misinformation.
- Provides a structured approach to communication, helping to manage the narrative and maintain control over public perception.

Efficiency:

- Speeds up the communication process during an incident, as pre-approved templates and scripts can be quickly customized and deployed.
- Reduces the time needed to draft messages from scratch, allowing the incident response team to focus on resolving the issue.

Compliance:

- Ensures that communications meet legal and regulatory requirements, as templates and scripts can be pre-approved by legal counsel.
- Helps to document the communication process for post-incident reviews and compliance audits.

Examples of Tailoring Communication Strategies

1. Minor Security Incident (e.g., Phishing Attempt)

Executives:

- **Communication:** "A phishing attempt was detected and blocked. No data was compromised, and the incident is under control. Further details will be provided in the weekly update."
- **Focus:** Assurance of control and minimal impact.

Customers:

- **Communication:** "We detected and blocked a phishing attempt targeting our email systems. No customer data was compromised. Please remain vigilant and report any suspicious emails."
- **Focus:** Transparency and reassurance.

2. Major Data Breach (e.g., Sensitive Data Compromise)

Executives:

- **Communication:** "We have experienced a data breach involving sensitive customer information. An incident response team has been activated, and we are working with external experts to mitigate the impact. An emergency meeting is scheduled for 2 PM to discuss further actions."
- **Focus:** Detailed impact analysis and strategic response planning.

Legal Counsel:

- **Communication:** "A data breach involving sensitive information has occurred. Attached are detailed logs and timelines of our response. We need your guidance on legal implications and regulatory compliance."
- **Focus:** Detailed documentation and compliance strategy.

Regulators:

- **Communication:** "We have experienced a data breach affecting sensitive customer data. We are currently assessing the full impact and will provide a detailed report within 48 hours as per regulatory requirements."
- **Focus:** Timely reporting and compliance.

Customers:

- **Communication:** "We regret to inform you that a data breach has occurred, affecting your personal information. We are taking immediate steps to address the situation and enhance our security measures. Please follow the instructions provided to protect your information."
- **Focus:** Transparency, reassurance, and actionable guidance.

Media:

- **Communication:** "Our organization has identified a data breach affecting customer information. We are working diligently to mitigate the impact and protect our customers. A press conference is scheduled for 4 PM to provide more details."
- **Focus:** Public statement and scheduled updates.

Conclusion

Effective communication during an information security incident is crucial for managing the situation, maintaining trust, and ensuring compliance. By understanding the different needs and preferences of internal and external stakeholders, organizations can tailor their communication strategies to provide relevant, timely, and accurate information. Developing and maintaining pre-approved communication templates and scripts ensures consistency, efficiency, and compliance. Through clear and strategic communication, organizations can navigate incidents more effectively and protect their reputation and stakeholder relationships.

Role of Media and Public Relations Management in Information Security Incidents

Media and public relations management play a critical role in minimizing reputational damage and negative publicity associated with information security incidents. Effective communication can mitigate the impact on the organization's brand, maintain stakeholder trust, and manage public perception.

Key Principles and Best Practices for Effective Crisis Communication

1. **Transparency:**
   - **Importance:** Being open and honest about the incident helps build and maintain trust with stakeholders.
   - **Practice:** Provide accurate and timely information about the incident, its impact, and the steps being taken to address it.
   - **Example:** A company experiencing a data breach issues a press release detailing the nature of the breach, the affected systems, and the actions being taken to mitigate the impact.
2. **Empathy:**
   - **Importance:** Demonstrating understanding and concern for those affected by the incident helps humanize the organization and fosters goodwill.
   - **Practice:** Acknowledge the inconvenience or harm caused to stakeholders and express genuine regret.

- **Example:** In a public statement, the CEO of a company affected by a security breach personally apologizes to customers for the breach and reassures them of the company's commitment to protecting their data.

3. **Proactivity:**
    - **Importance:** Proactively managing communications can help control the narrative and prevent the spread of misinformation.
    - **Practice:** Communicate early and often, providing regular updates as the situation evolves.
    - **Example:** During an ongoing cyberattack, a company issues daily updates on its website and social media channels to keep stakeholders informed about the status of the response efforts.

Examples of Using Social Media and Other Channels

1. **Monitoring Public Sentiment:**
    - **Tools:** Use social media monitoring tools like Hootsuite, Brandwatch, or Sprout Social to track public sentiment and identify emerging issues.
    - **Practice:** Monitor mentions of the company, incident, and related keywords to gauge public reaction and address concerns promptly.
    - **Example:** After a data breach, a company monitors social media for customer complaints and questions, responding promptly to reassure affected individuals and provide additional information.
2. **Responding to Misinformation:**
    - **Proactive Response:** Quickly address and correct any misinformation or rumors circulating about the incident.
    - **Example:** A company identifies a false rumor on Twitter claiming that all customer data has been stolen. The company immediately issues a clarifying statement on its social media channels, providing accurate information about the extent of the breach and the data affected.
3. **Engaging with Stakeholders:**
    - **Two-Way Communication:** Use social media and other channels to engage with stakeholders, answer questions, and provide support.
    - **Example:** A company sets up a dedicated helpdesk on its website and a hotline for customers to call with questions about the incident, and actively engages with users on social media to address their concerns.

Importance of Coordination with Internal Stakeholders

1. **Consistency:**
    - **Importance:** Consistent messaging across all communication channels is crucial to maintain credibility and avoid confusion.
    - **Practice:** Ensure that all internal stakeholders, including the incident response team, legal, compliance, and PR, are aligned on the communication strategy and key messages.
    - **Example:** Before issuing a public statement, a company holds a coordination meeting with representatives from the incident response team, legal, and PR to review and approve the messaging.
2. **Alignment:**
    - **Importance:** Aligning media and public relations efforts with the overall incident response strategy ensures that communications support the technical and operational response.
    - **Practice:** Integrate PR and media management into the incident response plan, and include PR representatives in incident response meetings.
    - **Example:** During a cybersecurity incident, the incident response manager includes the PR team in regular briefings to ensure they have up-to-date information to share with the public.
3. **Timely Information Sharing:**
    - **Importance:** Timely and accurate information sharing within the organization helps ensure that all stakeholders are informed and prepared to respond.

- **Practice:** Establish clear protocols for internal communication during an incident, including regular updates and information sharing.
- **Example:** A company sets up a secure internal communication channel for real-time updates from the incident response team, which the PR team uses to prepare timely public updates.

Best Practices for Crisis Communication

1. **Develop a Crisis Communication Plan:**
   - **Preparation:** Have a predefined crisis communication plan that outlines roles, responsibilities, and communication protocols for various types of incidents.
   - **Example:** The plan includes templates for press releases, social media posts, and FAQs, as well as contact information for key media outlets.
2. **Conduct Media Training:**
   - **Readiness:** Train key spokespeople on how to effectively communicate during a crisis, including how to handle difficult questions and maintain composure.
   - **Example:** The PR team conducts regular media training sessions for senior executives, including simulated press conferences and interview scenarios.
3. **Establish a Media Command Center:**
   - **Coordination:** Set up a centralized command center to manage media inquiries, monitor news coverage, and coordinate responses.
   - **Example:** During a major incident, the PR team operates from a designated command center equipped with monitoring tools, communication channels, and briefing materials.

Conclusion

Effective media and public relations management are essential for minimizing reputational damage and negative publicity during information security incidents. Key principles of crisis communication include transparency, empathy, and proactivity. Using social media and other channels to monitor and respond to public sentiment and misinformation helps maintain control of the narrative. Coordination with the incident response team and other internal stakeholders ensures consistency and alignment in messaging. By following these best practices, organizations can manage public perception, maintain stakeholder trust, and navigate the challenges of communicating during a crisis.

Incident Reporting and Compliance Requirements

Organizations must navigate a complex landscape of incident reporting and compliance requirements, including data breach notification laws, industry regulations, and contractual obligations. Compliance with these requirements is essential to avoid legal penalties, maintain stakeholder trust, and uphold organizational integrity.

Key Incident Reporting and Compliance Requirements

1. **Data Breach Notification Laws:**
   - **GDPR (General Data Protection Regulation):** Requires notification of data breaches to the relevant supervisory authority within 72 hours and communication to affected individuals if there is a high risk to their rights and freedoms.
   - **CCPA (California Consumer Privacy Act):** Requires businesses to notify California residents of data breaches involving their personal information.
   - **HIPAA (Health Insurance Portability and Accountability Act):** Mandates that covered entities notify affected individuals, the Secretary of Health and Human Services, and sometimes the media of breaches involving unsecured protected health information.
2. **Industry Regulations:**
   - **PCI DSS (Payment Card Industry Data Security Standard):** Requires organizations that handle payment card data to report security incidents to relevant stakeholders and maintain incident response and documentation procedures.

- SOX (Sarbanes-Oxley Act): Requires publicly traded companies to implement controls to ensure the integrity of financial reporting, including incident reporting related to data breaches that might impact financial data.

3. **Contractual Obligations:**
   - **Service Level Agreements (SLAs):** May require organizations to notify clients of incidents that affect the delivery of services or the confidentiality, integrity, and availability of client data.
   - **Vendor Contracts:** Often include clauses mandating the notification of incidents that impact the vendor's ability to deliver services securely.

Key Steps for Meeting Incident Reporting and Compliance Requirements

1. **Identifying Applicable Laws and Regulations:**
   - **Compliance Inventory:** Maintain an up-to-date inventory of all relevant laws, regulations, and contractual obligations that apply to the organization.
   - **Legal Consultation:** Consult with legal counsel to ensure a comprehensive understanding of applicable requirements.
2. **Assessing the Scope and Impact of the Incident:**
   - **Incident Categorization:** Categorize the incident based on severity, type, and the affected data.
   - **Impact Assessment:** Evaluate the potential impact on individuals, business operations, and compliance requirements.
   - **Data Inventory:** Identify the specific data involved in the incident, including personal, financial, and health information.
3. **Documenting and Submitting Required Reports and Notifications:**
   - **Documentation:** Maintain detailed records of the incident, including timeline, root cause analysis, impact assessment, and remediation efforts.
   - **Notification Templates:** Develop standardized templates for notifying regulatory authorities, affected individuals, and other stakeholders.
   - **Submission:** Ensure timely submission of reports and notifications in accordance with legal and contractual deadlines.

Best Practices for Meeting Compliance Requirements

1. **Establish an Incident Response Team (IRT):**
   - **Roles and Responsibilities:** Clearly define roles and responsibilities within the IRT, including legal, compliance, IT, and PR representatives.
   - **Training:** Provide regular training on incident response procedures and compliance requirements.
2. **Develop a Comprehensive Incident Response Plan:**
   - **Procedures:** Include detailed procedures for identifying, assessing, documenting, and reporting incidents.
   - **Communication Protocols:** Establish clear communication protocols for internal and external notifications.
3. **Leverage Incident Management Tools:**
   - **Automation:** Use incident management tools to automate compliance reporting and documentation processes.
   - **Integration:** Integrate these tools with existing systems (e.g., SIEM, ticketing systems) to streamline incident response and reporting.

Examples of Using Incident Management Tools

1. Incident Management Platforms:

- **ServiceNow:** Provides comprehensive incident management capabilities, including automated workflows for incident reporting, documentation, and compliance tracking.
- **Splunk Phantom:** Offers automation and orchestration of incident response processes, including the generation of compliance reports and notifications.

2. Compliance Reporting Automation:

- **Templates and Workflows:** Predefine templates and workflows for compliance reporting within the incident management tool.
- **Real-time Reporting:** Enable real-time reporting and updates to ensure timely submission of notifications to regulatory authorities and stakeholders.

Example Workflow Using ServiceNow:

1. **Incident Detection:** An incident is detected and logged in the ServiceNow platform.
2. **Classification and Categorization:** The incident is classified based on severity and type, triggering predefined workflows for compliance reporting.
3. **Impact Assessment:** The tool assists in performing an impact assessment, identifying affected data and systems.
4. **Automated Notifications:** Based on the impact assessment, ServiceNow automatically generates and sends notifications to relevant regulatory authorities, affected individuals, and internal stakeholders using predefined templates.
5. **Documentation:** All actions taken during the incident response are documented within the platform, creating an audit trail for compliance purposes.
6. **Post-Incident Review:** After resolution, a post-incident review is conducted, and lessons learned are documented for continuous improvement.

Conclusion

Meeting incident reporting and compliance requirements is essential for maintaining legal and regulatory compliance, protecting the organization's reputation, and ensuring transparency with stakeholders. Key steps include identifying applicable laws and regulations, assessing the scope and impact of incidents, and documenting and submitting required reports and notifications. Leveraging incident management tools and automation can streamline these processes, ensuring timely and accurate compliance reporting. By following best practices and using integrated tools, organizations can effectively manage incident reporting and compliance, minimizing the risk of non-compliance and associated penalties.

Case Study 1: Equifax Data Breach (2017)

Key Events:

- **Incident:** In September 2017, Equifax, one of the largest credit reporting agencies, announced a data breach that exposed personal information of approximately 147 million people.
- **Cause:** The breach was due to a vulnerability in the Apache Struts web application framework, which had a patch available but was not applied in a timely manner.
- **Discovery:** The breach was discovered by Equifax in July 2017, but it took six weeks to publicly disclose it.

Challenges:

- **Delayed Patch:** Failure to promptly apply the available patch for the Apache Struts vulnerability.
- **Poor Communication:** Delayed public disclosure and poor communication with affected individuals, leading to confusion and distrust.
- **Data Sensitivity:** The breach involved highly sensitive personal information, including Social Security numbers, birth dates, and addresses.

Outcomes:

- **Financial Losses:** Equifax faced significant financial costs, including $700 million in settlements and fines.
- **Reputational Damage:** The breach severely damaged Equifax's reputation and trust with consumers.
- **Regulatory Penalties:** Equifax faced regulatory scrutiny and penalties for failing to protect consumer data adequately.

Lessons Learned and Best Practices:

- **Timely Patching:** Organizations must prioritize the timely application of security patches to prevent exploitation of known vulnerabilities.

- **Effective Communication:** Clear and prompt communication with affected individuals is crucial in maintaining trust and managing the fallout from a breach.
- **Incident Preparedness:** Regularly update and test incident response plans to ensure quick and effective responses to breaches.

Case Study 2: Target Data Breach (2013)

Key Events:

- **Incident:** In December 2013, Target announced a data breach that affected 40 million credit and debit card accounts, and exposed personal information of up to 70 million customers.
- **Cause:** The breach was traced back to compromised credentials from a third-party HVAC vendor, which allowed attackers to infiltrate Target's network and install malware on point-of-sale (POS) systems.
- **Discovery:** The breach was discovered by Target's security team after being alerted by a third-party monitoring service.

Challenges:

- **Third-Party Risk:** The breach originated from a third-party vendor, highlighting the risks associated with supply chain security.
- **Detection and Response:** Despite having advanced security tools, Target's security team initially missed the breach indicators.
- **Customer Impact:** The breach compromised financial and personal information of millions of customers, leading to widespread concern and distrust.

Outcomes:

- **Financial Losses:** Target incurred over $200 million in costs related to the breach, including legal fees, settlements, and credit monitoring services.
- **Reputational Damage:** The breach harmed Target's reputation and resulted in a loss of consumer confidence.
- **Regulatory Scrutiny:** Target faced investigations and penalties from regulatory bodies for failing to protect consumer data.

Lessons Learned and Best Practices:

- **Third-Party Management:** Implement robust security measures for third-party vendors, including regular security assessments and monitoring.
- **Proactive Monitoring:** Utilize advanced threat detection tools and ensure security teams are adequately trained to recognize and respond to alerts.
- **Comprehensive Incident Response:** Develop and test incident response plans that include protocols for dealing with third-party breaches and minimizing customer impact.

Case Study 3: Sony Pictures Entertainment Hack (2014)

Key Events:

- **Incident:** In November 2014, Sony Pictures Entertainment suffered a devastating cyberattack that led to the theft and public release of confidential information, including employee records, unreleased films, and private emails.
- **Cause:** The attack was attributed to a sophisticated hacking group, reportedly in retaliation for the release of a controversial film.
- **Discovery:** The attack was discovered when employees found their computers inoperative, with a message demanding compliance with the attackers' demands.

Challenges:

- **Severe Disruption:** The attack caused significant operational disruption, with Sony Pictures temporarily losing access to its systems.
- **Data Exposure:** Sensitive internal communications and personal information were exposed, causing embarrassment and legal issues.

- **Response Coordination:** Coordinating a response to a large-scale, public-facing attack posed significant challenges.

Outcomes:

- **Financial Impact:** Sony Pictures faced substantial financial losses from the operational disruption, data recovery efforts, and legal expenses.
- **Reputational Damage:** The public release of private communications caused lasting reputational harm and strained relationships.
- **Legal Consequences:** The exposure of employee data led to lawsuits and regulatory scrutiny.

Lessons Learned and Best Practices:

- **Incident Preparedness:** Ensure robust incident response plans are in place and regularly tested, including protocols for large-scale attacks.
- **Employee Training:** Conduct regular security awareness training to help employees recognize and report suspicious activities.
- **Communication Strategy:** Develop a comprehensive communication strategy to manage public relations during and after an incident.

Case Study 4: Maersk NotPetya Attack (2017)

Key Events:

- **Incident:** In June 2017, Maersk, a global shipping company, was hit by the NotPetya ransomware, which disrupted its IT systems and operations worldwide.
- **Cause:** The ransomware spread via a compromised update of a widely used accounting software in Ukraine, impacting organizations globally.
- **Discovery:** The attack quickly spread through Maersk's network, crippling its operations, including booking systems and terminal operations.

Challenges:

- **Widespread Disruption:** The attack affected Maersk's global operations, causing significant logistical challenges and financial losses.
- **Data Recovery:** Recovering data and restoring systems was a massive undertaking, requiring collaboration with industry partners and vendors.
- **Communication:** Managing communication with customers, partners, and stakeholders during the widespread disruption was critical.

Outcomes:

- **Operational Impact:** Maersk experienced major operational disruptions, with some systems offline for weeks, resulting in significant financial losses.
- **Recovery Efforts:** The company undertook a massive recovery effort, eventually restoring operations by reformatting and rebuilding thousands of systems.
- **Reputational Impact:** Despite the disruption, Maersk's transparent communication helped maintain customer trust.

Lessons Learned and Best Practices:

- **Resilient Infrastructure:** Implement network segmentation and robust backup strategies to minimize the impact of widespread attacks.
- **Incident Coordination:** Establish a clear incident response plan that includes coordination with external partners and vendors for recovery efforts.
- **Transparent Communication:** Maintain open and honest communication with stakeholders during incidents to manage expectations and maintain trust.

Conclusion

These case studies highlight the critical importance of effective incident management and communication in minimizing the impact of information security incidents. Poor incident management can lead to severe financial losses, reputational damage, and regulatory penalties. Conversely, well-prepared and well-executed incident response plans can significantly mitigate the damage and help organizations recover more quickly. By learning from these real-world examples, organizations can implement best practices such as timely patching, robust third-party management, proactive monitoring, comprehensive incident response planning, resilient infrastructure, and transparent communication to enhance their incident management capabilities.

Real-World Examples and Scenarios of Information Security Incidents

Below are detailed examples and scenarios covering a range of information security incidents. Each example includes the specific characteristics and challenges of the incident, and guidance on how to effectively manage it using the concepts and techniques discussed.

Example 1: Phishing Attack (Minor Incident)

Scenario: An employee at a small financial firm receives an email that appears to be from a trusted vendor. The email contains a link that, when clicked, prompts the employee to enter their login credentials. Realizing the mistake, the employee reports the incident to the IT department.

Characteristics and Challenges:

- **Phishing Email:** A deceptive email designed to steal credentials.
- **Human Error:** Employee interaction with the phishing link.
- **Potential Exposure:** Risk of compromised account and data access.

Guidance:

1. **Identify:**
    - **Detection:** Use email filtering and monitoring tools to detect phishing emails.
    - **Employee Reports:** Encourage employees to report suspicious emails promptly.
2. **Investigate:**
    - **Log Analysis:** Review email server and web server logs to identify the source and destination of the phishing email.
    - **Forensic Analysis:** Check the compromised account for unauthorized access or changes.
3. **Contain:**
    - **Account Suspension:** Temporarily suspend the affected account to prevent further unauthorized access.
    - **Password Reset:** Require the employee to reset their password and enable multi-factor authentication (MFA).
4. **Recover:**
    - **System Scan:** Perform a thorough scan of the affected employee's workstation for malware.
    - **Awareness Training:** Provide refresher training to the employee and broader team on recognizing phishing attempts.
5. **Post-Incident Review:**
    - **Incident Documentation:** Document the incident details, response actions, and lessons learned.
    - **Policy Update:** Update the email security policy and reinforce the importance of reporting suspicious emails.

Example 2: Ransomware Attack (Moderate Incident)

Scenario: A medium-sized healthcare organization experiences a ransomware attack that encrypts critical patient data. The attackers demand a ransom payment for the decryption key. The incident disrupts operations and threatens patient care.

Characteristics and Challenges:

- **Ransomware:** Malware that encrypts data and demands payment.
- **Operational Disruption:** Impact on healthcare services and patient care.
- **Data Encryption:** Loss of access to critical data.

Guidance:

1. **Identify:**

  - **Detection:** Use endpoint protection and monitoring tools to detect ransomware activity.
  - **Alerting:** Ensure that the SIEM system generates alerts for unusual file encryption activities.
2. **Investigate:**
  - **Log Analysis:** Analyze logs from infected systems to determine the point of entry and spread of the ransomware.
  - **Network Forensics:** Examine network traffic to identify communication with the attacker's command and control server.
3. **Contain:**
  - **Network Isolation:** Disconnect affected systems from the network to prevent further spread.
  - **Quarantine:** Isolate infected devices and servers for further analysis.
4. **Recover:**
  - **Data Restoration:** Restore data from secure backups that were not affected by the ransomware.
  - **System Rebuild:** Rebuild infected systems from clean images and verify their integrity.
5. **Post-Incident Review:**
  - **Root Cause Analysis:** Use the "5 Whys" technique to identify the root cause of the infection (e.g., unpatched vulnerabilities).
  - **Improvement Plan:** Implement additional security measures, such as enhanced endpoint protection and regular backup testing.

Example 3: Data Breach (Major Incident)

Scenario: A large e-commerce company discovers that attackers have gained unauthorized access to its database containing customer payment information. The breach affects millions of customers and attracts significant media attention.

Characteristics and Challenges:

- **Data Breach:** Unauthorized access to sensitive customer data.
- **Large Scale:** Significant number of affected customers.
- **Public Scrutiny:** High media attention and potential regulatory fines.

Guidance:

1. **Identify:**
  - **Detection:** Use database activity monitoring tools to detect unusual access patterns.
  - **Threat Intelligence:** Leverage threat intelligence feeds to stay informed about emerging threats targeting the industry.
2. **Investigate:**
  - **Forensic Analysis:** Conduct a thorough forensic analysis to determine how the attackers gained access, what data was accessed, and for how long the breach went undetected.
  - **Log Correlation:** Correlate logs from different systems to trace the attacker's movements and actions.
3. **Contain:**
  - **Access Revocation:** Revoke unauthorized access and reset passwords for affected accounts.
  - **Patch Vulnerabilities:** Identify and patch any vulnerabilities that were exploited by the attackers.
4. **Recover:**
  - **Data Validation:** Validate the integrity of remaining data and ensure no further unauthorized access is possible.
  - **Customer Notification:** Notify affected customers and provide guidance on steps they should take, such as monitoring their financial accounts.
5. **Post-Incident Review:**
  - **Compliance Reporting:** Fulfill regulatory reporting requirements (e.g., GDPR, CCPA) by notifying relevant authorities.
  - **Media Management:** Coordinate with the PR team to manage public statements and address media inquiries transparently.
  - **Security Enhancements:** Implement long-term security enhancements, such as stronger encryption and more rigorous access controls.

Example 4: Insider Threat (Crisis Incident)

Scenario: A disgruntled employee at a technology company deliberately sabotages critical systems, causing a major outage and data loss. The incident affects the company's ability to deliver services and leads to significant financial losses.

Characteristics and Challenges:

- **Insider Threat:** Malicious actions by an employee with authorized access.
- **Service Disruption:** Major impact on business operations and service delivery.
- **Data Loss:** Loss of critical data and potential intellectual property.

Guidance:

1. **Identify:**
    - **Detection:** Use user and entity behavior analytics (UEBA) to detect abnormal behavior and potential insider threats.
    - **Employee Reporting:** Encourage employees to report suspicious behavior among colleagues.
2. **Investigate:**
    - **Access Logs:** Review access logs to identify unauthorized actions taken by the employee.
    - **Forensic Analysis:** Perform forensic analysis on the employee's workstation to gather evidence of sabotage.
3. **Contain:**
    - **Access Termination:** Immediately revoke the employee's access to all systems and physical premises.
    - **System Isolation:** Isolate affected systems to prevent further damage.
4. **Recover:**
    - **Data Recovery:** Restore data from secure backups and verify the integrity of the restored data.
    - **Service Restoration:** Work to restore affected services as quickly as possible to minimize downtime.
5. **Post-Incident Review:**
    - **Root Cause Analysis:** Use a fishbone diagram to identify contributing factors, such as lack of monitoring or insufficient access controls.
    - **Policy Revision:** Revise access control and monitoring policies to prevent future insider threats.
    - **Employee Support:** Implement programs to support employee well-being and address potential grievances proactively.

Conclusion

These real-world examples illustrate the spectrum of information security incidents, from minor phishing attacks to major data breaches and insider threats. By applying the concepts and techniques discussed, organizations can effectively identify, investigate, contain, and recover from such incidents. Regularly practicing and refining incident response procedures through hands-on scenarios reinforces key learning points and ensures readiness for real-world incidents.

Challenges and Considerations in Managing Information Security Incidents with Third-Party Service Providers

Managing information security incidents involving third-party service providers presents unique challenges and requires careful coordination and clear communication. Here are some key challenges and considerations:

Unique Challenges

1. Shared Responsibility:

- **Challenge:** Determining the division of responsibilities between the organization and the third-party service provider.
- **Consideration:** Both parties must understand their roles in incident detection, response, and remediation.

2. Visibility and Control:

- **Challenge:** Limited visibility into the third-party's infrastructure and operations can hinder timely incident detection and response.

- **Consideration:** Establish clear data sharing and monitoring protocols to ensure sufficient visibility.

3. Communication:

- **Challenge:** Effective communication is critical but can be complicated by differing priorities, procedures, and communication channels.
- **Consideration:** Develop and maintain clear communication channels and protocols for incident response.

4. Compliance and Regulatory Requirements:

- **Challenge:** Ensuring that third-party providers adhere to relevant legal and regulatory requirements.
- **Consideration:** Include compliance requirements in contracts and regularly audit third-party compliance.

5. Dependency on Third-Party Actions:

- **Challenge:** Relying on the third party for certain actions, such as patching vulnerabilities or providing logs, can delay incident response.
- **Consideration:** Clearly define and enforce service level agreements (SLAs) to ensure timely cooperation and response.

Importance of Clear Roles, Responsibilities, and Communication Channels

1. Establishing Clear Roles and Responsibilities:

- **Clarity:** Clearly define the roles and responsibilities of both the organization and the third-party provider in the incident response plan.
- **Accountability:** Assign accountability for specific tasks to ensure prompt and effective action.
- **Example:** Specify which party is responsible for initial incident detection, containment, and communication with affected stakeholders.

2. Ensuring Aligned and Integrated Incident Response Plans:

- **Alignment:** Ensure that the incident response plans of the organization and the third-party provider are aligned and compatible.
- **Integration:** Integrate the third-party's incident response procedures with the organization's plan to create a cohesive response strategy.
- **Example:** Conduct joint reviews of incident response plans to identify and address any gaps or inconsistencies.

3. Developing Effective Communication Channels:

- **Protocols:** Establish clear communication protocols, including escalation paths and points of contact, to streamline coordination.
- **Regular Updates:** Ensure regular updates and information sharing during an incident to keep all parties informed.
- **Example:** Create a communication matrix outlining key contacts, roles, and escalation paths for different types of incidents.

Using SLAs, Incident Response Playbooks, and Joint Exercises

1. Service Level Agreements (SLAs):

Role:

- SLAs define the expected service levels and response times for third-party providers, ensuring accountability and timely action during incidents.

Key Components:

- **Response Time:** Define maximum response times for different types of incidents.
- **Reporting Requirements:** Specify the frequency and format of incident reports.
- **Remediation Actions:** Outline the required remediation actions and timelines.

Example:

- An SLA with a cloud vendor might include a commitment to notify the organization within one hour of detecting a security breach and to provide detailed incident reports every 24 hours until resolution.

2. Incident Response Playbooks:

Role:

- Incident response playbooks provide detailed, step-by-step procedures for handling specific types of incidents, ensuring consistent and coordinated responses.

Key Components:

- **Scenarios:** Include detailed scenarios covering different types of incidents, such as data breaches, DDoS attacks, and malware infections.
- **Roles and Responsibilities:** Clearly define the roles and responsibilities of both the organization and the third-party provider.
- **Actions:** Specify the actions to be taken at each stage of the incident response process, from detection to recovery.

Example:

- A playbook for a ransomware attack might include steps for isolating infected systems, notifying the third-party security provider, conducting forensic analysis, and restoring data from backups.

3. Joint Exercises:

Role:

- Joint exercises simulate real-world incidents, helping to test and refine the incident response plans and coordination between the organization and third-party providers.

Types of Exercises:

- **Tabletop Exercises:** Simulate scenarios in a discussion-based format to evaluate response plans and decision-making processes.
- **Live Drills:** Conduct full-scale simulations of incidents to test the practical execution of response procedures and coordination.

Example:

- Conducting a joint tabletop exercise involving the organization, its cloud vendor, and managed security service provider to simulate a data breach scenario and evaluate the effectiveness of communication, coordination, and response efforts.

Examples of Improving Collaboration and Coordination

1. Regular Meetings and Reviews:

- Schedule regular meetings with third-party providers to review SLAs, incident response plans, and recent incidents. Use these meetings to identify areas for improvement and ensure ongoing alignment.

Example:

- Quarterly reviews with a cloud provider to assess compliance with SLAs, discuss recent security incidents, and update incident response procedures as needed.

2. Collaborative Incident Response Teams:

- Establish joint incident response teams that include representatives from the organization and third-party providers. This ensures seamless coordination and communication during incidents.

Example:

- Creating a joint incident response team with members from the organization's IT and security teams, the managed security service provider, and the cloud vendor to ensure a unified response to security incidents.

3. Shared Monitoring and Alerting:

- Implement shared monitoring and alerting systems that provide both the organization and third-party providers with real-time visibility into security events and incidents.

Example:

- Using a shared SIEM system that collects and correlates security data from both the organization's network and the cloud provider's infrastructure, enabling rapid detection and response to incidents.

Conclusion

Managing information security incidents involving third-party service providers requires addressing unique challenges related to shared responsibilities, visibility, communication, and compliance. Establishing clear roles, responsibilities, and communication channels is essential for effective incident management. Utilizing service level agreements (SLAs), incident response playbooks, and joint exercises can significantly improve collaboration and coordination with third parties during incidents. By fostering strong partnerships and ensuring alignment between internal and external incident response plans, organizations can enhance their overall security posture and mitigate the impact of security incidents more effectively.

The Role of Threat Intelligence in Information Security

Threat intelligence plays a critical role in enhancing an organization's capability to prevent, detect, and respond to information security incidents. It involves the collection, analysis, and dissemination of information about potential and actual threats to an organization's information systems. Effective threat intelligence enables organizations to anticipate, recognize, and mitigate threats more proactively and effectively.

Types and Sources of Threat Intelligence

1. **Open-Source Threat Intelligence (OSINT):**
    - **Description:** Publicly available information gathered from sources such as forums, blogs, social media, and government reports.
    - **Benefits:**
        - Free or low-cost.
        - Wide range of information sources.
        - Can provide early warnings of emerging threats.
    - **Challenges:**
        - May lack reliability and accuracy.
        - Requires significant effort to validate and analyze.
        - Volume of data can be overwhelming.
2. **Commercial Threat Intelligence:**
    - **Description:** Proprietary information provided by security vendors, often including advanced analytics and expert insights.
    - **Benefits:**
        - High quality and reliability.
        - Comprehensive and regularly updated.
        - Includes expert analysis and context.
    - **Challenges:**
        - Can be expensive.
        - May require integration with existing security tools and processes.
        - Potential dependency on vendor-specific formats and platforms.
3. **Industry-Specific Threat Intelligence:**
    - **Description:** Intelligence shared within specific industries or sectors through Information Sharing and Analysis Centers (ISACs) or similar organizations.
    - **Benefits:**
        - Highly relevant to specific industry threats.
        - Facilitates collaboration and information sharing among peers.
        - Often includes sector-specific best practices and mitigation strategies.
    - **Challenges:**
        - May have limited availability depending on the industry.
        - Requires active participation and contribution from members.
        - Can be less comprehensive compared to commercial feeds.

Integrating Threat Intelligence into Incident Management

1. Using Indicators of Compromise (IOCs):

- **Description:** IOCs are pieces of data that indicate potential malicious activity within a network or system (e.g., IP addresses, file hashes, URLs).

- **Integration:**
    - **SIEM Systems:** Integrate IOCs into SIEM systems to automate detection and correlation of suspicious activities.
        - Example: Feeding IOCs from threat intelligence feeds into a SIEM like Splunk to generate alerts when a known malicious IP address is detected.
    - **Endpoint Protection:** Use IOCs in endpoint detection and response (EDR) tools to identify and mitigate threats on endpoints.
        - Example: Configuring an EDR tool like CrowdStrike Falcon to block known malicious file hashes.

2. Threat Actor Profiles:

- **Description:** Detailed information about threat actors, including their tactics, techniques, and procedures (TTPs), motives, and historical activity.
- **Integration:**
    - **Incident Response Planning:** Use threat actor profiles to inform incident response strategies and prioritize containment efforts.
        - Example: During an incident, leveraging a threat actor profile to anticipate their next moves and deploy appropriate countermeasures.
    - **Training and Simulations:** Incorporate threat actor profiles into security training and simulation exercises.
        - Example: Using a known ransomware group's TTPs to create a realistic incident response drill.

3. Enrichment and Contextualization:

- **Description:** Adding context to raw threat data to improve understanding and decision-making.
- **Integration:**
    - **Automated Enrichment:** Use threat intelligence platforms (TIPs) to automatically enrich alerts with relevant threat intelligence.
        - Example: A TIP like ThreatConnect enriches SIEM alerts with additional context, such as associated threat actors and TTPs.
    - **Manual Analysis:** Security analysts use threat intelligence to investigate and understand the scope and impact of incidents.
        - Example: During an investigation, an analyst references threat intelligence reports to identify the likely threat actor and attack vector.

Benefits and Challenges of Integrating Threat Intelligence

Benefits:

1. **Proactive Defense:**
    - Anticipate and mitigate threats before they materialize.
    - Example: Blocking IP addresses known for command-and-control (C2) activity based on threat intelligence.
2. **Enhanced Detection and Response:**
    - Improve detection accuracy and response speed.
    - Example: Automatically correlating IOCs with network traffic to detect breaches early.
3. **Contextual Decision Making:**
    - Make informed decisions with context-rich information.
    - Example: Using threat actor profiles to prioritize response actions based on the threat actor's known behaviors.

Challenges:

1. **Data Overload:**
    - Managing and analyzing large volumes of threat data can be overwhelming.

- Solution: Use automated tools and platforms to filter and prioritize relevant intelligence.

2. **Integration Complexity:**
   - Integrating threat intelligence into existing security tools and processes can be complex.
   - Solution: Choose interoperable tools and establish clear integration workflows.
3. **Maintaining Relevance:**
   - Ensuring that threat intelligence remains up-to-date and relevant to the organization.
   - Solution: Regularly update feeds and validate intelligence sources.

Real-World Examples

Example 1: Using IOCs to Identify and Prioritize Incidents

Scenario: A financial institution receives an alert from its SIEM system indicating unusual activity from a known malicious IP address associated with a phishing campaign.

Steps:

1. **Integration:** The SIEM system ingests IOCs from multiple threat intelligence feeds.
2. **Detection:** The SIEM correlates network traffic logs with IOCs and generates an alert for suspicious activity.
3. **Investigation:** Security analysts review the alert and confirm that the IP address is linked to a known phishing campaign.
4. **Containment:** Analysts block the IP address at the firewall and isolate affected systems to prevent further spread.
5. **Recovery:** Conduct a thorough investigation and remove any malicious artifacts.
6. **Post-Incident Review:** Update incident response plans with lessons learned and review threat intelligence sources for accuracy and relevance.

Example 2: Using Threat Actor Profiles to Inform Containment Strategies

Scenario: A healthcare organization detects a ransomware infection on several critical systems.

Steps:

1. **Profile Analysis:** The incident response team references threat actor profiles to identify the ransomware group and their TTPs.
2. **Containment Strategy:** Based on the threat actor's known behaviors, the team prioritizes disconnecting infected systems and preventing lateral movement.
3. **Communication:** Inform internal stakeholders and, if necessary, regulatory bodies using predefined templates.
4. **Eradication:** Use decryption tools or restore from backups, following the threat actor's known encryption techniques.
5. **Recovery:** Validate that systems are clean and restore normal operations.
6. **Post-Incident Review:** Document the incident, refine detection rules, and update response strategies to account for new intelligence.

Conclusion

Integrating threat intelligence into an organization's security operations significantly enhances its ability to prevent, detect, and respond to information security incidents. By leveraging different types of threat intelligence—open-source, commercial, and industry-specific—and incorporating IOCs and threat actor profiles into incident management processes, organizations can improve their situational awareness and response capabilities. Despite challenges such as data overload and integration complexity, the benefits of a proactive, informed security posture are invaluable in today's dynamic threat landscape.

Importance of Employee Training and Awareness

Employee training and awareness are critical components of an organization's information security strategy. Employees often represent the first line of defense against security threats, and their behavior can significantly impact the overall security posture. Effective training and awareness programs help prevent security incidents and ensure employees are prepared to respond appropriately when incidents occur.

Key Elements of an Effective Security Awareness Program

1. Regular Training Sessions:

Content:

- **Basic Security Practices:** Password management, secure use of email, and safe web browsing habits.
- **Incident Response:** How to recognize and report potential security incidents.
- **Role-Specific Training:** Tailored content for different roles within the organization, addressing specific risks and responsibilities.

Frequency:

- Conduct training sessions at regular intervals (e.g., quarterly or semi-annually) to reinforce security concepts and keep employees updated on new threats.

Example:

- An annual cybersecurity training session for all employees, supplemented by quarterly updates on emerging threats and best practices.

2. Phishing Simulations:

Purpose:

- **Education:** Teach employees to recognize and respond to phishing attempts.
- **Assessment:** Evaluate the effectiveness of the training program and identify employees who may need additional training.

Implementation:

- Conduct regular phishing simulations, varying the types of phishing emails to cover different tactics used by attackers.
- Provide immediate feedback to employees who fall for the simulations, including tips on how to spot phishing attempts.

Example:

- A simulated phishing campaign where employees receive fake emails that mimic common phishing tactics. Those who click on links receive instant feedback and educational materials.

3. Ongoing Communication and Reinforcement:

Methods:

- **Newsletters:** Regular security newsletters that highlight recent incidents, new threats, and tips for staying secure.
- **Posters and Signage:** Visual reminders placed in common areas to reinforce key security messages.
- **Intranet Portal:** A dedicated section on the company's intranet with resources, guidelines, and updates on security policies.

Example:

- Monthly security newsletters that include real-world examples of security breaches, tips for avoiding phishing, and updates on company policies.

Tailoring Training Content and Delivery Methods

1. Different Roles and Levels of Technical Expertise:

Executive Leadership:

- **Focus:** High-level understanding of security risks, business impact, and strategic decision-making.
- **Delivery:** Short, focused sessions and executive briefings.

Technical Staff:

- **Focus:** In-depth technical training on specific security tools, incident response procedures, and threat analysis.
- **Delivery:** Hands-on workshops, technical webinars, and certification programs.

General Employees:

- **Focus:** Basic security awareness, recognizing phishing attempts, and reporting suspicious activities.
- **Delivery:** Interactive online modules, in-person training sessions, and simulated exercises.

Example:

- A multi-tiered training program where executives attend strategy-focused briefings, technical staff participate in hands-on workshops, and general employees complete interactive e-learning modules.

2. Measuring the Effectiveness of Training:

Metrics:

Completion Rates:

- Track the percentage of employees who complete the required training sessions.

Example:

- 95% of employees completed the annual cybersecurity training module.

Test Scores:

- Use quizzes and assessments to measure understanding of key concepts.

Example:

- The average test score on a post-training assessment increased from 70% to 85%.

Behavior Change:

- Monitor changes in behavior, such as a reduction in the number of employees clicking on phishing links.

Example:

- After implementing regular phishing simulations, the click-through rate on phishing emails dropped from 15% to 5%.

Incident Reporting:

- Track the number of security incidents reported by employees.

Example:

- An increase in the number of reported phishing attempts indicates greater awareness and vigilance among employees.

Examples of Effective Training Programs

1. Comprehensive Onboarding Training:

- **Description:** New employees receive a thorough introduction to the company's security policies, procedures, and expectations as part of their onboarding process.
- **Content:** Covers password policies, acceptable use of company resources, recognizing phishing emails, and incident reporting protocols.

Example:

- A new hire at a financial institution completes a mandatory security training module during their first week, followed by a quiz to ensure understanding.

2. Role-Based Training:

- **Description:** Employees receive training tailored to their specific roles and responsibilities.
- **Content:** Technical staff receive in-depth training on system vulnerabilities and incident response, while sales staff learn about securing customer data and recognizing social engineering attacks.

Example:

- IT staff participate in a hands-on workshop on network security and incident response, while customer service representatives receive training on safeguarding customer information.

3. Continuous Learning and Reinforcement:

- **Description:** Ongoing education through regular updates, reminders, and simulated exercises.
- **Content:** Monthly newsletters, periodic phishing simulations, and access to an online portal with security resources.

Example:

- Employees at a healthcare organization receive monthly security newsletters and participate in quarterly phishing simulations, with immediate feedback and additional training for those who fall for the simulations.

Conclusion

Employee training and awareness are fundamental to preventing and responding to information security incidents. An effective security awareness program includes regular training sessions, phishing simulations, and ongoing communication and reinforcement. Tailoring training content and delivery methods to different roles and levels of technical expertise ensures that all employees are adequately prepared to recognize and respond to security threats. Measuring the effectiveness of training through metrics such as completion rates, test scores, behavior change, and incident reporting helps organizations continuously improve their security posture. By fostering a culture of security awareness, organizations can significantly reduce the risk of security incidents and enhance their overall resilience.

Practice Questions and Quizzes on Threat Intelligence and Incident Management

Multiple-Choice Questions

1. **What is the primary purpose of threat intelligence in an organization's security strategy?**
    - A. To monitor employee activity
    - B. To anticipate and mitigate potential threats
    - C. To enforce password policies
    - D. To manage IT resources

Answer: B. To anticipate and mitigate potential threats

Explanation: Threat intelligence provides insights into potential threats, allowing organizations to take proactive measures to mitigate risks and enhance their security posture.

2. **Which of the following is NOT a typical source of open-source threat intelligence (OSINT)?**
    - A. Government reports
    - B. Social media
    - C. Proprietary security vendor reports
    - D. Public forums

Answer: C. Proprietary security vendor reports

Explanation: Proprietary security vendor reports are typically part of commercial threat intelligence offerings, not open-source intelligence.

3. **In the context of incident management, what are Indicators of Compromise (IOCs)?**
    - A. Data encryption techniques
    - B. Pieces of data that indicate a potential security breach
    - C. Methods for improving employee productivity
    - D. Policies for secure data handling

Answer: B. Pieces of data that indicate a potential security breach

Explanation: IOCs are specific pieces of data, such as IP addresses, file hashes, and URLs, that indicate potential malicious activity within a network or system.

4. **Which tool is commonly used for network traffic capture and analysis during an incident investigation?**
    - A. Splunk
    - B. Wireshark
    - C. ServiceNow
    - D. CrowdStrike Falcon

Answer: B. Wireshark

Explanation: Wireshark is a widely used tool for capturing and analyzing network traffic, helping investigators identify malicious activities and network anomalies.

5. **What is a key benefit of integrating threat intelligence with a SIEM system?**
    - A. Automated policy enforcement
    - B. Enhanced detection of suspicious activities through correlation of IOCs
    - C. Simplified network configuration
    - D. Improved employee training programs

Answer: B. Enhanced detection of suspicious activities through correlation of IOCs

Explanation: Integrating threat intelligence with a SIEM system enhances detection capabilities by correlating IOCs with network traffic and system logs, enabling quicker identification of potential threats.

Scenario-Based Questions

1. **Scenario:** A financial institution has detected multiple failed login attempts from an unknown IP address within a short period.

Question: Describe the steps the incident response team should take to identify, investigate, and respond to this potential threat. Include how threat intelligence could be used in this scenario.

Answer:

- **Identify:** Use the SIEM system to detect the multiple failed login attempts.
- **Investigate:**
  - Review the IP address against threat intelligence feeds to determine if it is associated with known malicious activity.
  - Correlate the failed login attempts with other network and system logs to identify any related suspicious activities.
- **Respond:**
  - Temporarily block the IP address to prevent further attempts.
  - Notify the affected user(s) and enforce a password reset if necessary.
  - Implement additional security measures, such as MFA, to protect user accounts.
- **Threat Intelligence Usage:**
  - Use threat intelligence to identify whether the IP address is linked to a known threat actor or campaign.
  - Update detection rules and alert thresholds based on the intelligence gathered.

2. **Scenario:** An e-commerce company discovers that a large volume of customer data has been exfiltrated from its network.

Question: Outline the incident response steps, focusing on containment, eradication, and recovery. Explain how threat intelligence can assist in determining the scope and impact of the breach.

Answer:

- **Containment:**
  - Isolate affected systems to prevent further data exfiltration.
  - Disable compromised accounts and reset passwords.
- **Eradication:**
  - Identify and remove the malicious software or backdoors used in the breach.
  - Patch vulnerabilities that were exploited by the attackers.
- **Recovery:**
  - Restore data from backups and ensure integrity.
  - Monitor systems for any signs of residual malicious activity.
- **Threat Intelligence Usage:**
  - Analyze threat intelligence to understand the methods used by the attackers and identify other potential targets.
  - Use IOCs from threat intelligence to scan the network for signs of the attackers' presence.
  - Determine the likely motive and targets of the attackers to better assess the impact of the breach.

Open-Ended Questions

1. **Explain the importance of maintaining a clear chain of custody during a forensic investigation. Provide an example of how mishandling evidence could affect the outcome of an incident response.**

Answer: Maintaining a clear chain of custody ensures that all evidence collected during a forensic investigation is properly documented, preserved, and handled. This is crucial for ensuring the integrity and admissibility of the evidence in legal proceedings. Mishandling evidence, such as failing to document who accessed the evidence and when, could lead to questions about its integrity and potentially render it inadmissible in court. For example, if a disk image taken during an investigation is not properly documented and someone without authorization accesses it, any findings from that disk image could be challenged, undermining the entire investigation.

2. **Discuss how automated incident response tools can enhance an organization's ability to manage security incidents. Provide specific examples of how these tools can be used to streamline and accelerate incident notifications and escalations.**

Answer: Automated incident response tools enhance an organization's ability to manage security incidents by streamlining and accelerating key processes, reducing the time required to detect, contain, and remediate threats. Examples include:

- **Automated Detection and Alerting:** SIEM systems can automatically correlate logs and IOCs, generating alerts when suspicious activities are detected.
- **Workflow Automation:** Tools like ServiceNow or IBM Resilient can automate incident response workflows, ensuring that notifications and escalations occur promptly according to predefined criteria.
- **Incident Orchestration:** Platforms like Splunk Phantom can automate the execution of response actions, such as isolating affected systems, blocking IP addresses, and notifying stakeholders via integrated communication channels (e.g., email, SMS, Slack). These tools enable faster and more efficient incident response, minimizing the potential impact of security incidents.

Detailed Explanations and References

Each question and answer is designed to reinforce key learning points and provide practical applications of the concepts covered. Here are some additional references to guide further study and exploration:

- **Threat Intelligence:**
  - "The Threat Intelligence Handbook" by Recorded Future.
  - SANS Institute's "Introduction to Cyber Threat Intelligence."
- **Incident Response:**
  - NIST Special Publication 800-61r2, "Computer Security Incident Handling Guide."
  - "Incident Response & Computer Forensics" by Jason Luttgens, Matthew Pepe, and Kevin Mandia.
- **Forensic Investigation:**
  - "Practical Digital Forensics" by Richard Boddington.
  - "Digital Forensics and Incident Response" by Gerard Johansen.

By completing these practice questions and quizzes, readers can solidify their understanding of threat intelligence and incident management, preparing them to apply these concepts effectively in real-world scenarios.

Role of Incident Management Metrics and Key Performance Indicators (KPIs)

Incident management metrics and KPIs are essential for measuring and improving the effectiveness and efficiency of an organization's incident response capabilities. They provide quantifiable data that can be analyzed to identify strengths, weaknesses, and opportunities for improvement in the incident management process. By systematically collecting, analyzing, and reporting these metrics, organizations can drive continuous improvement, ensure accountability, and demonstrate the value of incident management to stakeholders.

Common Metrics and KPIs for Incident Management

1. Mean Time to Detect (MTTD):

Definition:

- The average time taken to detect an incident from the moment it occurs.

Importance:

- Shorter MTTD indicates better monitoring and quicker identification of security issues, which is critical for minimizing potential damage.

Collection:

- Track the timestamp when an incident occurs and when it is first detected. Calculate the average detection time over a defined period.

Analysis:

- Compare MTTD across different types of incidents and over time to identify trends and areas for improvement.

Reporting:

- Report MTTD in regular security reports to stakeholders, highlighting progress and efforts to reduce detection time.

Example:

- If an organization detects incidents on average 2 hours after they occur, it can set a goal to reduce this to 1 hour by enhancing monitoring capabilities.

2. Mean Time to Respond (MTTR):

Definition:

- The average time taken to respond to an incident after it has been detected.

Importance:

- Shorter MTTR means quicker containment and remediation, reducing the overall impact of incidents.

Collection:

- Track the timestamp when an incident is detected and when response actions begin. Calculate the average response time over a defined period.

Analysis:

- Analyze MTTR to identify bottlenecks in the response process and assess the effectiveness of response strategies.

Reporting:

- Include MTTR in incident management reports to demonstrate the efficiency of the response process and identify areas for improvement.

Example:

- An organization with an MTTR of 3 hours aims to reduce this to 1 hour by streamlining its incident response procedures and enhancing team coordination.

3. Incident Resolution Rate:

Definition:

- The percentage of incidents that are successfully resolved within a specified time frame.

Importance:

- A high resolution rate indicates effective incident management and the ability to restore normal operations quickly.

Collection:

- Track the number of incidents and the number resolved within the target time frame. Calculate the resolution rate as a percentage.

Analysis:

- Evaluate the resolution rate across different incident types and time periods to identify trends and areas for improvement.

Reporting:

- Report resolution rates to stakeholders, showing the organization's ability to handle incidents effectively.

Example:

- If an organization resolves 80% of incidents within 24 hours, it can set a goal to increase this to 90% by improving response processes and resource allocation.

Collecting, Analyzing, and Reporting Metrics

1. Collection:

Tools and Systems:

- Utilize Security Information and Event Management (SIEM) systems, incident management software, and other monitoring tools to collect data on incident metrics.

Data Points:

- Collect data on incident occurrence times, detection times, response initiation times, resolution times, and other relevant details.

2. Analysis:

Trend Analysis:

- Analyze the collected data to identify trends over time, such as improvements or declines in MTTD and MTTR.

Root Cause Analysis:

- Conduct root cause analysis on incidents to understand underlying issues and identify areas for process improvement.

Benchmarking:

- Compare metrics against industry benchmarks and internal goals to assess performance and identify opportunities for improvement.

3. Reporting:

Regular Reports:

- Produce regular reports (e.g., monthly, quarterly) that summarize key metrics and highlight significant findings and trends.

Stakeholder Communication:

- Tailor reports to different stakeholders, providing high-level summaries for executives and detailed analysis for technical teams.

Visualization:

- Use visual aids such as charts, graphs, and dashboards to make the data easily understandable and actionable.

Continuous Improvement:

- Use the insights gained from the analysis to inform continuous improvement initiatives, such as refining detection techniques, optimizing response processes, and enhancing training programs.

Example of Using Metrics to Drive Continuous Improvement

Scenario:

- An organization has identified that its MTTD is higher than the industry benchmark, leading to delayed responses and increased impact from security incidents.

Actions:

- **Identify Gaps:** Conduct a thorough review of the current monitoring systems and processes to identify gaps and areas for enhancement.
- **Enhance Monitoring:** Implement advanced monitoring tools and threat intelligence feeds to improve the detection capabilities.
- **Training:** Provide additional training for the security operations team to recognize and respond to potential threats more quickly.
- **Automate Alerts:** Set up automated alerts for high-priority incidents to ensure immediate attention from the response team.

Results:

- After implementing these improvements, the organization tracks the new MTTD and finds it has decreased by 50%. This reduction leads to faster incident containment and less overall impact on the organization.

Reporting:

- The improved MTTD and other metrics are included in the next quarterly report to stakeholders, demonstrating the tangible benefits of the continuous improvement efforts and justifying further investments in security capabilities.

Conclusion

Incident management metrics and KPIs are vital tools for measuring and improving the effectiveness and efficiency of an organization's incident response capabilities. By systematically collecting, analyzing, and reporting on metrics such as MTTD, MTTR, and incident resolution rate, organizations can drive continuous improvement, ensure accountability, and demonstrate the value of their incident management efforts to stakeholders. Using these insights, organizations can refine their incident response strategies, enhance training programs, and optimize resource allocation to build a more resilient security posture.

Incident Response Orchestration and Automation

Incident response orchestration and automation involve using technology to streamline and enhance the processes involved in detecting, triaging, investigating, containing, and recovering from security incidents. This approach helps organizations improve the speed, consistency, and effectiveness of their incident response efforts by reducing manual tasks, standardizing workflows, and ensuring timely and coordinated responses.

Key Capabilities and Benefits

1. Workflow Automation:

- **Definition:** Automating repetitive and routine tasks within the incident response process.
- **Benefits:**
    - **Speed:** Accelerates response times by quickly executing predefined actions.
    - **Consistency:** Ensures that all incidents are handled using standardized procedures.
    - **Efficiency:** Frees up security analysts to focus on higher-value tasks.
- **Example:** Automatically isolating a compromised endpoint when malware is detected.

2. Case Management:

- **Definition:** Centralized management of incident details, actions taken, and communication.
- **Benefits:**
    - **Organization:** Keeps all incident-related information in one place.
    - **Collaboration:** Facilitates coordination among team members and stakeholders.
    - **Documentation:** Provides a complete record of the incident for compliance and post-incident review.
- **Example:** Using a platform to log all actions taken during a ransomware attack, from initial detection to final resolution.

3. Integration with Security Tools and Systems:

- **Definition:** Seamlessly connecting various security tools (e.g., SIEM, EDR, firewalls) to the orchestration platform.
- **Benefits:**
    - **Unified View:** Provides a comprehensive view of the security environment.
    - **Automation:** Enables automated responses based on correlated data from multiple sources.
    - **Efficiency:** Reduces the need for manual data aggregation and analysis.
- **Example:** Integrating a SIEM with an incident response platform to automatically trigger responses based on specific alerts.

Examples of Using Incident Response Orchestration and Automation Platforms

1. Detection and Triage:

- **Platform:** Splunk Phantom
- **Workflow:**
    1. **Integration:** Connects with SIEM to receive alerts.
    2. **Automated Triage:** Automatically prioritizes alerts based on predefined criteria (e.g., severity, asset value).
    3. **Notification:** Sends notifications to relevant stakeholders for high-priority incidents.
- **Benefit:** Quickly identifies and prioritizes the most critical threats, ensuring prompt attention.

2. Investigation:

- **Platform:** IBM Resilient
- **Workflow:**
    1. **Data Aggregation:** Automatically collects logs and contextual data from integrated security tools.
    2. **Analysis:** Uses machine learning to identify patterns and anomalies related to the incident.
    3. **Collaboration:** Enables analysts to collaborate within the platform, sharing insights and hypotheses.
- **Benefit:** Streamlines the investigation process, enabling faster and more accurate root cause analysis.

3. Containment:

- **Platform:** Palo Alto Networks Cortex XSOAR
- **Workflow:**
    1. **Detection:** Detects a malware infection via integrated EDR.
    2. **Automated Response:** Automatically isolates the infected endpoint from the network.
    3. **Validation:** Confirms isolation and notifies the incident response team.
- **Benefit:** Rapidly contains threats, minimizing the risk of lateral movement and further damage.

4. Recovery:

- **Platform:** ServiceNow Security Operations
- **Workflow:**
    1. **Task Assignment:** Assigns recovery tasks to relevant IT and security personnel.
    2. **Progress Tracking:** Tracks the progress of recovery efforts, providing real-time updates.
    3. **Post-Incident Review:** Automates the collection of data for post-incident analysis and reporting.
- **Benefit:** Ensures a coordinated recovery effort and comprehensive documentation for future reference.

Comprehensive Example Workflow

Scenario: A financial institution experiences a suspected phishing attack targeting its employees.

1. Detection:

- **Tool:** SIEM (Splunk)
- **Process:** Detects suspicious email activity and generates an alert.
- **Action:** Alert is sent to the orchestration platform (Splunk Phantom).

2. Triage:

- **Tool:** Splunk Phantom
- **Process:** Automatically triages the alert based on predefined criteria (e.g., high-priority due to potential data compromise).
- **Action:** Notifies the incident response team and creates a case.

3. Investigation:

- **Tool:** IBM Resilient
- **Process:** Aggregates data from the SIEM, email security, and endpoint protection tools.
- **Action:** Analysts review the collected data, identifying the source and scope of the phishing attempt.

4. Containment:

- **Tool:** Palo Alto Networks Cortex XSOAR
- **Process:** Detects compromised accounts and suspicious activity.
- **Action:** Automatically resets passwords for compromised accounts and blocks malicious IP addresses.

5. Recovery:

- **Tool:** ServiceNow Security Operations
- **Process:** Assigns tasks to IT to clean infected endpoints and restore affected systems.
- **Action:** Tracks the completion of recovery tasks and compiles a post-incident report.

6. Post-Incident Review:

- **Tool:** ServiceNow Security Operations

- **Process:** Automates the collection of all incident data and generates a report.
- **Action:** Schedules a review meeting to analyze the incident and update response strategies.

Conclusion

Incident response orchestration and automation significantly enhance the speed, consistency, and effectiveness of incident response processes. By leveraging workflow automation, case management, and integration with security tools, these platforms enable organizations to respond to incidents more quickly and efficiently. Examples such as automated triage, integrated investigations, rapid containment, and coordinated recovery demonstrate how these capabilities can streamline and optimize incident management processes. Implementing these solutions helps organizations stay ahead of threats and maintain a robust security posture.

Part V: CISM Exam Preparation:

CISM Exam Format Breakdown

1. Overview: The Certified Information Security Manager (CISM) exam is designed to assess the knowledge and skills required to manage, design, and oversee an enterprise's information security program. The exam is structured to test candidates on four domains crucial to information security management.

2. Exam Format:

- **Total Number of Questions:** 150 multiple-choice questions
- **Time Allocated:** 4 hours (240 minutes)
- **Question Distribution:** The questions are distributed across the four domains as follows:
    1. **Information Security Governance:** 24%
    2. **Information Risk Management:** 30%
    3. **Information Security Program Development and Management:** 27%
    4. **Information Security Incident Management:** 19%

3. Detailed Domain Breakdown:

Domain 1: Information Security Governance (24% - approximately 36 questions)

- Establish and maintain an information security governance framework.
- Develop and manage information security strategies.
- Oversee the information security governance processes and practices.

Domain 2: Information Risk Management (30% - approximately 45 questions)

- Identify and manage information security risks.
- Implement risk management frameworks and practices.
- Assess and mitigate threats and vulnerabilities.

Domain 3: Information Security Program Development and Management (27% - approximately 40 questions)

- Establish and manage the information security program.
- Align the program with business objectives and regulatory requirements.
- Implement security controls and practices.

Domain 4: Information Security Incident Management (19% - approximately 29 questions)

- Develop and maintain incident response plans.
- Coordinate and manage incident response activities.
- Conduct post-incident reviews and improve response capabilities.

4. Exam Administration:

- **Format:** The CISM exam is administered primarily through a computer-based testing (CBT) platform.
- **Testing Centers:** Available at designated testing centers worldwide, such as those operated by PSI.
- **Registration:** Candidates must register through ISACA's website and schedule their exam at an approved testing center.
- **Scoring:** The exam is scored on a scale of 200 to 800 points, with a passing score of 450.

5. Recent and Upcoming Changes:

- **Remote Proctoring:** Due to the COVID-19 pandemic, ISACA introduced the option for remote proctoring, allowing candidates to take the exam from home under strict supervision.
- **Exam Content Updates:** The CISM exam content is periodically updated to reflect changes in industry practices and emerging threats. The most recent update focused on integrating new trends and best practices in information security management.

6. Preparing for the Exam: Candidates are advised to:

- **Review the CISM Review Manual:** This comprehensive guide covers all four domains in depth.
- **Take Practice Exams:** Simulated exams can help familiarize candidates with the format and timing.
- **Join Study Groups:** Engaging with peers preparing for the exam can provide additional insights and support.

Conclusion

The CISM exam is a rigorous assessment of an individual's ability to manage and oversee information security programs. By understanding the exam format, question distribution, and administration process, candidates can better prepare and increase their chances of success. Staying informed about any changes to the exam structure or content is crucial for effective preparation.

Types of Questions on the CISM Exam

The CISM (Certified Information Security Manager) exam consists of various question types designed to assess candidates' knowledge and application of information security management concepts. The primary types of questions candidates can expect to encounter include multiple-choice, scenario-based, and case study questions.

1. Multiple-Choice Questions

Description:

- **Format:** Candidates are presented with a question and four answer options, from which they must select the correct or best answer.
- **Focus:** These questions test the candidate's knowledge of specific concepts, definitions, and principles related to information security management.

Example:

- **Question:** What is the primary purpose of an information security policy?
  - a) To define security roles and responsibilities
  - b) To specify technical configurations
  - c) To establish a framework for managing security risks
  - d) To outline disaster recovery procedures
- **Answer:** c) To establish a framework for managing security risks

Strategies:

- **Read Carefully:** Read the question and all answer choices thoroughly before selecting an answer.
- **Eliminate Wrong Answers:** Use the process of elimination to discard clearly incorrect answers, increasing the chances of choosing the correct one.
- **Focus on Keywords:** Pay attention to keywords and phrases in the question and answer choices that are central to the concept being tested.

2. Scenario-Based Questions

Description:

- **Format:** Candidates are given a scenario describing a specific situation or problem related to information security management. They must choose the best course of action or identify the most appropriate response based on the scenario.
- **Focus:** These questions assess the candidate's ability to apply theoretical knowledge to practical situations.

Example:

- **Question:** An organization has identified that its incident response plan is outdated and does not cover the latest types of cyber threats. As the CISM, what should be your first step in updating the plan?

- a) Conduct a business impact analysis
  - b) Review recent incident reports
  - c) Consult with external security experts
  - d) Schedule a meeting with the incident response team
- **Answer:** b) Review recent incident reports

Strategies:

- **Understand the Scenario:** Carefully read the scenario to fully understand the context and key issues.
- **Apply Knowledge:** Use your knowledge of best practices and principles to determine the most appropriate response.
- **Prioritize Actions:** Consider the logical sequence of actions and their impact on the situation described.

3. Case Study Questions

Description:

- **Format:** Candidates are presented with a detailed case study that includes multiple questions related to a complex, real-world situation. Each question within the case study may address different aspects of the scenario.
- **Focus:** These questions evaluate the candidate's comprehensive understanding and ability to manage complex information security issues.

Example:

- **Case Study:** A company has experienced a data breach that compromised customer information. The breach was caused by a phishing attack that targeted employees.
  - **Question 1:** What is the most important immediate action to take following the discovery of the breach?
    - a) Notify affected customers
    - b) Conduct a forensic analysis
    - c) Isolate compromised systems
    - d) Report the breach to regulators
  - **Answer:** c) Isolate compromised systems
  - **Question 2:** Which long-term strategy should the company implement to reduce the risk of future phishing attacks?
    - a) Increase network monitoring
    - b) Conduct regular security audits
    - c) Implement employee training programs
    - d) Upgrade firewall protections
  - **Answer:** c) Implement employee training programs

Strategies:

- **Analyze the Case:** Thoroughly review the case study details before attempting to answer the questions.
- **Synthesize Information:** Integrate information from different parts of the case study to form a holistic understanding.
- **Answer in Context:** Ensure that each answer is relevant to the specific context of the case study.

Question Format Variation Across Exam Sections

The CISM exam is divided into four domains:

1. **Information Security Governance**
2. **Information Risk Management**
3. **Information Security Program Development and Management**
4. **Information Security Incident Management**

Variation in Question Formats:

- **Information Security Governance:** May include multiple-choice questions focused on policies, roles, and responsibilities.

- **Information Risk Management:** Likely to have scenario-based questions assessing risk assessment and mitigation strategies.
- **Information Security Program Development and Management:** Could include both multiple-choice and case study questions evaluating program implementation and management skills.
- **Information Security Incident Management:** Often features scenario-based and case study questions to assess incident response and recovery capabilities.

Tips for Managing Time and Prioritizing Questions

1. Time Management:

- **Allocate Time:** Divide the total exam time by the number of questions to determine the average time available per question.
- **Monitor Progress:** Keep an eye on the clock and ensure you are progressing according to your time plan.
- **Flag and Skip:** If a question is taking too long, flag it and move on. Return to it after answering the easier questions.

2. Prioritization:

- **Answer Easy Questions First:** Quickly answer the questions you are confident about to secure those points.
- **Handle Complex Questions Next:** Spend more time on scenario-based and case study questions, as they require more analysis and critical thinking.
- **Review and Revise:** If time permits, review your answers, especially for flagged questions and those you were uncertain about.

3. Focus on Point Value:

- **Understand Weighting:** Some questions may have higher point values. Allocate more time and effort to these questions to maximize your score.

4. Stay Calm and Focused:

- **Stay Calm:** Maintain composure to think clearly and avoid careless mistakes.
- **Read Carefully:** Ensure you understand each question before answering.

Conclusion

The CISM exam includes multiple-choice, scenario-based, and case study questions, each requiring different strategies for effective tackling. By understanding the question formats and applying appropriate strategies, candidates can improve their performance across the exam's various domains. Effective time management and prioritization based on question complexity and point value are crucial for maximizing scores and achieving certification success.

CISM Exam Scoring and Passing Requirements

1. Minimum Passing Score:

- **Scale:** The CISM exam is scored on a scale from 200 to 800.
- **Passing Score:** To pass the exam, candidates must achieve a score of at least 450.

2. Question Weighting:

- Each question on the CISM exam contributes equally to the total score.
- There are no different weightings for different types of questions as all are multiple-choice.

3. Policy for Unanswered or Partially Completed Questions:

- **Unanswered Questions:** Questions that are not answered do not earn any points and do not negatively impact the score.
- **Partially Completed Questions:** Since all questions are multiple-choice with only one correct answer, partial credit is not applicable.

4. Exam Scoring Process:

- **Statistical Analysis and Equating:**
    - The scoring process includes statistical analysis to ensure that the exam is fair and consistent across different test forms and administrations.

    - **Equating:** This process adjusts for differences in difficulty across various versions of the exam, ensuring that scores are comparable regardless of when or where the exam is taken.
    - Equating ensures that a score of 450 on one version of the exam represents the same level of knowledge as a score of 450 on another version.
- **Raw Score to Scaled Score Conversion:**
    - The raw score (number of correct answers) is converted to a scaled score using a psychometric formula.
    - This ensures that the scaled scores reflect consistent levels of performance.

5. Historical Data on Passing Rates and Average Scores:

- **Passing Rates:** The passing rates for the CISM exam have varied over the years but generally range between 50% and 60%.
- **Average Scores:** While ISACA does not regularly publish average scores, anecdotal evidence and discussions in professional forums suggest that average passing scores tend to hover around the mid-500s.

Historical Data and Benchmarking

Example Historical Passing Rates:

- **2018:** Approximately 50-55% of candidates passed the CISM exam.
- **2019:** Approximately 50-60% of candidates passed the CISM exam.
- **2020:** The passing rate remained consistent with previous years, around 50-60%.
- **2021:** Similar trends continued with a passing rate of around 50-60%.

Benchmarking Performance:

- Candidates should aim for a comfortable margin above the passing score of 450 to ensure success.
- Regularly taking practice exams and scoring consistently in the 500-600 range can indicate good preparation and readiness for the actual exam.

Tips for Exam Preparation

1. **Understand the Domains:**
    - Focus on understanding the key concepts and practices within each of the four domains: Information Security Governance, Information Risk Management, Information Security Program Development and Management, and Information Security Incident Management.
2. **Practice Exams:**
    - Take multiple practice exams to become familiar with the format and types of questions.
    - Use practice exams to identify weak areas and focus study efforts accordingly.
3. **Study Materials:**
    - Use the CISM Review Manual and other ISACA-approved study resources.
    - Join study groups or online forums to discuss topics and share knowledge with peers.
4. **Time Management:**
    - Practice managing the 4-hour time limit to ensure that you can complete all 150 questions.
    - Develop a strategy for pacing yourself during the exam to avoid spending too much time on any single question.
5. **Review Key Concepts:**
    - Regularly review important concepts, frameworks, and best practices.
    - Make use of flashcards, summaries, and notes to reinforce learning.

Conclusion

Understanding the scoring and passing requirements for the CISM exam is crucial for effective preparation. Candidates need to achieve a scaled score of 450 to pass, with each multiple-choice question contributing equally to the total score. The use of statistical analysis and equating ensures fairness across different exam forms. Historical passing rates typically range between 50% and 60%, providing a benchmark for setting realistic expectations. By focusing on comprehensive study and consistent practice, candidates can enhance their chances of success on the CISM exam.

Optimizing the Exam Day Experience for the CISM Exam

As a seasoned CISM exam preparation expert, here are practical tips and advice to ensure you have the best possible experience on exam day.

Preparation Before Exam Day

1. Familiarize Yourself with the Testing Center:

- **Location:** Visit the testing center in advance to familiarize yourself with the location and reduce anxiety about finding it on exam day.
- **Procedures:** Review the testing center's procedures, such as check-in requirements and rules for what you can bring into the exam room.

2. Gather Necessary Identification and Materials:

- **Identification:** Ensure you have a valid government-issued photo ID. Some centers may require two forms of ID.
- **Materials:** Bring your exam confirmation email or admission ticket, if required. Know what is allowed in the testing room (e.g., earplugs, small snacks for breaks).

3. Plan Your Arrival:

- **Arrive Early:** Aim to arrive at least 30 minutes before the exam start time to account for traffic, parking, and the check-in process.
- **Rest Well:** Ensure you get a good night's sleep before the exam day to be alert and focused.

Managing Time Effectively During the Exam

1. Budget Time for Each Question:

- **Time Allocation:** The CISM exam typically consists of 150 questions to be completed in 4 hours. Allocate roughly 1.5 minutes per question.
- **Track Progress:** Regularly check the time and ensure you are on pace to complete all questions.

2. Mark and Review Difficult Questions:

- **Flagging Questions:** If you encounter difficult questions, flag them and move on to easier ones. This ensures you do not spend too much time on a single question.
- **Review:** After completing the exam, use any remaining time to review flagged questions and revise answers if necessary.

3. Take Strategic Breaks:

- **Scheduled Breaks:** Plan short breaks to rest your mind. This can help prevent fatigue and maintain concentration.
- **Stretch and Breathe:** Use breaks to stretch and take deep breaths to relax and recharge.

Minimizing Distractions and Staying Focused

1. Choose a Comfortable Seat:

- **Environment:** Select a seat away from high-traffic areas if possible. Make sure you are comfortable with your surroundings.

2. Use Provided Tools:

- **Noise-Cancelling Tools:** Use earplugs or noise-canceling headphones if allowed, to block out distractions.
- **Scratch Paper:** Utilize any scratch paper provided for note-taking and problem-solving.

3. Stay Positive and Confident:

- **Positive Mindset:** Remind yourself of your preparation and ability. Maintain a positive attitude and confidence in your knowledge.
- **Avoid Negative Thoughts:** Do not dwell on questions you are unsure about. Focus on the ones you can answer confidently.

Insider Tips and Tricks

1. Answer All Questions:

- **No Penalty for Guessing:** There is no penalty for wrong answers, so make sure to answer all questions, even if you have to guess.
- **Educated Guessing:** Use the process of elimination to make an educated guess when unsure.

2. Manage Stress:

- **Breathing Techniques:** Practice deep breathing techniques to manage stress and stay calm during the exam.
- **Visualization:** Visualize your success and the feeling of achieving your certification to boost your confidence.

3. Keep Hydrated and Energized:

- **Hydration:** Bring a bottle of water if allowed or ensure you drink enough water beforehand to stay hydrated.
- **Healthy Snacks:** Eat a light, nutritious meal before the exam to keep your energy levels stable.

4. Practice Relaxation:

- **Meditation:** Practice meditation or mindfulness exercises in the days leading up to the exam to improve focus and reduce anxiety.
- **Stretching:** Simple stretching exercises can help reduce physical tension and improve blood flow to your brain.

Conclusion

Optimizing your exam day experience involves careful preparation, effective time management, and strategies to maintain focus and confidence. By arriving early, being prepared with necessary identification and materials, and familiarizing yourself with the testing center procedures, you can start your exam day smoothly. Managing your time effectively during the exam by budgeting time for each question, marking difficult ones for review, and taking strategic breaks will help you stay on track. Minimizing distractions, maintaining a positive mindset, and using insider tips and tricks will further enhance your performance. With these strategies, you can confidently approach the CISM exam and increase your chances of success.

Importance of a Comprehensive and Realistic Study Plan for the CISM Exam

Creating a comprehensive and realistic study plan is critical for success in the CISM exam. A well-structured plan helps candidates manage their time effectively, stay focused on their goals, and systematically cover all necessary content areas. A study plan tailored to individual learning styles, schedules, and goals can make the preparation process more efficient and less stressful.

Step-by-Step Guide for Developing an Effective Study Plan

Step 1: Assess Current Knowledge and Skills

- **Self-Assessment:** Begin by evaluating your current understanding of the four CISM domains: Information Security Governance, Information Risk Management, Information Security Program Development and Management, and Information Security Incident Management.
- **Identify Gaps:** Use practice exams or diagnostic tests to identify strengths and weaknesses in each domain.

Step 2: Set Specific and Measurable Learning Objectives

- **Define Goals:** Set clear, specific, and achievable goals for what you want to accomplish in your study sessions.
    - Example: "Understand the principles of risk management by the end of week 2."
- **Measurable Outcomes:** Ensure your goals are measurable so you can track progress.
    - Example: "Score at least 80% on practice questions related to Information Security Governance."

Step 3: Allocate Time and Resources

- **Create a Schedule:** Develop a realistic study schedule that fits your lifestyle and commitments. Aim for consistent, daily study sessions rather than cramming.
    - Example: Study for 1-2 hours each weekday evening and 3-4 hours on weekends.
- **Prioritize Topics:** Allocate more time to areas where you have identified weaknesses.
    - Example: Spend extra time on Information Risk Management if it's a weaker area.
- **Plan Breaks:** Include regular breaks to avoid burnout and maintain productivity.

Step 4: Use a Variety of Study Materials and Methods

- **Textbooks:** Use comprehensive resources like the CISM Review Manual to cover theoretical concepts and frameworks.
- **Online Courses:** Enroll in online courses or webinars that provide structured learning and expert insights.
- **Practice Exams:** Regularly take practice exams to simulate test conditions, gauge your understanding, and build exam-taking stamina.
- **Study Groups:** Join study groups or forums to discuss challenging topics, share knowledge, and stay motivated.
- **Flashcards and Summaries:** Use flashcards for quick reviews of key terms and concepts and summaries to consolidate your learning.

Benefits of Using Diverse Study Materials and Methods

Textbooks:

- **Depth of Knowledge:** Provide comprehensive coverage of exam content.
- **Structured Learning:** Follow a logical progression of topics.
- **Reference Material:** Serve as a go-to resource for detailed explanations.

Online Courses:

- **Flexibility:** Allow you to study at your own pace and on your own schedule.
- **Interactive Learning:** Often include video lectures, quizzes, and discussion forums.

Practice Exams:

- **Assessment:** Help identify knowledge gaps and track progress.
- **Familiarity:** Familiarize you with the exam format and question types.
- **Confidence:** Build confidence and reduce exam anxiety through repeated practice.

Study Groups:

- **Collaboration:** Enable knowledge sharing and collaborative learning.
- **Accountability:** Provide motivation and accountability through peer support.
- **Diverse Perspectives:** Offer diverse insights and explanations on complex topics.

Flashcards and Summaries:

- **Memory Aids:** Enhance retention of key concepts through active recall.
- **Quick Reviews:** Allow for efficient and quick reviews, especially close to the exam date.

Sample Study Plan

Week 1-2: Information Security Governance

- **Self-Assessment:** Complete a diagnostic test for this domain.
- **Reading:** Chapters on governance from the CISM Review Manual.
- **Online Course:** Watch video lectures on information security governance.
- **Practice Questions:** Complete practice questions after each study session.
- **Summary Notes:** Create summary notes and flashcards.

Week 3-4: Information Risk Management

- **Self-Assessment:** Evaluate understanding through a practice test.
- **Reading:** Focus on risk management chapters.
- **Case Studies:** Review real-world case studies to understand application.
- **Practice Exams:** Take a full-length practice exam focusing on this domain.
- **Group Study:** Join a study group session to discuss risk management strategies.

Week 5-6: Information Security Program Development and Management

- **Reading:** Cover program development and management topics.
- **Online Course:** Participate in a webinar on security program management.
- **Practice Questions:** Regularly answer domain-specific questions.
- **Flashcards:** Use flashcards for key terms and concepts.

Week 7-8: Information Security Incident Management

- **Self-Assessment:** Identify areas needing improvement.
- **Reading:** Study incident management processes and best practices.
- **Simulations:** Participate in incident response simulations if available.
- **Practice Exams:** Complete practice questions and review incorrect answers.

Final Two Weeks: Review and Practice

- **Comprehensive Review:** Review all summary notes and flashcards.
- **Practice Exams:** Take multiple full-length practice exams.
- **Focus on Weak Areas:** Spend extra time on areas where scores are low.
- **Relaxation Techniques:** Practice relaxation and stress management techniques.

Conclusion

Creating a comprehensive and realistic study plan is essential for effectively preparing for the CISM exam. By assessing current knowledge, setting specific objectives, allocating time and resources, and using diverse study materials and methods, candidates can optimize their study efforts and improve their chances of success. Regular self-assessment and practice, combined with collaborative learning through study groups, will reinforce understanding and build confidence.

Proven Strategies for Effective Note-Taking, Retention, and Recall

Mastering complex information security concepts and terminology is crucial for success on the CISM exam. Here are some strategies and techniques to enhance note-taking, retention, and recall.

Note-Taking Strategies

1. Structured Notes:

- **Method:** Use a structured note-taking method such as the Cornell system. Divide your page into three sections: notes, cues, and summary.
  - **Notes:** During study sessions or lectures, write detailed notes in the main section.
  - **Cues:** After the session, write keywords or questions in the left-hand margin to trigger your memory.
  - **Summary:** At the bottom, write a brief summary of the page's content.
- **Example:** For a topic like "Risk Management," you might write detailed notes on risk assessment techniques, list keywords like "qualitative" and "quantitative" in the cues section, and summarize key points at the bottom.

2. Mind Maps:

- **Method:** Create visual diagrams that map out information hierarchically, starting with a central concept and branching out to related subtopics.
- **Example:** For "Incident Response," start with the central concept and branch out to subtopics such as "Preparation," "Detection," "Analysis," "Containment," "Eradication," and "Recovery."

3. Flashcards:

- **Method:** Use flashcards to capture key concepts, definitions, and examples. Write the term on one side and the definition or explanation on the other.
- **Example:**
  - **Front:** "MTTD (Mean Time to Detect)"
  - **Back:** "The average time taken to detect an incident from the moment it occurs."

4. Mnemonics:

- **Method:** Use mnemonic devices to help remember lists or complex concepts.
- **Example:** To remember the steps of the incident response process (Preparation, Detection, Analysis, Containment, Eradication, Recovery), use the mnemonic "Please Don't Ask Cats Ever Rest."

Retention and Recall Techniques

1. Active Recall:

- **Method:** Test yourself regularly by recalling information without looking at your notes. This strengthens memory and enhances retention.
- **Example:** After studying a topic, close your notes and write down everything you remember about it. Check your notes afterward to see what you missed.

2. Spaced Repetition:

- **Method:** Review information at increasing intervals over time. This helps move knowledge from short-term to long-term memory.
- **Example:** Use a spaced repetition system (SRS) app like Anki to schedule reviews of your flashcards. Review each card just before you are likely to forget it.

3. Summarization:

- **Method:** Summarize information in your own words. This forces you to process and understand the material deeply.
- **Example:** After reading a section on "Information Security Governance," summarize the main points in a paragraph without looking at your notes.

Creating Concise and Actionable Study Notes

1. Highlight Key Concepts:

- **Method:** Identify and highlight key concepts, definitions, and examples in your notes. Use different colors to categorize information.
- **Example:** Use yellow to highlight definitions, blue for key concepts, and green for examples.

2. Use Bullet Points:

- **Method:** Organize information using bullet points for easy scanning and quick review.
- **Example:** For "Risk Assessment," list the steps in bullet points:
    - Identify assets
    - Identify threats
    - Assess vulnerabilities
    - Determine risk levels

3. Incorporate Visual Aids:

- **Method:** Use diagrams, charts, and tables to visualize complex information.
- **Example:** Create a table to compare different risk assessment methods (qualitative vs. quantitative) with columns for advantages, disadvantages, and use cases.

4. Create Summary Sheets:

- **Method:** Summarize each chapter or topic on a single sheet of paper, focusing on the most critical information.
- **Example:** A summary sheet for "Information Security Policies" might include:
    - Definition of policies, procedures, and standards
    - Key elements of a security policy
    - Examples of real-world policies

Examples of Effective Note-Taking and Study Aids

1. Flashcards Example:

Front: "CIA Triad" **Back:** "Confidentiality: Ensures information is not disclosed to unauthorized individuals. Integrity: Ensures information is accurate and complete. Availability: Ensures information is accessible when needed."

2. Mind Map Example:

- **Central Concept:** "Information Security Governance"
    - **Branches:**
        - Policies and Standards
        - Roles and Responsibilities

- Compliance Requirements
- Risk Management
- Performance Measurement

3. Mnemonic Example:

- **Mnemonic for OSI Model Layers:** "All People Seem To Need Data Processing"
    - **Layers:** Application, Presentation, Session, Transport, Network, Data Link, Physical

Measuring the Effectiveness of Training

1. Completion Rates:

- **Method:** Track the percentage of completed training modules or study sessions.
- **Example:** 90% completion rate for flashcard reviews.

2. Test Scores:

- **Method:** Use quizzes and practice exams to measure understanding and retention.
- **Example:** Improved scores on practice exams from 70% to 85% after implementing spaced repetition.

3. Behavior Change:

- **Method:** Observe changes in behavior, such as improved ability to recall information during discussions or exams.
- **Example:** Increased accuracy and speed in answering scenario-based questions on the CISM practice tests.

Conclusion

Effective note-taking, retention, and recall of complex information security concepts are essential for CISM exam success. Using structured notes, mind maps, flashcards, and mnemonics can help organize and synthesize large amounts of information. Active recall and spaced repetition techniques enhance long-term retention and retrieval. By creating concise and actionable study notes, highlighting key concepts, and incorporating visual aids, candidates can optimize their study efforts. Measuring the effectiveness of these strategies through completion rates, test scores, and behavior changes ensures continuous improvement and readiness for the exam.

Importance of Leveraging Official ISACA Resources for CISM Exam Preparation

Using official ISACA resources, such as the **CISM Review Manual** and the **CISM Question, Answer, and Explanation (QAE) Database**, is critical for effective exam preparation. These resources are specifically designed to align with the CISM exam objectives and domains, ensuring that candidates cover all the necessary content comprehensively and accurately.

Overview of Official ISACA Resources

1. CISM Review Manual:

- **Content and Structure:**
    - The CISM Review Manual is divided into four sections, each corresponding to one of the CISM domains:
        1. Information Security Governance
        2. Information Risk Management
        3. Information Security Program Development and Management
        4. Information Security Incident Management
    - Each section includes detailed explanations of key concepts, principles, and practices relevant to the domain.
    - The manual also contains examples, diagrams, and references to support understanding.
- **Alignment with Exam Objectives:**
    - The content is directly aligned with the CISM exam objectives, ensuring comprehensive coverage of all topics that may be tested.
    - It includes key terms and definitions that are crucial for understanding the exam questions.

2. CISM Question, Answer, and Explanation (QAE) Database:

- **Content and Structure:**
    - The QAE Database contains a large collection of practice questions organized by domain.
    - Each question includes detailed explanations of the correct answer and why other options are incorrect.
    - Questions are designed to reflect the format and difficulty level of the actual exam.
- **Alignment with Exam Objectives:**
    - The questions cover the same domains as the exam, providing targeted practice on each area.
    - The explanations help deepen understanding of the concepts and improve critical thinking skills.

Tips and Strategies for Effectively Using Official ISACA Resources

1. Creating a Study Schedule:

- **Organize by Domain:**
    - Divide your study plan into sections corresponding to the four CISM domains.
    - Allocate sufficient time for each domain based on its weight in the exam and your proficiency.
- **Weekly Goals:**
    - Set weekly study goals, such as completing specific chapters from the CISM Review Manual and corresponding practice questions from the QAE Database.
- **Regular Review:**
    - Schedule regular review sessions to revisit difficult topics and reinforce your understanding.

2. Practicing with the QAE Questions:

- **Timed Conditions:**
    - Practice answering questions under timed conditions to simulate the actual exam environment.
    - This helps improve time management skills and reduces exam-day anxiety.
- **Analyze Explanations:**
    - After completing each set of questions, review the explanations thoroughly to understand the reasoning behind each answer.
    - Focus on why the correct answer is right and why the other options are wrong.

3. Cross-Referencing Key Concepts:

- **Integrated Learning:**
    - Cross-reference key concepts and terminology between the CISM Review Manual and the QAE Database.
    - This integrated approach reinforces learning and ensures you have a comprehensive understanding of the material.
- **Building Connections:**
    - Link related concepts across different domains to understand how they interact within the broader context of information security management.

4. Active Study Techniques:

- **Summarization:**
    - Create summaries of each chapter in your own words to reinforce understanding and retention.
- **Flashcards:**
    - Use flashcards for key terms and definitions to facilitate active recall.
- **Discussion and Teaching:**
    - Discuss complex topics with peers or study groups, or try teaching the concepts to someone else to solidify your understanding.

5. Regular Assessment and Adjustment:

- **Self-Assessment:**
    - Regularly assess your progress using practice exams from the QAE Database.
    - Identify areas of weakness and adjust your study plan accordingly.
- **Adaptation:**

- Be flexible with your study plan and adapt it based on your evolving understanding and comfort with the material.

Sample Study Plan Using Official ISACA Resources

Week 1-2: Information Security Governance

- **CISM Review Manual:**
  - Read and summarize chapters related to Information Security Governance.
- **QAE Database:**
  - Complete practice questions for this domain.
  - Review explanations for each question.

Week 3-4: Information Risk Management

- **CISM Review Manual:**
  - Study chapters on Information Risk Management.
- **QAE Database:**
  - Practice domain-specific questions.
  - Analyze detailed explanations to understand the logic behind each answer.

Week 5-6: Information Security Program Development and Management

- **CISM Review Manual:**
  - Focus on chapters covering Program Development and Management.
- **QAE Database:**
  - Answer practice questions.
  - Cross-reference key concepts with the Review Manual.

Week 7-8: Information Security Incident Management

- **CISM Review Manual:**
  - Review chapters on Incident Management.
- **QAE Database:**
  - Practice questions for this domain.
  - Pay special attention to incident response scenarios and strategies.

Final Two Weeks: Comprehensive Review and Practice Exams

- **Comprehensive Review:**
  - Go through summaries, flashcards, and notes for all domains.
- **Full-Length Practice Exams:**
  - Take full-length practice exams under timed conditions.
  - Review answers and explanations thoroughly.

Conclusion

Leveraging official ISACA resources like the CISM Review Manual and the QAE Database is essential for thorough and effective preparation for the CISM exam. These resources are specifically tailored to the exam content and provide comprehensive coverage of all necessary topics. By creating a structured study schedule, practicing with QAE questions, cross-referencing key concepts, and regularly assessing progress, candidates can enhance their understanding, improve their exam performance, and achieve certification success.

Benefits and Challenges of Participating in Study Groups and Online Forums

Benefits

1. Motivation and Accountability:

- **Motivation:** Being part of a study group can boost motivation, as you're surrounded by peers who share the same goal of passing the CISM exam. The group's collective energy can keep you focused and driven.
- **Accountability:** Regular group meetings and discussions create a sense of accountability. You're more likely to stay on track with your study schedule when others are counting on your participation and contributions.

2. Diverse Perspectives:

- **Enhanced Understanding:** Study groups bring together individuals with varied backgrounds and experiences, offering diverse perspectives on complex topics. This can deepen your understanding and introduce you to different approaches and insights.
- **Collaborative Learning:** Discussing and debating concepts with peers helps reinforce your knowledge and can clarify doubts. Collaborative problem-solving can lead to more robust solutions and a better grasp of the material.

3. Opportunities for Collaborative Learning and Problem-Solving:

- **Sharing Resources:** Group members can share study materials, practice questions, and other resources, providing a richer pool of information than studying alone.
- **Explaining Concepts:** Teaching and explaining concepts to others is a powerful way to solidify your understanding. Group members can help each other by explaining difficult topics in simpler terms.

Challenges

1. Misinformation:

- **Risk:** Study groups and online forums can sometimes spread incorrect information if members share unverified or misunderstood concepts.
- **Mitigation:** Always cross-check information from multiple reliable sources and encourage group members to do the same.

2. Distractions:

- **Risk:** Group meetings can occasionally veer off-topic, leading to wasted time and reduced study efficiency.
- **Mitigation:** Establish a clear agenda and goals for each meeting. Assign a facilitator to keep discussions focused and on track.

3. Coordination Issues:

- **Risk:** Scheduling regular meetings that accommodate everyone's availability can be challenging, especially with diverse time zones and commitments.
- **Mitigation:** Use scheduling tools to find common meeting times and consider rotating the schedule to accommodate different members.

Finding and Joining Study Groups

1. In-Person Study Groups:

- **Professional Networks:** Join local ISACA chapters or information security professional networks to find study groups in your area.
- **Workplace Groups:** If you have colleagues preparing for the CISM exam, form a study group at your workplace.
- **Educational Institutions:** Universities and training centers often facilitate study groups for professional certification exams.

2. Online Study Groups:

- **Social Media:** Join CISM-focused groups on LinkedIn, Facebook, or Reddit to connect with other exam candidates.
- **Online Forums:** Participate in online forums such as the ISACA community, where members discuss exam strategies and share resources.

- **Webinar Platforms:** Attend webinars and virtual study sessions hosted by training providers and certification organizations.

Maximizing the Value of Group Discussions and Activities

1. Be an Active Participant:

- **Engagement:** Actively participate in discussions, ask questions, and share your insights. Engagement enhances learning and contributes to the group's collective knowledge.
- **Preparation:** Come prepared to each meeting by reviewing the topics to be discussed and bringing any questions or challenges you encountered during your study sessions.

2. Utilize Collaborative Tools:

- **Shared Documents:** Use shared documents and collaborative platforms (e.g., Google Docs, OneDrive) to compile notes, resources, and practice questions.
- **Communication Tools:** Use tools like Slack, WhatsApp, or dedicated forums for ongoing communication and discussion between meetings.

3. Establish Clear Goals and Agendas:

- **Structured Meetings:** Set clear agendas for each meeting, outlining the topics to be covered and the goals to be achieved.
- **Roles:** Assign roles such as a facilitator, note-taker, or timekeeper to ensure meetings are productive and stay on track.

4. Encourage Diverse Contributions:

- **Inclusive Discussions:** Encourage all group members to contribute their perspectives and experiences. This can lead to richer discussions and a broader understanding of topics.
- **Peer Teaching:** Rotate the responsibility of explaining topics or leading discussions to enhance collaborative learning.

Tips for Active and Engaged Participation

1. Verify Information:

- **Critical Thinking:** Always verify information shared in the group through reliable sources such as official ISACA materials, textbooks, and reputable websites.
- **Question Assumptions:** Encourage group members to question and validate assumptions, fostering a culture of critical thinking.

2. Manage Time Effectively:

- **Focused Sessions:** Keep study sessions focused on the agenda. Use a timer if necessary to allocate specific times for each topic.
- **Breaks:** Schedule short breaks during longer meetings to maintain focus and prevent fatigue.

3. Balance Group and Individual Study:

- **Complementary Activities:** Use group study sessions to complement your individual study efforts. Group discussions can clarify doubts and reinforce learning, while individual study allows you to delve deeper into topics at your own pace.

4. Be Respectful and Supportive:

- **Respect:** Show respect for different opinions and perspectives. Constructive criticism should be encouraged, but it should always be respectful and supportive.
- **Encouragement:** Encourage and support group members, celebrating successes and providing motivation during challenging times.

Conclusion

Participating in study groups and online forums offers significant benefits for CISM exam preparation, including motivation, accountability, diverse perspectives, and collaborative learning opportunities. However, it also presents challenges such as the potential for misinformation and distractions. By actively engaging in group activities, verifying information, and utilizing collaborative tools, you can maximize the value of these study groups. Balancing group study with individual efforts and maintaining a respectful and supportive environment will further enhance your preparation and increase your chances of success on the CISM exam.

The Critical Role of Practice Exams in CISM Exam Preparation

Practice exams play a crucial role in assessing a candidate's readiness for the CISM exam. They provide a realistic simulation of the exam environment, allowing candidates to gauge their knowledge, identify areas for improvement, and develop effective strategies for taking the exam.

Benefits of Taking Multiple Practice Exams

1. Building Test-Taking Stamina:

- **Endurance:** The CISM exam lasts 4 hours, requiring sustained concentration and focus. Regular practice exams help build the stamina needed to maintain performance throughout the entire exam duration.
- **Familiarity:** Repeated exposure to the exam format reduces anxiety and increases confidence, making the actual exam experience less daunting.

2. Identifying Knowledge Gaps and Weaknesses:

- **Targeted Learning:** Practice exams highlight areas where the candidate's understanding is weak, enabling focused study on those topics.
- **Immediate Feedback:** Reviewing the answers and explanations immediately after completing a practice exam helps reinforce learning and correct misunderstandings.

3. Developing Effective Time Management and Problem-Solving Strategies:

- **Time Allocation:** Practice exams help candidates learn to allocate their time effectively across different sections and question types, preventing them from spending too long on any single question.
- **Strategic Approaches:** Regular practice helps in developing problem-solving strategies, such as eliminating incorrect answers quickly and making educated guesses when necessary.

Selecting High-Quality Practice Exams

1. Alignment with Exam Format and Content:

- **Structure:** Ensure that the practice exams follow the same format as the actual CISM exam, including the number of questions and the distribution across the four domains.
- **Relevance:** The content of the practice exams should closely match the topics and concepts covered in the CISM exam blueprint.
- **Difficulty:** Select practice exams that mirror the difficulty level of the actual exam to get an accurate sense of readiness.

2. Reliable Sources:

- **Official ISACA Practice Exams:** These are highly recommended as they are designed by the same organization that administers the CISM exam, ensuring a close match in content and difficulty.
- **Reputable Providers:** Use practice exams from reputable sources with positive reviews and endorsements from other CISM candidates.

Using Practice Exam Results to Adjust Study Plans

1. Analyze Performance:

- **Score Breakdown:** Review the scores in each domain to identify areas of strength and weakness.
- **Answer Explanations:** Study the explanations for both correct and incorrect answers to understand the reasoning behind them.

2. Adjust Study Plan:

- **Focus on Weak Areas:** Allocate more study time to domains or topics where scores were low.
- **Review Strong Areas:** Continue to review and practice strong areas to maintain and enhance understanding.
- **Revisit Resources:** Use the CISM Review Manual, QAE Database, and other study materials to reinforce knowledge in weak areas.

3. Continuous Improvement:

- **Regular Practice:** Take multiple practice exams at regular intervals to track progress and adjust study strategies.
- **Simulate Exam Conditions:** Practice under timed conditions to build exam-day endurance and reduce anxiety.
- **Iterative Learning:** Use the feedback from each practice exam to refine the study plan continuously, ensuring all areas are thoroughly covered.

Step-by-Step Guide to Incorporate Practice Exams into Study Plan

1. Initial Assessment:

- **Baseline Practice Exam:** Take an initial practice exam to establish a baseline score and identify knowledge gaps.
- **Analysis:** Review the results to determine areas needing improvement.

2. Ongoing Study and Practice:

- **Regular Practice:** Schedule practice exams every 1-2 weeks to monitor progress and adjust the study plan.
- **Targeted Review:** After each practice exam, focus on weak areas identified in the results.
- **Balanced Study:** Ensure that the study plan covers all domains adequately, revisiting stronger areas periodically to maintain proficiency.

3. Final Preparation:

- **Simulate Exam Conditions:** In the final weeks before the exam, take full-length practice exams under strict timed conditions to simulate the actual exam environment.
- **Comprehensive Review:** Use the results from these practice exams to conduct a comprehensive review of all domains, focusing on any remaining weak areas.

Conclusion

Practice exams are an essential component of CISM exam preparation. They help build test-taking stamina, identify knowledge gaps, and develop effective time management and problem-solving strategies. By selecting high-quality practice exams that closely match the format, content, and difficulty of the actual CISM exam, and by using the results to continuously adjust and refine the study plan, candidates can enhance their readiness and increase their chances of success on the exam.

Analyzing Practice Exam Results for CISM Exam Preparation

Analyzing practice exam results is crucial for identifying areas of improvement in test-taking skills and domain knowledge. By systematically reviewing and categorizing missed questions, identifying root causes of errors, and developing targeted strategies, you can enhance your performance and build confidence for the actual exam.

Step-by-Step Guide for Analyzing Practice Exam Results

1. Collect and Organize Results:

- **Compile Results:** Gather all your practice exam results in one place. This can be a physical notebook, spreadsheet, or dedicated exam prep software.
- **Record Details:** Note the date of the exam, overall score, scores for each domain, and specific questions you got wrong.

2. Review Missed Questions:

- **Identify Patterns:** Look for recurring types of errors or specific domains where you consistently miss questions.
- **Categorize Errors:** Categorize missed questions based on the reason for the error, such as:
  - Lack of knowledge
  - Misinterpretation of the question
  - Time pressure
  - Careless mistakes

3. Identify Root Causes:

- **Lack of Knowledge:** If a question was missed due to not knowing the material, identify the specific concept or topic.
- **Misinterpretation:** If the error was due to misunderstanding the question, analyze why the question was confusing. Was it the wording, the context, or the presence of distractors?
- **Time Pressure:** Determine if time management issues caused the error. Did you run out of time or rush through the question?
- **Careless Mistakes:** Identify if the mistake was due to oversight or lack of attention to detail.

4. Develop Targeted Strategies:

- **Address Knowledge Gaps:**
    - **Review Materials:** Revisit textbooks, study guides, and notes for topics where knowledge gaps were identified.
    - **Supplement Learning:** Use additional resources like online courses, webinars, or tutoring if needed.
- **Improve Interpretation Skills:**
    - **Practice Reading Comprehension:** Practice interpreting complex questions and identifying key information.
    - **Analyze Question Structure:** Study how questions are worded and what they are specifically asking for.
- **Enhance Time Management:**
    - **Timed Practice Tests:** Take timed practice exams to get accustomed to the pressure and pace.
    - **Pacing Techniques:** Learn to pace yourself, allocating specific amounts of time to different sections or question types.
- **Reduce Careless Mistakes:**
    - **Double-Check Answers:** Develop a habit of reviewing your answers before moving on.
    - **Stay Focused:** Practice mindfulness and concentration techniques to maintain focus during the exam.

Tracking Progress and Performance Over Time

1. Establish Baselines:

- **Initial Scores:** Record your scores from the first few practice exams to establish a baseline for overall performance and domain-specific knowledge.

2. Use Metrics:

- **Overall Score:** Track your overall score for each practice exam to monitor general improvement.
- **Domain-Specific Scores:** Break down your scores by domain (Information Security Governance, Information Risk Management, Information Security Program Development and Management, Information Security Incident Management) to identify specific areas of strength and weakness.
- **Question Type Accuracy:** Analyze your accuracy for different types of questions (multiple-choice, scenario-based, case study) to see which formats you need to focus on.

3. Monitor Trends:

- **Improvement Trends:** Look for upward trends in your scores, indicating progress.
- **Plateaus:** Identify any plateaus where scores are not improving, suggesting a need for a change in study strategy.
- **Regression:** Be aware of any regressions in scores, which may indicate knowledge decay or misunderstanding of new material.

4. Adjust Study Plan:

- **Target Weak Areas:** Allocate more study time to weaker domains and question types.
- **Reassess Strategies:** If certain strategies are not yielding improvement, reassess and adjust them. For example, if time management is still an issue, try different pacing techniques or practice more under timed conditions.

5. Build Confidence:

- **Celebrate Progress:** Acknowledge improvements and milestones to build confidence.
- **Simulate Exam Conditions:** Regularly take full-length practice exams under simulated exam conditions to build endurance and familiarity with the exam format.

Example of Analyzing Practice Exam Results

Initial Analysis:

- **Overall Score:** 70%
- **Domain Scores:** Governance: 75%, Risk Management: 65%, Program Development: 60%, Incident Management: 80%
- **Common Errors:** Misinterpretation of scenario-based questions, frequent mistakes in Program Development questions, and occasional time management issues.

Action Plan:

- **Knowledge Gaps:** Focus on reviewing materials for the Program Development domain.
- **Interpretation Skills:** Practice more scenario-based questions, paying attention to context and key details.
- **Time Management:** Take timed practice tests and practice pacing techniques.
- **Track Improvement:** After a month, take another full-length practice exam to gauge progress and adjust strategies as needed.

Conclusion

Analyzing practice exam results systematically helps identify patterns, trends, and opportunities for improvement in both test-taking skills and domain knowledge. By categorizing missed questions, identifying root causes of errors, and developing targeted strategies, you can address weaknesses and enhance overall performance. Tracking progress over time using metrics like overall scores, domain-specific scores, and question type accuracy ensures continuous improvement and builds confidence for the actual CISM exam. Implement these strategies to optimize your study efforts and increase your chances of exam success.

The Critical Role of Practice Exams in CISM Exam Preparation

Practice exams play a crucial role in assessing a candidate's readiness for the CISM exam. They provide a realistic simulation of the exam environment, allowing candidates to gauge their knowledge, identify areas for improvement, and develop effective strategies for taking the exam.

Benefits of Taking Multiple Practice Exams

1. Building Test-Taking Stamina:

- **Endurance:** The CISM exam lasts 4 hours, requiring sustained concentration and focus. Regular practice exams help build the stamina needed to maintain performance throughout the entire exam duration.
- **Familiarity:** Repeated exposure to the exam format reduces anxiety and increases confidence, making the actual exam experience less daunting.

2. Identifying Knowledge Gaps and Weaknesses:

- **Targeted Learning:** Practice exams highlight areas where the candidate's understanding is weak, enabling focused study on those topics.
- **Immediate Feedback:** Reviewing the answers and explanations immediately after completing a practice exam helps reinforce learning and correct misunderstandings.

3. Developing Effective Time Management and Problem-Solving Strategies:

- **Time Allocation:** Practice exams help candidates learn to allocate their time effectively across different sections and question types, preventing them from spending too long on any single question.
- **Strategic Approaches:** Regular practice helps in developing problem-solving strategies, such as eliminating incorrect answers quickly and making educated guesses when necessary.

Selecting High-Quality Practice Exams

1. Alignment with Exam Format and Content:

- **Structure:** Ensure that the practice exams follow the same format as the actual CISM exam, including the number of questions and the distribution across the four domains.
- **Relevance:** The content of the practice exams should closely match the topics and concepts covered in the CISM exam blueprint.
- **Difficulty:** Select practice exams that mirror the difficulty level of the actual exam to get an accurate sense of readiness.

2. Reliable Sources:

- **Official ISACA Practice Exams:** These are highly recommended as they are designed by the same organization that administers the CISM exam, ensuring a close match in content and difficulty.
- **Reputable Providers:** Use practice exams from reputable sources with positive reviews and endorsements from other CISM candidates.

Using Practice Exam Results to Adjust Study Plans

1. Analyze Performance:

- **Score Breakdown:** Review the scores in each domain to identify areas of strength and weakness.
- **Answer Explanations:** Study the explanations for both correct and incorrect answers to understand the reasoning behind them.

2. Adjust Study Plan:

- **Focus on Weak Areas:** Allocate more study time to domains or topics where scores were low.
- **Review Strong Areas:** Continue to review and practice strong areas to maintain and enhance understanding.
- **Revisit Resources:** Use the CISM Review Manual, QAE Database, and other study materials to reinforce knowledge in weak areas.

3. Continuous Improvement:

- **Regular Practice:** Take multiple practice exams at regular intervals to track progress and adjust study strategies.
- **Simulate Exam Conditions:** Practice under timed conditions to build exam-day endurance and reduce anxiety.
- **Iterative Learning:** Use the feedback from each practice exam to refine the study plan continuously, ensuring all areas are thoroughly covered.

Step-by-Step Guide to Incorporate Practice Exams into Study Plan

1. Initial Assessment:

- **Baseline Practice Exam:** Take an initial practice exam to establish a baseline score and identify knowledge gaps.
- **Analysis:** Review the results to determine areas needing improvement.

2. Ongoing Study and Practice:

- **Regular Practice:** Schedule practice exams every 1-2 weeks to monitor progress and adjust the study plan.
- **Targeted Review:** After each practice exam, focus on weak areas identified in the results.
- **Balanced Study:** Ensure that the study plan covers all domains adequately, revisiting stronger areas periodically to maintain proficiency.

3. Final Preparation:

- **Simulate Exam Conditions:** In the final weeks before the exam, take full-length practice exams under strict timed conditions to simulate the actual exam environment.
- **Comprehensive Review:** Use the results from these practice exams to conduct a comprehensive review of all domains, focusing on any remaining weak areas.

Conclusion

Practice exams are an essential component of CISM exam preparation. They help build test-taking stamina, identify knowledge gaps, and develop effective time management and problem-solving strategies. By selecting high-quality

practice exams that closely match the format, content, and difficulty of the actual CISM exam, and by using the results to continuously adjust and refine the study plan, candidates can enhance their readiness and increase their chances of success on the exam.
- Emphasize the importance of effective time management during the CISM exam, given the limited time available and the complexity of the questions. Provide specific strategies and techniques for optimizing time usage, such as reading questions carefully and thoroughly, eliminating clearly incorrect answer choices, and making educated guesses when necessary. Discuss the trade-offs between speed and accuracy, and provide guidance on how to strike the right balance based on one's individual strengths and weaknesses. Offer tips for managing the psychological and physical aspects of time pressure, such as maintaining a steady pace, taking deep breaths, and staying focused on the present moment.

The Importance of Effective Time Management During the CISM Exam

Effective time management is crucial during the CISM exam due to the limited time available and the complexity of the questions. With 150 questions to answer in 4 hours, candidates need to manage their time efficiently to ensure they can address all questions thoughtfully and thoroughly.

Strategies and Techniques for Optimizing Time Usage

1. Reading Questions Carefully and Thoroughly:

- **Initial Read:** Read each question slowly and carefully to understand exactly what is being asked.
- **Key Terms:** Pay attention to key terms and phrases that indicate the focus of the question (e.g., "most likely," "best describes," "except").
- **Context:** Understand the context and scenario provided, as many questions are scenario-based and require critical thinking.

2. Eliminating Clearly Incorrect Answer Choices:

- **Process of Elimination:** Quickly eliminate any answer choices that are obviously incorrect or irrelevant.
- **Narrow Down:** This approach increases the odds of selecting the correct answer from the remaining options.

3. Making Educated Guesses:

- **Reasoned Guessing:** If unsure about an answer after eliminating incorrect choices, make an educated guess based on your knowledge and understanding.
- **No Penalty:** Remember that there is no penalty for guessing on the CISM exam, so it is better to answer all questions rather than leave any blank.

Balancing Speed and Accuracy

1. Trade-offs Between Speed and Accuracy:

- **Speed:** Rushing through questions can lead to careless mistakes and misinterpretation of the question.
- **Accuracy:** Taking too much time on each question can result in not completing the exam.

2. Striking the Right Balance:

- **Pacing:** Develop a pacing strategy by dividing the total time by the number of questions (approximately 1.6 minutes per question).
- **Timed Practice:** Use practice exams to determine your natural pace and adjust accordingly.
- **Time Allocation:** Allocate more time for complex or high-weight questions and less time for straightforward ones.

Tips for Managing Psychological and Physical Aspects of Time Pressure

1. Maintaining a Steady Pace:

- **Regular Check-ins:** Periodically check the time to ensure you are on track, but avoid constant clock-watching.
- **Section Goals:** Set mini-goals for completing sections of the exam within certain time frames.

2. Staying Focused on the Present Moment:

- **Mindfulness:** Practice mindfulness techniques to stay focused on the current question rather than worrying about previous or upcoming ones.
- **Deep Breaths:** Take deep breaths to stay calm and clear-headed.

3. Physical and Mental Endurance:

- **Hydration:** Stay hydrated but avoid excessive drinking to minimize the need for breaks.
- **Breaks:** If allowed, take short breaks to stretch and relax without losing too much time.

Sample Time Management Plan

1. Initial 10 Minutes:

- **Quick Scan:** Briefly scan through the exam to get an overview and note any particularly challenging sections.
- **Easy Wins:** Answer a few easy questions to build confidence and momentum.

2. Next 3 Hours:

- **Balanced Pacing:** Aim to complete 75 questions (half the exam) in the first 2 hours, then the remaining 75 in the next 2 hours.
- **Focused Attention:** Spend approximately 1.6 minutes per question but be flexible based on complexity.

3. Final 50 Minutes:

- **Review:** Use remaining time to review flagged questions and make final checks.
- **Completion:** Ensure all questions are answered, making educated guesses where necessary.

Conclusion

Effective time management is critical for success in the CISM exam. By reading questions carefully, eliminating clearly incorrect answers, making educated guesses, and balancing speed with accuracy, candidates can optimize their performance. Managing psychological and physical aspects of time pressure through steady pacing, mindfulness, and breaks helps maintain focus and endurance. Developing and practicing a time management plan tailored to individual strengths and weaknesses will enhance the likelihood of completing the exam successfully within the allotted time.

Managing Exam Anxiety and Stress During CISM Exam Preparation

Understanding Exam Anxiety and Its Impact

Prevalence and Impact:

- Exam anxiety is a common experience among test-takers and can significantly affect performance. Stress and anxiety can lead to physical, emotional, and cognitive symptoms that hinder effective study and test-taking abilities.

Symptoms of Exam Anxiety

Physiological Symptoms:

- **Racing Heartbeat:** Feeling your heart pound or beat rapidly.
- **Sweaty Palms:** Excessive sweating, particularly on the palms.
- **Nausea or Upset Stomach:** Feeling sick or experiencing stomach discomfort.
- **Shortness of Breath:** Difficulty breathing or feeling like you can't get enough air.

Psychological Symptoms:

- **Racing Thoughts:** Inability to control or slow down thoughts.
- **Difficulty Concentrating:** Struggling to focus on study material or exam questions.
- **Negative Thinking:** Persistent thoughts of failure or inadequacy.
- **Restlessness:** Feeling jittery or unable to sit still.

Strategies for Managing Exam Anxiety

1. Preparation and Planning:

- **Early Preparation:** Start studying well in advance to avoid last-minute cramming, which can increase stress.
- **Structured Study Plan:** Create a study schedule that breaks down the material into manageable chunks. Stick to the plan to ensure comprehensive coverage of all topics.

2. Relaxation and Stress-Reduction Techniques:

Deep Breathing:

- **Method:** Practice deep breathing exercises to calm the nervous system. Inhale deeply through the nose, hold for a few seconds, and exhale slowly through the mouth.
- **Example:** Before starting a study session or during the exam, take a few minutes to focus on your breath and perform deep breathing exercises.

Progressive Muscle Relaxation (PMR):

- **Method:** Tense and then relax different muscle groups in your body, starting from the toes and working up to the head.
- **Example:** During a break in the exam, tense your leg muscles for a few seconds, then release. Repeat with other muscle groups to reduce physical tension.

Positive Self-Talk:

- **Method:** Replace negative thoughts with positive affirmations and encouragements.
- **Example:** Remind yourself, "I am well-prepared for this exam," or "I can handle this challenge."

Mindfulness and Meditation:

- **Method:** Practice mindfulness or meditation to stay present and reduce anxiety.
- **Example:** Spend 10 minutes each day meditating, focusing on your breath, and letting go of anxious thoughts.

3. Self-Care and Stress Management:

Healthy Lifestyle:

- **Nutrition:** Eat balanced meals rich in nutrients to support brain function.
- **Sleep:** Aim for 7-9 hours of quality sleep each night to ensure your mind and body are well-rested.
- **Exercise:** Engage in regular physical activity to reduce stress and improve mood.

Realistic Expectations:

- **Set Achievable Goals:** Break down your study goals into realistic and achievable tasks to avoid feeling overwhelmed.
- **Acceptance:** Accept that some anxiety is normal and can be managed with the right strategies.

4. Seeking Support:

Family and Friends:

- **Talk It Out:** Share your feelings and concerns with trusted family members or friends. Their support can provide comfort and reassurance.
- **Study Partners:** Study with peers or join a study group to gain different perspectives and reduce feelings of isolation.

Professional Help:

- **Counseling:** If anxiety becomes overwhelming, consider seeking help from a counselor or psychologist who can provide professional strategies for managing stress.

5. Practical Exam-Day Tips:

Arrive Early:

- **Familiarity:** Arrive at the exam center early to familiarize yourself with the surroundings and reduce last-minute stress.
- **Relaxation:** Use the extra time to perform relaxation exercises before the exam starts.

Strategic Breaks:

- **Short Breaks:** Take short breaks during the exam to stretch, breathe deeply, and relax your mind.
- **Hydration:** Drink water during breaks to stay hydrated and focused.

Focus on the Present:

- **Question at Hand:** Concentrate on one question at a time rather than worrying about the entire exam.

- **Avoid Rushing:** Read each question carefully and avoid rushing through the answers.

Example of a Relaxation Routine

Before Studying or the Exam:

1. **Deep Breathing:** Spend 5 minutes on deep breathing exercises.
2. **Progressive Muscle Relaxation:** Spend another 5 minutes tensing and relaxing different muscle groups.
3. **Positive Self-Talk:** Take a moment to affirm your preparation and capabilities.

During Breaks:

1. **Stretching:** Stand up, stretch your arms and legs to release physical tension.
2. **Deep Breathing:** Take a few deep breaths to calm your mind.
3. **Hydration:** Drink some water to stay hydrated.

Conclusion

Managing exam anxiety and stress is essential for effective CISM exam preparation. By recognizing the symptoms and implementing practical strategies such as deep breathing, progressive muscle relaxation, and positive self-talk, you can reduce the intensity and duration of anxiety. Maintaining a healthy lifestyle, setting realistic expectations, and seeking support from family, friends, and professionals are also crucial. Employ these techniques to stay calm and focused, ensuring you perform your best on exam day.

Receiving and Interpreting CISM Exam Results

1. Timeline for Score Reporting:

- **Immediate Preliminary Results:** For computer-based tests (CBT), preliminary results are typically provided immediately after completing the exam.
- **Official Results:** Official results are usually released within 10 business days after the exam date. Candidates receive an email notification once their results are available.

2. Format and Content of the Score Report:

- **Overall Score:** The score report includes a scaled score ranging from 200 to 800. A score of 450 or higher is required to pass.
- **Domain-Level Performance:** The report provides a breakdown of performance across the four domains of the CISM exam:
    1. Information Security Governance
    2. Information Risk Management
    3. Information Security Program Development and Management
    4. Information Security Incident Management
- **Performance Indicators:** Each domain score is accompanied by performance indicators such as "below proficiency," "proficient," or "above proficiency."

3. Meaning of Different Score Components:

- **Overall Score:** Reflects the candidate's general competency in information security management. A scaled score of 450 or above indicates a pass.
- **Domain-Level Performance:** Indicates the candidate's strengths and weaknesses across the specific domains, providing insights into areas that may require further study or improvement.

Determining the Passing Score

1. Standard Setting and Statistical Equating:

- **Standard Setting:** The passing score is determined through a standard-setting process that involves subject matter experts defining the minimum level of competence required.
- **Statistical Equating:** This process ensures that scores are comparable across different exam administrations. It adjusts for variations in exam difficulty, ensuring that a scaled score of 450 represents the same level of knowledge and proficiency, regardless of when the exam was taken.

2. Equating and Fairness:

- The use of statistical equating ensures that the passing score reflects a consistent standard of knowledge and proficiency across different test forms and administrations.

Interpreting and Using the Score Report

1. Identifying Strengths and Weaknesses:

- **Domain Performance:** Use the domain-level performance indicators to identify areas where you performed well and areas needing improvement.
- **Focused Review:** Concentrate on domains where your performance was "below proficiency" or "proficient" but not "above proficiency."

2. Informing Future Study and Professional Development:

- **Targeted Study:** Develop a study plan that focuses on weaker domains, using resources such as the CISM Review Manual, QAE Database, and additional training courses.
- **Professional Development:** Consider professional development opportunities such as workshops, seminars, or advanced certifications to enhance your knowledge and skills in weaker areas.

Guidance on Interpreting the Score Report

1. Immediate Actions:

- **Celebrate Success:** If you passed, celebrate your achievement and consider how the CISM certification can advance your career.
- **Plan for Retake:** If you did not pass, use the score report to identify weak areas and plan your study strategy for a retake.

2. Long-Term Development:

- **Continuous Learning:** Even if you passed, continuous learning is essential. Use your score report to guide ongoing education and training efforts.
- **Career Goals:** Align your study and professional development plans with your career goals, leveraging your CISM certification to pursue advanced roles in information security management.

Example Interpretation and Action Plan

Scenario: You received an overall score of 430 and the following domain-level performance:

- Information Security Governance: Below Proficiency
- Information Risk Management: Proficient
- Information Security Program Development and Management: Below Proficiency
- Information Security Incident Management: Proficient

Action Plan:

1. **Focused Study:** Allocate more time to study Information Security Governance and Information Security Program Development and Management.
    - **Resources:** Use the CISM Review Manual and QAE Database to revisit these domains.
    - **Supplemental Learning:** Consider additional resources like online courses, webinars, and study groups focused on these areas.
2. **Practice Exams:** Take additional practice exams to gauge progress and adjust your study plan as needed.
    - **Timed Conditions:** Simulate exam conditions to improve time management and reduce anxiety.
3. **Professional Development:**
    - **Workshops and Seminars:** Attend workshops and seminars that focus on governance and program development.
    - **Mentorship:** Seek mentorship or peer support from experienced information security managers.
4. **Retake Strategy:**
    - **Preparation Timeline:** Plan a study schedule that allows for thorough review and practice before scheduling a retake.
    - **Confidence Building:** Use practice exams to build confidence and ensure readiness for the retake.

Conclusion

Receiving and interpreting CISM exam results is a critical step in your certification journey. Understanding the timeline for score reporting, the format and content of the score report, and the meaning of different score components helps you make informed decisions about your study and professional development plans. By leveraging your score report to identify strengths and weaknesses, you can focus your efforts on areas needing improvement and continue to build your expertise in information security management.

Next Steps for Candidates Who Pass the CISM Exam

Congratulations on passing the CISM exam! Earning this prestigious certification is a significant achievement. Here are the next steps to claim, activate, and maintain your CISM credential, as well as an overview of the benefits and responsibilities that come with it.

Claiming and Activating the CISM Credential

1. Submit the CISM Application:

- **Application Form:** After passing the exam, you need to complete and submit the CISM Certification Application. This form is available on the ISACA website.
- **Experience Requirements:** Verify that you meet the work experience requirements. You need at least five years of work experience in information security management. Up to two years can be waived if you meet certain conditions (e.g., holding another certification, having a master's degree in a related field).

2. Documentation:

- **Proof of Experience:** Provide detailed documentation of your work experience, including job descriptions, roles, and responsibilities, signed by a supervisor.
- **Education Waivers (if applicable):** Submit proof of education or other certifications to qualify for experience waivers.

3. Fees:

- **Application Fee:** Pay the non-refundable application fee when you submit your application. The fee varies depending on whether you are an ISACA member.

4. Agreements:

- **Code of Professional Ethics:** Agree to abide by the ISACA Code of Professional Ethics, which sets forth the principles of conduct for information security professionals.
- **Continuing Professional Education (CPE):** Agree to the CISM Continuing Education Policy, which requires ongoing professional development to maintain your certification.

Benefits and Privileges of CISM Certification

1. Access to Exclusive Resources:

- **ISACA Membership:** Gain access to ISACA's vast resources, including research, publications, and the latest industry insights.
- **Online Communities:** Participate in exclusive forums and online communities where you can engage with other CISM professionals.

2. Networking Opportunities:

- **Conferences and Events:** Attend ISACA conferences, chapter meetings, and other events to network with industry leaders and peers.
- **Professional Networks:** Join local and global professional networks, opening doors to career opportunities and collaborations.

3. Career Advancement:

- **Recognition:** The CISM certification is recognized globally as a mark of excellence in information security management.
- **Career Growth:** Enhance your career prospects and qualify for senior positions in information security management, such as Chief Information Security Officer (CISO) or Security Consultant.
- **Salary Potential:** Certified professionals often command higher salaries and have better job stability.

Maintaining the CISM Certification

1. Continuing Professional Education (CPE):

- **Earning CPE Credits:** You must earn a minimum of 20 CPE credits annually and a total of 120 CPE credits over three years. CPE activities include attending conferences, participating in training courses, teaching, and publishing articles.
- **Reporting CPE Credits:** Annually report your CPE activities to ISACA, detailing how each activity contributed to your professional development.
- **Record Keeping:** Maintain records of your CPE activities, including certificates, receipts, and other documentation, for potential audit by ISACA.

2. Adhering to the ISACA Code of Professional Ethics:

- **Professional Conduct:** Continue to adhere to the ethical guidelines outlined in the ISACA Code of Professional Ethics. This includes maintaining confidentiality, integrity, and professional behavior.
- **Compliance:** Ensure compliance with all relevant laws and regulations in your professional practice.

3. Recertification Process:

- **Annual Maintenance Fee:** Pay the annual CISM maintenance fee to keep your certification active.
- **Submit Recertification Application:** Every three years, submit a recertification application demonstrating that you have met the CPE requirements and adhered to the ISACA Code of Professional Ethics.

Tips for Successful Certification Maintenance

1. Stay Engaged:

- **Professional Networks:** Stay active in professional networks and participate in relevant events and discussions.
- **ISACA Resources:** Regularly check ISACA's website and publications for updates on CPE opportunities and industry trends.

2. Plan Your CPE Activities:

- **Annual Goals:** Set annual goals for earning CPE credits, ensuring a balanced mix of activities such as attending conferences, taking courses, and contributing to publications.
- **Record and Report Promptly:** Keep detailed records of your CPE activities and report them promptly to avoid last-minute scrambles at the end of the year.

3. Seek Support:

- **Employer Support:** Discuss your CISM certification and CPE requirements with your employer. Many organizations support professional development through funding and providing time off for training and conferences.
- **Peer Support:** Collaborate with other CISM-certified professionals to share knowledge, resources, and opportunities for earning CPE credits.

Conclusion

Successfully passing the CISM exam is a significant milestone in your professional journey. To claim and activate your CISM credential, ensure you meet the experience requirements, submit the necessary documentation, and adhere to ISACA's professional standards. Enjoy the benefits of CISM certification, including access to exclusive resources, networking opportunities, and career advancement potential. Maintain your certification through continuous professional education, adherence to the ISACA Code of Professional Ethics, and active engagement in the information security community. With these steps, you can maximize the value of your CISM certification and continue to grow as a leader in information security management.

CISM Recertification Requirements

Maintaining the CISM certification requires ongoing professional development through Continuing Professional Education (CPE) activities. This ensures that certified professionals stay current with emerging trends, best practices, and evolving industry standards.

Number and Types of CPE Credits Required

1. Annual and Three-Year Requirements:

- **Annual Requirement:** A minimum of 20 CPE hours must be earned each year.
- **Three-Year Requirement:** A total of at least 120 CPE hours must be earned over a three-year reporting cycle.

2. Types of CPE Activities:

- **Professional Education:** Attending conferences, seminars, workshops, and training courses.
- **Knowledge Contributions:** Publishing articles, books, or research papers in the field of information security.
- **Self-Study:** Completing online courses, webinars, or self-paced learning modules.
- **Professional Meetings:** Participating in ISACA chapter meetings or other relevant professional organizations.
- **Volunteering:** Serving on ISACA boards, committees, or as an exam proctor.
- **Teaching and Presenting:** Delivering presentations or teaching courses related to information security.

Reporting Cycle and Deadlines

1. Reporting Cycle:

- The CISM certification follows a three-year reporting cycle, with CPE credits being tracked annually.

2. Deadlines:

- **Annual Submission:** CPE credits must be reported annually to maintain active certification status.
- **Three-Year Submission:** By the end of each three-year cycle, a total of 120 CPE hours must be submitted.

Process for Submitting and Verifying CPE Activities

1. Submission Process:

- **Online Submission:** CPE activities are submitted through the ISACA website via the MyISACA portal.
- **Documentation:** Maintain documentation of all CPE activities, including certificates of completion, attendance records, and published works.

2. Verification Process:

- **Audit:** ISACA may audit CPE submissions. Certified professionals should retain documentation for at least 12 months after the end of the three-year reporting cycle.
- **Supporting Evidence:** Ensure that all submitted activities can be verified with appropriate evidence, such as receipts, certificates, or letters from event organizers.

Examples of Eligible CPE Activities

1. **Attending Conferences:**
   - **Example:** Attending the annual ISACA conference, which provides numerous sessions and workshops eligible for CPE credits.
2. **Completing Training Courses:**
   - **Example:** Enrolling in an advanced cybersecurity training course from a recognized provider.
3. **Publishing Articles:**
   - **Example:** Writing an article on information security governance for a peer-reviewed journal.
4. **Volunteering for ISACA Committees:**
   - **Example:** Serving as a member of an ISACA chapter board or committee.

Benefits of Actively Engaging in CPE Activities

1. Staying Current with Emerging Trends and Best Practices:

- **Knowledge Update:** Regular participation in CPE activities ensures that professionals remain up-to-date with the latest developments in information security.
- **Skill Enhancement:** Continuous learning helps professionals acquire new skills and improve existing ones.

2. Expanding Professional Network:

- **Networking Opportunities:** Attending conferences, seminars, and professional meetings provides opportunities to connect with peers, industry leaders, and potential mentors.

- **Collaborative Learning:** Engaging with the professional community fosters collaborative learning and knowledge sharing.

3. **Demonstrating Commitment to Ongoing Learning and Growth:**
   - **Professional Credibility:** Actively pursuing CPE activities demonstrates a commitment to maintaining and enhancing professional competence.
   - **Career Advancement:** Continuous professional development can lead to new career opportunities, promotions, and recognition within the industry.

Conclusion

Maintaining the CISM certification requires a proactive approach to professional development through CPE activities. By fulfilling the annual and three-year CPE requirements, certified professionals ensure they stay current with industry trends, expand their professional network, and demonstrate a commitment to ongoing learning and growth. Engaging in a variety of eligible CPE activities, such as attending conferences, completing training courses, publishing articles, and volunteering, not only meets the certification requirements but also enriches professional expertise and career prospects.

Guidance and Support for Candidates Who Do Not Pass the CISM Exam on Their First Attempt

Failing the CISM exam on the first attempt can be disheartening, but it does not define your abilities or potential as an information security professional. Here's a step-by-step guide to help you analyze your exam performance, identify areas for improvement, and prepare for future attempts, along with tips for managing the emotional and psychological challenges of exam retakes.

Step-by-Step Guide for Analyzing Exam Performance

1. **Review Your Score Report:**
   - **Detailed Feedback:** Examine the score report provided by ISACA, which breaks down your performance by domain. Identify which areas you scored lowest in.
   - **Domain Analysis:** Pay attention to the specific domains where you need improvement (Information Security Governance, Information Risk Management, Information Security Program Development and Management, Information Security Incident Management).
2. **Identify Areas for Improvement:**
   - **Knowledge Gaps:** Determine which concepts or topics you were unfamiliar with or found difficult.
   - **Question Types:** Identify whether certain types of questions (e.g., scenario-based, multiple-choice) were more challenging.
   - **Exam Strategies:** Reflect on your time management, approach to difficult questions, and any areas where you felt underprepared.
3. **Seek Feedback:**
   - **Mentors and Peers:** Discuss your exam experience with mentors, peers, or colleagues who have passed the CISM exam. They can provide insights and advice on how to improve.
   - **Study Groups:** Join or re-engage with study groups to get different perspectives on complex topics and to benefit from group study sessions.

Developing a Targeted Study Plan

1. **Set Specific Goals:**
   - **SMART Goals:** Set specific, measurable, achievable, relevant, and time-bound (SMART) goals for your next study period.
   - **Focus Areas:** Prioritize the domains and topics where you scored the lowest.
2. **Create a Study Schedule:**
   - **Regular Study Sessions:** Plan regular study sessions and stick to the schedule. Consistent study habits are key to retention and understanding.

- **Balanced Approach:** Allocate more time to weaker areas but ensure you still review stronger areas to maintain a balanced knowledge base.

3. **Utilize Varied Study Resources:**
   - **Official ISACA Materials:** Use official ISACA study guides, practice questions, and other recommended resources.
   - **Supplementary Resources:** Incorporate additional study aids such as online courses, webinars, and books from reputable sources.
4. **Practice with Purpose:**
   - **Mock Exams:** Take full-length practice exams under timed conditions to simulate the actual exam experience and improve time management.
   - **Review Mistakes:** After each practice exam, thoroughly review the questions you missed and understand why the correct answers are right.

Maintaining a Growth Mindset

1. **Embrace the Learning Process:**
   - **Continuous Improvement:** View the failed attempt as an opportunity to learn and grow. Every mistake is a chance to improve your understanding.
   - **Positive Attitude:** Maintain a positive attitude and remind yourself that many successful professionals have faced similar setbacks.
2. **Seek Support:**
   - **Study Groups:** Re-engage with study groups or join new ones to benefit from collective knowledge and moral support.
   - **Mentorship:** Seek mentorship from certified professionals who can provide guidance, encouragement, and study tips.

Managing Emotional and Psychological Challenges

1. **Dealing with Disappointment:**
   - **Acceptance:** Accept that it's normal to feel disappointed, but don't dwell on it. Acknowledge your feelings and then refocus on your goals.
   - **Perspective:** Remember that a single exam does not define your career or potential. Many successful professionals have faced and overcome similar challenges.
2. **Rebuilding Confidence:**
   - **Small Wins:** Celebrate small achievements during your preparation, such as mastering a difficult concept or improving your practice test scores.
   - **Positive Affirmations:** Use positive affirmations to build confidence. Remind yourself of your strengths and past successes.
3. **Staying Motivated:**
   - **End Goal:** Keep the end goal in mind – earning your CISM certification and advancing your career.
   - **Reward System:** Set up a reward system for yourself to celebrate milestones and keep motivation high.

Practical Tips for Exam Retakes

1. **Structured Revision:**
   - **Focused Study Sessions:** Break down your study sessions into manageable chunks, focusing on one domain or topic at a time.
   - **Active Learning:** Engage in active learning techniques such as teaching concepts to others, discussing with peers, and applying concepts in real-world scenarios.
2. **Time Management:**
   - **Simulate Exam Conditions:** Practice taking exams in a simulated environment to improve time management and reduce anxiety.

- **Pacing:** Develop a strategy for pacing yourself during the exam. Allocate specific times for each section and stick to it.

3. Health and Well-being:

- **Balanced Lifestyle:** Maintain a balanced lifestyle with proper nutrition, exercise, and adequate sleep.
- **Stress Management:** Incorporate stress management techniques such as meditation, deep breathing exercises, and breaks to recharge.

Conclusion

Failing the CISM exam on your first attempt is not a setback but a stepping stone to success. By systematically analyzing your exam performance, identifying areas for improvement, and developing a targeted study plan, you can improve your chances of success in future attempts. Maintaining a growth mindset, seeking support, and managing emotional and psychological challenges are crucial for staying motivated and confident. With perseverance, dedication, and the right strategies, you will achieve your goal of becoming a Certified Information Security Manager.

The Importance of Continuing Professional Education (CPE) and Skill Development

Continuing Professional Education (CPE) and ongoing skill development are critical for staying relevant, competitive, and effective in the rapidly evolving field of information security management. With constant advancements in technology, evolving regulatory landscapes, and new threats emerging, professionals must continuously update their knowledge and skills to manage these changes effectively.

Key Areas and Topics for Ongoing Learning and Growth

1. **Emerging Technologies:**
    - **Importance:** Understanding new technologies is essential for anticipating and mitigating potential security risks.
    - **Topics:** Artificial Intelligence (AI), Machine Learning (ML), Internet of Things (IoT), blockchain, and cloud computing.
    - **Example:** Learning how AI can be used to enhance threat detection and response.
2. **Regulatory Compliance:**
    - **Importance:** Staying current with laws and regulations ensures that organizations remain compliant and avoid legal penalties.
    - **Topics:** General Data Protection Regulation (GDPR), Health Insurance Portability and Accountability Act (HIPAA), and other industry-specific regulations.
    - **Example:** Understanding the implications of GDPR for data protection practices.
3. **Risk Management Frameworks:**
    - **Importance:** Effective risk management is crucial for identifying, assessing, and mitigating risks.
    - **Topics:** NIST Risk Management Framework (RMF), ISO/IEC 27001, and COSO.
    - **Example:** Implementing the NIST RMF to improve organizational risk management processes.
4. **Leadership and Communication Skills:**
    - **Importance:** Strong leadership and communication skills are necessary for effectively managing teams and influencing stakeholders.
    - **Topics:** Strategic planning, team management, and stakeholder communication.
    - **Example:** Enhancing skills in presenting security strategies to executive leadership.

High-Quality CPE Resources and Opportunities

1. **Industry Conferences:**
    - **Example:** ISACA conferences, RSA Conference, Black Hat, and DEF CON.
    - **Benefits:** Networking opportunities, exposure to the latest industry trends, and access to expert sessions.
2. **Online Courses:**
    - **Example:** Courses from platforms like Coursera, edX, and Udacity, as well as ISACA's own online training resources.
    - **Benefits:** Flexibility to learn at your own pace and access to a wide range of topics.

3. **Professional Associations:**
   - **Example:** ISACA, $(ISC)^2$, SANS Institute, and ISSA.
   - **Benefits:** Access to member-exclusive resources, certification programs, and networking events.
4. **Peer-Reviewed Publications:**
   - **Example:** Journals and magazines such as the ISACA Journal, IEEE Security & Privacy, and InfoSec Institute's resources.
   - **Benefits:** In-depth research articles and case studies on cutting-edge topics.

Setting Personal and Professional Development Goals

1. **Goal Setting:**
   - **Personal Goals:** Identify specific skills or knowledge areas to improve.
   - **Professional Goals:** Align learning objectives with career aspirations, such as aspiring to a leadership role or specializing in a niche area of information security.
2. **Stretch Assignments and Leadership Opportunities:**
   - **Importance:** Taking on challenging projects or leadership roles helps build new skills and demonstrates initiative.
   - **Example:** Volunteering to lead a cybersecurity project or mentoring junior staff.
3. **Continuous Assessment and Adaptation:**
   - **Assessment:** Regularly evaluate your skills and knowledge against industry standards and emerging trends.
   - **Adaptation:** Adjust your learning and development plan to address any gaps or new interests.
   - **Example:** Periodically review and update your professional development plan to ensure it aligns with the latest industry requirements and personal career goals.

Conclusion

Continuing professional education and skill development beyond the CISM certification are essential for maintaining relevance and competitiveness in the field of information security management. Key areas for ongoing learning include emerging technologies, regulatory compliance, risk management frameworks, and leadership skills. Leveraging high-quality CPE resources such as industry conferences, online courses, professional associations, and peer-reviewed publications can provide valuable insights and learning opportunities. Setting personal and professional development goals, seeking stretch assignments, and continuously assessing and adapting skills will ensure that professionals stay ahead of the curve and meet the changing needs of the profession.

The Role of Professional Networking and Mentorship in Supporting Growth and Success as a CISM-Certified Information Security Manager

Networking and mentorship are pivotal for the ongoing growth and success of a CISM-certified information security manager. Engaging with professional networks and seeking mentorship can provide numerous benefits, including knowledge sharing, career advancement, and personal development.

Benefits of Professional Networking

1. Knowledge Sharing and Best Practices:

- **Access to Expertise:** Networking with peers and industry leaders exposes you to diverse perspectives and expertise. You can learn about the latest trends, tools, and techniques in information security management.
- **Resource Exchange:** Sharing resources such as articles, research papers, and tools helps keep you updated and improves your skill set.

2. Collaboration on Projects and Initiatives:

- **Joint Ventures:** Networking can lead to opportunities for collaboration on projects, research, or initiatives, enhancing your professional portfolio and visibility in the industry.
- **Problem-Solving:** Engaging with others allows you to seek advice and solutions for challenges you face in your role, leading to more effective problem-solving.

3. Building Relationships:

- **Professional Relationships:** Developing relationships with peers and industry leaders can open doors to new career opportunities, partnerships, and collaborations.
- **Support System:** A strong professional network provides a support system for sharing experiences, advice, and encouragement.

Participating in ISACA Chapters and Online Communities

1. **ISACA Chapters:**
    - **Local Engagement:** Join your local ISACA chapter to participate in events, meetings, and workshops. These provide opportunities to network with local professionals and stay informed about regional issues and solutions.
    - **Leadership Opportunities:** Volunteering for chapter committees or leadership roles can enhance your skills, visibility, and professional reputation.
2. **Special Interest Groups (SIGs):**
    - **Focused Discussions:** Participate in ISACA SIGs that focus on specific areas of interest or expertise, such as cloud security, risk management, or data privacy.
    - **Knowledge Exchange:** SIGs provide a platform for deep dives into specialized topics, allowing you to stay ahead in niche areas of information security.
3. **Online Communities:**
    - **Forums and Discussion Groups:** Engage in online forums and discussion groups on platforms like ISACA's Engage, LinkedIn, or Reddit to share experiences, ask questions, and offer advice.
    - **Webinars and Virtual Meetups:** Attend webinars and virtual meetups to learn from experts and interact with professionals worldwide.

Tips for Effective Networking

1. **Attend Events:**
    - **Conferences and Seminars:** Attend industry conferences, seminars, and workshops to meet other professionals and learn about the latest developments in the field.
    - **Networking Events:** Participate in networking events and social gatherings organized by professional associations like ISACA.
2. **Volunteer for Committees:**
    - **Committee Membership:** Join committees or working groups within your professional organization to contribute to initiatives and build relationships with peers.
    - **Event Organization:** Volunteer to help organize events, which can increase your visibility and expand your network.
3. **Leverage Social Media and Online Platforms:**
    - **Professional Profiles:** Maintain an active and updated profile on LinkedIn and other professional networks.
    - **Engage and Share:** Regularly share insights, articles, and updates on social media to engage with your network and demonstrate thought leadership.
    - **Online Courses and Groups:** Participate in online courses and groups to meet like-minded professionals and expand your knowledge.

The Value of Mentorship

1. **Seeking Mentorship:**
    - **Guidance and Advice:** A mentor provides guidance, advice, and support, helping you navigate your career path and overcome challenges.
    - **Professional Growth:** Learning from a mentor's experiences and insights can accelerate your professional growth and development.
2. **Serving as a Mentor:**
    - **Giving Back:** Mentoring others allows you to give back to the profession by helping develop the next generation of information security leaders.

- **Gaining Perspectives:** Mentoring provides new perspectives and insights, enriching your own understanding and approach to information security.
- **Leadership Development:** Serving as a mentor enhances your leadership skills and reinforces your knowledge and expertise.

Tips for Effective Mentorship

1. Finding a Mentor:

- **Identify Potential Mentors:** Look for experienced professionals in your network or industry who align with your career goals and values.
- **Approach Professionally:** Approach potential mentors respectfully and professionally, explaining why you seek their guidance and how you hope to benefit from their mentorship.

2. Being a Good Mentee:

- **Be Receptive:** Be open to feedback and willing to learn from your mentor's experiences and advice.
- **Set Clear Goals:** Define clear goals and expectations for the mentorship relationship, ensuring both parties understand the objectives.

3. Being a Good Mentor:

- **Listen and Understand:** Actively listen to your mentee and understand their goals, challenges, and aspirations.
- **Provide Constructive Feedback:** Offer constructive feedback and actionable advice to help your mentee grow and succeed.
- **Encourage and Support:** Encourage your mentee to take on new challenges and support them in their professional development.

Conclusion

Professional networking and mentorship are essential for the ongoing growth and success of a CISM-certified information security manager. Actively participating in ISACA chapters, special interest groups, and online communities provides opportunities for knowledge sharing, collaboration, and building valuable relationships. Effective networking involves attending events, volunteering for committees, and leveraging social media. Mentorship, whether seeking or providing it, offers significant benefits in terms of guidance, new perspectives, and leadership development. By engaging in these activities, you can enhance your professional journey, contribute to the information security community, and develop the next generation of leaders.

Career Paths and Opportunities for CISM-Certified Professionals

CISM-certified professionals have a wide range of career paths available to them, each offering different opportunities based on their skills, interests, and experience. The certification demonstrates a high level of expertise in information security management, making it highly valuable for various roles in the field.

Common Roles and Responsibilities

1. **Information Security Manager:**
    - **Responsibilities:** Oversee and manage an organization's information security program, develop and implement security policies and procedures, ensure compliance with regulatory requirements, and manage security incidents.
    - **Skills Needed:** Strong understanding of security frameworks, risk management, incident response, and compliance. Leadership and communication skills are essential for managing teams and interacting with stakeholders.
2. **Security Architect:**
    - **Responsibilities:** Design and implement security solutions to protect an organization's IT infrastructure, perform security assessments and audits, develop security architecture standards, and ensure that security is integrated into all aspects of IT projects.
    - **Skills Needed:** In-depth knowledge of security technologies and protocols, network security, and secure software development. Requires both technical expertise and strategic planning abilities.

3. **Risk and Compliance Manager:**
   - **Responsibilities:** Identify and assess security risks, develop and implement risk management strategies, ensure compliance with laws and regulations, conduct audits, and report on security risks to senior management.
   - **Skills Needed:** Proficiency in risk assessment methodologies, compliance requirements (e.g., GDPR, HIPAA), and audit processes. Strong analytical skills and attention to detail are crucial.
4. **Chief Information Security Officer (CISO):**
   - **Responsibilities:** Develop and lead the organization's information security strategy, oversee the security program, manage the security budget, report to the executive team, and ensure alignment of security initiatives with business objectives.
   - **Skills Needed:** Extensive experience in information security management, strategic planning, leadership, and communication. CISOs must be able to influence and drive security culture across the organization.

Key Factors Influencing Career Progression and Success

1. **Industry and Organizational Context:**
   - **Industry:** Different industries (e.g., finance, healthcare, technology) have varying security requirements and regulatory landscapes. Understanding the specific needs of your industry can enhance career opportunities.
   - **Organization Size:** Career opportunities and roles can differ significantly between small businesses and large enterprises. Larger organizations may offer more specialized roles, while smaller ones may require a broader skill set.
2. **Technical and Business Skills:**
   - **Technical Skills:** Staying current with emerging technologies and security threats is essential. Continuous learning and certification in areas such as cloud security, AI, and machine learning can be advantageous.
   - **Business Acumen:** Understanding the business side of security, including how security initiatives support organizational goals, is critical for career advancement. Skills in project management, budgeting, and strategic planning are valuable.
3. **Leadership and Communication Abilities:**
   - **Leadership:** Effective leadership skills are essential for managing teams, driving security initiatives, and fostering a security-aware culture.
   - **Communication:** Clear communication skills are necessary for articulating security risks and strategies to non-technical stakeholders, including executives and board members.

Guidance on Assessing and Pursuing Career Options

1. **Conduct Informational Interviews:**
   - **Purpose:** Gain insights into different roles and industries, understand the day-to-day responsibilities, and learn about the career paths of professionals in your desired role.
   - **How:** Reach out to industry professionals through LinkedIn, professional associations, or networking events. Prepare thoughtful questions about their career journey, challenges, and advice for someone entering the field.
2. **Building a Strong Personal Brand:**
   - **Online Presence:** Maintain an updated LinkedIn profile, share relevant content, and engage with the information security community.
   - **Thought Leadership:** Contribute to industry publications, speak at conferences, and participate in webinars to establish yourself as an expert in the field.
3. **Leveraging Professional Networks and Resources:**
   - **Professional Associations:** Join organizations like ISACA, $(ISC)^2$, and local security chapters to access resources, attend events, and expand your network.
   - **Mentorship:** Seek mentors who can provide guidance, support, and career advice. A mentor can help navigate challenges and open doors to new opportunities.

Example Career Path

Starting Position: Information Security Analyst

- **Responsibilities:** Monitor security alerts, conduct vulnerability assessments, assist with incident response, and support compliance efforts.
- **Skills Developed:** Technical proficiency, foundational knowledge of security practices, and initial exposure to risk management and compliance.

Mid-Level Position: Information Security Manager

- **Responsibilities:** Oversee the security team, develop security policies, manage security projects, and ensure regulatory compliance.
- **Skills Developed:** Leadership, strategic planning, in-depth understanding of security frameworks, and experience in managing security incidents.

Advanced Position: Security Architect

- **Responsibilities:** Design security solutions, conduct security architecture reviews, integrate security into IT projects, and perform threat modeling.
- **Skills Developed:** Advanced technical skills, strategic and tactical planning, and collaboration with IT and business units.

Senior Position: Chief Information Security Officer (CISO)

- **Responsibilities:** Lead the security program, develop the security strategy, manage the security budget, report to the executive team, and influence security culture.
- **Skills Developed:** Executive leadership, business alignment, communication with board members, and comprehensive knowledge of information security management.

Conclusion

CISM-certified professionals have diverse career paths available to them, including roles such as Information Security Manager, Security Architect, Risk and Compliance Manager, and CISO. Success in these roles depends on a combination of industry knowledge, technical and business skills, and leadership abilities. By conducting informational interviews, building a strong personal brand, and leveraging professional networks and resources, professionals can effectively assess and pursue their desired career paths. Setting personal and professional development goals, seeking out challenging assignments, and continuously updating skills and knowledge are essential for staying relevant and competitive in the dynamic field of information security management.

Staying Informed and Engaged with the Broader Information Security Community

Importance of Staying Informed and Engaged

Staying informed and engaged with the broader information security community is crucial for CISM-certified professionals. The field of information security is dynamic, with constant advancements and emerging challenges. Engaging with the community helps professionals keep up-to-date with the latest trends, share best practices, and collaborate on solutions to common problems.

Key Industry Trends, Challenges, and Opportunities

1. Evolving Threat Landscape:

- **Trend:** Cyber threats are continuously evolving, with sophisticated attack methods such as advanced persistent threats (APTs), ransomware, and zero-day exploits becoming more prevalent.
- **Challenge:** Staying ahead of attackers requires constant vigilance, ongoing education, and the adoption of advanced security technologies.
- **Opportunity:** There is a growing demand for skilled professionals who can develop and implement proactive security measures and incident response strategies.

2. Growing Importance of Privacy and Data Protection:

- **Trend:** With the increasing amount of personal data being collected, privacy and data protection have become critical concerns.

- **Challenge:** Compliance with regulations such as GDPR, CCPA, and other data protection laws requires robust policies and practices.
- **Opportunity:** Organizations need experts who can navigate complex regulatory environments, ensuring compliance while maintaining strong security postures.

3. **Convergence of Information Security with Other Business Functions:**
   - **Trend:** Information security is increasingly integrated with other business functions, such as risk management, compliance, and IT operations.
   - **Challenge:** Ensuring seamless collaboration and alignment across departments to achieve comprehensive security.
   - **Opportunity:** CISM-certified professionals can lead initiatives that bridge gaps between security and business objectives, enhancing overall organizational resilience.

Role of CISM-Certified Professionals in Shaping the Future of the Field

1. **Thought Leadership:**
   - **Influence:** CISM-certified professionals can influence the direction of the field by sharing insights, research, and innovative practices.
   - **Example:** Publishing articles, presenting at conferences, and participating in webinars to disseminate knowledge and drive discussions on emerging issues.
2. **Advocacy:**
   - **Policy Development:** Engage in advocacy efforts to shape policies and regulations that impact the information security landscape.
   - **Example:** Collaborating with industry associations, regulatory bodies, and government agencies to contribute to the development of security standards and frameworks.
3. **Collaboration:**
   - **Community Engagement:** Collaborate with other stakeholders, including peers, industry leaders, and academic institutions, to address common challenges and advance the field.
   - **Example:** Participating in industry working groups, joint research projects, and multi-stakeholder initiatives to share knowledge and develop comprehensive solutions.

Staying Informed and Engaged

1. **Attending Industry Events:**
   - **Conferences:** Attend major industry conferences such as RSA Conference, Black Hat, and ISACA's own conferences. These events offer opportunities to learn about the latest developments, network with peers, and gain insights from experts.
   - **Workshops and Seminars:** Participate in workshops and seminars that focus on specific areas of interest or emerging issues in information security.
2. **Participating in Research and Policy Initiatives:**
   - **Research Projects:** Contribute to or lead research projects that explore new technologies, threat vectors, and security strategies.
   - **Policy Development:** Engage with policy initiatives at local, national, or international levels to help shape regulations and standards.
3. **Contributing to Online Discussions and Publications:**
   - **Forums and Discussion Groups:** Join online forums, discussion groups, and social media communities related to information security. Engage in discussions, ask questions, and share your expertise.
   - **Writing and Publishing:** Write articles, whitepapers, and blog posts on current issues, trends, and best practices in information security. Contribute to industry publications and journals.

Examples of Engagement

1. **ISACA Engage Platform:**

- **Networking:** Use ISACA's Engage platform to connect with other professionals, participate in discussions, and access exclusive resources.
- **Collaboration:** Join special interest groups and working groups that focus on topics relevant to your expertise and interests.

2. Industry Associations:

- **Membership:** Become a member of professional associations such as ISACA, $(ISC)^2$, and the Information Systems Security Association (ISSA).
- **Committees:** Volunteer for committees or leadership roles within these associations to influence their direction and contribute to the community.

3. Continuous Learning:

- **Online Courses:** Enroll in online courses and certifications that focus on new technologies, emerging threats, and advanced security techniques.
- **Webinars and Podcasts:** Regularly listen to webinars and podcasts featuring industry experts discussing current trends and challenges.

Conclusion

Staying informed and engaged with the broader information security community is essential for CISM-certified professionals to remain relevant and effective in their roles. By understanding key industry trends, participating in professional networking and mentorship, and contributing to thought leadership and policy development, CISM-certified professionals can shape the future of the field. Engaging with industry events, research initiatives, and online discussions enhances knowledge, fosters collaboration, and drives continuous improvement in information security practices. Through these efforts, professionals can not only advance their careers but also contribute to the overall resilience and security of their organizations and the broader industry.

Conclusion:

Key Takeaways and Learning Objectives from the CISM Study Guide

The CISM study guide covers essential concepts, frameworks, and best practices needed to succeed on the CISM exam and excel in the field of information security management. Below is a summary of the key takeaways and learning objectives from each section, organized by the four domains covered in the exam.

Domain 1: Information Security Governance

Key Takeaways:

- **Governance Framework:** Establish and maintain an information security governance framework and supporting processes to ensure that the information security strategy aligns with organizational goals and objectives.
- **Policies and Procedures:** Develop, approve, and enforce information security policies, standards, and procedures.
- **Roles and Responsibilities:** Define and manage roles, responsibilities, and accountabilities to support information security governance.
- **Strategic Alignment:** Ensure information security strategies align with business objectives, and establish mechanisms for executive oversight and support.

Learning Objectives:

- Understand the components of an effective information security governance framework.
- Learn how to develop and implement security policies and procedures.
- Gain knowledge of aligning security initiatives with organizational goals.
- Recognize the importance of executive support and strategic alignment in information security governance.

Domain 2: Information Risk Management

Key Takeaways:

- **Risk Assessment:** Identify and evaluate information security risks to achieve business objectives.
- **Risk Mitigation:** Implement risk management practices to mitigate identified risks.
- **Risk Monitoring:** Continuously monitor and review risk management practices to ensure their effectiveness.
- **Compliance:** Ensure that risk management practices comply with relevant laws, regulations, and policies.

Learning Objectives:

- Master the processes for identifying, assessing, and evaluating risks.
- Understand various risk mitigation strategies and controls.
- Learn how to develop and implement risk management practices.
- Know how to ensure compliance with legal and regulatory requirements.

Domain 3: Information Security Program Development and Management

Key Takeaways:

- **Program Development:** Establish and manage the information security program to align with organizational goals.
- **Security Controls:** Implement and manage security controls to protect information assets.
- **Resource Management:** Ensure that the information security program has adequate resources, including personnel, tools, and budget.
- **Performance Measurement:** Establish metrics and reporting mechanisms to measure the effectiveness of the information security program.

Learning Objectives:

- Understand how to develop and manage an information security program.
- Learn about different types of security controls and their implementation.
- Gain skills in resource management for security initiatives.
- Develop the ability to measure and report on the effectiveness of the security program.

Domain 4: Information Security Incident Management

Key Takeaways:

- **Incident Response Plan:** Develop and implement an incident response plan to ensure timely and effective response to security incidents.
- **Detection and Analysis:** Detect, identify, and analyze security incidents.
- **Response and Recovery:** Coordinate and manage incident response activities to minimize impact and ensure recovery.
- **Post-Incident Activities:** Conduct post-incident reviews and continuous improvement to enhance future incident response efforts.

Learning Objectives:

- Learn how to develop and implement an effective incident response plan.
- Understand the processes for detecting and analyzing security incidents.
- Gain knowledge of coordinating and managing incident response activities.
- Know how to conduct post-incident reviews and improve incident response capabilities.

Interconnectedness and Importance of Domains

Holistic Approach:

- **Integration:** These four domains are interconnected, each playing a critical role in achieving a comprehensive and effective information security program.
- **Strategic Alignment:** Information security governance sets the foundation, ensuring that all security initiatives align with business objectives.
- **Risk Management:** Effective risk management practices protect the organization from potential threats and vulnerabilities.

- **Program Management:** Developing and managing a robust security program ensures the implementation of appropriate security controls and resource allocation.
- **Incident Response:** A well-prepared incident response capability minimizes the impact of security incidents and ensures rapid recovery.

Importance:

- A holistic approach to information security management integrates these domains, creating a resilient and adaptive security posture.
- Understanding the interconnectedness of these domains helps professionals design and implement security strategies that support and protect organizational goals.

Conclusion

Mastering the critical concepts, frameworks, and best practices within each domain of the CISM exam is essential for success. The four domains—Information Security Governance, Information Risk Management, Information Security Program Development and Management, and Information Security Incident Management—are interdependent and collectively ensure a robust and effective information security program. By focusing on these key takeaways and learning objectives, candidates can prepare effectively for the CISM exam and excel in their roles as information security managers.

The Importance of Continuous Learning and Professional Development in Information Security Management

Continuous learning and professional development are crucial for information security professionals, particularly in the rapidly evolving field of information security management. While the CISM certification provides a strong foundation, the dynamic nature of the threat landscape, emerging technologies, and regulatory changes necessitates ongoing education and skill enhancement.

Rapid Pace of Change and Evolution in Information Security

1. Evolving Threat Landscape:

- **Increasing Sophistication of Attacks:** Cyber threats are becoming more sophisticated, with attackers employing advanced techniques such as AI-driven attacks, deep fakes, and polymorphic malware.
- **New Threat Vectors:** The rise of Internet of Things (IoT) devices, remote work, and digital transformation initiatives introduce new vulnerabilities and attack surfaces.

2. Technological Advancements:

- **Cloud Security:** The adoption of cloud services is growing, requiring a deep understanding of cloud security principles, shared responsibility models, and best practices for securing cloud environments.
- **Artificial Intelligence and Machine Learning:** These technologies are both tools for improving security (e.g., threat detection and response) and new attack vectors that require novel defensive strategies.

3. Regulatory Environment:

- **Data Protection and Privacy Regulations:** Regulations such as GDPR, CCPA, and others are continuously evolving, necessitating a thorough understanding of compliance requirements and their implications for information security.
- **Cross-Border Data Flows:** The globalization of business and data flows introduces complexities in managing compliance with various international regulations.

Emerging Trends and Challenges

1. Cloud Security:

- **Importance:** As organizations increasingly migrate to the cloud, securing cloud infrastructure, applications, and data becomes paramount.
- **Challenges:** Understanding the shared responsibility model, implementing effective access controls, and managing cloud-specific threats.
- **Role of CISM Professionals:** Lead initiatives to develop and enforce robust cloud security policies, ensure compliance with regulatory standards, and train staff on best practices for cloud security.

2. **Convergence of Information Security with Privacy and Data Protection:**
    - **Importance:** Data privacy and protection are integral to information security, with overlapping goals and requirements.
    - **Challenges:** Ensuring compliance with diverse regulations while maintaining strong security measures.
    - **Role of CISM Professionals:** Develop integrated security and privacy frameworks, advocate for data protection best practices, and collaborate with legal and compliance teams to align security and privacy initiatives.
3. **Increasing Sophistication and Impact of Cyber Attacks:**
    - **Importance:** The scale and impact of cyber attacks are growing, affecting not only financial stability but also reputational and operational aspects of organizations.
    - **Challenges:** Staying ahead of attackers through proactive threat intelligence, advanced detection and response capabilities, and continuous monitoring.
    - **Role of CISM Professionals:** Implement advanced threat intelligence programs, lead incident response teams, and foster a culture of security awareness across the organization.

Role of CISM-Certified Professionals in Driving the Future of the Field

1. **Leadership and Advocacy:**
    - **Thought Leadership:** Share knowledge and insights through articles, webinars, and conference presentations. Influence the direction of the field by contributing to the development of best practices and standards.
    - **Policy Development:** Engage in policy development at the organizational, national, and international levels. Advocate for robust security policies and practices that address emerging threats and challenges.
2. **Continuous Professional Development:**
    - **Advanced Certifications and Courses:** Pursue advanced certifications such as CISSP, CEH, or specialized courses in areas like cloud security, AI, and privacy.
    - **Ongoing Education:** Enroll in university courses, attend workshops, and participate in professional development programs to stay current with the latest advancements in the field.
3. **Active Participation in Professional Communities:**
    - **Networking and Collaboration:** Engage with professional communities, such as ISACA chapters, to network with peers, share experiences, and collaborate on projects.
    - **Mentorship:** Mentor less experienced professionals, helping them navigate their career paths and develop their skills. This not only benefits the mentees but also reinforces the mentor's own knowledge and leadership abilities.

Examples of Continuous Learning and Professional Development

1. **Keeping Up with Emerging Technologies:**
    - **Example:** Enroll in courses on cloud security platforms like AWS, Azure, or Google Cloud to understand the unique security challenges and solutions in these environments.
    - **Outcome:** Enhance your ability to secure cloud infrastructure, guide cloud migrations, and ensure compliance with cloud security standards.
2. **Staying Updated on Regulatory Changes:**
    - **Example:** Attend webinars and workshops on new data protection regulations, such as updates to GDPR or the introduction of new privacy laws in various jurisdictions.
    - **Outcome:** Ensure your organization remains compliant with evolving regulations and can adapt quickly to new legal requirements.
3. **Engaging in Threat Intelligence Sharing:**
    - **Example:** Participate in threat intelligence sharing platforms and communities, such as Information Sharing and Analysis Centers (ISACs) or the Cyber Threat Alliance (CTA).
    - **Outcome:** Gain access to the latest threat intelligence, improve your organization's defensive capabilities, and contribute to the broader security community's efforts to combat cyber threats.

Conclusion

Continuous learning and professional development are essential for information security professionals to stay current and adaptable in the ever-evolving field of information security management. The rapid pace of change in the threat landscape, technologies, and regulatory environments demands a commitment to ongoing education and skill enhancement. By engaging with emerging trends, advocating for robust security practices, and actively participating in professional communities, CISM-certified professionals can lead the way in addressing the challenges and opportunities in information security. Through continuous learning, they can drive the future direction of the field and ensure their organizations remain resilient against evolving threats.

Applying CISM Knowledge and Skills in Real-World Scenarios

Leveraging CISM knowledge and skills in real-world scenarios involves translating theoretical concepts into practical applications to address security challenges. Successful information security managers and leaders demonstrate how to apply these skills effectively to achieve significant benefits in various areas such as risk reduction, compliance, business enablement, and incident response. Below are some case studies, success stories, and lessons learned from CISM-certified professionals across different industries, organization types, and geographic regions.

Case Studies and Success Stories

1. Risk Reduction in a Financial Institution

Case Study:

- **Organization:** A mid-sized bank facing frequent phishing and malware attacks.
- **Challenge:** High volume of phishing attempts and malware infections leading to potential data breaches and financial loss.
- **CISM Application:** The CISM-certified security manager implemented a comprehensive risk management program. This included deploying advanced threat detection tools, conducting regular security awareness training for employees, and enhancing email filtering systems.
- **Outcome:** The bank saw a 60% reduction in phishing incidents and a significant decrease in malware infections. The improved risk management practices also led to better compliance with financial regulations.

Key Success Factors:

- **Proactive Risk Management:** Identifying and addressing potential risks before they become incidents.
- **Employee Training:** Ensuring staff are aware of security threats and know how to respond appropriately.

2. Compliance Achievement in Healthcare

Case Study:

- **Organization:** A large hospital network required to comply with HIPAA regulations.
- **Challenge:** Ensuring compliance across multiple locations with varying levels of existing security measures.
- **CISM Application:** The CISM-certified Chief Information Security Officer (CISO) led the development of a unified information security program. This included standardizing security policies, conducting regular compliance audits, and implementing encryption and access control measures.
- **Outcome:** The hospital network achieved full HIPAA compliance, significantly reducing the risk of data breaches and fines. Patient data protection improved, leading to increased trust from patients and stakeholders.

Key Success Factors:

- **Standardization:** Creating consistent security policies and procedures across all locations.
- **Regular Audits:** Continuously monitoring and auditing for compliance.

3. Business Enablement in Technology Sector

Case Study:

- **Organization:** A tech startup developing a new cloud-based service.
- **Challenge:** Balancing the need for rapid development with robust security measures.

- **CISM Application:** The CISM-certified Security Architect integrated security into the development lifecycle through secure coding practices, regular security assessments, and automated security testing tools.
- **Outcome:** The startup successfully launched its service on schedule, with security integrated from the ground up. This proactive approach not only protected the service from vulnerabilities but also became a selling point for security-conscious customers.

Key Success Factors:

- **Security Integration:** Embedding security into every phase of the development lifecycle.
- **Automation:** Using automated tools to streamline security testing and reduce manual efforts.

4. Incident Response in Retail

Case Study:

- **Organization:** A global retail chain experiencing a significant data breach.
- **Challenge:** Rapidly identifying and containing the breach to minimize damage.
- **CISM Application:** The CISM-certified Incident Manager activated the incident response plan, coordinated with internal and external stakeholders, and utilized advanced forensic tools to investigate the breach.
- **Outcome:** The breach was contained within 48 hours, and a comprehensive post-incident analysis was conducted. Lessons learned were integrated into the security program, leading to improved incident response capabilities and stronger defenses against future attacks.

Key Success Factors:

- **Rapid Response:** Quickly activating the incident response plan to minimize damage.
- **Post-Incident Review:** Learning from incidents to strengthen future defenses.

Key Success Factors and Challenges in Implementing Effective Security Programs

1. Gaining Executive Buy-In and Support

- **Importance:** Executive support is crucial for securing the necessary resources and prioritizing security initiatives.
- **Strategies:**
  - **Communication:** Clearly articulate the value of security initiatives in terms of business impact.
  - **Metrics:** Use metrics and reports to demonstrate the effectiveness of security measures and their alignment with business goals.

2. Aligning with Business Objectives and Strategies

- **Importance:** Security initiatives should support and enable business objectives, not hinder them.
- **Strategies:**
  - **Integration:** Integrate security planning with business strategy development.
  - **Collaboration:** Work closely with other business units to understand their goals and how security can support them.

3. Fostering a Culture of Security Awareness and Accountability

- **Importance:** A security-aware culture ensures that all employees understand their role in protecting the organization.
- **Strategies:**
  - **Training:** Regularly conduct security awareness training and simulations.
  - **Engagement:** Encourage reporting of suspicious activities and reward proactive security behaviors.

Guidance on Assessing and Pursuing Career Options

1. Conduct Informational Interviews:

- **Purpose:** Gain insights into different roles and industries, understand day-to-day responsibilities, and learn about career paths from experienced professionals.
- **How:** Reach out to industry professionals via LinkedIn, professional associations, or networking events. Prepare questions to understand their career journey, challenges, and advice.

2. Building a Strong Personal Brand:

- **Online Presence:** Maintain an updated LinkedIn profile, share relevant content, and engage with the information security community.
- **Thought Leadership:** Contribute to industry publications, speak at conferences, and participate in webinars to establish yourself as an expert.

3. Leveraging Professional Networks and Resources:

- **Professional Associations:** Join organizations like ISACA, (ISC)², SANS Institute, and ISSA to access resources, attend events, and expand your network.
- **Mentorship:** Seek mentors who can provide guidance, support, and career advice.

Conclusion

Applying CISM knowledge and skills in real-world scenarios involves addressing security challenges through practical solutions, strategic planning, and continuous improvement. Case studies and success stories demonstrate the tangible benefits of effective information security management, including risk reduction, compliance achievement, business enablement, and rapid incident response. Key success factors such as gaining executive buy-in, aligning security with business objectives, and fostering a culture of security awareness are critical for implementing and managing effective security programs. By conducting informational interviews, building a strong personal brand, and leveraging professional networks, CISM-certified professionals can assess and pursue diverse career opportunities and achieve success in the dynamic field of information security management.

Words of Encouragement and Motivation for CISM Exam Candidates

Preparing for the CISM exam is a significant undertaking that requires dedication, time, and effort. As you embark on this journey, remember the profound value and importance of your work in safeguarding organizations and individuals from the ever-growing threats of the cyber world. Your commitment to achieving the CISM certification not only reflects your dedication to professional excellence but also highlights your role in protecting critical information and systems.

Recognizing Your Dedication

1. Acknowledging the Effort:

- **Time Investment:** The countless hours you spend studying, attending courses, and engaging with practice questions are a testament to your determination and perseverance.
- **Balancing Act:** Balancing work, personal life, and exam preparation is no small feat. Your ability to manage these demands speaks volumes about your resilience and commitment.

2. The Importance of Your Work:

- **Protecting Assets:** As a future CISM-certified professional, you play a crucial role in protecting your organization's valuable assets and sensitive information.
- **Mitigating Risks:** Your expertise helps mitigate risks, prevent breaches, and ensure business continuity, making a significant impact on the security landscape.

The Value of the CISM Certification

1. Career Advancement:

- **Opportunities:** Earning the CISM certification opens doors to advanced career opportunities, leadership roles, and increased earning potential.
- **Recognition:** The CISM credential is globally recognized and respected, signifying your expertise and commitment to information security management.

2. Leadership and Impact:

- **Influence:** As a CISM-certified professional, you will have the opportunity to influence organizational policies, lead security initiatives, and drive strategic decisions.
- **Contribution:** Your work will contribute to creating safer, more secure environments for organizations and individuals alike.

Staying Focused and Resilient

1. Focus and Commitment:

- **Stay the Course:** Keep your eye on the prize. The path to certification may be challenging, but the rewards are well worth the effort.
- **Dedicated Routine:** Establish a consistent study routine and stick to it. Consistency and discipline are key to mastering the material.

2. Seeking Support:

- **Peers and Mentors:** Don't hesitate to reach out to peers, mentors, and study groups. Their support, insights, and encouragement can be invaluable.
- **Professional Networks:** Engage with professional networks and online communities to share experiences, ask questions, and stay motivated.

3. Celebrating Progress:

- **Milestones:** Celebrate your achievements along the way, whether it's completing a difficult chapter, acing a practice test, or simply maintaining your study schedule.
- **Positive Reinforcement:** Recognize the progress you've made and use it as fuel to keep going. Each step forward is a step closer to your goal.

Words of Motivation

1. Believe in Yourself:

- **Confidence:** Trust in your abilities and the hard work you've put in. You are capable and prepared.
- **Resilience:** Embrace the challenges and setbacks as opportunities for growth. Your resilience and perseverance will see you through.

2. Embrace the Journey:

- **Learning Experience:** View this journey as more than just passing an exam. It's an opportunity to deepen your knowledge, enhance your skills, and grow professionally.
- **Long-Term Goals:** Remember why you started this journey. The long-term benefits of earning your CISM certification will far outweigh the temporary difficulties.

3. You Are Not Alone:

- **Shared Journey:** Many have walked this path before you and have succeeded. Draw strength from their stories and know that you are part of a larger community.
- **Support System:** Lean on your support system – friends, family, colleagues. They are rooting for your success and are there to help you along the way.

Conclusion

As you prepare for the CISM exam, keep in mind the significant impact of your work in protecting against cyber threats and the immense opportunities that await you. Stay focused, committed, and resilient, seeking support and celebrating your progress along the way. Your dedication and perseverance will not only help you achieve the prestigious CISM certification but also position you as a leader in the field of information security management. Believe in yourself, embrace the journey, and continue striving towards your goal. You've got this!

Call to Action: Continue Your Learning and Growth Beyond the CISM Certification

Achieving the CISM certification is a significant milestone in your career, but it is only the beginning of your journey in the dynamic and ever-evolving field of information security. To stay relevant, competitive, and effective, it is essential to actively engage in continuous learning and growth. By contributing to the broader information security community, you not only enhance your own skills and knowledge but also help advance the profession as a whole.

Engage in the Information Security Community

Join Professional Associations and Networks:

- **ISACA and Local Chapters:** Become an active member of ISACA and participate in your local chapter's events and activities. This provides opportunities for networking, professional development, and staying updated on the latest trends and best practices.
- **Other Associations:** Consider joining additional professional organizations such as $(ISC)^2$, SANS Institute, ISSA, and OWASP.

Attend Industry Conferences and Events:

- **Conferences:** Attend major industry conferences like the RSA Conference, Black Hat, DEF CON, and ISACA's annual conferences. These events offer valuable learning opportunities, hands-on workshops, and the chance to network with peers and industry leaders.
- **Local Events:** Participate in local and regional cybersecurity events, meetups, and seminars to stay engaged with the community and learn from nearby experts.

Pursue Additional Certifications and Training:

- **Certifications:** Enhance your credentials by pursuing other relevant certifications such as CISSP, CRISC, CEH, or specialized certifications in cloud security, penetration testing, or data privacy.
- **Training:** Continuously seek out training opportunities, including online courses, boot camps, and workshops, to stay abreast of emerging technologies and evolving threats.

Share Your Knowledge and Expertise

Mentoring:

- **Guide New Professionals:** Become a mentor to those new to the field. Share your experiences, provide career advice, and help them navigate the challenges of information security.
- **Develop Leadership:** Encourage and develop the next generation of information security leaders by providing them with the tools and knowledge they need to succeed.

Writing and Speaking:

- **Publications:** Write articles, whitepapers, or books on information security topics. Share your insights and contribute to the body of knowledge in the field.
- **Speaking Engagements:** Speak at conferences, webinars, and local events. Sharing your expertise publicly enhances your reputation and helps educate others.

Give Back to the Profession

Volunteer Work:

- **ISACA Committees:** Serve on ISACA committees, boards, or working groups. Volunteering within professional organizations helps shape the future of the profession.
- **Community Outreach:** Participate in cybersecurity awareness programs, local community initiatives, or educational outreach to promote information security practices.

Advocacy and Collaboration:

- **Policy Advocacy:** Engage in advocacy efforts to influence information security policies and regulations. Your expertise can help shape better security practices and standards.
- **Academic Collaboration:** Collaborate with academic institutions by guest lecturing, advising on curriculum development, or supporting research projects. This helps bridge the gap between academia and industry.

Importance of Giving Back and Developing Future Leaders

Giving back to the profession is crucial for its continuous improvement and sustainability. By actively contributing to the community, you:

- **Enhance Collective Knowledge:** Share your expertise to help others learn and grow, thereby raising the overall competency of the field.
- **Build a Strong Network:** Develop valuable connections with other professionals, which can lead to collaborative opportunities and career advancement.

- **Inspire and Mentor:** Empower the next generation of information security professionals to become effective leaders and innovators.

Conclusion

Your journey in information security does not end with the CISM certification. By actively engaging in continuous learning, participating in professional communities, and sharing your expertise, you can significantly impact your career and the field of information security. Join professional associations, attend industry events, pursue further education, and give back through mentoring and volunteer work. Together, we can advance the profession, foster a culture of security, and develop the leaders of tomorrow.

Final Message of Inspiration and Empowerment

As you stand on the brink of earning your CISM certification, remember the profound responsibility and critical role you are about to undertake. As an information security manager, you will be the guardian of your organization's most valuable assets, ensuring the confidentiality, integrity, and availability of information that is vital to its success. Your work will not only protect data and systems but also build the trust and resilience needed for a secure digital future.

Embracing the Challenges and Opportunities

1. Navigating the Complex Landscape:

- **Challenges Ahead:** The world of information security is ever-changing, with new threats and vulnerabilities emerging constantly. You will face complex challenges that require innovative solutions and steadfast determination.
- **Opportunities to Lead:** With these challenges come opportunities to lead and make a significant impact. Your expertise will be crucial in shaping the strategies and policies that safeguard your organization.

2. The Need for Strong, Ethical Leadership:

- **Visionary Leadership:** The future of information security depends on leaders who are not only skilled and knowledgeable but also ethical and visionary. Your decisions and actions will set the tone for your team and organization.
- **Ethical Responsibility:** Uphold the highest standards of integrity and professionalism. Your ethical leadership will inspire trust and confidence, both within your organization and in the wider community.

Charting Your Path to Success

1. Embrace Your Unique Strengths:

- **Individual Strengths:** Recognize and embrace your unique strengths, passions, and perspectives. These qualities will distinguish you as a leader and help you navigate your career path.
- **Personal Growth:** Continuously seek opportunities for personal and professional growth. Stay curious, open-minded, and committed to lifelong learning.

2. Make a Lasting Impact:

- **Transformative Role:** As a CISM-certified professional, you have the power to transform your organization's security posture and contribute to a safer digital world.
- **Inspire Others:** Use your knowledge and experience to mentor and inspire others in the field. Your leadership can cultivate a new generation of security professionals committed to excellence and integrity.

3. Build a Resilient Future:

- **Resilient Systems:** Focus on building resilient systems and processes that can withstand and adapt to evolving threats.
- **Secure Digital Future:** Your work is foundational to creating a secure digital future where innovation can thrive, and individuals and organizations can operate with confidence.

Final Encouragement

As you prepare to take your place as a leader in information security, know that you are stepping into a role of immense importance and potential. Embrace the challenges with courage, seize the opportunities with enthusiasm, and lead with integrity and vision. Your journey as a CISM-certified professional is just beginning, and the impact you will make is boundless.

Believe in your capabilities, stay true to your values, and chart your path with determination and purpose. The future of information security is bright, and it is in your hands to shape it. You are not just earning a certification; you are becoming a beacon of security, trust, and leadership in a digital world that needs you. Go forth and make a difference – the world is counting on you.

Practice Test Questions

Introduction to the CISM Practice Exam Section

Welcome to the practice test section of your CISM (Certified Information Security Manager) Exam Prep STUDY GUIDE. This section is designed to help you deepen your understanding of key concepts and assess your readiness for the CISM exam.

Why We Provide Instant Feedback

1. **Instant Feedback**: By having the answer and explanation readily available, you can quickly assess your understanding of each concept. If you answered correctly, the explanation will reinforce your knowledge. If you answered incorrectly, you can immediately learn from your mistake and clarify any misunderstandings.
2. **Efficient Learning**: Providing answers and explanations directly after each question eliminates the need to flip back and forth between the questions and an answer key. This streamlined approach allows you to focus on the content and maintain your momentum as you progress through the practice test.
3. **Enhanced Retention**: Research has shown that receiving immediate feedback on your responses can significantly improve learning and retention. By reviewing the answer and explanation right after answering a question, you'll be more likely to remember the information and apply it effectively in the future.

Tips for Using This Practice Test

- **Use a Piece of Paper to Cover the Answers**: To simulate a real test environment and test your knowledge without any hints, use a piece of paper or another object to cover the answers as you attempt each question. Reveal the answer and explanation only after you have made your choice.
- **Repeated Topics**: Some important topics might be covered several times in different ways. This repetition is intentional to ensure you have a robust understanding of critical concepts.

1. As you work through the questions, remember that the goal is not just to get the right answer but to understand why it is the right answer. This practice will help you build a strong foundation of knowledge and skills necessary for the CISM exam and your future career in information security management. Good luck, and let's get started!

Which of the following best describes the primary role of information security governance in an organization?
a. Ensuring compliance with legal and regulatory requirements
b. Implementing technical controls to protect information assets
c. Aligning information security strategies with business objectives
d. Conducting periodic vulnerability assessments and penetration testing

Answer: c. Aligning information security strategies with business objectives. Explanation: Information security governance is the process of establishing and maintaining a framework that ensures information security strategies and objectives are aligned with and support the organization's business goals. While compliance, technical controls, and vulnerability assessments are important aspects of information security, they are not the primary focus of governance.

2. An organization's Board of Directors has requested a presentation on the current state of information security. Which of the following metrics would be most relevant to include in the presentation?
a. The number of security incidents detected and resolved in the past quarter
b. The percentage of employees who have completed the annual security awareness training
c. The average time it takes to patch critical vulnerabilities across all systems
d. The alignment of the information security program with the organization's risk appetite

Answer: d. The alignment of the information security program with the organization's risk appetite. Explanation: When presenting to the Board of Directors, it is crucial to focus on metrics that demonstrate how the information security program supports the organization's overall risk management strategy and business objectives. While operational metrics like incident counts, training completion rates, and patching times are important, they are less strategic and may not provide the high-level insight the Board requires.

3. Which of the following is the most important factor to consider when developing an information security policy?
a. The length and format of the policy document
b. The technical controls required to enforce the policy
c. The alignment of the policy with the organization's risk appetite and business objectives
d. The frequency with which the policy will be reviewed and updated

Answer: c. The alignment of the policy with the organization's risk appetite and business objectives. Explanation: An effective information security policy must be tailored to the organization's specific risk tolerance and support its overall business goals. The policy should provide a clear direction and set of expectations for managing information security risks in a way that enables the business to operate effectively. While the length, format, technical controls, and review frequency are important considerations, they are secondary to ensuring the policy is aligned with the organization's risk appetite and objectives.

4. Which of the following is the most effective way to ensure that information security policies and procedures are consistently followed by employees?
a. Conducting annual security awareness training sessions
b. Implementing strict disciplinary measures for policy violations
c. Embedding security requirements into business processes and workflows
d. Regularly reminding employees of their security responsibilities via email

Answer: c. Embedding security requirements into business processes and workflows. Explanation: While training, disciplinary measures, and regular reminders can help promote security awareness and compliance, the most effective way to ensure consistent adherence to policies and procedures is to integrate security requirements directly into employees' daily work processes. By making security an integral part of how work gets done, rather than an additional task or afterthought, organizations can create a culture of security and minimize the risk of human error or non-compliance.

5. Which of the following is the most important consideration when prioritizing information security investments?
a. The total cost of the investment
b. The ease of implementing the proposed security controls
c. The alignment of the investment with the organization's risk management strategy
d. The popularity of the security technology or vendor in the market

Answer: c. The alignment of the investment with the organization's risk management strategy. Explanation: When making investment decisions, it is crucial to prioritize security initiatives that align with the organization's overall risk management strategy and address the most significant threats to the business. While cost, ease of implementation, and market trends are factors to consider, they should not drive the decision-making process. Instead, investments should be based on a clear understanding of the organization's risk landscape and the specific controls needed to mitigate those risks effectively.

6. An organization has experienced a significant data breach involving the personal information of its customers. Which of the following is the most important step to take in the immediate aftermath of the breach?
a. Conducting a thorough root cause analysis to determine how the breach occurred
b. Notifying affected customers and providing them with guidance on protective measures
c. Implementing additional security controls to prevent future breaches

d. Issuing a public statement to minimize reputational damage

Answer: b. Notifying affected customers and providing them with guidance on protective measures. Explanation: In the wake of a data breach, the top priority should be to notify affected individuals as quickly as possible and provide them with clear guidance on steps they can take to protect themselves from potential harm, such as identity theft or fraud. While root cause analysis, additional security controls, and public relations are important, they should not take precedence over ensuring that impacted customers are informed and supported.

7. Which of the following is the most important factor to consider when developing an incident response plan?
a. The technical expertise of the incident response team members
b. The alignment of the plan with industry best practices and standards
c. The integration of the plan with the organization's overall business continuity strategy
d. The frequency with which the plan is tested and updated

Answer: c. The integration of the plan with the organization's overall business continuity strategy. Explanation: An effective incident response plan must be closely aligned with the organization's broader business continuity and disaster recovery strategies to ensure that security incidents can be managed in a way that minimizes disruption to critical business processes. The plan should take into account the organization's specific business requirements, risk tolerance, and recovery time objectives. While the expertise of the response team, alignment with standards, and regular testing are important, they should support the overall goal of maintaining business continuity in the face of an incident.

8. Which of the following metrics is most useful for evaluating the effectiveness of an organization's security awareness training program?
a. The number of employees who have completed the training
b. The percentage of employees who passed the post-training quiz
c. The reduction in security incidents caused by human error
d. The feedback from employees on the quality of the training content

Answer: c. The reduction in security incidents caused by human error. Explanation: While completion rates, quiz scores, and employee feedback can provide insights into the reach and perceived quality of a security awareness training program, the ultimate measure of its effectiveness is the extent to which it changes behavior and reduces risk. By tracking the number of security incidents that can be attributed to human error over time, organizations can assess whether their training efforts are having a meaningful impact on employee behavior and overall security posture.

9. An organization is considering outsourcing its security operations center (SOC) to a managed security service provider (MSSP). Which of the following is the most important factor to consider when selecting an MSSP?
a. The MSSP's market share and reputation in the industry
b. The specific security technologies and tools used by the MSSP
c. The MSSP's ability to customize its services to the organization's unique needs and risk profile
d. The cost of the MSSP's services compared to other providers

Answer: c. The MSSP's ability to customize its services to the organization's unique needs and risk profile. Explanation: When outsourcing critical security functions like SOC operations, it is essential to choose a provider that can tailor its services to the organization's specific security requirements, risk landscape, and business objectives. A one-size-fits-all approach is unlikely to be effective, as each organization faces unique challenges and requires a customized strategy. While factors like market reputation, technology stack, and cost are important, they should be secondary to finding a provider that can serve as a true partner in managing the organization's specific security needs.

10. Which of the following is the most effective way to ensure that third-party vendors and business partners comply with an organization's information security policies and standards?
a. Requiring vendors to sign non-disclosure agreements (NDAs) before sharing any sensitive information
b. Conducting annual security audits of vendors' practices and systems
c. Incorporating specific security requirements and service level agreements (SLAs) into vendor contracts
d. Providing vendors with access to the organization's security awareness training materials

Answer: c. Incorporating specific security requirements and service level agreements (SLAs) into vendor contracts. Explanation: To hold third-party vendors accountable for adhering to the organization's security policies and standards, it is essential to establish clear expectations and requirements upfront as part of the contractual agreement. This should include specific security controls, performance metrics, reporting obligations, and consequences for non-compliance. While NDAs, audits, and training can help support vendor security management, they are not as effective as legally binding contract terms in ensuring ongoing compliance.

11. Which of the following best describes the primary goal of information security governance?
a. Ensuring compliance with legal and regulatory requirements
b. Implementing technical controls to protect information assets
c. Aligning information security strategies with business objectives
d. Conducting periodic vulnerability assessments and penetration testing

Answer: c. Aligning information security strategies with business objectives. Explanation: Information security governance aims to ensure that an organization's information security strategies and practices are aligned with and support its overall business objectives. This involves establishing a framework for making informed decisions about information security risks, investments, and priorities based on the organization's specific goals, risk appetite, and compliance obligations.

12. Which of the following is the most important outcome of effective information security governance?
a. Reduced costs associated with security technology investments
b. Increased stakeholder confidence in the organization's ability to protect sensitive information
c. Improved compliance with industry-specific security standards and regulations
d. Enhanced technical capabilities to detect and respond to security incidents

Answer: b. Increased stakeholder confidence in the organization's ability to protect sensitive information. Explanation: The ultimate goal of information security governance is to assure stakeholders (e.g., customers, shareholders, regulators) that the organization is effectively managing information security risks and protecting sensitive data. While cost optimization, compliance, and technical capabilities are important enablers of effective governance, they are not the primary outcomes that governance seeks to achieve.

13. Which of the following is a key principle of effective information security governance?
a. Centralized decision-making and control over all security activities
b. Separation of duties between security and IT operations teams
c. Alignment of security strategies with the organization's risk appetite and business objectives
d. Prioritization of security investments based on the latest industry trends and technologies

Answer: c. Alignment of security strategies with the organization's risk appetite and business objectives. Explanation: A fundamental principle of effective information security governance is ensuring that security strategies, policies, and decisions are aligned with the organization's overall risk tolerance and business goals. This requires a clear understanding of the organization's risk landscape, as well as ongoing communication and collaboration between security leaders and business stakeholders to ensure that security practices enable rather than hinder the achievement of business objectives.

14. Which of the following is the most important factor in gaining executive support for information security governance initiatives?
a. Presenting a detailed technical analysis of the organization's security vulnerabilities
b. Demonstrating the potential cost savings associated with improved security practices
c. Highlighting the reputational and financial risks associated with security breaches or non-compliance
d. Comparing the organization's security posture to that of its competitors

Answer: c. Highlighting the reputational and financial risks associated with security breaches or non-compliance. Explanation: To secure executive buy-in for information security governance, it is essential to communicate the business impact of security risks in terms that resonate with senior leaders. This often involves emphasizing the potential reputational damage, financial losses, legal liabilities, and operational disruptions that could result from a major security incident or compliance failure, rather than focusing on technical vulnerabilities or cost savings alone.

15. Which of the following is the most effective way to ensure that information security governance is an ongoing, continuous process?
a. Conducting annual security audits and assessments
b. Implementing automated security monitoring and reporting tools
c. Establishing clear roles, responsibilities, and accountability for security decision-making
d. Providing regular security awareness training to all employees

Answer: c. Establishing clear roles, responsibilities, and accountability for security decision-making. Explanation: While audits, monitoring, and training are important components of a comprehensive security program, the key to ensuring continuous governance is establishing clear ownership and accountability for security decisions and outcomes. This involves defining specific roles and responsibilities for security leadership, as well as implementing processes for ongoing communication, reporting, and performance measurement to ensure that governance activities are consistently carried out and adapted as needed over time.

16. Which of the following metrics is most useful for assessing the effectiveness of an organization's information security governance program?
a. The number of security incidents detected and resolved each month
b. The percentage of systems and applications that have been patched and updated
c. The level of alignment between security initiatives and the organization's risk management strategy
d. The number of employees who have completed security awareness training

Answer: c. The level of alignment between security initiatives and the organization's risk management strategy. Explanation: The primary goal of information security governance is to ensure that security practices are aligned with and support the organization's overall risk management approach. Therefore, the most relevant metric for evaluating governance effectiveness is the degree to which security initiatives and investments are prioritized and implemented in accordance with the organization's risk appetite, tolerance, and business objectives, rather than operational metrics like incident counts or patching rates.

17. Which of the following is the most significant challenge in implementing effective information security governance?
a. The rapid pace of change in the technology and threat landscape
b. The complexity and scale of modern enterprise IT environments
c. The lack of standardized frameworks and best practices for security governance

d. The difficulty in aligning security goals with business objectives and risk management strategies

Answer: d. The difficulty in aligning security goals with business objectives and risk management strategies. Explanation: While factors like technological change, environmental complexity, and the absence of clear standards can certainly complicate governance efforts, the most fundamental challenge is often the disconnect between security and business priorities. Security leaders may struggle to translate technical risks into business terms, while business leaders may view security as a barrier to innovation and growth. Overcoming this misalignment requires ongoing communication, education, and collaboration to ensure that security is treated as a strategic enabler rather than a necessary evil.

18. Which of the following is the most important competency for an effective information security governance leader?
a. Deep technical expertise in security tools and technologies
b. Strong project management and organizational skills
c. Excellent communication and relationship-building abilities
d. Extensive knowledge of regulatory compliance requirements

Answer: c. Excellent communication and relationship-building abilities. Explanation: While technical knowledge, project management acumen, and compliance expertise are certainly valuable, the most critical skill for a security governance leader is the ability to communicate effectively with a wide range of stakeholders and build productive relationships across the organization. Governance requires influencing and collaborating with individuals at all levels, from board members and executives to business unit leaders and IT staff, in order to drive alignment, secure resources, and effect change.

19. Which of the following statements best describes the relationship between information security governance and IT governance?
a. Information security governance and IT governance are essentially the same things.
b. Information security governance is a subset of IT governance, focused specifically on security issues.
c. IT governance is a subset of information security governance, focused specifically on technology issues.
d. Information security governance and IT governance are separate but interdependent disciplines.

Answer: d. Information security governance and IT governance are separate but interdependent disciplines. Explanation: While information security governance and IT governance are closely related and often overlap, they are distinct disciplines with different focuses. IT governance broadly addresses the management and oversight of an organization's IT resources, investments, and performance, while information security governance specifically addresses the management and oversight of information security risks, policies, and programs. Effective security governance requires close coordination with IT governance to ensure that security considerations are integrated into overall IT strategy and decision-making, but it also involves engagement with other governance functions such as corporate governance, risk management, and compliance.

20. Which of the following is the most important outcome of aligning information security governance with enterprise risk management (ERM)?
a. Improved coordination and information sharing between security and risk management teams
b. Increased visibility and understanding of security risks among senior executives and board members
c. Enhanced ability to prioritize and allocate resources to the most critical security risks
d. Greater assurance that security practices are consistent with the organization's overall risk tolerance

Answer: d. Greater assurance that security practices are consistent with the organization's overall risk tolerance. Explanation: The primary benefit of aligning information security governance with ERM is ensuring that security risks are managed in a way that is consistent with the organization's broader risk appetite and tolerance. By integrating security into the overall ERM framework, organizations can ensure that security risks are assessed, prioritized, and treated in the context of other enterprise risks, rather than in isolation. This helps to ensure that security investments and practices are appropriate given the organization's specific risk profile and business objectives, and that security risk management is an integral part of the organization's overall risk management strategy.

21. Which of the following is NOT a key component of an information security governance framework?
a. Risk management
b. Compliance management
c. Incident response procedures
d. Performance measurement

Answer: c. Incident response procedures. Explanation: While incident response is a critical part of an overall information security program, it is not typically considered a core component of a governance framework. Governance focuses on the high-level management and oversight of the information security function, including risk management, compliance management, and performance measurement. Incident response, on the other hand, is a more tactical and operational process that falls under the broader umbrella of security management.

22. Which of the following is the primary role of the Board of Directors in an information security governance framework?
a. Developing and implementing security policies and procedures
b. Conducting regular vulnerability assessments and penetration tests
c. Providing oversight and strategic direction for the information security program
d. Investigating and responding to security incidents and breaches

Answer: c. Providing oversight and strategic direction for the information security program. Explanation: In an effective information security governance framework, the Board of Directors is responsible for providing high-level oversight and guidance to ensure that the organization's security program is aligned with its overall strategy and risk appetite. This includes reviewing and approving security policies, setting performance expectations, and monitoring the effectiveness of the program. The Board typically delegates the day-to-day management and implementation of security controls to the executive leadership team and security practitioners.

23. Which of the following is the most important benefit of having a well-defined information security governance framework?
a. Ensuring compliance with all applicable laws and regulations
b. Preventing all security incidents and breaches from occurring
c. Aligning security practices with the organization's risk tolerance and business objectives
d. Minimizing the costs associated with implementing and maintaining security controls

Answer: c. Aligning security practices with the organization's risk tolerance and business objectives. Explanation: The primary purpose of an information security governance framework is to ensure that an organization's security practices are consistent with its overall risk management strategy and business goals. A well-defined framework provides a structure for making informed decisions about security investments, policies, and priorities based on the organization's specific risk profile and objectives. While compliance, incident prevention, and cost optimization are important considerations, they are not the ultimate goals of a governance framework.

24. Which of the following is a key role of security policies in an information security governance framework?
a. Providing detailed technical specifications for implementing security controls
b. Establishing clear expectations and guidelines for acceptable use of information assets

c. Ensuring complete protection against all possible security threats and vulnerabilities
d. Eliminating the need for security awareness training and education programs

Answer: b. Establishing clear expectations and guidelines for acceptable use of information assets. Explanation: Security policies are a critical component of an information security governance framework, as they set the foundation for how an organization manages and protects its information assets. Policies establish clear rules, responsibilities, and expectations for the acceptable use of systems, data, and other resources, and provide a basis for holding individuals accountable for their security-related actions. While policies may reference technical controls and standards, their primary purpose is to provide high-level guidance and direction, not detailed implementation specifications.

25. Which of the following metrics is most useful for measuring the effectiveness of an information security governance framework?
a. The number of security incidents detected and prevented each year
b. The percentage of employees who have completed mandatory security awareness training
c. The level of alignment between security initiatives and the organization's risk appetite and business objectives
d. The frequency with which security policies and procedures are reviewed and updated

Answer: c. The level of alignment between security initiatives and the organization's risk appetite and business objectives. Explanation: The effectiveness of an information security governance framework should be measured by the degree to which it enables an organization to manage security risks in a way that supports its overall business strategy and goals. Metrics that focus on the alignment between security practices and the organization's risk tolerance, such as the percentage of high-priority risks that have been adequately mitigated or the level of stakeholder confidence in the security program, are more meaningful indicators of governance effectiveness than operational metrics like incident counts or training completion rates.

26. Which of the following is a key responsibility of senior management in an information security governance framework?
a. Conducting regular security audits and assessments
b. Developing and implementing tactical security controls and procedures
c. Allocating adequate resources and funding to support the security program
d. Responding to security incidents and breaches as they occur

Answer: c. Allocating adequate resources and funding to support the security program. Explanation: In an information security governance framework, senior management is responsible for ensuring that the security program has the necessary resources, including personnel, technology, and funding, to effectively manage risks and support business objectives. This includes developing and approving security budgets, prioritizing investments based on risk and value, and ensuring that security initiatives are adequately staffed and supported. While senior management may also be involved in overseeing audits, control implementation, and incident response, these responsibilities are typically delegated to other roles within the security organization.

27. Which of the following is the most important factor in ensuring the success of an information security governance framework?
a. Implementing the latest security technologies and tools
b. Achieving 100% compliance with all applicable laws and regulations
c. Obtaining buy-in and support from senior leadership and the Board of Directors
d. Hiring a large team of highly skilled security professionals

Answer: c. Obtaining buy-in and support from senior leadership and the Board of Directors. Explanation: The effectiveness of an information security governance framework depends heavily on the level of support and engagement from an organization's top leadership. Without clear direction, oversight, and resources from the Board and senior management, even the most well-designed governance framework will struggle to achieve its objectives. Securing executive buy-in requires ongoing communication and education to ensure that leaders understand the business impact of security risks and the value of a strong governance program.

28. Which of the following statements best describes the relationship between an information security governance framework and a risk management framework?
a. An information security governance framework and a risk management framework are the same things.
b. An information security governance framework is a subset of a risk management framework.
c. A risk management framework is a subset of an information security governance framework.
d. An information security governance framework and a risk management framework are separate but closely related.

Answer: d. An information security governance framework and a risk management framework are separate but closely related. Explanation: While an information security governance framework and a risk management framework are distinct, they are highly interdependent. A governance framework establishes the overall structure and processes for managing an organization's security program, while a risk management framework provides a specific methodology for identifying, assessing, and treating risks. Effective security governance requires the integration of risk management principles and practices to ensure that security decisions are risk-based and aligned with business objectives.

29. Which of the following is the most important aspect of an information security governance framework for ensuring compliance with relevant laws and regulations?
a. Conducting regular compliance audits and assessments
b. Implementing technical controls to prevent compliance violations
c. Providing compliance training to all employees and stakeholders
d. Establishing clear policies and oversight processes for managing compliance obligations

Answer: d. Establishing clear policies and oversight processes for managing compliance obligations. Explanation: While audits, technical controls, and training are all important components of a compliance program, the foundation of effective compliance management within a governance framework is the establishment of clear policies, roles, and responsibilities for meeting legal and regulatory requirements. This includes defining the specific compliance obligations that apply to the organization, assigning ownership and accountability for ensuring compliance, and implementing processes for monitoring, reporting, and enforcing adherence to policies and standards.

30. Which of the following is a key benefit of integrating information security governance with broader IT governance and corporate governance frameworks?
a. Reducing the overall cost and complexity of governance processes
b. Eliminating the need for dedicated security governance resources and oversight
c. Ensuring that security considerations are incorporated into enterprise-wide decision-making
d. Allowing security teams to operate independently from other business functions

Answer: c. Ensuring that security considerations are incorporated into enterprise-wide decision-making. Explanation: Integrating information security governance with other governance frameworks helps to ensure that security is not treated as a siloed or isolated function, but rather as an integral part of an organization's overall business strategy and operations. By aligning security governance with IT and corporate governance processes, organizations can ensure that security risks and requirements are consistently considered in the context of broader technology, financial, and operational decisions. This promotes a more holistic and effective approach to risk management and helps to embed security into the fabric of the business.

31. An organization's Board of Directors has requested a presentation on the alignment of the company's information security program with its overall business strategy. Which of the following topics would be most important to include in the presentation?
a. A detailed technical overview of the organization's security architecture and controls
b. A comparison of the organization's security budget and staffing levels to industry benchmarks
c. An analysis of how the security program supports the organization's key business objectives and risk management priorities
d. A summary of the latest cybersecurity threats and trends, and their potential impact on the organization

Answer: c. An analysis of how the security program supports the organization's key business objectives and risk management priorities. Explanation: When communicating with the Board about the alignment of security with business objectives, it is essential to focus on the strategic value and impact of the security program, rather than technical details or operational metrics. The Board is primarily interested in understanding how security investments and initiatives help to enable the organization's core business goals, manage its key risks, and support its overall mission and values. Providing specific examples and metrics that demonstrate this alignment is key to securing the Board's buy-in and support for the security program.

32. Which of the following is the most effective way to ensure that information security is consistently considered in the development of new business initiatives and strategies?
a. Requiring all business plans to undergo a formal security review and approval process
b. Educating business leaders on the latest cybersecurity risks and trends
c. Embedding security professionals within business units to provide ongoing guidance and support
d. Conducting regular security audits and assessments of business processes and systems

Answer: c. Embedding security professionals within business units to provide ongoing guidance and support. Explanation: While security reviews, education, and audits are all important components of a comprehensive security program, the most effective way to ensure that security is consistently integrated into business decision-making is to have security professionals directly involved in the day-to-day operations and initiatives of each business unit. By working side-by-side with business leaders and teams, security professionals can proactively identify and address potential risks, provide real-time guidance and support, and help to build a culture of security awareness and accountability throughout the organization.

33. An organization is considering implementing a new customer-facing web application that will collect and store sensitive personal information. Which of the following is the most important consideration from an information security perspective?
a. The potential revenue and market share that the application could generate
b. The level of technical complexity and novelty of the application's features and functionality
c. The alignment of the application's security requirements with the organization's overall risk appetite and tolerance
d. The speed and agility with which the application can be developed and launched

Answer: c. The alignment of the application's security requirements with the organization's overall risk appetite and tolerance. Explanation: When evaluating the security implications of a new business initiative, such as a customer-facing web application, the most critical factor is whether the associated risks are acceptable given the organization's overall risk management strategy and priorities. This requires a clear understanding of the specific security requirements and controls needed to protect sensitive data, as well as an assessment of how those requirements align with the organization's risk appetite and tolerance thresholds. While factors such as revenue potential, technical complexity, and time-to-market are important business considerations, they should not override the need to ensure that security risks are effectively managed in line with the organization's overall risk posture.

34. Which of the following metrics would be most useful for communicating the business value of an information security program to senior executives?
a. The number of security incidents detected and prevented each month
b. The percentage of systems and applications that have been patched and updated
c. The reduction in the organization's cyber insurance premiums due to improved security practices
d. The average time required to detect and contain security incidents

Answer: c. The reduction in the organization's cyber insurance premiums due to improved security practices. Explanation: When seeking to demonstrate the business value of an information security program to senior executives, it is important to use metrics that translate security performance into financial and strategic terms. One powerful example is the potential cost savings associated with reducing the organization's cyber insurance premiums through improved security practices. By implementing effective controls and demonstrating a strong security posture, organizations can often negotiate lower premiums or more favorable coverage terms with their insurers. This directly impacts the bottom line and provides a tangible measure of the return on security investments. Other metrics, such as incident counts or patching rates, may be useful for operational purposes but are less effective at communicating the strategic value of security to business leaders.

35. Which of the following is the most significant challenge in aligning information security with business objectives?
a. The technical complexity and rapid evolution of cybersecurity threats and technologies
b. The lack of standardized metrics and frameworks for measuring security performance and value
c. The competing priorities and incentives of different stakeholders within the organization
d. The difficulty in quantifying the full financial and reputational costs of security incidents and breaches

Answer: c. The competing priorities and incentives of different stakeholders within the organization. Explanation: One of the main obstacles to achieving alignment between security and business objectives is the often-conflicting interests and motivations of various stakeholders, such as business unit leaders, IT teams, legal and compliance departments, and security professionals. Each group may have its own goals, metrics, and decision-making processes that prioritize different aspects of security or business performance. For example, business leaders may be primarily focused on revenue growth and time-to-market, while security teams may prioritize risk reduction and control effectiveness. Balancing these competing priorities and finding ways to incentivize collaboration and shared accountability is a key challenge in driving true alignment between security and the business.

36. An organization has recently suffered a major data breach that has resulted in significant financial losses and reputational damage. Which of the following actions would be most important for the information security team to take to help restore trust and confidence among customers and stakeholders?
a. Conducting a thorough root cause analysis and technical investigation of the breach
b. Implementing new security controls and technologies to prevent future incidents
c. Providing transparent and timely communication about the breach and the organization's response efforts
d. Terminating or disciplining employees who were responsible for the security failures that led to the breach

Answer: c. Providing transparent and timely communication about the breach and the organization's response efforts. Explanation: In the aftermath of a major security incident, one of the most critical factors in maintaining the trust and support of customers, partners, and other stakeholders is the quality and timeliness of the organization's communication and transparency. While technical investigations, control improvements, and accountability measures are all important elements of the response process, the top priority from a business perspective should be providing clear, accurate, and empathetic information about what happened, how it is being addressed, and what steps are being taken to prevent future incidents. This may involve a combination of public statements, individual notifications, and ongoing updates that demonstrate the organization's commitment to security and to making things right for those affected by the breach.

37. Which of the following is the most effective way to build a culture of security awareness and responsibility among employees across an organization?
a. Conducting mandatory annual security training sessions for all employees
b. Sending regular security update emails and newsletters to all employees
c. Integrating security goals and metrics into employee performance evaluations and incentives
d. Requiring employees to sign acceptable use policies and other security agreements

Answer: c. Integrating security goals and metrics into employee performance evaluations and incentives. Explanation: While training, communication, and policies are important components of a security awareness program, the most powerful way to drive lasting behavior change and accountability is to embed security into the organization's performance management and incentive structures. By including specific security objectives and metrics in employee evaluations and tying them to compensation, promotions, and other rewards, organizations can send a clear message that security is a core responsibility and value for all employees, not just the security team. This approach helps to create a sense of shared ownership and motivation for security, and encourages employees to prioritize security considerations in their day-to-day work and decision-making.

38. An organization is evaluating potential vendors for a new cloud-based software service that will store and process sensitive customer data. Which of the following factors should be given the highest priority in the selection process from an information security perspective?
a. The vendor's market share and reputation in the industry
b. The cost and scalability of the vendor's service offerings
c. The vendor's ability to meet the organization's specific security and compliance requirements
d. The speed and ease of implementation of the vendor's solution

Answer: c. The vendor's ability to meet the organization's specific security and compliance requirements. Explanation: When selecting a third-party vendor or service provider that will have access to sensitive data, the primary consideration from a security standpoint should be the vendor's capacity and commitment to meeting the organization's unique security and compliance needs. This includes evaluating the vendor's security controls, data handling practices, incident response capabilities, and adherence to relevant industry standards and regulations. It may also involve assessing the vendor's willingness to customize its offerings or enter into specific contractual agreements to ensure alignment with the organization's security policies and risk management framework. While factors such as cost, performance, and market presence are certainly important, they should not take precedence over the fundamental requirement of protecting the confidentiality, integrity, and availability of the organization's data.

39. Which of the following statements best describes the role of information security in enabling an organization's digital transformation and innovation initiatives?
a. Security is a necessary but separate function that should not interfere with or slow down digital transformation efforts.
b. Security is an integral part of digital transformation and should be embedded into all aspects of the innovation process.
c. Security is primarily a compliance and regulatory requirement that must be met to allow digital transformation to proceed.
d. Security is a technical discipline that focuses on protecting systems and data, while digital transformation is a business strategy.

Answer: b. Security is an integral part of digital transformation and should be embedded into all aspects of the innovation process. Explanation: In today's digital business environment, information security cannot be treated as a siloed or separate function from an organization's overall strategy and operations. To be successful and sustainable, digital transformation and innovation initiatives must be built on a foundation of strong security practices that enable trust, resilience, and agility. This means integrating security considerations and expertise into every stage of the innovation lifecycle, from ideation and design to development, testing, and deployment. By working closely with business and technology teams to identify and manage risks, implement secure architectures and controls, and build security into the fabric of new products, services, and processes, information security professionals can help to accelerate and support digital transformation efforts while also protecting the organization's critical assets and stakeholders.

40. An organization's marketing department has proposed a new initiative to collect and analyze customer data from various sources to personalize advertising and improve targeting. Which of the following would be the most important consideration for the information security team in evaluating this proposal?
a. The potential revenue and competitive advantages that could be gained from the initiative
b. The technical feasibility and complexity of implementing the necessary data collection and analysis tools
c. The alignment of the initiative with the organization's data governance and privacy policies and risk appetite
d. The level of interest and demand from customers for more personalized and targeted advertising

Answer: c. The alignment of the initiative with the organization's data governance and privacy policies and risk appetite. Explanation: When assessing the security implications of a new data-driven business initiative, such as personalized advertising, the primary focus should be on ensuring that the collection, use, and protection of customer data aligns with the organization's established data governance framework, privacy policies, and overall risk management strategy. This includes evaluating the specific types and sources of data being collected, the purposes for which it will be used, the consent and notification mechanisms for customers, and the controls in place to safeguard data throughout its lifecycle. It also involves considering the potential risks and liabilities associated with the initiative, such as data breaches, regulatory violations, or reputational damage, and determining whether they fall within the organization's acceptable risk tolerance levels. While the business benefits and technical aspects of the initiative are certainly relevant, they should be weighed against the fundamental need to uphold the organization's commitments and obligations to protecting customer privacy and security.

41. Which of the following best describes the primary role of the Information Security Manager in governance?
a. Developing and implementing technical security controls and solutions
b. Conducting periodic vulnerability assessments and penetration tests
c. Providing strategic guidance and oversight to ensure the security program aligns with business objectives
d. Investigating and responding to security incidents and breaches

Answer: c. Providing strategic guidance and oversight to ensure the security program aligns with business objectives. Explanation: The Information Security Manager plays a critical role in governance by serving as a strategic leader and advisor who ensures that the organization's security program supports its overall goals and risk management priorities. This involves working closely with senior executives, the Board of Directors, and other key stakeholders to understand the organization's business objectives, risk appetite, and compliance obligations, and to develop and implement a security strategy that enables the achievement of those objectives. While the Information Security Manager may also be involved in overseeing technical controls, assessments, and incident response, these tactical responsibilities are secondary to the primary governance role of providing strategic direction and alignment.

42. Which of the following is the most important competency for an effective Information Security Manager in fulfilling their governance responsibilities?
a. Deep technical expertise in security tools and technologies
b. Strong project management and organizational skills
c. Excellent communication and relationship-building abilities
d. Extensive knowledge of regulatory compliance requirements

Answer: c. Excellent communication and relationship-building abilities. Explanation: To be effective in their governance role, an Information Security Manager must be able to communicate clearly and persuasively with a wide range of stakeholders, including executives, Board members, business unit leaders, IT teams, and external partners. They must be able to translate complex technical risks into business terms, articulate the strategic value of security investments, and build consensus and support for security initiatives. This requires strong interpersonal skills, emotional intelligence, and the ability to establish trust and credibility with stakeholders at all levels of the organization. While technical expertise, project management skills, and compliance knowledge are certainly important, they are not sufficient on their own to drive the kind of strategic alignment and influence that is essential for effective security governance.

43. Which of the following is the most important responsibility of the Information Security Manager in developing and maintaining an information security governance framework?
a. Defining and documenting security policies, procedures, and standards
b. Conducting regular security audits and assessments to identify gaps and weaknesses
c. Implementing and managing security technologies and tools
d. Aligning security goals and initiatives with the organization's overall business objectives and risk management strategy

Answer: d. Aligning security goals and initiatives with the organization's overall business objectives and risk management strategy. Explanation: The key to developing an effective information security governance framework is ensuring that it is closely aligned with the organization's broader strategic priorities and risk management approach. As the primary owner and driver of the framework, the Information Security Manager must take the lead in understanding the organization's business goals, risk appetite, and compliance obligations, and translating those into a set of security objectives, policies, and initiatives that support and enable the achievement of those goals. This involves ongoing communication and collaboration with senior leaders and stakeholders across the organization to ensure that security is not seen as a standalone or siloed function, but rather as an integral part of the overall business strategy and operations.

44. Which of the following metrics would be most useful for the Information Security Manager to track and report on as part of their governance responsibilities?
a. The number of security incidents detected and resolved each month
b. The percentage of systems and applications that have been patched and updated
c. The level of alignment between security initiatives and the organization's risk appetite and business objectives
d. The number of employees who have completed security awareness training

Answer: c. The level of alignment between security initiatives and the organization's risk appetite and business objectives. Explanation: As a strategic leader and advisor, the Information Security Manager should focus on metrics that demonstrate the value and effectiveness of the security program in supporting the organization's overall goals and risk management priorities. One of the most important indicators of this alignment is the degree to which security investments and initiatives are prioritized and implemented based on their relevance and impact to the organization's specific risk appetite and business objectives. By tracking and reporting on metrics such as the percentage of high-priority risks that have been addressed, the level of senior leadership engagement and support for security, and the contribution of security to key business outcomes, the Information Security Manager can help to build credibility and justify the ongoing investment in security.

45. Which of the following is the most significant challenge for the Information Security Manager in ensuring effective governance of third-party relationships and supply chain security?
a. Conducting thorough due diligence and risk assessments of potential vendors and partners
b. Implementing technical controls and monitoring solutions to detect and prevent security incidents
c. Ensuring clear contractual terms and service level agreements that hold third parties accountable for security

d. Aligning third-party security practices with the organization's internal policies and risk management framework

Answer: d. Aligning third-party security practices with the organization's internal policies and risk management framework. Explanation: One of the key governance challenges for the Information Security Manager is extending the organization's security policies, standards, and controls to third-party relationships and ensuring consistency and alignment across the entire supply chain. This requires a holistic approach that goes beyond simply conducting one-time assessments or implementing point solutions, and instead focuses on building a shared understanding and commitment to security with vendors and partners. The Information Security Manager must work closely with procurement, legal, and business teams to establish clear expectations and requirements for third-party security, and to implement ongoing monitoring, auditing, and collaboration processes to ensure that those requirements are being met. This may involve developing common risk assessment frameworks, sharing threat intelligence and best practices, and participating in joint incident response planning and testing.

46. In the event of a major security incident or data breach, what is the primary role of the Information Security Manager in the organization's crisis management and response efforts?
a. Leading the technical investigation and forensic analysis of the incident
b. Coordinating with legal and public relations teams to manage external communications and disclosures
c. Providing strategic guidance and support to senior leaders to ensure an effective and coordinated response
d. Implementing emergency security controls and measures to contain and mitigate the impact of the incident

Answer: c. Providing strategic guidance and support to senior leaders to ensure an effective and coordinated response. Explanation: In a crisis situation, the Information Security Manager's primary responsibility is to serve as a strategic advisor and liaison to senior leadership, helping to guide and coordinate the organization's overall response and recovery efforts. This involves providing clear and timely information and recommendations to executives and the Board on the scope and impact of the incident, the key risks and priorities for response, and the resources and support needed from across the organization. The Information Security Manager must also work closely with other key functions, such as legal, HR, communications, and customer service, to ensure a consistent and effective approach to managing the incident and mitigating its consequences. While the Information Security Manager may also be involved in overseeing technical investigations and implementing control measures, these tactical responsibilities should not distract from the critical governance role of providing strategic direction and support to leadership.

47. Which of the following is the most effective way for the Information Security Manager to build and maintain strong relationships with key stakeholders across the organization?
a. Regularly attending department meetings and events to share updates on security initiatives and gather feedback
b. Providing detailed technical reports and metrics on security performance and compliance
c. Developing a clear and compelling communication strategy that articulates the value and importance of security
d. Offering training and education sessions to help stakeholders understand and support security best practices

Answer: c. Developing a clear and compelling communication strategy that articulates the value and importance of security. Explanation: To be effective in their governance role, the Information Security Manager must be able to build trust, credibility, and influence with stakeholders at all levels of the organization. This requires a proactive and strategic approach to communication that goes beyond simply sharing information or delivering training, and instead focuses on engaging stakeholders in a meaningful dialogue about the value and importance of security to the business. The Information Security Manager should develop a clear and compelling narrative that explains how security supports and enables the organization's goals and objectives, and how it helps to protect the interests of customers, employees, and other key stakeholders. This narrative should be tailored to the specific needs and concerns of different audiences, and should be delivered through a variety of channels and formats, such as executive briefings, town hall meetings, newsletters, and social media. By consistently communicating the strategic value of security and building strong relationships with stakeholders, the Information Security Manager can help to create a culture of shared ownership and accountability for security across the organization.

48. How can the Information Security Manager effectively advocate for and justify investments in security initiatives and resources to senior leadership and the Board?
a. By presenting detailed cost-benefit analyses and ROI projections for each proposed investment
b. By highlighting the potential legal and regulatory risks and penalties associated with security failures or non-compliance
c. By aligning security investment proposals with the organization's overall business strategy and risk management priorities
d. By comparing the organization's security spending and capabilities to industry benchmarks and best practices

Answer: c. By aligning security investment proposals with the organization's overall business strategy and risk management priorities. Explanation: To secure the necessary funding and support for security initiatives, the Information Security Manager must be able to clearly articulate how those initiatives contribute to the organization's overall success and risk resilience. This requires a deep understanding of the organization's business objectives, competitive landscape, and risk appetite, and the ability to translate security risks and opportunities into strategic terms that resonate with senior leaders and the Board. Rather than focusing solely on the technical merits or compliance requirements of a particular security investment, the Information Security Manager should frame the proposal in the context of how it supports and enables the organization's key priorities, such as entering new markets, launching new products or services, or improving customer trust and loyalty. By demonstrating the strategic alignment and value of security investments, the Information Security Manager can help to build a compelling business case and gain the buy-in and support of key decision-makers.

49. Which of the following is the most important factor in determining the appropriate level of involvement and oversight of the Information Security Manager in the organization's overall risk management and decision-making processes?
a. The size and complexity of the organization's IT infrastructure and security environment
b. The regulatory and compliance requirements applicable to the organization's industry and geographic locations
c. The maturity and effectiveness of the organization's existing risk management and governance frameworks
d. The level of risk associated with the organization's business activities and the potential impact of security incidents

Answer: d. The level of risk associated with the organization's business activities and the potential impact of security incidents. Explanation: The extent to which the Information Security Manager is involved in and provides oversight of the organization's broader risk management and decision-making processes should be based on the level of risk and potential impact associated with security issues. In organizations where security risks are highly relevant and consequential to the overall business strategy and operations, such as those in heavily regulated industries, those dealing with highly sensitive data, or those with a high public profile, the Information Security Manager should have a more prominent and influential role in governance and risk management. This may involve serving on executive risk committees, providing regular briefings to the Board, and being consulted on major business decisions and initiatives. In contrast, in organizations where security risks are less material or where there are well-established risk management and governance processes in place, the Information Security Manager may have a more limited or advisory role. Ultimately, the key is to ensure that the level of security governance is commensurate with the level of risk and importance to the business.

50. Which of the following best describes the ideal reporting structure and relationship between the Information Security Manager and other senior executives and governance bodies?
a. The Information Security Manager should report directly to the CEO or Board of Directors to ensure adequate visibility and support for security

b. The Information Security Manager should report to the CIO or IT leadership to ensure close alignment with technology strategy and operations
c. The Information Security Manager should report to the CFO or finance leadership to ensure adequate oversight and control over security spending and risk management
d. The Information Security Manager should have a dotted-line or matrix reporting relationship to multiple executives and governance bodies based on the specific security issues and initiatives involved

Answer: d. The Information Security Manager should have a dotted-line or matrix reporting relationship to multiple executives and governance bodies based on the specific security issues and initiatives involved. Explanation: Given the cross-functional and strategic nature of the Information Security Manager's role, it is important that they have strong relationships and alignment with a variety of senior leaders and governance bodies across the organization. While the specific reporting structure may vary depending on the organization's size, industry, and culture, a matrix or dotted-line approach that allows the Information Security Manager to work closely with multiple stakeholders is often most effective. This may involve reporting directly to the CIO or CISO for operational purposes, while also having regular interactions and accountability to the CFO, COO, and other executives on matters related to risk management, compliance, and business strategy. Additionally, the Information Security Manager should have a direct line of communication to the Board of Directors or relevant Board committees, such as the Risk or Audit Committee, to ensure adequate oversight and support for the security program. By fostering a collaborative and integrated approach to security governance, the Information Security Manager can help to ensure that security is a shared responsibility and priority across the entire organization.

51. Which of the following best describes the primary purpose of an information security policy?
a. To provide detailed technical specifications for implementing security controls and solutions
b. To establish high-level principles, guidelines, and expectations for managing information security risks
c. To ensure compliance with all applicable laws, regulations, and industry standards
d. To document the specific procedures and steps for responding to security incidents and breaches

Answer: b. To establish high-level principles, guidelines, and expectations for managing information security risks. Explanation: An information security policy is a strategic document that sets forth the organization's overall approach, direction, and priorities for managing information security risks. It defines the scope and objectives of the security program, the roles and responsibilities of key stakeholders, and the guiding principles and standards that should be followed. While policies may reference specific laws, regulations, or controls, their primary purpose is to provide a high-level framework for making consistent and effective security decisions across the organization.

52. What is the most important factor to consider when determining the scope and applicability of an information security policy?
a. The size and complexity of the organization's IT infrastructure and security environment
b. The regulatory and compliance requirements applicable to the organization's industry and geographic locations
c. The sensitivity and criticality of the information assets and systems covered by the policy
d. The preferences and expectations of key stakeholders, such as executives, customers, and partners

Answer: c. The sensitivity and criticality of the information assets and systems covered by the policy. Explanation: The scope and applicability of an information security policy should be based primarily on the level of risk associated with the specific information assets, systems, and processes that the policy is intended to protect. This requires a clear understanding and classification of the organization's data and systems based on their sensitivity, criticality, and potential impact if compromised. Assets that are deemed to be of high value or importance, such as intellectual property, financial data, or customer information, may require more stringent and comprehensive policy coverage than those that are less sensitive or critical. By aligning policy scope with risk levels, organizations can ensure that their security efforts are prioritized and proportionate to the specific threats and vulnerabilities they face.

53. Which of the following is the most effective approach for ensuring that information security policies are consistently followed and enforced across the organization?
a. Conducting regular security awareness training sessions for all employees
b. Implementing technical controls and monitoring solutions to detect and prevent policy violations
c. Defining clear consequences and disciplinary measures for policy non-compliance
d. Integrating security policies and procedures into business processes and workflows

Answer: d. Integrating security policies and procedures into business processes and workflows. Explanation: While training, technical controls, and enforcement measures are all important components of a policy compliance program, the most effective way to ensure consistent adherence to security policies is to embed them into the day-to-day operations and routines of the organization. This means translating high-level policy statements into specific procedures, guidelines, and standards that are tailored to the unique needs and contexts of different business units, functions, and roles. By making security an integral part of how work gets done, rather than an additional task or afterthought, organizations can foster a culture of continuous compliance and risk management.

54. Which of the following is the most important consideration when developing procedures to support the implementation of an information security policy?
a. Ensuring that the procedures are comprehensive and cover all possible scenarios and exceptions
b. Aligning the procedures with industry best practices and standards, such as ISO 27001 or NIST SP 800-53
c. Involving a wide range of stakeholders, including IT, legal, HR, and business units, in the procedure development process
d. Balancing the need for security with the operational efficiency and productivity of the business

Answer: d. Balancing the need for security with the operational efficiency and productivity of the business. Explanation: When developing procedures to implement security policies, it is critical to strike the right balance between risk management and business enablement. Procedures that are overly complex, restrictive, or burdensome can lead to employee frustration, workarounds, and even resistance to security measures. On the other hand, procedures that are too lax or incomplete can leave the organization exposed to unacceptable risks. The key is to design procedures that are clear, practical, and adaptable to the specific needs and constraints of different business processes and user groups. This requires close collaboration between security teams and business stakeholders to ensure that security requirements are integrated seamlessly into workflows and that any necessary trade-offs or exceptions are carefully evaluated and managed.

54. What is the primary difference between security standards and security procedures?
a. Standards are mandatory, while procedures are optional
b. Standards are high-level and general, while procedures are detailed and specific
c. Standards are externally focused, while procedures are internally focused
d. Standards are technical in nature, while procedures are operational in nature

Answer: b. Standards are high-level and general, while procedures are detailed and specific. Explanation: In the context of information security policies, standards and procedures serve different but complementary purposes. Standards establish the minimum requirements, specifications, or best practices that must be met in order to achieve a desired level of security. They provide a consistent and measurable basis for assessing and comparing security performance across different systems, processes, or organizations. Procedures, on the other hand, provide the detailed steps, instructions, and guidelines for actually implementing and operationalizing the standards in a specific context. They translate the high-level requirements of standards into concrete actions and responsibilities that can be carried out by individuals or teams. Together, standards and procedures help to ensure that security policies are not just aspirational statements, but are effectively and consistently put into practice.

55. Which of the following is the most important benefit of using a formal policy development lifecycle methodology, such as the PDCA (Plan-Do-Check-Act) model?
a. It ensures that policies are completely aligned with industry standards and best practices
b. It helps to identify and prioritize the most critical security risks and vulnerabilities
c. It provides a structured and repeatable process for creating, reviewing, and updating policies
d. It guarantees that policies will be fully understood and accepted by all stakeholders

Answer: c. It provides a structured and repeatable process for creating, reviewing, and updating policies. Explanation: A formal policy development lifecycle methodology, such as the PDCA model, provides a systematic and disciplined approach to managing the entire policy process, from initial planning and drafting through implementation, monitoring, and continuous improvement. By following a standardized set of steps and checkpoints, organizations can ensure that their policies are developed in a consistent, efficient, and effective manner, and that they remain up-to-date and relevant over time. This helps to reduce the risk of policy gaps, conflicts, or inconsistencies, and to promote a more proactive and coordinated approach to security governance. While a lifecycle methodology can certainly help to align policies with standards, prioritize risks, and engage stakeholders, its primary benefit is in providing a structured foundation for the ongoing management and optimization of the policy framework.

56. What is the most common pitfall or challenge in implementing information security policies and procedures?
a. Failing to adequately communicate and explain the policies to employees and stakeholders
b. Underestimating the time, resources, and costs required to develop and maintain policies
c. Focusing too much on technical controls and solutions, rather than on people and processes
d. Not regularly reviewing and updating policies to keep pace with changing risks and requirements

Answer: a. Failing to adequately communicate and explain the policies to employees and stakeholders. Explanation: One of the most significant barriers to effective policy implementation is a lack of clear, consistent, and engaging communication about the policies and their importance to the organization. Too often, policies are simply written and published without sufficient attention to how they will be disseminated, explained, and reinforced to the people who need to follow them. This can lead to confusion, misinterpretation, or even outright resistance among employees and stakeholders who may not understand the purpose, benefits, or expectations of the policies. To overcome this challenge, organizations must develop a comprehensive communication plan that includes a variety of channels, formats, and messages tailored to different audiences and contexts. This may involve training sessions, e-learning modules, posters, videos, newsletters, and other creative approaches to raising awareness and building buy-in for the policies and procedures.

57. Which of the following is the most effective way to ensure that information security policies and procedures remain relevant and effective over time?
a. Conducting an annual review and update of all policies and procedures
b. Establishing a dedicated policy management team or function within the organization
c. Implementing automated policy management and enforcement tools and technologies
d. Continuously monitoring and assessing the implementation and effectiveness of policies and procedures

Answer: d. Continuously monitoring and assessing the implementation and effectiveness of policies and procedures. Explanation: Given the rapidly evolving nature of information security risks and requirements, it is essential that policies and procedures are not treated as static or one-time documents, but rather as living and dynamic tools that are continuously monitored, assessed, and adapted to changing circumstances. This requires a proactive and data-driven approach to policy management that goes beyond periodic reviews or audits, and instead focuses on real-time visibility and feedback on how policies are being implemented and whether they are achieving their intended outcomes. By establishing metrics, dashboards, and reporting mechanisms to track policy compliance, effectiveness, and impact, organizations can quickly identify and respond to gaps, issues, or opportunities for improvement. They can also use this data to inform more targeted and timely updates to policies and procedures, as well as to demonstrate the value and progress of their security programs to stakeholders.

58. What is the role of security architecture and design principles in the development and implementation of information security policies and procedures?
a. Security architecture and design principles are not directly relevant to policy and procedure development
b. Security architecture and design principles should be used to determine the specific technical controls and solutions required by policies and procedures
c. Security architecture and design principles provide a framework for aligning policies and procedures with the organization's overall security strategy and goals
d. Security architecture and design principles are only applicable to the development of technical standards and guidelines, not policies and procedures

Answer: c. Security architecture and design principles provide a framework for aligning policies and procedures with the organization's overall security strategy and goals. Explanation: Security architecture and design principles, such as defense-in-depth, least privilege, and fail-safe defaults, are not just technical concepts, but also fundamental guiding principles that should inform the development and implementation of policies and procedures. They provide a coherent and consistent framework for making decisions about the types of policies and procedures that are needed, the level of detail and specificity required, and the way in which they should be structured and organized. By aligning policies and procedures with architectural principles, organizations can ensure that they are not only internally consistent and mutually reinforcing, but also support the overall security strategy and risk management goals of the enterprise. This helps to create a more unified and integrated approach to security governance, rather than a piecemeal or siloed one.

59. What is the most important consideration when developing exception processes for information security policies and procedures?
a. Ensuring that exceptions are granted only in rare and justifiable circumstances
b. Documenting and tracking all exceptions in a centralized repository or system
c. Involving senior management or the Board in the review and approval of exceptions
d. Establishing clear criteria and procedures for evaluating and managing the risks associated with exceptions

Answer: d. Establishing clear criteria and procedures for evaluating and managing the risks associated with exceptions. Explanation: While it is important to carefully control and limit the granting of exceptions to security policies and procedures, it is equally important to recognize that exceptions are sometimes necessary and appropriate to meet legitimate business needs or to respond to unique or unforeseen circumstances. The key is to have a well-defined and disciplined process for evaluating, approving, and managing exceptions that takes into account the specific risks and trade-offs involved. This should include clear criteria for determining when exceptions may be warranted, based on factors such as the criticality of the asset or process, the potential impact and likelihood of the risk, and the feasibility and cost of alternative mitigations. It should also include procedures for documenting, tracking, and periodically reviewing exceptions to ensure that they remain justified and effective over time, and that any additional controls or monitoring measures are properly implemented. By treating exceptions not as ad hoc or arbitrary decisions, but as an integral part of the overall risk management framework, organizations can strike a better balance between security and business agility.

60. Which of the following best describes the relationship between information security policies, procedures, and standards?
a. Policies are high-level statements of management's intent, procedures provide specific operational steps, and standards define the minimum acceptable level of security
b. Policies, procedures, and standards are interchangeable terms that refer to the same set of documented security requirements

c. Policies are mandatory, procedures are recommended, and standards are optional best practices
d. Policies apply to the entire organization, procedures apply to specific departments or functions, and standards apply to external third parties

Answer: a. Policies are high-level statements of management's intent, procedures provide specific operational steps, and standards define the minimum acceptable level of security. Explanation: In the hierarchy of information security documentation, policies sit at the top as the most high-level and strategic statements of an organization's security objectives, principles, and responsibilities. Procedures provide the next level of detail, translating policies into specific operational steps and instructions for implementation. Standards, which may be based on industry best practices or regulatory requirements, define the minimum acceptable level of security that must be met across the organization. Together, policies, procedures, and standards form a comprehensive and integrated framework for managing information security risks and outcomes.

61. Which of the following is the primary purpose of information security policies?
a. To define the technical controls and configurations required to secure systems and data
b. To establish management's expectations and requirements for protecting the confidentiality, integrity, and availability of information assets
c. To provide step-by-step instructions for implementing and maintaining security measures
d. To ensure compliance with all applicable laws, regulations, and contractual obligations

Answer: b. To establish management's expectations and requirements for protecting the confidentiality, integrity, and availability of information assets. Explanation: The main objective of information security policies is to articulate management's strategic intent, direction, and priorities for safeguarding the organization's information assets. Policies set the tone and expectations for security at the highest level, and provide a basis for making consistent and effective decisions about security risks, controls, and investments. While policies may reference specific legal or contractual requirements, their primary focus is on defining the organization's own security objectives and principles, based on its unique business needs, risk tolerance, and values.

62. What is the main difference between information security policies and procedures?
a. Policies are written by senior management, while procedures are written by operational staff
b. Policies are reviewed and updated annually, while procedures are updated continuously
c. Policies are enforceable and mandatory, while procedures are optional and discretionary
d. Policies provide high-level guidance and direction, while procedures provide detailed instructions and steps for implementation

Answer: d. Policies provide high-level guidance and direction, while procedures provide detailed instructions and steps for implementation. Explanation: Policies and procedures are complementary but distinct components of an information security program. Policies establish the overall framework and requirements for security, while procedures provide the specifics of how those requirements should be implemented and operationalized on a day-to-day basis. Procedures take the high-level statements of policies and break them down into actionable steps, roles, and responsibilities that can be followed by individuals and teams. Without clear procedures, policies risk being seen as abstract or aspirational, rather than as practical and enforceable standards of behavior.

63. Which of the following is an example of an information security standard?
a. A document that outlines the acceptable use of the organization's email system
b. A set of step-by-step instructions for configuring firewall rules and access controls
c. A requirement that all employees must use strong passwords and change them every 90 days
d. A high-level statement of the organization's commitment to protecting customer privacy

Answer: c. A requirement that all employees must use strong passwords and change them every 90 days. Explanation: Information security standards specify the minimum acceptable level of security that must be consistently implemented across the organization. They are typically more specific and prescriptive than policies, but less detailed and procedural than procedures. Standards often take the form of technical or operational requirements, such as password complexity rules, encryption strength, or access control settings, that must be met in order to be considered compliant with policies and to adequately protect information assets.

64. Which of the following is the most effective approach for communicating information security policies to employees and stakeholders?
a. Posting policies on the organization's intranet or shared drive for self-service access
b. Emailing policies to all employees and requiring them to acknowledge receipt and understanding
c. Incorporating policy awareness and training into new hire orientation and annual refresher programs
d. All of the above

Answer: d. All of the above. Explanation: Effective communication of information security policies requires a multi-faceted approach that leverages various channels and formats to reach and engage different audiences. Posting policies on a centralized repository, such as an intranet or shared drive, ensures that they are always accessible and up-to-date, and can be easily referenced by employees as needed. Emailing policies and requiring acknowledgment helps to ensure that employees have received and read them, and provides a record of their acceptance. Incorporating policy awareness and training into orientation and ongoing education programs helps to reinforce key messages, answer questions, and promote a culture of security awareness and compliance. Together, these approaches create a comprehensive and layered communication strategy that maximizes the impact and effectiveness of policy dissemination.

65. What is the primary benefit of aligning an organization's information security policies with industry standards and frameworks, such as ISO 27001 or NIST SP 800-53?
a. It ensures that the organization's policies are 100% compliant with all legal and regulatory requirements
b. It eliminates the need for the organization to develop its own customized policies and procedures
c. It provides a benchmark for measuring the completeness and effectiveness of the organization's policies against best practices
d. It automatically certifies the organization's policies as being secure and effective

Answer: c. It provides a benchmark for measuring the completeness and effectiveness of the organization's policies against best practices. Explanation: Industry standards and frameworks provide a valuable reference point for developing and assessing an organization's information security policies. By aligning with widely accepted and validated best practices, organizations can ensure that their policies are comprehensive, consistent, and effective in managing information security risks. Standards and frameworks can also help organizations to identify gaps or areas for improvement in their policies, based on a systematic and objective evaluation of their controls and processes. However, it is important to recognize that alignment with standards does not guarantee compliance with legal or regulatory requirements, nor does it eliminate the need for organizations to tailor their policies to their specific business needs and risk environment.

66. Which of the following is the most important factor to consider when determining the appropriate level of detail and specificity to include in information security procedures?
a. The technical complexity of the systems and processes being protected
b. The size and structure of the organization and its IT department
c. The level of risk associated with the information assets and processes being protected
d. The preferences and expectations of senior management and the Board of Directors

Answer: c. The level of risk associated with the information assets and processes being protected. Explanation: The level of detail and specificity in information security procedures should be proportional to the level of risk associated with the assets and processes they are designed to protect. Procedures for high-risk or critical assets, such as those containing sensitive data or supporting essential business functions, may require more granular and prescriptive steps to ensure that all necessary controls and safeguards are properly implemented. Conversely, procedures for lower-risk assets may be more general and flexible, allowing for greater discretion and adaptation to local needs. The key is to strike the right balance between providing sufficient guidance to mitigate risks and allowing for practical implementation and use by the intended audience.

67. What is the role of information security policies, procedures, and standards in the overall risk management framework of an organization?
a. They are the primary means by which an organization identifies and assesses its information security risks
b. They are the only controls that an organization needs to implement in order to manage its information security risks
c. They provide the foundation for the consistent and effective implementation of information security controls across the organization
d. They are optional tools that an organization may choose to use or not use depending on its risk tolerance and budget

Answer: c. They provide the foundation for the consistent and effective implementation of information security controls across the organization. Explanation: Information security policies, procedures, and standards are essential components of an organization's overall risk management framework. They provide the basis for identifying, prioritizing, and mitigating information security risks in a consistent and repeatable manner across the entire organization. Policies establish the high-level objectives and requirements for risk management, while procedures and standards translate those requirements into specific controls and actions that can be implemented and monitored. Together, they help to ensure that an organization's risk management efforts are comprehensive, coordinated, and effective in reducing the likelihood and impact of security incidents. However, policies, procedures, and standards are not the only elements of a risk management framework, which also includes risk assessment, risk treatment, risk monitoring, and risk communication processes.

68. What is the most common challenge in developing and implementing information security policies, procedures, and standards?
a. Keeping up with the rapid pace of change in technology and business processes
b. Obtaining buy-in and support from senior management and business stakeholders
c. Ensuring that policies, procedures, and standards are consistently followed and enforced
d. All of the above

Answer: d. All of the above. Explanation: Developing and implementing effective information security policies, procedures, and standards is a complex and ongoing process that involves multiple challenges. One of the biggest challenges is keeping policies, procedures, and standards up-to-date and relevant in the face of constantly evolving technologies, threats, and business requirements. This requires regular review, assessment, and updating of documentation to ensure that it remains aligned with current risks and needs. Another challenge is securing the necessary buy-in, resources, and support from senior management and business stakeholders, who may view security as a cost or barrier to productivity and innovation. Effective communication, education, and collaboration are essential to demonstrate the value and importance of policies, procedures, and standards in enabling the organization's goals and objectives. Finally, ensuring consistent adherence to policies, procedures, and standards across a complex and distributed organization is an ongoing challenge that requires a combination of training, awareness, monitoring, and enforcement measures. Addressing these challenges requires a proactive, risk-based, and collaborative approach to policy development and implementation.

69. What is the difference between a policy exception and a policy violation?

a. An exception is a temporary deviation from a policy that is approved by management, while a violation is an unauthorized deviation that may result in disciplinary action
b. An exception is a permanent change to a policy that is approved by the Board of Directors, while a violation is a temporary deviation that is approved by management
c. An exception is an acceptable risk that is identified and documented as part of the policy development process, while a violation is an unacceptable risk that is identified after the policy has been implemented
d. There is no difference between a policy exception and a policy violation

Answer: a. An exception is a temporary deviation from a policy that is approved by management, while a violation is an unauthorized deviation that may result in disciplinary action. Explanation: A policy exception is a situation in which an individual or group is granted permission to deviate from a specific policy requirement for a limited time and scope, based on a documented and approved business justification. Exceptions are typically reviewed and approved by management, and may be subject to additional controls or monitoring to mitigate any associated risks. A policy violation, on the other hand, is an unauthorized or unapproved deviation from a policy that occurs without proper justification or approval. Violations may be intentional or unintentional, but in either case, they represent a failure to adhere to the organization's established security requirements and may result in disciplinary action or other consequences. It is important for organizations to have clear processes and criteria for granting and managing policy exceptions, as well as for detecting and responding to policy violations, in order to maintain the integrity and effectiveness of their security program.

70. Which of the following best describes the purpose of the policy development life cycle?
a. To ensure that policies are developed quickly and efficiently without the need for extensive review or revision
b. To provide a structured and repeatable process for creating, implementing, and maintaining effective information security policies
c. To eliminate the need for input or collaboration from stakeholders outside of the information security team
d. To guarantee that policies will never need to be updated or changed once they are initially developed

Answer: b. To provide a structured and repeatable process for creating, implementing, and maintaining effective information security policies. Explanation: The policy development life cycle is a framework that outlines the key stages and activities involved in creating and managing information security policies over time. The purpose of the life cycle is to ensure that policies are developed in a systematic, consistent, and effective manner, with appropriate input and oversight from relevant stakeholders. The life cycle typically includes stages such as planning, drafting, reviewing, approving, communicating, implementing, monitoring, and updating policies, with specific tasks and deliverables associated with each stage. By following a structured life cycle approach, organizations can ensure that their policies are well-designed, aligned with business needs, and responsive to changing risks and requirements.

71. What is the first stage of the policy development life cycle?
a. Drafting the policy document
b. Identifying the need for a new or updated policy
c. Obtaining approval from senior management
d. Communicating the policy to employees and stakeholders

Answer: b. Identifying the need for a new or updated policy. Explanation: The first stage of the policy development life cycle is the planning or initiation phase, which involves identifying the need for a new or updated policy. This need may be driven by various factors, such as changes in the organization's risk environment, new legal or regulatory requirements, incidents or audit findings, or shifts in business strategies or priorities. The planning stage involves defining the scope, objectives, and stakeholders for the policy, as well as securing the necessary resources and support for the development process. This stage sets the foundation for the rest of the life cycle and ensures that the policy is aligned with the organization's overall goals and priorities.

72. Which of the following is the most important activity during the policy drafting stage of the life cycle?
a. Conducting a thorough risk assessment to identify the specific threats and vulnerabilities that the policy should address
b. Reviewing and incorporating feedback from all relevant stakeholders, including business units, IT, legal, and HR
c. Ensuring that the policy is written in clear, concise, and non-technical language that can be easily understood by all employees
d. Obtaining formal approval and sign-off from senior management and the Board of Directors

Answer: c. Ensuring that the policy is written in clear, concise, and non-technical language that can be easily understood by all employees. Explanation: While all of the activities mentioned are important during the policy drafting stage, the most critical is ensuring that the policy is written in a way that is accessible and understandable to the intended audience. Policies that are overly technical, legalistic, or confusing are less likely to be read, understood, and followed by employees, which undermines their effectiveness. Clear and concise language, with definitions of key terms and specific examples, helps to ensure that the policy is easily communicated and enforced. Incorporating feedback from stakeholders and aligning with risk assessments are also important, but the primary goal of the drafting stage is to produce a document that effectively conveys the organization's security requirements and expectations to all employees.

73. What is the purpose of the policy review and approval stage of the life cycle?
a. To ensure that the policy is technically feasible and can be implemented using existing security controls and technologies
b. To verify that the policy is consistent with the organization's overall risk management strategy and risk appetite
c. To obtain buy-in and support from all employees and stakeholders who will be affected by the policy
d. To identify and correct any errors, inconsistencies, or conflicts in the policy document before it is finalized

Answer: d. To identify and correct any errors, inconsistencies, or conflicts in the policy document before it is finalized. Explanation: The main objective of the policy review and approval stage is to ensure that the policy document is complete, accurate, and consistent before it is officially adopted and implemented. This stage typically involves a formal review process in which the draft policy is circulated to key stakeholders, such as IT, legal, HR, and business unit leaders, for feedback and validation. The review process helps to identify any errors, omissions, or contradictions in the policy, as well as any potential operational or legal issues that need to be addressed. Once all feedback is incorporated and the policy is finalized, it is typically submitted to senior management or the Board for formal approval and sign-off. While the review and approval stage also helps to build consensus and support for the policy, its primary focus is on ensuring the quality and integrity of the policy document itself.

74. Which of the following is the most effective way to communicate a new or updated information security policy to employees?
a. Sending a copy of the policy document to all employees via email and requiring them to acknowledge receipt
b. Posting the policy document on the organization's intranet or shared drive for employees to access on their own
c. Conducting mandatory training sessions that explain the key requirements and expectations of the policy
d. Including a brief summary of the policy in the organization's monthly newsletter or company-wide announcements

Answer: c. Conducting mandatory training sessions that explain the key requirements and expectations of the policy. Explanation: While all of the communication methods mentioned can be useful for raising awareness about a new or updated policy, the most effective approach is to provide employees with direct, interactive training on the policy's content and implications. Training sessions, whether conducted in-person or online, allow employees to ask questions, clarify expectations, and discuss how the policy applies to their specific roles and responsibilities. Training also helps to reinforce the importance and priority of the policy, and provides a mechanism for verifying that employees understand and agree to comply with its requirements. Passively distributing the policy document or posting it on the intranet may not ensure that employees actually read and internalize the policy, while brief summaries may not provide sufficient detail or context. A combination of training and other communication methods is often the most effective approach for ensuring widespread awareness and adoption of the policy.

75. What is the main goal of the policy implementation stage of the life cycle?
a. To develop and deploy the specific technical controls and safeguards needed to enforce the policy requirements
b. To integrate the policy requirements into the organization's business processes, procedures, and employee performance metrics
c. To monitor and measure the effectiveness of the policy in reducing information security risks and incidents
d. To provide ongoing training and awareness to employees to ensure that they continue to understand and follow the policy

Answer: b. To integrate the policy requirements into the organization's business processes, procedures, and employee performance metrics. Explanation: The primary objective of the policy implementation stage is to ensure that the policy is not just a document on a shelf, but is actually put into practice and integrated into the day-to-day operations of the organization. This involves translating the high-level policy statements into specific procedures, guidelines, and standards that can be easily followed and measured by employees and teams. It also involves aligning the policy with existing business processes and systems, and establishing clear roles, responsibilities, and accountability for compliance. Some key activities during the implementation stage may include updating job descriptions and performance goals to include policy-related duties, integrating policy requirements into system and application development processes, and establishing metrics and reporting mechanisms to track policy adoption and effectiveness. While technical controls and ongoing training are certainly important aspects of policy implementation, the main focus is on embedding the policy into the fabric of the organization's culture and operations.

76. What is the purpose of the policy monitoring and enforcement stage of the life cycle?
a. To continuously assess the organization's compliance with the policy requirements and identify any gaps or violations
b. To develop and implement new technical controls and countermeasures to address emerging threats and vulnerabilities
c. To review and update the policy document to ensure that it remains relevant and effective over time
d. To provide additional training and awareness to employees who are found to be non-compliant with the policy

Answer: a. To continuously assess the organization's compliance with the policy requirements and identify any gaps or violations. Explanation: The main objective of the policy monitoring and enforcement stage is to ensure that the organization is consistently meeting the requirements and expectations set forth in the policy, and to detect and respond to any deviations or violations. This involves establishing processes and tools for continuously monitoring key indicators of policy compliance, such as system configurations, access logs, and user behavior, and comparing them against the policy standards. It also involves defining clear protocols for investigating and responding to potential violations, including escalation procedures, disciplinary measures, and remediation steps. The goal is to identify and address policy gaps or failures as quickly as possible, before they can lead to more serious security incidents or risks. While policy monitoring and enforcement may involve some technical controls and employee training, its primary focus is on verifying and maintaining the organization's adherence to its established security policies and practices.

77. Which of the following is the most important consideration when determining the appropriate frequency and scope of policy reviews and updates?
a. The size and complexity of the organization and its IT environment
b. The preferences and opinions of senior management and the Board of Directors
c. The rate of change in the external threat landscape and regulatory environment
d. The available budget and resources for policy development and management activities

Answer: c. The rate of change in the external threat landscape and regulatory environment. Explanation: The most critical factor in determining how often and extensively an organization should review and update its information security policies is the pace of change in the external environment that affects its risk exposure and compliance obligations. In today's rapidly evolving digital landscape, new technologies, threats, and regulations are emerging all the time, and organizations need to ensure that their policies keep pace with these changes to remain effective and relevant. For example, the rise of cloud computing, mobile devices, and social media has introduced new risks and challenges that may not have been addressed in older policies, while new laws and standards such as GDPR, CCPA, and NIST have imposed new requirements and expectations for data protection and privacy. Organizations should establish a regular schedule for reviewing and updating their policies based on a proactive assessment of these external factors, rather than relying solely on internal considerations such as organizational size, management preferences, or resource constraints. The goal is to ensure that policies are always aligned with the current realities and best practices of information security, and are able to effectively mitigate the most relevant and pressing risks facing the organization.

78. What is the role of metrics and key performance indicators (KPIs) in the policy development life cycle?
a. Metrics and KPIs are not relevant to the policy development life cycle and should not be used
b. Metrics and KPIs are used to determine the specific content and requirements of information security policies
c. Metrics and KPIs are used to track and demonstrate the effectiveness and value of information security policies over time
d. Metrics and KPIs are used to punish employees who fail to comply with information security policies

Answer: c. Metrics and KPIs are used to track and demonstrate the effectiveness and value of information security policies over time. Explanation: Metrics and KPIs play a crucial role in the policy development life cycle by providing a way to measure and communicate the performance and impact of information security policies in a quantifiable and objective manner. By defining specific, measurable, and relevant indicators of policy effectiveness, such as the number of security incidents, the level of employee compliance, or the reduction in risk exposure, organizations can track the success of their policies over time and identify areas for improvement. Metrics and KPIs can also help to demonstrate the value and importance of information security policies to senior management and other stakeholders, by showing how they contribute to the organization's overall goals and objectives. This can help to build support and justify investment in ongoing policy development and management activities. It is important to note that metrics and KPIs should be carefully chosen and aligned with the specific goals and requirements of each policy, and should be regularly reviewed and updated as part of the overall policy life cycle. They should also be used as a tool for continuous improvement and learning, rather than as a means of punishment or blame.

79. Which of the following best describes the relationship between the policy development life cycle and an organization's overall information security program?
a. The policy development life cycle is a separate and independent process from the overall information security program
b. The policy development life cycle is the only component of an organization's overall information security program
c. The policy development life cycle is a critical foundation and driver of an organization's overall information security program
d. The policy development life cycle is an optional best practice that organizations may choose to follow or not

Answer: c. The policy development life cycle is a critical foundation and driver of an organization's overall information security program. Explanation: The policy development life cycle is not just a standalone process, but is a fundamental and integral part of an organization's broader information security program. Policies provide the essential framework and direction for all other aspects of information security, including risk management, technical controls, incident response, and user awareness. They establish the organization's overall approach, priorities, and expectations for protecting its information assets, and provide a common language and reference point for all stakeholders involved in security. The policy development life cycle ensures that policies are created, implemented, and maintained in a consistent, effective, and agile manner, and that they remain aligned with the organization's evolving business needs and risk landscape. In this sense, the policy life cycle is the foundation upon which the rest of the information security program is built, and is a key enabler and driver of its success. An organization's security program cannot be truly effective or sustainable without a robust and well-managed policy development process at its core.

80. Which of the following best describes the purpose of the policy development life cycle?
a. To ensure that policies are developed quickly and efficiently without the need for extensive review or revision
b. To provide a structured and repeatable process for creating, implementing, and maintaining effective information security policies
c. To eliminate the need for input or collaboration from stakeholders outside of the information security team
d. To guarantee that policies will never need to be updated or changed once they are initially developed

Answer: b. To provide a structured and repeatable process for creating, implementing, and maintaining effective information security policies. Explanation: The policy development life cycle is a framework that outlines the key stages and activities involved in creating and managing information security policies over time. The purpose of the life cycle is to ensure that policies are developed in a systematic, consistent, and effective manner, with appropriate input and oversight from relevant stakeholders. The life cycle typically includes stages such as planning, drafting, reviewing, approving, communicating, implementing, monitoring, and updating policies, with specific tasks and deliverables associated with each stage. By following a structured life cycle approach, organizations can ensure that their policies are well-designed, aligned with business needs, and responsive to changing risks and requirements.

81. What is the first stage of the policy development life cycle?
a. Drafting the policy document
b. Identifying the need for a new or updated policy
c. Obtaining approval from senior management
d. Communicating the policy to employees and stakeholders

Answer: b. Identifying the need for a new or updated policy. Explanation: The first stage of the policy development life cycle is the planning or initiation phase, which involves identifying the need for a new or updated policy. This need may be driven by various factors, such as changes in the organization's risk environment, new legal or regulatory requirements, incidents or audit findings, or shifts in business strategies or priorities. The planning stage involves defining the scope, objectives, and stakeholders for the policy, as well as securing the necessary resources and support for the development process. This stage sets the foundation for the rest of the life cycle and ensures that the policy is aligned with the organization's overall goals and priorities.

82. Which of the following is the most important activity during the policy drafting stage of the life cycle?
a. Conducting a thorough risk assessment to identify the specific threats and vulnerabilities that the policy should address
b. Reviewing and incorporating feedback from all relevant stakeholders, including business units, IT, legal, and HR
c. Ensuring that the policy is written in clear, concise, and non-technical language that can be easily understood by all employees
d. Obtaining formal approval and sign-off from senior management and the Board of Directors

Answer: c. Ensuring that the policy is written in clear, concise, and non-technical language that can be easily understood by all employees. Explanation: While all of the activities mentioned are important during the policy drafting stage, the most critical is ensuring that the policy is written in a way that is accessible and understandable to the intended audience. Policies that are overly technical, legalistic, or confusing are less likely to be read, understood, and followed by employees, which undermines their effectiveness. Clear and concise language, with definitions of key terms and specific examples, helps to ensure that the policy is easily communicated and enforced. Incorporating feedback from stakeholders and aligning with risk assessments are also important, but the primary goal of the drafting stage is to produce a document that effectively conveys the organization's security requirements and expectations to all employees.

83. What is the purpose of the policy review and approval stage of the life cycle?
a. To ensure that the policy is technically feasible and can be implemented using existing security controls and technologies
b. To verify that the policy is consistent with the organization's overall risk management strategy and risk appetite
c. To obtain buy-in and support from all employees and stakeholders who will be affected by the policy
d. To identify and correct any errors, inconsistencies, or conflicts in the policy document before it is finalized

Answer: d. To identify and correct any errors, inconsistencies, or conflicts in the policy document before it is finalized. Explanation: The main objective of the policy review and approval stage is to ensure that the policy document is complete, accurate, and consistent before it is officially adopted and implemented. This stage typically involves a formal review process in which the draft policy is circulated to key stakeholders, such as IT, legal, HR, and business unit leaders, for feedback and validation. The review process helps to identify any errors, omissions, or contradictions in the policy, as well as any potential operational or legal issues that need to be addressed. Once all feedback is incorporated and the policy is finalized, it is typically submitted to senior management or the Board for formal approval and sign-off. While the review and approval stage also helps to build consensus and support for the policy, its primary focus is on ensuring the quality and integrity of the policy document itself.

84. Which of the following is the most effective way to communicate a new or updated information security policy to employees?
a. Sending a copy of the policy document to all employees via email and requiring them to acknowledge receipt
b. Posting the policy document on the organization's intranet or shared drive for employees to access on their own
c. Conducting mandatory training sessions that explain the key requirements and expectations of the policy
d. Including a brief summary of the policy in the organization's monthly newsletter or company-wide announcements

Answer: c. Conducting mandatory training sessions that explain the key requirements and expectations of the policy. Explanation: While all of the communication methods mentioned can be useful for raising awareness about a new or updated policy, the most effective approach is to provide employees with direct, interactive training on the policy's content and implications. Training sessions, whether conducted in-person or online, allow employees to ask questions, clarify expectations, and discuss how the policy applies to their specific roles and responsibilities. Training also helps to reinforce the importance and priority of the policy, and provides a mechanism for verifying that employees understand and agree to comply with its requirements. Passively distributing the policy document or posting it on the intranet may not ensure that employees actually read and internalize the policy, while brief summaries may not provide sufficient detail or context. A combination of training and other communication methods is often the most effective approach for ensuring widespread awareness and adoption of the policy.

85. What is the main goal of the policy implementation stage of the life cycle?
a. To develop and deploy the specific technical controls and safeguards needed to enforce the policy requirements
b. To integrate the policy requirements into the organization's business processes, procedures, and employee performance metrics
c. To monitor and measure the effectiveness of the policy in reducing information security risks and incidents
d. To provide ongoing training and awareness to employees to ensure that they continue to understand and follow the policy

Answer: b. To integrate the policy requirements into the organization's business processes, procedures, and employee performance metrics. Explanation: The primary objective of the policy implementation stage is to ensure that the policy is not just a document on a shelf, but is actually put into practice and integrated into the day-to-day operations of the organization. This involves translating the high-level policy statements into specific procedures, guidelines, and standards that can be easily followed and measured by employees and teams. It also involves aligning the policy with existing business processes and systems, and establishing clear roles, responsibilities, and accountability for compliance. Some key activities during the implementation stage may include updating job descriptions and performance goals to include policy-related duties, integrating policy requirements into system and application development processes, and establishing metrics and reporting mechanisms to track policy adoption and effectiveness. While technical controls and ongoing training are certainly important aspects of policy implementation, the main focus is on embedding the policy into the fabric of the organization's culture and operations.

86. What is the purpose of the policy monitoring and enforcement stage of the life cycle?
a. To continuously assess the organization's compliance with the policy requirements and identify any gaps or violations
b. To develop and implement new technical controls and countermeasures to address emerging threats and vulnerabilities
c. To review and update the policy document to ensure that it remains relevant and effective over time
d. To provide additional training and awareness to employees who are found to be non-compliant with the policy

Answer: a. To continuously assess the organization's compliance with the policy requirements and identify any gaps or violations. Explanation: The main objective of the policy monitoring and enforcement stage is to ensure that the organization is consistently meeting the requirements and expectations set forth in the policy, and to detect and respond to any deviations or violations. This involves establishing processes and tools for continuously monitoring key indicators of policy compliance, such as system configurations, access logs, and user behavior, and comparing them against the policy standards. It also involves defining clear protocols for investigating and responding to potential violations, including escalation procedures, disciplinary measures, and remediation steps. The goal is to identify and address policy gaps or failures as quickly as possible, before they can lead to more serious security incidents or risks. While policy monitoring and enforcement may involve some technical controls and employee training, its primary focus is on verifying and maintaining the organization's adherence to its established security policies and practices.

87. Which of the following is the most important consideration when determining the appropriate frequency and scope of policy reviews and updates?
a. The size and complexity of the organization and its IT environment
b. The preferences and opinions of senior management and the Board of Directors
c. The rate of change in the external threat landscape and regulatory environment
d. The available budget and resources for policy development and management activities

Answer: c. The rate of change in the external threat landscape and regulatory environment. Explanation: The most critical factor in determining how often and extensively an organization should review and update its information security policies is the pace of change in the external environment that affects its risk exposure and compliance obligations. In today's rapidly evolving digital landscape, new technologies, threats, and regulations are emerging all the time, and organizations need to ensure that their policies keep pace with these changes to remain effective and relevant. For example, the rise of cloud computing, mobile devices, and social media has introduced new risks and challenges that may not have been addressed in older policies, while new laws and standards such as GDPR, CCPA, and NIST have imposed new requirements and expectations for data protection and privacy. Organizations should establish a regular schedule for reviewing and updating their policies based on a proactive assessment of these external factors, rather than relying solely on internal considerations such as organizational size, management preferences, or resource constraints. The goal is to ensure that policies are always aligned with the current realities and best practices of information security, and are able to effectively mitigate the most relevant and pressing risks facing the organization.

88. What is the role of metrics and key performance indicators (KPIs) in the policy development life cycle?
a. Metrics and KPIs are not relevant to the policy development life cycle and should not be used
b. Metrics and KPIs are used to determine the specific content and requirements of information security policies
c. Metrics and KPIs are used to track and demonstrate the effectiveness and value of information security policies over time
d. Metrics and KPIs are used to punish employees who fail to comply with information security policies

Answer: c. Metrics and KPIs are used to track and demonstrate the effectiveness and value of information security policies over time. Explanation: Metrics and KPIs play a crucial role in the policy development life cycle by providing a way to measure and communicate the performance and impact of information security policies in a quantifiable and objective manner. By defining specific, measurable, and relevant indicators of policy effectiveness, such as the number of security incidents, the level of employee compliance, or the reduction in risk exposure, organizations can track the success of their policies over time and identify areas for improvement. Metrics and KPIs can also help to demonstrate the value and importance of information security policies to senior management and other stakeholders, by showing how they contribute to the organization's overall goals and objectives. This can help to build support and justify investment in ongoing policy development and management activities. It is important to note that metrics and KPIs should be carefully chosen and aligned with the specific goals and requirements of each policy, and should be regularly reviewed and updated as part of the overall policy life cycle. They should also be used as a tool for continuous improvement and learning, rather than as a means of punishment or blame.

89. Which of the following best describes the relationship between the policy development life cycle and an organization's overall information security program?
a. The policy development life cycle is a separate and independent process from the overall information security program
b. The policy development life cycle is the only component of an organization's overall information security program
c. The policy development life cycle is a critical foundation and driver of an organization's overall information security program
d. The policy development life cycle is an optional best practice that organizations may choose to follow or not

Answer: c. The policy development life cycle is a critical foundation and driver of an organization's overall information security program. Explanation: The policy development life cycle is not just a standalone process, but is a fundamental and integral part of an organization's broader information security program. Policies provide the essential framework and direction for all other aspects of information security, including risk management, technical controls, incident response, and user awareness. They establish the organization's overall approach, priorities, and expectations for protecting its information assets, and provide a common language and reference point for all stakeholders involved in security. The policy development life cycle ensures that policies are created, implemented, and maintained in a consistent, effective, and agile manner, and that they remain aligned with the organization's evolving business needs and risk landscape. In this sense, the policy life cycle is the foundation upon which the rest of the information security program is built, and is a key enabler and driver of its success. An organization's security program cannot be truly effective or sustainable without a robust and well-managed policy development process at its core.

90. An organization has recently implemented a new information security policy that requires all employees to use multi-factor authentication (MFA) when accessing company systems and data. However, the IT department has reported that many employees are not complying with the policy and are still using simple passwords. Which of the following is the most effective approach for improving compliance with the MFA policy?
a. Sending out a company-wide email reminding employees of the importance of using MFA and the consequences of non-compliance
b. Disabling access to company systems for any employee who fails to set up MFA within a specified timeframe
c. Providing additional training and support to help employees understand and implement MFA on their devices

d. Implementing technical controls that automatically enforce MFA for all user accounts and prevent access without it

Answer: d. Implementing technical controls that automatically enforce MFA for all user accounts and prevent access without it. Explanation: While communication, training, and consequences can all play a role in improving policy compliance, the most effective way to ensure that a critical security control like MFA is consistently used is to enforce it through technical means. By configuring systems and applications to require MFA by default and preventing access for users who have not set it up, the organization can eliminate the risk of non-compliance and ensure a baseline level of protection. This approach is more reliable and scalable than relying on individual employees to follow the policy on their own, and reduces the burden on IT staff to monitor and enforce compliance manually. Of course, technical enforcement should be complemented by clear communication and training to help employees understand the reason for the policy and how to comply with it, but it should be the primary mechanism for ensuring consistent implementation.

91. An organization has a well-established information security policy that prohibits the use of personal devices for work purposes. However, during a recent audit, it was discovered that several employees in the sales department have been using their personal smartphones to access and store customer data, in violation of the policy. Which of the following is the most appropriate response to this situation?
a. Immediately terminating the employment of the individuals involved in the policy violation
b. Conducting a thorough investigation to determine the extent and cause of the violation, and taking appropriate corrective and preventive actions
c. Revising the policy to allow the use of personal devices, as long as they are properly secured and managed
d. Ignoring the violation, as the productivity benefits of using personal devices outweigh the potential security risks

Answer: b. Conducting a thorough investigation to determine the extent and cause of the violation, and taking appropriate corrective and preventive actions. Explanation: When a policy violation is discovered, it is important to respond in a way that is proportionate, fair, and effective in preventing future occurrences. Immediately terminating the individuals involved may be an overreaction, especially if the violation was unintentional or if there are extenuating circumstances. On the other hand, ignoring the violation or changing the policy to allow the behavior sends the message that the policy is not important or enforceable. The best approach is to conduct a thorough investigation to understand the full scope and context of the violation, including how long it has been occurring, how many employees and customers are affected, and what factors may have contributed to the behavior. Based on the findings, the organization can take appropriate corrective actions, such as disciplinary measures, remediation efforts, and policy updates, as well as preventive actions, such as additional training, monitoring, and technical controls, to reduce the risk of future violations.

92. A multinational corporation has a global information security policy that requires all employees to complete an annual online training course on data protection and privacy. The policy states that employees who fail to complete the training by the specified deadline will have their network access suspended until the training is completed. However, the organization has been experiencing high rates of non-compliance, particularly among employees in certain regions and business units. Which of the following factors is most likely contributing to the non-compliance issue?
a. The training course is too long and complex for employees to complete in a timely manner
b. The consequences for non-compliance are not consistently enforced across the organization
c. The policy and training requirements are not adequately communicated and explained to employees
d. The cultural and operational differences among different regions and business units are not taken into account in the policy and training design

Answer: d. The cultural and operational differences among different regions and business units are not taken into account in the policy and training design. Explanation: When implementing a global policy and training program, it is important to recognize and accommodate the diverse needs, expectations, and constraints of employees in different parts of the organization. A one-size-fits-all approach may not be effective or appropriate for all regions and business units, due to differences in language, culture, technology infrastructure, regulatory requirements, and work practices. For example, employees in some regions may have limited access to computers or internet connectivity, making it difficult to complete an online training course. Employees in certain business units, such as manufacturing or field operations, may have different job roles and risk profiles than those in corporate offices, requiring a different type of training content and format. To improve compliance and effectiveness, the organization should consider tailoring the policy and training to the specific needs and contexts of each region and business unit, while still maintaining a consistent overall framework and set of standards. This may involve providing translated content, offline training options, role-based training modules, and local support resources. The organization should also engage with regional and business unit leaders to understand their unique challenges and requirements, and to secure their buy-in and support for the policy and training implementation.

93. An organization has implemented a data classification policy that requires all employees to label and handle information assets according to their level of sensitivity and criticality. The policy defines three classification levels: Confidential, Internal Use Only, and Public. However, a recent audit has revealed that many employees are not consistently applying the correct classification labels to their documents and emails, leading to potential data leakage and compliance risks. Which of the following is the most effective way to improve the accuracy and consistency of data classification across the organization?
a. Providing additional training and guidance to employees on how to determine the appropriate classification level for different types of information
b. Implementing automated tools and workflows that suggest or enforce the appropriate classification level based on the content and context of the information
c. Conducting regular audits and spot checks to identify and correct classification errors, and providing feedback to employees on their performance
d. Simplifying the classification scheme to only two levels, such as Sensitive and Non-Sensitive, to reduce confusion and ambiguity

Answer: b. Implementing automated tools and workflows that suggest or enforce the appropriate classification level based on the content and context of the information. Explanation: While training, auditing, and simplification can all help to improve the accuracy and consistency of data classification, the most scalable and reliable approach is to use technology to automate and guide the classification process as much as possible. By implementing tools that can scan and analyze the content and metadata of documents and emails, and suggest or apply the appropriate classification label based on predefined rules and patterns, organizations can reduce the burden on individual employees to make subjective and error-prone classification decisions. For example, a tool might be configured to automatically classify any document containing certain keywords, such as "confidential" or "proprietary", as Confidential, or to prompt the user to confirm the classification if the content appears to be sensitive but is not labeled as such. Automated classification tools can also help to enforce consistency and compliance with the organization's policies and standards, by preventing the mislabeling or mishandling of sensitive information. Of course, automated tools should be complemented by clear policies, training, and auditing to ensure that employees understand their responsibilities and are held accountable for their actions. But by leveraging technology to streamline and standardize the classification process, organizations can significantly improve the accuracy, efficiency, and effectiveness of their data protection efforts.

94. An organization has a strict password policy that requires all employees to use complex passwords that are at least 12 characters long, include a mix of uppercase and lowercase letters, numbers, and special characters, and are changed every 90 days. However, the IT department has received numerous complaints from employees that the policy is too burdensome and is hindering their productivity. They argue that the frequent password changes and complexity requirements are causing them to forget their passwords and waste time on password resets. Which of the following is the best approach for balancing the security benefits of the password policy with the usability and productivity needs of the employees?

a. Relaxing the password complexity and expiration requirements to make the policy more user-friendly and reduce the burden on employees
b. Providing employees with a password management tool that can generate and store complex passwords securely, and automatically fill them in when needed
c. Conducting a thorough risk assessment to determine if the current password policy is appropriate and effective given the organization's specific security needs and threats
d. Replacing password-based authentication with alternative methods, such as biometric or token-based authentication, that are more secure and user-friendly

Answer: c. Conducting a thorough risk assessment to determine if the current password policy is appropriate and effective given the organization's specific security needs and threats. Explanation: While the other options presented may have some merit in certain situations, the best approach in this case is to take a step back and reassess the password policy in the context of the organization's overall risk posture and security requirements. Complex password policies like the one described can be effective in preventing unauthorized access and protecting sensitive data, but they can also have unintended consequences if they are not well-aligned with the needs and capabilities of the users. By conducting a risk assessment, the organization can evaluate the specific threats and vulnerabilities it faces, the likelihood and impact of password-related incidents, and the costs and benefits of different password policy options. The assessment should also consider factors such as the sensitivity of the data being protected, the technical and operational feasibility of the policy requirements, and the potential impact on user productivity and satisfaction. Based on the results of the assessment, the organization may determine that the current policy is appropriate and necessary, or that it needs to be modified to better balance security and usability. For example, the organization might decide to keep the complexity requirements but extend the password expiration period to 180 days, or to provide employees with password management tools to help them cope with the policy. The key is to make an informed decision based on a thorough understanding of the risks and tradeoffs involved, rather than simply reacting to user complaints or implementing a one-size-fits-all solution.

95. An organization has recently experienced a security incident in which an employee fell victim to a phishing attack and inadvertently downloaded malware onto their company-issued laptop. The malware was able to spread to other systems on the network and exfiltrate sensitive data before it was detected and contained. In response to the incident, the organization's CISO has proposed implementing a new security awareness training program that includes regular phishing simulations to test employees' ability to recognize and report suspicious emails. However, some managers have expressed concerns that the simulations could be seen as a form of entrapment and could damage employee morale and trust. Which of the following is the most appropriate way to address these concerns while still achieving the goals of the training program?
a. Making participation in the phishing simulations mandatory for all employees, and tying performance on the simulations to annual performance reviews and bonuses
b. Conducting the phishing simulations secretly, without informing employees that they are being tested, in order to get a more accurate measure of their real-world behavior
c. Emphasizing the positive aspects of the training program, such as the opportunity to learn and practice important skills, and providing rewards and recognition for employees who perform well on the simulations
d. Involving employees in the design and implementation of the training program, and soliciting their feedback and input on how to make the simulations fair, relevant, and engaging

Answer: d. Involving employees in the design and implementation of the training program, and soliciting their feedback and input on how to make the simulations fair, relevant, and engaging. Explanation: Phishing simulations can be a powerful tool for raising awareness and changing behavior around email security, but they can also be perceived as punitive, manipulative, or unrealistic if they are not implemented in a thoughtful and transparent manner. To avoid these negative unintended consequences, it is important to involve employees as active participants and stakeholders in the training program, rather than simply subjecting them to it. This means communicating clearly and honestly about the purpose, scope, and logistics of the simulations, and giving employees a voice in shaping how they are conducted. For example, the organization could convene a cross-functional working group of employees to help design the simulation scenarios, based on their real-world experiences and knowledge of the organization's email practices and culture. The organization could also survey employees to gather their input on the frequency, difficulty, and relevance of the simulations, and use this feedback to continuously improve the program over time. By engaging employees as partners in the training process, the organization can build trust, buy-in, and a shared sense of responsibility for email security. This approach is more likely to lead to sustainable behavior change and a positive security culture than a top-down, compliance-driven approach that treats employees as passive recipients of training.

96. An organization has a mobile device policy that requires all employees to use company-issued smartphones and tablets for work purposes, and prohibits the use of personal devices to access company data and systems. The policy also requires all mobile devices to be encrypted, password-protected, and remotely manageable by the IT department. Recently, a senior executive at the organization has requested an exception to the policy, stating that they prefer to use their personal smartphone for work and do not want to carry two devices. The executive argues that they are very careful with their device and that the convenience and productivity benefits of using their own device outweigh the potential security risks. Which of the following is the most appropriate way for the information security team to respond to this request?
a. Granting the exception request, as the executive is a senior leader and should be trusted to make their own decisions about mobile device usage
b. Denying the exception request, as making exceptions for certain individuals would undermine the consistency and effectiveness of the mobile device policy
c. Evaluating the specific risks and benefits of the exception request, and determining if any additional security controls or monitoring measures could be put in place to mitigate the risks
d. Recommending that the organization revisit and update its mobile device policy to allow for the use of personal devices, as long as they meet certain security and management requirements

Answer: c. Evaluating the specific risks and benefits of the exception request, and determining if any additional security controls or monitoring measures could be put in place to mitigate the risks. Explanation: Exceptions to security policies can be a difficult and sensitive issue, particularly when they involve senior leaders or other influential individuals within the organization. On one hand, making exceptions for certain individuals can create a perception of unfairness or double standards, and can undermine the credibility and effectiveness of the policies. On the other hand, rigidly enforcing policies without considering the specific needs and circumstances of individual users can lead to frustration, workarounds, and loss of productivity. In this case, the best approach is to carefully evaluate the exception request on its own merits, and to determine if there are any ways to accommodate the executive's needs while still maintaining an acceptable level of security. This may involve conducting a risk assessment to identify the specific threats and vulnerabilities associated with the use of a personal device, and determining if any additional security controls or monitoring measures could be put in place to mitigate those risks. For example, the organization might require the executive to install a mobile device management (MDM) solution on their personal device, which would allow the IT department to enforce certain security policies and remotely wipe the device if it is lost or stolen. The organization might also require the executive to sign a personal device usage agreement that outlines their responsibilities and obligations for securing and protecting company data on their device. By taking a risk-based, case-by-case approach to exception requests, the organization can demonstrate its commitment to security while also being responsive to the needs of its users. Of course, any exceptions should be carefully documented and regularly reviewed to ensure that they are still appropriate and effective over time.

97. An organization has a data retention policy that requires all business records and documents to be retained for a specified period of time, based on their content and purpose, and then securely deleted or destroyed when they are no longer needed. The policy is designed to ensure compliance with legal and regulatory requirements, as well as to reduce the risk of data breaches and other security incidents. However, a recent audit has found that many employees are not following the retention schedule and are keeping documents and emails indefinitely, often because they are unsure of what they are allowed to delete or because they feel that the information may be useful in the future.

Which of the following is the most effective way to improve compliance with the data retention policy and reduce the risk of over-retention?

a. Providing employees with clear and specific guidance on what types of information need to be retained and for how long, and what can be safely deleted

b. Implementing automated retention and deletion workflows that enforce the policy based on predefined rules and criteria, and notify employees when action is required

c. Conducting regular audits and spot checks to identify instances of over-retention, and taking disciplinary action against employees who violate the policy

d. Encouraging employees to use their own judgment and discretion when deciding what information to retain or delete, as they are in the best position to determine the business value and risk of the data

Answer: b. Implementing automated retention and deletion workflows that enforce the policy based on predefined rules and criteria, and notify employees when action is required. Explanation: Data retention is a complex and often overlooked aspect of information security and compliance, but it is critical for reducing the risk and cost of over-retention. When organizations keep data for longer than necessary, they increase the potential for data breaches, legal liabilities, and storage and management costs. They also make it harder to find and use the information that is truly important and valuable for the business. While providing guidance and training to employees on retention requirements is certainly important, it is not sufficient to ensure consistent and reliable compliance with the policy. Employees may still struggle to interpret and apply the retention rules to their specific data sets, or may simply forget or neglect to delete data when required. Audits and penalties can help to identify and deter non-compliance, but they are reactive and do not prevent the problem from occurring in the first place. The most effective solution is to automate the retention and deletion process as much as possible, using technology to enforce the policy based on predefined rules and criteria. For example, the organization could implement a data classification and retention management system that automatically tags and categorizes data based on its content and metadata, and applies the appropriate retention and deletion schedules based on the organization's policy. The system could also send notifications and reminders to data owners when action is required, such as reviewing

98. An organization that processes credit card transactions is subject to the Payment Card Industry Data Security Standard (PCI DSS). Which of the following is the most critical requirement for ensuring compliance with PCI DSS?

a. Implementing strong access controls and user authentication mechanisms

b. Encrypting all credit card data at rest and in transit

c. Conducting regular vulnerability scans and penetration tests

d. Developing and maintaining a comprehensive information security policy

Answer: b. Encrypting all credit card data at rest and in transit. Explanation: While all of the options listed are important components of PCI DSS compliance, the most critical requirement is the encryption of credit card data. PCI DSS mandates that all sensitive cardholder data must be encrypted using strong cryptographic algorithms both when it is stored (at rest) and when it is transmitted over networks (in transit). This helps to protect the data from unauthorized access or disclosure, even if other security controls fail. Access controls, vulnerability testing, and security policies are also essential for PCI DSS compliance, but they are not sufficient on their own to protect cardholder data if it is not properly encrypted.

99. An organization that operates in the healthcare industry is subject to the Health Insurance Portability and Accountability Act (HIPAA). Which of the following is the most important step for ensuring compliance with HIPAA's Privacy Rule?

a. Implementing strong technical safeguards to protect electronic protected health information (ePHI)

b. Providing regular training to employees on HIPAA privacy and security requirements

c. Conducting a thorough risk assessment to identify potential vulnerabilities and threats to ePHI

d. Developing and implementing comprehensive policies and procedures for handling and protecting ePHI

Answer: d. Developing and implementing comprehensive policies and procedures for handling and protecting ePHI. Explanation: The HIPAA Privacy Rule sets forth specific requirements for how covered entities (such as healthcare providers and health plans) must handle and protect individuals' protected health information (PHI). While technical safeguards, employee training, and risk assessments are all important aspects of HIPAA compliance, the most critical step is to develop and implement clear, comprehensive policies and procedures that govern the use, disclosure, and protection of PHI. These policies and procedures must address issues such as patient rights, data access and amendment, breach notification, and business associate agreements, and must be regularly reviewed and updated to ensure ongoing compliance with HIPAA regulations. Without a strong policy framework in place, an organization may struggle to consistently and effectively safeguard PHI, even if it has robust technical controls and well-trained employees.

100. An organization that handles personal data of European Union (EU) citizens is subject to the General Data Protection Regulation (GDPR). Which of the following is the most important principle of GDPR that organizations must adhere to when processing personal data?
a. Data minimization - collecting and retaining only the minimum amount of personal data necessary for the specified purpose
b. Storage limitation - retaining personal data only for as long as necessary to fulfill the specified purpose
c. Integrity and confidentiality - protecting personal data from unauthorized access, alteration, or destruction
d. Lawfulness, fairness, and transparency - processing personal data in a lawful, fair, and transparent manner

Answer: d. Lawfulness, fairness, and transparency - processing personal data in a lawful, fair, and transparent manner. Explanation: While all of the principles listed are important aspects of GDPR compliance, the most fundamental principle is that personal data must be processed lawfully, fairly, and transparently. This means that organizations must have a legal basis for collecting and using personal data (such as consent, contract, or legitimate interest), must be clear and upfront with individuals about how their data will be used, and must handle the data in a way that is fair and not deceptive or misleading. The principles of data minimization, storage limitation, and security are all designed to support and reinforce this overarching principle of lawful, fair, and transparent processing. Without a solid foundation of lawfulness and transparency, an organization's data practices may be seen as unethical or non-compliant, even if they are technically secure and minimally invasive.

101. An organization has entered into a contract with a third-party service provider that will have access to the organization's sensitive data. Which of the following is the most critical security requirement that should be included in the contract?
a. The service provider must have a SOC 2 Type II certification
b. The service provider must agree to regular security audits by the organization
c. The service provider must indemnify the organization against any data breaches or security incidents
d. The service provider must implement specific technical and administrative safeguards to protect the organization's data

Answer: d. The service provider must implement specific technical and administrative safeguards to protect the organization's data. Explanation: When entrusting sensitive data to a third-party service provider, it is essential to ensure that the provider has appropriate security measures in place to protect that data. While certifications, audits, and legal protections can provide some level of assurance, the most critical requirement is that the contract specifies the specific technical and administrative safeguards that the provider must implement to secure the organization's data. These may include requirements for encryption, access controls, monitoring, incident response, and employee training, among others. By clearly defining these requirements in the contract, the organization can hold the provider accountable for maintaining a robust security posture and can ensure that its data is being protected in accordance with its own security standards and risk tolerance. Certifications and audits can help to verify compliance with these requirements, but they are not a substitute for clearly defined contractual obligations.

102. An organization is subject to a new state law that requires it to notify individuals within 30 days of discovering a data breach involving their personal information. Which of the following is the most important step the organization should take to ensure compliance with this requirement?
a. Implementing strong technical controls to prevent data breaches from occurring in the first place
b. Conducting regular security awareness training for employees to help them identify and report potential breaches
c. Developing and testing an incident response plan that includes clear procedures for breach notification
d. Purchasing cyber insurance to cover the costs of breach notification and any associated legal liabilities

Answer: c. Developing and testing an incident response plan that includes clear procedures for breach notification. Explanation: While preventing breaches, training employees, and mitigating financial risks are all important aspects of an organization's overall security strategy, the most critical step for complying with breach notification laws is to have a well-defined and well-rehearsed incident response plan in place. This plan should include clear procedures for identifying, investigating, and containing potential breaches, as well as for assessing the scope and impact of the breach and determining whether notification is required under applicable laws and regulations. The plan should also specify the roles and responsibilities of key personnel, the timeline and methods for notifying affected individuals and regulators, and the steps for providing support and remediation to those affected. By thoroughly documenting and testing these procedures in advance, the organization can ensure that it is prepared to respond quickly and effectively to a breach and meet its legal obligations for notification, even in the face of a rapidly evolving and high-pressure situation.

103. An organization operates in a highly regulated industry and is subject to multiple compliance requirements, including HIPAA, PCI DSS, and SOX. Which of the following is the most effective approach for managing and tracking compliance across all of these different frameworks?
a. Conducting separate, siloed compliance assessments and audits for each individual framework
b. Implementing a unified governance, risk, and compliance (GRC) platform that integrates and maps requirements across frameworks
c. Outsourcing compliance management to a qualified third-party service provider
d. Relying on manual processes and spreadsheets to track and document compliance activities

Answer: b. Implementing a unified governance, risk, and compliance (GRC) platform that integrates and maps requirements across frameworks. Explanation: Managing compliance with multiple, overlapping regulatory frameworks can be a complex and time-consuming task, particularly for organizations in heavily regulated industries. While conducting separate assessments, outsourcing compliance, or using manual tracking methods may be sufficient for small-scale or low-risk situations, the most effective approach for managing complex compliance requirements is to implement a unified GRC platform. A GRC platform provides a centralized, automated system for mapping and harmonizing requirements across different frameworks, identifying common controls and processes, and tracking the status of compliance activities and assessments. By integrating compliance management into a single, cohesive program, a GRC platform can help organizations to streamline their efforts, reduce duplication and inconsistency, and improve visibility and reporting to stakeholders. It can also enable more proactive and strategic compliance management, by providing insights into risk trends, control effectiveness, and areas for improvement.

104. An organization has determined that it is not currently in compliance with certain provisions of the GDPR, which applies to its processing of EU customer data. Which of the following is the most appropriate course of action for addressing this non-compliance?
a. Ignoring the non-compliance and hoping that regulators do not notice or take enforcement action
b. Conducting a risk assessment to determine the potential impact and likelihood of enforcement action, and deciding whether to accept the risk or take corrective action
c. Immediately ceasing all processing of EU customer data until full compliance can be achieved
d. Developing and implementing a prioritized plan for remediating the non-compliance, based on the severity and scope of the issues identified

Answer: d. Developing and implementing a prioritized plan for remediating the non-compliance, based on the severity and scope of the issues identified. Explanation: When an organization discovers that it is not in compliance with a legal or regulatory requirement, such as GDPR, it is important to take prompt and appropriate action to address the non-compliance. Ignoring the issue or simply accepting the risk is not a responsible or effective approach, as it exposes the organization to potential enforcement action, reputational damage, and loss of customer trust. Ceasing all processing activities may be necessary in extreme cases of non-compliance, but it is often not practical or proportionate, particularly if the non-compliance is limited in scope or severity. The most appropriate course of action is typically to develop a prioritized plan for remediating the non-compliance, based on a thorough assessment of the specific issues identified. This plan should prioritize the most critical and urgent issues, such as those that pose the greatest risk to individuals' rights and freedoms, and should outline specific steps for addressing each issue, along with timelines, resources, and accountability. The plan should also include measures for preventing future non-compliance, such as updating policies and procedures, implementing new controls, and providing additional training to employees. By proactively and systematically addressing non-compliance in this way, organizations can demonstrate their commitment to data protection and minimize the risk of enforcement action or reputational harm.

105. An organization has received a request from a customer to exercise their right to data portability under GDPR. Which of the following is the most important consideration when responding to this request?
a. Verifying the identity of the customer making the request to ensure that the data is not disclosed to an unauthorized party
b. Determining whether the requested data falls within the scope of the data portability right and whether any exemptions apply
c. Ensuring that the data is provided to the customer in a structured, commonly used, and machine-readable format
d. Complying with the request within the required timeframe of one month, or three months if the request is complex

Answer: b. Determining whether the requested data falls within the scope of the data portability right and whether any exemptions apply. Explanation: The right to data portability under GDPR gives individuals the right to receive their personal data in a structured, commonly used, and machine-readable format, and to transmit that data to another controller without hindrance. However, this right only applies to certain types of personal data and processing activities, and there are several important exemptions and limitations that organizations need to consider when responding to a portability request. For example, the right only applies to data that the individual has provided to the controller, and that is processed based on the individual's consent or on a contract. It does not apply to data that is processed based on other legal grounds, such as legitimate interests or legal obligations. Additionally, the right may be limited or restricted if it would adversely affect the rights and freedoms of others, or if it would be technically infeasible or disproportionately difficult for the controller to comply. Therefore, the most important step in responding to a portability request is to carefully assess whether the requested data falls within the scope of the right, and whether any exemptions or limitations apply. This requires a thorough understanding of the specific data elements and processing activities involved, as well as the broader context and potential impacts of the request. While verifying the identity of the requestor, providing the data in an appropriate format, and complying with the required timeframes are all important aspects of fulfilling a portability request, they are secondary to the initial determination of whether the request is valid and applicable under GDPR.

106. An organization has entered into a contract with a cloud service provider to store and process sensitive customer data. Which of the following contract provisions is most important for ensuring that the organization retains control over the data and can comply with its legal and regulatory obligations?
a. A requirement for the provider to maintain specific technical and organizational security measures to protect the data
b. A clause specifying that the organization retains ownership and control over the data, and that the provider must use the data only as instructed by the organization
c. A provision allowing the organization to audit the provider's security practices and controls on a regular basis
d. An indemnification clause requiring the provider to compensate the organization for any losses or damages resulting from a data breach or security incident

Answer: b. A clause specifying that the organization retains ownership and control over the data, and that the provider must use the data only as instructed by the organization. Explanation: When outsourcing data processing activities to a third-party service provider, such as a cloud provider, it is critical for the organization to ensure that it retains ultimate control over the data and can fulfill its legal and regulatory obligations with respect to that data. One of the most important ways to achieve this is through clear and explicit contract language that specifies the organization's ownership and control over the data, and that limits the provider's use and disclosure of the data to only what is necessary to perform the contracted services. This type of clause, often referred to as a "data ownership and control" or "data use and disclosure" clause, helps to establish the organization as the data controller and the provider as a data processor, with specific responsibilities and limitations under applicable data protection laws and regulations. By retaining ownership and control over the data, the organization can ensure that it has the ability to comply with data subject rights requests, breach notification requirements, and other legal obligations, even when the data is being processed by a third party. While security requirements, audit rights, and indemnification provisions are also important components of a robust service provider contract, they are ultimately in service of the broader goal of maintaining the organization's control and accountability over its data.

107. An organization has determined that it needs to appoint a Data Protection Officer (DPO) to comply with GDPR requirements. Which of the following factors should be given the most weight when selecting a DPO?
a. The individual's knowledge and experience with the organization's specific business operations and data processing activities
b. The individual's formal education and professional certifications in data protection and privacy, such as CIPP or CIPM
c. The individual's ability to work independently and report directly to the highest level of management within the organization
d. The individual's technical expertise in implementing and managing security controls and technologies

Answer: c. The individual's ability to work independently and report directly to the highest level of management within the organization. Explanation: The role of the Data Protection Officer (DPO) under GDPR is to act as an independent, expert advisor and oversight function for an organization's data protection activities. The DPO is responsible for monitoring compliance with GDPR, providing advice and recommendations to the organization, and serving as a point of contact for data subjects and supervisory authorities. Given the critical importance of this role, the most important factor to consider when selecting a DPO is their ability to operate with a high degree of autonomy and independence within the organization, and to have direct access to and support from the highest levels of management. This independence is essential for ensuring that the DPO can effectively perform their duties without undue influence or interference from other business or operational interests, and can raise concerns or issues directly with decision-makers when necessary. While knowledge of the organization's specific operations, formal education and certifications in data protection, and technical security expertise are all valuable qualities for a DPO, they are ultimately less important than the individual's ability to act as an objective, credible, and empowered advocate for data protection within the organization. The GDPR itself emphasizes the importance of independence and direct reporting lines for the DPO role, and organizations should prioritize these factors when selecting and positioning their DPO.

108.An organization that processes the personal data of European Union (EU) citizens is subject to which of the following regulations?
a. The Health Insurance Portability and Accountability Act (HIPAA)
b. The Payment Card Industry Data Security Standard (PCI DSS)
c. The General Data Protection Regulation (GDPR)
d. The Sarbanes-Oxley Act (SOX)

Answer: c. The General Data Protection Regulation (GDPR). Explanation: The GDPR is a comprehensive data protection law that applies to any organization that processes the personal data of EU citizens, regardless of where the organization is located. It sets strict requirements for how personal data must be collected, used, and protected, and gives individuals certain rights over their data. HIPAA applies specifically to protected health information in the United States healthcare industry, PCI DSS applies to organizations that handle credit card data, and SOX applies to financial reporting and internal controls for publicly traded companies in the United States.

109. Which of the following is a key principle of the GDPR?
a. Data subjects have the right to receive their personal data in a structured, commonly used, and machine-readable format
b. Personal data can be collected and processed without the explicit consent of the data subject, as long as it is for a legitimate business purpose
c. Organizations are not required to report data breaches to supervisory authorities or affected individuals
d. Data protection impact assessments are optional and only recommended for high-risk processing activities

Answer: a. Data subjects have the right to receive their personal data in a structured, commonly used, and machine-readable format. Explanation: The right to data portability is one of the key rights granted to individuals under the GDPR. It allows data subjects to receive a copy of their personal data in a structured, commonly used, and machine-readable format, and to transmit that data to another controller without hindrance. This right aims to give individuals more control over their personal data and to facilitate data sharing and competition between services. The other options are incorrect statements about the GDPR: explicit consent is generally required for processing personal data, data breaches must be reported to authorities and individuals in certain circumstances, and data protection impact assessments are mandatory for high-risk processing activities.

110. Under HIPAA, which of the following is an example of protected health information (PHI)?
a. An individual's name and address
b. An individual's social security number
c. An individual's medical record number and diagnosis code
d. An individual's employment history and salary information

Answer: c. An individual's medical record number and diagnosis code. Explanation: Protected health information (PHI) under HIPAA includes any individually identifiable health information that is created, received, or maintained by a covered entity (such as a healthcare provider or health plan) or its business associates. This includes information about an individual's physical or mental health condition, the provision of healthcare services, and payment for those services. A medical record number and diagnosis code, when combined with other identifying information, would constitute PHI. While names, addresses, and social security numbers can be considered identifying information, they are not necessarily PHI on their own unless they are linked to health information. Employment and salary information is not typically considered PHI unless it is part of an individual's health records.

111. Which of the following HIPAA rules establishes requirements for the use and disclosure of PHI?
a. The Privacy Rule
b. The Security Rule
c. The Enforcement Rule
d. The Breach Notification Rule

Answer: a. The Privacy Rule. Explanation: The HIPAA Privacy Rule sets national standards for the protection of individuals' PHI by covered entities and their business associates. It establishes the permitted uses and disclosures of PHI, the rights of individuals with respect to their PHI, and the administrative requirements for covered entities to implement privacy policies and procedures. The Security Rule focuses specifically on the safeguarding of electronic PHI, the Enforcement Rule sets forth the enforcement procedures and penalties for HIPAA violations, and the Breach

Notification Rule requires covered entities to notify individuals and authorities in the event of a breach of unsecured PHI.

112. Which of the following is a requirement of the Sarbanes-Oxley Act (SOX)?
a. Establishing and maintaining an adequate system of internal control over financial reporting
b. Encrypting all sensitive financial data in transit and at rest
c. Conducting annual penetration testing of financial systems and networks
d. Appointing a Chief Privacy Officer to oversee compliance with data protection regulations

Answer: a. Establishing and maintaining an adequate system of internal control over financial reporting. Explanation: The Sarbanes-Oxley Act (SOX) was enacted in 2002 to protect investors and improve the accuracy and reliability of corporate financial disclosures. One of the key requirements of SOX is that publicly traded companies must establish and maintain an adequate system of internal control over financial reporting (ICFR). This means implementing policies, procedures, and practices to ensure that financial statements are accurate, complete, and fairly presented in accordance with generally accepted accounting principles (GAAP). Companies must also assess and report on the effectiveness of their ICFR annually. While information security controls such as encryption and penetration testing are important for protecting financial data and systems, they are not specifically required by SOX. Similarly, while data protection and privacy are important considerations for financial institutions, SOX does not mandate the appointment of a Chief Privacy Officer.

113. Under the Payment Card Industry Data Security Standard (PCI DSS), which of the following is a requirement for protecting stored cardholder data?
a. Encrypting cardholder data using strong cryptography
b. Storing cardholder data only on systems that are not connected to the internet
c. Masking all but the last four digits of the primary account number (PAN) when displaying cardholder data
d. Retaining cardholder data for at least five years for auditing and compliance purposes

Answer: a. Encrypting cardholder data using strong cryptography. Explanation: The PCI DSS is a set of security standards designed to ensure that all companies that accept, process, store, or transmit credit card information maintain a secure environment. One of the key requirements of the PCI DSS is that stored cardholder data must be protected using strong cryptography, such as AES-256 or RSA-2048. This helps to ensure that even if an attacker gains access to the stored data, they will not be able to read or use it without the encryption key. While the PCI DSS does require masking of the PAN when displayed (option c), this is a separate requirement from encryption of stored data. Storing cardholder data only on isolated systems (option b) is not sufficient on its own to meet PCI DSS requirements, and retaining cardholder data for extended periods (option d) is discouraged and subject to additional security requirements.

114. Which of the following is a key difference between the European Union's GDPR and the California Consumer Privacy Act (CCPA)?
a. The GDPR applies only to companies based in the EU, while the CCPA applies to any company doing business in California
b. The GDPR requires explicit consent for processing personal data, while the CCPA allows for implied consent in certain circumstances
c. The GDPR imposes higher fines for violations than the CCPA
d. The GDPR does not provide for a private right of action, while the CCPA allows individuals to sue companies for certain violations

Answer: d. The GDPR does not provide for a private right of action, while the CCPA allows individuals to sue companies for certain violations. Explanation: While both the GDPR and the CCPA are comprehensive data protection regulations that give individuals certain rights over their personal data, there are some key differences between the two laws. One significant difference is that the CCPA provides for a private right of action, which means that individuals can sue companies directly for certain violations of the law, such as data breaches resulting from inadequate security measures. The GDPR, on the other hand, does not provide for a private right of action, and enforcement is handled primarily by supervisory authorities. Both the GDPR and the CCPA have extraterritorial reach and can apply to companies outside of the EU and California, respectively, if they process the personal data of individuals in those jurisdictions (option a). Both laws also generally require explicit consent for processing personal data, with some limited exceptions (option b). While the GDPR does impose higher maximum fines than the CCPA (up to 4% of global annual revenue or €20 million, whichever is higher), the CCPA also has significant penalties of up to $7,500 per intentional violation (option c).

115. Which of the following is a requirement of the HIPAA Security Rule?
a. Implementing access controls to limit access to electronic PHI to authorized users only
b. Conducting annual privacy training for all employees who handle PHI
c. Obtaining patient consent before sharing PHI with other healthcare providers for treatment purposes
d. Providing patients with a copy of their PHI within 30 days of a request

Answer: a. Implementing access controls to limit access to electronic PHI to authorized users only. Explanation: The HIPAA Security Rule sets forth specific requirements for safeguarding electronic PHI (ePHI) that is created, received, maintained, or transmitted by covered entities and their business associates. One of the key requirements of the Security Rule is the implementation of access controls, which are technical policies and procedures that allow only authorized users to access ePHI. This includes measures such as unique user identification, emergency access procedures, automatic logoff, and encryption and decryption of ePHI. Annual privacy training (option b) is a requirement of the HIPAA Privacy Rule, not the Security Rule. Obtaining patient consent for treatment disclosures (option c) is also a Privacy Rule requirement, with some exceptions for emergencies and other specific circumstances. Providing patients with a copy of their PHI within a certain timeframe (option d) is a right granted by the Privacy Rule, but the specific timeframe is 30 days with a possible 30-day extension, not 30 days as stated in the option.

116. Which of the following is a requirement of the Gramm-Leach-Bliley Act (GLBA) for financial institutions?
a. Implementing a comprehensive information security program to protect customer data
b. Providing customers with an annual privacy notice explaining the institution's data collection and sharing practices
c. Obtaining customer consent before sharing their nonpublic personal information with nonaffiliated third parties
d. All of the above

Answer: d. All of the above. Explanation: The Gramm-Leach-Bliley Act (GLBA) is a U.S. law that requires financial institutions to protect the privacy and security of customer data. The law has three main components: the Financial Privacy Rule, the Safeguards Rule, and the Pretexting provisions. The Financial Privacy Rule requires financial institutions to provide customers with a privacy notice at the time of establishing a relationship and annually thereafter, explaining the institution's policies and practices for collecting, using, and sharing customer data (option b). The notice must also give customers the right to opt out of having their nonpublic personal information shared with nonaffiliated third parties, with some exceptions (option c). The Safeguards Rule requires financial institutions to implement a comprehensive written information security program that includes administrative, technical, and physical safeguards to protect the confidentiality, integrity, and availability of customer data (option a). The Pretexting provisions prohibit the use of false pretenses to obtain customer data from financial institutions. Therefore, all of the options listed are requirements of the GLBA for financial institutions.

117. Which of the following is a key principle of the OECD Guidelines on the Protection of Privacy and Transborder Flows of Personal Data?
a. Personal data should be collected and processed only with the knowledge and consent of the data subject
b. Personal data should be retained indefinitely to ensure its availability for future uses

c. Personal data should be shared freely across borders to facilitate global commerce and innovation
d. Personal data should be used for any purpose that the collecting organization deems appropriate

Answer: a. Personal data should be collected and processed only with the knowledge and consent of the data subject. Explanation: The Organization for Economic Cooperation and Development (OECD) Guidelines on the Protection of Privacy and Transborder Flows of Personal Data, also known as the OECD Privacy Framework, is a set of principles and guidelines for the protection of personal data that has been adopted by many countries and organizations around the world. One of the key principles of the OECD Privacy Framework is the Collection Limitation Principle, which states that personal data should be collected by lawful and fair means, and where appropriate, with the knowledge or consent of the data subject. This principle aims to ensure that individuals are aware of and have control over the collection and use of their personal data. The other options are not consistent with the principles of the OECD Privacy Framework. Personal data should be retained only as long as necessary to fulfill the purposes for which it was collected (option b), and should not be used for purposes beyond those for which it was originally collected without the consent of the data subject (option d). While the OECD Privacy Framework does recognize the importance of transborder data flows for global commerce and innovation, it also emphasizes the need for appropriate safeguards and limitations on such flows to protect individual privacy (option c).

118. An organization is entering into a contract with a cloud service provider to store and process sensitive customer data. Which of the following is the most important security requirement to include in the contract?
a. The provider must have a SOC 2 Type II certification
b. The provider must agree to allow the organization to conduct annual on-site security audits
c. The provider must include specific data protection provisions, such as data encryption and access controls
d. The provider must indemnify the organization against any data breaches or security incidents

Answer: c. The provider must include specific data protection provisions, such as data encryption and access controls. Explanation: When outsourcing sensitive data processing to a third-party provider, it is critical to ensure that the contract includes specific security requirements to protect the data. These requirements should align with the organization's own security policies and standards, as well as any applicable legal or regulatory requirements. Data protection provisions such as encryption, access controls, and incident response procedures are essential for mitigating the risk of unauthorized access, use, or disclosure of the data. While certifications (option a), audit rights (option b), and indemnification clauses (option d) can provide additional assurance and protection, they are not a substitute for clear and enforceable contractual requirements for securing the data itself.

119. An organization is negotiating a contract with a vendor that will have access to the organization's confidential information. Which of the following is the most appropriate way to address the confidentiality requirements in the contract?
a. Including a broad confidentiality clause that prohibits the vendor from disclosing any information related to the organization
b. Specifying the exact types of information that are considered confidential and the permitted uses and disclosures of that information
c. Requiring the vendor to obtain the organization's written consent before disclosing any information to third parties
d. Relying on the vendor's standard confidentiality agreement without any modifications or additions

Answer: b. Specifying the exact types of information that are considered confidential and the permitted uses and disclosures of that information. Explanation: When addressing confidentiality requirements in a contract, it is important to be as specific and detailed as possible about what information is covered and how it can be used and disclosed. A broad or vague confidentiality clause (option a) may be difficult to interpret and enforce, and may not provide sufficient protection for the organization's most sensitive information. Similarly, relying on the vendor's standard confidentiality agreement (option d) may not adequately address the organization's specific needs and risks.

Requiring written consent for all disclosures (option c) may be impractical and may not account for necessary or permitted disclosures, such as those required by law. The best approach is to clearly define the scope of confidential information and the specific circumstances under which it can be used or disclosed, such as for the purpose of performing the contracted services or as required by a court order. This helps to ensure that both parties have a clear understanding of their obligations and can be held accountable for any breaches of confidentiality.

120. An organization has entered into a contract with a service provider that includes a requirement for the provider to maintain specific security controls and standards. Which of the following is the most effective way to ensure that the provider is complying with these requirements?
a. Relying on the provider's self-assessments and attestations of compliance
b. Conducting periodic third-party audits of the provider's security practices and controls
c. Requiring the provider to submit monthly compliance reports to the organization
d. Terminating the contract immediately if any non-compliance is discovered

Answer: b. Conducting periodic third-party audits of the provider's security practices and controls. Explanation: While contractual security requirements are an important first step in ensuring that service providers maintain appropriate safeguards for the organization's data and systems, it is equally important to verify and validate the provider's compliance with those requirements on an ongoing basis. Self-assessments and attestations (option a) can be useful for demonstrating the provider's commitment to security, but they may not provide an objective or comprehensive view of the provider's actual practices and controls. Monthly compliance reports (option c) can help to track the provider's progress and identify potential issues, but they may not be sufficient to detect or prevent non-compliance. Terminating the contract immediately for any non-compliance (option d) may be an overreaction and may not allow for the opportunity to remediate or mitigate the issue. The most effective approach is to conduct periodic independent audits of the provider's security program, using a qualified third-party assessor. These audits can provide a more thorough and objective evaluation of the provider's compliance with contractual requirements, as well as identify any gaps or weaknesses that need to be addressed. The frequency and scope of the audits should be based on the level of risk associated with the services being provided and the sensitivity of the data involved.

121. An organization is outsourcing its customer support function to a third-party service provider. Which of the following is the most important consideration when addressing data privacy requirements in the contract?
a. Specifying the minimum retention period for customer data collected by the provider
b. Requiring the provider to obtain explicit consent from customers before collecting their data
c. Defining the specific purposes for which the provider is permitted to use customer data
d. Mandating that the provider delete all customer data immediately upon termination of the contract

Answer: c. Defining the specific purposes for which the provider is permitted to use customer data. Explanation: When outsourcing functions that involve the collection and processing of customer data, it is critical to ensure that the contract includes clear and specific requirements for protecting the privacy of that data. One of the most important considerations is specifying the purposes for which the provider is allowed to use the data, and prohibiting any uses that are not necessary for the performance of the contracted services. This helps to ensure that the provider is only using the data in ways that are consistent with the organization's privacy policies and applicable laws and regulations. Specifying retention periods (option a) is important for ensuring that data is not kept longer than necessary, but it does not address the purposes for which the data can be used during that retention period. Requiring explicit consent (option b) is a good practice for transparency and user control, but it may not be practical or necessary in all cases, depending on the nature of the services being provided and the legal basis for processing the data. Mandating immediate deletion of data upon termination (option d) can help to prevent unauthorized use or disclosure after the contract ends, but it may not be feasible or appropriate in all cases, such as where the data is needed for legal or regulatory purposes. The key is to carefully define and limit the purposes for which the provider can use the data, and to ensure that those purposes align with the organization's privacy obligations and user expectations.

122. An organization is entering into a contract with a cloud service provider that will be processing personal data on behalf of the organization. Under the European Union's General Data Protection Regulation (GDPR), which of the following is the organization considered in relation to the provider?
a. Data controller
b. Data processor
c. Data protection officer
d. Data subject

Answer: a. Data controller. Explanation: Under the GDPR, the organization that determines the purposes and means of processing personal data is considered the "data controller," while the entity that processes the data on behalf of the controller is considered the "data processor." In this scenario, the organization is the data controller because it is outsourcing the processing of personal data to the cloud service provider and retains control over the purposes and means of that processing. The cloud service provider is the data processor because it is processing the data on behalf of and under the instructions of the organization. The data protection officer (option c) is a specific role required by the GDPR for certain organizations, but it is not a general designation for parties in a data processing relationship. The data subject (option d) is the individual whose personal data is being processed, not the organization or the provider. It is important for the organization to understand its role and responsibilities as a data controller, including ensuring that the contract with the provider includes appropriate data protection clauses and safeguards, as required by the GDPR.

123. An organization has entered into a contract with a vendor that includes specific security and privacy requirements. Which of the following is the most appropriate way to address the vendor's liability for breaches of these requirements?
a. Requiring the vendor to indemnify the organization for any losses or damages resulting from a breach
b. Capping the vendor's liability at the total amount paid under the contract
c. Excluding any liability for the vendor, as the organization is ultimately responsible for its own security and privacy
d. Requiring the vendor to maintain a specific level of cybersecurity insurance coverage

Answer: a. Requiring the vendor to indemnify the organization for any losses or damages resulting from a breach. Explanation: When including security and privacy requirements in a contract with a vendor, it is important to also address the consequences and remedies for any breaches of those requirements. One common approach is to require the vendor to indemnify the organization for any losses, damages, or liabilities that result from the vendor's failure to comply with the specified requirements. This helps to ensure that the vendor is held accountable for any harm caused by its actions or omissions, and that the organization is protected from bearing the full cost of any incidents or breaches. Capping the vendor's liability (option b) may limit the organization's potential recovery and may not provide sufficient incentive for the vendor to maintain strong security and privacy practices. Excluding vendor liability altogether (option c) may leave the organization without recourse in the event of a breach, and may not reflect the shared responsibility between the parties for protecting the data and systems involved. Requiring cybersecurity insurance (option d) can provide additional financial protection, but it does not address the specific allocation of liability between the parties or the vendor's underlying obligations to comply with the contractual requirements. Indemnification clauses can be a powerful tool for managing vendor risk, but they should be carefully drafted and negotiated to ensure that they are enforceable and aligned with the organization's overall risk management strategy.

124. An organization is negotiating a service level agreement (SLA) with a cloud service provider. Which of the following is the most important metric to include in the SLA from an information security perspective?
a. Uptime percentage for the cloud services
b. Response time for customer support inquiries
c. Time to resolve security incidents and vulnerabilities
d. Frequency of feature updates and enhancements

Answer: c. Time to resolve security incidents and vulnerabilities. Explanation: A service level agreement (SLA) is a contractual commitment between a service provider and a customer that defines the expected level of service and the consequences for failing to meet those expectations. When negotiating an SLA with a cloud service provider, it is important to include metrics that are relevant to the security and availability of the services being provided. While uptime percentage (option a) is a common metric for ensuring the overall reliability and accessibility of the services, it does not specifically address the provider's responsiveness to security issues. Response time for customer support (option b) is important for general service quality, but it may not be directly related to security incidents or vulnerabilities. Frequency of feature updates (option d) can be relevant for ensuring that the services remain current and competitive, but it is not a primary security consideration. The most important security metric to include in the SLA is the time to resolve security incidents and vulnerabilities (option c). This metric establishes clear expectations for how quickly the provider must investigate, contain, and remediate any security issues that arise, and helps to ensure that the organization's data and systems are protected from ongoing risks or threats. The SLA should specify the maximum acceptable timeframes for different severity levels of incidents and vulnerabilities, as well as the penalties or remedies for failing to meet those timeframes. This can help to hold the provider accountable for maintaining a strong security posture and minimizing the impact of any security events.

125. An organization is outsourcing its payment processing function to a third-party service provider. Which of the following is the most important requirement to include in the contract to ensure compliance with the Payment Card Industry Data Security Standard (PCI DSS)?
a. The provider must maintain a current PCI DSS Attestation of Compliance (AOC)
b. The provider must use end-to-end encryption for all payment card data
c. The provider must store all payment card data in a secure, offline environment
d. The provider must implement multi-factor authentication for all access to payment card data

Answer: a. The provider must maintain a current PCI DSS Attestation of Compliance (AOC). Explanation: The Payment Card Industry Data Security Standard (PCI DSS) is a set of security requirements for organizations that accept, process, store, or transmit payment card data. When outsourcing payment processing functions to a third-party service provider, it is critical to ensure that the provider is fully compliant with the PCI DSS and can demonstrate that compliance to the organization and its acquiring bank. The most important requirement to include in the contract is that the provider must maintain a current PCI DSS Attestation of Compliance (AOC), which is a formal certification by a qualified security assessor (QSA) that the provider has met all of the applicable PCI DSS requirements. The AOC provides assurance that the provider has implemented the necessary security controls and practices to protect payment card data, and that it has been independently validated against the PCI DSS standards. While end-to-end encryption (option b), secure storage (option c), and multi-factor authentication (option d) are all important security measures that can help to protect payment card data, they are not sufficient on their own to demonstrate full PCI DSS compliance. The AOC is the most comprehensive and authoritative way to ensure that the provider is meeting its obligations under the PCI DSS and can be trusted to handle the organization's payment card data securely.

126. An organization is entering into a contract with a service provider that will have access to the organization's intellectual property (IP). Which of the following is the most important consideration when addressing IP protection in the contract?
a. Requiring the provider to obtain the organization's written consent before using or disclosing any IP
b. Specifying the ownership and licensing rights for any IP developed or modified by the provider under the contract
c. Mandating that the provider implement specific technical and administrative safeguards to protect the organization's IP
d. Prohibiting the provider from filing any patents or other IP registrations related to the services provided under the contract

Answer: b. Specifying the ownership and licensing rights for any IP developed or modified by the provider under the contract. Explanation: When engaging a service provider that will have access to the organization's intellectual property (IP), it is important to clearly define and protect the organization's rights and interests in that IP. One of the most critical considerations is specifying the ownership and licensing rights for any IP that is developed or modified by the provider in the course of performing the contracted services. This includes any new inventions, designs, software, or other creative works that may be created using or incorporating the organization's existing IP. The contract should clearly state that the organization retains ownership of its pre-existing IP, as well as any improvements or derivatives of that IP, and that the provider is only granted a limited license to use that IP for the purposes of the contract. The contract should also address the ownership and licensing of any new IP that is developed by the provider specifically for the organization, and should ensure that the organization has the necessary rights to use and exploit that IP as needed. Requiring written consent for IP use and disclosure (option a) can help to prevent unauthorized sharing or misuse of the organization's IP, but it does not address the underlying ownership and licensing issues. Mandating specific safeguards (option c) is important for protecting the confidentiality and integrity of the IP, but it does not establish the legal rights and obligations of the parties. Prohibiting the provider from filing IP registrations (option d) may be appropriate in some cases to prevent the provider from claiming ownership of the organization's IP, but it does not affirmatively grant the organization the rights it needs to use and control its own IP. A clear and comprehensive IP clause is essential for any contract involving the sharing or development of valuable intellectual assets.

127. An organization is using a third-party service provider to collect and process personal data from its customers. Under the European Union's General Data Protection Regulation (GDPR), which of the following is the most important requirement for the contract between the organization and the provider?
a. The contract must include a detailed description of the technical security measures implemented by the provider
b. The contract must specify the procedures for the provider to notify the organization in the event of a data breach
c. The contract must require the provider to obtain explicit consent from customers before collecting their personal data
d. The contract must include mandatory data protection clauses that set out the provider's obligations as a data processor

Answer: d. The contract must include mandatory data protection clauses that set out the provider's obligations as a data processor. Explanation: Under the GDPR, when an organization (the data controller) engages a third-party service provider (the data processor) to process personal data on its behalf, the contract between the parties must include certain mandatory data protection clauses. These clauses are specified in Article 28 of the GDPR and are designed to ensure that the data processor complies with the GDPR's requirements and safeguards the rights and freedoms of the data subjects. The mandatory clauses must address issues such as the scope and nature of the processing, the duration of the processing, the types of personal data and categories of data subjects involved, the obligations and rights of the data controller, and the specific measures that the data processor must implement to ensure the security and confidentiality of the personal data. While technical security measures (option a), breach notification procedures (option b), and consent mechanisms (option c) are all important elements of GDPR compliance, they are not the most critical requirements for the contract between the controller and processor. The GDPR places the primary responsibility for obtaining consent and implementing security measures on the data controller, not the data processor. The data processor's main obligations are to act only on the instructions of the controller, to implement appropriate technical and organizational measures to protect the personal data, and to assist the controller in fulfilling its own obligations under the GDPR. The mandatory data protection clauses are the key mechanism for ensuring that these obligations are clearly defined and legally binding on the data processor.

128. Which of the following best describes the primary purpose of compliance monitoring in an information security program?
a. To identify and correct security vulnerabilities before they can be exploited
b. To ensure that security policies, procedures, and controls are being consistently followed and are effective
c. To investigate and respond to security incidents and data breaches
d. To train employees on security best practices and their roles and responsibilities

Answer: b. To ensure that security policies, procedures, and controls are being consistently followed and are effective. Explanation: Compliance monitoring is the process of continuously assessing an organization's adherence to its own security policies, as well as to external laws, regulations, and standards. The main goal of compliance monitoring is to verify that the security measures and practices defined in the organization's policies and procedures are being consistently implemented and are operating effectively to mitigate risks and protect sensitive data. While identifying vulnerabilities (option a), responding to incidents (option c), and training employees (option d) are all important aspects of an information security program, they are not the primary focus of compliance monitoring. Compliance monitoring is more concerned with ensuring that the organization is doing what it says it will do in terms of security, and that its security controls are functioning as intended.

129. Which of the following is the most effective method for monitoring compliance with security policies and procedures?
a. Conducting annual security audits and assessments
b. Implementing automated compliance monitoring tools and dashboards
c. Reviewing system logs and access reports on an ad-hoc basis
d. Relying on employee self-reporting of policy violations or security incidents

Answer: b. Implementing automated compliance monitoring tools and dashboards. Explanation: While all of the methods listed can play a role in compliance monitoring, the most effective approach is to use automated tools and dashboards that provide continuous, real-time visibility into the organization's security posture and policy adherence. Automated compliance monitoring solutions can be configured to track specific security controls, configurations, and user activities, and to alert security teams to any deviations or anomalies. They can also provide centralized dashboards and reports that give a comprehensive view of compliance status across the entire organization, and that can be easily shared with auditors and regulators. Annual audits (option a) are important for in-depth assessments and independent validation, but they provide only a point-in-time snapshot and may miss ongoing or emerging compliance issues. Ad-hoc log reviews (option c) can be useful for investigating specific incidents or concerns, but they are not a systematic or proactive approach to compliance monitoring. Employee self-reporting (option d) is an unreliable and incomplete method, as it depends on individuals' awareness, willingness, and ability to report issues accurately and promptly. Automated tools provide the most consistent, comprehensive, and efficient way to monitor compliance on an ongoing basis.

130. Which of the following is the most important factor to consider when selecting security metrics and key performance indicators (KPIs) for compliance reporting?
a. The availability of data and the ease of collecting and analyzing the metrics
b. The alignment of the metrics with the organization's overall business objectives and risk management strategies
c. The preferences and expectations of external auditors and regulators
d. The ability of the metrics to showcase the success and effectiveness of the security program

Answer: b. The alignment of the metrics with the organization's overall business objectives and risk management strategies. Explanation: When choosing security metrics and KPIs for compliance reporting, it is critical to ensure that they are meaningful, relevant, and aligned with the organization's broader goals and priorities. The metrics should provide insights into how well the security program is supporting and enabling the business, and how effectively it is managing and mitigating the organization's key risks. They should be tied to specific business outcomes and objectives, such as reducing the frequency and impact of security incidents, improving the efficiency and reliability of security processes, and enhancing customer trust and satisfaction. Metrics that are chosen solely based on the availability of data or the ease of collection (option a) may not provide a true picture of the security program's performance or value. Metrics that are designed to meet the expectations of auditors and regulators (option c) are important for demonstrating compliance, but they may not be sufficient to drive continuous improvement and risk reduction. Metrics that are selected to showcase the success of the security program (option d) may present a biased or incomplete view, and may not identify areas for improvement or investment. By aligning metrics with business objectives and risk management strategies, organizations can ensure that their compliance reporting is both meaningful and actionable, and that it supports data-driven decision making and accountability.

131. Which of the following is the most effective way to communicate compliance status and metrics to senior management and the board?
a. Presenting detailed technical reports and data analysis at regular board meetings
b. Providing high-level dashboards and executive summaries that highlight key risks, trends, and actions
c. Conducting annual compliance training sessions for senior leaders and board members
d. Distributing monthly compliance newsletters and updates via email

Answer: b. Providing high-level dashboards and executive summaries that highlight key risks, trends, and actions. Explanation: When reporting compliance status and metrics to senior management and the board, it is important to provide information that is clear, concise, and relevant to their roles and responsibilities. Senior leaders and board members typically do not have the time or expertise to review detailed technical reports or data analysis (option a), and may not find this level of detail meaningful or actionable. Annual training sessions (option c) and monthly newsletters (option d) can be useful for raising awareness and providing general education, but they are not the most effective way to convey specific compliance status and metrics on a regular basis. The most effective approach is to provide high-level dashboards and executive summaries that present a clear and compelling picture of the organization's compliance posture, key risks and trends, and priority actions and initiatives. These dashboards should be visually engaging and easy to understand, using graphs, charts, and color-coding to highlight important information. They should also include brief narratives and explanations that provide context and interpretation for the data, and that link the compliance metrics to the organization's overall business objectives and risk management strategies. By providing this type of strategic, actionable compliance reporting, security leaders can help senior management and the board to make informed decisions and to exercise effective oversight of the security program.

132. Which of the following is the most important consideration when establishing the frequency and timing of compliance monitoring activities?
a. The availability of resources and budget for monitoring and reporting
b. The expectations and requirements of external auditors and regulators
c. The criticality and sensitivity of the systems and data being monitored
d. The preferences and schedules of the security team and other stakeholders

Answer: c. The criticality and sensitivity of the systems and data being monitored. Explanation: When determining how often and when to conduct compliance monitoring activities, the most important factor to consider is the level of risk associated with the systems, applications, and data being monitored. Systems and data that are critical to the organization's operations, that handle highly sensitive or regulated information, or that are exposed to significant threats and vulnerabilities should be monitored more frequently and thoroughly than those with lower risk profiles. For example, systems that process financial transactions, store personal data, or support essential business functions may require continuous or daily monitoring, while less critical systems may be monitored weekly or monthly. The frequency and timing of monitoring should be based on a risk assessment that takes into account the potential impact of a compliance failure or security breach, as well as the likelihood and sophistication of threats and vulnerabilities. Resource availability and budgets (option a) are important practical considerations, but they should not drive the fundamental risk-based approach to compliance monitoring. External requirements and expectations (option b) should be factored into the monitoring plan, but they may not fully reflect the organization's specific risk landscape and priorities. Stakeholder preferences and schedules (option d) should be accommodated where possible, but they should not override the risk-based rationale for the monitoring frequency and timing. By aligning monitoring activities with risk levels, organizations can ensure that they are allocating their resources and efforts effectively to mitigate the most significant compliance and security risks.

133. Which of the following is the most effective way to ensure that compliance monitoring results are actionable and lead to continuous improvement?
a. Assigning ownership and accountability for each compliance metric and control to specific individuals or teams
b. Establishing clear thresholds and triggers for escalation and remediation based on the severity and impact of compliance issues
c. Integrating compliance monitoring data with other security and risk management data to provide a more comprehensive view
d. Automating compliance monitoring processes and reports to reduce manual effort and improve consistency

Answer: b. Establishing clear thresholds and triggers for escalation and remediation based on the severity and impact of compliance issues. Explanation: Compliance monitoring is not an end in itself, but rather a means to identify and address risks and gaps in an organization's security posture. To ensure that compliance monitoring results are actionable and lead to meaningful improvements, it is essential to establish clear thresholds and triggers for escalation and remediation based on the severity and potential impact of the issues identified. This involves defining specific criteria and metrics that indicate when a compliance issue requires immediate attention and action, such as a critical control failure, a high-risk vulnerability, or a repeated policy violation. It also involves setting up automated alerts and notifications that are sent to the appropriate stakeholders and decision-makers when these thresholds are exceeded, along with clear guidance on the expected response and remediation steps. By embedding these thresholds and triggers into the compliance monitoring process, organizations can ensure that issues are promptly identified, prioritized, and addressed based on their relative importance and urgency. While assigning ownership and accountability (option a), integrating data (option c), and automating processes (option d) can all contribute to the effectiveness and efficiency of compliance monitoring, they are not sufficient on their own to ensure that results are acted upon and that improvements are made. Clear escalation and remediation criteria are the key to driving accountability and action based on compliance monitoring insights.

134. Which of the following is the most significant challenge in implementing an effective compliance monitoring and reporting program?
a. Identifying and agreeing on the most meaningful and relevant compliance metrics and KPIs
b. Collecting and analyzing compliance data from multiple disparate systems and sources
c. Communicating compliance results and priorities to different stakeholders with varying levels of technical knowledge and interest
d. Balancing the need for comprehensive compliance monitoring with the potential impact on system performance and user productivity

Answer: b. Collecting and analyzing compliance data from multiple disparate systems and sources. Explanation: One of the biggest obstacles to effective compliance monitoring and reporting is the complexity and fragmentation of an organization's IT environment. Most organizations today have a wide range of systems, applications, devices, and data sources that are relevant to compliance, each with its own logging, monitoring, and reporting capabilities. Collecting and consolidating compliance data from these disparate sources can be a significant technical and logistical challenge, requiring the use of specialized tools, APIs, and connectors to extract, transform, and load the data into a centralized repository or platform. Once the data is collected, it must be normalized, correlated, and analyzed to identify trends, patterns, and anomalies that may indicate compliance issues or risks. This requires sophisticated data analytics and visualization capabilities, as well as domain expertise to interpret and contextualize the results. While defining relevant metrics (option a), communicating results (option c), and balancing monitoring with performance (option d) are all important considerations in compliance monitoring and reporting, they are typically less complex and time-consuming than the underlying data collection and analysis challenges. Organizations that can effectively overcome these data challenges, through the use of automation, integration, and advanced analytics tools, are better positioned to implement comprehensive and reliable compliance monitoring and reporting programs.

135. Which of the following compliance metrics is most useful for measuring the effectiveness of an organization's security awareness and training program?
a. The percentage of employees who have completed the annual security awareness training
b. The number of security incidents caused by human error or policy violations
c. The results of periodic phishing simulations and other behavioral assessments
d. The feedback and satisfaction scores from employee surveys and evaluations

Answer: b. The number of security incidents caused by human error or policy violations. Explanation: While all of the metrics listed can provide valuable insights into the effectiveness of a security awareness and training program, the most direct and meaningful measure is the number of actual security incidents that are caused by human error, negligence, or non-compliance. This metric provides a clear and tangible indication of how well employees are understanding, retaining, and applying the knowledge and skills they have learned in the training program. If the number of human-related incidents is high or increasing, it suggests that the training is not effectively changing behavior or reducing risk, and that additional or different approaches may be needed. The completion rate of the training (option a) is a useful measure of participation and coverage, but it does not necessarily indicate whether the training is having the desired impact on behavior and risk reduction. Phishing simulation results (option c) can provide a more specific and realistic assessment of employees' ability to recognize and respond to common social engineering tactics, but they are just one aspect of a comprehensive awareness program. Employee feedback and satisfaction scores (option d) can help to gauge the quality and relevance of the training content and delivery, but they are subjective measures that may not directly correlate with actual security outcomes. By focusing on the number of human-related incidents as the primary metric, organizations can more accurately assess the real-world effectiveness of their awareness and training efforts, and prioritize improvements based on the most significant risks and gaps.

136. Which of the following is the most important step in responding to a compliance violation or gap identified through monitoring activities?
a. Conducting a root cause analysis to determine the underlying factors that led to the violation or gap
b. Implementing immediate corrective actions to remediate the specific issue and prevent further occurrences
c. Reporting the violation or gap to senior management and the board, along with a plan for addressing it
d. Updating policies, procedures, and controls to reflect the lessons learned from the violation or gap

Answer: b. Implementing immediate corrective actions to remediate the specific issue and prevent further occurrences. Explanation: When a compliance violation or gap is identified through monitoring activities, the most critical and time-sensitive step is to take immediate action to remediate the issue and prevent further damage or exposure. This may involve a range of corrective measures, depending on the nature and severity of the issue, such as:

- Blocking or disabling access to compromised systems or data
- Patching or fixing vulnerabilities or misconfigurations
- Revoking or changing user credentials and privileges
- Restoring or recovering data from backups
- Notifying affected stakeholders and authorities
- Activating incident response and business continuity plans

The goal of these immediate actions is to contain and mitigate the risk as quickly and effectively as possible, and to prevent the issue from escalating or spreading further. While conducting a root cause analysis (option a), reporting to senior management (option c), and updating policies and controls (option d) are all important follow-up steps in the response process, they should not delay or distract from the urgent need to address the issue at hand. In fact, taking swift and decisive corrective action can help to demonstrate the organization's commitment to compliance and security, and can reduce the potential impact and liability of the violation or gap. By prioritizing immediate remediation, organizations can minimize the damage and duration of compliance issues, and can lay the groundwork for a more thorough and strategic response that addresses the underlying root causes and systemic weaknesses.

137. Which of the following is the most effective way to validate the accuracy and completeness of compliance monitoring data and reports?
a. Conducting manual reviews and spot checks of the data and reports on a regular basis
b. Comparing the monitoring data and reports to external benchmarks and industry standards
c. Implementing automated data quality and integrity checks within the monitoring and reporting tools
d. Engaging an independent third party to audit and verify the monitoring data and reports

Answer: c. Implementing automated data quality and integrity checks within the monitoring and reporting tools. Explanation: Compliance monitoring and reporting is only as effective as the accuracy and reliability of the underlying data and analytics. If the data is incomplete, inconsistent, or incorrect, it can lead to false positives, false negatives, and misguided decisions and actions. To ensure the integrity and trustworthiness of compliance monitoring data and reports, the most effective approach is to implement automated data quality and integrity checks within the monitoring and reporting tools themselves. These checks can include:

- Data validation rules that ensure that data fields are complete, properly formatted, and within expected ranges
- Data reconciliation processes that compare data across different sources and systems to identify discrepancies and anomalies
- Data lineage and provenance tracking that documents the origin, transformation, and flow of data through the monitoring and reporting pipeline
- Data security and access controls that prevent unauthorized modification or deletion of data
- Data backup and recovery mechanisms that ensure data can be restored in case of loss or corruption

By embedding these automated checks and controls into the monitoring and reporting tools, organizations can proactively detect and prevent data quality issues, and can have greater confidence in the accuracy and completeness of their compliance reports and insights. While manual reviews (option a), external benchmarking (option b), and third-party audits (option d) can provide additional layers of validation and assurance, they are typically more time-consuming, costly, and reactive than automated data quality checks. By making data integrity a core feature of the compliance monitoring and reporting process, organizations can reduce the risk of false or misleading results, and can make more informed and effective decisions based on reliable and trustworthy data.

138. Which of the following is the most significant potential consequence of non-compliance with the Payment Card Industry Data Security Standard (PCI DSS) for an organization that processes credit card transactions?
a. Increased risk of data breaches and cyber attacks
b. Damage to the organization's reputation and customer trust
c. Financial penalties and fines imposed by credit card companies and banks
d. Suspension or termination of the organization's ability to accept credit card payments

Answer: d. Suspension or termination of the organization's ability to accept credit card payments. Explanation: While non-compliance with PCI DSS can lead to various negative consequences, such as increased security risks (option a), reputational damage (option b), and financial penalties (option c), the most severe and potentially devastating consequence is the possibility of losing the ability to process credit card transactions altogether. If an organization is found to be non-compliant with PCI DSS, the credit card companies and acquiring banks may decide to suspend or terminate the organization's merchant account and payment processing privileges, effectively cutting off a critical revenue stream and business capability. This can be particularly catastrophic for organizations that rely heavily on credit card transactions, such as retailers, hospitality businesses, and online service providers. The financial and operational impact of not being able to accept credit card payments can far outweigh the costs of fines and penalties, and can threaten the very survival of the business. Therefore, maintaining compliance with PCI DSS is not just a matter of avoiding negative consequences, but of preserving the fundamental ability to conduct business and generate revenue in today's digital economy.

139. Which of the following is a potential legal consequence of non-compliance with the European Union's General Data Protection Regulation (GDPR) for an organization that processes the personal data of EU citizens?
a. Imprisonment of the organization's executives and senior management
b. Seizure of the organization's assets and property by EU authorities
c. Revocation of the organization's business license and right to operate in the EU
d. Administrative fines of up to €20 million or 4% of the organization's global annual revenue, whichever is higher

Answer: d. Administrative fines of up to €20 million or 4% of the organization's global annual revenue, whichever is higher. Explanation: The GDPR is a comprehensive and stringent data protection law that applies to any organization that collects, processes, or stores the personal data of EU citizens, regardless of where the organization is based. One of the key enforcement mechanisms of the GDPR is the power of supervisory authorities to impose significant administrative fines on organizations that violate the law's requirements. The maximum fine that can be levied under the GDPR is €20 million or 4% of the organization's total worldwide annual revenue for the preceding financial year, whichever is higher. This means that for large multinational corporations, the potential financial impact of GDPR non-compliance can be enormous, running into hundreds of millions or even billions of euros. While the GDPR does provide for other legal consequences, such as warnings, reprimands, and orders to suspend data processing, it does not explicitly authorize the imprisonment of individuals (option a), the seizure of assets (option b), or the revocation of business licenses (option c) as penalties for non-compliance. The administrative fines are the primary legal and financial deterrent for organizations to ensure they comply with the GDPR's requirements for data protection, transparency, and accountability.

140. Which of the following is a common organizational consequence of non-compliance with information security policies and regulations?
a. Increased budget and resources for the information security department
b. Improved collaboration and communication between the information security team and other business units
c. Disciplinary action against employees who violate security policies, up to and including termination of employment
d. Greater support and buy-in from senior management for information security initiatives and priorities

Answer: c. Disciplinary action against employees who violate security policies, up to and including termination of employment. Explanation: One of the most direct and visible consequences of non-compliance with an organization's information security policies and procedures is the potential for disciplinary action against the individuals responsible for the violations. Depending on the severity and frequency of the non-compliance, and the specific terms of the organization's HR and security policies, disciplinary action can range from verbal or written warnings to more serious measures such as fines, suspensions, or even termination of employment. The purpose of disciplinary action is to hold employees accountable for their security-related behavior and decisions, and to deter future non-compliance by demonstrating that there are real and meaningful consequences for violating the organization's security rules and expectations. While non-compliance can sometimes lead to increased budget and resources for security (option a), improved collaboration with other teams (option b), or greater management support (option d), these are typically more indirect and longer-term consequences that depend on how the organization responds to and learns from the non-compliance incident. Disciplinary action, on the other hand, is a more immediate and targeted consequence that directly addresses the root cause of the non-compliance at the individual level, and sends a clear message about the importance of adhering to the organization's security policies and standards.

141. Which of the following is a potential consequence of non-compliance with industry-specific regulations, such as HIPAA for healthcare organizations or SOX for publicly traded companies?
a. Increased scrutiny and oversight from regulatory agencies and authorities
b. Mandatory public disclosure of the organization's security policies and practices
c. Restriction on the organization's ability to collect and use customer data for marketing purposes
d. Requirement to implement specific security technologies and solutions, such as encryption or multi-factor authentication

Answer: a. Increased scrutiny and oversight from regulatory agencies and authorities. Explanation: Many industries are subject to specific laws and regulations that impose additional requirements and obligations for information security and data protection, beyond the general legal and ethical standards that apply to all organizations. Examples include HIPAA for healthcare providers and plans, SOX for publicly traded companies, GLBA for financial institutions, and FERPA for educational institutions. Non-compliance with these industry-specific regulations can trigger a range of consequences, but one of the most significant is the likelihood of increased scrutiny and oversight from the relevant regulatory agencies and authorities. This can take the form of more frequent or in-depth audits, investigations, and inspections, as well as requests for additional documentation, reporting, and remediation of identified deficiencies. The goal of this increased oversight is to ensure that the organization takes the necessary steps to address the non-compliance and prevent future violations, and to protect the interests and rights of the individuals and stakeholders affected by the organization's security practices. While some industry-specific regulations may require public disclosure of certain security practices (option b), restrict certain data collection and use (option c), or mandate specific security controls (option d), these are typically more prescriptive and narrow consequences that vary by regulation and context. Increased regulatory scrutiny and oversight, on the other hand, is a more general and pervasive consequence of non-compliance that can apply across different industries and regulations, and can have a significant impact on an organization's reputation, operations, and bottom line.

142. Which of the following is a potential financial consequence of a major data breach or security incident resulting from non-compliance with information security standards and best practices?
a. Increased sales and revenue due to heightened customer awareness and interest in the organization's products and services
b. Reduced stock price and market valuation due to investor concerns and loss of confidence in the organization's management and governance
c. Improved credit rating and borrowing terms due to the organization's demonstrated commitment to addressing and resolving security issues
d. Decreased insurance premiums and coverage limits due to the organization's higher risk profile and claims history

Answer: b. Reduced stock price and market valuation due to investor concerns and loss of confidence in the organization's management and governance. Explanation: A major data breach or security incident can have severe and long-lasting financial consequences for an organization, particularly if it is found to be the result of non-compliance with established security standards and best practices. One of the most significant potential impacts is a reduction in the organization's stock price and market valuation, as investors react to the news of the breach and the perceived mismanagement of security risks and responsibilities. Investors may lose confidence in the organization's ability to protect its assets and reputation, and may view the breach as a sign of broader governance and leadership failures. This loss of investor confidence can lead to a sell-off of the organization's stock, driving down its price and market capitalization. In some cases, the financial impact of a breach can be so severe that it threatens the organization's ability to continue as a going concern, or makes it a target for lawsuits, regulatory actions, or takeover attempts. While a breach may sometimes lead to short-term increases in sales or revenue (option a) due to heightened public attention and interest, this is typically a temporary and unpredictable effect that does not offset the longer-term financial damage. Similarly, while a breach may prompt an organization to invest in and improve its security posture, this is unlikely to result in immediate improvements in credit rating or borrowing terms (option c), or reductions in insurance costs (option d), given the increased risk and uncertainty associated with the organization's security practices and vulnerabilities.

143. Which of the following is a potential reputational consequence of non-compliance with data privacy regulations, such as GDPR or CCPA?
a. Increased trust and loyalty from customers who value the organization's transparency and accountability
b. Improved relationships and partnerships with other organizations who view the non-compliance as a sign of the organization's flexibility and adaptability
c. Enhanced brand recognition and market differentiation due to the organization's unique and innovative approach to data privacy

d. Negative media coverage and public criticism of the organization's data handling practices and commitment to user privacy

Answer: d. Negative media coverage and public criticism of the organization's data handling practices and commitment to user privacy. Explanation: Data privacy has become an increasingly important and sensitive issue for individuals, organizations, and society as a whole, as the amount and sensitivity of personal data being collected, processed, and shared continues to grow. Regulations such as GDPR and CCPA have been enacted to give individuals greater control over their personal data, and to hold organizations accountable for their data handling practices and obligations. Non-compliance with these regulations can have significant reputational consequences for organizations, as it may be seen as a betrayal of customer trust and a failure to respect individual privacy rights. Negative media coverage and public criticism are common outcomes of data privacy non-compliance, as journalists, activists, and concerned citizens draw attention to the organization's practices and demand greater transparency, accountability, and reform. This negative publicity can damage the organization's brand image and reputation, erode customer loyalty and trust, and deter potential customers and partners from engaging with the organization. While compliance with data privacy regulations may sometimes be seen as a burden or constraint on organizations, it is increasingly recognized as a fundamental expectation and responsibility in today's digital age. Organizations that prioritize and demonstrate their commitment to data privacy, through transparent and accountable practices, are more likely to build and maintain positive reputations and relationships with their customers and stakeholders (option a). Non-compliance, on the other hand, is unlikely to be viewed as a sign of flexibility or adaptability (option b), or as a unique or innovative approach to data privacy (option c), but rather as a failure to meet basic legal and ethical standards for protecting personal data.

144. Which of the following is a potential operational consequence of non-compliance with information security policies and controls?
a. Streamlined and optimized business processes due to the removal of unnecessary security barriers and restrictions
b. Increased efficiency and productivity of employees who are no longer burdened by complex and time-consuming security procedures
c. Improved system performance and availability due to the reduction of security-related overhead and latency
d. Disruption or interruption of critical business functions and services due to security incidents or data breaches

Answer: d. Disruption or interruption of critical business functions and services due to security incidents or data breaches. Explanation: Information security policies and controls are designed to protect an organization's systems, data, and operations from various threats and risks, such as unauthorized access, malware, phishing, and social engineering. Non-compliance with these policies and controls can leave an organization vulnerable to security incidents and data breaches that can have severe operational consequences. If critical systems or data are compromised, corrupted, or rendered unavailable due to a security incident, it can disrupt or interrupt the organization's ability to carry out its essential business functions and services. This can lead to lost productivity, missed deadlines, dissatisfied customers, and damaged relationships with partners and suppliers. In some cases, the operational impact of a security incident can be so severe that it threatens the organization's ability to continue operating, or requires significant time and resources to recover and resume normal operations. While some may argue that security policies and controls can create operational inefficiencies or barriers (option a), or that non-compliance can lead to greater productivity or performance (options b and c), these are typically short-sighted and misguided views that do not account for the long-term risks and costs of inadequate security. In reality, effective security policies and controls are essential for ensuring the reliability, integrity, and continuity of an organization's operations, and for protecting against the potentially catastrophic consequences of security incidents and breaches.

145. Which of the following is a potential legal consequence of non-compliance with contractual security requirements in a vendor or partner agreement?
a. Criminal prosecution and imprisonment of the organization's executives and senior management
b. Seizure of the organization's intellectual property and trade secrets by the vendor or partner

c. Termination of the contract and potential litigation for breach of contract and damages
d. Requirement to provide the vendor or partner with access to the organization's security policies and controls for ongoing monitoring and auditing

Answer: c. Termination of the contract and potential litigation for breach of contract and damages. Explanation: When an organization enters into a contract or agreement with a vendor, partner, or customer, it may be required to comply with specific security requirements or standards as a condition of the contract. These requirements may be designed to protect the other party's data, systems, or interests, or to ensure compatibility and interoperability between the parties' security practices and controls. Non-compliance with these contractual security requirements can be treated as a breach of contract, and can trigger various legal consequences depending on the specific terms and conditions of the agreement. One of the most common consequences is the termination of the contract by the other party, who may view the non-compliance as a material breach that undermines the purpose and value of the agreement. Termination can result in the loss of business, revenue, or access to critical resources or capabilities provided by the vendor or partner. In addition to termination, the other party may also seek legal remedies for breach of contract, such as monetary damages, injunctive relief, or specific performance. This can lead to costly and time-consuming litigation that diverts resources and attention away from the organization's core business activities. While non-compliance with contractual security requirements could potentially lead to criminal charges (option a) or intellectual property disputes (option b) in extreme cases, these are typically less common and direct consequences than termination and breach of contract. Similarly, while some contracts may require ongoing security audits or monitoring (option d), this is typically a proactive measure to prevent or detect non-compliance, rather than a consequence of non-compliance itself.

146. Which of the following is a potential regulatory consequence of non-compliance with security breach notification laws, such as those required by HIPAA or state data breach statutes?
a. Mandatory public apology and admission of wrongdoing by the organization's CEO or senior leadership
b. Requirement to provide free credit monitoring and identity theft protection services to all affected individuals for a minimum of five years
c. Prohibition on the organization's ability to collect, process, or store personal data for a specified period of time
d. Investigation and enforcement action by the relevant regulatory agency, including potential fines, penalties, and corrective action plans

Answer: d. Investigation and enforcement action by the relevant regulatory agency, including potential fines, penalties, and corrective action plans. Explanation: Many laws and regulations, such as HIPAA and state data breach notification statutes, require organizations to notify affected individuals, regulatory agencies, and/or law enforcement in the event of a security breach that compromises personal data. These notification requirements are designed to ensure that individuals are aware of the breach and can take appropriate steps to protect themselves from potential harm, such as identity theft or fraud. They also allow regulators to investigate the cause and impact of the breach, and to hold organizations accountable for any non-compliance or negligence that may have contributed to the incident. Failure to comply with breach notification requirements can result in regulatory investigations and enforcement actions by the relevant agencies, such as the Department of Health and Human Services (HHS) for HIPAA violations or state attorneys general for violations of state data breach laws. These enforcement actions can include a range of consequences, such as:

- Civil or criminal fines and penalties, which can vary depending on the severity and duration of the non-compliance
- Corrective action plans or consent decrees, which require the organization to take specific steps to remediate the non-compliance and prevent future violations
- Increased regulatory scrutiny and oversight, including more frequent audits, inspections, or reporting requirements
- Public disclosure of the non-compliance and enforcement action, which can damage the organization's reputation and credibility

While some breach notification laws may require organizations to provide credit monitoring or identity protection services to affected individuals (option b), this is typically a separate requirement from the notification itself, and may not be mandatory in all cases. Public apologies (option a) or prohibitions on data collection (option c) are not typically direct regulatory consequences of non-compliance with breach notification laws, but may be voluntary or court-ordered remedies in some cases.

147. Which of the following is a potential ethical consequence of non-compliance with industry codes of conduct or professional standards related to information security?
a. Increased respect and admiration from peers and colleagues who view the non-compliance as a sign of the individual's independence and creativity
b. Greater opportunities for career advancement and leadership roles due to the individual's willingness to take risks and challenge established norms
c. Loss of professional certifications or memberships, and potential exclusion from future employment or business opportunities in the field
d. Enhanced personal brand and reputation as a thought leader and innovator in the information security community

Answer: c. Loss of professional certifications or memberships, and potential exclusion from future employment or business opportunities in the field. Explanation: Information security professionals are expected to adhere to various industry codes of conduct and professional standards that establish the ethical and behavioral norms for the field. These standards may be set by professional associations, certification bodies, or other industry groups, and cover issues

148. An organization is conducting a risk assessment for its e-commerce platform. Which of the following is the most appropriate risk identification technique to identify potential security threats and vulnerabilities?
a. Business impact analysis (BIA)
b. Annualized loss expectancy (ALE) calculation
c. Threat modeling using a framework like STRIDE or DREAD
d. Quantitative risk analysis using Monte Carlo simulations

Answer: c. Threat modeling using a framework like STRIDE or DREAD. Explanation: Threat modeling is a structured approach to identifying and analyzing potential security threats and vulnerabilities in a system or application. It involves systematically examining the system from an attacker's perspective and identifying the different ways in which the system could be compromised or exploited. Frameworks like STRIDE (Spoofing, Tampering, Repudiation, Information Disclosure, Denial of Service, Elevation of Privilege) and DREAD (Damage, Reproducibility, Exploitability, Affected Users, Discoverability) provide a standardized way to categorize and prioritize threats based on their characteristics and potential impact. Threat modeling is particularly useful for identifying risks in complex, multi-layered systems like e-commerce platforms, where there are many potential entry points and attack vectors. Business impact analysis (option a) is a related but distinct technique that focuses on identifying and quantifying the potential consequences of a disruption or outage, rather than the specific threats that could cause it. Annualized loss expectancy (option b) and Monte Carlo simulations (option d) are quantitative risk analysis methods that are used to estimate the financial impact of risks, but they do not directly identify the underlying threats and vulnerabilities.

149. An organization has identified a critical security risk related to its mobile device management (MDM) system. The risk has a high likelihood of occurrence and could result in a severe data breach if exploited. Which of the following is the most appropriate risk treatment option for this scenario?
a. Risk acceptance
b. Risk avoidance
c. Risk mitigation
d. Risk transfer

Answer: c. Risk mitigation. Explanation: Risk mitigation involves taking steps to reduce the likelihood or impact of a risk to an acceptable level. It is the most appropriate risk treatment option when a risk has been identified as high likelihood and high impact, and when the risk cannot be avoided or transferred. In the scenario described, the risk related to the MDM system is critical and could result in a severe data breach, so it requires immediate attention and action to mitigate the risk. Mitigation measures could include implementing additional security controls, such as stronger authentication and encryption, as well as improving monitoring and incident response capabilities. Risk acceptance (option a) is not appropriate for a high likelihood, high impact risk, as it would leave the organization exposed to a significant threat without any proactive measures to address it. Risk avoidance (option b) may not be feasible or practical in this case, as the MDM system is likely a critical part of the organization's mobile strategy and cannot be easily eliminated or replaced. Risk transfer (option d), such as through cyber insurance, can help to manage the financial impact of a breach, but it does not directly address the underlying vulnerability or prevent the breach from occurring in the first place.

150. Which of the following is a key benefit of using quantitative risk analysis methods, such as Monte Carlo simulations or value at risk (VaR) models?
a. They provide a more accurate and precise estimate of risk exposure than qualitative methods
b. They are easier to communicate and explain to non-technical stakeholders than qualitative methods
c. They require less time and effort to perform than qualitative methods
d. They are more suitable for identifying and prioritizing risks than qualitative methods

Answer: a. They provide a more accurate and precise estimate of risk exposure than qualitative methods. Explanation: Quantitative risk analysis methods use numerical data and statistical techniques to estimate the probability and impact of risks in monetary terms. By assigning specific values and ranges to risk variables, such as the likelihood of occurrence, the potential cost of a breach, and the effectiveness of controls, quantitative methods can provide a more granular and precise estimate of an organization's overall risk exposure. This can help organizations to make more informed decisions about risk prioritization, resource allocation, and risk treatment options. Monte Carlo simulations, for example, use random sampling and probability distributions to model the range of possible outcomes and scenarios for a given risk, taking into account the variability and uncertainty in the input variables. Value at risk (VaR) models estimate the maximum potential loss that an organization could incur over a given time period, at a given confidence level, based on historical data and statistical analysis. While quantitative methods can provide more precision and accuracy than qualitative methods, they are not necessarily easier to communicate or explain to non-technical stakeholders (option b), as they often involve complex mathematical concepts and assumptions. They also typically require more time, effort, and specialized expertise to perform than qualitative methods (option c), as they involve gathering and analyzing large amounts of data and running multiple simulations or models. Finally, while quantitative methods can be used to prioritize risks based on their estimated impact and likelihood, they are not inherently more suitable for identifying risks than qualitative methods (option d), as they still rely on the same underlying process of threat modeling and vulnerability assessment.

151. An organization is implementing a risk management framework based on the ISO 31000 standard. Which of the following is a key principle of effective risk management according to the standard?
a. Risk management should be a standalone process that is separate from other business activities
b. Risk management should be focused primarily on financial risks and impacts
c. Risk management should be transparent and inclusive, involving stakeholders throughout the process
d. Risk management should rely primarily on historical data and past incidents to identify and assess risks

Answer: c. Risk management should be transparent and inclusive, involving stakeholders throughout the process. Explanation: ISO 31000 is a widely recognized international standard that provides guidelines and principles for effective risk management. One of the key principles emphasized in the standard is that risk management should be transparent and inclusive, involving stakeholders at all levels of the organization and throughout the risk management process. This principle recognizes that risk management is not just the responsibility of a single department or function, but rather a collaborative effort that requires input and participation from a wide range of stakeholders, including business units, IT, legal, compliance, and external partners. Transparency means that the risk management process should be clearly documented, communicated, and understood by all stakeholders, with roles, responsibilities, and accountability clearly defined. Inclusivity means that stakeholders should be actively engaged in identifying, assessing, and mitigating risks, and that their perspectives and concerns should be taken into account in decision-making. By involving stakeholders throughout the process, organizations can ensure that risk management is aligned with business objectives, that potential risks and impacts are thoroughly considered, and that risk treatment plans are practical and effective. The standard emphasizes that risk management should be integrated into all organizational activities and decision-making processes (option a), not treated as a standalone or isolated function. It also stresses that risk management should consider a wide range of risks, including strategic, operational, financial, and reputational risks (option b), not just financial impacts. Finally, while historical data and past incidents can be useful inputs into the risk management process, the standard emphasizes the importance of forward-looking and proactive risk identification and assessment (option d), rather than relying solely on reactive or retrospective approaches.

152. An organization has identified a high-risk vulnerability in its web application that could allow attackers to gain unauthorized access to sensitive customer data. The organization is considering two potential risk treatment options: implementing a web application firewall (WAF) to block exploits of the vulnerability, or redesigning the application to eliminate the vulnerability altogether. Which of the following factors should be given the most weight in deciding between these two options?
a. The cost and complexity of implementing and maintaining each option
b. The preferences and opinions of the web application development team
c. The potential impact and consequences of a successful exploit of the vulnerability
d. The industry best practices and standards for web application security

Answer: c. The potential impact and consequences of a successful exploit of the vulnerability. Explanation: When deciding between different risk treatment options, the most important factor to consider is the potential impact and consequences of the risk being addressed. In this scenario, the vulnerability in the web application could allow attackers to gain unauthorized access to sensitive customer data, which could have severe consequences for the organization, such as:

- Financial losses from lawsuits, fines, and settlements related to the data breach
- Reputational damage and loss of customer trust and loyalty
- Regulatory investigations and enforcement actions for non-compliance with data protection laws
- Operational disruptions and costs associated with incident response and remediation

Given the high stakes involved, the organization should prioritize the risk treatment option that provides the most effective and reliable protection against the vulnerability, even if it may be more costly or complex to implement. In this case, redesigning the application to eliminate the vulnerability altogether would provide a more fundamental and long-term solution than simply blocking exploits with a WAF. While a WAF can be an effective short-term mitigation measure, it may not be sufficient to prevent all possible attack vectors and may require ongoing tuning and maintenance to keep up with evolving threats. Redesigning the application, on the other hand, can address the root cause of the vulnerability and provide a more robust and future-proof solution. The cost and complexity of each option (option a) should certainly be considered in the decision-making process, but should not be the primary driver if the potential impact of the risk is severe. The preferences and opinions of the development team (option b) should also be taken into account, but should not override the objective assessment of risk and the need for effective risk treatment. Industry best practices and standards (option d) can provide valuable guidance and benchmarks for web application security, but should be adapted to the specific context and risk profile of the organization.

153. An organization is using the NIST Cybersecurity Framework (CSF) to guide its risk management program. Which of the following is a key function of the framework?

a. Identify
b. Protect
c. Detect
d. All of the above

Answer: d. All of the above. Explanation: The NIST Cybersecurity Framework (CSF) is a comprehensive and widely-used framework for managing and reducing cybersecurity risks. It is organized around five core functions that represent the key stages and activities of an effective risk management program:

1. Identify: This function involves understanding the organization's business context, resources, and risk landscape, and using this information to develop a risk management strategy and prioritize risk management activities. Key activities include asset management, business environment analysis, governance, and risk assessment.

2. Protect: This function involves implementing appropriate safeguards and controls to prevent, limit, or contain the impact of potential cybersecurity events. Key activities include access control, awareness and training, data security, information protection processes and procedures, maintenance, and protective technology.

3. Detect: This function involves implementing appropriate activities to identify the occurrence of cybersecurity events in a timely manner. Key activities include anomalies and events detection, continuous security monitoring, and detection processes.

4. Respond: This function involves implementing appropriate activities to take action regarding a detected cybersecurity incident, and to contain its impact. Key activities include response planning, communications, analysis, mitigation, and improvements.

5. Recover: This function involves implementing appropriate activities to restore capabilities or services that were impaired due to a cybersecurity incident, and to ensure resilience and recovery planning. Key activities include recovery planning, improvements, and communications.

All five functions are critical and interdependent components of an effective risk management program, and should be implemented in a continuous and iterative manner. The framework emphasizes the importance of aligning risk management activities with business objectives and priorities, and of involving stakeholders throughout the process to ensure a shared understanding of risks and responsibilities. By providing a common language and structure for risk management, the NIST CSF helps organizations to assess their current risk posture, identify gaps and opportunities for improvement, and communicate their risk management approach to internal and external stakeholders.

154. An organization is conducting a business impact analysis (BIA) as part of its risk management program. Which of the following is the primary purpose of a BIA?
a. To identify and prioritize the organization's most critical business processes and assets
b. To estimate the financial losses that could result from a disruption or outage of critical processes and assets
c. To determine the maximum tolerable downtime (MTD) for each critical process and asset
d. All of the above

Answer: d. All of the above. Explanation: A business impact analysis (BIA) is a key component of an organization's risk management and business continuity planning process. The primary purpose of a BIA is to identify and prioritize the organization's most critical business processes, services, and assets, and to assess the potential impact of a disruption or outage on these critical elements. This information is used to guide the development of strategies and plans to prevent, mitigate, and recover from potential incidents and ensure the continuity of essential operations. The main objectives of a BIA include:

1. Identifying and prioritizing critical business processes and assets (option a): This involves working with business units and stakeholders to identify the processes, services, and assets that are most essential to the organization's mission, revenue, reputation, and regulatory compliance. Criticality is typically assessed based on factors such as the severity of impact, the time sensitivity of the process, the availability of alternatives or workarounds, and the interdependencies with other processes and systems.

2. Estimating the financial and operational impact of a disruption (option b): For each critical process and asset, the BIA estimates the potential losses and costs that could result from a disruption or outage, such as lost revenue, increased expenses, regulatory fines, and customer attrition. This helps the organization to quantify its risk exposure and prioritize its risk management and continuity planning efforts based on the potential business impact.

3. Determining the maximum tolerable downtime (MTD) for each critical process and asset (option c): The MTD is the maximum amount of time that a critical process or asset can be unavailable before the impact becomes unacceptable to the organization. This metric is used to set recovery time objectives (RTOs) and recovery point objectives (RPOs) for business continuity and disaster recovery planning, and to guide the selection and implementation of appropriate continuity strategies and solutions.

By conducting a comprehensive BIA, organizations can gain a clear understanding of their most critical business processes and assets, the potential impact of disruptions, and the recovery requirements and priorities. This information is essential for developing effective risk management and business continuity strategies that are aligned with the organization's overall business objectives and risk appetite. The BIA should be reviewed and updated regularly to ensure that it remains current and relevant in the face of changing business and risk landscapes.

155. An organization has identified a critical third-party service provider that has access to sensitive customer data. Which of the following is the most important step the organization should take to manage the risks associated with this third-party relationship?
a. Conducting a thorough due diligence assessment of the provider's security controls and practices before engaging in the relationship
b. Requiring the provider to sign a non-disclosure agreement (NDA) to protect the confidentiality of the data
c. Implementing technical controls to monitor and restrict the provider's access to the data on an ongoing basis
d. Establishing clear contractual terms and service level agreements (SLAs) that specify the provider's security obligations and liabilities

Answer: a. Conducting a thorough due diligence assessment of the provider's security controls and practices before engaging in the relationship. Explanation: Third-party relationships, such as those with service providers, vendors, and partners, can introduce significant risks to an organization's information security and data protection posture. These risks can arise from a variety of factors, such as the provider's own security practices and controls, the nature and sensitivity of the data being shared, and the level of access and control granted to the provider. To effectively manage these risks, the most important step an organization should take is to conduct a thorough due diligence assessment of the provider's security controls and practices before engaging in the relationship. This assessment should cover a wide range of areas, such as:

- The provider's information security policies, procedures, and standards
- The provider's technical and administrative safeguards for protecting data, such as encryption, access controls, and monitoring
- The provider's incident response and business continuity plans and capabilities
- The provider's compliance with relevant laws, regulations, and industry standards, such as GDPR, HIPAA, and PCI DSS
- The provider's hiring and training practices for ensuring the security awareness and competence of its personnel
- The provider's third-party relationships and supply chain security practices
- The provider's history of security incidents, breaches, and regulatory actions

By conducting a comprehensive due diligence assessment, the organization can gain a clear understanding of the provider's security posture and identify any potential gaps, weaknesses, or risks that need to be addressed before proceeding with the relationship. This assessment can also help the organization to negotiate appropriate contractual terms and SLAs (option d) that clearly define the provider's security obligations and liabilities, and provide a basis for ongoing monitoring and enforcement. While NDAs (option b) and technical controls (option c) can be important tools for protecting the confidentiality and integrity of the data shared with the provider, they are not sufficient on their own to address the broader range of risks associated with third-party relationships. A thorough due diligence assessment is the foundation for a risk-based and proactive approach to managing third-party security risks throughout the lifecycle of the relationship.

156. An organization is conducting a risk assessment for its critical IT infrastructure. Which of the following is a key advantage of using quantitative risk assessment methods over qualitative methods?
a. Quantitative methods are more efficient and require less time and resources to perform
b. Quantitative methods provide a more precise and objective measure of risk exposure in monetary terms
c. Quantitative methods are easier to communicate and understand for non-technical stakeholders
d. Quantitative methods are better suited for identifying and prioritizing risks based on their potential impact

Answer: b. Quantitative methods provide a more precise and objective measure of risk exposure in monetary terms. Explanation: Quantitative risk assessment methods use numerical data, statistical analysis, and mathematical models to estimate the probability and impact of risks in financial terms. By assigning specific monetary values to risk factors, such as the cost of a security incident or the value of an asset, quantitative methods can provide a more precise and objective measure of an organization's overall risk exposure. This allows organizations to prioritize risks based on their potential financial impact, and to make more informed decisions about risk treatment options and resource allocation. Quantitative methods can also help organizations to perform cost-benefit analysis and to justify security investments based on their expected return on investment (ROI). While quantitative methods can be more time-consuming and resource-intensive than qualitative methods (option a), they provide a more rigorous and defensible approach to risk measurement and decision-making. Quantitative results can be more challenging to communicate to non-technical stakeholders (option c), as they often involve complex statistical concepts and formulas, but they provide a more concrete and actionable basis for risk management than qualitative ratings or rankings. Quantitative methods can be used to prioritize risks based on their monetary impact (option d), but they are not inherently better suited for risk identification than qualitative methods, which can also be used to identify potential risk scenarios and factors.

157. Which of the following is a key limitation of using qualitative risk assessment methods?
a. Qualitative methods are too complex and time-consuming for most organizations to implement effectively
b. Qualitative methods do not provide sufficient detail or granularity to support risk-based decision making
c. Qualitative methods rely heavily on subjective judgments and opinions, which can vary widely among different stakeholders
d. Qualitative methods are not compatible with most risk management frameworks and standards

Answer: c. Qualitative methods rely heavily on subjective judgments and opinions, which can vary widely among different stakeholders. Explanation: Qualitative risk assessment methods use descriptive categories or ratings, such as high, medium, or low, to characterize the likelihood and impact of risks. These ratings are typically based on expert judgment, historical data, or best practices, and are used to prioritize risks and guide risk treatment decisions. While qualitative methods can be useful for quickly identifying and categorizing risks, they have several limitations compared to quantitative methods. One of the main limitations is that qualitative ratings are inherently subjective and can vary widely depending on the knowledge, experience, and biases of the individuals involved in the assessment process. Different stakeholders may have different perceptions of what constitutes a high or low risk, based on their own roles, responsibilities, and risk tolerance. This can lead to inconsistencies and disagreements in risk prioritization and decision-making, and can make it difficult to compare and aggregate risks across different parts of the organization. Qualitative methods are generally less complex and time-consuming than quantitative methods (option a), as they do not require extensive data collection and analysis. However, they can still provide sufficient detail and granularity to support risk-based decision making (option b), especially when used in combination with other risk management techniques such as scenario analysis or root cause analysis. Qualitative methods are also compatible with most risk management frameworks and standards (option d), which often provide guidance on how to define and apply risk rating scales and criteria.

158. An organization is considering using a combination of quantitative and qualitative risk assessment methods for its information security risk management program. Which of the following is a key benefit of using a hybrid approach?
a. A hybrid approach eliminates the need for subjective judgments and ensures complete objectivity in risk assessment
b. A hybrid approach allows organizations to assess all possible risks, regardless of their likelihood or impact
c. A hybrid approach provides a more comprehensive and balanced view of risks, leveraging the strengths of both quantitative and qualitative methods
d. A hybrid approach is always more cost-effective and efficient than using either quantitative or qualitative methods alone

Answer: c. A hybrid approach provides a more comprehensive and balanced view of risks, leveraging the strengths of both quantitative and qualitative methods. Explanation: While quantitative and qualitative risk assessment methods each have their own strengths and limitations, many organizations choose to use a combination of both approaches to gain a more comprehensive and balanced view of their risk landscape. A hybrid approach allows organizations to leverage the precision and objectivity of quantitative methods for risks that can be easily measured and monetized, while using qualitative methods for risks that are more difficult to quantify or that require more contextual understanding. For example, an organization might use quantitative methods to estimate the financial impact of a data breach based on historical data and industry benchmarks, while using qualitative methods to assess the reputational impact of the breach based on the sensitivity of the data and the expectations of key stakeholders. By combining both approaches, organizations can gain a more nuanced and multifaceted view of their risks, and can make more informed decisions about risk prioritization and treatment. A hybrid approach does not necessarily eliminate the need for subjective judgments (option a), as qualitative methods still rely on expert opinions and assumptions to some extent. However, it can help to validate and calibrate those judgments against quantitative data and models, and can provide a more robust basis for risk-based decision making. A hybrid approach also does not allow organizations to assess all possible risks (option b), as there will always be some level of uncertainty and unknowns in risk assessment. However, it can help organizations to focus their efforts on the most critical and impactful risks, and to allocate their resources more effectively. A hybrid approach may not always be more cost-effective or efficient than using either approach alone (option d), as it may require more time, skills, and tools to implement and integrate both methods. However, the benefits of a more comprehensive and balanced risk assessment may outweigh the additional costs and efforts in the long run.

159. An organization has conducted a qualitative risk assessment for its IT infrastructure and has identified a risk as "high" based on its potential impact and likelihood. Which of the following is the most appropriate next step for managing this risk?
a. Accepting the risk and taking no further action, as high risks are an inherent part of doing business
b. Conducting a more detailed quantitative analysis to estimate the potential financial impact of the risk
c. Implementing immediate risk mitigation measures to reduce the likelihood or impact of the risk
d. Transferring the risk to a third-party insurance provider or service provider

Answer: b. Conducting a more detailed quantitative analysis to estimate the potential financial impact of the risk. Explanation: When a qualitative risk assessment identifies a risk as "high," it indicates that the risk has a significant potential impact on the organization and a high likelihood of occurring. However, the qualitative rating alone does not provide enough information to determine the most appropriate risk treatment strategy, as it does not quantify the potential financial or operational impact of the risk. In this case, the most appropriate next step is to conduct a more detailed quantitative analysis to estimate the potential costs and losses associated with the risk, such as the cost of downtime, data loss, legal liabilities, or reputational damage. This analysis can help the organization to better understand the magnitude and urgency of the risk, and to prioritize it against other risks and initiatives. It can also provide a basis for cost-benefit analysis and ROI calculations for different risk treatment options. Accepting the risk and taking no further action (option a) is not a viable option for high risks, as it exposes the organization to unacceptable levels of potential harm and liability. Immediate mitigation measures (option c) may be necessary in some cases, especially if the risk poses an imminent threat to critical assets or operations. However, without a quantitative understanding of the risk, the organization may over- or under-invest in mitigation efforts, or may not select the most effective or efficient measures. Transferring the risk to a third party (option d) may be an appropriate risk treatment option in some cases, but it should be based on a careful analysis of the costs and benefits of risk transfer, as well as the capabilities and reliability of the third party. A quantitative analysis can help the organization to determine whether risk transfer is a cost-effective and feasible option, and to negotiate appropriate terms and conditions with the third party.

160. An organization is using a risk matrix to prioritize its information security risks based on their likelihood and impact. Which of the following is a key limitation of using a risk matrix for risk assessment?
a. Risk matrices do not take into account the inherent uncertainty and variability of risk likelihood and impact estimates
b. Risk matrices do not provide a quantitative measure of risk exposure or potential losses
c. Risk matrices can lead to an overemphasis on high-likelihood, low-impact risks at the expense of low-likelihood, high-impact risks
d. All of the above

Answer: d. All of the above. Explanation: A risk matrix is a commonly used tool for qualitative risk assessment and prioritization. It typically consists of a grid with likelihood on one axis and impact on the other, and risks are plotted on the grid based on their estimated likelihood and impact ratings. The matrix is often color-coded to highlight the most significant risks, such as red for high likelihood and high impact, yellow for medium likelihood and medium impact, and green for low likelihood and low impact. While risk matrices can be a useful starting point for risk assessment and communication, they have several key limitations that organizations should be aware of:

1. Risk matrices do not take into account the inherent uncertainty and variability of risk likelihood and impact estimates (option a). The ratings used in a risk matrix are often based on subjective judgments and assumptions, which can vary widely among different stakeholders and change over time as new information becomes available. Risk matrices do not typically provide a way to quantify or communicate this uncertainty, which can lead to a false sense of precision and confidence in risk prioritization.

2. Risk matrices do not provide a quantitative measure of risk exposure or potential losses (option b). The color-coding used in a risk matrix is a qualitative representation of risk severity, but it does not convey the actual magnitude or scale of potential impacts in terms of financial, operational, or reputational losses. This can make it difficult for organizations to make informed decisions about risk treatment options and resource allocation, as they may not have a clear understanding of the costs and benefits of different mitigation strategies.

3. Risk matrices can lead to an overemphasis on high-likelihood, low-impact risks at the expense of low-likelihood, high-impact risks (option c). The visual nature of a risk matrix can draw attention to the top-right corner of the grid, where risks with high likelihood and high impact are typically plotted. However, this can obscure the importance of risks in the bottom-right corner, which may have a low likelihood but a catastrophic impact if they occur. Organizations may underestimate or overlook these "black swan" events, which can be the most damaging and difficult to recover from.

To mitigate these limitations, organizations should use risk matrices as part of a broader risk assessment and management process that incorporates other techniques such as quantitative analysis, scenario planning, and stakeholder consultation. They should also regularly review and update their risk matrices to reflect changes in the risk landscape and to validate the assumptions and judgments underlying the ratings. Finally, they should use risk matrices as a communication and prioritization tool, but not as the sole basis for risk treatment decisions or resource allocation.

161. An organization has identified a critical risk to its confidential customer data and has decided to conduct a quantitative risk assessment to estimate the potential financial impact of a data breach. Which of the following is the most important factor to consider when selecting a quantitative risk assessment methodology?
a. The availability and quality of historical data on similar data breaches and their costs
b. The preferences and familiarity of the risk assessment team with different methodologies
c. The level of detail and complexity of the methodology, regardless of its applicability to the specific risk scenario
d. The cost and time required to implement the methodology, regardless of its effectiveness in estimating risk exposure

Answer: a. The availability and quality of historical data on similar data breaches and their costs. Explanation: When conducting a quantitative risk assessment, the accuracy and reliability of the results depend heavily on the quality and relevance of the input data used in the analysis. This is particularly true for estimating the potential financial impact of a risk scenario, such as a data breach, which can involve complex and variable costs such as incident response, legal liabilities, customer compensation, and reputational damage. To select an appropriate quantitative risk assessment methodology, the most important factor to consider is the availability and quality of historical data on similar data breaches and their associated costs. This data can come from a variety of sources, such as industry benchmarks, case studies, claims databases, or the organization's own incident records. The data should be as specific and comparable to the risk scenario as possible, taking into account factors such as the type and volume of data involved, the cause and scope of the breach, the regulatory and legal environment, and the industry and market context. The more relevant and reliable the historical data, the more accurate and actionable the risk assessment results will be. The preferences and familiarity of the risk assessment team (option b) should be a secondary consideration, as the team can be trained and supported in using a new methodology if it is the most appropriate for the risk scenario. The level of detail and complexity of the methodology (option c) should be balanced with its applicability and feasibility for the specific risk scenario, as a highly detailed and complex methodology may not necessarily provide more accurate or useful results if it is not well-suited to the available data and resources. The cost and time required to implement the methodology (option d) should also be balanced with its effectiveness in estimating risk exposure, as a cheaper or faster methodology may not be worth the investment if it does not provide reliable or actionable results. Ultimately, the selection of a quantitative risk assessment methodology should be based on a careful consideration of the specific risk scenario, the available data and resources, and the intended use and audience of the risk assessment results.

162. An organization is using a combination of quantitative and qualitative risk assessment methods to prioritize its information security risks. Which of the following is a key challenge in integrating the results of these different methods?
a. Quantitative and qualitative risk assessments use different terminologies and metrics, making it difficult to compare and aggregate their results
b. Quantitative risk assessments are always more accurate and reliable than qualitative assessments, so the qualitative results should be disregarded
c. Qualitative risk assessments are always more comprehensive and nuanced than quantitative assessments, so the quantitative results should be disregarded
d. Quantitative and qualitative risk assessments are fundamentally incompatible and should never be used together in the same risk management program

Answer: a. Quantitative and qualitative risk assessments use different terminologies and metrics, making it difficult to compare and aggregate their results. Explanation: While using a combination of quantitative and qualitative risk assessment methods can provide a more comprehensive and balanced view of an organization's risk landscape, integrating the results of these different methods can be challenging. One of the key challenges is that quantitative and qualitative assessments often use different terminologies, scales, and metrics to describe and measure risks, making it difficult to directly compare and aggregate their results. For example, a quantitative assessment may express risk exposure in terms of dollar amounts or probabilities, while a qualitative assessment may use ratings such as high, medium, or low, or colors such as red, yellow, or green. To integrate these results, organizations need to establish a common framework or taxonomy that maps the different terminologies and metrics to a consistent set of risk categories and priorities. This may involve normalizing or converting the quantitative results into qualitative ratings, or vice versa, based on predefined thresholds or ranges. It may also involve weighting or prioritizing the results based on their relative importance or confidence levels, and using visualization tools such as risk heat maps or dashboards to provide a unified view of the risk landscape. While quantitative assessments are often more precise and objective than qualitative assessments, they are not always more accurate or reliable (option b), as they depend on the quality and relevance of the input data and assumptions used in the analysis. Similarly, while qualitative assessments can provide more contextual and nuanced insights than quantitative assessments, they are not always more comprehensive or valid (option c), as they rely on subjective judgments and opinions that may be biased or inconsistent. Quantitative and qualitative assessments are not fundamentally incompatible (option d), but rather complementary and synergistic, as they provide different perspectives and insights on the same risk scenarios. The key is to carefully design and execute the risk assessment process to ensure that the different methods are aligned, validated, and integrated in a meaningful and actionable way.

163. Which of the following is the primary purpose of conducting a Business Impact Analysis (BIA) as part of an organization's risk management program?
a. To identify and prioritize the organization's most critical assets, processes, and dependencies
b. To estimate the financial losses that could result from security incidents and data breaches
c. To determine the appropriate level of investment in cybersecurity controls and technologies
d. To assess the effectiveness of the organization's incident response and business continuity plans

Answer: a. To identify and prioritize the organization's most critical assets, processes, and dependencies. Explanation: A Business Impact Analysis (BIA) is a systematic process for identifying and prioritizing an organization's most critical business functions, assets, and resources, and assessing the potential impact of disruptions to those elements. The primary purpose of a BIA is to provide a foundation for risk management and business continuity planning by determining which assets and processes are essential to the organization's survival and success, and how quickly they need to be restored in the event of an incident. By understanding the criticality and dependencies of different business elements, organizations can make informed decisions about risk mitigation, resource allocation, and continuity strategies. While a BIA may include estimates of financial losses (option b), these are typically a secondary output used to quantify and communicate the potential impact of disruptions. A BIA is not directly focused on determining cybersecurity investments (option c) or assessing incident response and continuity plans (option d), although its results can inform those decisions as part of a broader risk management program.

164. Which of the following is a key step in the Business Impact Analysis (BIA) process?
a. Identifying and documenting the organization's key stakeholders and their contact information
b. Analyzing the organization's financial statements and budget to determine the cost of downtime
c. Conducting interviews and workshops with business unit leaders to gather data on critical processes and dependencies
d. Reviewing the organization's insurance policies to determine the coverage for business interruptions and losses

Answer: c. Conducting interviews and workshops with business unit leaders to gather data on critical processes and dependencies. Explanation: One of the key steps in conducting a Business Impact Analysis (BIA) is to engage with business unit leaders and subject matter experts to gather data on the organization's critical processes, assets, and dependencies. This typically involves a combination of interviews, workshops, and surveys to elicit information on the inputs, outputs, resources, and timing requirements of each process, as well as the potential impact of disruptions on the organization's operations, reputation, and financial performance. By directly involving business stakeholders in the BIA process, organizations can ensure that the analysis is based on accurate and relevant data, and that the results are validated and accepted by those who will be responsible for implementing continuity strategies. Identifying stakeholders and their contact information (option a) is an important preparatory step for the BIA, but it is not a core component of the analysis itself. Analyzing financial statements (option b) and reviewing insurance policies (option d) may provide useful context and inputs for the BIA, but they are not sufficient on their own to identify and prioritize critical business processes and dependencies.

165. Which of the following metrics is typically used in a Business Impact Analysis (BIA) to determine the criticality and priority of a business process?
a. The number of employees involved in the process
b. The maximum tolerable downtime (MTD) for the process
c. The historical frequency and duration of disruptions to the process
d. The level of customer satisfaction with the outputs of the process

Answer: b. The maximum tolerable downtime (MTD) for the process. Explanation: The maximum tolerable downtime (MTD) is a key metric used in Business Impact Analysis (BIA) to determine the criticality and priority of a business process. The MTD represents the maximum amount of time that a process can be disrupted before the impact becomes unacceptable to the organization, based on factors such as financial losses, regulatory compliance, and reputational damage. Processes with shorter MTDs are typically considered more critical and are given higher priority for continuity planning and resource allocation. For example, a process with an MTD of 24 hours would be considered more critical than a process with an MTD of 1 week, all other factors being equal. The MTD is used to establish recovery time objectives (RTOs) and recovery point objectives (RPOs) for each process, which guide the development and implementation of continuity strategies and solutions. The number of employees involved in a process (option a) may be a useful data point for understanding the resource requirements and dependencies of the process, but it does not directly indicate the criticality of the process. The historical frequency and duration of disruptions (option c) can provide valuable context for risk assessment and continuity planning, but they are not a direct measure of the process's importance or urgency. Customer satisfaction (option d) is an important consideration for many processes, but it is not typically used as a primary metric for determining criticality in a BIA.

166. An organization has conducted a Business Impact Analysis (BIA) and has identified a critical business process with a maximum tolerable downtime (MTD) of 4 hours. Which of the following is the most appropriate recovery time objective (RTO) for this process?
a. 1 hour
b. 4 hours
c. 8 hours
d. 24 hours

Answer: a. 1 hour. Explanation: The recovery time objective (RTO) is a key metric used in Business Impact Analysis (BIA) and business continuity planning to specify the maximum amount of time allowed for the recovery of a critical process after a disruption occurs. The RTO is typically set based on the maximum tolerable downtime (MTD) identified in the BIA, but it is usually shorter than the MTD to provide a margin of safety and to ensure that the process is restored before the impact becomes unacceptable. In this case, if the MTD for the critical process is 4 hours, the most appropriate RTO would be less than 4 hours to ensure that the process is recovered within the tolerable timeframe. An RTO of 1 hour (option a) would provide a reasonable buffer and would help to minimize the impact of the disruption on the organization's operations and stakeholders. An RTO of 4 hours (option b) would be equal to the MTD and would not provide any margin for error or unexpected complications in the recovery process. An RTO of 8 hours or 24 hours (options c and d) would exceed the MTD and would not be appropriate for a critical process that cannot tolerate more than 4 hours of downtime. The specific RTO for a given process should be based on a careful analysis of the process's requirements, dependencies, and recovery capabilities, as well as the organization's risk appetite and continuity objectives.

167. Which of the following is a common challenge in conducting a Business Impact Analysis (BIA) across multiple business units and locations?
a. Obtaining accurate and consistent data on the criticality and dependencies of business processes
b. Identifying the maximum tolerable downtime (MTD) for each process
c. Estimating the financial impact of disruptions to each process
d. Determining the appropriate recovery strategies and solutions for each process

Answer: a. Obtaining accurate and consistent data on the criticality and dependencies of business processes. Explanation: One of the most common challenges in conducting a Business Impact Analysis (BIA) across multiple business units and locations is obtaining accurate and consistent data on the criticality and dependencies of business processes. This challenge arises from several factors, such as:

- Different business units may have different understandings and definitions of what constitutes a critical process, based on their specific roles, objectives, and stakeholders.
- Business processes may span multiple units and locations, making it difficult to identify and map all the inputs, outputs, and dependencies involved.
- Business units may have different levels of maturity and sophistication in documenting and measuring their processes, leading to gaps and inconsistencies in the data.
- Stakeholders may have different perceptions and biases about the importance and urgency of their processes, leading to subjective and conflicting assessments.

To overcome these challenges, organizations need to establish a clear and consistent framework for defining and assessing the criticality and dependencies of business processes, and ensure that all stakeholders are trained and aligned on the framework. This may involve developing standardized templates, taxonomies, and metrics for capturing and analyzing process data, as well as conducting cross-functional workshops and validation sessions to identify and reconcile any discrepancies or gaps in the data. Identifying the MTD (option b), estimating financial impacts (option c), and determining recovery strategies (option d) are all important components of the BIA, but they typically rely on having accurate and consistent data on the criticality and dependencies of the processes being analyzed. Without a solid foundation of process data, these other aspects of the BIA may be incomplete, inconsistent, or unreliable.

168. Which of the following is a key benefit of using a structured and repeatable methodology for conducting a Business Impact Analysis (BIA)?
a. It ensures that all possible disruption scenarios and impacts are identified and analyzed, regardless of their likelihood or severity
b. It eliminates the need for subjective judgments and estimates in determining the criticality and priority of business processes
c. It provides a consistent and defensible approach for justifying investments in continuity and recovery solutions
d. It guarantees that the organization will be able to recover from any disruption within the maximum tolerable downtime (MTD) for each process

Answer: c. It provides a consistent and defensible approach for justifying investments in continuity and recovery solutions. Explanation: Using a structured and repeatable methodology for conducting a Business Impact Analysis (BIA) provides several benefits for an organization's risk management and business continuity program. One of the key benefits is that it provides a consistent and defensible approach for justifying investments in continuity and recovery solutions. By following a standardized process for identifying and prioritizing critical business processes, and quantifying the potential impact of disruptions, a BIA methodology helps organizations to make informed and rational decisions about where to allocate resources and how to prioritize continuity strategies. A structured BIA methodology enables organizations to:

- Demonstrate due diligence and best practices in assessing and managing business continuity risks

- Communicate the value and importance of continuity investments to senior leadership and other stakeholders
- Benchmark their continuity capabilities against industry standards and peer organizations
- Comply with regulatory and contractual requirements for business continuity planning

While a structured BIA methodology can help organizations to identify and analyze a wide range of disruption scenarios and impacts, it does not guarantee that all possible scenarios will be identified (option a), as there is always some degree of uncertainty and unpredictability in risk assessment. Similarly, while a structured methodology can help to reduce subjectivity and bias in the BIA process, it does not completely eliminate the need for expert judgment and estimation (option b), particularly in determining the likelihood and impact of different scenarios. Finally, while a structured BIA methodology can help organizations to establish recovery objectives and strategies, it does not guarantee that the organization will be able to meet those objectives in every scenario (option d), as the actual recovery time will depend on a variety of factors such as the nature and extent of the disruption, the effectiveness of the continuity plans, and the availability of resources and capabilities.

169. An organization has conducted a Business Impact Analysis (BIA) and has identified several critical processes with short maximum tolerable downtimes (MTDs) and high financial impacts. However, the organization has limited resources and budget for implementing continuity and recovery solutions. Which of the following is the most appropriate approach for prioritizing investments based on the BIA results?
a. Prioritize the processes with the highest historical frequency of disruptions, as they are most likely to require recovery in the future
b. Prioritize the processes with the longest MTDs, as they provide the most flexibility and time for implementing solutions
c. Prioritize the processes with the highest financial impacts, as they represent the greatest potential losses and risks to the organization
d. Prioritize the processes with the largest number of employees and customers, as they have the greatest visibility and reputational impact

Answer: c. Prioritize the processes with the highest financial impacts, as they represent the greatest potential losses and risks to the organization. Explanation: When an organization has limited resources and budget for implementing continuity and recovery solutions, it is important to prioritize investments based on the results of the Business Impact Analysis (BIA) in order to maximize the risk reduction and value achieved. One of the most effective approaches for prioritization is to focus on the processes with the highest financial impacts, as they represent the greatest potential losses and risks to the organization in the event of a disruption. By quantifying the financial impact of each process based on factors such as lost revenue, increased expenses, regulatory fines, and customer churn, the BIA provides a clear and objective basis for comparing the relative importance and urgency of different processes. Processes with higher financial impacts should generally receive higher priority for continuity investments, as they have the greatest potential to impact the organization's bottom line and long-term viability. Prioritizing based on historical frequency of disruptions (option a) may not be the most effective approach, as past disruptions may not be indicative of future risks, and processes with low frequency but high impact may still require significant investment. Prioritizing based on MTDs (option b) may not always align with the organization's risk appetite and continuity objectives, as some processes with longer MTDs may still have high financial or strategic importance. Prioritizing based on the number of employees and customers (option d) may be a useful secondary consideration for reputational and stakeholder management purposes, but it should not override the primary focus on financial impact and risk. Ultimately, the prioritization approach should be based on a holistic analysis of the BIA results, as well as the organization's specific risk profile, business objectives, and resource constraints. The approach should be reviewed and updated regularly to ensure that it remains aligned with changing business and risk landscapes.

170. Which of the following is a key output of a Business Impact Analysis (BIA) that can be used to inform an organization's disaster recovery planning efforts?
a. A list of the organization's critical suppliers and vendors
b. A map of the organization's network topology and infrastructure

c. A set of recovery time objectives (RTOs) for each critical process
d. A schedule of planned maintenance and upgrade activities for key systems

Answer: c. A set of recovery time objectives (RTOs) for each critical process. Explanation: One of the key outputs of a Business Impact Analysis (BIA) that is directly relevant to an organization's disaster recovery planning is a set of recovery time objectives (RTOs) for each critical process. The RTO is a metric that specifies the maximum amount of time allowed for the recovery of a process after a disruption occurs, based on the process's maximum tolerable downtime (MTD) and other factors such as dependencies and resource requirements. The RTOs established in the BIA provide critical input for the design and implementation of disaster recovery strategies and solutions, as they help to:

- Determine the required level of redundancy, resilience, and failover for each process and its supporting systems and infrastructure
- Prioritize the order and timing of recovery activities based on the criticality and urgency of each process
- Identify the need for alternative processing sites, backup data and systems, and other continuity capabilities
- Establish metrics and targets for testing and validating the effectiveness of disaster recovery plans and procedures

By aligning the disaster recovery planning efforts with the RTOs established in the BIA, organizations can ensure that their recovery capabilities are commensurate with the business requirements and risk appetite for each critical process. This helps to optimize the allocation of resources and minimize the impact and duration of disruptions. While a list of critical suppliers and vendors (option a) is an important input for the BIA and can help to identify external dependencies and risks, it is not a direct output of the BIA itself. Similarly, while a map of the organization's network topology and infrastructure (option b) is a valuable tool for disaster recovery planning, it is typically developed separately from the BIA. Finally, while a schedule of planned maintenance and upgrade activities (option d) is an important consideration for ensuring the availability and performance of key systems, it is not a specific output of the BIA process.

171. An organization has recently completed a Business Impact Analysis (BIA) and has identified several gaps and inconsistencies in the results across different business units and processes. Which of the following is the most appropriate next step for validating and refining the BIA results?
a. Conducting a risk assessment to identify and quantify the likelihood and impact of different disruption scenarios
b. Reviewing the organization's insurance policies to determine the coverage and limitations for business interruption losses
c. Facilitating a series of workshops with business unit leaders and subject matter experts to review and validate the BIA data and assumptions
d. Implementing a set of continuity and recovery solutions based on the current BIA results, and then updating the BIA based on the effectiveness of those solutions

Answer: c. Facilitating a series of workshops with business unit leaders and subject matter experts to review and validate the BIA data and assumptions. Explanation: Conducting a Business Impact Analysis (BIA) is an iterative process that requires ongoing validation and refinement to ensure that the results are accurate, consistent, and actionable. When gaps and inconsistencies are identified in the initial BIA results, the most appropriate next step is to facilitate a series of workshops with business unit leaders and subject matter experts to review and validate the data and assumptions used in the analysis. These workshops provide an opportunity to:

- Clarify any misunderstandings or discrepancies in the data collected from different sources
- Challenge and refine the assumptions and estimates used to determine the criticality, dependencies, and impact of each process
- Identify any missing or overlooked processes, assets, or stakeholders that should be included in the analysis
- Build consensus and buy-in among business stakeholders for the BIA results and their implications for continuity planning

By actively engaging business stakeholders in the validation process, organizations can ensure that the BIA results are credible, comprehensive, and aligned with the actual needs and priorities of the business. This helps to increase the likelihood that the BIA will be used effectively to drive continuity and recovery decisions and investments. Conducting a risk assessment (option a) is a complementary activity that can help to inform and refine the BIA, but it is not a substitute for validating the BIA data and assumptions with business stakeholders. Similarly, reviewing insurance policies (option b) can provide useful information for quantifying the financial impact of disruptions, but it does not address the underlying accuracy and consistency of the BIA results.

172. Which of the following is the primary purpose of a risk register in an information security risk management program?
a. To identify and document all possible risks, regardless of their likelihood or impact
b. To prioritize risks based on their potential impact and the effectiveness of existing controls
c. To assign ownership and accountability for each risk to specific individuals or teams
d. To track the status and progress of risk mitigation activities over time

Answer: b. To prioritize risks based on their potential impact and the effectiveness of existing controls. Explanation: A risk register is a key tool used in information security risk management to document and prioritize identified risks. The primary purpose of a risk register is to provide a structured and consistent approach for assessing and comparing the relative importance and urgency of different risks, based on factors such as their potential impact on the organization's objectives, the likelihood of occurrence, and the effectiveness of existing controls. By prioritizing risks in the register, organizations can focus their resources and efforts on the most significant and pressing risks, and make informed decisions about risk treatment options. While a risk register should aim to be comprehensive in identifying relevant risks (option a), it is not practical or useful to document every possible risk without considering its materiality or significance. Assigning risk ownership (option c) is an important step in risk management, but it is not the primary purpose of the risk register itself. Tracking the status and progress of risk mitigation activities (option d) is a valuable use of the risk register, but it is a secondary purpose that follows from the initial prioritization of risks.

173. Which of the following criteria should be used to determine the priority of a risk in a risk register?
a. The preferences and concerns of individual stakeholders
b. The historical frequency and impact of similar risks in the past
c. The alignment of the risk with the organization's strategic objectives
d. The availability of resources and budget to mitigate the risk

Answer: c. The alignment of the risk with the organization's strategic objectives. Explanation: When prioritizing risks in a risk register, one of the most important criteria to consider is the alignment of each risk with the organization's strategic objectives. Risks that have the potential to significantly impact or disrupt the achievement of the organization's goals and priorities should generally be given higher priority than those that are less directly relevant or impactful. This approach ensures that risk management efforts are focused on the areas that are most critical to the organization's success and helps to justify the allocation of resources and attention to mitigating these risks. While the preferences and concerns of individual stakeholders (option a) should be considered in risk prioritization, they should not be the primary or sole criteria, as they may not always align with the broader organizational perspective. The historical frequency and impact of similar risks (option b) can provide useful context and data for assessing risk, but they should not be the only factors considered, as the risk landscape is constantly evolving and past events may not be predictive of future risks. The availability of resources and budget (option d) is an important practical consideration in risk management, but it should not drive risk prioritization decisions, as high-priority risks may require additional resources to be allocated or reallocated from other areas.

174. Which of the following is an example of a quantitative risk prioritization technique that can be used in conjunction with a risk register?
a. Risk appetite statements

b. Risk heat maps
c. Risk likelihood and impact ratings
d. Annualized loss expectancy (ALE)

Answer: d. Annualized loss expectancy (ALE). Explanation: Annualized loss expectancy (ALE) is a quantitative risk prioritization technique that can be used in conjunction with a risk register. ALE is calculated by multiplying the potential loss from a risk event by the frequency or probability of occurrence, and expressing the result as an annualized financial value. For example, if a data breach is estimated to cost the organization $1 million per occurrence, and the probability of a breach occurring in a given year is 10%, the ALE would be $100,000 ($1 million x 10%). ALE provides a standardized and objective way to compare and prioritize risks based on their potential financial impact, and helps organizations to make risk treatment decisions based on cost-benefit analysis. Risk appetite statements (option a) are qualitative expressions of an organization's willingness to accept or tolerate different levels of risk, but they do not provide a specific prioritization of individual risks. Risk heat maps (option b) are visual tools that plot risks on a grid based on their likelihood and impact ratings, but they are typically qualitative or semi-quantitative in nature. Risk likelihood and impact ratings (option c) are used to assess and prioritize risks, but they are usually expressed as qualitative scales (e.g., high, medium, low) rather than quantitative values.

175. An organization has identified a new risk that has a high potential impact but a low likelihood of occurrence. Which of the following is the most appropriate risk treatment option for this scenario?
a. Accepting the risk and taking no further action
b. Transferring the risk to a third party through insurance or outsourcing
c. Mitigating the risk through the implementation of additional controls
d. Avoiding the risk by discontinuing the associated activity or process

Answer: c. Mitigating the risk through the implementation of additional controls. Explanation: When a risk has a high potential impact but a low likelihood of occurrence, the most appropriate risk treatment option is usually to mitigate the risk by implementing additional controls or safeguards. This approach seeks to reduce the potential impact of the risk to an acceptable level, without necessarily eliminating the risk entirely. By focusing on impact mitigation rather than likelihood reduction, organizations can prioritize their resources and efforts on the risks that have the greatest potential to cause harm or disruption, even if they are less likely to occur. Accepting the risk (option a) may not be appropriate in this case, as the high potential impact suggests that the risk exceeds the organization's risk appetite and tolerance thresholds. Transferring the risk (option b) may be a viable option in some cases, but it does not address the underlying vulnerability or exposure, and may not be cost-effective or feasible for all types of risks. Avoiding the risk (option d) may be necessary in extreme cases where the potential impact is catastrophic and cannot be effectively mitigated, but it should be a last resort, as it may require significant changes to the organization's operations and strategies.

176. Which of the following is a common pitfall or mistake in risk prioritization that can lead to suboptimal risk management decisions?
a. Prioritizing risks based on their potential financial impact rather than their strategic relevance
b. Overestimating the effectiveness of existing controls in mitigating risks
c. Involving too many stakeholders in the risk prioritization process
d. Updating and reviewing the risk register too frequently to keep up with changing business and threat landscapes

Answer: b. Overestimating the effectiveness of existing controls in mitigating risks. Explanation: One of the most common pitfalls or mistakes in risk prioritization is overestimating the effectiveness of existing controls in mitigating risks. This can lead to a false sense of security and an underestimation of the residual risk exposure, resulting in suboptimal risk management decisions. When assessing the priority of risks in the risk register, it is important to critically evaluate the design, implementation, and operating effectiveness of the controls that are in place to mitigate each risk. This evaluation should consider factors such as:

- The inherent limitations and weaknesses of each control type (e.g., preventive, detective, corrective)
- The maturity and consistency of control execution across the organization
- The potential for control circumvention or override by insiders or attackers
- The adequacy of control monitoring and testing to identify and correct deficiencies

By taking a realistic and evidence-based approach to control effectiveness assessment, organizations can ensure that risk prioritization decisions are based on a true understanding of the residual risk exposure, rather than an overreliance on the mere existence of controls. Prioritizing risks based on financial impact (option a) is a valid and commonly used approach, as it helps to focus risk management efforts on the areas that have the greatest potential to impact the organization's bottom line. However, it should be balanced with consideration of strategic relevance and other risk criteria. Involving multiple stakeholders in risk prioritization (option c) is generally a good practice, as it helps to ensure that different perspectives and expertise are considered, and that risk decisions are aligned with business needs. Updating and reviewing the risk register frequently (option d) is important to keep up with the dynamic nature of risk, and should not be considered a pitfall or mistake.

177. Which of the following is a benefit of using a standardized risk rating scale or matrix in a risk register?
a. It eliminates the need for qualitative risk assessments and expert judgment
b. It ensures that all risks are treated equally, regardless of their context or impact
c. It allows for the objective comparison and aggregation of risks across different business units and risk categories
d. It predicts the actual likelihood and impact of risks with a high degree of accuracy and precision

Answer: c. It allows for the objective comparison and aggregation of risks across different business units and risk categories. Explanation: Using a standardized risk rating scale or matrix in a risk register provides several benefits for an organization's risk management program. One of the key benefits is that it allows for the objective comparison and aggregation of risks across different business units, functions, and risk categories. By using a consistent set of criteria and ratings for assessing the likelihood and impact of risks, a standardized scale helps to normalize risk data and make it more comparable and actionable. This is particularly important for organizations with complex or distributed operations, where risks may be identified and managed by different teams using different methodologies or terminology. A standardized scale provides a common language and framework for communicating and prioritizing risks, and enables the organization to develop a more holistic and integrated view of its risk profile. This can help to identify trends, patterns, and interdependencies among risks, and support more strategic and proactive risk management decision making. A standardized risk rating scale does not eliminate the need for qualitative risk assessments and expert judgment (option a), as these are still important inputs into the risk prioritization process. It also does not ensure that all risks are treated equally (option b), as the context and impact of each risk should still be considered in determining the appropriate risk response. Finally, while a standardized scale can provide a structured and consistent approach to risk assessment, it does not necessarily predict the actual likelihood and impact of risks with a high degree of accuracy or precision (option d), as risk is inherently uncertain and variable.

178. An organization has implemented a risk register as part of its enterprise risk management program. Which of the following is a key factor in ensuring that the risk register remains an effective and valuable tool over time?
a. Assigning ownership of the risk register to a single individual or function within the organization
b. Limiting access to the risk register to only senior management and the board of directors
c. Regularly reviewing and updating the risk register based on changes in the business and risk landscape
d. Automating the risk register process through the use of specialized software or tools

Answer: c. Regularly reviewing and updating the risk register based on changes in the business and risk landscape. Explanation: A risk register is a living document that should be continuously updated and refined to reflect changes in an organization's business operations, strategic objectives, and risk environment. To ensure that the risk register remains an effective and valuable tool over time, it is critical to establish a regular process for reviewing and updating the register based on new information and insights. This process should involve:

- Monitoring internal and external risk indicators and events that may impact the organization's risk profile
- Assessing the continued relevance and validity of the risks documented in the register
- Identifying new or emerging risks that may need to be added to the register
- Updating the ratings and prioritization of risks based on changes in likelihood, impact, or control effectiveness
- Reviewing the progress and effectiveness of risk mitigation plans and adjusting them as needed
- Communicating risk updates and changes to relevant stakeholders and decision-makers

By institutionalizing a regular risk review and update process, organizations can ensure that their risk register remains a dynamic and actionable tool for risk management, rather than a static or stale document. This helps to maintain the credibility and usefulness of the risk register, and supports more timely and informed risk decision making. Assigning ownership of the risk register to a single individual or function (option a) can help to ensure accountability and consistency in risk management, but it should not preclude the involvement and input of other stakeholders in the risk review and update process. Limiting access to the risk register (option b) may be appropriate for highly sensitive or confidential risks, but in general, the risk register should be accessible to those who need it to perform their risk management responsibilities. Automating the risk register process (option d) can help to streamline and standardize risk data collection and reporting, but it is not a substitute for the human judgment and analysis required to effectively review and update the register.

179. Which of the following is a potential consequence of not regularly reviewing and updating a risk register?
a. Overallocation of resources to risk mitigation activities that are no longer relevant or impactful
b. Increased efficiency and speed in identifying and responding to new or emerging risks
c. Greater alignment between risk management activities and the organization's strategic objectives
d. Enhanced credibility and trust in the risk management program among stakeholders

Answer: a. Overallocation of resources to risk mitigation activities that are no longer relevant or impactful.
Explanation: One of the main purposes of a risk register is to prioritize and allocate resources to the most significant and pressing risks facing an organization. However, if the risk register is not regularly reviewed and updated to reflect changes in the business and risk landscape, it can lead to the overallocation of resources to risk mitigation activities that are no longer relevant or impactful. For example, if a risk that was previously rated as high priority has been effectively mitigated through the implementation of controls, but the risk register has not been updated to reflect this change, the organization may continue to allocate time, money, and personnel to addressing the risk, even though it is no longer a significant threat. Similarly, if new risks emerge that are not captured in the risk register, the organization may not allocate sufficient resources to mitigating these risks, leaving it exposed to potential harm or disruption. Over time, this misalignment between risk management activities and the actual risk profile of the organization can lead to inefficiencies, wasted resources, and a false sense of security. It can also undermine the credibility and effectiveness of the risk management program, as stakeholders may lose confidence in the ability of the program to identify and address the most important risks. To avoid these negative consequences, it is important to establish a regular cadence of risk register reviews and updates, and to ensure that the register remains a living and dynamic tool for risk management. This enables the organization to be more agile and responsive to changing risk conditions (option b), while also maintaining alignment with its strategic objectives (option c) and building trust and credibility with stakeholders (option d).

180. An organization's risk register has identified a large number of risks across multiple business units and risk categories. Which of the following is the most effective approach for prioritizing and managing these risks?
a. Addressing the risks in the order in which they were identified and documented in the risk register
b. Focusing on the risks that have the highest likelihood of occurrence, regardless of their potential impact
c. Prioritizing the risks based on their alignment with the organization's risk appetite and tolerance statements

d. Deferring the prioritization and management of risks until additional resources and budget become available

Answer: c. Prioritizing the risks based on their alignment with the organization's risk appetite and tolerance statements. Explanation: When an organization's risk register contains a large number of diverse risks, it can be challenging to determine which risks should be prioritized for management attention and resources. To ensure that risk management efforts are focused on the most important and relevant risks, the most effective approach is to prioritize the risks based on their alignment with the organization's risk appetite and tolerance statements. Risk appetite and tolerance statements are formal expressions of an organization's willingness to accept or tolerate different levels and types of risk in pursuit of its strategic objectives. They provide a framework for risk decision making by setting boundaries and thresholds for acceptable risk exposure, and by defining the organization's preferred risk posture and response strategies. By prioritizing risks based on their alignment with these statements, organizations can ensure that they are managing risks in a way that is consistent with their overall risk management philosophy and business goals. This approach helps to:

- Focus resources and attention on the risks that have the greatest potential to impact the organization's ability to achieve its objectives
- Ensure that risk management activities are proportionate to the risk exposure and the organization's risk capacity and capabilities
- Provide a clear and consistent basis for risk escalation, reporting, and governance
- Enable more proactive and strategic risk management, rather than reactive and ad hoc responses

Addressing risks in the order in which they were identified (option a) may not be the most effective approach, as it does not take into account the relative importance or urgency of the risks. Focusing solely on high-likelihood risks (option b) may not be sufficient, as it ignores the potential impact of low-likelihood but high-consequence risks. Deferring risk prioritization and management (option d) is not a viable option, as it leaves the organization exposed to unmitigated risks and may lead to missed opportunities for risk reduction and value creation. By aligning risk prioritization with risk appetite and tolerance, organizations can make more informed and effective risk management decisions that support the achievement of their strategic objectives.

181. An organization is implementing a risk management framework based on the ISO 31000 standard. Which of the following is the first step in the risk management process according to the standard?
a. Establishing the context
b. Conducting a risk assessment
c. Developing a risk treatment plan
d. Monitoring and reviewing risks

Answer: a. Establishing the context. Explanation: The ISO 31000 standard provides a comprehensive framework for managing risks across an organization. The risk management process outlined in the standard begins with establishing the context, which involves defining the internal and external parameters that the organization must consider when managing risk. This includes understanding the organization's objectives, stakeholders, risk criteria, and risk appetite. Establishing the context sets the foundation for the subsequent steps in the risk management process and ensures that risk management activities are aligned with the organization's goals and values. Conducting a risk assessment (option b) is the next step after establishing the context, and involves identifying, analyzing, and evaluating risks. Developing a risk treatment plan (option c) and monitoring and reviewing risks (option d) are important subsequent steps, but they are not the starting point of the risk management process according to ISO 31000.

182. Which of the following risk management frameworks is specifically focused on managing information security risks?
a. COSO Enterprise Risk Management Framework
b. ISO 31000 Risk Management Standard

c. NIST Risk Management Framework (RMF)
d. Basel III Framework for Bank Risk Management

Answer: c. NIST Risk Management Framework (RMF). Explanation: The NIST Risk Management Framework (RMF) is a comprehensive approach to managing information security risks in organizations. It provides a structured process for identifying, assessing, and mitigating risks to an organization's information systems and data. The RMF is based on the NIST Special Publication 800-37, which outlines a six-step process for managing information security risks: categorize, select, implement, assess, authorize, and monitor. The RMF is widely used in the US federal government and is increasingly being adopted by private sector organizations as well. The COSO Enterprise Risk Management Framework (option a) is a broader framework that addresses all types of risks facing an organization, not just information security risks. The ISO 31000 standard (option b) is a general risk management standard that can be applied to any type of risk, including information security risks, but it is not specifically focused on information security. The Basel III Framework (option d) is a set of international banking regulations that address financial risks, such as credit risk and liquidity risk, but it does not directly address information security risks.

183. An organization is using the NIST Cybersecurity Framework (CSF) to guide its risk management program. Which of the following is not one of the core functions of the CSF?
a. Identify
b. Protect
c. Transfer
d. Detect

Answer: c. Transfer. Explanation: The NIST Cybersecurity Framework (CSF) is a voluntary framework that provides a common language and methodology for managing and reducing cybersecurity risks. The CSF is organized around five core functions that represent the key pillars of an organization's cybersecurity risk management program: Identify, Protect, Detect, Respond, and Recover. The Identify function involves understanding the organization's systems, assets, and risk landscape. The Protect function involves implementing safeguards to ensure the confidentiality, integrity, and availability of information assets. The Detect function involves identifying the occurrence of cybersecurity events in a timely manner. The Respond function involves taking action regarding detected cybersecurity incidents. The Recover function involves maintaining plans for resilience and restoring capabilities or services that were impaired due to a cybersecurity incident. Transfer (option c) is not one of the core functions of the CSF. Risk transfer is a common risk management strategy that involves shifting the financial impact of a risk to another party, such as through insurance or contracts, but it is not a core function of the CSF.

184. An organization is conducting a risk assessment as part of its risk management process. Which of the following is the most appropriate method for identifying risks in this context?
a. Reviewing past incident reports and audit findings
b. Conducting vulnerability scans and penetration tests
c. Brainstorming sessions with stakeholders
d. All of the above

Answer: d. All of the above. Explanation: Risk identification is a critical step in the risk assessment process, as it involves determining what could go wrong, how it could happen, and what the potential consequences could be. To ensure a comprehensive and effective risk identification process, organizations should use a combination of methods and sources, including:

- Reviewing past incident reports, audit findings, and other historical data to identify trends, patterns, and lessons learned (option a)

- Conducting vulnerability scans, penetration tests, and other technical assessments to identify weaknesses and potential attack vectors (option b)
- Facilitating brainstorming sessions, workshops, and interviews with stakeholders to gather diverse perspectives and insights on risks (option c)
- Analyzing industry and threat intelligence reports to identify emerging risks and best practices
- Reviewing legal, regulatory, and contractual requirements to identify compliance risks and obligations

Using a multi-faceted approach to risk identification helps to ensure that all relevant risks are captured and considered in the risk assessment process. Relying on a single method or source may result in an incomplete or biased view of the risk landscape, leading to suboptimal risk management decisions. Therefore, the most appropriate answer is "All of the above" (option d), as it recognizes the value of using a combination of methods and sources for effective risk identification.

185. An organization has identified a critical risk related to its supply chain and is evaluating potential risk treatment options. Which of the following is not a valid risk treatment option according to the ISO 31000 standard?
a. Avoiding the risk
b. Accepting the risk
c. Sharing the risk
d. Enhancing the risk

Answer: d. Enhancing the risk. Explanation: According to the ISO 31000 standard, there are four main risk treatment options that organizations can consider when deciding how to respond to an identified risk:

1. Avoiding the risk: This involves deciding not to start or continue with the activity that gives rise to the risk, or removing the source of the risk altogether.

2. Accepting or retaining the risk: This involves making an informed decision to take on the risk and bear the potential consequences, often because the cost or effort of treating the risk outweighs the potential benefits.

3. Reducing or mitigating the risk: This involves implementing controls, safeguards, or countermeasures to reduce the likelihood or impact of the risk to an acceptable level.

4. Sharing or transferring the risk: This involves shifting some or all of the risk to another party, such as through insurance, contracts, or outsourcing arrangements.

Enhancing the risk (option d) is not a valid risk treatment option according to ISO 31000, as it implies deliberately increasing the level of risk exposure, which is contrary to the goal of risk management. While there may be cases where an organization chooses to accept a higher level of risk in pursuit of a strategic opportunity or objective, this would still fall under the category of accepting or retaining the risk (option b), rather than enhancing it. The ISO 31000 standard emphasizes that risk treatment options should be selected and implemented based on a careful analysis of their feasibility, effectiveness, and alignment with the organization's risk appetite and tolerance levels.

186. An organization is implementing a risk management methodology based on the OCTAVE (Operationally Critical Threat, Asset, and Vulnerability Evaluation) framework. Which of the following is a key principle of the OCTAVE approach?
a. Focusing on technical vulnerabilities and attack vectors
b. Relying primarily on quantitative risk analysis methods
c. Emphasizing the role of senior management in risk decision-making
d. Outsourcing risk assessments to external experts and consultants

Answer: c. Emphasizing the role of senior management in risk decision-making. Explanation: OCTAVE (Operationally Critical Threat, Asset, and Vulnerability Evaluation) is a risk-based strategic assessment and planning methodology for information security. It was developed by the Software Engineering Institute (SEI) at Carnegie Mellon University and has been widely adopted by organizations across various industries. One of the key principles of the OCTAVE approach is the emphasis on the role of senior management in risk decision-making. OCTAVE recognizes that effective risk management requires the active involvement and support of an organization's leadership, as they are ultimately responsible for setting risk priorities, allocating resources, and ensuring alignment with business objectives. The OCTAVE methodology includes specific activities and outputs designed to engage senior management in the risk management process, such as:

- Defining the organization's risk measurement criteria and risk tolerance levels
- Identifying and prioritizing critical assets and their security requirements
- Reviewing and approving risk assessment results and risk treatment plans
- Communicating risk management strategies and decisions to stakeholders

By involving senior management in these key risk management activities, OCTAVE helps to ensure that risk decisions are based on a strategic understanding of the organization's goals, values, and constraints, rather than solely on technical or operational considerations. This principle is in contrast to approaches that focus primarily on technical vulnerabilities and attack vectors (option a), rely mainly on quantitative risk analysis methods (option b), or outsource risk assessments to external experts (option d), which may not adequately consider the broader organizational context and leadership perspective.

187. An organization has conducted a risk assessment and has identified several high-priority risks that require treatment. Which of the following is the most important factor to consider when selecting and implementing risk treatment options?
a. The cost and resource requirements of each treatment option
b. The preferences and opinions of individual stakeholders and business units
c. The potential effectiveness of each treatment option in reducing the risk to an acceptable level
d. The ease and speed of implementing each treatment option

Answer: c. The potential effectiveness of each treatment option in reducing the risk to an acceptable level. Explanation: When selecting and implementing risk treatment options, the most important factor to consider is the potential effectiveness of each option in reducing the identified risks to an acceptable level. The primary goal of risk treatment is to modify the risk by changing the likelihood or impact of the risk event, or by changing the organization's exposure to the risk. Therefore, the selected treatment options should be based on a careful analysis of their ability to mitigate the risk and bring it within the organization's risk appetite and tolerance levels. This analysis should consider factors such as:

- The specific risk scenarios and threats being addressed
- The root causes and contributing factors of the risk
- The strengths and limitations of different treatment options, such as controls, safeguards, or risk transfer mechanisms
- The interactions and dependencies among different treatment options and risks
- The residual risk remaining after the treatment is implemented

While the cost and resource requirements of each treatment option (option a) are certainly important considerations, they should not be the primary driver of risk treatment decisions. The most cost-effective or resource-efficient option may not always be the most effective in reducing the risk to an acceptable level. Similarly, while the preferences and opinions of individual stakeholders (option b) should be considered and incorporated into the risk treatment process, they should not override the objective assessment of risk reduction effectiveness. The ease and speed of implementation (option d) are also relevant factors, particularly in cases where time is of the essence, but they should not take precedence over the effectiveness of the treatment in addressing the risk. Ultimately, the selection and implementation of risk treatment options should be guided by a risk-based and evidence-based approach that prioritizes the most effective measures for reducing the organization's risk exposure.

188. An organization is using a combination of quantitative and qualitative risk analysis methods as part of its risk management process. Which of the following is an example of a qualitative risk analysis technique?
a. Monte Carlo simulation
b. Failure Mode and Effects Analysis (FMEA)
c. Sensitivity analysis
d. Delphi method

Answer: d. Delphi method. Explanation: Qualitative risk analysis techniques are used to prioritize and characterize risks based on their probability and impact, using descriptive scales and expert judgment. These techniques are often used when numerical data is not available or when the risks are difficult to quantify. Examples of qualitative risk analysis techniques include:

- Risk probability and impact assessment
- Risk categorization and ranking
- Risk urgency assessment
- Delphi method

The Delphi method (option d) is a structured communication technique that relies on a panel of experts to provide input and reach consensus on the likelihood and impact of risks. The experts are asked to provide their opinions anonymously and iteratively, with the results aggregated and shared back with the group until a consensus is reached. The Delphi method is particularly useful for assessing risks that are complex, ambiguous, or uncertain, and for incorporating diverse perspectives and expertise into the risk analysis process. Monte Carlo simulation (option a) and sensitivity analysis (option c) are examples of quantitative risk analysis techniques that use numerical models and statistical methods to estimate the probability and impact of risks. These techniques are used when sufficient data is available to support mathematical modeling and simulation. Failure Mode and Effects Analysis (FMEA) (option b) is a structured approach to identifying and prioritizing potential failure modes and their effects on a system or process. While FMEA can involve both qualitative and quantitative elements, it is primarily focused on identifying and analyzing specific failure scenarios rather than providing an overall assessment of risk likelihood and impact.

189. An organization is implementing a risk management framework and is considering using risk indicators to monitor and communicate its risk profile. Which of the following is the most important characteristic of effective risk indicators?
a. They are based on easily available and inexpensive data sources
b. They are complex and sophisticated, requiring specialized expertise to interpret
c. They are directly tied to the organization's risk appetite and tolerance statements
d. They are static and consistent, providing a stable view of the risk profile over time

Answer: c. They are directly tied to the organization's risk appetite and tolerance statements. Explanation: Risk indicators are metrics or measures that provide insight into an organization's risk profile and help to monitor changes in risk exposure over time. Effective risk indicators should be:

- Relevant: They should be directly tied to the organization's key risks and risk management objectives, and should provide meaningful and actionable information for decision-making.
- Measurable: They should be based on reliable and timely data that can be consistently collected and analyzed over time.

- Predictive: They should be forward-looking and provide early warning signals of potential risk events or trends, rather than just reflecting past performance.
- Comparable: They should be standardized and consistent across the organization, allowing for benchmarking and trend analysis.
- Communicable: They should be easily understandable and interpretable by stakeholders, and should be presented in a clear and concise format.

One of the most important characteristics of effective risk indicators is that they are directly tied to the organization's risk appetite and tolerance statements (option c). Risk appetite and tolerance statements define the level and type of risk that an organization is willing to accept in pursuit of its objectives, and set the boundaries and thresholds for acceptable risk exposure. Risk indicators should be designed to monitor and measure the organization's risk profile against these statements, and to alert management when risk levels are approaching or exceeding the defined thresholds. This helps to ensure that risk management activities are aligned with the organization's overall risk strategy and that risk decisions are based on a clear understanding of the organization's risk capacity and preferences. While ease of data collection (option a), complexity and sophistication (option b), and stability over time (option d) are all relevant considerations in the design and implementation of risk indicators, they are not as critical as the alignment with risk appetite and tolerance statements in ensuring the effectiveness and value of the indicators for risk management purposes.

190. An organization has recently experienced a significant risk event that resulted in financial and reputational damage. Which of the following is the most appropriate risk management activity to undertake in response to this event?
a. Conducting a root cause analysis to identify the underlying factors that contributed to the event
b. Updating the organization's risk register to include the newly identified risk
c. Implementing additional controls and safeguards to prevent similar events from occurring in the future
d. Communicating the details of the event to external stakeholders and regulators

Answer: a. Conducting a root cause analysis to identify the underlying factors that contributed to the event.
Explanation: When an organization experiences a significant risk event, such as a major incident, breach, or failure, it is important to undertake a thorough and systematic review of the event to identify the root causes and contributing factors. This process, known as a root cause analysis, involves:

- Gathering and analyzing data and evidence related to the event, such as logs, reports, and interviews with stakeholders
- Identifying the sequence of events and actions that led up to the event
- Determining the underlying causal factors, such as human errors, system failures, or process weaknesses
- Evaluating the effectiveness of existing controls and risk management measures in preventing or mitigating the event
- Developing recommendations for corrective and preventive actions to address the identified root causes and prevent similar events from occurring in the future

Conducting a root cause analysis is the most appropriate risk management activity to undertake in response to a significant risk event, as it provides a structured and objective approach to learning from the event and improving the organization's risk management practices. Updating the risk register (option b) is an important step in documenting and tracking the newly identified risk, but it does not address the underlying causes of the event. Implementing additional controls and safeguards (option c) may be necessary based on the findings of the root cause analysis, but it should not be the first or only response to the event. Communicating the details of the event to external stakeholders (option d) may be required for transparency and accountability purposes, but it is not a risk management activity in itself and should be carefully planned and executed based on the organization's communication strategy and legal/regulatory obligations. The insights and lessons learned from the root cause analysis should inform the organization's overall risk management strategy and help to drive continuous improvement in risk identification, assessment, and treatment practices.

191. An organization is implementing a risk management framework based on ISO 27005. Which of the following is the FIRST step in the risk assessment process according to this standard?
a. risk identification
b. risk analysis
c. risk evaluation
d. context establishment

Answer: d. context establishment. Explanation: ISO 27005 specifies context establishment as the initial step in the risk assessment process. This involves defining the scope, boundaries, and risk criteria for the assessment. Risk identification, analysis, and evaluation are subsequent steps that build upon the established context.

192. A company is adopting the NIST Risk Management Framework (RMF) for its information systems. Which document is required to move from the Categorize step to the Select step in the RMF?
a. system security plan
b. risk assessment report
c. plan of action and milestones
d. security assessment report

Answer: a. system security plan. Explanation: In the NIST RMF, the system security plan (SSP) is developed in the Categorize step and is a prerequisite for moving to the Select step, where security controls are selected based on the system categorization. The risk assessment report, plan of action and milestones, and security assessment report are developed in later stages of the RMF.

192. During the risk analysis phase of ISO 27005, which of the following is used to determine the potential consequences of a risk?
a. risk appetite
b. risk criteria
c. risk treatment plan
d. risk ownership

Answer: b. risk criteria. Explanation: In ISO 27005, risk criteria are defined during context establishment and used during risk analysis to evaluate the significance of risks. Consequences are assessed against these predefined criteria. Risk appetite is the amount of risk an organization is willing to accept, while a risk treatment plan outlines actions to mitigate risks. Risk ownership refers to assigning responsibility for managing a particular risk.

193. Under the NIST Risk Management Framework (RMF), which step involves determining the impact level (low, moderate, high) for a system based on the potential worst-case impact of a breach?
a. Categorize
b. Select
c. Implement
d. Assess

Answer: a. Categorize. Explanation: The first step in the NIST RMF is Categorize, where systems are categorized based on a FIPS 199 impact analysis. This involves assessing the confidentiality, integrity, and availability requirements and determining the potential impact (low, moderate, high) of a breach. The Select, Implement, and Assess steps focus on identifying, implementing, and assessing security controls based on the assigned categorization.

194. Which of the following risk treatment options involves sharing the potential benefits and losses associated with a risk with another party?
a. risk avoidance
b. risk transfer
c. risk mitigation
d. risk acceptance

Answer: b. risk transfer. Explanation: Risk transfer is a risk treatment option that involves sharing or transferring the potential consequences (both positive and negative) of a risk to another party, often through insurance or contracts. Risk avoidance seeks to eliminate the risk entirely, while risk mitigation aims to reduce the likelihood or impact of the risk. Risk acceptance means deciding to take no action and accepting the potential consequences.

195. An organization has identified a critical vulnerability in its web application. The risk has been assessed as having a high likelihood and high impact. Which risk treatment option is MOST appropriate in this scenario?
a. risk acceptance
b. risk avoidance
c. risk sharing
d. risk mitigation

Answer: d. risk mitigation. Explanation: Given the high likelihood and high impact of the risk, the most appropriate treatment option is risk mitigation. This involves taking actions to reduce the probability of the vulnerability being exploited or to minimize the impact if it does occur. Accepting such a critical risk or simply transferring it to another party would not be prudent. Complete avoidance may not be feasible if the web application is essential to business operations.

196. According to ISO 27005, which of the following is an output of the risk identification phase?
a. risk treatment plan
b. risk assessment report
c. list of prioritized risks
d. list of potential threats

Answer: d. list of potential threats. Explanation: In ISO 27005, the risk identification phase involves identifying sources of risk, areas of impact, events, and their potential consequences. The output of this phase is a comprehensive list of risks, often in the form of potential threats that could exploit vulnerabilities. The risk treatment plan and risk assessment report are developed in later phases, while the list of prioritized risks is an output of the risk evaluation phase.

196. Under the NIST Risk Management Framework (RMF), which step involves developing, implementing, and documenting security controls for a system?
a. Categorize
b. Select
c. Implement
d. Monitor

Answer: c. Implement. Explanation: In the NIST RMF, the Implement step is where security controls that were selected in the previous step are actually put into action. This involves configuring, enabling, and documenting the controls according to the system security plan. The Categorize step focuses on system categorization, Select involves choosing the appropriate controls, and Monitor is an ongoing phase to maintain visibility into control effectiveness.

197. An organization is using a risk assessment methodology that calculates risk scores based on the product of likelihood and impact values. A particular risk has been assessed as having a likelihood of 3 (on a scale of 1-5) and an impact of 4 (on a scale of 1-5). What is the resulting risk score?
a. 7
b. 9
c. 12
d. 15

Answer: c. 12. Explanation: The risk score is calculated by multiplying the likelihood value (3) by the impact value (4), resulting in a score of 12. This type of scoring is common in risk assessment methodologies, providing a way to quantify and prioritize risks. A higher score indicates a more significant risk that may require more immediate attention and robust treatment measures.

198. During the risk evaluation phase of ISO 27005, risks are prioritized based on a comparison of their analysis results against which of the following?
a. risk treatment options
b. risk assessment methodology
c. risk criteria
d. risk management framework

Answer: c. risk criteria. Explanation: In ISO 27005, risks are evaluated by comparing the results of the risk analysis against the risk criteria established during context establishment. These criteria define the thresholds and priorities for risk treatment. The evaluation determines whether a risk is acceptable or requires treatment. The risk treatment options, assessment methodology, and overall risk management framework inform the evaluation but are not the direct basis for prioritization.

199. An organization has identified a risk associated with a legacy system that stores sensitive customer data. The system is nearing end-of-life, and the vendor will no longer provide security updates. Which risk treatment option is MOST appropriate?
a. risk acceptance
b. risk mitigation
c. risk transfer
d. risk avoidance

Answer: d. risk avoidance. Explanation: Given the sensitive nature of the data and the lack of ongoing security support, the most appropriate risk treatment is avoidance. This would involve decommissioning the legacy system and migrating the data to a modern, secure platform. Accepting the risk or simply mitigating it with compensating controls may not be sufficient given the potential impact of a breach. Transferring the risk to a third party does not address the underlying issue of an unsupported system.

200. A company is considering outsourcing its data center operations to a cloud service provider. Which risk treatment option does this represent?
a. risk mitigation
b. risk acceptance
c. risk avoidance
d. risk transfer

Answer: d. risk transfer. Explanation: Outsourcing the data center to a cloud provider is an example of risk transfer. The company is transferring the risks associated with operating and securing the data center to the cloud provider. However, it's important to note that while the day-to-day operational risks are transferred, the company still retains responsibility for ensuring the provider meets required security standards. Risk mitigation would involve implementing controls to reduce risk, acceptance means taking no action, and avoidance would be deciding not to outsource at all.

201. An e-commerce company has identified a high risk of distributed denial-of-service (DDoS) attacks against its website. Which combination of risk treatment options is likely to be most effective?
a. risk acceptance and risk transfer
b. risk mitigation and risk transfer
c. risk avoidance and risk acceptance
d. risk mitigation and risk avoidance

Answer: b. risk mitigation and risk transfer. Explanation: For a high-risk threat like DDoS attacks, a combination of mitigation and transfer is often the most effective approach. Mitigation measures could include implementing DDoS protection services, increasing network capacity, and developing an incident response plan. Transferring some of the risk could involve using a content delivery network (CDN) or cloud-based DDoS mitigation service, which can absorb and filter attack traffic. Accepting such a high risk is not prudent, and completely avoiding it may not be realistic for an e-commerce business.

202. An organization has decided to accept a particular risk related to the use of employee-owned mobile devices. What is a key consideration when documenting this decision?
a. risk ownership
b. risk probability
c. risk impact
d. risk appetite

Answer: d. risk appetite. Explanation: When an organization decides to accept a risk, it's important to document this decision in the context of the organization's risk appetite. Risk appetite is the amount and type of risk an organization is willing to accept in pursuit of its objectives. The decision to accept the risk of employee-owned devices should align with this appetite and be approved by appropriate stakeholders. Risk ownership, probability, and impact are important factors in assessing the risk but are not the primary considerations in documenting risk acceptance.

203. A company has identified a risk related to the potential failure of a critical business application. The risk has been assessed as having a low likelihood but a high impact. Which risk treatment option is MOST appropriate?
a. risk acceptance
b. risk transfer
c. risk mitigation
d. risk avoidance

Answer: c. risk mitigation. Explanation: Although the likelihood of the risk is low, the high potential impact warrants proactive treatment. Risk mitigation is the most appropriate option, which could involve measures such as implementing redundant systems, developing a comprehensive business continuity plan, and regularly testing failover procedures. Accepting such a high-impact risk or transferring it to a third party may not adequately protect the business. Complete avoidance may not be feasible if the application is critical to operations.

204. An organization has identified a compliance risk related to a new data privacy regulation. The risk involves potential fines for non-compliance. Which risk treatment option is MOST appropriate?
a. risk transfer

b. risk acceptance
c. risk mitigation
d. risk avoidance

Answer: c. risk mitigation. Explanation: For regulatory compliance risks, mitigation is often the most appropriate treatment option. This involves taking steps to ensure compliance with the new data privacy regulation, such as updating policies and procedures, conducting staff training, and implementing necessary technical controls. Transferring the risk (e.g., through insurance) may help with potential fines but does not address the underlying compliance issue. Accepting the risk of non-compliance is not advisable, and complete avoidance may not be realistic if the regulation applies to the organization's core business activities.

205. During the risk treatment process, an organization identifies a third-party service that can be used to outsource a high-risk business function. What is a key consideration when evaluating this risk transfer option?
a. service level agreements (SLAs)
b. risk ownership
c. risk appetite
d. risk probability

Answer: a. service level agreements (SLAs). Explanation: When transferring a risk to a third-party service provider, it's crucial to establish clear service level agreements (SLAs). SLAs define the specific responsibilities of the service provider, the expected level of service, and the consequences for not meeting those expectations. This helps ensure that the risk is effectively managed by the third party and that the organization's interests are protected. While risk ownership will change with the transfer, and the risk probability and organizational risk appetite should be considered, the SLAs are the key mechanism for defining the terms of the risk transfer.

206. An organization has decided to avoid a particular risk by discontinuing a product line. What is an important consideration when implementing this risk avoidance strategy?
a. risk probability
b. risk transfer options
c. risk acceptance criteria
d. business impact analysis

Answer: d. business impact analysis. Explanation: When deciding to avoid a risk by discontinuing a product line, it's important to conduct a thorough business impact analysis (BIA). The BIA assesses the potential operational, financial, and reputational consequences of the discontinuation. This includes evaluating the impact on revenue, customer relationships, market share, and interdependencies with other products or services. The BIA helps ensure that the decision to avoid the risk is well-informed and that appropriate strategies are put in place to manage the transition. Risk probability, transfer options, and acceptance criteria are less relevant considerations for a risk avoidance decision.

207. A company has identified a risk related to the use of a particular software vendor. The risk involves potential security vulnerabilities in the vendor's products. Which risk treatment option is MOST appropriate?
a. risk avoidance
b. risk acceptance
c. risk mitigation
d. risk transfer

Answer: c. risk mitigation. Explanation: For risks related to software vulnerabilities, risk mitigation is often the most appropriate treatment option. Mitigation measures could include regularly patching and updating the software, implementing compensating security controls, and closely monitoring the vendor's security advisories and incident response. Completely avoiding the risk by switching vendors may not be practical if the software is critical to business operations. Accepting the risk without any mitigation is not advisable given the potential impact of a security breach. Transferring the risk to a third party does not address the underlying vulnerability issue.

207. An organization has implemented a risk treatment plan that includes a combination of mitigation, transfer, and acceptance strategies. What is the next key step in the risk management process?
a. risk identification
b. risk assessment
c. risk monitoring and review
d. risk communication

Answer: c. risk monitoring and review. Explanation: After implementing a risk treatment plan, the next critical step is ongoing risk monitoring and review. This involves regularly assessing the effectiveness of the treatment measures, identifying any changes in the risk landscape, and adjusting the treatment plan as needed. Continuous monitoring helps ensure that risks remain within acceptable levels and that the organization can respond quickly to any new or evolving threats. Risk identification and assessment are earlier stages in the risk management process, while risk communication is an ongoing activity throughout the process.

208. An organization is implementing risk mitigation controls for its web-based customer portal. Which of the following is an example of a detective control?
a. requiring strong, complex passwords for user accounts
b. implementing a web application firewall (WAF)
c. logging and monitoring user activities
d. encrypting sensitive data in transit and at rest

Answer: c. logging and monitoring user activities. Explanation: Detective controls are designed to identify and alert on security events or anomalies after they have occurred. Logging and monitoring user activities, such as login attempts, transactions, and data access, is a key detective control that helps identify potential security incidents. Requiring strong passwords and encrypting data are preventive controls that aim to prevent incidents from occurring. A web application firewall is also a preventive control that filters out malicious traffic before it reaches the application.

209. An organization is implementing risk mitigation controls for its mobile device management (MDM) system. Which of the following is an example of a corrective control?
a. remotely wiping a lost or stolen device
b. enforcing device encryption
c. restricting installation of unapproved apps
d. requiring multi-factor authentication for device enrollment

Answer: a. remotely wiping a lost or stolen device. Explanation: Corrective controls are designed to minimize the impact of a security incident after it has been detected. Remotely wiping a lost or stolen device is a corrective control that helps prevent unauthorized access to sensitive data on the device. Enforcing device encryption and restricting unapproved apps are preventive controls that help prevent incidents from occurring. Requiring multi-factor authentication for enrollment is a preventive control that ensures only authorized devices are added to the MDM system.

210. An organization is implementing risk mitigation controls for its industrial control systems (ICS). Which of the following is an example of a compensating control?
a. segmenting ICS networks from corporate networks

b. implementing role-based access control (RBAC) for ICS assets
c. conducting regular vulnerability scans of ICS components
d. providing additional employee training on ICS security best practices

Answer: d. providing additional employee training on ICS security best practices. Explanation: Compensating controls are alternative controls that are implemented when the primary control is not feasible or practical. In the context of ICS security, providing additional employee training on security best practices can help compensate for technical limitations or legacy systems that may be difficult to secure. Network segmentation, role-based access control, and vulnerability scanning are all examples of primary controls that directly address ICS security risks.

211. An organization is implementing risk mitigation controls for its cloud-based infrastructure. Which of the following is an example of a preventive control?
a. enabling cloud provider's disaster recovery options
b. implementing cloud security posture management (CSPM) tools
c. conducting regular penetration testing of cloud resources
d. enforcing multi-factor authentication for privileged user accounts

Answer: d. enforcing multi-factor authentication for privileged user accounts. Explanation: Preventive controls are designed to prevent security incidents from occurring. Enforcing multi-factor authentication for privileged user accounts, such as administrators and developers, is a critical preventive control in cloud environments. It adds an extra layer of security beyond just passwords, making it much harder for attackers to gain unauthorized access. Enabling disaster recovery options is a corrective control, while CSPM tools and penetration testing are detective controls that identify potential vulnerabilities or misconfigurations.

212. An organization is implementing risk mitigation controls for its remote workforce. Which of the following is an example of an administrative control?
a. providing secure virtual private network (VPN) access
b. enforcing endpoint encryption on employee devices
c. implementing data loss prevention (DLP) software
d. establishing acceptable use policies for remote work

Answer: d. establishing acceptable use policies for remote work. Explanation: Administrative controls are policies, procedures, and guidelines that govern how people interact with systems and data. Establishing clear acceptable use policies for remote work is an important administrative control. These policies define expectations and responsibilities for employees working remotely, such as handling sensitive data, using secure connections, and reporting incidents. VPN access and endpoint encryption are technical controls, while DLP software is a detective control.

213. An organization is implementing risk mitigation controls for its Internet of Things (IoT) devices. Which of the following is an example of a physical control?
a. requiring unique, complex passwords for each IoT device
b. regularly patching and updating IoT device firmware
c. securing physical access to IoT device locations
d. monitoring IoT device network traffic for anomalies

Answer: c. securing physical access to IoT device locations. Explanation: Physical controls are measures that restrict and monitor physical access to systems and environments. For IoT devices, securing the physical locations where they are installed is a crucial physical control. This could involve measures like locked enclosures, surveillance cameras, or access control systems. Requiring strong passwords and regularly patching firmware are logical/technical controls, while monitoring network traffic is a detective control.

214. An organization is implementing risk mitigation controls for its third-party vendors. Which of the following is an example of a preventive control?
a. conducting regular security audits of vendors
b. requiring vendors to comply with the organization's security policies
c. monitoring vendor access to the organization's systems
d. establishing incident response procedures for vendor-related incidents

Answer: b. requiring vendors to comply with the organization's security policies. Explanation: Preventive controls aim to prevent security incidents from occurring, and requiring vendors to adhere to the organization's security policies and standards is a key preventive measure. This ensures that vendors have appropriate security controls in place and reduces the risk of introducing vulnerabilities through third-party interactions. Regular audits and access monitoring are detective controls, while incident response procedures are corrective controls.

215. An organization is implementing risk mitigation controls for its software development lifecycle (SDLC). Which of the following is an example of a corrective control?
a. conducting code reviews and security testing
b. implementing secure coding practices and guidelines
c. rolling back to a previous version in case of a security incident
d. training developers on application security best practices

Answer: c. rolling back to a previous version in case of a security incident. Explanation: Corrective controls are designed to minimize the impact of a security incident after it has been detected. In the context of the SDLC, having the ability to quickly roll back to a previous, stable version of an application in case of a security breach is a key corrective control. It allows the organization to mitigate the immediate impact while the incident is being investigated and resolved. Code reviews, secure coding practices, and developer training are all preventive controls that help avoid vulnerabilities in the first place.

216. An organization is implementing risk mitigation controls for its data center. Which of the following is an example of a detective control?
a. implementing multi-factor authentication for data center access
b. installing environmental monitoring systems (e.g., temperature, humidity)
c. conducting regular fire drills and emergency response exercises
d. encrypting data at rest on storage devices

Answer: b. installing environmental monitoring systems (e.g., temperature, humidity). Explanation: Detective controls are designed to identify and alert on potential issues or anomalies. In a data center context, installing environmental monitoring systems to track temperature, humidity, and other conditions is a key detective control. These systems can alert staff to potential issues before they cause damage to equipment or disrupt operations. Multi-factor authentication is a preventive control, while fire drills and data encryption are corrective and preventive controls, respectively.

217. An organization is implementing risk mitigation controls for its bring your own device (BYOD) program. Which of the following is an example of a compensating control?
a. implementing mobile device management (MDM) software
b. requiring employees to sign a BYOD acceptable use agreement
c. providing company-owned devices for high-risk roles or tasks

d. conducting regular security awareness training for BYOD users

Answer: c. providing company-owned devices for high-risk roles or tasks. Explanation: Compensating controls are alternative measures put in place when the primary control is not feasible or practical. In a BYOD context, providing company-owned devices for employees in high-risk roles or handling sensitive tasks can help compensate for the inherent risks of personal devices. This allows the organization to maintain tighter control and security for critical assets. MDM software is a preventive control, while acceptable use agreements and security awareness training are administrative controls.

218. An organization has implemented a risk management program and wants to ensure its ongoing effectiveness. Which of the following is the PRIMARY purpose of continuous risk monitoring and review?
a. identifying new risks that have emerged since the initial risk assessment
b. ensuring that risk mitigation controls are operating as intended
c. updating the organization's risk appetite and tolerance levels
d. communicating risk information to stakeholders and decision-makers

Answer: b. ensuring that risk mitigation controls are operating as intended. Explanation: The primary purpose of continuous risk monitoring and review is to verify that the implemented risk mitigation controls continue to operate effectively over time. While identifying new risks, updating risk appetite, and communicating risk information are all important activities, the main focus of monitoring is to ensure that the controls are functioning as designed and that the organization's risk posture remains within acceptable levels. Monitoring helps detect control failures or changes in the risk environment that may require adjustments to the risk management strategy.

219. In the context of continuous risk monitoring, what is the significance of establishing key risk indicators (KRIs)?
a. KRIs help prioritize which risks should be mitigated first
b. KRIs provide a quantitative measure of the organization's overall risk exposure
c. KRIs trigger alerts when predefined risk thresholds are exceeded
d. KRIs determine the appropriate risk response strategy for each identified risk

Answer: c. KRIs trigger alerts when predefined risk thresholds are exceeded. Explanation: Key risk indicators (KRIs) are metrics that provide an early signal of increasing risk exposure in a particular area. They are used in continuous monitoring to proactively identify when risks are approaching or exceeding predefined thresholds, triggering alerts for further investigation or action. KRIs help organizations stay within their risk appetite by providing a forward-looking view of potential issues. While KRIs can inform prioritization and response decisions, their primary role is to serve as an early warning system, not to quantify overall risk exposure or determine the specific risk response strategy.

220. An organization conducts quarterly risk assessments as part of its continuous monitoring program. Which of the following is a KEY benefit of this approach?
a. identifying risks that were missed during the initial risk assessment
b. ensuring that all identified risks are completely eliminated
c. detecting changes in the risk environment and control effectiveness
d. reducing the overall cost of the risk management program

Answer: c. detecting changes in the risk environment and control effectiveness. Explanation: Conducting regular risk assessments, such as on a quarterly basis, allows organizations to detect changes in both the internal and external risk environment. This includes identifying new threats, vulnerabilities, or business changes that may impact the organization's risk profile. Regular assessments also help verify whether existing controls remain effective over time. While these assessments may identify previously overlooked risks, the primary benefit is maintaining a current understanding of the risk landscape. Complete risk elimination is not a realistic goal, and while cost reduction is beneficial, it is not the main driver for continuous monitoring.

221. Which of the following is a KEY challenge in implementing continuous risk monitoring and review?
a. defining clear roles and responsibilities for risk monitoring activities
b. integrating risk monitoring data from multiple sources and systems
c. communicating risk information to non-technical stakeholders
d. ensuring that all risk mitigation controls are implemented as planned

Answer: b. integrating risk monitoring data from multiple sources and systems. Explanation: One of the main challenges in continuous risk monitoring is effectively integrating and correlating data from various security tools, systems, and processes across the organization. This can include log data, vulnerability scans, threat intelligence feeds, and more. Consolidating this data into a meaningful view of the organization's risk posture can be complex, often requiring specialized tools and expertise. While defining clear roles, communicating to stakeholders, and ensuring control implementation are all important, the technical challenge of data integration is often the most significant hurdle in establishing an effective monitoring program.

222. What is the PRIMARY role of risk metrics in the context of continuous risk monitoring and review?
a. to quantify the likelihood and impact of individual risks
b. to track the implementation status of risk mitigation controls
c. to measure the overall effectiveness of the risk management program
d. to compare the organization's risk profile to industry benchmarks

Answer: c. to measure the overall effectiveness of the risk management program. Explanation: In continuous monitoring, risk metrics serve as key performance indicators (KPIs) that help measure the ongoing effectiveness and maturity of the organization's risk management program as a whole. These metrics can include things like the number of incidents detected and resolved, the time to respond to and mitigate risks, and the percentage of controls operating effectively. While risk metrics can also help quantify individual risks, track control implementation, and enable industry comparisons, their primary purpose in monitoring is to provide a high-level view of the risk management program's performance over time, enabling continuous improvement.

223. An organization wants to establish a risk dashboard as part of its continuous monitoring program. Which of the following is a KEY consideration when designing this dashboard?
a. including all possible risk metrics and data points
b. focusing on historical risk data rather than real-time information
c. tailoring the dashboard to the needs of different stakeholder groups
d. using a standalone tool that is separate from other risk management systems

Answer: c. tailoring the dashboard to the needs of different stakeholder groups. Explanation: When designing a risk dashboard for continuous monitoring, it's crucial to consider the information needs of various stakeholders. Senior executives may require a high-level view of key risk indicators and trends, while operational teams may need more detailed data on specific controls and incidents. Tailoring the dashboard to these different audiences helps ensure that the right information is available to support decision-making at each level. Including all possible metrics can lead to information overload, while focusing solely on historical data limits the ability to respond to emerging risks. Integrating the dashboard with other risk management tools, rather than using a standalone system, helps provide a more comprehensive view.

224. In the context of continuous risk monitoring, what is the significance of establishing risk thresholds and alert levels?

a. to prioritize which risks should be addressed first based on their severity
b. to determine when to escalate risks to senior management for decision-making
c. to automate the implementation of risk mitigation controls based on predefined criteria
d. to trigger notifications when risks exceed the organization's risk appetite or tolerance

Answer: d. to trigger notifications when risks exceed the organization's risk appetite or tolerance. Explanation: Risk thresholds and alert levels are used in continuous monitoring to define when a risk has exceeded the organization's predetermined risk appetite or tolerance. When these thresholds are breached, automated alerts notify relevant stakeholders, prompting further investigation and potential action. This helps ensure that risks are proactively managed and kept within acceptable boundaries. While thresholds can inform prioritization and escalation decisions, their primary purpose is to serve as a trigger for action, not to directly determine priorities or automate control implementation.

225. What is the role of trend analysis in continuous risk monitoring and review?
a. to identify patterns and changes in the organization's risk profile over time
b. to determine the root cause of individual risk events or incidents
c. to forecast future risks based on historical data and projections
d. to benchmark the organization's risk management performance against peers

Answer: a. to identify patterns and changes in the organization's risk profile over time. Explanation: Trend analysis is a key technique used in continuous risk monitoring to identify patterns, changes, and emerging issues in the organization's risk landscape over time. By tracking key risk indicators and metrics, organizations can spot trends such as an increasing frequency of security incidents, a rise in vendor risks, or a shift in the types of threats facing the organization. This helps inform proactive decision-making and risk response. While trend analysis can provide insights for root cause analysis, forecasting, and benchmarking, its primary value in monitoring is to surface changes that may signal the need for adjustments to the risk management strategy.

226. Which of the following is a KEY benefit of integrating continuous risk monitoring with an organization's incident response processes?
a. reducing the overall number of security incidents and breaches
b. minimizing the time and resources required for incident investigations
c. improving the organization's ability to detect and respond to emerging threats
d. eliminating the need for a dedicated incident response team

Answer: c. improving the organization's ability to detect and respond to emerging threats. Explanation: Integrating continuous risk monitoring with incident response processes helps organizations more quickly detect and respond to emerging threats and risk events. Monitoring activities such as log analysis, threat intelligence, and anomaly detection can provide early warning signs of potential incidents, triggering a rapid response. This integration enhances an organization's overall security posture and resilience. While effective monitoring and response can help reduce the frequency and impact of incidents, it does not eliminate them entirely. Monitoring data can help streamline investigations, but it does not replace the need for thorough incident analysis. A dedicated incident response capability remains critical even with robust monitoring in place.

227. An organization conducts an annual review of its risk management program as part of its continuous improvement efforts. Which of the following is a KEY input to this review process?
a. results of employee surveys on risk awareness and culture
b. financial data on the costs and benefits of risk mitigation controls
c. feedback from external stakeholders such as customers and regulators
d. data and insights from ongoing risk monitoring and measurement activities

Answer: d. data and insights from ongoing risk monitoring and measurement activities. Explanation: The results and insights generated from an organization's continuous risk monitoring activities are a crucial input to the periodic review and improvement of the overall risk management program. Monitoring data provides a fact-based view of the program's performance, including the effectiveness of controls, trends in the risk landscape, and the status of key risk indicators. This data helps identify gaps, weaknesses, and opportunities for enhancement. While employee surveys, financial analyses, and external stakeholder feedback can all provide valuable perspectives, the monitoring data offers the most direct and objective measure of the program's ongoing effectiveness and maturity.

228. An information security manager is preparing a presentation for the board of directors on the organization's cybersecurity risk management program. Which of the following is the MOST important consideration when tailoring the content for this audience?
a. including detailed technical information about specific security controls
b. focusing on the business impact and strategic implications of cybersecurity risks
c. providing a comprehensive list of all identified risks and their mitigation plans
d. comparing the organization's risk management approach to industry benchmarks

Answer: b. focusing on the business impact and strategic implications of cybersecurity risks. Explanation: When communicating with the board of directors, it's crucial to frame cybersecurity risks in terms of their potential impact on the organization's strategic objectives, financial performance, and reputation. The board is primarily concerned with the big-picture implications of risk management, rather than the technical details of specific controls or a comprehensive list of all identified risks. While industry comparisons can provide useful context, the main focus should be on how the risk management program aligns with and supports the organization's overall business strategy.

229. Which of the following is a KEY challenge when communicating risk management concepts to non-technical stakeholders?
a. translating technical risk data into business-relevant terms and metrics
b. ensuring that all stakeholders have a detailed understanding of the risk assessment methodology
c. providing stakeholders with access to raw data from security tools and systems
d. involving stakeholders in the selection and implementation of risk mitigation controls

Answer: a. translating technical risk data into business-relevant terms and metrics. Explanation: One of the main challenges in communicating risk management concepts to non-technical audiences is effectively translating technical risk data, such as vulnerability scan results or threat intelligence, into terms and metrics that are meaningful from a business perspective. This may involve framing risks in terms of potential financial losses, operational disruptions, or reputational damage. While providing some level of methodological transparency is important, stakeholders don't necessarily need a deep understanding of the technical details. Providing raw tool data or involving stakeholders in control selection are less critical for effective communication.

230. An information security manager is preparing a risk report for the organization's audit committee. Which of the following is MOST important to include in this report?
a. a detailed description of the organization's risk assessment methodology
b. an overview of the top risks and their potential impact on the organization
c. a comprehensive list of all risk mitigation controls and their implementation status
d. a comparison of the organization's risk profile to industry benchmarks and standards

Answer: b. an overview of the top risks and their potential impact on the organization. Explanation: When reporting to the audit committee, the focus should be on providing a clear, concise summary of the most significant risks facing the organization and their potential impact on key business objectives. The committee needs to understand the top risks in order to provide effective oversight and guidance. While some information on the risk assessment methodology and mitigation controls may be relevant for context, a detailed description or comprehensive list is likely too granular for this audience. Industry comparisons can be insightful but should not be the main focus of the report.

231. In the context of communicating risk management concepts, what is the primary purpose of using risk scenarios or case studies?
a. to provide a detailed, technical explanation of how specific threats exploit vulnerabilities
b. to demonstrate the organization's compliance with industry standards and regulations
c. to help stakeholders understand the potential real-world impact of identified risks
d. to justify the cost and resource requirements of the risk management program

Answer: c. to help stakeholders understand the potential real-world impact of identified risks. Explanation: Risk scenarios and case studies are powerful communication tools because they help make abstract risks more tangible and relatable for stakeholders. By walking through a realistic example of how a particular risk could play out and the resulting consequences, stakeholders can better grasp the importance of managing that risk effectively. Scenarios focus on the business impact of risks, rather than the technical details of how they manifest. While scenarios can highlight the importance of compliance and justify risk management investments, their primary purpose is to build understanding and engagement among stakeholders.

232. Which of the following is a KEY benefit of regularly communicating risk management insights and activities to stakeholders?
a. reducing the overall cost of the risk management program
b. ensuring that all identified risks are completely eliminated
c. fostering a culture of risk awareness and shared responsibility
d. transferring accountability for risk management to business leaders

Answer: c. fostering a culture of risk awareness and shared responsibility. Explanation: Regular, effective communication about risk management helps promote a culture where all stakeholders understand their role in managing risk and are actively engaged in the process. By sharing insights and updates, the risk management function can build trust, transparency, and a sense of shared ownership across the organization. This cultural shift is critical for embedding risk management into day-to-day decision-making and operations. While communication can help optimize risk management investments and mitigate risks, it doesn't necessarily reduce overall costs or eliminate all risks entirely. Communication also does not transfer accountability, as ultimate responsibility for risk management still rests with leadership.

233. An information security manager is creating a risk dashboard for senior executives. Which of the following is the MOST important consideration when selecting metrics and data points to include?
a. focusing on metrics that are easy to collect and report, even if they are less relevant
b. including as many metrics as possible to provide a comprehensive view of the risk landscape
c. selecting metrics that are aligned with the organization's key business objectives and risk appetite
d. prioritizing metrics that showcase the success and value of the risk management program

Answer: c. selecting metrics that are aligned with the organization's key business objectives and risk appetite. Explanation: When designing a risk dashboard for senior executives, it's crucial to choose metrics that are directly relevant to the organization's strategic goals and risk tolerance. Executives need a clear, concise picture of how well the organization is managing the risks that matter most to the business. Metrics should be carefully curated based on their significance, not just their availability or quantity. While ease of collection and reporting are important considerations, they should not trump relevance. Similarly, while it's valuable to highlight the risk management program's successes, the dashboard should provide an objective view, not just a promotional tool.

234. Which of the following is MOST important for an information security manager to consider when communicating with business unit leaders about risk management?
a. using a formal, one-way communication style to establish authority and expertise
b. providing detailed information on the technical aspects of risk assessment and mitigation
c. focusing solely on the risks and control gaps that require the most urgent attention
d. framing risk management as a collaborative process that supports business objectives

Answer: d. framing risk management as a collaborative process that supports business objectives. Explanation: When engaging with business unit leaders, it's essential to position risk management as a partnership that helps the business achieve its goals, not as a separate, imposing process. Effective communication involves framing risk discussions in terms of how managing risks can enable business success, innovation, and competitive advantage. A collaborative, two-way dialogue that invites input and feedback from business leaders is more impactful than a formal, one-way information push. While some technical detail may be necessary, the focus should be on the business implications of risks, not just the technical aspects. Balancing discussions of risks and gaps with recognition of what's working well is also important for building trust and engagement.

235. In the context of communicating risk management concepts, what is the primary purpose of using quantitative risk metrics and data visualizations?
a. to provide a definitive, objective measure of the organization's overall risk exposure
b. to help stakeholders quickly understand and engage with complex risk information
c. to demonstrate the sophistication and maturity of the risk management program
d. to ensure that all risk decisions are based solely on mathematical calculations

Answer: b. to help stakeholders quickly understand and engage with complex risk information. Explanation: Quantitative risk metrics and data visualizations, such as risk heat maps or dashboards, are valuable communication tools because they can simplify complex risk data into a more accessible, understandable format. By translating risk information into visual, numerical terms, these techniques help stakeholders quickly grasp the key insights and engage in more meaningful discussions about risk management. While quantitative metrics can provide a measure of objectivity, they are not a definitive, absolute measure of risk. They are a decision support tool, not a replacement for judgment and qualitative considerations. The primary purpose of these techniques is to aid understanding and communication, not to showcase the risk management program or to reduce all decisions to pure mathematical calculations.

236. Which of the following is a KEY consideration when communicating risk management concepts to external stakeholders, such as regulators or customers?
a. providing a detailed, technical description of the organization's risk assessment methodology
b. emphasizing the organization's compliance with relevant standards and regulations
c. highlighting the competitive advantages of the organization's risk management approach
d. focusing on the specific risks and control gaps that are most relevant to the stakeholder's concerns

Answer: d. focusing on the specific risks and control gaps that are most relevant to the stakeholder's concerns. Explanation: When communicating with external stakeholders, it's important to tailor the message to their specific interests and concerns. Regulators, for example, will be primarily focused on the organization's management of compliance and regulatory risks, while customers may be more interested in data privacy and security risks. By addressing the risks and issues that matter most to each stakeholder group, the organization can demonstrate its understanding and build trust. While compliance is important to highlight, it should not be the sole focus. Similarly, while some high-level information on methodology and competitive differentiation may provide useful context, delving into technical details or extensive comparisons is likely to be less effective than a targeted, relevant discussion of key risks and how they are being managed.

237. An information security manager is preparing to communicate the results of a recent risk assessment to the organization's risk committee. Which of the following is MOST important to consider when planning this communication?
a. providing a detailed description of the risk assessment process and methodology
b. including a comprehensive list of all identified risks, regardless of significance
c. focusing on the key findings, trends, and recommended actions
d. comparing the organization's risk assessment results to industry benchmarks

Answer: c. focusing on the key findings, trends, and recommended actions. Explanation: When communicating risk assessment results to a risk committee, the priority should be on clearly conveying the most significant insights and outcomes. This includes highlighting the top risks identified, any notable trends or changes in the risk landscape, and the key actions recommended to address these risks. The committee needs a concise, actionable summary to inform their oversight and decision-making. While some high-level information on the assessment process and methodology can provide useful context, a detailed description is likely too in-the-weeds for this audience. Similarly, providing a comprehensive list of all identified risks can obscure the most important findings. Industry comparisons may offer helpful perspective but should not be the main focus of the communication.

238. An information security manager is preparing to present the organization's cybersecurity risk management strategy to the board of directors. Which of the following is the MOST important consideration when tailoring the presentation for this audience?
a. providing detailed technical information about the organization's security controls and technologies
b. focusing on the business impact and strategic implications of cybersecurity risks and investments
c. including a comprehensive list of all identified risks and their associated mitigation plans
d. comparing the organization's cybersecurity posture and risk management approach to industry peers

Answer: b. focusing on the business impact and strategic implications of cybersecurity risks and investments. Explanation: When communicating with the board of directors, it's crucial to frame cybersecurity risks and the risk management strategy in terms of their alignment with and impact on the organization's overall business objectives, strategy, and performance. The board is primarily concerned with how cybersecurity risks could affect strategic goals, financial outcomes, competitive advantage, and brand reputation. They need to understand the business case for cybersecurity investments and how the risk management approach supports organizational resilience and success. Technical details, exhaustive risk lists, and peer comparisons may provide useful context but should not be the main focus for this high-level, strategically-oriented audience.

239. Which of the following is the MOST effective approach for an information security manager to take when communicating with business unit leaders about cybersecurity risks?
a. emphasizing the technical complexity and sophistication of cybersecurity threats and controls
b. highlighting the potential negative consequences and liabilities associated with cybersecurity breaches
c. framing cybersecurity risk management as a business enabler and competitive advantage
d. focusing the discussion solely on the cybersecurity risks and vulnerabilities within the business unit's systems and processes

Answer: c. framing cybersecurity risk management as a business enabler and competitive advantage. Explanation: When engaging business unit leaders, it's important to position cybersecurity risk management as a strategic partner that helps the business achieve its goals and objectives. By framing the conversation around how effectively managing cybersecurity risks can enable business innovation, growth, and competitive differentiation, the information security manager can build buy-in and collaboration. While it's important to discuss potential consequences and unit-specific risks, focusing too heavily on the negative or getting overly technical can be counterproductive. The key is to emphasize the business value and benefits of proactive, integrated risk management, not just the threats and vulnerabilities.

240. An information security manager is preparing a cybersecurity risk report for the organization's audit committee. Which of the following should be the PRIMARY focus of this report?
a. a detailed description of the organization's cybersecurity risk assessment methodology and process
b. an overview of the most significant cybersecurity risks and their potential impact on the organization
c. a comprehensive inventory of all the organization's cybersecurity controls and their implementation status
d. a comparison of the organization's cybersecurity risk posture against industry benchmarks and standards

Answer: b. an overview of the most significant cybersecurity risks and their potential impact on the organization. Explanation: When reporting to the audit committee, the main objective should be to provide a clear, concise summary of the top cybersecurity risks facing the organization and the potential consequences of those risks on business operations, financial performance, compliance, and reputation. The committee needs this high-level risk overview to effectively fulfill their oversight responsibilities and ensure the organization's risk management efforts are focused on the most material issues. While information on methodology, controls, and industry comparisons can provide valuable context, diving too deep into these details can obscure the key risk insights the committee needs to know.

241. Which of the following is the LEAST effective technique for an information security manager to use when communicating cybersecurity risks to non-technical stakeholders?
a. translating technical risk data into business-oriented metrics and terminology
b. using real-world examples and scenarios to illustrate the potential impact of cybersecurity risks
c. providing detailed network diagrams and data flow charts to explain potential attack paths
d. employing data visualization techniques like risk heat maps and dashboards to convey risk levels

Answer: c. providing detailed network diagrams and data flow charts to explain potential attack paths. Explanation: When communicating with non-technical audiences, it's important to avoid overly technical jargon, details, and visuals that may be confusing or overwhelming. Detailed network diagrams and data flow charts, while useful for technical planning and analysis, are likely to be too complex and "in the weeds" for business stakeholders. Instead, it's more effective to translate cybersecurity risks into terms and concepts that align with business concerns, such as financial impact, operational disruption, and reputational damage. Real-world examples, scenarios, and visual aids like heat maps and dashboards can help make the risks more tangible and understandable, without getting bogged down in technical minutiae.

242. An information security manager is meeting with the organization's marketing team to discuss cybersecurity risks related to a new customer-facing mobile application. Which of the following should be the PRIMARY focus of this discussion?
a. the technical details of the mobile application's authentication and encryption mechanisms
b. the specific compliance requirements and regulatory standards applicable to the mobile application data
c. the potential reputational and customer trust implications of a cybersecurity breach in the mobile application
d. the development timeline and budget constraints for implementing cybersecurity controls in the mobile application

Answer: c. the potential reputational and customer trust implications of a cybersecurity breach in the mobile application. Explanation: When discussing cybersecurity risks with the marketing team, it's crucial to frame the conversation around the potential impact on customer relationships, brand perception, and market competitiveness. Marketing is primarily concerned with building and maintaining customer trust and loyalty, so highlighting how a security breach could erode that trust and tarnish the organization's reputation will help get their attention and support for cybersecurity risk management. While compliance, technical controls, and project constraints are all important considerations, they are likely secondary to the customer-facing implications for the marketing audience.

243. Which of the following is the MOST important factor for an information security manager to consider when selecting metrics and data points to include in a cybersecurity risk dashboard for senior executives?
a. the ease and simplicity of collecting and reporting the data, even if it is less directly relevant to key business risks
b. the comprehensiveness of the metrics in covering all possible cybersecurity risks, regardless of their likelihood or impact
c. the alignment of the metrics with the organization's strategic objectives, risk appetite, and key performance indicators
d. the ability of the metrics to showcase the success and value of the cybersecurity team's efforts and initiatives

Answer: c. the alignment of the metrics with the organization's strategic objectives, risk appetite, and key performance indicators. Explanation: When designing a cybersecurity risk dashboard for senior executives, the most critical consideration is choosing metrics that directly tie to the organization's strategic goals, risk tolerance, and key measures of business performance. Executives need a dashboard that provides a clear, concise picture of the cybersecurity risks that matter most to the organization's success and how well those risks are being managed. The metrics should be carefully selected based on their relevance and significance, not just their ease of collection or reporting. While it's important to be comprehensive, the dashboard should focus on the most material risks, not every possible threat. And while highlighting the cybersecurity team's accomplishments has value, the primary purpose of the dashboard should be to provide executives with an objective, business-focused view of the risk landscape.

244. An information security manager is preparing to communicate the results of a cybersecurity risk assessment to software developers and engineers. Which of the following is the MOST important consideration when tailoring this communication for a technical audience?
a. avoiding technical jargon and details in favor of high-level, business-oriented language
b. providing an in-depth explanation of the risk assessment methodology, including data sources and analysis techniques used
c. focusing on the specific technical vulnerabilities identified and their potential exploit scenarios
d. comparing the organization's technical cybersecurity controls and practices to industry standards and best practices

Answer: c. focusing on the specific technical vulnerabilities identified and their potential exploit scenarios. Explanation: When communicating risk assessment results to a technical audience like software developers and engineers, it's important to provide details that are relevant to their domain expertise and responsibilities. This includes discussing the specific technical vulnerabilities discovered, how they could potentially be exploited, and what the resulting impact could be. By providing this level of technical detail, the information security manager can help the technical teams understand the risks in terms that are meaningful to them and engage them in developing targeted mitigation strategies. In contrast to communications with business stakeholders, technical audiences will expect and appreciate a deeper dive into the technical aspects of the risks and controls. However, the focus should still be on the most significant and actionable findings, not an exhaustive exploration of every issue or a lengthy methodology description.

245. Which of the following is the MOST effective way for an information security manager to build buy-in and support for cybersecurity risk management initiatives among business unit leaders?
a. emphasizing the potential legal and regulatory consequences of not adequately addressing cybersecurity risks
b. providing detailed technical information about the sophistication and complexity of current cybersecurity threats
c. framing cybersecurity risk management as a business enabler that supports the achievement of strategic objectives
d. highlighting the cost and resource requirements associated with implementing and maintaining cybersecurity controls

Answer: c. framing cybersecurity risk management as a business enabler that supports the achievement of strategic objectives. Explanation: To gain the support and engagement of business unit leaders, it's essential to position cybersecurity risk management as a strategic partner that helps the business succeed, not as a compliance burden or cost center. By communicating how managing cybersecurity risks can enable the business to innovate, grow, and compete more effectively, the information security manager can demonstrate the value and relevance of cybersecurity to each unit's goals and objectives. While it's important to discuss potential consequences and resource needs, focusing too heavily on the negative aspects or getting overly technical can be counterproductive. The key is to shift the conversation from cybersecurity as a necessary evil to cybersecurity as a business imperative and competitive advantage.

246. An information security manager is meeting with the organization's human resources (HR) team to discuss cybersecurity awareness training for employees. Which of the following should be the PRIMARY focus of this discussion?
a. the technical details of common cyber attack techniques, like phishing and malware
b. the specific compliance and regulatory requirements related to employee cybersecurity training
c. the importance of employee cybersecurity awareness in protecting the organization's sensitive data and systems
d. the logistical details of scheduling and delivering the cybersecurity training sessions to all employees

Answer: c. the importance of employee cybersecurity awareness in protecting the organization's sensitive data and systems. Explanation: When engaging the HR team about cybersecurity awareness training, the main objective should be to help them understand the critical role that employees play in safeguarding the organization's information assets and infrastructure. By focusing on how well-trained, vigilant employees can serve as a strong first line of defense against cyber threats, the information security manager can get HR's buy-in and support for making cybersecurity training a priority. While it's useful to cover some high-level examples of common attack techniques, diving too deep into technical details may be less effective for this audience. Similarly, while compliance requirements and logistics are important considerations, they should not overshadow the fundamental message about the importance and value of employee awareness.

247. An information security manager is presenting to the organization's finance team about the budget and resources needed for cybersecurity risk management. Which of the following is the MOST important point to emphasize in this presentation?
a. the alignment of cybersecurity investments with the organization's overall risk management strategy and priorities
b. the technical superiority and advanced features of the cybersecurity tools and technologies being proposed
c. the potential cost savings and efficiencies that could result from implementing the proposed cybersecurity measures
d. the fact that the requested budget and resources are in line with industry benchmarks and peer organizations' spending

Answer: a. the alignment of cybersecurity investments with the organization's overall risk management strategy and priorities. Explanation: When discussing cybersecurity budgets and resources with the finance team, it's crucial to demonstrate how the proposed investments directly support and align with the organization's broader risk management approach and strategic goals. By showing how cybersecurity is an integral part of the organization's overall risk posture and business objectives, the information security manager can justify the funding and resources as essential, not optional. While potential cost savings, technical capabilities, and industry benchmarks can all be persuasive points, the primary focus should be on positioning cybersecurity as a strategic investment that enables the organization to manage its risks effectively and responsibly.

248. An information security manager is preparing to present the results of a comprehensive risk assessment to the organization's senior leadership team. Which of the following should be the PRIMARY focus of the presentation?
a. a detailed description of the risk assessment methodology, including data sources and analysis techniques used

b. a comprehensive list of all identified risks, along with their likelihood, impact, and risk scores
c. an overview of the most significant risks, their potential business impact, and recommended mitigation strategies
d. a comparison of the organization's risk profile against industry benchmarks and standards

Answer: c. an overview of the most significant risks, their potential business impact, and recommended mitigation strategies. Explanation: When presenting risk assessment results to senior leadership, the main objective should be to provide a clear, concise summary of the top risks facing the organization, the potential consequences of those risks on business objectives and performance, and the key actions recommended to address them. Senior leaders need this high-level, actionable information to make informed decisions about risk management priorities and investments. While details on methodology and a comprehensive risk inventory can provide useful context, they should not distract from the key insights and recommendations that leadership needs to know. Industry comparisons may offer perspective but are less critical than a focus on the organization's specific, most significant risks.

249. Which of the following is the MOST effective way to present the results of a quantitative risk assessment to a non-technical audience?
a. providing the detailed mathematical formulas and calculations used to determine risk scores and values
b. presenting the raw data and risk scores in large, complex spreadsheets and tables
c. using data visualization techniques, such as risk heat maps and dashboards, to illustrate risk levels and priorities
d. focusing primarily on the risk assessment methodology and process, rather than the specific risk findings

Answer: c. using data visualization techniques, such as risk heat maps and dashboards, to illustrate risk levels and priorities. Explanation: When presenting quantitative risk assessment results to non-technical stakeholders, it's important to translate the numerical data into visual formats that are easy to understand and interpret. Data visualization tools like risk heat maps, which use color-coding to represent risk severity, and interactive dashboards, which allow users to explore risk data at different levels of detail, can help make complex risk information more accessible and engaging for a general business audience. Detailed mathematical formulas and large, raw data tables are likely to be overwhelming and confusing for non-technical viewers. And while it's useful to provide some context on the assessment approach, the primary focus should be on clearly communicating the risk findings and their business implications, not on the methodology itself.

250. An information security manager is presenting the results of a risk assessment to the organization's board of directors. Which of the following should be AVOIDED in this presentation?
a. highlighting the potential strategic and reputational impact of the identified risks
b. providing a high-level overview of the risk assessment process and methodology
c. using technical jargon and detailed descriptions of specific vulnerabilities and attack scenarios
d. proposing risk mitigation strategies and investments aligned with the organization's business objectives

Answer: c. using technical jargon and detailed descriptions of specific vulnerabilities and attack scenarios. Explanation: When communicating with the board of directors, it's crucial to focus on the strategic, big-picture implications of the risk assessment findings and to avoid getting bogged down in technical details. The board needs to understand how the identified risks could impact the organization's key objectives, competitive position, and reputation, not the intricacies of specific vulnerabilities or attack vectors. Using technical jargon and diving too deep into the weeds of particular risk scenarios can obscure the high-level insights and recommendations that the board needs to provide effective oversight and guidance. It's important to provide some context on the risk assessment process, but the emphasis should be on the business-relevant results and risk management strategies, not the technical minutiae.

251. Which of the following is the MOST important consideration when presenting risk assessment results to an audience that includes both technical and non-technical stakeholders?
a. using a highly technical, detailed approach to ensure the accuracy and completeness of the information presented

b. focusing solely on the non-technical stakeholders and avoiding any technical content that may confuse or overwhelm them
c. splitting the presentation into separate technical and non-technical sections to cater to each audience independently
d. balancing the level of technical detail with clear explanations of the business context and impact of the risks

Answer: d. balancing the level of technical detail with clear explanations of the business context and impact of the risks. Explanation: When presenting to a mixed audience of technical and non-technical stakeholders, it's important to strike a balance that engages and informs both groups. This means providing enough technical detail to satisfy the interests and expertise of the technical audience, while also clearly explaining what the risks mean from a business perspective for the non-technical participants. One effective approach is to structure the presentation around the business impact and strategic implications of the risks, while using clear, concise language and relatable examples to make the technical aspects more accessible to a general audience. It's also helpful to provide additional technical details in an appendix or separate handout for those who want to dive deeper. The key is to avoid either overwhelming non-technical stakeholders with jargon-heavy content or underwhelming technical staff with an overly simplified, non-technical focus.

252. An information security manager is presenting the results of a risk assessment to the organization's compliance and legal teams. Which of the following should be the PRIMARY focus of this presentation?
a. the technical details of the vulnerabilities identified and their potential exploit scenarios
b. the potential legal liabilities and regulatory compliance implications of the identified risks
c. the estimated costs and resource requirements for implementing risk mitigation measures
d. the risk assessment methodology and how it aligns with industry standards and best practices

Answer: b. the potential legal liabilities and regulatory compliance implications of the identified risks. Explanation: When communicating risk assessment results to compliance and legal stakeholders, it's crucial to focus on how the identified risks may impact the organization's ability to meet its legal obligations and regulatory requirements. This audience will be primarily concerned with understanding which risks could lead to potential compliance breaches, legal liabilities, fines, or reputational damage if not properly addressed. While it's important to provide some high-level information on the types of vulnerabilities found and the overall risk assessment approach, detailed technical exploit scenarios or cost estimates for mitigation are likely to be of secondary interest for this group. The key is to frame the risk findings in terms of their implications for the organization's compliance posture and legal risk exposure.

253. Which of the following is the LEAST effective technique for presenting risk assessment results to senior executives?
a. highlighting the top risks and their potential impact on the organization's strategic objectives and key performance indicators
b. using storytelling and real-world examples to illustrate the business implications of the identified risks
c. providing a detailed, step-by-step walkthrough of the risk assessment methodology, including all data sources and analysis techniques used
d. presenting risk insights and metrics in a clear, concise executive summary format

Answer: c. providing a detailed, step-by-step walkthrough of the risk assessment methodology, including all data sources and analysis techniques used. Explanation: When presenting risk assessment results to senior executives, it's important to focus on the key insights and outcomes that are most relevant to their strategic decision-making responsibilities. Executives need a clear, concise understanding of the top risks facing the organization, the potential business impact of those risks, and the recommended actions to mitigate them. Storytelling and real-world examples can be powerful tools for making the risk findings more tangible and relatable for a leadership audience. And presenting the key points in an executive summary format, with clear visuals and metrics, can help make the information more accessible and actionable. In contrast, providing a detailed, step-by-step walkthrough of the risk assessment methodology itself is likely to be less effective for this audience. While it's useful to provide some high-level context on the approach, diving too deep into the technical details of the data sources and analysis techniques used can distract from the key risk insights and recommendations that executives need to know.

254. An information security manager is presenting the results of a risk assessment to the organization's IT operations and security teams. Which of the following should be the MAIN focus of this presentation?
a. the high-level business impact and strategic implications of the identified risks
b. the specific technical vulnerabilities and threats identified, along with recommended mitigation actions
c. the risk assessment methodology and how it compares to other industry-standard approaches
d. the estimated costs and resource requirements for implementing the recommended risk mitigation measures

Answer: b. the specific technical vulnerabilities and threats identified, along with recommended mitigation actions. Explanation: When presenting risk assessment results to IT operations and security teams, it's important to focus on the technical details and actionable insights that are most relevant to their day-to-day responsibilities. These teams will be primarily interested in understanding the specific vulnerabilities, misconfigurations, and threats that were identified during the assessment, along with the recommended technical controls and mitigations to address them. While it's useful to provide some high-level context on the business impact of the risks and the overall risk assessment methodology, diving too deep into strategic implications or cost estimates may be less effective for this technically-oriented audience. The key is to provide the IT and security staff with the tactical information they need to take action and strengthen the organization's security posture.

255. Which of the following is the MOST important factor to consider when prioritizing risks to highlight in a risk assessment results presentation?
a. the ease and cost-effectiveness of implementing mitigation measures for each risk
b. the alignment of each risk with the organization's strategic objectives and risk appetite
c. the novelty and sophistication of the threats or vulnerabilities associated with each risk
d. the level of technical detail and complexity involved in explaining each risk to the audience

Answer: b. the alignment of each risk with the organization's strategic objectives and risk appetite. Explanation: When deciding which risks to prioritize in a risk assessment results presentation, the most critical consideration is the relevance and significance of each risk to the organization's key goals, objectives, and overall risk tolerance. Risks that have the potential to significantly impact the organization's ability to achieve its strategic aims, or that exceed the defined risk appetite levels, should be given top priority in the presentation. While factors such as the ease of mitigation, the novelty of the threats, and the technical complexity of the risks are all important considerations, they are secondary to the fundamental alignment with the organization's strategic priorities and risk management approach. Highlighting risks that are highly relevant to the organization's specific context and risk profile will help ensure that the presentation focuses on the most impactful and actionable insights for the audience.

256. An information security manager is presenting risk assessment results to a mixed audience that includes business unit leaders, IT staff, and compliance personnel. Which of the following is the BEST way to structure and deliver the presentation?
a. using a highly technical, detailed approach that emphasizes the specific vulnerabilities and attack scenarios identified
b. focusing solely on the high-level business risks and impacts, without any reference to the underlying technical issues
c. organizing the presentation by risk category (e.g., strategic, operational, financial) rather than by business unit or system
d. employing a layered approach that starts with the key business risks and recommendations, then allows for optional deep-dives into technical details

Answer: d. employing a layered approach that starts with the key business risks and recommendations, then allows for optional deep-dives into technical details. Explanation: When presenting risk assessment results to a diverse audience with varying levels of technical expertise and business focus, it's important to use a layered approach that provides relevant and accessible information for all participants. One effective strategy is to structure the core presentation around the key business risks, impacts, and recommendations that are most relevant to the majority of the audience. This high-level overview should be presented in clear, concise terms that all stakeholders can understand, regardless of their technical background. Then, for those audience members who want or need more detailed technical information, the presentation can include optional "deep-dive" sections or appendices that provide more granular data on specific vulnerabilities, threats, or mitigation strategies. This layered approach allows the main presentation to remain focused and engaging for the full audience, while still providing opportunities for technical staff and other interested parties to explore the underlying details. Organizing the content by business risk category, rather than by business unit or system, can also help make the presentation more relevant and actionable for a cross-functional audience.

257. Which of the following is the MOST effective way to conclude a risk assessment results presentation to senior executives?
a. with a detailed recap of the risk assessment methodology and process steps followed
b. with a comprehensive list of all identified risks, prioritized by risk score or severity level
c. with a clear call-to-action on the top risk mitigation priorities and next steps for the organization
d. with a comparison of the organization's risk profile to industry benchmarks and peer organizations

Answer: c. with a clear call-to-action on the top risk mitigation priorities and next steps for the organization. Explanation: When concluding a risk assessment results presentation to senior executives, the most important objective is to leave the audience with a clear understanding of the key takeaways and a sense of urgency and direction for the risk management actions needed. Ending with a strong call-to-action that highlights the top risk mitigation priorities and outlines specific next steps for the organization can help galvanize executive support and drive meaningful change. This action-oriented conclusion should focus on the most critical risks and recommendations that require leadership attention and resources, rather than presenting an exhaustive list of all identified issues. While it's useful to provide some high-level recap of the risk assessment process and industry context throughout the presentation, diving too deep into methodological details or comparative benchmarks at the end can dilute the impact of the key messages. The goal is to conclude with a clear, compelling case for the risk management actions needed to protect and support the organization's strategic objectives.

258. An information security manager is seeking to obtain buy-in and support from senior executives for a new enterprise-wide risk management program. Which of the following is the MOST effective approach to take?
a. emphasizing the technical complexity and sophistication of the proposed risk management tools and processes
b. highlighting the potential negative consequences and liabilities of not implementing the program
c. focusing on how the program aligns with and supports the organization's strategic objectives and business priorities
d. providing detailed cost estimates and resource requirements for implementing the program

Answer: c. focusing on how the program aligns with and supports the organization's strategic objectives and business priorities. Explanation: When seeking executive buy-in for a risk management initiative, it's crucial to frame the program in terms of its strategic value and alignment with the organization's key goals and priorities. Senior leaders are most likely to support initiatives that they see as directly contributing to the success and resilience of the business. By emphasizing how the risk management program will help the organization achieve its objectives, protect its assets and reputation, and make more informed decisions, the information security manager can build a compelling case for investment and support. While it's important to discuss potential consequences, costs, and technical capabilities, these factors are secondary to the fundamental alignment with business strategy.

259. Which of the following is the LEAST effective way for an information security manager to build support for risk management initiatives among business unit leaders?
a. engaging business unit leaders in the risk assessment process to ensure their perspectives and concerns are addressed
b. framing risk management as a business enabler that helps the units achieve their objectives and innovate safely
c. providing regular updates and reports on risk management activities and outcomes relevant to each business unit
d. emphasizing the technical complexity and compliance requirements of risk management processes and controls

Answer: d. emphasizing the technical complexity and compliance requirements of risk management processes and controls. Explanation: When seeking to build support and engagement for risk management among business unit leaders, it's important to focus on the business benefits and relevance of the initiatives, rather than the technical or compliance aspects. Business leaders are more likely to embrace risk management when they see it as a strategic partner that helps them achieve their goals and objectives, not as a bureaucratic or technical burden. Engaging business units in the risk assessment process, framing risk management as a business enabler, and providing regular, relevant updates are all effective ways to build understanding, trust, and collaboration. However, emphasizing the complexity of risk management processes or the compliance requirements can make the initiatives seem more onerous and less valuable from a business perspective.

260. An information security manager is presenting a business case for investing in a new risk management technology solution. Which of the following is the MOST important factor to emphasize in the business case?
a. the potential cost savings and efficiencies that the solution can provide over time
b. the technical superiority and advanced features of the solution compared to alternatives
c. the alignment of the solution with the organization's overall risk management strategy and objectives
d. the use of the solution by peer organizations and industry leaders

Answer: c. the alignment of the solution with the organization's overall risk management strategy and objectives. Explanation: When making a business case for a risk management technology investment, the most critical factor to highlight is how the solution aligns with and supports the organization's overarching risk management approach and goals. The proposed technology should be positioned as an enabler of the organization's risk management strategy, helping to streamline processes, enhance decision-making, and improve overall risk posture. While potential cost savings, technical capabilities, and peer adoption are all relevant considerations, they should be framed in the context of how they contribute to the strategic risk management objectives. Ultimately, senior stakeholders are most likely to support investments that are clearly tied to the organization's risk management priorities and direction.

261. Which of the following is the BEST way for an information security manager to obtain buy-in from the legal and compliance teams for a proposed risk management initiative?
a. emphasizing how the initiative will reduce the workload and responsibilities of the legal and compliance teams
b. highlighting how the initiative aligns with and supports the organization's legal and compliance obligations
c. providing detailed technical information about the risk management tools and processes involved in the initiative
d. focusing on the potential cost savings and efficiencies that the initiative can provide to the organization

Answer: b. highlighting how the initiative aligns with and supports the organization's legal and compliance obligations. Explanation: When seeking buy-in from legal and compliance stakeholders for a risk management initiative, it's essential to demonstrate how the proposed activities will help the organization meet its regulatory requirements and mitigate legal risks. These teams are primarily concerned with ensuring that the organization operates within the bounds of applicable laws, regulations, and ethical standards. By framing the risk management initiative as a means of strengthening compliance, reducing legal exposures, and demonstrating due diligence, the information security manager can tap into the core priorities and motivations of the legal and compliance functions. While potential cost savings and process efficiencies are certainly relevant, they are likely to be secondary considerations for these stakeholders compared to the compliance and risk mitigation benefits.

262. An information security manager is seeking to build support for risk management initiatives among the organization's software development teams. Which of the following is the MOST effective approach to take?
a. emphasizing the importance of compliance with regulatory standards and industry best practices for secure software development
b. highlighting the potential negative consequences and liabilities associated with security vulnerabilities in the organization's software products
c. focusing on how integrating risk management practices into the software development lifecycle can improve product quality, reliability, and customer satisfaction
d. providing detailed technical information about the software security testing tools and processes that will be implemented as part of the risk management initiatives

Answer: c. focusing on how integrating risk management practices into the software development lifecycle can improve product quality, reliability, and customer satisfaction. Explanation: When seeking to build support for risk management among software development teams, it's important to frame the initiatives in terms of their benefits for the quality, reliability, and market success of the software products being developed. Developers are often motivated by the desire to create high-quality, innovative solutions that meet customer needs and expectations. By highlighting how risk management practices, such as threat modeling, secure coding, and security testing, can help identify and mitigate defects and vulnerabilities early in the development process, the information security manager can align risk management with the development teams' core goals and priorities. While compliance and potential consequences are certainly relevant, focusing too heavily on these aspects may make risk management seem like an external constraint or burden, rather than an integral part of the development process. Similarly, providing detailed technical information about security tools and processes is important, but should be balanced with a focus on the broader benefits for product quality and customer satisfaction.

263. Which of the following is the MOST important factor for an information security manager to consider when seeking to obtain buy-in for risk management initiatives from IT operations teams?
a. the potential impact of risk management activities on system performance and availability
b. the alignment of risk management initiatives with IT service management (ITSM) frameworks and processes
c. the opportunities for IT staff to acquire new skills and certifications related to risk management
d. the potential for risk management tools and processes to create additional workload and complexity for IT teams

Answer: a. the potential impact of risk management activities on system performance and availability. Explanation: When seeking buy-in from IT operations teams for risk management initiatives, one of the most critical considerations is how the proposed activities may affect the performance, availability, and stability of the systems and services that IT is responsible for maintaining. IT operations staff are often primarily focused on ensuring that systems run smoothly and meet agreed-upon service levels. If risk management initiatives are perceived as potentially disrupting operations or degrading performance, IT teams may be resistant to their implementation. To obtain buy-in, the information security manager should emphasize how the risk management measures will be designed and executed in a way that minimizes operational impact and supports the overall goals of system reliability and uptime. This may involve highlighting the use of non-intrusive monitoring tools, scheduling activities during maintenance windows, and establishing clear communication and coordination processes between security and operations teams. While alignment with ITSM frameworks, skill development opportunities, and workload considerations are all relevant factors, the fundamental priority for most IT operations teams will be ensuring that risk management does not compromise their ability to deliver stable, high-performing systems and services.

264. An information security manager is seeking to build support for implementing a new risk assessment methodology across the organization. Which of the following is the LEAST effective approach to take?

a. conducting pilot risk assessments using the new methodology to demonstrate its value and feasibility
b. providing training and educational resources to help stakeholders understand the new methodology and its benefits
c. seeking input and feedback from stakeholders on how to tailor the methodology to the organization's specific needs and context
d. mandating the use of the new methodology through a top-down directive from senior leadership

Answer: d. mandating the use of the new methodology through a top-down directive from senior leadership. Explanation: When seeking to build broad organizational support for a new risk assessment methodology, a top-down, directive approach is often less effective than a more collaborative, iterative process of engagement and education. Simply mandating the use of the new methodology through senior leadership authority may create resistance and resentment among stakeholders who feel that the change is being imposed upon them without their input or buy-in. A more effective approach is to work with stakeholders to build understanding, trust, and ownership in the new methodology over time. This may involve conducting pilot assessments to demonstrate the methodology's value and practicality, providing training and resources to help stakeholders learn and adopt the new approach, and actively seeking feedback and suggestions on how to customize the methodology to fit the organization's unique risk landscape and culture. By engaging stakeholders as partners in the implementation process, rather than simply dictating the change from the top down, the information security manager can help build a sense of shared commitment and accountability for the success of the new risk assessment approach.

265. Which of the following is the MOST important message for an information security manager to convey when communicating the value of risk management to business stakeholders?
a. risk management helps the organization comply with legal and regulatory requirements and avoid penalties
b. risk management enables the organization to pursue its strategic objectives and opportunities with greater confidence and resilience
c. risk management demonstrates to customers, partners, and investors that the organization takes security and privacy seriously
d. risk management reduces the workload and stress on individual employees by providing clear guidance and processes for managing risks

Answer: b. risk management enables the organization to pursue its strategic objectives and opportunities with greater confidence and resilience. Explanation: When communicating the value of risk management to business stakeholders, the most compelling and effective message is often one that ties risk management directly to the achievement of the organization's strategic goals and objectives. By framing risk management as an enabler of business success, rather than just a compliance or security function, the information security manager can help stakeholders understand how effective risk management supports innovation, growth, and competitive advantage. The key is to emphasize that by identifying, assessing, and mitigating potential risks and uncertainties, the organization can make more informed decisions, seize opportunities with greater confidence, and bounce back more quickly from disruptions or setbacks. In other words, risk management is not just about avoiding negative outcomes, but about creating the resilience and adaptability needed to thrive in an uncertain and dynamic business environment. While compliance, customer trust, and employee workload are all relevant benefits of risk management, they are typically secondary to the fundamental value proposition of enabling the organization to pursue its mission and vision with greater clarity, confidence, and agility.

266. An information security manager is trying to obtain support and resources for a new risk management initiative during a time of budget constraints and competing priorities. Which of the following is the BEST approach to take?
a. focusing on the potential long-term cost savings and efficiencies that the initiative can provide
b. emphasizing the dire consequences and potential legal liabilities of not implementing the initiative
c. aligning the initiative with the organization's most critical strategic objectives and risk priorities
d. proposing a scaled-down, phased approach to implementing the initiative over time

Answer: c. aligning the initiative with the organization's most critical strategic objectives and risk priorities. Explanation: In a context of limited resources and competing demands, the most effective way for an information security manager to obtain support for a new risk management initiative is to demonstrate how the initiative directly aligns with and supports the organization's most pressing strategic goals and risk management priorities. By framing the initiative as a targeted, high-impact investment that addresses the risks and opportunities that are most material to the organization's success, the manager can make a compelling case for prioritization and funding, even in a constrained environment. This requires a deep understanding of the organization's strategic landscape, as well as the ability to articulate how the risk management initiative will help the organization navigate and thrive in that landscape. While potential cost savings, legal considerations, and phased implementation approaches are all relevant factors to consider, they are unlikely to be as persuasive as a clear, direct link to the organization's core strategic objectives and risk priorities. Ultimately, senior leaders and decision-makers are more likely to allocate scarce resources to initiatives that they see as essential to the organization's ability to achieve its mission and create value, even in tough times.

267. Which of the following is the MOST effective way for an information security manager to build grass-roots support and engagement for risk management among employees at all levels of the organization?
a. conducting mandatory, company-wide training sessions on risk management policies and procedures
b. sending regular email updates and newsletters highlighting risk management activities and successes
c. establishing a network of risk management champions or liaisons within each business unit or department
d. implementing an incentive or reward program for employees who demonstrate good risk management practices

Answer: c. establishing a network of risk management champions or liaisons within each business unit or department. Explanation: To build widespread, bottom-up support and engagement for risk management across the organization, one of the most effective strategies is to establish a distributed network of risk management advocates or ambassadors embedded within each major business unit, department, or location. These champions or liaisons serve as a vital link between the central risk management function and the front-line employees who are often best positioned to identify, assess, and mitigate risks in their day-to-day work. By appointing and empowering a diverse group of influential and respected employees to promote risk management within their own teams and peer networks, the information security manager can help create a sense of local ownership and accountability for risk management, rather than it being seen as a distant, top-down mandate. The risk management liaisons can help to contextualize and translate risk management concepts and practices for their specific operational contexts, as well as to surface and communicate local risk concerns and ideas back to the central risk management team. While training, communication, and incentive programs can all play important roles in building risk management awareness and motivation, they are often less powerful than the direct, personal influence and example of trusted peers and leaders within employees' immediate work environments. A well-functioning risk liaison network can help to embed and normalize risk management as an integral part of the organization's culture and operations, rather than as a separate, imposed set of requirements.

268. An organization is establishing a risk ownership and accountability structure for its information security program. Which of the following is the MOST important consideration in determining risk ownership?
a. the technical expertise and qualifications of the potential risk owner
b. the seniority and authority of the potential risk owner within the organization
c. the alignment of the risk with the potential owner's roles and responsibilities
d. the willingness and availability of the potential risk owner to take on the role

Answer: c. the alignment of the risk with the potential owner's roles and responsibilities. Explanation: When determining risk ownership, the most critical factor is ensuring that the designated owner has the appropriate level of responsibility, authority, and accountability for managing the specific risk in question. Effective risk ownership requires a clear and logical alignment between the nature of the risk and the roles, objectives, and decision-making purview of the owner. The risk should fall within the owner's sphere of influence and control, so that they have the necessary levers and resources to assess, treat, and monitor the risk over time. While factors such as technical expertise, seniority, and willingness are certainly relevant considerations, they are secondary to the fundamental requirement of aligning risk ownership with organizational roles and responsibilities.

269. Which of the following is the PRIMARY role of a risk owner in an information security risk management program?
a. to identify and assess all potential risks within their area of responsibility
b. to implement and maintain all risk mitigation controls and safeguards
c. to monitor and report on the effectiveness of risk treatment activities
d. to ensure that risks are managed in accordance with the organization's risk appetite and tolerance

Answer: d. to ensure that risks are managed in accordance with the organization's risk appetite and tolerance. Explanation: The primary responsibility of a risk owner is to ensure that the risks within their purview are effectively managed in alignment with the organization's overall risk appetite and tolerance levels. This requires a clear understanding of the organization's risk management strategy, objectives, and criteria, as well as the specific risk treatment plans and targets established for each owned risk. The risk owner is accountable for making informed decisions about risk treatment options, allocating resources and responsibilities for implementing controls, and monitoring risk levels and control effectiveness over time. While risk identification, control implementation, and monitoring activities are all important aspects of the risk owner's role, their ultimate accountability is for ensuring that risks are maintained at an acceptable level in relation to the organization's risk appetite and business objectives.

270. In an information security risk management context, which of the following BEST describes the concept of risk appetite?
a. the amount of risk an organization must take to achieve its strategic objectives
b. the level of risk an organization is willing to accept in pursuit of its objectives
c. the maximum amount of risk an organization can handle without significant harm
d. the minimum level of risk an organization needs to maintain to stay competitive

Answer: b. the level of risk an organization is willing to accept in pursuit of its objectives. Explanation: Risk appetite refers to the types and amount of risk an organization is prepared to tolerate or accept in the process of pursuing its strategic goals and creating value. It represents a conscious, strategic decision about how much uncertainty and potential loss the organization is willing to take on, given its objectives, stakeholder expectations, and organizational capacity. Risk appetite is typically expressed as a series of statements or measures that define acceptable risk levels across different categories or areas of the business. By clearly articulating its risk appetite, an organization provides guidance and boundaries for risk-taking and risk treatment decisions at all levels. It's important to note that risk appetite is not the same as risk capacity (the maximum risk the organization can absorb) or risk need (the minimum risk required to operate), but rather a strategic choice aligned with the organization's risk culture, values, and objectives.

271. Which of the following is the MOST effective way to ensure clear risk ownership and accountability across an organization?
a. defining and communicating risk ownership roles and responsibilities in policies and procedures
b. assigning risk ownership to the most senior executive in each business unit or department
c. distributing risk ownership evenly across all employees to promote shared responsibility
d. rotating risk ownership assignments periodically to build broad risk management expertise

Answer: a. defining and communicating risk ownership roles and responsibilities in policies and procedures. Explanation: To establish clear and effective risk ownership and accountability throughout an organization, the most important step is to formally define and document the specific roles, responsibilities, and expectations associated with risk ownership in the organization's risk management policies, procedures, and governance structures. This includes specifying the criteria for assigning risk ownership, the key activities and decision-making authorities of risk owners, the reporting and escalation lines for risk-related matters, and the performance measures and accountability mechanisms for risk owners. By codifying risk ownership in official organizational policies and processes, and communicating these expectations consistently to all stakeholders, the organization creates a transparent, systematic, and enforceable framework for risk ownership and accountability. While factors such as seniority, distribution, and rotation of risk ownership assignments can play a role in building an effective risk culture, they are not as fundamental as having a clear, documented, and well-communicated governance structure for risk ownership roles and responsibilities.

272. In the context of information security risk management, which of the following is the PRIMARY purpose of a risk register?
a. to prioritize risks based on their potential impact and likelihood
b. to assign ownership and accountability for each identified risk
c. to document and track the status of risks throughout their lifecycle
d. to calculate the overall risk score and risk appetite of the organization

Answer: c. to document and track the status of risks throughout their lifecycle. Explanation: A risk register is a central repository and management tool used to capture, document, and monitor key information about an organization's identified risks throughout their lifecycle. Its primary purpose is to provide a structured and consistent way to record and track the status of each risk, from initial identification through assessment, treatment, and ongoing monitoring. A typical risk register includes details such as risk descriptions, owners, categories, impact and likelihood ratings, treatment plans, control implementation status, and review dates. By serving as a comprehensive and up-to-date inventory of an organization's risk landscape, the risk register enables risk owners, managers, and stakeholders to maintain a clear and shared understanding of the risk management process and the current state of each managed risk. While the risk register can certainly help to inform risk prioritization, ownership assignment, and overall risk scoring and appetite setting, its core function is to provide a systematic means of documenting and tracking risks over time, to ensure that they are effectively and accountably managed in accordance with the organization's risk management framework.

273. Which of the following is the MOST important factor in promoting effective risk ownership and accountability in an organization?
a. implementing advanced risk management software and analytics tools
b. conducting frequent risk assessments and audits to identify control gaps and weaknesses
c. establishing clear performance metrics and incentives for risk management responsibilities
d. fostering a culture of proactive risk awareness, communication, and collaboration

Answer: d. fostering a culture of proactive risk awareness, communication, and collaboration. Explanation: While factors such as technology, assessment processes, and performance management can certainly support and enable effective risk ownership and accountability, the most fundamental driver is the underlying organizational culture and mindset around risk. A culture that encourages open communication, proactive identification and escalation of risks, cross-functional collaboration in risk treatment, and continuous learning and improvement is essential for embedding risk ownership and accountability into the fabric of the organization. In such a culture, risk management is seen not as a separate, compliance-driven activity, but as an integral part of every role and decision-making process. Risk owners feel empowered and motivated to take a proactive, long-term view of risk management, and are supported by a network of engaged stakeholders across the organization. Cultivating this type of risk-aware culture requires strong leadership, consistent messaging, and reinforcement of risk management principles and behaviors at all levels. It also involves creating a psychologically safe environment where individuals feel comfortable raising concerns, admitting mistakes, and challenging assumptions. Without this foundation of a proactive, collaborative risk culture, even the most sophisticated tools, processes, and incentives will struggle to drive genuine ownership and accountability for risk management outcomes.

274. In an information security risk management context, what is the PRIMARY difference between risk appetite and risk tolerance?
a. risk appetite is set by senior management, while risk tolerance is set by operational teams
b. risk appetite applies to strategic risks, while risk tolerance applies to operational risks
c. risk appetite is a qualitative measure, while risk tolerance is a quantitative measure
d. risk appetite is a high-level statement, while risk tolerance defines specific acceptable risk levels

Answer: d. risk appetite is a high-level statement, while risk tolerance defines specific acceptable risk levels. Explanation: While risk appetite and risk tolerance are closely related concepts, they differ in terms of their level of specificity and granularity. Risk appetite is a high-level, strategic expression of the types and amount of risk an organization is willing to accept in pursuit of its objectives. It sets the overall tone and direction for risk-taking and risk management across the organization. In contrast, risk tolerance represents the specific, measurable boundaries or thresholds for acceptable risk exposure within each risk category or area. Risk tolerance translates the high-level risk appetite into operational terms, defining the maximum level of risk the organization is prepared to tolerate in relation to each of its key risk indicators or metrics. For example, an organization may have a general risk appetite statement of "low to moderate risk" for cybersecurity, but set specific risk tolerance levels such as "less than 5% of systems with critical vulnerabilities" or "less than 1 data breach per year". Together, risk appetite and risk tolerance provide a framework for making consistent, aligned risk decisions and ensuring that risks are managed within acceptable boundaries across the organization.

275. Which of the following is the MOST effective way for an organization to ensure that risk owners have the necessary knowledge, skills, and resources to fulfill their responsibilities?
a. providing regular risk management training and certification opportunities
b. automating risk management processes and decision-making with advanced software tools
c. assigning risk ownership to the most experienced and senior staff in each area
d. establishing a centralized risk management function to support and guide risk owners

Answer: a. providing regular risk management training and certification opportunities. Explanation: To enable risk owners to effectively perform their roles and responsibilities, the most important investment an organization can make is in their risk management knowledge, skills, and capabilities. Providing regular, high-quality training and development opportunities is crucial for ensuring that risk owners have the necessary competencies and expertise to identify, assess, treat, and monitor risks in their areas of responsibility. This may include a mix of internal and external training programs, workshops, simulations, and certifications covering topics such as risk assessment methodologies, control design and implementation, risk reporting and communication, and industry-specific risk domains. By prioritizing continuous risk management learning and skill-building for risk owners, the organization demonstrates its commitment to risk management excellence and empowers risk owners to stay current with evolving risk landscapes and best practices. While factors such as technology, seniority, and centralized support can certainly assist risk owners in their duties, they are not a substitute for the core knowledge and capabilities that come from focused, ongoing training and professional development in risk management.

276. An organization has identified a significant risk related to a critical business process, but is struggling to identify an appropriate risk owner. Which of the following is the BEST course of action?
a. assign ownership to the most senior executive responsible for the overall business function
b. assign ownership to the individual contributor most familiar with the specific process
c. assign ownership collectively to the entire team responsible for executing the process
d. escalate the risk to the board of directors to determine the appropriate owner

Answer: a. assign ownership to the most senior executive responsible for the overall business function. Explanation: When a clear risk owner cannot be readily identified for a significant risk, the best approach is typically to assign ownership to the highest-level executive with overall responsibility and accountability for the business function or area in which the risk resides. This executive, such as a vice president or director, should have the necessary authority, resources, and cross-functional perspective to effectively oversee the management of the risk and to coordinate risk treatment activities across the relevant teams and processes. While the executive may not have the most detailed technical knowledge of the specific process, they are in the best position to ensure that the risk is given appropriate attention and priority, and to make informed decisions about risk treatment options and resource allocation. Assigning ownership to an individual contributor or team may not provide sufficient authority or scope to manage a significant, cross-cutting risk, while escalating to the board level may not be necessary or appropriate for operational risk management decisions. The key is to find the right balance of seniority, accountability, and operational knowledge to drive effective risk ownership and mitigation.

277. Which of the following is the PRIMARY benefit of establishing clear risk ownership and accountability in an organization?
a. reducing the overall number and severity of risks facing the organization
b. enabling faster and more efficient risk assessment and mitigation processes
c. promoting proactive risk identification and treatment by those closest to the risks
d. demonstrating compliance with regulatory and industry risk management standards

Answer: c. promoting proactive risk identification and treatment by those closest to the risks. Explanation: The primary value of establishing clear risk ownership and accountability lies in its ability to drive proactive, timely, and effective risk management by the individuals and teams who are most knowledgeable about and impacted by the risks in question. When risk owners are clearly defined and empowered, they are more likely to take a hands-on, day-to-day approach to identifying, assessing, and mitigating risks as an integral part of their regular responsibilities and decision-making processes. They are better positioned to spot emerging risks, implement practical and sustainable risk controls, and adapt risk management strategies to changing business and operational realities. In contrast, without clear risk ownership, risk management can become a reactive, siloed, or compliance-driven exercise that is disconnected from the real-world challenges and opportunities facing the organization. While clear risk ownership can certainly contribute to a reduction in risk exposure, more efficient risk processes, and better regulatory compliance, its most significant impact is in fostering a culture of proactive, embedded risk management at the front lines of the organization, where risks are most visible and manageable.

278. An organization is developing its information security program and considering different frameworks to align with. Which of the following is the MOST important factor to consider when selecting a framework?
a. the popularity and adoption rate of the framework among industry peers
b. the level of technical detail and prescriptiveness provided by the framework
c. the alignment of the framework with the organization's business objectives and risk profile
d. the cost and resource requirements for implementing the framework

Answer: c. the alignment of the framework with the organization's business objectives and risk profile. Explanation: When selecting a framework to guide the development of an information security program, the most critical consideration is how well the framework aligns with the unique business context, objectives, and risk landscape of the organization. The chosen framework should provide a structure and approach that supports the organization's strategic priorities, regulatory requirements, and risk management goals. It should be adaptable to the organization's size, industry, technology environment, and risk appetite. Factors such as popularity, technical detail, and implementation costs are important, but secondary to the fundamental alignment between the framework and the organization's specific needs and circumstances. A well-aligned framework will help ensure that the information security program is focused, relevant, and effective in managing the risks that matter most to the business.

279. Which of the following is the PRIMARY role of senior management in the development and implementation of an information security program?

a. to provide detailed technical guidance on security controls and technologies
b. to set the overall direction and priorities for the program based on business objectives and risk appetite
c. to directly manage the day-to-day activities and operations of the security team
d. to serve as the primary point of contact for external stakeholders on security matters

Answer: b. to set the overall direction and priorities for the program based on business objectives and risk appetite. Explanation: The primary responsibility of senior management in an information security program is to establish the strategic vision, goals, and risk parameters that guide the program's development and execution. This includes defining the program's alignment with business objectives, setting the organization's risk appetite and tolerance levels, allocating resources and budget, and communicating the importance of information security to all stakeholders. Senior management provides the top-down leadership and support necessary to ensure that the program has the visibility, authority, and resources to be effective. While senior managers may provide high-level input on technical strategies and serve as escalation points for major issues or incidents, they typically delegate the detailed technical decision-making and day-to-day program management to the CISO and security team. Their role is to empower and oversee the program at a strategic level, not to get involved in operational details.

280. An organization is implementing an information security program and wants to ensure that security is integrated into all aspects of its operations. Which of the following is the MOST effective approach to achieve this goal?
a. conducting annual security awareness training for all employees
b. implementing a comprehensive set of technical security controls and tools
c. appointing a dedicated security champion within each business unit and functional area
d. requiring all new projects and initiatives to undergo a formal security review and approval process

Answer: c. appointing a dedicated security champion within each business unit and functional area. Explanation: To truly embed security into all facets of an organization's operations, one of the most powerful strategies is to establish a network of security champions or liaisons within each major business unit, department, and location. These champions serve as the local faces and voices of the security program, promoting security awareness, best practices, and collaboration within their respective areas. They act as a bridge between the central security team and the front-line employees, helping to translate security policies and requirements into practical, context-specific guidance. By having dedicated security advocates embedded throughout the organization, security becomes a shared responsibility and an integral part of everyone's job, rather than a separate, centralized function. While training, technology, and processes are certainly important components of a comprehensive security program, they alone cannot create the kind of pervasive, culturally-ingrained approach to security that having a distributed network of champions can foster.

281. Which of the following is the MOST important factor to consider when setting goals and objectives for an information security program?
a. the available budget and resources for implementing security measures
b. the latest threat trends and attack techniques reported by security vendors and media
c. the regulatory compliance requirements applicable to the organization's industry and locations
d. the organization's overall business strategy, risk appetite, and key performance indicators

Answer: d. the organization's overall business strategy, risk appetite, and key performance indicators. Explanation: When establishing goals and objectives for an information security program, the most critical input should be the organization's overarching business context and priorities. The security program's aims should be directly aligned with and supportive of the organization's mission, vision, and strategic objectives. They should reflect the organization's risk appetite and tolerance, focusing on the most significant threats and vulnerabilities that could impact the achievement of business goals. The program's success measures should be tied to key performance indicators that matter to the business, such as uptime, customer satisfaction, and regulatory compliance. While factors like budget, threat trends, and regulatory requirements are certainly important considerations, they should be viewed through the lens of how they affect the organization's ability to achieve its core objectives. By grounding the security program in the broader business context, security leaders can ensure that their efforts are targeted, relevant, and value-driven.

282. An organization wants to promote a culture of proactive security risk management among its employees. Which of the following is likely to be the LEAST effective approach?
a. incorporating security performance metrics into employee evaluations and incentives
b. providing regular security awareness training and simulations to all staff
c. encouraging employees to report potential security risks and incidents without fear of retribution
d. implementing strict disciplinary measures for employees who violate security policies

Answer: d. implementing strict disciplinary measures for employees who violate security policies. Explanation: While holding employees accountable for adhering to security policies is important, a heavy-handed focus on punishment and discipline is unlikely to foster a culture of proactive, voluntary engagement in security risk management. Fear of consequences can actually discourage employees from reporting risks, incidents, or mistakes, driving security issues underground. A more effective approach is to create a positive, supportive environment that encourages and rewards security awareness and participation. This can include providing regular training and education to build security skills and confidence, incorporating security metrics into performance evaluations and incentives to reinforce desired behaviors, and establishing clear, safe channels for reporting security concerns without fear of blame or retaliation. The goal is to make security a shared responsibility and a source of pride and empowerment for employees, not a burden or a threat. When employees feel trusted, respected, and motivated to contribute to the organization's security posture, they are more likely to act as proactive risk managers in their day-to-day work.

283. Which of the following is the PRIMARY purpose of conducting regular security risk assessments as part of an information security program?
a. to identify all possible security risks facing the organization, regardless of likelihood or impact
b. to prioritize security investments based on the latest threat trends and vendor product offerings
c. to demonstrate compliance with regulatory standards and avoid potential fines or penalties
d. to understand the organization's current risk profile and inform risk treatment decision-making

Answer: d. to understand the organization's current risk profile and inform risk treatment decision-making. Explanation: The main objective of conducting regular security risk assessments is to provide a clear, up-to-date picture of the organization's risk landscape and to guide informed decision-making about risk management priorities and strategies. Through systematic identification, analysis, and evaluation of risks, assessments help organizations understand their most significant areas of exposure, the potential impacts of those risks on business objectives, and the effectiveness of existing controls. This intelligence enables security leaders and stakeholders to make targeted, risk-based decisions about where to focus resources and efforts for maximum risk reduction and business value. While risk assessments can certainly help organizations identify a wide range of potential risks, prioritize investments, and demonstrate regulatory compliance, their primary purpose is to provide the necessary insights to proactively manage and treat risks in alignment with the organization's specific risk appetite, tolerance, and objectives.

284. An organization is developing a set of key performance indicators (KPIs) to measure the effectiveness of its information security program. Which of the following is the MOST important characteristic of effective KPIs?
a. focusing on technical metrics like the number of vulnerabilities patched or incidents resolved
b. aligning with industry benchmarks and peer performance data for comparability
c. measuring outcomes that are directly tied to business objectives and risk reduction goals
d. capturing a wide range of data points across all areas of the security program

Answer: c. measuring outcomes that are directly tied to business objectives and risk reduction goals. Explanation: The most critical attribute of effective security KPIs is their alignment with and relevance to the organization's specific business goals and risk management priorities. Rather than simply tracking activity or output metrics (like number of patches or incidents), or comparing to generic industry benchmarks, the most meaningful KPIs measure outcomes that demonstrate the real-world impact and value of the security program. This means focusing on indicators that show how security efforts are reducing risk exposure, supporting business continuity and resilience, enabling regulatory compliance, improving customer trust, or otherwise contributing to the achievement of strategic objectives. By tying KPIs to business outcomes, security leaders can better communicate the value of their programs to executive stakeholders, make data-driven decisions about resource allocation and priorities, and continuously monitor and improve their efforts to maximize business impact. While operational metrics and industry comparisons can provide useful context and insights, they should be secondary to KPIs that directly measure the program's effectiveness in achieving the organization's unique security and business goals.

285. Which of the following is the MOST important consideration when developing security policies and procedures for an organization?
a. ensuring that policies are as comprehensive and detailed as possible to cover all potential scenarios
b. aligning policies with the latest technical standards and best practices published by industry bodies
c. tailoring policies to the organization's specific business context, culture, and risk appetite
d. making sure that policies are strict and inflexible to minimize the risk of non-compliance

Answer: c. tailoring policies to the organization's specific business context, culture, and risk appetite. Explanation: The most critical factor in developing effective security policies and procedures is ensuring that they are appropriately customized to the unique characteristics, needs, and constraints of the organization. This includes considering the organization's industry, regulatory environment, risk profile, business objectives, technology landscape, and cultural norms. Policies should be aligned with the organization's overall risk appetite and tolerance, providing clear guidance on acceptable and unacceptable behaviors and practices. They should be practical, understandable, and implementable given the organization's existing processes, systems, and resources. While it's important for policies to be comprehensive and aligned with industry standards and best practices, they should not be overly complex, rigid, or disconnected from the realities of the organization's operations. Policies that are too cumbersome, strict, or ill-suited to the organization's context are less likely to be followed and may actually hinder rather than enable effective security practices. The key is to strike a balance between providing clear, consistent guidelines and allowing for flexibility and adaptation to the organization's specific circumstances.

286. An organization wants to implement a security awareness and training program for its employees. Which of the following is likely to be the MOST effective approach?
a. providing one-size-fits-all training content to all employees on an annual basis
b. focusing training efforts primarily on technical staff and developers who work directly with systems and applications
c. using a variety of training methods and materials tailored to different roles, learning styles, and risk profiles
d. emphasizing the disciplinary consequences of non-compliance with security policies

Answer: c. using a variety of training methods and materials tailored to different roles, learning styles, and risk profiles. Explanation: To maximize the impact and effectiveness of a security awareness and training program, it's important to recognize that different employees have different learning needs, preferences, and job-specific security responsibilities. A one-size-fits-all approach, delivered infrequently or focused solely on technical staff, is unlikely to engage and resonate with all employees. Instead, the most successful programs typically employ a diverse mix of training content, formats, and channels that are tailored to the unique roles, risks, and learning styles of different audience segments. This can include a combination of in-person workshops, online modules, simulations, games, posters, newsletters, and other creative methods that make security learning relevant, interactive, and memorable for each employee. By segmenting and personalizing training efforts, organizations can ensure that all employees receive the knowledge and skills they need to fulfill their specific security responsibilities, whether they are executives handling sensitive data, customer service representatives detecting social engineering attempts, or IT administrators configuring critical systems. The key is to create a continuous, adaptive, and engaging learning experience that empowers all employees to be active participants in the organization's security culture.

287. Which of the following metrics is likely to be the MOST useful for communicating the value and effectiveness of an information security program to senior business stakeholders?
a. the number of security incidents detected and resolved each month
b. the percentage of systems with known vulnerabilities that have been patched
c. the reduction in overall business risk exposure and impact achieved through security efforts
d. the number of security policies and procedures that have been developed and implemented

Answer: c. the reduction in overall business risk exposure and impact achieved through security efforts. Explanation: When communicating the value and effectiveness of an information security program to senior business leaders, it's crucial to use metrics that are directly tied to the organization's strategic priorities and risk management goals. While operational metrics like the number of incidents resolved, vulnerabilities patched, or policies implemented can provide useful insights into the program's activities and coverage, they don't necessarily demonstrate the real-world impact and benefit of those efforts to the business. The most compelling metric for executive stakeholders is typically the measurable reduction in the organization's overall risk exposure and potential business impact that can be attributed to the security program's initiatives. This can be expressed in terms of avoided financial losses, maintained business continuity, protected reputation, or enabled strategic objectives. By quantifying and articulating the risk reduction and business value achieved, security leaders can show a clear return on investment and strategic alignment of their programs. This helps to justify continued support and resources, and positions security as a key enabler rather than a cost center. Metrics that focus on outcomes and business impact, rather than just activity or technical performance, are essential for demonstrating the strategic relevance and effectiveness of the security program to senior decision-makers.

288. An organization is defining the scope and objectives of its information security program. Which of the following is the MOST important factor to consider?
a. the latest cybersecurity threat trends and attack techniques
b. the organization's overall business strategy, risk appetite, and regulatory environment
c. the available budget and resources for implementing security controls and technologies
d. the preferences and priorities of the IT department and security team

Answer: b. the organization's overall business strategy, risk appetite, and regulatory environment. Explanation: When establishing the scope and objectives of an information security program, the primary driver should be the organization's unique business context and requirements. The program's goals and priorities should be directly aligned with the organization's strategic objectives, industry-specific regulatory obligations, and defined risk appetite and tolerance levels. By grounding the program in the broader business landscape, security leaders can ensure that their efforts are targeted, relevant, and supportive of the organization's success. While factors like current threat trends, available resources, and the preferences of the security team are important considerations, they should be evaluated in light of the overarching business needs and direction. The key is to develop a security program that enables the organization to achieve its objectives while managing risk to acceptable levels.

289. Which of the following should be the PRIMARY goal of an information security program?
a. to eliminate all cybersecurity risks and vulnerabilities facing the organization
b. to support the organization's business objectives by managing information risks to acceptable levels
c. to implement the most advanced and comprehensive security controls and technologies available
d. to achieve compliance with all applicable laws, regulations, and industry standards

Answer: b. to support the organization's business objectives by managing information risks to acceptable levels. Explanation: The fundamental purpose of an information security program is to enable the organization to pursue its mission and strategic goals while protecting the confidentiality, integrity, and availability of its information assets to an acceptable degree. Rather than aiming for absolute security or compliance, the program should focus on implementing risk management practices that are commensurate with the organization's specific risk appetite, tolerance, and business priorities. This involves identifying, assessing, and treating risks in a way that balances the need for security with the practical realities of the organization's resources, constraints, and objectives. While striving to minimize risks and vulnerabilities, comply with relevant requirements, and leverage appropriate controls and technologies are all important aspects of a security program, they should be in service of the larger goal of supporting the organization's overall success and resilience.

290. An organization is defining the objectives of its information security program. Which of the following is LEAST likely to be a primary objective?
a. protecting the confidentiality, integrity, and availability of the organization's information assets
b. ensuring compliance with relevant laws, regulations, and contractual obligations
c. implementing the most cutting-edge security technologies and solutions available in the market
d. supporting the organization's business goals and risk management strategies

Answer: c. implementing the most cutting-edge security technologies and solutions available in the market. Explanation: While leveraging appropriate security technologies and solutions is certainly an important element of an effective information security program, it is typically not a primary objective in and of itself. The program's goals should be focused on achieving specific outcomes and benefits for the organization, such as protecting critical information assets, meeting compliance requirements, and enabling business objectives, rather than on implementing technology for its own sake. The selection and implementation of security controls and tools should be based on a careful assessment of the organization's unique risks, requirements, and resources, not simply on chasing the latest market trends or innovations. A mature security program recognizes that technology is just one component of a comprehensive risk management approach that also includes people, processes, and policies. Overemphasizing technology without aligning it to clear business and risk management priorities can lead to inefficient, ineffective, and unsustainable security practices.

291. Which of the following is the MOST important consideration when defining the scope of an information security program?
a. including all possible information assets and systems, regardless of their criticality or sensitivity
b. aligning the scope with the organization's risk assessment results and business priorities
c. ensuring that the scope is as broad and comprehensive as possible to cover all potential risks
d. focusing primarily on externally-facing systems and assets that are visible to customers and partners

Answer: b. aligning the scope with the organization's risk assessment results and business priorities. Explanation: When determining the scope of an information security program, the key is to focus on the information assets, systems, and processes that are most critical to the organization's operations, objectives, and risk profile. This requires a risk-based approach that prioritizes resources and efforts based on the results of a thorough risk assessment, which identifies the organization's most significant threats, vulnerabilities, and potential impacts. The scope should also align with the organization's overall business strategy and priorities, ensuring that security initiatives are targeted to the areas that are most essential to the organization's success and resilience. While it's important for the scope to be comprehensive enough to address the full range of relevant risks, it should not be so broad that it dilutes the program's effectiveness or exceeds the organization's realistic capacity to manage. Focusing solely on externally-facing assets or trying to cover every possible system and data point can lead to an inefficient and unsustainable program that fails to prioritize the most critical risks and business needs.

292. An organization wants to ensure that its information security program objectives are achievable and measurable. Which of the following is the BEST approach?
a. setting objectives that are aspirational and challenging to motivate the security team to perform at a high level
b. defining objectives that are broad and flexible to allow for adaptation to changing circumstances over time
c. establishing objectives that are specific, measurable, attainable, relevant, and time-bound (SMART)
d. creating objectives that are focused primarily on meeting compliance requirements and avoiding regulatory penalties

Answer: c. establishing objectives that are specific, measurable, attainable, relevant, and time-bound (SMART). Explanation: To develop information security program objectives that are both achievable and measurable, it's important to follow the SMART framework. This means crafting objectives that are:

- Specific: clearly defined and focused on a particular outcome or result
- Measurable: quantifiable and trackable using specific metrics or key performance indicators (KPIs)
- Attainable: realistic and achievable given the organization's resources, constraints, and capabilities
- Relevant: aligned with and supportive of the organization's overall business strategy, risk management priorities, and regulatory requirements
- Time-bound: associated with specific deadlines or timeframes for completion

By setting SMART objectives, security leaders can establish clear, concrete targets that guide program planning, execution, and evaluation. Measurable objectives enable the program to demonstrate progress, value, and accountability to stakeholders. Attainable and relevant objectives ensure that the program is focused on outcomes that are both feasible and impactful for the organization. Time-bound objectives create a sense of urgency and momentum for achieving results. In contrast, objectives that are overly aspirational, vague, compliance-driven, or untethered from the organization's practical realities are less likely to be effective drivers of a successful security program.

293. Which of the following is the MOST effective way to align an information security program's objectives with the organization's broader risk management framework?
a. mapping the security program objectives to specific risk categories and tolerance levels defined in the risk management framework
b. ensuring that the security program objectives are reviewed and approved by the risk management committee or function
c. incorporating risk management terminology and concepts into the wording of the security program objectives
d. requiring the security team to provide regular reports on risk management activities and metrics to senior leadership

Answer: a. mapping the security program objectives to specific risk categories and tolerance levels defined in the risk management framework. Explanation: To effectively integrate an information security program into the organization's overall risk management approach, it's essential to establish a clear and explicit linkage between the program's objectives and the specific risk domains, priorities, and parameters defined in the organizational risk management framework. This involves identifying the key risk categories and subcategories that are relevant to information security (such as data breaches, system disruptions, intellectual property theft, etc.), and aligning the security program objectives to the organization's defined risk appetite and tolerance levels for each of those categories. By mapping program objectives to concrete risk management targets and thresholds, security leaders can ensure that their initiatives are focused on the most critical risk areas and are measurable against the organization's overall risk posture. This alignment helps to position the security program as a key component of the organization's governance, risk, and compliance (GRC) efforts, rather than as a siloed or ancillary function. While practices like collaborative planning with risk management teams, incorporating risk terminology, and providing risk-related reporting are all valuable, they are not as fundamental as directly tying program objectives to the risk management framework itself.

294. Which of the following should be the FIRST step in defining the scope and objectives of an information security program?
a. conducting a comprehensive inventory of all information assets and systems across the organization
b. benchmarking the organization's current security posture against industry peers and best practices
c. identifying and engaging key stakeholders to understand business priorities and risk perceptions
d. developing a detailed roadmap and timeline for implementing security controls and technologies

Answer: c. identifying and engaging key stakeholders to understand business priorities and risk perceptions. Explanation: Before diving into technical assessments, benchmarking, or implementation planning, the critical first step in establishing an effective information security program is to engage with key stakeholders across the organization to gather insights on business objectives, risk concerns, and expectations for the program. This stakeholder engagement process should include senior executives, business unit leaders, IT and operations managers, legal and compliance representatives, and other relevant decision-makers and influencers. The goal is to build a clear understanding of the organization's strategic priorities, regulatory requirements, risk appetite, and perceived security needs and gaps. These stakeholder perspectives should inform the scoping and objective-setting process, ensuring that the program is aligned with and responsive to the organization's unique business context and risk landscape. By starting with this business-centric, collaborative approach, security leaders can lay the foundation for a program that is not only technically sound but also organizationally relevant and credible. Conducting asset inventories, benchmarking exercises, and implementation planning are important subsequent steps, but they should be guided by the insights and priorities surfaced through initial stakeholder engagement.

295. An organization is establishing an information security program and wants to prioritize its efforts based on risk. Which of the following is the MOST important factor to consider when assessing risk?
a. the potential financial impact of a security incident or breach
b. the likelihood of a particular threat or vulnerability being exploited
c. the reputational damage that could result from a security failure
d. the alignment of each risk with the organization's strategic objectives and risk appetite

Answer: d. the alignment of each risk with the organization's strategic objectives and risk appetite. Explanation: While factors like financial impact, likelihood of occurrence, and reputational damage are certainly important considerations in risk assessment, the most critical lens for prioritizing information security risks is their relationship to the organization's overall strategy, goals, and risk appetite. A truly risk-based approach to scoping and driving an information security program requires a deep understanding of which risks pose the greatest potential to disrupt or derail the organization's core objectives and outcomes. This means looking beyond generic impact and probability measures to consider the specific business context and risk parameters within which the organization operates. Risks that may seem significant based on financial or reputational metrics alone may be less critical when evaluated against the organization's defined risk appetite and tolerance levels in different areas. Conversely, risks that appear relatively minor in isolation may be elevated in priority if they align with the organization's most essential strategic assets, processes, or stakeholder concerns. By grounding risk assessment in a holistic view of the organization's risk profile and business priorities, security leaders can ensure that program efforts are targeted to the areas that matter most for organizational success and resilience.

296. Which of the following is LEAST important to consider when defining the objectives of an information security program?
a. the organization's mission, vision, and values
b. the current cybersecurity threat landscape and attack trends
c. the organization's industry-specific regulatory and compliance requirements
d. the organization's risk management strategy and risk appetite statements

Answer: b. the current cybersecurity threat landscape and attack trends. Explanation: While staying informed about the evolving cybersecurity threat landscape and emerging attack techniques is certainly valuable for shaping tactical security priorities and controls, it is not as fundamental as other business-centric factors when defining the high-level objectives of an information security program. The program's objectives should be primarily driven by the organization's unique mission, values, regulatory environment, and risk management approach, rather than by generic or external threat trends alone. Overemphasizing current attack patterns or media-hyped threats can lead to a reactive, threat-centric program that is misaligned with the organization's specific risk profile and business needs. The most effective security programs are those that are anchored in a clear understanding of the organization's strategic goals, cultural principles, compliance obligations, and risk appetite, and that use this business context to guide risk assessment, prioritization, and mitigation efforts. While threat intelligence and trend analysis can help refine the program's tactical focus and inform control selection, they should not be the main drivers of the program's overarching objectives and direction.

297. Which of the following is the BEST way to ensure that an information security program's scope and objectives remain aligned with the organization's changing business needs over time?
a. conducting annual reviews and updates of the program scope and objectives with key stakeholders
b. automating security processes and technologies to adapt to changing requirements and conditions
c. outsourcing security functions to external service providers with expertise in evolving business landscapes
d. implementing a rigid change management process that prevents alterations to the program scope and objectives

Answer: a. conducting annual reviews and updates of the program scope and objectives with key stakeholders. Explanation: To maintain alignment between an information security program and the organization's dynamic business environment, it's essential to establish a regular cadence of review and adjustment with key stakeholders. This should involve, at minimum, an annual process of reassessing the program's scope and objectives in light of any changes to the organization's strategies, priorities, risks, or external context. The review should engage senior leaders, business unit representatives, and other relevant decision-makers to gather input on evolving needs, expectations, and constraints. The goal is to ensure that the program remains relevant, responsive, and value-driven as the business landscape shifts. By institutionalizing this collaborative, iterative approach to program planning and alignment, security leaders can build agility and resilience into the fabric of the program. While practices like automation, outsourcing, and change management can help operationalize program adaptability, they are not as crucial as the fundamental governance process of ongoing stakeholder engagement and realignment. A rigid, static program that is not regularly calibrated to changing business realities will quickly lose effectiveness and credibility, no matter how efficient its technical implementation may be.

298. An organization is developing its information security program and wants to ensure that it covers all critical areas. Which of the following is NOT one of the main components of a comprehensive information security program?
a. governance and policy
b. incident response and recovery
c. compliance and audit
d. marketing and public relations

Answer: d. marketing and public relations. Explanation: While effective communication and stakeholder engagement are certainly important for the success of an information security program, the core components typically do not include marketing or public relations functions. The main pillars of a comprehensive program are governance and policy (establishing the program's structure, authority, and guiding principles), risk assessment and management (identifying, evaluating, and treating risks), asset and data protection (implementing controls to safeguard information assets), incident response and recovery (detecting, investigating, and resolving security incidents), compliance and audit (ensuring adherence to legal, regulatory, and contractual requirements), and awareness and training (educating and empowering employees to support security goals). These components cover the essential operational, technical, and human aspects of information security, rather than public-facing communication or promotion.

299. Which of the following is the PRIMARY purpose of information security policies in an organization?
a. to demonstrate compliance with legal and regulatory requirements
b. to provide detailed technical instructions for implementing security controls
c. to establish management's expectations and requirements for protecting information assets
d. to assign specific roles and responsibilities to individual security team members

Answer: c. to establish management's expectations and requirements for protecting information assets. Explanation: The fundamental role of information security policies is to articulate the organization's official position, priorities, and parameters for safeguarding its information resources. Policies serve as the strategic foundation and authority for the entire information security program, communicating senior leadership's risk appetite, protection goals, and organizational mandates. They establish the high-level expectations, principles, and rules that guide all security-related decisions and actions across the enterprise. While policies can help demonstrate compliance, provide implementation guidance, and designate roles and responsibilities, these are secondary to their primary purpose of defining the organization's formal stance and approach to information security at a governance level. Effective policies should be clear, concise, and aligned with business objectives, providing a unifying framework and direction for all subsequent security activities and controls.

300. Which of the following is MOST important for ensuring the effectiveness of an information security awareness and training program?
a. covering a comprehensive set of technical security topics and concepts
b. delivering training through a single, standardized method and format for all employees
c. aligning training content and approaches with the organization's specific risks, culture, and audience needs
d. minimizing the time and resources required for employees to complete training activities

Answer: c. aligning training content and approaches with the organization's specific risks, culture, and audience needs. Explanation: To be truly effective, an information security awareness and training program must be tailored to the unique characteristics, priorities, and learning preferences of the organization and its employees. The content and delivery of training should be directly informed by the organization's risk assessment results, identifying the most critical knowledge gaps and behavioral vulnerabilities that need to be addressed. The program should also be designed with the organization's culture and workforce demographics in mind, using language, examples, and formats that resonate with different employee groups and learning styles. A one-size-fits-all approach that focuses solely on technical comprehensiveness or efficiency is unlikely to engage and motivate all employees to adopt secure practices. The key is to make training relevant, relatable, and accessible to each audience, reflecting their specific job roles, risk exposures, and organizational context. By customizing training to the organization's distinct needs and nuances, security leaders can maximize its impact and value in driving real behavioral change and risk reduction.

301. Which of the following is the MOST critical success factor for an information security incident response and recovery program?
a. having a large and highly skilled incident response team
b. investing in the most advanced threat detection and forensics technologies
c. establishing clear roles, responsibilities, and communication channels before an incident occurs
d. conducting frequent, unannounced incident response simulations and drills

Answer: c. establishing clear roles, responsibilities, and communication channels before an incident occurs. Explanation: While factors like team skills, technology investments, and regular testing are all important for effective incident response, the most crucial foundation is a well-defined and well-communicated plan that clarifies roles, responsibilities, and coordination processes in advance of an actual incident. In the high-pressure, time-sensitive context of a security breach or disruption, confusion and conflicts over who is in charge, who needs to be involved, and how information should flow can significantly hinder the speed and effectiveness of response efforts. A robust incident response plan should spell out the specific roles and decision-making authorities of different stakeholders (such as IT, legal, HR, communications, and executive teams), the protocols and timelines for escalation and reporting, and the methods and channels for internal and external communication. By establishing and socializing this governance framework before an incident hits, organizations can ensure that everyone knows their part and can work together seamlessly to investigate, contain, and recover from a breach. Having a clear, coordinated plan is more important than the size of the response team, the sophistication of the tools, or the frequency of drills, as it provides the essential structure and alignment for all other response capabilities and activities.

302. Which of the following is the PRIMARY goal of information security risk assessments?
a. to identify all possible threats and vulnerabilities, regardless of likelihood or impact
b. to calculate the precise financial costs and benefits of different security investments
c. to benchmark the organization's security posture against industry peers and standards
d. to understand the organization's current risk profile and prioritize mitigation efforts

Answer: d. to understand the organization's current risk profile and prioritize mitigation efforts. Explanation: The main objective of conducting information security risk assessments is to provide a clear, comprehensive picture of the organization's risk landscape, enabling informed decision-making about risk treatment and resource allocation. Through systematic identification, analysis, and evaluation of threats, vulnerabilities, and impacts, risk assessments help organizations understand their most significant areas of exposure and potential harm, as well as the effectiveness of existing controls. This intelligence allows security leaders to prioritize risks based on their alignment with business objectives, regulatory requirements, and organizational risk appetite, focusing mitigation efforts on the areas that pose the greatest danger or opportunity. While risk assessments may involve identifying a wide range of possible risk scenarios, estimating financial implications, and comparing the organization's risk posture to industry benchmarks, these activities are in service of the larger goal of generating actionable insights to drive targeted, risk-based security strategies and investments. The key outcome of an assessment is not a laundry list of risks, a precise financial forecast, or a competitive scorecard, but a sharpened understanding of the organization's unique risk profile and priorities, enabling proactive, pragmatic, and business-aligned risk management.

303. Which of the following is LEAST important for demonstrating compliance with information security laws, regulations, and standards?
a. maintaining detailed documentation of security policies, procedures, and controls
b. conducting regular internal audits and risk assessments to identify compliance gaps
c. achieving certification or accreditation under relevant industry standards (e.g., ISO 27001, SOC 2)
d. investing in the latest cutting-edge security technologies and solutions

Answer: d. investing in the latest cutting-edge security technologies and solutions. Explanation: While keeping up with technological advancements and implementing effective security tools and controls are certainly important for an overall security program, they are not the most critical factors for demonstrating compliance with specific legal, regulatory, or industry requirements. Compliance is primarily about adhering to defined sets of rules, standards, and best practices, and being able to provide evidence of that adherence. This evidence typically takes the form of documentation (such as policies, procedures, control descriptions, and audit trails), assessments (such as internal audits, risk analyses, and gap assessments), and third-party validations (such as certifications, accreditations, or audit reports). Investing in cutting-edge technology may help improve the organization's security posture, but it does not inherently prove compliance with any particular set of requirements. In fact, an overemphasis on technology without corresponding attention to documentation, assessment, and governance can actually undermine compliance efforts. The key is to align security controls and processes with applicable compliance frameworks, and to maintain a consistent, auditable record of that alignment over time.

304. What is the MOST important factor in determining the appropriate frequency and scope of information security compliance audits?

a. the size and complexity of the organization's IT infrastructure and systems
b. the budget and resources available for conducting audits and assessments
c. the requirements and expectations of relevant legal, regulatory, and contractual obligations
d. the preferences and availability of the internal audit team or external assessors

Answer: c. the requirements and expectations of relevant legal, regulatory, and contractual obligations. Explanation: The primary driver for the timing and extent of information security compliance audits should be the specific mandates and guidelines established by the laws, regulations, standards, and contracts to which the organization is subject. Different compliance regimes often have explicit requirements or recommendations for the frequency and rigor of audits and assessments, based on factors such as the sensitivity of the data involved, the criticality of the systems and processes, and the level of risk exposure. For example, the Payment Card Industry Data Security Standard (PCI DSS) requires annual audits for organizations processing large volumes of credit card transactions, while the Health Insurance Portability and Accountability Act (HIPAA) calls for periodic assessments based on an organization's risk analysis. Contractual obligations with customers, partners, or suppliers may also specify particular audit frequencies or scopes. While factors like organizational complexity, resource availability, and assessor preferences may influence the practicalities of audit planning and execution, they should not override the fundamental compliance requirements and expectations. The key is to understand and align with the audit demands of the organization's specific regulatory and contractual environment, and to build a sustainable and defensible audit program around those demands.

305. Which of the following is the BEST approach for integrating information security risk management into an organization's enterprise risk management (ERM) program?
a. conducting separate, siloed risk assessments and reporting processes for information security and other risk domains
b. assigning ownership and accountability for information security risks to the IT department or CISO alone
c. aligning information security risk criteria, assessment methods, and reporting with the overall ERM framework and governance
d. prioritizing information security risks and controls over other enterprise risk areas

Answer: c. aligning information security risk criteria, assessment methods, and reporting with the overall ERM framework and governance. Explanation: To effectively incorporate information security risk management into an organization's broader ERM program, it's essential to harmonize the approaches, criteria, and communication channels used for identifying, evaluating, and reporting on information security risks with those used for other enterprise risk domains (such as financial, operational, legal, and reputational risks). This means adopting consistent risk assessment methodologies, impact and likelihood rating scales, risk appetite and tolerance definitions, and reporting templates and frequencies across all risk areas, in accordance with the organization's overarching ERM framework and governance structure. By using a common language and process for risk management, the organization can more easily compare, prioritize, and treat risks across different domains, ensuring that information security risks are considered alongside and in relation to other critical enterprise risks. Conducting isolated assessments, assigning narrow ownership, or prioritizing information security risks in a vacuum can lead to a fragmented, inefficient, and potentially conflicting view of organizational risk. The key is to embed information security risk management as a core component of a unified, holistic, and business-aligned ERM program, with clear roles, relationships, and communication flows among all risk stakeholders.

306. Which of the following is MOST essential for the long-term success and sustainability of an information security program?
a. implementing the most advanced and comprehensive set of security controls and technologies
b. achieving and maintaining compliance with all applicable laws, regulations, and standards
c. fostering a culture of shared responsibility and proactive risk management across the organization
d. securing a large, dedicated budget and team for the information security function

Answer: c. fostering a culture of shared responsibility and proactive risk management across the organization. Explanation: While technical controls, compliance, and resource allocation are certainly important elements of an effective information security program, the most fundamental factor for long-term success is the creation of a pervasive, ingrained culture of security awareness, ownership, and action throughout the organization. A strong security culture is one where every employee, from the boardroom to the front lines, understands their role and responsibility in protecting the organization's information assets, and where secure behaviors and decisions are instinctive and habitual, not just imposed or enforced. In a culture of shared responsibility, security is not seen as a barrier or a burden, but as an essential enabler of business objectives and an integral part of everyone's job. This mindset of proactive risk management, where potential issues are anticipated, reported, and mitigated early and often, can help the organization stay ahead of evolving threats and prevent major incidents or breaches. Cultivating this type of resilient, risk-aware culture requires ongoing education, communication, and reinforcement from leadership, as well as the integration of security considerations into all aspects of organizational strategy, governance, and operations. Ultimately, a deeply embedded security culture can be more powerful and sustainable than any specific control, compliance program, or budget line item.

307. Which of the following is the MOST important characteristic of effective information security policies and procedures?
a. they are developed and maintained solely by the information security team
b. they are as comprehensive and detailed as possible, covering every potential scenario
c. they are aligned with the organization's business objectives, risk appetite, and culture
d. they are based on the most stringent and prescriptive industry standards and frameworks

Answer: c. they are aligned with the organization's business objectives, risk appetite, and culture. Explanation: The most critical attribute of successful information security policies and procedures is their alignment and compatibility with the unique goals, constraints, and context of the organization they are meant to serve. Policies and procedures should be tailored to the specific risks, regulatory requirements, strategic priorities, and cultural norms of the organization, striking a balance between security and business needs. They should reflect the organization's risk appetite and tolerance, focusing on the most critical assets and threats while allowing for flexibility and innovation in other areas. They should be written in clear, concise language that resonates with the organization's communication style and values, and that can be easily understood and followed by all employees. Overly generic, complex, or stringent policies that are disconnected from the organization's realities are likely to be ignored, circumvented, or resisted, undermining their effectiveness and credibility. Effective policies and procedures are not one-size-fits-all or set in stone, but rather living documents that evolve with the organization's changing needs and circumstances, through ongoing collaboration and feedback from stakeholders across the business. The key is to craft policies and procedures that are not only technically sound but also organizationally relevant, practical, and sustainable.

308. An organization is developing its information security program and wants to ensure that it supports the company's overall business objectives. Which of the following is the MOST important consideration for aligning the program with business goals?
a. implementing the most advanced and costly security controls available in the market
b. achieving compliance with all applicable laws, regulations, and industry standards
c. understanding the organization's strategic priorities, key assets, and risk appetite
d. hiring a large team of highly skilled security professionals with diverse technical expertise

Answer: c. understanding the organization's strategic priorities, key assets, and risk appetite. Explanation: The foundation of an effective, business-aligned information security program is a deep understanding of the organization's specific goals, values, constraints, and risk environment. The program should be designed to protect and enable the most critical assets, processes, and relationships that drive the organization's success and competitive advantage. This requires close collaboration with business leaders to identify strategic priorities, value chains, and risk appetites, and to tailor security efforts accordingly. A program that is overly focused on generic compliance checklists, cutting-edge technologies, or expert personnel without a clear grounding in the unique business context is likely to be seen as a costly barrier rather than a strategic partner. Alignment starts with understanding and empathy for the business, not just security for security's sake.

309. Which of the following is the BEST way to ensure that an information security program is aligned with the organization's risk appetite?
a. conducting annual risk assessments and presenting the results to senior management
b. implementing a comprehensive set of security controls based on industry best practices
c. defining and communicating risk appetite statements in collaboration with business stakeholders
d. purchasing cyber insurance policies to transfer residual risks to third-party providers

Answer: c. defining and communicating risk appetite statements in collaboration with business stakeholders. Explanation: An organization's risk appetite is the amount and type of risk it is willing to accept in pursuit of its objectives. Aligning an information security program with risk appetite requires a clear, shared understanding and articulation of the organization's risk thresholds and priorities. This is best achieved through the collaborative development and dissemination of formal risk appetite statements that define acceptable levels of risk across different categories, such as data confidentiality, system availability, and regulatory compliance. These statements should be crafted with input from senior leaders, business unit managers, and other key stakeholders to ensure they reflect the organization's strategic priorities, values, and constraints. They should be reviewed and updated regularly as the business and risk landscape evolves. While risk assessments, control frameworks, and risk transfer mechanisms are important tools for managing risk, they are not a substitute for a well-defined and well-communicated risk appetite. Without a clear "north star" of risk tolerance and prioritization, an information security program can become misaligned, inefficient, and ineffective in supporting business goals.

310. An organization has defined its risk appetite and wants to ensure that its information security program is focused on the most critical risks. Which of the following is the MOST important input to this prioritization process?
a. the latest cybersecurity threat trends and attack vectors published by industry analysts
b. the results of vulnerability scans and penetration tests conducted on the organization's systems
c. the information gathered from interviews and workshops with business and IT stakeholders
d. the budget and resource constraints of the information security department

Answer: c. the information gathered from interviews and workshops with business and IT stakeholders. Explanation: To effectively prioritize information security risks and align the security program with the organization's risk appetite, it's essential to gather input and insights from a wide range of internal stakeholders. This includes conducting structured interviews, workshops, and surveys with senior executives, business unit leaders, IT managers, legal and compliance officers, and other key personnel to understand their perspectives on the organization's critical assets, processes, and dependencies, as well as their concerns and priorities related to information risks. These stakeholder engagement activities provide valuable context and validation for the results of technical risk assessments, vulnerability scans, and threat intelligence analysis. They help ensure that the security program is focused on protecting what matters most to the business, not just what is most vulnerable or most hyped in the media. Budgets and resources are important considerations for prioritization, but they should be informed by a clear understanding of business priorities and risk appetite, not the other way around. The key is to ground risk prioritization in a holistic view of the organization's unique risk landscape and tolerance levels, as defined by the people who know the business best.

311. Which of the following is the LEAST effective way to communicate the alignment of an information security program with business goals and risk appetite?
a. conducting regular briefings and discussions with senior leadership and the board of directors
b. developing and distributing concise, non-technical program summaries and status reports
c. including relevant business context and risk considerations in all security policies and procedures
d. using complex technical jargon and detailed security metrics in all program communications

Answer: d. using complex technical jargon and detailed security metrics in all program communications. Explanation: When communicating the business alignment and value of an information security program, it's important to use language, concepts, and measures that resonate with the target audience. For senior leaders, board members, and other non-technical stakeholders, this means focusing on high-level, strategic themes and outcomes rather than diving into the weeds of technical vulnerabilities, controls, and metrics. While detailed technical information is important for managing and improving the program internally, it can be confusing, overwhelming, or irrelevant for business audiences. Instead, communications should highlight how the program supports and enables the organization's key objectives, mitigates risks to critical assets and processes, and complies with relevant laws and regulations. Metrics should be translated into business terms, such as potential financial impacts, customer satisfaction scores, or competitive advantages. Program summaries and status reports should be concise, visually engaging, and free of jargon and acronyms. The goal is to build understanding, trust, and advocacy for the program among business stakeholders, not to impress them with technical depth and complexity.

312. An organization wants to integrate its information security program with its enterprise risk management (ERM) framework. Which of the following is the MOST important step in this integration process?
a. conducting separate risk assessments for information security and other risk domains
b. developing a unified risk taxonomy and assessment methodology across all risk areas
c. assigning ownership of information security risks to the IT department or CISO
d. prioritizing information security risks over other types of business risks

Answer: b. developing a unified risk taxonomy and assessment methodology across all risk areas. Explanation: To effectively integrate an information security program with an organization's broader ERM framework, it's essential to establish a common language, structure, and process for identifying, assessing, and managing risks across all domains. This starts with creating a unified risk taxonomy that defines a consistent set of risk categories, sub-categories, and definitions that can be applied to information security risks as well as other types of risks, such as financial, operational, legal, and reputational risks. The taxonomy should be aligned with industry standards and best practices, but customized to the organization's specific business context and objectives. Next, a standardized risk assessment methodology should be developed and implemented across all risk areas, including information security. This methodology should define common criteria and scales for evaluating risk likelihood and impact, as well as consistent processes and templates for risk identification, analysis, evaluation, treatment, and monitoring. Conducting isolated risk assessments, assigning siloed risk ownership, or prioritizing certain risks in a vacuum can lead to a fragmented and ineffective approach to risk management. The key is to enable a holistic, integrated view of risk across the enterprise, with information security risks considered alongside and in relation to other critical risks.

313. Which of the following is the BEST way to ensure that an information security program remains aligned with changing business goals and risk appetite over time?
a. conducting annual risk assessments and program reviews with limited stakeholder involvement
b. implementing a rigid change management process that discourages updates to program policies and procedures
c. establishing a governance structure that includes regular input and oversight from senior business leaders
d. relying on automated security tools and technologies to adapt to changing requirements and threats

Answer: c. establishing a governance structure that includes regular input and oversight from senior business leaders. Explanation: To maintain alignment between an information security program and the organization's evolving business objectives and risk landscape, it's critical to establish a robust governance framework that enables ongoing collaboration, communication, and adaptation. This framework should include formal mechanisms for soliciting input and feedback from senior business leaders and other key stakeholders on a regular basis, such as quarterly program reviews, risk committee meetings, and strategy sessions. These engagements provide opportunities to reassess the program's priorities, performance, and resource needs in light of changing business goals, market conditions, and risk profiles. They also help ensure that the program remains visible, accountable, and relevant to the organization's top decision-makers. In addition to senior-level oversight, effective governance also involves clear roles, responsibilities, and decision-making authorities for program management and execution, as well as defined processes for policy review, incident escalation, and risk reporting. While periodic risk assessments, flexible change management, and adaptive technologies are all important enablers of program alignment, they are not a substitute for a strong governance foundation that keeps the program anchored to business priorities and risk appetite over time.

314. An organization has recently updated its business strategy and risk appetite, and wants to ensure that its information security program is aligned with these changes. Which of the following is the MOST important action to take?
a. conducting a gap analysis between the current program and industry best practices
b. reviewing and updating the program's policies, procedures, and controls based on the new business context
c. implementing new security technologies and tools to address emerging threats and vulnerabilities
d. providing additional training and resources to the information security team to improve their skills and knowledge

Answer: b. reviewing and updating the program's policies, procedures, and controls based on the new business context. Explanation: When an organization's business strategy and risk appetite undergo significant changes, it's essential to revisit and realign the information security program to ensure it remains relevant, effective, and supportive of the new objectives and priorities. This requires a comprehensive review and update of the program's foundational elements, such as its policies, procedures, standards, guidelines, and controls, to reflect the revised business context and risk parameters. The review should involve a close examination of how the changes in strategy and risk appetite impact the organization's critical assets, processes, and relationships, as well as its regulatory and contractual obligations. Policies and procedures may need to be modified to accommodate new business initiatives, technologies, or partnerships, while still maintaining an appropriate level of security and compliance. Controls may need to be strengthened, relaxed, or re-prioritized based on the updated risk assessment and treatment plan. While gap analyses, technology investments, and team training can all help improve the program's maturity and effectiveness, they should be driven by a clear understanding of the new business and risk environment, not conducted in isolation. The key is to proactively adapt the program to align with the organization's changing needs and expectations.

315. Which of the following is the MOST important benefit of aligning an information security program with business goals and risk appetite?
a. reducing the overall cost and complexity of the program by eliminating unnecessary controls and processes
b. improving the program's ability to prevent and detect all possible security incidents and breaches
c. enhancing the program's credibility and influence among business stakeholders by demonstrating its strategic value
d. increasing the program's budget and resources by showcasing its technical sophistication and expertise

Answer: c. enhancing the program's credibility and influence among business stakeholders by demonstrating its strategic value. Explanation: The primary advantage of closely aligning an information security program with an organization's business objectives and risk appetite is the increased visibility, trust, and support the program can gain from key stakeholders across the enterprise. When the program is able to clearly articulate and demonstrate how it enables and protects the organization's most critical assets, processes, and goals, it is more likely to be seen as a strategic partner and value driver, rather than a cost center or compliance burden. By speaking the language of business risk and performance, the program can build credibility and influence among senior leaders, board members, and business unit managers. This, in turn, can lead to greater buy-in and collaboration for security initiatives, as well as more informed and risk-based decision-making at all levels of the organization. While cost optimization, breach prevention, and resource allocation are all important considerations for an information security program, they are ultimately dependent on the program's ability to establish its relevance and worth to the business. Alignment is the foundation for effectiveness, efficiency, and impact.

316. An organization's information security program has been aligned with its business objectives and risk appetite for several years, but recent changes in the market and regulatory environment have created new challenges and opportunities. Which of the following is the BEST approach for the program to adapt to these changes?
a. conducting a comprehensive overhaul of the program's policies, procedures, and controls to align with industry best practices
b. engaging with business stakeholders to understand the implications of the changes and update the program accordingly
c. investing in the latest security technologies and tools to address emerging threats and compliance requirements
d. outsourcing the program to a third-party provider with expertise in the new market and regulatory landscape

Answer: b. engaging with business stakeholders to understand the implications of the changes and update the program accordingly. Explanation: When faced with significant changes in the external environment, such as new market dynamics, competitive pressures, or regulatory requirements, an information security program must be able to quickly and effectively adapt its strategies, priorities, and activities to remain aligned with the organization's evolving needs and goals. The best way to do this is through proactive, ongoing engagement with business stakeholders to understand the nature and impact of the changes on the organization's objectives, risks, and constraints. This involves regular dialogues and collaborations with senior leaders, business unit managers, legal and compliance teams, and other key functions to gather insights and perspectives on the new challenges and opportunities facing the organization. These engagements should inform a targeted review and update of the program's policies, procedures, controls, and metrics to ensure they remain relevant and effective in the new context. While benchmarking against industry practices, acquiring new technologies, and leveraging external expertise can all be valuable inputs to the program's adaptation process, they should be driven by a clear understanding of the specific business implications and priorities arising from the environmental changes. The key is to maintain a tight feedback loop between the program and the business to enable continuous alignment and optimization.

317. Which of the following metrics is MOST useful for demonstrating the alignment of an information security program with business goals and risk appetite?
a. the number of security incidents and breaches prevented or detected by the program
b. the percentage of systems and applications that have been patched and updated to the latest versions
c. the level of compliance with relevant security standards and regulations, as measured by audit results
d. the reduction in overall business risk exposure and potential impact, as assessed by senior stakeholders

Answer: d. the reduction in overall business risk exposure and potential impact, as assessed by senior stakeholders. Explanation: To effectively measure and communicate the alignment of an information security program with an organization's business objectives and risk appetite, it's essential to use metrics that are meaningful and relevant to senior business stakeholders. While technical measures such as the number of incidents prevented, systems patched, or compliance gaps closed can provide useful insights into the program's operational effectiveness and efficiency, they don't necessarily translate into tangible business outcomes or risk reduction. The most compelling metric for demonstrating the program's strategic value and alignment is the degree to which it has helped to mitigate the organization's overall risk exposure and potential impact, as perceived and validated by senior leaders and decision-makers. This can be assessed through regular surveys, interviews, and workshops with executives and board members to gather their qualitative and quantitative feedback on how well the program is supporting the organization's risk management goals and risk appetite. By tracking and reporting on this senior stakeholder assessment over time, the program can show a clear and direct link between its activities and the organization's risk posture and business performance. This, in turn, can help build trust, credibility, and support for the program among the organization's top leaders and influencers.

318. An organization is establishing a governance structure for its information security program. Which of the following is the MOST important role of the board of directors in this structure?
a. approving the detailed technical implementation of security controls and technologies

b. providing strategic oversight and guidance to ensure alignment with business objectives and risk appetite
c. conducting regular vulnerability assessments and penetration tests to identify security weaknesses
d. developing and enforcing specific security policies, procedures, and standards for the organization

Answer: b. providing strategic oversight and guidance to ensure alignment with business objectives and risk appetite. Explanation: The primary responsibility of the board of directors in the governance of an information security program is to provide high-level strategic direction, oversight, and accountability to ensure that the program is aligned with and supportive of the organization's overall business goals, risk management priorities, and risk appetite. This involves setting clear expectations and priorities for the program, approving the program's budget and resource allocation, monitoring the program's performance and effectiveness, and ensuring that significant risks and issues are being appropriately managed and escalated. The board should not be involved in the detailed technical implementation or operational management of the program, but rather should focus on the strategic questions of whether the program is adequately protecting the organization's critical assets and enabling its key objectives. Regular interaction and reporting between the board and the senior information security leadership is essential for maintaining this strategic alignment and oversight.

319. Which of the following is the MOST important characteristic of an effective information security steering committee?
a. it is composed primarily of technical security experts and IT managers
b. it meets infrequently, only when major security incidents or decisions arise
c. it has representation from key business functions and senior management
d. it has decision-making authority over all aspects of the security program budget and resources

Answer: c. it has representation from key business functions and senior management. Explanation: An information security steering committee is a critical component of an organization's security program governance structure, providing cross-functional oversight, guidance, and decision-making to ensure that the program is aligned with and accountable to the needs of the business. To be effective in this role, the committee must include representatives from the major business units, as well as senior executives with the authority to make strategic decisions and commit resources. This diverse membership ensures that the committee has a comprehensive understanding of the organization's risks, priorities, and constraints, and can provide informed direction and support for the security program. While technical security and IT leaders should certainly be included, they should not dominate the committee, as its focus should be on business risk management rather than technical implementation details. Regular, frequent meetings are also important for maintaining the committee's engagement and responsiveness, rather than convening only for crises or major decisions. The committee's authority should be focused on strategic governance matters, such as approving program plans, policies, and budgets, rather than operational security management.

320. In the context of information security program governance, what is the PRIMARY purpose of a security charter or mandate?
a. to define the specific technical controls and countermeasures to be implemented by the program
b. to establish the roles, responsibilities, and authority of the security function within the organization
c. to identify the individuals who will be held accountable for security incidents and breaches
d. to document the results of the organization's most recent security risk assessment and audit

Answer: b. to establish the roles, responsibilities, and authority of the security function within the organization. Explanation: A security charter or mandate is a foundational document in the governance of an information security program, serving to formally define and legitimize the purpose, scope, and authority of the security function within the organization. It articulates the mission and objectives of the security program, the roles and responsibilities of key security positions and committees, the reporting and accountability lines for security matters, and the high-level policies and principles that guide security decision-making. The charter is typically approved by senior leadership and the board of directors, providing the security team with the necessary organizational standing and empowerment to carry out its duties effectively. It helps to clarify the relationship and boundaries between the security function and other parts of the organization, and serves as a reference point for communicating and enforcing security expectations and requirements. While the charter may reference high-level control objectives or risk management principles, it does not typically include detailed technical specifications or assessment results, as these are covered in separate documents.

321. Which of the following is the BEST way to ensure that an organization's information security policies and standards remain current and relevant over time?
a. reviewing and updating them annually, regardless of changes in the business or technology environment
b. relying on automated policy management tools to identify and suggest necessary revisions
c. establishing a regular review cycle that includes input and validation from key business stakeholders
d. delegating responsibility for policy maintenance to the legal and compliance functions

Answer: c. establishing a regular review cycle that includes input and validation from key business stakeholders. Explanation: Information security policies and standards are critical governance mechanisms for establishing and communicating the organization's expectations, requirements, and guidelines for protecting its information assets. However, to remain effective and relevant, these documents must be regularly reviewed and updated to reflect changes in the organization's business objectives, risk environment, regulatory obligations, and technological landscape. The best way to ensure this ongoing alignment is to establish a formal review cycle that includes input and validation from key stakeholders across the organization, not just within the security function. This should involve representatives from business units, IT, legal, compliance, HR, and other relevant groups, who can provide diverse perspectives on the practical implications and feasibility of the policies and standards. The review process should be conducted at least annually, and more frequently if significant changes occur in the business or risk environment. Automated tools and templates can help streamline the process, but should not replace the need for human judgment and collaboration. Delegating policy maintenance to a single function, such as legal or compliance, can result in a narrow, siloed view that may not adequately reflect the broader needs and realities of the organization.

322. Which of the following is the MOST important factor to consider when determining the appropriate reporting and communication channels for an organization's information security program?
a. the technical complexity and sophistication of the security technologies and controls being used
b. the preferences and communication styles of the individual security team members and leaders
c. the existing organizational structure, culture, and decision-making processes
d. the frequency and severity of security incidents and breaches experienced by the organization

Answer: c. the existing organizational structure, culture, and decision-making processes. Explanation: Effective communication and reporting are essential for the success and credibility of an information security program, ensuring that relevant stakeholders are kept informed and engaged, and that important risks and issues are escalated and addressed in a timely manner. When designing the communication and reporting channels for the program, it's critical to consider the broader organizational context in which the program operates, including the formal hierarchy, lines of authority, and accountability, as well as the informal networks, norms, and expectations that shape how information flows and decisions are made. The program's communication and reporting mechanisms should be aligned with and leverage the organization's existing structures and processes, rather than creating separate or conflicting channels. This may involve using established management meetings, executive committees, and board reports to convey security updates and priorities, as well as tapping into cross-functional working groups, communities of practice, and social networks to build relationships and gather input. The specific technologies, personalities, and incidents involved in the program are less important than ensuring that the right people are getting the right information at the right time, in a way that is consistent with the organization's overall communication culture and decision-making style.

323. Which of the following is the PRIMARY role of information security policies in the governance of an information security program?
a. to provide detailed technical specifications for the implementation of security controls and countermeasures
b. to define the high-level principles, expectations, and requirements for protecting the organization's information assets
c. to assign specific roles and responsibilities to individual security team members and stakeholders
d. to document the results of security risk assessments, audits, and incident investigations

Answer: b. to define the high-level principles, expectations, and requirements for protecting the organization's information assets. Explanation: Information security policies are a critical component of the governance framework for an organization's security program, serving to articulate the strategic objectives, guiding principles, and mandatory requirements for safeguarding the confidentiality, integrity, and availability of the organization's information resources. Policies establish the foundational rules, standards, and guidelines that direct and constrain security-related decisions and behaviors across the organization, from high-level risk management strategies to day-to-day operational practices. They communicate the organization's security priorities, risk appetite, and compliance obligations, and provide a consistent reference point for aligning security efforts with business goals. While policies may assign general roles and responsibilities for policy implementation and enforcement, they typically do not include detailed technical specifications, audit results, or personnel assignments, which are addressed in separate procedures, plans, and job descriptions. The primary purpose of policies is to set the overall tone and direction for the security program, defining "what" needs to be done and "why," rather than prescribing "how" it should be done.

324. In the context of information security program governance, what is the main difference between policies, standards, and procedures?
a. policies are mandatory, while standards and procedures are optional
b. policies are technical, while standards and procedures are non-technical
c. policies are strategic, while standards and procedures are tactical and operational
d. policies apply to the entire organization, while standards and procedures apply only to the security team

Answer: c. policies are strategic, while standards and procedures are tactical and operational. Explanation: While policies, standards, and procedures are all important components of an information security program's governance framework, they serve distinct purposes and operate at different levels of detail and specificity. Policies are the highest-level governance documents, establishing the overall principles, objectives, and requirements for the security program. They are strategic in nature, focusing on the "what" and "why" of security, and are typically broad in scope, applying to the entire organization. Standards, on the other hand, are more specific and tactical, providing detailed criteria and guidelines for the consistent implementation of security controls across the organization. They define the "how" of security, often in technical terms, and may be mandatory or recommended, depending on the organization's risk appetite and compliance requirements. Procedures are the most detailed and operational level of documentation, describing the step-by-step processes and actions required to implement and maintain specific security controls or activities. They are typically focused on the day-to-day responsibilities of individual security team members or system owners. All three types of documents are important for effective security governance, but they have different levels of abstraction and granularity, and are intended for different audiences and purposes within the organization.

325. Which of the following is the MOST effective way to measure and report on the performance of an information security program to senior management and the board of directors?
a. focusing on technical metrics, such as the number of vulnerabilities patched or incidents detected
b. providing detailed descriptions of the specific security controls and technologies being implemented
c. highlighting the program's alignment with and impact on business objectives and risk management priorities
d. comparing the program's budget and resources to industry benchmarks and best practices

Answer: c. highlighting the program's alignment with and impact on business objectives and risk management priorities. Explanation: When communicating the performance and value of an information security program to senior leaders and the board, it's essential to focus on metrics and messages that are meaningful and relevant to their strategic priorities and concerns. While technical metrics, control descriptions, budget comparisons, and other operational details are important for managing the program internally, they often fail to resonate with executive audiences who are more interested in the big-picture implications of security for the business. The most effective way to engage and inform these stakeholders is to emphasize how the security program aligns with and supports the organization's overall strategy, risk management goals, and key performance indicators. This involves translating security metrics into business terms, such as the potential financial impact of cyber risks, the level of compliance with regulatory requirements, the degree of customer trust and satisfaction, or the ability to enable new digital initiatives. It also involves highlighting the program's contributions to critical business outcomes, such as reducing the likelihood and impact of disruptions, protecting intellectual property and competitive advantages, and strengthening organizational resilience. By framing security performance in the context of business objectives and risks, the program can demonstrate its strategic relevance and value, and build credibility and support among senior decision-makers.

326. Which of the following is the PRIMARY purpose of conducting regular information security audits and assessments as part of a program governance framework?
a. to identify and punish employees who are not complying with security policies and procedures
b. to provide evidence of the organization's compliance with legal and regulatory requirements
c. to evaluate the effectiveness of the security program and identify areas for improvement
d. to justify increases in the security program's budget and resources

Answer: c. to evaluate the effectiveness of the security program and identify areas for improvement. Explanation: Information security audits and assessments are important governance mechanisms for providing independent, objective evaluation and assurance of the design and operation of an organization's security controls, processes, and policies. The primary goal of these activities is to measure the effectiveness of the security program in achieving its stated objectives, managing risks to an acceptable level, and complying with relevant standards and requirements. By regularly examining the program's performance and identifying gaps, weaknesses, and opportunities for improvement, audits and assessments help to ensure that the program remains aligned with the organization's evolving business needs, risk landscape, and best practices. While audit results can certainly be used to demonstrate compliance, enforce accountability, and support resource requests, these are secondary benefits. The main purpose is to provide actionable insights and recommendations for continuously monitoring, adapting, and enhancing the security program over time, as part of a robust governance and risk management framework. Audits and assessments should be seen as constructive tools for learning and growth, rather than as punitive or purely compliance-driven exercises.

327. Which of the following is the MOST important factor to consider when determining the appropriate level of authority and independence for an organization's information security function?
a. the size and complexity of the organization's IT infrastructure and systems
b. the personal leadership style and preferences of the senior security executive or CISO
c. the organization's overall risk management philosophy and governance structure
d. the frequency and severity of security incidents and breaches experienced by the organization

Answer: c. the organization's overall risk management philosophy and governance structure. Explanation: The level of authority and independence granted to an organization's information security function should be primarily based on the organization's overarching approach to risk management and governance, rather than on technical, personal, or reactive factors. In organizations with a strong commitment to proactive, enterprise-wide risk management, the security function is typically positioned as a strategic partner and enabler, with a direct reporting line to senior leadership and the board, and with sufficient autonomy and resources to influence and enforce security policies and practices across the organization. This allows the security team to provide objective, unbiased advice and oversight, and to escalate important risks and issues without undue pressure or interference from other business or IT interests. In contrast, organizations with a more siloed, compliance-focused approach to risk management may view security as a technical or operational concern, buried within the IT department or with limited visibility and clout. The maturity and effectiveness of the organization's overall governance framework, including its risk appetite, decision-making processes, and accountability structures, should inform the appropriate level of empowerment and independence for the security function. Factors such as system complexity, leadership personalities, and past incidents can influence the specific tactics and priorities of the security team, but should not dictate its fundamental role and standing within the organization.

328. An organization is implementing a data loss prevention (DLP) solution to protect sensitive information from unauthorized disclosure. Which of the following is the MOST important consideration when selecting and configuring DLP controls?
a. the volume and velocity of data being processed and stored by the organization
b. the specific types and locations of sensitive data that need to be protected
c. the technical compatibility of the DLP solution with the organization's existing security tools
d. the preferences and user experience of employees and business partners

Answer: b. the specific types and locations of sensitive data that need to be protected. Explanation: The primary goal of a DLP solution is to identify, monitor, and control the movement and use of sensitive data across an organization's networks, systems, and applications. To be effective, DLP controls must be carefully aligned with the unique characteristics and requirements of the data they are meant to protect. This requires a clear understanding and classification of the different types of sensitive information that exist within the organization, such as personally identifiable information (PII), financial data, intellectual property, and regulated content. It also requires a comprehensive inventory and mapping of where this data resides, including databases, file shares, cloud services, and endpoints. With this information, the organization can define and implement DLP policies and rules that are tailored to the specific risks and workflows associated with each data type and location, ensuring that controls are appropriately granular and contextual. While factors such as data volume, technical integration, and user experience are important considerations for DLP deployment, they should be secondary to the fundamental alignment of controls with the organization's sensitive data landscape.

329. Which of the following is the BEST approach for ensuring that security controls remain effective and relevant over time?
a. implementing a diverse set of controls from multiple vendors and products
b. configuring controls to be as strict and restrictive as possible to minimize risk
c. establishing a continuous monitoring and improvement process for controls
d. relying on automated tools and artificial intelligence to adapt controls to changing threats

Answer: c. establishing a continuous monitoring and improvement process for controls. Explanation: Security controls are not set-and-forget mechanisms, but rather require ongoing monitoring, measurement, and adjustment to ensure that they remain aligned with the organization's evolving risks, requirements, and environment. A key principle of effective security control management is continuous improvement, which involves regularly assessing the performance and effectiveness of controls, identifying gaps and weaknesses, and implementing enhancements and updates as needed. This requires establishing a formal process and governance structure for control monitoring and optimization, including defining key performance indicators (KPIs), conducting periodic audits and assessments, analyzing security events and incidents, and gathering feedback from stakeholders. By institutionalizing this process, organizations can proactively identify and respond to changes in their threat landscape, technology stack, business processes, and regulatory obligations, and can ensure that their controls continue to provide the necessary level of protection and value over time. While a multi-layered control architecture, strict configurations, and automated tools can all contribute to control effectiveness, they are not a substitute for a systematic, data-driven approach to continuous monitoring and improvement.

330. An organization is implementing a privileged access management (PAM) solution to control and monitor the use of administrative accounts. Which of the following is the MOST important technical control to include in the PAM architecture?
a. multi-factor authentication for all privileged account access
b. detailed logging and reporting of privileged account activities
c. automatic provisioning and deprovisioning of privileged accounts
d. integration with the organization's identity and access management (IAM) system

Answer: a. multi-factor authentication for all privileged account access. Explanation: Privileged accounts, such as administrator, root, and service accounts, pose a significant risk to organizations due to their high levels of access and authority over critical systems and data. If compromised or misused, privileged accounts can enable attackers to steal sensitive information, disrupt operations, and cause widespread damage. Therefore, one of the most important technical controls for mitigating privileged access risk is strong authentication, specifically multi-factor authentication (MFA). MFA requires users to provide two or more distinct forms of identification, such as a password, a security token, and a biometric factor, before being granted access to a privileged account. This greatly reduces the risk of unauthorized access, even if a password is compromised or guessed. While logging, provisioning, and IAM integration are all important components of a comprehensive PAM solution, they are detective and supportive controls that do not directly prevent unauthorized access in the same way that MFA does. MFA is a crucial preventive control that should be a foundational element of any PAM architecture, providing a strong first line of defense against privilege misuse and compromise.

331. Which of the following is the PRIMARY benefit of implementing a security information and event management (SIEM) system?
a. preventing security incidents and breaches from occurring
b. providing a centralized view and analysis of security data from multiple sources
c. automating the enforcement of security policies and controls across the organization
d. replacing the need for other security monitoring and detection tools

Answer: b. providing a centralized view and analysis of security data from multiple sources. Explanation: A SIEM system is a critical tool for security monitoring, threat detection, and incident response, allowing organizations to collect, aggregate, and analyze large volumes of security-related data from diverse sources, such as network devices, servers, applications, and security controls. The primary value of a SIEM is its ability to provide a unified, real-time view of an organization's security posture, enabling security teams to quickly identify and investigate potential threats and anomalies that may be hidden in disparate log files and alerts. By correlating and contextualizing data from multiple sources, a SIEM can help detect patterns and relationships that indicate malicious activity, such as failed login attempts across multiple systems or unusual traffic flows between network segments. This centralized visibility and intelligence enables organizations to prioritize and respond to security events more efficiently and effectively, reducing the time and impact of incidents. While a SIEM can support policy enforcement and incident prevention by providing actionable insights, it is primarily a detective and investigative tool, not a preventive or automated control. It also does not replace the need for other specialized security tools, but rather integrates and enhances their value by providing a holistic, cross-functional view of security data.

332. An organization is implementing a web application firewall (WAF) to protect its e-commerce platform from common web-based attacks. Which of the following is the MOST important consideration when configuring WAF rules and policies?
a. blocking all traffic from countries and regions that are known sources of web-based attacks
b. aligning rules and policies with the specific application architecture and business logic
c. configuring the WAF to inspect and filter all incoming and outgoing web traffic
d. enabling all available WAF rules and signatures to provide maximum protection

Answer: b. aligning rules and policies with the specific application architecture and business logic. Explanation: A WAF is a specialized security control that sits in front of web applications and monitors, filters, and blocks potentially malicious HTTP/HTTPS traffic, such as SQL injection, cross-site scripting (XSS), and other common web-based attacks. To be effective, WAF rules and policies must be carefully tuned and customized to the unique characteristics and requirements of the specific web application being protected. This involves a deep understanding of the application's architecture, functionality, and business logic, including its URL structure, input fields, cookies, and other application-specific elements. Generic or overly broad WAF rules can result in false positives, blocking legitimate traffic and disrupting user experience. Overly permissive rules can result in false negatives, allowing attacks to slip through. The key is to strike a balance between security and usability by defining granular, context-aware rules that are aligned with the expected behavior and risk profile of the application. While IP-based geoblocking, full traffic inspection, and comprehensive rule sets can be useful in certain scenarios, they should be applied judiciously based on the specific needs and constraints of the application, rather than as one-size-fits-all solutions.

333. Which of the following is the BEST approach for integrating security controls into an organization's software development lifecycle (SDLC)?
a. conducting security testing and code review only after the application has been fully developed
b. outsourcing all security-related aspects of the SDLC to a third-party service provider
c. implementing security controls and practices at every stage of the SDLC, from requirements to deployment
d. relying on developers to incorporate security best practices into their coding without additional oversight

Answer: c. implementing security controls and practices at every stage of the SDLC, from requirements to deployment. Explanation: Integrating security into the SDLC is a critical aspect of building secure software and minimizing the risk of vulnerabilities and defects. The most effective approach is to embed security controls and practices throughout the entire SDLC, from the earliest stages of planning and design to the final stages of testing and deployment. This means incorporating security requirements and risk assessments into the initial project scoping and specification, designing security architecture and controls into the application structure and logic, performing secure coding and code review during the development phase, conducting comprehensive security testing and vulnerability scans before release, and implementing secure configuration and deployment processes. By making security an integral part of every stage of the SDLC, organizations can identify and mitigate risks early and often, when they are less costly and disruptive to fix. Waiting until the end of the development process to address security, outsourcing security responsibilities, or relying solely on developer discretion are all reactive and insufficient approaches that can lead to significant security gaps and technical debt. A proactive, integrated approach to secure software development requires a combination of people, processes, and tools working together seamlessly across the SDLC.

334. An organization is implementing data encryption to protect sensitive information both at rest and in transit. Which of the following is the MOST important factor to consider when selecting an encryption algorithm and key management approach?
a. the processing power and storage capacity of the systems that will be performing the encryption
b. the preferences and familiarity of the IT and security teams with specific encryption technologies
c. the level of security and assurance provided by the encryption algorithm and key management standards
d. the cost and licensing model of the encryption software and hardware components

Answer: c. the level of security and assurance provided by the encryption algorithm and key management standards. Explanation: Encryption is a fundamental security control for protecting the confidentiality and integrity of sensitive data, both when it is stored (at rest) and when it is transmitted (in transit). The effectiveness of encryption depends on the strength and reliability of the underlying cryptographic algorithms and key management practices used. When selecting an encryption approach, the most critical consideration is the level of security and assurance provided by the specific algorithms and standards chosen. This means evaluating the cryptographic strength, computational complexity, and attack resistance of different encryption algorithms, such as AES, RSA, and elliptic curve cryptography, based on their key sizes, mathematical properties, and public scrutiny. It also means assessing the robustness and trustworthiness of the key management practices, such as key generation, distribution, storage, rotation, and revocation, based on established standards and best practices, such as NIST SP 800-57. Factors such as system performance, team familiarity, and solution cost are important practical considerations, but they should not override the fundamental security and assurance requirements for protecting sensitive data. The goal is to select encryption and key management approaches that are well-vetted, widely-accepted, and appropriately strong for the organization's specific data protection needs and risk tolerance.

335. Which of the following is the PRIMARY reason for implementing network segmentation as a security control?
a. to improve network performance and reduce latency between different parts of the network
b. to limit the potential impact and scope of a security breach or compromise
c. to simplify network administration and management tasks for IT staff
d. to ensure compliance with industry-specific security standards and regulations

Answer: b. to limit the potential impact and scope of a security breach or compromise. Explanation: Network segmentation is a security architecture and control strategy that involves dividing a network into smaller, isolated sub-networks or zones based on different security levels, business functions, or trust boundaries. The primary goal of segmentation is to contain and minimize the blast radius of a potential security incident, such as a malware outbreak, data breach, or insider attack. By separating critical assets, sensitive data, and high-risk systems into different network segments with strict access controls and monitoring, organizations can prevent attackers from easily moving laterally across the network and escalating their privileges. Segmentation also helps to enforce the principle of least privilege, ensuring that users and systems can only access the specific resources and services they need to perform their roles, rather than having broad, unrestricted access to the entire network. While segmentation can have secondary benefits for network performance, management efficiency, and compliance, these are not the main drivers for its use as a security control. The fundamental value of segmentation lies in its ability to compartmentalize and isolate security risks, reducing the overall attack surface and impact of compromise.

336. Which of the following is the MOST effective way to ensure that security controls are properly implemented and operating as intended?
a. relying on vendor documentation and product specifications to validate control effectiveness
b. conducting periodic vulnerability scans and penetration tests to identify control weaknesses
c. performing regular security audits and assessments using a risk-based approach
d. implementing automated security orchestration and response tools to monitor control behavior

Answer: c. performing regular security audits and assessments using a risk-based approach. Explanation: Verifying the proper implementation and operation of security controls is a critical aspect of security assurance and risk management. The most effective way to achieve this assurance is through a combination of regular security audits and assessments that systematically evaluate the design, deployment, and performance of controls against established standards, policies, and best practices. Audits and assessments should be conducted using a risk-based approach, focusing on the controls and systems that are most critical to the organization's security posture and business objectives. This involves a comprehensive review of control documentation, configurations, and outputs, as well as hands-on testing and observation of control behavior in real-world scenarios. Audits and assessments should be performed by qualified and objective personnel, either internally or through third-party services, to provide an independent and unbiased view of control effectiveness. While vendor documentation, vulnerability scans, and automated tools can provide useful inputs and insights for control validation, they are not sufficient on their own to ensure comprehensive and reliable assurance. Regular, risk-based audits and assessments are essential for identifying control gaps, weaknesses, and improvement opportunities, and for driving continuous enhancement of the organization's security posture.

337. An organization is selecting a suite of security controls to protect its cloud-based infrastructure and applications. Which of the following is the MOST important consideration when choosing cloud security controls?

a. the geographic location and data residency requirements of the cloud service provider
b. the specific shared responsibility model and security capabilities of the cloud platform
c. the brand reputation and market share of the cloud security vendor or product
d. the compatibility and integration of the cloud security controls with on-premises systems

Answer: b. the specific shared responsibility model and security capabilities of the cloud platform. Explanation: When implementing security controls in a cloud computing environment, it's essential to understand and align with the unique security responsibilities and capabilities of the specific cloud platform being used. Cloud security operates under a shared responsibility model, where the cloud service provider (CSP) is responsible for securing the underlying infrastructure and services, while the customer is responsible for securing their own data, applications, and access. The exact delineation of responsibilities varies depending on the cloud service model (IaaS, PaaS, SaaS) and the specific CSP's terms and conditions. Therefore, when selecting cloud security controls, organizations must carefully consider the native security features and services offered by the CSP, such as identity and access management, encryption, logging, and monitoring, and how they can be leveraged and extended to meet the organization's specific security requirements. Controls should be chosen and configured to complement and integrate with the CSP's security capabilities, rather than duplicate or conflict with them. Factors such as data location, vendor reputation, and on-premises compatibility are important, but secondary to the fundamental alignment with the CSP's shared responsibility model and platform security architecture.

338. An organization is developing a comprehensive security control framework to protect its information assets. Which of the following is an example of a technical security control?
a. conducting background checks on new employees
b. implementing multi-factor authentication for system access
c. providing security awareness training to all staff
d. restricting physical access to the data center

Answer: b. implementing multi-factor authentication for system access. Explanation: Technical security controls are safeguards that are implemented using technology to protect the confidentiality, integrity, and availability of information systems and data. Examples include firewalls, intrusion detection systems, encryption, and access controls. Multi-factor authentication, which requires users to provide two or more forms of identification (such as a password and a fingerprint) to gain system access, is a strong technical control for preventing unauthorized access. Background checks, security training, and physical access restrictions are important, but they are considered administrative and physical controls, respectively, rather than technical controls.

339. Which of the following is the PRIMARY objective of administrative security controls?
a. to prevent unauthorized physical access to sensitive facilities and equipment
b. to define and enforce policies, procedures, and guidelines for secure behavior
c. to detect and respond to security incidents and breaches in real-time
d. to implement technical safeguards such as firewalls and encryption

Answer: b. to define and enforce policies, procedures, and guidelines for secure behavior. Explanation: Administrative security controls, also known as management controls, are focused on establishing the policies, procedures, standards, and guidelines that govern secure practices within an organization. These controls define the rules and expectations for acceptable use of systems, handling of sensitive data, incident reporting, and other security-related behaviors. Examples include security policies, risk assessments, audits, and training programs. The primary goal of administrative controls is to provide a formal framework for managing and enforcing security in a consistent, organization-wide manner. They are distinct from technical controls, which use technology to enforce security, and physical controls, which secure tangible assets and facilities. While administrative controls can guide incident response and other security processes, their main objective is to prevent security issues by defining and regulating secure conduct.

340. An organization is implementing security controls to protect its sensitive data from insider threats. Which of the following is the BEST example of a preventive administrative control for mitigating insider risk?
a. monitoring employee system activity and access patterns for anomalies
b. encrypting sensitive data both at rest and in transit
c. conducting regular security awareness training for all staff
d. performing background checks and security clearances for new hires

Answer: d. performing background checks and security clearances for new hires. Explanation: Insider threats, which involve malicious or negligent actions by employees and other trusted insiders, are a significant risk to organizations' sensitive data. One of the most effective ways to prevent insider incidents is through rigorous screening and vetting of personnel, especially those with access to critical systems and data. Background checks and security clearances are preventive administrative controls that help organizations identify and filter out individuals with criminal histories, financial problems, or other risk factors that could make them more likely to steal or misuse data. By carefully evaluating the trustworthiness and reliability of new hires and periodically re-screening existing staff, organizations can reduce the likelihood of insider breaches. While monitoring, encryption, and training are all important controls for detecting, protecting, and educating against insider threats, they are detective, technical, and corrective controls, respectively, rather than preventive administrative measures. Pre-employment screening is a proactive, policy-based control that addresses insider risk at its source.

341. Which of the following is the PRIMARY advantage of technical security controls over administrative and physical controls?
a. they are more cost-effective and easier to implement than other types of controls
b. they can automatically prevent, detect, and respond to security incidents without human intervention
c. they provide a visible deterrent to potential attackers and malicious insiders
d. they are more reliable and effective than human-based controls

Answer: b. they can automatically prevent, detect, and respond to security incidents without human intervention. Explanation: The primary benefit of technical security controls is their ability to enforce security policies and rules consistently and continuously, without relying on human judgment, awareness, or action. Technical controls such as firewalls, intrusion prevention systems, and access control mechanisms can automatically block unauthorized traffic, detect and alert on suspicious activity, and terminate malicious processes or sessions in real-time. This allows organizations to maintain a strong security posture even in the face of complex, fast-moving threats and large-scale, distributed environments. In contrast, administrative controls rely on human understanding and compliance with policies and procedures, which can be inconsistent or error-prone. Physical controls provide a visible deterrent and protect physical assets, but cannot prevent or detect logical attacks. While technical controls can be costly and complex to implement, they are generally more scalable, reliable, and responsive than manual controls. However, the most effective security programs use a combination of administrative, technical, and physical controls in a layered, defense-in-depth approach.

342. An organization is classifying its security controls based on their function and purpose. Which of the following is the BEST example of a detective technical control?
a. a firewall that blocks unauthorized network traffic based on predefined rules
b. an intrusion detection system that monitors network activity for signs of malicious behavior
c. an access control system that requires users to authenticate with a smart card and PIN
d. an encryption system that scrambles sensitive data to prevent unauthorized access

Answer: b. an intrusion detection system that monitors network activity for signs of malicious behavior. Explanation: Detective controls are designed to identify and alert on security incidents or policy violations that have already occurred or are in progress. They provide visibility into the organization's security posture and enable timely response and investigation. Intrusion detection systems (IDS) are a prime example of detective technical controls. They continuously monitor network traffic and system activity, looking for patterns or signatures that indicate potential attacks, compromises, or anomalies. When a suspicious event is detected, the IDS generates an alert for security staff to investigate and respond. Firewalls and access controls are preventive controls that aim to stop unauthorized activity before it occurs, while encryption is a corrective control that protects data from being accessed or used improperly. Detective controls like IDS complement preventive and corrective measures by providing a means of identifying and reacting to security issues that have evaded or bypassed other defenses.

343. An organization is implementing security controls to protect its physical assets and facilities. Which of the following is the BEST example of a corrective physical control?
a. security guards who patrol the premises and monitor surveillance cameras
b. fire suppression systems that automatically extinguish fires in the data center
c. badges and access cards that restrict entry to authorized personnel only
d. fences and barriers that deter intruders and prevent unauthorized access

Answer: b. fire suppression systems that automatically extinguish fires in the data center. Explanation: Corrective controls are designed to minimize the impact and damage of security incidents or disasters that have already occurred. They help organizations recover from and restore normal operations after an adverse event. In the context of physical security, fire suppression systems are a key example of corrective controls. These systems, which include sprinklers, gas discharge, and other mechanisms, automatically detect and extinguish fires in critical facilities like data centers, limiting the spread of damage and allowing for swift recovery. While security guards, access cards, and fences are important physical controls, they are primarily preventive in nature, seeking to deter and block unauthorized access to facilities. Fire suppression is a reactive control that kicks in after a fire has started, to minimize its impact. Other examples of corrective physical controls include backup power generators, disaster recovery sites, and incident response teams. These controls are essential for organizational resilience and continuity in the face of physical disruptions.

344. An organization is reviewing its security controls to identify gaps and overlaps. Which of the following is an example of a control that fulfills both preventive and detective functions?
a. security information and event management (SIEM) system
b. data loss prevention (DLP) solution
c. security awareness training program
d. backup and disaster recovery plan

Answer: b. data loss prevention (DLP) solution. Explanation: While many security controls are designed to serve a single primary function (preventive, detective, corrective), some controls can fulfill multiple roles simultaneously. Data loss prevention (DLP) solutions are a prime example of a control that provides both preventive and detective capabilities. DLP tools monitor and analyze data in use, in motion, and at rest across an organization's networks, endpoints, and storage systems. They use predefined policies and rules to identify sensitive or regulated data and to detect and prevent unauthorized or suspicious data access, transfer, or exfiltration attempts. The preventive function of DLP is to block risky data actions before they can result in a breach or compliance violation. The detective function is to generate alerts and reports on data usage patterns and anomalies for further investigation. SIEM systems are primarily detective, while training programs and backup plans are preventive and corrective, respectively. By combining preventive and detective features, DLP provides a more comprehensive and proactive approach to data protection than single-function controls.

345. Which of the following is the MOST important consideration when selecting and implementing administrative security controls?
a. the technical compatibility and interoperability of the controls with existing systems
b. the alignment of the controls with the organization's culture, values, and risk tolerance

c. the initial and ongoing costs of implementing and maintaining the controls
d. the availability of skilled personnel to operate and manage the controls

Answer: b. the alignment of the controls with the organization's culture, values, and risk tolerance. Explanation: Administrative security controls are the policies, procedures, standards, and guidelines that define and govern secure behavior within an organization. To be effective, these controls must be carefully tailored to the specific needs, goals, and characteristics of the organization and its people. The most critical factor in selecting and implementing administrative controls is ensuring that they align with the organization's culture, values, and risk tolerance. Controls that are overly restrictive, burdensome, or incompatible with the way people work are likely to be resisted, circumvented, or ignored, undermining their intended purpose. On the other hand, controls that are too lax or misaligned with the organization's risk appetite may fail to provide adequate protection or compliance. Effective administrative controls strike a balance between security and usability, and are designed with the organization's unique context and priorities in mind. While technical compatibility, cost, and personnel considerations are certainly important, they are secondary to the fundamental alignment of controls with the human and organizational factors that drive behavior and risk.

346. Which of the following is the PRIMARY reason why administrative security controls are often considered the foundation of an organization's security program?
a. they are the easiest and least expensive type of control to implement and maintain
b. they provide the policies and procedures that guide the implementation of all other controls
c. they are the most effective type of control for preventing and detecting security incidents
d. they are required by law and industry regulations for most organizations

Answer: b. they provide the policies and procedures that guide the implementation of all other controls. Explanation: Administrative security controls, also known as management controls, are often considered the bedrock of an organization's security program because they establish the overarching framework and direction for all other security efforts. Administrative controls include the high-level policies, standards, guidelines, and procedures that define the organization's security objectives, risk appetite, roles and responsibilities, and expected behaviors. They provide the strategic and governance foundation upon which technical and physical controls are selected, implemented, and operated. Without clear and comprehensive administrative controls, an organization's security posture can become fragmented, inconsistent, and misaligned with its overall goals and risk management priorities. Effective administrative controls ensure that security is approached in a holistic, coordinated, and risk-based manner across the entire organization. While administrative controls are not always the easiest, cheapest, or most directly effective type of control, they are essential for creating a coherent and sustainable security program that enables an organization to achieve its mission while managing risk to acceptable levels.

347. Which of the following BEST describes the relationship between administrative, technical, and physical security controls?
a. they are independent and distinct categories that should be implemented separately
b. they are hierarchical, with administrative controls directing technical controls and technical controls directing physical controls
c. they are complementary and interdependent, working together to provide layered security
d. they are interchangeable and redundant, providing the same types of protection

Answer: c. they are complementary and interdependent, working together to provide layered security. Explanation: Administrative, technical, and physical security controls are not isolated or competing categories, but rather mutually reinforcing and synergistic components of a comprehensive, defense-in-depth security strategy. Each type of control plays a unique and critical role in protecting an organization's assets, systems, and data, but they are most effective when used in combination and coordination with one another. Administrative controls provide the policies, procedures, and management oversight that guide the selection, implementation, and operation of technical and physical controls. Technical controls provide the automated mechanisms and safeguards that enforce administrative policies and protect against cyber threats. Physical controls provide the tangible barriers and monitoring that secure facilities, equipment, and personnel from physical threats. Together, these controls create multiple layers of protection that compensate for the weaknesses and gaps of any single control type. For example, a strong password policy (administrative) is more effective when combined with multi-factor authentication (technical) and physical access restrictions to sensitive areas. This principle of layered, multidimensional security is essential for defending against the wide range of threats facing modern organizations.

348. An organization is selecting security controls to mitigate the risk of data breaches. Which of the following is the MOST important factor to consider in the selection process?
a. the cost and complexity of implementing and maintaining the controls
b. the alignment of the controls with industry best practices and standards
c. the effectiveness of the controls in addressing the specific threats and vulnerabilities facing the organization
d. the popularity and market share of the vendors offering the control solutions

Answer: c. the effectiveness of the controls in addressing the specific threats and vulnerabilities facing the organization. Explanation: When selecting security controls, the most critical consideration is how well the controls mitigate the unique risks facing the organization. Controls should be chosen based on a thorough understanding of the organization's threat landscape, attack surface, and vulnerability profile, as identified through risk assessments and threat intelligence. The goal is to prioritize controls that provide the greatest risk reduction and business value, targeting the most likely and impactful threats and weaknesses. While factors such as cost, complexity, compliance, and vendor reputation are important, they should be secondary to the fundamental alignment of controls with the organization's specific risk profile and security needs. A control that is inexpensive, popular, or standards-compliant may still be ineffective if it does not address the most relevant and pressing threats to the organization's assets and operations.

349. An organization is prioritizing the implementation of security controls based on risk. Which of the following should be the PRIMARY input to the prioritization process?
a. the expected cost and resource requirements for implementing each control
b. the results of vulnerability scans and penetration tests on the organization's systems
c. the level of risk associated with each control, as determined by a formal risk assessment
d. the availability and expertise of staff to manage and maintain each control

Answer: c. the level of risk associated with each control, as determined by a formal risk assessment. Explanation: Risk-based prioritization is a key principle of effective security control selection and implementation. It involves focusing resources and efforts on the controls that provide the greatest reduction in risk, based on a systematic assessment of the likelihood and impact of different threats and vulnerabilities. A formal risk assessment, which identifies, analyzes, and evaluates the organization's risk landscape, should be the primary driver for control prioritization. The assessment results, including risk scores, rankings, and treatment recommendations, provide an objective and defensible basis for determining which controls are most critical and urgent to implement. While factors such as cost, feasibility, and staff availability are certainly important considerations, they should be evaluated in the context of the risk assessment findings, not as independent or primary drivers. Vulnerability scans and penetration tests can provide valuable input to the risk assessment process, but they alone do not provide a comprehensive or prioritized view of risk. The key is to use risk assessment as the central framework for making informed, risk-based decisions about control selection and implementation.

350. An organization has identified a set of potential security controls to implement, but has limited budget and resources. Which of the following is the BEST approach for prioritizing the controls?
a. implementing the controls that are least expensive and easiest to deploy, regardless of their risk impact

b. focusing on controls that address the threats and vulnerabilities with the highest likelihood of occurrence
c. prioritizing controls that mitigate the risks with the greatest potential impact to the organization
d. selecting controls that balance risk reduction with cost and feasibility, based on a risk-benefit analysis

Answer: d. selecting controls that balance risk reduction with cost and feasibility, based on a risk-benefit analysis. Explanation: In situations where resources are constrained, it's important to prioritize security controls based on a careful analysis of their costs, benefits, and risks. A risk-benefit analysis is a systematic approach for evaluating and comparing the expected risk reduction of each control against its total cost of ownership and operational feasibility. This involves quantifying factors such as the likelihood and impact of the risks addressed by each control, the upfront and ongoing costs of implementation and maintenance, the availability of necessary skills and tools, and the potential disruption to business processes. By weighing these factors, organizations can identify the controls that provide the greatest risk reduction per unit of cost and effort, optimizing the allocation of limited resources. Simply selecting the cheapest or easiest controls, or focusing solely on likelihood or impact, can lead to suboptimal risk management decisions. A balanced, risk-benefit approach ensures that the organization is getting the most value and protection from its security investments.

351. An organization is implementing security controls to comply with a new industry regulation. Which of the following is the MOST important consideration when selecting the controls?
a. the specific requirements and standards mandated by the regulation
b. the level of risk associated with non-compliance, as determined by a risk assessment
c. the availability of pre-built, regulation-specific control templates from vendors
d. the existing security controls and practices already in place at the organization

Answer: a. the specific requirements and standards mandated by the regulation. Explanation: When the primary driver for implementing security controls is compliance with an industry regulation, the most critical factor to consider is the specific set of requirements and standards prescribed by the regulation itself. Regulations often have detailed and explicit criteria for the types of controls that must be in place, the level of protection they must provide, and the evidence needed to demonstrate compliance. Organizations should carefully review and interpret the regulatory text, guidance documents, and any applicable standards or frameworks referenced by the regulation. The goal is to ensure that the selected controls fully align with and satisfy the letter and spirit of the regulatory requirements, minimizing the risk of non-compliance and penalties. While risk assessments, vendor templates, and existing controls can certainly inform and support the selection process, they should not override or substitute for the direct regulatory mandates. Compliance is about meeting a defined set of external expectations, not just managing internal risks or leveraging available solutions.

352. An organization is selecting security controls to protect against advanced persistent threats (APTs). Which of the following is the MOST important factor to consider?
a. the ability of the controls to prevent all possible attack vectors and entry points
b. the integration and interoperability of the controls with the organization's existing security tools
c. the level of visibility and context provided by the controls for detecting and responding to APT activity
d. the total cost and complexity of deploying and managing the controls across the organization

Answer: c. the level of visibility and context provided by the controls for detecting and responding to APT activity. Explanation: Advanced persistent threats (APTs) are highly sophisticated, targeted attacks that use stealthy and continuous techniques to gain and maintain unauthorized access to an organization's networks and systems. Given the complex and evolving nature of APTs, it is virtually impossible for any single control or combination of controls to completely prevent all possible attack vectors and entry points. Instead, the most critical capability for defending against APTs is the ability to quickly and accurately detect, investigate, and respond to APT activity at any stage of the attack lifecycle. This requires controls that provide deep, real-time visibility into the organization's environment, assets, and user and entity behavior. Controls should be able to collect, correlate, and analyze diverse security telemetry, providing contextual alerts and forensic evidence for identifying and scoping APT incidents. They should enable proactive threat hunting and rapid incident response workflows. While integration, cost, and coverage are important considerations, they are secondary to the fundamental need for controls that can help the organization detect, understand, and contain APTs before they can achieve their objectives.

353. An organization is prioritizing the implementation of security controls to protect its most critical assets. Which of the following is the BEST approach for identifying those critical assets?
a. conducting a vulnerability scan to identify the systems with the most technical weaknesses
b. reviewing the organization's inventory of hardware and software components
c. performing a business impact analysis to determine the assets most essential to the organization's mission and operations
d. surveying end-users to understand which assets they consider most important for their day-to-day work

Answer: c. performing a business impact analysis to determine the assets most essential to the organization's mission and operations. Explanation: To effectively prioritize security controls and investments, it's crucial to have a clear and comprehensive understanding of the organization's most critical assets—the systems, data, and processes that are essential to achieving its mission, delivering value, and maintaining competitive advantage. The best way to identify these assets is through a formal business impact analysis (BIA). A BIA is a systematic process for evaluating the potential consequences of a disruption to an organization's operations, reputation, and finances. It involves working closely with business stakeholders to map out and prioritize the organization's key products, services, and supporting infrastructure. Through workshops, interviews, and data analysis, the BIA determines the maximum tolerable downtime, recovery time objectives, and recovery point objectives for each critical asset, based on its importance to the organization's goals and legal/contractual obligations. The BIA results provide a risk-informed, business-driven basis for prioritizing assets and allocating security resources. While vulnerability scans, inventories, and user surveys can provide useful inputs, they do not capture the full business context and criticality of assets like a BIA does.

354. An organization has identified a set of high-priority security controls to implement, but is unsure of the most effective sequence and timeline for rolling them out. Which of the following is the BEST approach for developing an implementation plan?
a. deploying the controls that are fastest and easiest to implement first, to show quick progress and gain momentum
b. rolling out all the controls simultaneously to maximize efficiency and avoid gaps in coverage
c. starting with the controls that address the highest-likelihood threats, and then moving on to lower-likelihood threats
d. grouping the controls into logical phases based on dependencies, resources, and business impact, and then sequencing the phases

Answer: d. grouping the controls into logical phases based on dependencies, resources, and business impact, and then sequencing the phases. Explanation: Once an organization has prioritized a set of security controls to implement, the next step is to develop a rational and achievable plan for rolling them out. The most effective approach is to group the controls into logical phases or workstreams based on a variety of factors, and then sequence the phases in a way that optimizes the balance between risk reduction, resource utilization, and operational continuity. Factors to consider when grouping controls include technical dependencies (controls that rely on others being in place first), resource constraints (controls that compete for the same budget, skills, or tools), and business impact (controls that affect critical assets or processes). The goal is to create a set of coherent, manageable phases that can be implemented in a logical order, with each phase delivering incremental risk reduction and building towards the overall target state. Implementing the easiest controls first, or all controls at once, or solely based on likelihood, can lead to fragmented, inefficient, or disruptive rollouts that fail to optimize risk mitigation and business value over time. A phased, risk-informed approach provides a structured and adaptive way to implement controls in a complex and dynamic environment.

355. An organization is selecting security controls to protect its cloud-based assets and services. Which of the following is the MOST important factor to consider?
a. the geographic location and legal jurisdiction of the cloud data centers
b. the specific shared responsibility model and security capabilities of the cloud provider
c. the level of interoperability between the cloud controls and the organization's on-premises controls
d. the cost and pricing structure of the cloud security services and features

Answer: b. the specific shared responsibility model and security capabilities of the cloud provider. Explanation: When implementing security controls in a cloud environment, it's essential to understand and align with the unique security responsibilities and capabilities of the cloud service provider (CSP). Cloud security operates under a shared responsibility model, where the CSP is responsible for securing the underlying infrastructure and services, while the customer is responsible for securing their own data, applications, and access. The exact division of responsibilities varies depending on the cloud service model (IaaS, PaaS, SaaS) and the specific provider's terms and conditions. Therefore, when selecting cloud security controls, organizations must carefully consider what native security features and services are offered by the CSP, and how they can be leveraged and extended to meet the organization's specific security requirements. Controls should be chosen and configured to complement and integrate with the CSP's security capabilities, rather than duplicate or conflict with them. Factors such as data location, control interoperability, and pricing are important, but secondary to the fundamental alignment with the CSP's shared responsibility model and security architecture. The key is to design a cohesive, layered security approach that optimizes the combination of CSP and customer controls.

356. An organization is prioritizing the implementation of security controls based on a recent risk assessment. Which of the following should be the HIGHEST priority for control implementation?
a. risks with a low likelihood of occurrence but a high potential impact
b. risks that have been previously identified in past assessments but not yet remediated
c. risks that can be mitigated by low-cost, open-source security tools
d. risks with a high residual risk score after considering existing controls

Answer: d. risks with a high residual risk score after considering existing controls. Explanation: Risk assessments provide a structured and objective way to identify, analyze, and prioritize an organization's risk landscape. One of the key outputs of a risk assessment is a set of residual risk scores for each identified risk, which represent the remaining level of risk after considering the effectiveness of any existing controls. Residual risk scores are typically calculated by multiplying the likelihood and impact of each risk, and then subtracting the mitigating effect of current controls. Risks with high residual risk scores are those that pose the greatest threat to the organization, either because they are highly likely and impactful, or because they are not adequately covered by existing defenses. Therefore, when prioritizing control implementations based on a risk assessment, the highest priority should be given to addressing risks with high residual risk scores, as they represent the most significant and urgent gaps in the organization's security posture. Focusing solely on high-impact or low-cost or previously-identified risks may not provide the most risk reduction value if those risks are already well-controlled or unlikely to occur. The key is to target the risks that are most critical and unmitigated, based on a holistic and quantitative assessment of the current risk and control environment.

357. An organization is selecting security controls to protect against insider threats. Which of the following is the MOST important consideration?
a. the ability of the controls to completely prevent all insider threat activity
b. the level of integration between the controls and the organization's HR and legal processes
c. the balance between security and privacy struck by the controls for monitoring employee behavior
d. the cost and scalability of the controls for large and complex user populations

Answer: c. the balance between security and privacy struck by the controls for monitoring employee behavior. Explanation: Insider threats, which involve malicious or unintentional actions by trusted employees and partners, are a significant and growing risk to organizations. Insiders have valid access to sensitive systems and data, and their activity can be difficult to distinguish from legitimate work. To effectively mitigate insider threats, organizations must implement controls that provide visibility and context into user behavior, enabling the detection and investigation of suspicious or risky actions. However, these controls must be carefully designed and governed to strike an appropriate balance between security and privacy. Overly invasive or indiscriminate monitoring can violate employee privacy, damage morale and trust, and run afoul of legal and regulatory requirements. On the other hand, overly limited or selective monitoring can leave dangerous blind spots and fail to deter or detect insider misconduct. The most important consideration for insider threat controls is finding a middle ground that protects the organization's critical assets and interests while respecting the legitimate privacy expectations and rights of employees. This requires close collaboration with HR, legal, and ethics stakeholders to define clear, transparent, and proportional monitoring policies and procedures, and to implement controls with granular, risk-based targeting and strong access controls and oversight. The goal is not perfect prevention or total surveillance, but rather a nuanced, context-aware approach that balances security and privacy in a sustainable and defensible way.

358. An organization is implementing a data loss prevention (DLP) solution to protect sensitive information. Which of the following is the MOST important consideration when deploying DLP controls?
a. maximizing the volume and types of data scanned by the DLP system
b. tuning DLP policies and rules to balance security and business productivity
c. integrating the DLP system with as many other security tools as possible
d. achieving full coverage of all the organization's endpoints and cloud services from day one

Answer: b. tuning DLP policies and rules to balance security and business productivity. Explanation: While broad coverage, integration, and scalability are important factors for DLP success, the most critical aspect of implementation is carefully configuring the system's detection and enforcement rules to strike the right balance between data protection and business enablement. Overly broad or strict rules can generate excessive false positives, blocking legitimate data use and frustrating end users. Overly narrow or lax rules can miss real data leaks and fail to mitigate risk. Effective DLP deployment requires close collaboration with data owners and business process experts to define policies that reflect the organization's true data sensitivity, usage patterns, and risk appetite. Rules should be granular, contextual, and regularly tuned based on feedback and evolving needs.

359. Which of the following is the BEST way to test the effectiveness of security awareness training controls?
a. conducting a penetration test of the organization's network perimeter defenses
b. administering a multiple-choice quiz to all employees immediately after the training
c. performing a social engineering exercise to assess employee susceptibility to phishing attempts
d. monitoring security incident metrics for a reduction in human-caused breaches

Answer: c. performing a social engineering exercise to assess employee susceptibility to phishing attempts. Explanation: Security awareness training aims to educate employees about cybersecurity risks and best practices, with the goal of reducing human-related vulnerabilities. While quizzes and incident metrics can provide some indication of training effectiveness, the most direct and realistic way to assess whether employees have internalized and applied the lessons is through controlled social engineering tests. These involve sending simulated phishing emails or staging other pretexting scenarios to see how employees respond in real-world situations. A well-designed exercise will mimic common attack techniques, measure key behaviors (e.g., click rates, reporting rates), and provide targeted feedback and remediation. Penetration testing focuses on technical controls and does not directly assess human awareness and decision-making.

360. An organization has implemented a set of security controls based on a risk assessment. Which of the following is the MOST important next step?

a. conducting a penetration test to attempt to bypass or defeat the controls
b. documenting the controls in policies and procedures for auditors and regulators
c. performing a business impact analysis to prioritize the controls for ongoing maintenance
d. developing metrics and key risk indicators to measure the effectiveness of the controls over time

Answer: d. developing metrics and key risk indicators to measure the effectiveness of the controls over time. Explanation: Implementing security controls is not a one-time event, but rather an ongoing process of monitoring, measurement, and adjustment. To ensure that controls remain effective and aligned with the organization's risk posture over time, it's essential to establish a continuous feedback loop of metrics and indicators. This involves defining specific, measurable, and actionable criteria for each control, such as reduced incident counts, faster detection times, or lower vulnerability scores. By regularly collecting and analyzing this data, organizations can track the performance of controls, identify gaps and improvement opportunities, and make data-driven decisions about control optimization and investment. While penetration testing, documentation, and impact analysis are all valuable control management practices, they are point-in-time activities that do not provide the ongoing visibility and insight of a robust metrics program.

361. An organization is testing the efficacy of its security information and event management (SIEM) system. Which of the following is the BEST approach?
a. reviewing the SIEM system's out-of-the-box correlation rules and alerts
b. conducting a vulnerability scan of the SIEM system's underlying infrastructure
c. measuring the volume of raw event data ingested by the SIEM system per day
d. running a series of simulated attack scenarios and assessing the SIEM system's detection and response capabilities

Answer: d. running a series of simulated attack scenarios and assessing the SIEM system's detection and response capabilities. Explanation: A SIEM system's primary purpose is to detect and prioritize potential security incidents by collecting, aggregating, and analyzing log data from across an organization's environment. The most effective way to test a SIEM's efficacy is through realistic, end-to-end attack simulations that stress the system's ability to identify, correlate, and alert on malicious activity. These scenarios should be based on the organization's key threats and risk scenarios, and should span the full attack lifecycle from initial compromise to data exfiltration or destruction. By measuring the SIEM's performance in terms of true and false positives, alert prioritization, analyst workflow, and response times, organizations can validate that the system is properly tuned and providing the expected level of risk reduction. Simply reviewing static rules, scanning for vulnerabilities, or measuring data volume does not provide a true test of the SIEM's real-world detection and response capabilities.

362. An organization has deployed a set of endpoint detection and response (EDR) agents across its corporate laptops and desktops. Which of the following is the MOST important consideration when testing the EDR controls?
a. ensuring that the EDR agents do not cause any degradation in endpoint performance or user productivity
b. verifying that the EDR agents are properly collecting and forwarding endpoint telemetry to the central management console
c. validating that the EDR agents can detect and block a comprehensive set of known malware samples and behavioral indicators
d. checking that the EDR agents are configured according to the vendor's recommended best practices and templates

Answer: c. validating that the EDR agents can detect and block a comprehensive set of known malware samples and behavioral indicators. Explanation: The primary function of an EDR solution is to identify and contain threats on endpoints by continuously monitoring and analyzing system activity for signs of malicious behavior. When testing EDR controls, the most critical objective is to verify that the agents can effectively detect and block a wide range of known and unknown threats, including malware, fileless attacks, and living-off-the-land techniques. This involves executing a diverse set of malware samples and attack simulations on representative endpoints and measuring the EDR's ability to identify and disrupt the malicious activity in real-time. The test cases should span different threat vectors, tactics, and techniques, and should include both signature-based and behavioral detections. While factors such as performance overhead, telemetry collection, and vendor compliance are important, they are secondary to the core threat detection and response capabilities that ultimately determine the EDR's effectiveness in reducing endpoint risk.

363. An organization is implementing a privileged access management (PAM) solution to control and monitor the use of administrative accounts. Which of the following is the MOST important aspect to test during the PAM deployment?
a. the ability to automatically discover and onboard all privileged accounts across the organization
b. the granularity and flexibility of the PAM solution's role-based access control (RBAC) model
c. the security and redundancy of the PAM solution's underlying infrastructure and data stores
d. the end-to-end workflow for requesting, approving, and auditing privileged access sessions

Answer: d. the end-to-end workflow for requesting, approving, and auditing privileged access sessions. Explanation: A PAM solution's primary objective is to enforce least privilege and accountability for the use of sensitive administrative accounts. The most critical aspect to validate during PAM testing is the complete lifecycle of privileged access, from request to review. This includes verifying that users can easily request access through a self-service portal, that requests are routed to the appropriate approvers based on predefined policies, that approvals are properly documented and time-limited, that active sessions are monitored and recorded, and that post-session reviews are conducted to detect and investigate any anomalies or misuse. The testing should cover both routine and emergency access scenarios, and should involve a representative sample of privileged account types and use cases. While account discovery, RBAC design, and infrastructure security are important facets of PAM, they are foundational elements that support, but do not directly ensure, the core access control and auditing functions that PAM is meant to provide.

364. An organization has deployed a web application firewall (WAF) to protect its e-commerce site. Which of the following is the BEST way to test the WAF's effectiveness?
a. conducting a penetration test of the WAF infrastructure to identify any misconfigurations or vulnerabilities
b. scanning the web application for common OWASP Top 10 vulnerabilities before and after the WAF deployment
c. replaying a sample of real-world application traffic through the WAF and measuring the blocking rate
d. executing a series of targeted application-layer attacks and assessing the WAF's detection and prevention capabilities

Answer: d. executing a series of targeted application-layer attacks and assessing the WAF's detection and prevention capabilities. Explanation: A WAF's main purpose is to detect and block common web-based attacks, such as SQL injection, cross-site scripting (XSS), and session hijacking, before they reach the protected application. The most direct and comprehensive way to gauge a WAF's effectiveness is by subjecting it to a battery of realistic, application-specific attack payloads and techniques, and validating that the WAF correctly identifies and stops the malicious requests without blocking legitimate traffic. The test cases should be derived from the OWASP Top 10, but should be customized to the unique parameters, logic, and potential vulnerabilities of the particular application. They should span different HTTP methods, parameters, encodings, and evasion techniques. While penetration testing, vulnerability scanning, and traffic replay can provide useful insights, they do not fully exercise the WAF's core detection and blocking capabilities against actual attack patterns.

365. An organization is testing the secure configuration of its cloud-based virtual machine (VM) instances. Which of the following is the MOST important configuration setting to validate?
a. the allocation of sufficient CPU and memory resources to each VM instance
b. the application of the latest operating system and application patches to each VM instance
c. the restriction of network access to each VM instance based on the principle of least privilege
d. the encryption of data stored on each VM instance's virtual disks

Answer: c. the restriction of network access to each VM instance based on the principle of least privilege. Explanation: When deploying virtual machines in a cloud environment, one of the most critical security considerations is properly constraining their network connectivity to minimize the attack surface and lateral movement potential. Each VM should be configured with the minimum network access required for its specific function, using a combination of network security groups, firewalls, and access control lists. The default stance should be to deny all traffic, with rules only allowing specific source IPs, ports, and protocols as needed. This is particularly important for VMs hosting sensitive data or critical applications. During testing, the network access policies for each VM should be carefully reviewed and validated, both in terms of the configured rulesets and the actual observed traffic flows. Any overly broad or permissive access should be identified and remediated. While patching, resource allocation, and disk encryption are also important security controls, they are secondary to the fundamental network isolation and segmentation that is the first line of defense for cloud VMs.

366. An organization has implemented a comprehensive security awareness training program for its employees. Which of the following is the BEST way to measure the long-term effectiveness of the training?
a. comparing the number of security incidents caused by human error before and after the training
b. conducting periodic phishing simulations and tracking the click and reporting rates over time
c. administering annual knowledge assessments to test employees' understanding and retention of key concepts
d. monitoring the completion and attestation rates for the training modules across the organization

Answer: b. conducting periodic phishing simulations and tracking the click and reporting rates over time. Explanation: The ultimate goal of security awareness training is to change employee behaviors and reduce human-related risks to the organization. While knowledge assessments, completion tracking, and incident metrics can provide some indication of training impact, the most direct and meaningful way to gauge long-term effectiveness is through regular, real-world phishing tests. By sending simulated phishing emails to employees on an ongoing basis (e.g., monthly or quarterly), and measuring the percentage who click on malicious links or attachments and the percentage who report the emails to security, organizations can assess the actual, sustained impact of the training on two key behaviors: susceptibility to phishing and proactive reporting. Tracking these metrics over time, and comparing them to pre-training baselines and industry benchmarks, provides a quantitative, outcome-focused way to evaluate the training's efficacy and identify areas for improvement. It's important to view phishing tests not as a "gotcha" exercise, but as a way to reinforce and measure the application of training concepts in realistic scenarios.

367. An organization has deployed a multi-factor authentication (MFA) solution for remote access to its corporate applications. Which of the following is the MOST important factor to consider when testing the MFA implementation?
a. the ease of enrolling and managing MFA credentials for new and existing users
b. the variety and strength of supported MFA methods (e.g., hardware tokens, mobile push, biometrics)
c. the reliability and availability of the MFA service provider or infrastructure
d. the end-user experience and performance impact of the MFA prompts and workflows

Answer: b. the variety and strength of supported MFA methods (e.g., hardware tokens, mobile push, biometrics). Explanation: The primary purpose of MFA is to strengthen authentication security by requiring multiple, independent factors beyond just a password. The most critical aspect to validate when testing an MFA solution is the robustness and appropriateness of the specific factors and methods used. The National Institute of Standards and Technology (NIST) defines three main categories of authentication factors: something you know (e.g., password), something you have (e.g., token), and something you are (e.g., fingerprint). A strong MFA implementation should support at least two different categories, and should use factors that are resistant to common attacks such as phishing, theft, and forgery. During testing, the supported MFA methods should be carefully assessed for their security properties, such as the use of cryptographic algorithms, the resistance to cloning or tampering, and the binding to the user's identity. The user experience, enrollment process, and backend reliability are important usability and operations considerations, but they are secondary to the core security and assurance provided by the chosen MFA methods.

368. An organization has implemented a set of security controls based on its risk assessment. Which of the following is the MOST important ongoing activity to ensure the controls remain effective?
a. conducting annual penetration tests to identify any gaps or weaknesses in the controls
b. monitoring and analyzing key risk indicators (KRIs) and metrics associated with each control
c. performing quarterly vulnerability scans to detect any new or unpatched vulnerabilities
d. reviewing and updating the control documentation and procedures on a regular basis

Answer: b. monitoring and analyzing key risk indicators (KRIs) and metrics associated with each control. Explanation: Security controls are not static mechanisms, but rather dynamic tools that must be continually monitored, measured, and adjusted to remain effective in a changing risk landscape. The most critical activity for ensuring the ongoing efficacy of controls is to define and track a set of key risk indicators (KRIs) and metrics that provide insight into the performance and impact of each control over time. KRIs are quantifiable data points that provide an early signal of increasing risk exposure or control weakness, such as an uptick in failed login attempts or a drop in patch compliance rates. Metrics provide a more comprehensive view of control effectiveness, such as the percentage of high-risk vulnerabilities mitigated or the mean time to detect and respond to incidents. By regularly collecting, analyzing, and reporting on these indicators, organizations can proactively identify control gaps and take corrective action before major issues occur. While penetration testing, vulnerability scanning, and documentation reviews are important periodic activities, they provide point-in-time assessments rather than the continuous, data-driven visibility of a robust KRI and metric program.

369. Which of the following is the BEST approach for monitoring the effectiveness of access control policies and mechanisms?
a. conducting monthly access reviews to verify that user permissions align with job roles and responsibilities
b. analyzing security logs to identify any unauthorized access attempts or suspicious user behavior
c. performing regular penetration tests to attempt to bypass or escalate access controls
d. surveying users to assess their understanding and compliance with access control procedures

Answer: b. analyzing security logs to identify any unauthorized access attempts or suspicious user behavior. Explanation: Access controls are critical security measures that ensure users can only access the specific resources and actions they need to perform their jobs. To effectively monitor the ongoing performance and impact of these controls, organizations must leverage the wealth of data generated by security logs and events. By collecting and analyzing login records, permission changes, resource accesses, and other user activities across systems and applications, security teams can detect patterns and anomalies that may indicate access control violations or misconfigurations. This can include failed login attempts, access from unusual locations or devices, privilege escalation, or data exfiltration. Advanced security analytics tools can help identify and prioritize high-risk events, and enable rapid investigation and response. While access reviews, penetration tests, and user surveys can provide valuable periodic checkpoints, they do not offer the real-time, comprehensive visibility into actual user behavior that log analysis provides. Logs serve as the essential audit trail and early warning system for access control effectiveness.

370. An organization has deployed a data loss prevention (DLP) solution to protect sensitive information. Which of the following metrics is MOST important for measuring the effectiveness of the DLP controls?
a. the number of DLP policies and rules configured in the system
b. the volume of data scanned and analyzed by the DLP system on a daily basis
c. the percentage of DLP alerts that are investigated and resolved within the target timeframe
d. the reduction in the number of sensitive data incidents and breaches over time

Answer: d. the reduction in the number of sensitive data incidents and breaches over time. Explanation: The ultimate goal of a DLP program is to prevent the unauthorized disclosure, modification, or destruction of sensitive information. While operational metrics such as the number of policies, volume of data scanned, and alert resolution time are important for assessing the efficiency and coverage of the DLP system, they do not directly measure the effectiveness of the controls in achieving the desired outcome. The most meaningful metric for gauging DLP success is the actual change in the frequency and severity of sensitive data incidents and breaches over time. By tracking the number, type, and impact of data loss events before and after the DLP implementation, organizations can quantify the risk reduction and business value provided by the controls. A downward trend in incidents, particularly those resulting from insider threats or external attacks, is a strong indicator that the DLP system is effectively identifying and blocking risky data activities. It's important to supplement this outcome metric with root cause analysis and lessons learned to continuously refine DLP policies and processes.

371. Which of the following is the BEST way to validate the effectiveness of security awareness and training controls?
a. tracking the percentage of employees who complete the required training courses on time
b. conducting periodic phishing simulations and measuring the click and reporting rates
c. administering quizzes and assessments to test employee understanding of key concepts
d. monitoring the number of security incidents caused by human error or policy violations

Answer: b. conducting periodic phishing simulations and measuring the click and reporting rates. Explanation: Security awareness and training programs aim to educate employees about cyber threats and best practices, with the goal of reducing human-related risks to the organization. While completion rates, quiz scores, and incident counts can provide some indication of training impact, the most direct and realistic way to assess the actual change in employee behavior is through simulated phishing exercises. Phishing remains one of the most common and effective tactics used by attackers to compromise organizations, and employee susceptibility to phishing is a key indicator of overall security awareness. By regularly sending mock phishing emails and tracking the percentage of employees who click on malicious links or attachments, as well as the percentage who report the emails to security, organizations can measure the real-world effectiveness of their training over time. A decrease in click rates and an increase in reporting rates demonstrate that employees are applying the lessons learned to identify and respond to potential threats. Phishing simulations also provide a valuable opportunity for targeted, hands-on learning and reinforcement.

372. An organization is monitoring the effectiveness of its incident response processes and capabilities. Which of the following metrics is MOST important to track and analyze?
a. the number of security alerts generated by detection tools and systems
b. the percentage of security incidents that are categorized as high severity or critical
c. the mean time to detect, investigate, and contain security incidents
d. the total number of hours spent by the incident response team investigating and resolving incidents

Answer: c. the mean time to detect, investigate, and contain security incidents. Explanation: The primary objective of an incident response program is to minimize the impact and duration of security incidents by ensuring rapid detection, analysis, containment, and recovery. While the volume and severity of alerts and incidents are important context measures, the most critical metric for assessing the effectiveness and efficiency of incident response is the average cycle time for key phases of the incident lifecycle. This includes the mean time to detect (MTTD) an incident from the initial compromise, the mean time to investigate (MTTI) and triage the incident to determine its scope and severity, and the mean time to contain (MTTC) the incident by isolating and neutralizing the threat. Together, these measures provide a holistic view of the organization's ability to quickly identify, understand, and disrupt security incidents before they can cause significant harm. Tracking and trending these metrics over time can help identify bottlenecks, optimize processes, and justify investments in detection and response capabilities. The total hours spent by the team is more of an efficiency or resource utilization metric, rather than a direct measure of incident response outcomes.

373. An organization has implemented a vulnerability management program to identify and remediate weaknesses in its systems and applications. Which of the following metrics is MOST important for measuring the effectiveness of the program?
a. the total number of vulnerabilities identified across the environment

b. the percentage of systems and applications covered by the vulnerability scans
c. the average severity level of the vulnerabilities identified
d. the mean time to remediate critical and high-risk vulnerabilities

Answer: d. the mean time to remediate critical and high-risk vulnerabilities. Explanation: The goal of vulnerability management is not just to discover vulnerabilities, but to effectively prioritize and mitigate them based on their potential risk to the organization. While metrics such as the total number, coverage, and average severity of vulnerabilities provide useful context, the most important measure of program effectiveness is the speed and consistency with which the most critical vulnerabilities are actually remediated. The mean time to remediate (MTTR) for critical and high-risk vulnerabilities is a key performance indicator that reflects the organization's ability to efficiently triage, prioritize, and patch or mitigate the vulnerabilities that pose the greatest threat to its assets and operations. A low and decreasing MTTR indicates that the organization is proactively managing its vulnerability risk, while a high or increasing MTTR suggests that the remediation process is falling behind the discovery process. It's important to track MTTR by severity level, as well as by other factors such as asset criticality and patch complexity, to ensure that remediation efforts are properly focused and resourced.

374. An organization is evaluating the effectiveness of its security monitoring and analytics capabilities. Which of the following is the BEST approach to assess the accuracy and relevance of the security alerts generated?
a. reviewing a sample of alerts to determine if they represent actual security incidents or false positives
b. comparing the total number of alerts generated to industry benchmarks and peer organizations
c. measuring the percentage of alerts that are investigated and resolved within the target timeframe
d. analyzing the correlation and context provided by the alerts to identify broader attack patterns and campaigns

Answer: a. reviewing a sample of alerts to determine if they represent actual security incidents or false positives. Explanation: Security monitoring and analytics tools, such as SIEM and UEBA systems, are designed to detect and prioritize potential security incidents by analyzing large volumes of log and event data from across the organization's environment. However, the effectiveness of these tools depends heavily on the accuracy and relevance of the alerts they generate. A high volume of false positive alerts can overwhelm security teams and distract from real threats, while a high volume of false negative alerts can result in missed or delayed detection of actual incidents. To assess the signal-to-noise ratio of security alerts, the best approach is to conduct regular, in-depth reviews of a representative sample of alerts to determine their validity and actionability. This involves investigating the underlying events and data that triggered each alert, and classifying them as true positives (actual incidents), false positives (benign activity), or false negatives (missed incidents). By measuring and tracking the percentage of true positives over time, organizations can tune their detection rules and thresholds to optimize accuracy and minimize wasted effort. While total alert volume, resolution time, and correlation are useful efficiency and context measures, they do not directly assess the fundamental quality and fidelity of the alerts themselves.

375. An organization has deployed a suite of endpoint detection and response (EDR) tools to monitor and protect its user devices. Which of the following is the MOST important factor to consider when evaluating the effectiveness of the EDR controls?
a. the percentage of endpoints that have the EDR agent installed and active
b. the frequency and depth of endpoint scans performed by the EDR tools
c. the ability of the EDR tools to detect and block known and unknown threats in real-time
d. the integration and interoperability of the EDR tools with other security systems and processes

Answer: c. the ability of the EDR tools to detect and block known and unknown threats in real-time. Explanation: The primary purpose of EDR tools is to provide real-time visibility and protection against threats at the endpoint level, where users interact with applications and data. While agent coverage, scan frequency, and integration are important operational considerations, the most critical measure of EDR effectiveness is the ability to accurately identify and disrupt malicious activity as it occurs, before it can cause harm. This includes detecting and blocking both known threats, such as malware and exploits, and unknown or emerging threats, such as fileless attacks and living-off-the-land techniques. To assess this capability, organizations should conduct regular testing and validation of their EDR tools using a mix of real-world attack simulations, threat intelligence, and retrospective analysis. This can involve executing a range of malware samples, attack frameworks, and adversary tactics to see how well the EDR tools detect and respond, as well as reviewing past incidents and alerts to identify any missed or delayed detections. The goal is to continuously measure and improve the accuracy, speed, and coverage of the EDR tools in identifying and containing actual endpoint threats, rather than just their deployment and integration metrics.

376. An organization is measuring the effectiveness of its security controls using a variety of metrics and key risk indicators (KRIs). Which of the following is the MOST important characteristic of effective KRIs?
a. they are easy to collect and report using automated tools and processes
b. they are directly aligned with specific business objectives and risk appetite statements
c. they provide a comprehensive and detailed view of all security risks and controls
d. they are based on industry standards and benchmarks for security measurement

Answer: b. they are directly aligned with specific business objectives and risk appetite statements. Explanation: Key risk indicators (KRIs) are metrics that provide an early signal of increasing risk exposure in a particular area of the business. They are used to monitor changes in risk levels and trigger appropriate responses before risks exceed acceptable thresholds. To be effective, KRIs must be carefully selected and defined to align with the organization's specific business goals, risk appetite, and risk management strategies. Each KRI should be tied to a clear risk outcome or objective, such as preventing data breaches, maintaining system availability, or complying with regulations. They should also be calibrated to the organization's stated risk tolerance in each area, so that they provide meaningful and actionable insight into when risks are approaching or exceeding limits. Effective KRIs are typically forward-looking, predictive measures that help organizations anticipate and manage risk proactively, rather than just reacting to incidents after the fact. While factors such as ease of collection, comprehensiveness, and alignment with industry standards are desirable attributes for KRIs, they are secondary to the fundamental requirement of business and risk relevance. KRIs that are not directly linked to the organization's specific risk profile and priorities may be less useful for driving risk-informed decision making and action.

377. An organization has implemented a set of security controls and is monitoring their effectiveness using various metrics. Which of the following is the BEST approach for communicating the results of the monitoring program to senior leadership?
a. providing detailed technical reports on the status and configuration of each control
b. presenting a high-level dashboard of key metrics and trends aligned with business objectives
c. conducting regular in-depth briefings on the latest threat intelligence and attack techniques
d. sharing raw security data and event logs for independent analysis and interpretation

Answer: b. presenting a high-level dashboard of key metrics and trends aligned with business objectives. Explanation: Effective communication of security control effectiveness to senior leadership requires translating technical security metrics into business-relevant insights and outcomes. While detailed technical reports, threat intelligence briefings, and raw data dumps may be useful for operational security teams, they are often too granular, complex, and disconnected from business context to be meaningful for executive decision-makers. The best approach is to develop a concise, visual dashboard that highlights a carefully chosen set of key metrics and trends that align with the organization's overall business objectives and risk management priorities. This dashboard should provide a clear, intuitive view of the current state and trajectory of the security program, using language and concepts that resonate with leadership. For example, instead of reporting on the number of vulnerabilities patched or incidents handled, the dashboard might show the percentage of critical systems meeting the organization's risk threshold, or the reduction in potential financial losses from cyber incidents over time. The goal is to tell a compelling story of how the security controls are enabling the business to operate and innovate securely, and where targeted improvements or investments may be needed. Regular reviews of the dashboard with leadership can help drive strategic alignment, risk-informed decision making, and continuous improvement of the security program.

378. An organization is initiating a large-scale security project to implement a new enterprise-wide access control system. Which of the following is the MOST important factor to consider when selecting a project manager?
a. their technical expertise and certification in the specific access control technology being implemented
b. their experience and track record in successfully delivering similar-sized security projects on time and within budget
c. their seniority and position within the organization's IT department and leadership hierarchy
d. their familiarity and relationships with the key vendors and suppliers involved in the project

Answer: b. their experience and track record in successfully delivering similar-sized security projects on time and within budget. Explanation: When selecting a project manager for a major security initiative, the most critical qualification is demonstrated experience and success in leading comparable projects to completion, while meeting the defined scope, schedule, budget, and quality objectives. A proven track record of effective project management, including the ability to plan, organize, execute, monitor, and control all project activities and resources, is more important than deep technical expertise in the specific security domain or technology. While technical knowledge is certainly valuable, it is not sufficient on its own to ensure the complex coordination, communication, and problem-solving skills needed to drive a large project to success. Seniority, vendor relationships, and other factors may be relevant considerations, but they are secondary to the fundamental project management competencies and experience required for the role. The Project Management Institute (PMI) identifies several core areas of expertise for successful project managers, including integration, scope, time, cost, quality, human resource, communications, risk, procurement, and stakeholder management (PMBOK Guide, 6th Edition, 2017). A strong candidate will have a demonstrable history of applying these skills to deliver results in a similar project context.

379. An information security team is planning a major software upgrade project that will impact multiple business units across the organization. Which of the following is the BEST approach for identifying and engaging project stakeholders?
a. reviewing the organizational chart and including the most senior executive from each impacted department
b. conducting a stakeholder analysis to identify and prioritize individuals and groups based on their interest and influence in the project
c. relying on the project sponsor to determine and communicate with the key stakeholders as needed throughout the project lifecycle
d. sending a broad announcement to all employees in the impacted departments and inviting them to participate in the project

Answer: b. conducting a stakeholder analysis to identify and prioritize individuals and groups based on their interest and influence in the project. Explanation: Effective stakeholder engagement is critical to the success of any security project, particularly those with broad organizational impact. Stakeholders are individuals, groups, or organizations that can affect or be affected by the project's outcomes, and may include executive sponsors, business process owners, end-users, technical teams, external partners, and others. The best approach for identifying and prioritizing stakeholders is to conduct a systematic stakeholder analysis early in the project planning phase. This involves brainstorming a comprehensive list of potential stakeholders, and then assessing each one based on their level of interest (how much they care about or are impacted by the project) and influence (how much power or authority they have over the project's direction and resources). Stakeholders can then be mapped into a matrix or grid, with high interest/high influence stakeholders requiring the most proactive engagement and communication throughout the project. Simply including senior executives, relying on the sponsor, or broadcasting to all employees does not provide the nuanced understanding and targeted engagement needed for effective stakeholder management. The Project Management Institute provides a detailed framework for stakeholder identification and analysis in the PMBOK Guide (6th Edition, 2017, Section 13.1).

380. An organization is implementing a new security information and event management (SIEM) system as part of a larger security operations improvement project. Which of the following is the MOST important consideration when developing the project schedule?
a. ensuring that the schedule includes detailed tasks and timelines for every possible activity and deliverable
b. building contingency and buffer time into the schedule to account for potential delays or issues
c. aligning the schedule with the availability and preferences of the key technical resources and vendors
d. focusing on the critical path activities that directly impact the project's end date and objectives

Answer: d. focusing on the critical path activities that directly impact the project's end date and objectives. Explanation: When developing a project schedule, it's essential to identify and prioritize the activities that are most critical to achieving the project's overall goals and timeline. These "critical path" activities are the longest sequence of dependent tasks that determine the minimum time required to complete the project, and where any delays will directly impact the final delivery date. In a SIEM implementation project, examples of critical path activities might include defining requirements, selecting and procuring the solution, installing and configuring the system, integrating data sources, developing correlation rules, and testing end-to-end functionality. By carefully planning and managing these key tasks, and their associated dependencies and resources, the project team can ensure that the project stays on track and delivers the expected outcomes. While comprehensive task planning, risk buffering, and resource scheduling are all important aspects of effective project management, they should not come at the expense of a clear focus on the critical path. Over-planning, over-buffering, or over-accommodating stakeholder preferences can lead to schedule bloat and inefficiency. The Project Management Institute provides guidance on critical path method and schedule development in the PMBOK Guide (6th Edition, 2017, Section 6.5).

381. An information security department is experiencing high turnover and low morale among its project management staff. Which of the following is the BEST strategy for improving retention and engagement of these critical resources?
a. offering competitive salaries and benefits packages to match or exceed industry standards
b. providing opportunities for skill development, career progression, and meaningful work within the organization
c. implementing strict performance management and accountability measures to weed out low performers
d. recruiting new project managers from outside the organization to bring fresh perspectives and energy

Answer: b. providing opportunities for skill development, career progression, and meaningful work within the organization. Explanation: While competitive compensation, performance management, and external recruiting can all play a role in building and maintaining a strong project management team, the most effective long-term strategy for retention and engagement is to create an environment that supports professional growth, advancement, and purpose. Project managers, like most knowledge workers, are often motivated by opportunities to learn new skills, take on new challenges, and make a tangible impact through their work. Organizations that provide clear career paths, training and development programs, and exposure to diverse and meaningful projects are more likely to attract and retain top talent. This can include offering project management certification sponsorship, rotating assignments across different business areas, involving project managers in strategic planning and decision making, and recognizing and rewarding high performance and potential. By investing in the ongoing development and engagement of project managers, organizations can build a loyal, motivated, and high-performing team that is equipped to deliver successful security projects and drive continuous improvement. The Project Management Institute emphasizes the importance of talent management and development in its Talent Triangle framework, which includes technical project management, leadership, and strategic and business management skills (PMI Talent Triangle, 2021).

382. An organization is implementing a new cloud security platform and has assigned a senior security architect as the technical lead for the project. Which of the following is the MOST important responsibility of the technical lead?
a. ensuring that the selected platform meets all of the organization's functional and non-functional requirements
b. making all key technical decisions and communicating them to the project team and stakeholders

c. providing subject matter expertise and guidance to the project team, while collaborating with other experts and stakeholders to make informed decisions
d. independently designing and implementing the platform configuration and integration without input from others

Answer: c. providing subject matter expertise and guidance to the project team, while collaborating with other experts and stakeholders to make informed decisions. Explanation: The primary role of a technical lead on a security project is to provide deep domain knowledge, experience, and guidance to help the project team make sound technical decisions and deliver a high-quality, fit-for-purpose solution. This includes understanding and articulating the technical requirements, constraints, and trade-offs of the project, and ensuring that the selected technologies, architectures, and designs align with the organization's security goals and standards. However, the technical lead should not work in isolation or make unilateral decisions without input and buy-in from other experts and stakeholders. Effective technical leadership involves close collaboration and communication with the project manager, business owners, end-users, vendors, and other subject matter experts to gather diverse perspectives, validate assumptions, and build consensus around technical approaches. The technical lead should foster a team culture of openness, creativity, and shared ownership, while still providing clear direction and accountability for technical outcomes. Balancing expert judgement with inclusive decision making is key to driving technical excellence and project success. The Project Management Institute highlights the importance of collaborative leadership and team building in its Project Manager Competency Development Framework (PMCDF, 3rd Edition, 2017).

383. An information security project team is experiencing delays and cost overruns due to scope creep and changing requirements from stakeholders. Which of the following is the BEST approach for managing these challenges?
a. accommodating all stakeholder requests to ensure their satisfaction and continued support for the project
b. enforcing strict change control processes and rejecting any new requirements that deviate from the original project plan
c. engaging stakeholders to prioritize and align requirements with project objectives, while using agile practices to adapt to changing needs
d. cutting features and functionality from the project scope to meet the original budget and timeline commitments

Answer: c. engaging stakeholders to prioritize and align requirements with project objectives, while using agile practices to adapt to changing needs. Explanation: Scope creep and changing requirements are common challenges in information security projects, where the complex and dynamic nature of the threat landscape, business environment, and technology ecosystem can make it difficult to define and stick to a fixed set of deliverables. While it's important to have a clear and agreed-upon project scope and plan, attempting to rigidly enforce the original requirements or blindly accepting all stakeholder requests can lead to misalignment, dissatisfaction, and project failure. The best approach is to proactively engage stakeholders to continuously validate and prioritize requirements based on their alignment with the project's key objectives and value proposition. This involves regular stakeholder meetings, demos, and feedback loops to ensure that the project stays focused on the most critical and relevant outcomes, while also being flexible enough to adapt to evolving needs and constraints. Agile project management methodologies, such as Scrum or Kanban, can be particularly useful for managing changing requirements, by delivering value in short, iterative cycles and using empirical feedback to adjust plans and priorities. Cutting features or sacrificing quality to meet arbitrary deadlines or budgets is rarely a sustainable solution, and can lead to technical debt and stakeholder frustration. The Project Management Institute provides guidance on scope management and agile practices in the PMBOK Guide (6th Edition, 2017, Sections 5 and 6).

384. An organization is planning a major security infrastructure upgrade project and needs to secure funding and resources from executive leadership. Which of the following is the MOST important information to include in the project business case?
a. a detailed technical architecture diagram and bill of materials for the proposed solution
b. a comprehensive risk assessment and mitigation plan for all potential project failures and issues
c. a clear articulation of the project's alignment with and impact on the organization's strategic goals and objectives

d. a comparison of the project's costs and benefits to industry benchmarks and best practices

Answer: c. a clear articulation of the project's alignment with and impact on the organization's strategic goals and objectives. Explanation: When seeking executive sponsorship and investment for a security project, it's critical to frame the project in terms of its strategic value and business outcomes, not just its technical merits or risk mitigation features. While the technical details, risk management plans, and industry comparisons are important supporting information, the most compelling business case will focus on how the project directly supports and enables the organization's top-level goals, objectives, and key results. This requires understanding the organization's strategic priorities, such as increasing revenue, reducing costs, improving customer satisfaction, or enabling innovation, and explicitly mapping the project's deliverables and benefits to those drivers. For example, a security infrastructure upgrade might be positioned as a way to improve system performance and availability, thereby increasing productivity and reducing downtime costs. Or it might be framed as a necessary foundation for launching new digital products and services, thereby supporting growth and competitive advantage. By clearly articulating the strategic alignment and impact of the project, in terms that resonate with executive stakeholders, the project team can build a strong case for prioritization and funding. The Project Management Institute emphasizes the importance of strategic alignment and benefits realization in its Standard for Project Management (4th Edition, 2017).

385. An information security project manager is assigned to lead a high-profile initiative with a tight deadline and limited budget. Which of the following is the BEST approach for managing project risks and issues?
a. avoiding all risks by carefully planning and controlling all project activities and outcomes
b. accepting all risks and dealing with issues reactively as they occur, in order to meet the project constraints
c. identifying, assessing, and prioritizing risks and issues, and developing proactive response plans for the most critical ones
d. transferring all risks to third-party vendors and service providers through contracts and service level agreements

Answer: c. identifying, assessing, and prioritizing risks and issues, and developing proactive response plans for the most critical ones. Explanation: Effective risk and issue management is essential for delivering successful security projects, particularly in challenging environments with tight constraints and high stakes. While it may be tempting to try to avoid all risks through rigorous planning and control, or to simply react to issues as they arise in order to meet deadlines and budgets, these approaches are rarely effective or sustainable in the face of complex and dynamic project realities. Similarly, attempting to transfer all risks to external parties may not be feasible or advisable, given the shared responsibilities and interdependencies involved in most security projects. The best approach is to proactively identify, assess, and prioritize risks and issues based on their likelihood and potential impact on the project's objectives, and to develop targeted response strategies for the most critical ones. This involves engaging stakeholders to surface and validate risks and issues, using qualitative and quantitative techniques to analyze and rank them, and creating practical action plans to prevent, mitigate, or contingency plan for the highest priority items. Regularly monitoring and communicating risks and issues, and adjusting plans as needed based on changing circumstances, is also key. The Project Management Institute provides a comprehensive framework for project risk management in the PMBOK Guide (6th Edition, 2017, Section 11).

386. An organization is implementing a new data loss prevention (DLP) solution as part of a broader information protection program. Which of the following is the MOST important factor to consider when allocating project resources?
a. ensuring that the project team includes representatives from all departments and levels of the organization
b. assigning the most experienced and senior security engineers to lead the technical implementation and configuration
c. balancing the skills and capacity of the project team with the complexity and criticality of the project tasks and deliverables
d. minimizing the size and cost of the project team by leveraging external consultants and contractors for key roles

Answer: c. balancing the skills and capacity of the project team with the complexity and criticality of the project tasks and deliverables. Explanation: Effective resource allocation is critical for ensuring that security projects are staffed with the right mix of knowledge, experience, and bandwidth to deliver high-quality results on time and within budget. When assigning resources to a complex and critical project like a DLP implementation, it's important to carefully consider the specific skills, competencies, and workload of each team member in relation to the project's requirements and priorities. This involves breaking down the project into its component tasks and deliverables, assessing the level of expertise and effort required for each one, and matching them with the available talent pool. The goal is to ensure that the most critical and complex work is assigned to the most capable and available resources, while also providing opportunities for growth and development. Simply including representatives from all areas, relying on seniority, or minimizing costs through external sourcing may not result in the optimal mix of skills and capacity for the project's needs. Over-allocation or under-allocation of resources can lead to burnout, delays, and quality issues. The Project Management Institute provides guidance on human resource management and capacity planning in the PMBOK Guide (6th Edition, 2017, Section 9).

387. An information security project is nearing completion and preparing for final delivery and closeout. Which of the following is the MOST important activity to ensure a smooth transition and ongoing success?
a. conducting a comprehensive post-implementation review and lessons learned exercise with the project team and stakeholders
b. developing and executing a detailed transition plan that includes knowledge transfer, support handoff, and operational readiness testing
c. celebrating the project's success and recognizing the contributions of individual team members and supporters
d. archiving all project documents and artifacts in a centralized repository for future reference and auditing purposes

Answer: b. developing and executing a detailed transition plan that includes knowledge transfer, support handoff, and operational readiness testing. Explanation: While post-project reviews, celebrations, and documentation are all valuable closeout activities, the most critical factor for ensuring the long-term success and value of a security project is a well-planned and executed transition to operations. This involves creating and following a comprehensive plan that addresses all aspects of moving the project deliverables into the live production environment and preparing the organization to effectively own, operate, and support the new capabilities on an ongoing basis. Key elements of an effective transition plan include:
- Knowledge transfer: Documenting and communicating the design, configuration, and usage of the delivered solution to the relevant operational teams and stakeholders, through training, workshops, and hands-on sessions.
- Support handoff: Defining and implementing clear roles, responsibilities, and processes for incident management, change management, and continuous improvement of the solution, in collaboration with the service desk, IT operations, and other support functions.
- Operational readiness testing: Conducting thorough testing and validation of the solution in the production environment, including system integration, performance, security, and user acceptance testing, to ensure that it meets all functional and non-functional requirements and is fit for purpose.
- Hypercare and stabilization: Providing enhanced monitoring, support, and issue resolution during the initial post-launch period, to quickly identify and address any problems or gaps, and to ensure a stable and reliable operation.

388. An organization is implementing a complex, enterprise-wide security transformation program. Which project management methodology is BEST suited for this type of initiative?
a. Waterfall, which follows a linear, sequential approach with distinct phases and milestones
b. Agile, which uses iterative, incremental delivery with close collaboration and rapid feedback loops
c. PRINCE2, which provides a highly structured, process-based framework for directing and controlling projects
d. Critical Path Method (CPM), which focuses on identifying and managing the longest sequence of dependent tasks

Answer: b. Agile, which uses iterative, incremental delivery with close collaboration and rapid feedback loops. Explanation: For large-scale, complex security transformation programs, Agile methodologies like Scrum or Kanban are often the most effective approach. Agile emphasizes delivering value in short, iterative cycles, with close collaboration between cross-functional teams and stakeholders. This allows for rapid feedback, learning, and adaptation in the face of changing requirements, risks, and constraints. By breaking down the program into smaller, manageable increments, Agile helps manage complexity, reduce uncertainty, and deliver tangible results faster. Waterfall's linear, phased approach can be too rigid and slow for dynamic, multi-faceted security initiatives. PRINCE2's process-heavy framework may add overhead and bureaucracy. CPM's focus on critical path scheduling may not adequately address the people and adaptive aspects of transformation. Agile's principles of transparency, inspection, and adaptation align well with the governance, risk, and compliance goals of security programs (Agile Alliance, 2001).

389. An information security project team is struggling with misunderstandings and conflicts between the technical and business stakeholders. Which project management methodology element is MOST important for addressing this challenge?
a. Work Breakdown Structure (WBS), which decomposes the project scope into manageable tasks and deliverables
b. Gantt Chart, which provides a visual timeline of project activities, dependencies, and milestones
c. RACI Matrix, which defines the roles and responsibilities of project stakeholders for each task and decision
d. Risk Register, which identifies and assesses potential project threats and mitigation strategies

Answer: c. RACI Matrix, which defines the roles and responsibilities of project stakeholders for each task and decision. Explanation: Effective stakeholder engagement and communication is critical for aligning diverse interests and perspectives on security projects. A RACI (Responsible, Accountable, Consulted, Informed) matrix is a powerful tool for clarifying and agreeing on the specific roles and responsibilities of each stakeholder group for key project activities and decisions. By explicitly defining who is responsible for doing the work, who is accountable for the outcomes, who needs to be consulted for input and feedback, and who needs to be kept informed of progress and changes, a RACI helps ensure clear expectations, efficient decision making, and productive collaboration. It surfaces and resolves potential conflicts or gaps in understanding, and provides a common reference point for the project team and stakeholders. While a WBS, Gantt chart, and risk register are valuable project planning and control tools, they do not directly address the interpersonal and organizational dynamics of stakeholder alignment like a RACI does. The Project Management Institute highlights the importance of RACI matrices in the PMBOK Guide (6th Edition, 2017, Section 9.1.2.1).

390. An organization is launching a new security incident response program and wants to ensure rapid, flexible delivery and continuous improvement. Which project management methodology is BEST aligned with these goals?
a. Waterfall, which emphasizes upfront planning, documentation, and sequential execution of project phases
b. Lean, which focuses on maximizing value and minimizing waste through process optimization and standardization
c. Six Sigma, which uses statistical methods to measure and control quality and reduce defects and variation
d. DevOps, which integrates development and operations practices to enable fast, frequent delivery and learning

Answer: d. DevOps, which integrates development and operations practices to enable fast, frequent delivery and learning. Explanation: For time-critical, evolving initiatives like security incident response, DevOps provides a highly relevant and applicable project management approach. DevOps seeks to break down silos between development and operations teams, and enable rapid, reliable, and repeatable delivery of software and services through automation, collaboration, and continuous feedback. Key DevOps practices, such as continuous integration and delivery (CI/CD), infrastructure as code (IaC), monitoring and logging, and blameless post-mortems, can be adapted to the incident response context to enable agile, adaptive, and learning-driven improvements. For example, CI/CD pipelines can be used to automatically test and deploy incident response playbooks and tools, IaC can be used to quickly spin up and tear down forensic environments, and post-mortems can be used to identify and share lessons learned from each incident. Waterfall's heavy upfront planning and linear execution may be too slow and inflexible for the dynamic nature of incident response. Lean and Six Sigma, while useful for optimizing and stabilizing processes, may not fully address the speed and adaptability demands of incident response. DevOps' focus on rapid feedback, experimentation, and learning aligns well with the continuous improvement goals of an agile incident response program (Google, n.d., "Site Reliability Engineering (SRE) Book").

391. An information security team is planning a major data center migration project and needs to ensure strict control over costs, timelines, and deliverables. Which project management methodology is MOST appropriate for this type of project?
a. Agile Scrum, which uses short, time-boxed sprints to deliver working product increments
b. Lean Kanban, which visualizes and optimizes workflows using a board with work-in-progress limits
c. PRINCE2, which provides a structured, stage-based framework for managing project scope, schedule, and resources
d. Critical Chain Project Management (CCPM), which focuses on managing resource constraints and dependencies

Answer: c. PRINCE2, which provides a structured, stage-based framework for managing project scope, schedule, and resources. Explanation: For projects with well-defined, stable requirements and a strong emphasis on predictability and control, the PRINCE2 (PRojects IN Controlled Environments) methodology can be a good fit. PRINCE2 is a process-based approach that provides a comprehensive framework for organizing and governing projects across their lifecycle, from initiation to closure. It defines clear roles and responsibilities, such as the project board, project manager, and team managers, and prescribes a set of integrated processes and themes for managing scope, schedule, cost, quality, risk, and other project dimensions. PRINCE2's stage-based approach, with formal approvals and gate reviews between each stage, helps ensure tight alignment and control of project deliverables against agreed-upon business cases and baselines. For a security project like a data center migration, where the scope and requirements are well-understood upfront, and the stakes for cost and timeline overruns are high, PRINCE2 can provide the necessary rigor and discipline. Agile Scrum and Lean Kanban are better suited for projects with dynamic, evolving requirements where the focus is on adaptability and speed. CCPM's focus on resource optimization may not be as critical as overall project control and governance for this type of initiative. The AXELOS PRINCE2 manual (2017) provides detailed guidance on applying the methodology.

392. A security software development project is experiencing delays and quality issues due to unpredictable and changing requirements from stakeholders. Which project management methodology principle is MOST relevant for addressing this challenge?
a. Managing by exception, which allows the project manager to handle deviations from the plan within defined tolerances
b. Progressive elaboration, which allows for the gradual refinement and detailing of requirements over the project lifecycle
c. Earned value management, which measures project progress and performance against the planned budget and schedule
d. Integrated change control, which assesses and approves proposed changes to the project scope, schedule, or cost baselines

Answer: b. Progressive elaboration, which allows for the gradual refinement and detailing of requirements over the project lifecycle. Explanation: In software development projects, it is common for requirements to evolve and emerge over time, as stakeholders gain new insights and priorities change. Attempting to fully define and lock down all requirements upfront can lead to delays, rework, and stakeholder dissatisfaction. The principle of progressive elaboration, which is a key tenet of iterative and incremental project management methodologies like Agile, recognizes that requirements may be high-level and uncertain at the beginning of a project, and become clearer and more detailed as the project progresses through multiple iterations or phases. By allowing for the gradual discovery and refinement of requirements, in close collaboration with stakeholders, progressive elaboration helps manage the inherent uncertainty and changeability of software projects. It enables the project team to adapt and respond to new information, while still maintaining a clear vision and direction for the overall project outcomes. Managing by exception, earned value management, and integrated change control are valuable project management techniques, but they focus more on controlling deviations and changes to an established plan, rather than embracing the evolutionary nature of requirements like progressive elaboration does. The Project Management Institute's PMBOK Guide (6th Edition, 2017, Section 1.2.4.2) and Agile Practice Guide (2017) discuss the principle of progressive elaboration.

393. An organization is outsourcing a critical security operations function to a managed security service provider (MSSP) and needs to ensure clear accountability and performance management. Which project management methodology element is MOST important to include in the contract and service level agreement (SLA)?
a. Work Breakdown Structure (WBS), which defines the detailed tasks, deliverables, and acceptance criteria for the services
b. Risk Management Plan, which identifies the key service delivery risks and specifies the mitigation and contingency strategies
c. Quality Management Plan, which establishes the quality standards, metrics, and control processes for the services
d. Requirements Traceability Matrix, which maps the service requirements to the specific contract provisions and SLA clauses

Answer: d. Requirements Traceability Matrix, which maps the service requirements to the specific contract provisions and SLA clauses. Explanation: When outsourcing critical security functions to an MSSP, it is essential to have a clear, comprehensive, and enforceable contract and SLA that defines the roles, responsibilities, and expectations for service delivery. A key tool for ensuring alignment and accountability between the service requirements and the legal agreements is a Requirements Traceability Matrix (RTM). An RTM is a document that maps each specific service requirement, such as the scope, performance levels, quality standards, reporting obligations, and penalties, to the corresponding clauses and provisions in the contract and SLA. It helps ensure that all requirements are adequately covered and flow down to the vendor, and that there is a clear basis for measuring and enforcing compliance. An RTM also facilitates change management and dispute resolution, by providing a shared reference point for the requirements and their contractual implications. While a WBS, Risk Management Plan, and Quality Management Plan are important components of the outsourcing project management framework, they focus more on the internal planning and control of the service delivery, rather than the external alignment with the legal agreements like an RTM does. The Project Management Institute's PMBOK Guide (6th Edition, 2017, Section 5.2.3.1) highlights the importance of requirements traceability in project scope management.

394. An agile security project team is using user stories and story points for requirements definition and estimation. Which project management methodology element is MOST important for ensuring accurate and reliable story point estimates?
a. Velocity tracking, which measures the average number of story points completed per sprint
b. Planning poker, which involves the team collaboratively estimating story points using specialized card decks
c. Definition of Done (DoD), which specifies the acceptance criteria and quality standards for user stories
d. Relative sizing, which estimates story points based on the perceived complexity and effort relative to other stories

Answer: d. Relative sizing, which estimates story points based on the perceived complexity and effort relative to other stories. Explanation: In agile project management, story points are a unit of measure used to estimate the relative size and complexity of user stories or requirements. Unlike traditional time-based estimates, story points represent the team's collective assessment of how much work is involved in completing a story, based on factors such as complexity, uncertainty, and dependencies. The key to accurate and consistent story point estimation is the practice of relative sizing. Relative sizing involves comparing the size and complexity of a story to other stories the team has previously completed or is familiar with. By focusing on the relative differences between stories, rather than trying to estimate absolute hours or days, the team can arrive at more reliable and meaningful estimates that account for their specific context and capabilities. Techniques like planning poker, which facilitate collaborative estimation through structured discussions and consensus-building, can support relative sizing. However, the fundamental principle of relative estimation, based on past experience and comparative judgment, is the most critical factor. Velocity tracking and

Definition of Done are important agile practices for planning and quality assurance, respectively, but they are more about measuring and validating the outcomes of estimation, rather than the estimation process itself. The Scaled Agile Framework (SAFe) provides guidance on relative estimation and story pointing (SAFe 5.0, "Agile Estimating and Planning").

395. A security project manager is using earned value management (EVM) to track and report project performance. Which EVM metric is MOST important for predicting whether the project will be completed within the approved budget?
a. Schedule Performance Index (SPI), which measures the efficiency of the project schedule
b. Cost Performance Index (CPI), which measures the efficiency of the project spending
c. Planned Value (PV), which measures the approved budget for the work scheduled to be completed
d. Actual Cost (AC), which measures the actual costs incurred for the work completed

Answer: b. Cost Performance Index (CPI), which measures the efficiency of the project spending. Explanation: Earned Value Management (EVM) is a project management technique that integrates scope, schedule, and cost data to provide a holistic view of project performance and progress. It compares the planned work and budget to the actual work completed and costs incurred, using a set of standardized metrics and formulas. The most critical EVM metric for predicting a project's cost outcome is the Cost Performance Index (CPI). CPI is calculated by dividing the Earned Value (EV), which represents the budgeted cost of the work actually performed, by the Actual Cost (AC) of that work. A CPI of 1 means the project is exactly on budget, a CPI greater than 1 means the project is under budget, and a CPI less than 1 means the project is over budget. By tracking CPI over time, project managers can identify trends and variances in cost efficiency, and forecast whether the project is likely to finish within the approved budget. While metrics like SPI, PV, and AC provide important schedule and cost insights, they do not directly predict the overall cost outcome like CPI does. The Project Management Institute's PMBOK Guide (6th Edition, 2017, Section 7.4.2.2) provides detailed guidance on CPI and other EVM metrics and formulas.

396. A security project team is using a Kanban board to visualize and manage their workflow. Which Kanban metric is MOST important for identifying and addressing bottlenecks and flow issues?
a. Cycle Time, which measures the total time from when a work item starts until it is completed
b. Throughput, which measures the number of work items completed per unit of time
c. Work in Progress (WIP), which measures the number of work items currently being worked on
d. Lead Time, which measures the total time from when a work item is requested until it is delivered

Answer: c. Work in Progress (WIP), which measures the number of work items currently being worked on. Explanation: Kanban is a lean project management methodology that focuses on visualizing and optimizing the flow of work through a system. A key principle of Kanban is to limit the amount of work in progress (WIP) at any given time, to prevent overload, bottlenecks, and waste. By setting explicit WIP limits for each stage of the workflow, and tracking the actual WIP against those limits, Kanban teams can identify and address flow problems. For example, if the WIP for a particular stage, such as testing or deployment, is consistently at or above the limit, it may indicate a bottleneck or constraint that is slowing down the overall throughput. By investigating the root causes of the WIP buildup, such as lack of resources, skills, or automation, the team can take corrective actions to improve the flow. Metrics like cycle time, throughput, and lead time are important for measuring the efficiency and predictability of the overall workflow, but they are lagging indicators that reflect the outcomes of WIP management. WIP is the leading indicator that directly influences the other metrics and provides the most actionable insights for continuous improvement. The Kanban Guide for Scrum Teams (2018) and the Kanban Maturity Model (KMM) provide guidance on WIP limits and other Kanban practices.

397. An organization is developing its annual cybersecurity budget and wants to ensure optimal allocation of resources. Which of the following is the MOST important factor to consider when prioritizing budget items?
a. the total cost of ownership (TCO) of each security tool and technology

b. the alignment of each budget item with the organization's risk management strategy and business objectives
c. the preferences and recommendations of the IT and security team members
d. the industry benchmarks and best practices for security spending in the organization's sector

Answer: b. the alignment of each budget item with the organization's risk management strategy and business objectives. Explanation: Effective cybersecurity budgeting requires a risk-based, business-aligned approach that prioritizes investments based on their criticality to the organization's overall security posture and strategic goals. The most important factor to consider is how each proposed budget item, such as a new security control, program, or initiative, supports the organization's risk management strategy and enables its core business objectives. This involves assessing the potential risk reduction and business value of each item in relation to the organization's risk appetite, threat landscape, regulatory requirements, and strategic priorities. Items that address the highest priority risks and have the greatest impact on the confidentiality, integrity, and availability of critical assets and processes should receive the top funding. While TCO, team preferences, and industry benchmarks can provide useful cost and context data, they should not be the primary drivers of budgeting decisions. The key is to optimize the allocation of limited resources based on a clear understanding of the organization's specific risk profile and business needs. ISACA's COBIT 2019 framework provides guidance on aligning enterprise and IT goals, including information security goals, with organizational strategy and risk priorities (COBIT 2019 Framework, "Governance and Management Objectives").

398. An information security manager is requesting budget approval for a new incident response platform. Which of the following is the MOST important information to include in the budget justification?
a. the technical features and capabilities of the platform, compared to other market options
b. the estimated return on investment (ROI) and cost savings from implementing the platform
c. the risks and potential business impacts of not implementing the platform
d. the compatibility and integration of the platform with the organization's existing security tools

Answer: c. the risks and potential business impacts of not implementing the platform. Explanation: When seeking budget approval for a security investment, it is critical to articulate the business case in terms of the risks and impacts that the investment will help mitigate or prevent. For an incident response platform, this means highlighting the potential consequences of not having effective capabilities to detect, investigate, and contain security incidents, such as data breaches, system outages, reputational damage, financial losses, and regulatory penalties. By quantifying the likelihood and magnitude of these risks, and the expected risk reduction from the platform, the security manager can demonstrate the necessity and value of the investment to the business. This risk-based justification should be the primary focus of the budget request, as it directly aligns with the organization's overall risk management and business continuity priorities. Information about the platform's features, costs, and integration, while important for due diligence and implementation planning, are secondary to the fundamental risk and impact considerations. The ISO/IEC 27014:2013 standard on governance of information security emphasizes the importance of using business impact assessments to inform information security investment decisions (ISO/IEC 27014:2013, Section 6.2).

399. An organization's cybersecurity program is facing budget constraints and needs to optimize its resource allocation. Which of the following is the BEST approach for identifying cost savings opportunities?
a. conducting a comprehensive review of all security tools and technologies to identify unused or underutilized licenses
b. implementing across-the-board budget cuts for all security projects and initiatives
c. outsourcing all non-critical security functions to lower-cost service providers
d. performing a risk-based cost-benefit analysis of each security control and process

Answer: d. performing a risk-based cost-benefit analysis of each security control and process. Explanation: In a resource-constrained environment, it is essential to make informed, data-driven decisions about where to allocate limited cybersecurity funds for maximum risk reduction and business value. The best approach is to conduct a systematic cost-benefit analysis of each existing and proposed security control and process, using a risk-based framework. This involves assessing the total costs of each item, including direct expenses, indirect costs, and opportunity costs, and comparing them to the expected benefits, such as reduced risk exposure, improved compliance, and enhanced operational efficiency. By quantifying and prioritizing the risk-adjusted return on investment (RAROI) of each item, the organization can identify the areas of highest impact and lowest relative cost, and make targeted optimizations. While license optimization, across-the-board cuts, and outsourcing can provide some short-term cost savings, they do not address the fundamental question of which controls and processes are most critical and cost-effective for managing the organization's specific risks. A risk-based cost-benefit approach enables more strategic and sustainable resource allocation decisions. The NIST SP 800-55 Revision 1 provides guidance on measuring the effectiveness and efficiency of information security controls, including cost-benefit analysis (NIST SP 800-55 Rev. 1, Section 6.1).

400. A security operations team is requesting additional staff to handle the increasing volume of security alerts and incidents. Which of the following metrics is MOST important to include in the staffing justification?
a. the number of security alerts generated per day by the organization's monitoring tools
b. the percentage of security alerts that are false positives or low severity
c. the average time required to triage, investigate, and resolve each security incident
d. the ratio of security staff to total employees in the organization

Answer: c. the average time required to triage, investigate, and resolve each security incident. Explanation: When requesting additional staff for security operations, it is important to provide data-driven evidence of the workload and performance challenges facing the current team. The most relevant and compelling metric is the average time required to handle each security incident, from initial alert to final resolution. This metric directly reflects the efficiency and effectiveness of the security operations process, and the capacity of the team to keep up with the demand. If the average handling time is consistently exceeding the target service level agreements (SLAs) or industry benchmarks, it indicates a resource gap that may warrant additional staffing. By quantifying the time requirements and potential improvements from adding staff, the team can make a strong business case for the investment. Metrics like alert volume, false positive rate, and staff-to-employee ratio, while useful for context, do not directly measure the impact of staffing levels on incident response outcomes. The key is to focus on metrics that demonstrate how additional resources will help the team meet its critical performance objectives and reduce risk to the business. The NIST SP 800-61 Revision 2 provides guidance on incident handling metrics and staffing models (NIST SP 800-61 Rev. 2, Section 3.4.2).

401. An organization is implementing a new security awareness and training program and needs to allocate resources for content development and delivery. Which of the following is the MOST important factor to consider when estimating the resource requirements?
a. the total number of employees in the organization who will receive the training
b. the delivery format and frequency of the training (e.g. online, in-person, annual, quarterly)
c. the specific topics and learning objectives to be covered in the training
d. the availability and skills of internal staff to develop and deliver the training content

Answer: c. the specific topics and learning objectives to be covered in the training. Explanation: When planning and budgeting for a security awareness and training program, the most critical factor to consider is the scope and depth of the content itself. The specific topics, skills, and behaviors to be taught will drive the level of effort and expertise required for content development and delivery. For example, a training program that covers a wide range of technical and non-technical topics, from secure coding practices to social engineering awareness, will require more resources than a program focused on a single compliance or policy area. Similarly, a program that aims to build advanced, role-specific skills will require more in-depth and interactive content than a program focused on general awareness and basic secure behaviors. By clearly defining the learning objectives and outcomes for each target audience, the organization can estimate the time, skills, and tools needed to create and deliver effective training materials. Factors like audience size, delivery mode, and internal capabilities are important for scaling and sourcing the program, but should be based on the fundamental content requirements. The NIST SP 800-50 provides guidance on designing and budgeting for security awareness and training programs (NIST SP 800-50, Section 3.2).

402. An information security team is evaluating two different endpoint detection and response (EDR) solutions and needs to select the most cost-effective option. Which of the following is the MOST important financial metric to consider in the evaluation?
a. the upfront capital expense (CAPEX) of purchasing and deploying each solution
b. the recurring operational expense (OPEX) of licensing, maintaining, and supporting each solution
c. the projected cost savings and cost avoidance from each solution over its lifecycle
d. the total cost of ownership (TCO) of each solution, including both CAPEX and OPEX

Answer: d. the total cost of ownership (TCO) of each solution, including both CAPEX and OPEX. Explanation: When comparing the cost-effectiveness of different security solutions, it is essential to consider the full lifecycle costs, not just the initial purchase price or the ongoing maintenance fees. The total cost of ownership (TCO) is a comprehensive financial metric that includes both the upfront capital expenses (CAPEX) and the recurring operational expenses (OPEX) of a solution over its expected lifespan. CAPEX typically includes costs such as hardware, software licenses, implementation services, and training, while OPEX includes costs such as subscription fees, maintenance contracts, support services, and internal labor for managing the solution. By calculating the TCO for each EDR option, the team can make an apples-to-apples comparison of the long-term financial impact and value. The TCO analysis should also factor in any expected cost savings or avoidance from the solution, such as reduced incident response efforts or prevented data breach costs, to give a more complete picture of the return on investment (ROI). Focusing solely on CAPEX, OPEX, or savings metrics may not capture the full economic profile and trade-offs of each option. The ISACA Information Security Business Case Development guide provides a framework for calculating and comparing the TCO and ROI of security investments (ISACA ISBCD, Section 5.2).

403. An organization is allocating its annual cybersecurity budget and needs to decide how much to spend on proactive risk mitigation versus reactive incident response. Which of the following is the BEST approach for determining the optimal balance?
a. allocating an equal amount to both mitigation and response, to ensure adequate coverage of both areas
b. allocating the majority of the budget to mitigation, to minimize the likelihood and impact of incidents
c. allocating the majority of the budget to response, to maximize the speed and effectiveness of incident handling
d. allocating the budget based on a risk assessment and cost-benefit analysis of mitigation and response options

Answer: d. allocating the budget based on a risk assessment and cost-benefit analysis of mitigation and response options. Explanation: Determining the optimal balance between proactive and reactive security spending requires a data-driven, risk-based approach that considers the organization's unique threat landscape, risk tolerance, and business priorities. The best way to allocate the budget is to conduct a comprehensive risk assessment that identifies the most critical assets, the most likely and impactful threats, and the potential consequences of successful attacks. Based on this assessment, the organization can evaluate the costs and benefits of different risk mitigation and incident response strategies, and prioritize investments that provide the greatest risk reduction and business value. This may involve a mix of proactive measures, such as vulnerability management, security training, and threat intelligence, and reactive measures, such as incident response planning, forensic tools, and crisis communication. The key is to use quantitative risk analysis and cost-benefit modeling to determine the optimal allocation that balances risk prevention and impact minimization, given the available resources. Arbitrary or fixed ratios, such as 50-50 or 80-20, may not reflect the organization's specific risk profile and priorities. The ISO/IEC 27005:2018 standard provides guidance on information security risk management, including risk assessment and treatment decision-making (ISO/IEC 27005:2018, Section 8.3).

404. A cybersecurity vendor is offering a new threat intelligence service and claims it will provide a high return on investment (ROI) for the organization. Which of the following is the MOST important factor to consider when evaluating the vendor's ROI claim?
a. the number of threat indicators and alerts provided by the service on a daily or weekly basis
b. the accuracy and relevance of the threat intelligence to the organization's specific industry and technology environment
c. the cost of the service compared to other threat intelligence providers in the market
d. the marketing materials and case studies provided by the vendor to support their ROI claim

Answer: b. the accuracy and relevance of the threat intelligence to the organization's specific industry and technology environment. Explanation: When assessing the potential ROI of a threat intelligence service, the most critical factor is the quality and applicability of the intelligence to the organization's unique risk context. Threat intelligence is only valuable if it provides timely, accurate, and actionable insights into the specific threats and attack vectors that are most likely to target the organization, based on its industry, geography, technology stack, and business model. A service that generates a high volume of generic, false positive, or irrelevant alerts may actually create more work and cost for the security team, rather than delivering efficiency and risk reduction benefits. To properly evaluate the vendor's ROI claim, the organization should request samples and demos of the intelligence, and assess how well it aligns with and informs their existing threat models, defense strategies, and incident response playbooks. The organization should also validate the vendor's data sources, analytics, and delivery mechanisms, and compare them to their internal threat intelligence capabilities and gaps. Factors like indicator volume, service cost, and marketing claims are less reliable predictors of ROI than the actual relevance and usefulness of the intelligence in the organization's specific environment. The SANS Threat Intelligence Consumption poster provides guidance on selecting and evaluating threat intelligence service for maximum ROI (SANS Threat Intelligence Consumption, Version 1.0).

405. An organization is considering outsourcing some of its security operations center (SOC) functions to a managed security service provider (MSSP) to reduce costs and improve efficiency. Which of the following is the MOST important factor to consider when making the outsourcing decision?
a. the upfront and ongoing costs of the MSSP services compared to the current in-house SOC costs
b. the service level agreements (SLAs) and key performance indicators (KPIs) offered by the MSSP for incident detection and response times
c. the ability of the MSSP to integrate with the organization's existing security tools and processes
d. the potential risks and long-term strategic implications of relying on a third-party for critical security functions

Answer: d. the potential risks and long-term strategic implications of relying on a third-party for critical security functions. Explanation: While cost savings, performance improvement, and operational integration are important considerations when evaluating MSSP outsourcing options, the most crucial factor is the strategic and risk-based assessment of the long-term implications of the decision. Outsourcing critical SOC functions, such as security monitoring, incident triage, and threat hunting, to a third-party provider involves a significant transfer of control and responsibility for the organization's security posture. This can create new risks and dependencies, such as reduced visibility and agility, increased exposure to vendor security incidents, and loss of in-house skills and knowledge. The organization must carefully weigh these risks against the potential benefits, and consider the long-term impact on its ability to manage and adapt to evolving threats and business needs. This requires a holistic, multi-stakeholder analysis of the organization's security strategy, risk appetite, regulatory requirements, and core competencies, not just a financial or operational assessment. The decision should align with the organization's overall sourcing and risk management principles, and include provisions for vendor governance, performance management, and exit planning. The ISACA Information Security Sourcing guide provides a framework for evaluating and managing information security outsourcing decisions and relationships (ISACA ISS, Section 3.2).

406. An organization is implementing a risk-based approach to cybersecurity budgeting and needs to prioritize investments based on the likelihood and impact of different threats. Which of the following is the MOST important input to the risk assessment process?
a. the annual reports and financial statements of the organization, to determine the potential financial impact of security incidents
b. the results of vulnerability scans and penetration tests, to identify the most likely attack vectors and weaknesses
c. the insights and judgments of experienced security professionals, based on their knowledge of the threat landscape and the organization's environment
d. the historical data and trends on security incidents and losses in the organization's industry and peer group

Answer: c. the insights and judgments of experienced security professionals, based on their knowledge of the threat landscape and the organization's environment. Explanation: Conducting a risk assessment to inform cybersecurity budgeting decisions requires a combination of quantitative data analysis and qualitative expert judgment. While factors like financial impact, technical vulnerabilities, and historical trends can provide valuable inputs and context, the most critical element is the professional insights and opinions of seasoned security practitioners who deeply understand the organization's specific threat landscape, risk profile, and defense capabilities. These experts, such as the CISO, security architects, and threat intelligence analysts, bring a wealth of knowledge and experience about the tactics, techniques, and procedures (TTPs) of different threat actors, the likelihood and impact of different attack scenarios, and the effectiveness and gaps of the organization's current security controls. They can provide nuanced, contextual assessments of the risk levels and priorities that go beyond simple quantitative metrics or benchmarks. Their judgments, supported by relevant data points and analysis, should be the primary driver of the risk assessment results and recommendations. The NIST SP 800-30 Revision 1 emphasizes the importance of leveraging subject matter expertise and experience in the risk assessment process, alongside empirical data gathering and analysis (NIST SP 800-30 Rev. 1, Section 2.

407. An organization is outsourcing its customer support function to a third-party service provider. Which of the following is the MOST important security consideration when selecting and onboarding the provider?
a. the provider's compliance with relevant industry standards and regulations, such as ISO 27001 and GDPR
b. the provider's ability to integrate with the organization's existing customer relationship management (CRM) system
c. the provider's physical security controls for protecting customer data, such as access controls and surveillance
d. the provider's pricing model and service level agreements (SLAs) for customer support performance metrics

Answer: a. the provider's compliance with relevant industry standards and regulations, such as ISO 27001 and GDPR. Explanation: When outsourcing a critical business function like customer support, which involves access to sensitive customer data, the most important security factor to consider is the third-party provider's adherence to applicable information security and privacy standards and regulations. Compliance with widely-accepted frameworks like ISO/IEC 27001 for information security management and GDPR for data protection demonstrates that the provider has implemented robust security controls and practices to safeguard customer information. It provides assurance that the provider has been independently audited and certified to meet rigorous security requirements, reducing the risk of data breaches, unauthorized access, or misuse. While factors like system integration, physical security, and service performance are important considerations, they are not as foundational as the provider's overall security posture and regulatory compliance. The organization should carefully review the provider's compliance certifications, audit reports, and security policies, and include specific security and privacy requirements in the service contract and service level agreement (SLA). The ISACA Information Security Sourcing guide provides detailed guidance on evaluating and managing the security risks of third-party relationships (ISACA ISS, Section 5).

408. An organization is assessing the information security risks of a critical software supplier that has access to sensitive corporate data. Which of the following is the BEST method for evaluating the supplier's security controls and practices?
a. reviewing the supplier's website and marketing materials for information about their security program and policies

b. conducting an on-site audit of the supplier's security controls, processes, and documentation
c. requesting copies of the supplier's SOC 2 Type II and ISO 27001 certification reports
d. asking the supplier to complete a detailed security questionnaire and self-assessment

Answer: c. requesting copies of the supplier's SOC 2 Type II and ISO 27001 certification reports. Explanation: When assessing the security posture of a third-party supplier, particularly one with access to sensitive data, it is important to obtain objective, independent evidence of the supplier's security controls and practices. The most reliable and efficient method is to request the supplier's relevant security audit and certification reports, such as a SOC 2 Type II report and an ISO/IEC 27001 certificate. A SOC 2 Type II report provides detailed information and assurance about the design and operating effectiveness of the supplier's security, availability, processing integrity, confidentiality, and privacy controls over a period of time, based on a rigorous independent audit against the AICPA Trust Services Criteria. An ISO/IEC 27001 certificate demonstrates that the supplier has implemented a comprehensive information security management system (ISMS) that meets the requirements of the international standard, as verified by an accredited certification body. Reviewing these reports provides a more thorough and trustworthy assessment than relying on the supplier's self-reported information or conducting a limited, point-in-time audit. However, the organization should still carefully review and verify the reports, and follow up with the supplier on any gaps or issues identified. The NIST SP 800-161 provides guidance on assessing and managing the security risks of third-party suppliers and contractors (NIST SP 800-161, Section 2.2).

409. An organization is negotiating a service level agreement (SLA) with a cloud service provider for hosting its mission-critical applications. Which of the following is the MOST important security metric to include in the SLA?
a. the maximum allowable downtime and recovery time objective (RTO) for the hosted applications
b. the frequency and scope of vulnerability scans and penetration tests performed by the provider
c. the percentage of the provider's staff who have completed background checks and security training
d. the encryption algorithms and key lengths used by the provider for data at rest and in transit

Answer: a. the maximum allowable downtime and recovery time objective (RTO) for the hosted applications. Explanation: When outsourcing mission-critical applications to a cloud service provider, the most crucial security consideration is ensuring the continuous availability and resilience of the applications. Downtime can result in significant business disruption, financial losses, and reputational damage. Therefore, the most important security metric to include in the cloud service level agreement (SLA) is the maximum allowable downtime and recovery time objective (RTO) for the hosted applications. The maximum allowable downtime specifies the total amount of time the applications can be unavailable over a given period, such as a month or year, before the provider incurs penalties or remedies. The RTO specifies the maximum amount of time it should take the provider to restore the applications to full functionality after an outage. These metrics establish clear, measurable expectations and accountability for the provider's performance and help mitigate the risk of prolonged disruptions. While other security measures like vulnerability testing, personnel screening, and encryption are important, they are more tactical and preventive in nature, rather than directly ensuring the availability and recoverability of the applications. The Cloud Standards Customer Council provides guidance on developing cloud SLAs that include key security metrics and requirements (CSCC Cloud SLA Guide, Version 1).

410. An organization is implementing a vendor risk management program to assess and monitor the security practices of its third-party suppliers. Which of the following is the MOST important step in establishing an effective program?
a. conducting an initial risk assessment of all existing suppliers to identify and prioritize high-risk vendors
b. developing a standardized vendor security questionnaire and assessment process
c. implementing a vendor risk management software platform to automate assessments and workflows
d. defining clear roles and responsibilities for vendor risk management activities across the organization

Answer: d. defining clear roles and responsibilities for vendor risk management activities across the organization. Explanation: While conducting initial risk assessments, developing standardized assessment processes, and implementing automation tools are all important components of a vendor risk management program, the most critical foundational step is establishing clear governance and accountability for the program. This involves defining the specific roles, responsibilities, and decision-making authorities for vendor risk management activities across the different functions and levels of the organization, such as procurement, legal, IT, security, and senior management. A well-defined governance structure ensures that vendor risk is consistently and effectively managed throughout the vendor lifecycle, from selection and onboarding to ongoing monitoring and off-boarding. It also promotes cross-functional collaboration, communication, and oversight, and helps ensure that vendor risk management aligns with the organization's overall risk management strategy and objectives. Without clear ownership and accountability, vendor risk management can become fragmented, reactive, and ineffective, leading to gaps and inconsistencies in risk identification, assessment, and mitigation. The NIST SP 800-161 emphasizes the importance of establishing a governance structure and risk management processes for third-party suppliers and contractors (NIST SP 800-161, Section 3).

411. An organization has discovered that one of its vendors has suffered a data breach involving the organization's sensitive data. Which of the following is the MOST important immediate action for the organization to take?
a. terminating the vendor contract and seeking legal remedies for the breach
b. publicly disclosing the breach and notifying affected customers and stakeholders
c. activating the organization's incident response plan and assessing the scope and impact of the breach
d. conducting a root cause analysis of the breach and identifying corrective actions for the vendor

Answer: c. activating the organization's incident response plan and assessing the scope and impact of the breach. Explanation: When a vendor suffers a data breach involving an organization's data, the most critical immediate priority is to contain and assess the potential impact of the breach on the organization and its stakeholders. This requires quickly activating the organization's incident response plan and procedures, which should include specific steps for managing third-party breaches. The incident response team should work closely with the vendor to gather information about the nature, scope, and timeline of the breach, and determine what specific data and systems were affected. They should also assess the potential consequences of the breach, such as regulatory violations, financial losses, or reputational damage, and identify any urgent mitigation or notification requirements. While actions like terminating the vendor contract, public disclosure, and root cause analysis may be necessary depending on the severity and circumstances of the breach, they are not the most time-sensitive priorities in the immediate aftermath of the incident. The focus should be on triaging the situation, limiting further damage, and understanding the full impact before taking broader response and recovery actions. The NIST SP 800-61 Revision 2 provides guidance on handling third-party data breaches as part of an incident response process (NIST SP 800-61 Rev. 2, Section 2.3.2).

412. An organization is assessing the security risks of a proposed new cloud service provider. Which of the following is the MOST important factor to consider in the risk assessment?
a. the provider's financial stability and market share in the cloud services industry
b. the provider's service level agreements (SLAs) and customer support offerings
c. the provider's data center locations and physical security measures
d. the provider's shared responsibility model and security controls for the cloud platform

Answer: d. the provider's shared responsibility model and security controls for the cloud platform. Explanation: When evaluating the security risks of a cloud service provider, the most critical aspect to examine is how the provider allocates and implements security responsibilities and controls within its cloud platform. Cloud security operates under a shared responsibility model, where the provider is responsible for securing the underlying infrastructure and services, while the customer is responsible for securing their own data, applications, and access. The exact division of responsibilities varies depending on the cloud service model (IaaS, PaaS, SaaS) and the specific provider's architecture and policies. Therefore, it is essential to clearly understand and assess the provider's security controls, configurations, and practices at each layer of the cloud stack, and how they interface with the customer's own security measures. This includes evaluating the provider's access management, network segmentation, data encryption, logging and monitoring, incident response, and other key security functions, and how they are implemented and maintained across the cloud environment. Factors like the provider's financial health, service quality, and physical security are important, but secondary to the core technical and operational security of the cloud platform itself. The Cloud Security Alliance (CSA) Cloud Controls Matrix provides a framework for assessing the security controls of cloud service providers (CSA CCM, Version 4).

413. An organization is outsourcing its software development to a third-party vendor and needs to ensure the security of the development process and deliverables. Which of the following is the MOST important requirement to include in the vendor contract?
a. the vendor's compliance with the organization's secure coding standards and practices
b. the vendor's use of static code analysis tools to identify and remediate vulnerabilities
c. the vendor's participation in regular security awareness training for its development team
d. the vendor's agreement to indemnify the organization for any security breaches or damages

Answer: a. the vendor's compliance with the organization's secure coding standards and practices. Explanation: When outsourcing software development to a third-party vendor, it is critical to establish clear and enforceable expectations for the security of the development process and outputs. The most fundamental and impactful requirement is for the vendor to adhere to the organization's own secure coding standards and practices throughout the software development lifecycle (SDLC). Secure coding standards define the specific rules, guidelines, and best practices for writing secure code and avoiding common vulnerabilities, such as input validation, error handling, and access control. They help ensure that security is consistently built into the software from the ground up, rather than bolted on later. By contractually obligating the vendor to follow the organization's secure coding standards, and providing them with the necessary training and resources to do so, the organization can maintain control and visibility over the security of the outsourced code. While other measures like using code scanning tools, providing security training, and establishing liability provisions can help reinforce and incentivize secure development, they are not as directly tied to the actual quality and security of the code itself. The OWASP Secure Coding Practices Quick Reference Guide provides an example of secure coding standards that can be adapted and incorporated into vendor contracts (OWASP SCP, Version 2.0).

414. An organization is evaluating a potential new vendor for a critical business process and needs to assess the vendor's security posture. Which of the following is the LEAST reliable source of information for the assessment?
a. the vendor's responses to the organization's security questionnaire and due diligence requests
b. the vendor's SOC 2 Type II report and ISO 27001 certification status
c. feedback and references from the vendor's other customers in similar industries
d. the vendor's website and marketing materials describing their security program and practices

Answer: d. the vendor's website and marketing materials describing their security program and practices. Explanation: When assessing the security posture of a potential vendor, it is important to gather objective, verifiable, and trustworthy information from multiple sources. The vendor's own website and marketing content is often the least reliable source, as it is designed to promote and sell the vendor's services, rather than provide a transparent and balanced view of their security capabilities and gaps. Vendors may exaggerate or selectively present their security measures, certifications, and track record, without fully disclosing the limitations, exceptions, or past incidents. While the vendor's website can provide useful background information and claims to investigate further, it should not be relied upon as a primary or definitive source for security assessment. More credible and substantive sources include the vendor's responses to specific security questionnaires and due diligence requests, which can be validated and clarified through follow-up discussions; the vendor's third-party security audit reports and certifications, which provide independent assurance of their controls; and feedback from the vendor's current or past customers, who can share their real-world experiences and lessons learned. The NIST SP 800-161 provides guidance on collecting and analyzing vendor security information from various sources as part of a supply chain risk management program (NIST SP 800-161, Section 2.2.1).

415. An organization has recently terminated a contract with a third-party service provider due to repeated security breaches and non-compliance issues. Which of the following is the MOST important step to take after the termination to mitigate further risks?
a. conducting a lessons learned review to identify the root causes and gaps in the vendor management process
b. updating the organization's vendor selection and onboarding criteria to prevent similar issues in the future
c. verifying that the former provider has securely destroyed or returned all of the organization's data and assets
d. notifying relevant stakeholders and authorities about the termination and the reasons behind it

Answer: c. verifying that the former provider has securely destroyed or returned all of the organization's data and assets. Explanation: When terminating a relationship with a third-party service provider, especially due to security and compliance failures, the most critical immediate priority is to ensure that the organization's sensitive data, intellectual property, and other assets are properly secured and disposed of by the provider. This is essential to prevent further breaches, leaks, or misuse of the organization's information after the contract ends. The organization should have clear contractual provisions and procedures for data and asset handling upon termination, including requirements for the provider to promptly and securely return, destroy, or transfer all relevant materials according to the organization's instructions and standards. The organization should verify and document the provider's compliance with these requirements, such as by receiving certificates of destruction, conducting audits or inspections, or using data loss prevention (DLP) tools. Only after the organization's assets are confirmed to be fully secured should it turn to other post-termination activities, such as conducting lessons learned reviews, updating vendor management processes, or notifying stakeholders. These are important steps for preventing future issues and maintaining transparency, but they are not as time-sensitive and critical as ensuring the safe and complete off-boarding of the organization's assets from the terminated provider. The ISACA Information Security Sourcing guide provides a checklist of key considerations and actions for securely terminating vendor relationships (ISACA ISS, Appendix D).

416. An organization is implementing a third-party risk management program and needs to prioritize its efforts based on the criticality and sensitivity of the data and systems accessed by each vendor. Which of the following is the MOST appropriate framework for this prioritization?
a. the NIST Cybersecurity Framework (CSF)'s five core functions of Identify, Protect, Detect, Respond, and Recover
b. the ISO/IEC 27001 standard's 14 security domains and 114 controls
c. the Cloud Security Alliance (CSA)'s Cloud Controls Matrix (CCM)
d. the organization's own data classification policy and schema

Answer: d. the organization's own data classification policy and schema. Explanation: When prioritizing third-party risk management efforts, the most relevant and appropriate framework is the organization's internal data classification policy and schema. Data classification is the process of categorizing an organization's information assets based on their level of sensitivity, criticality, and risk, and defining the corresponding security requirements and handling procedures for each category. A typical data classification schema includes levels such as Public, Internal, Confidential, and Restricted, with increasing security controls and restrictions for each level. By mapping each vendor's access and interaction with the organization's data and systems to the appropriate classification level, the organization can objectively and consistently assess the inherent risk and priority of that vendor relationship. Vendors with access to highly sensitive or critical data and systems, such as Confidential or Restricted information, would be considered higher risk and higher priority for more rigorous and frequent security assessments, monitoring, and controls. The data classification framework provides a clear, organization-specific basis for risk-based vendor prioritization and resource allocation. While other frameworks like NIST CSF, ISO/IEC 27001, and CSA CCM provide valuable guidance and best practices for managing vendor security risks, they are not as directly tied to the unique data and system risks of each organization and vendor relationship.

417. An organization is implementing a new information security program and needs to ensure that its staff has the necessary skills and knowledge to support the program. Which of the following is the BEST approach for the information security manager to take?
a. Conduct a skills assessment to identify gaps and develop a training plan to address them
b. Hire new staff with the required skills and knowledge to replace existing staff
c. Outsource all information security functions to a third-party provider
d. Assume that existing staff already have the necessary skills and knowledge

Answer: a. Conduct a skills assessment to identify gaps and develop a training plan to address them. Explanation: The best approach is to assess the current skills and knowledge of the staff, identify any gaps, and then develop a targeted training plan to address those gaps. This ensures that existing staff are given the opportunity to acquire the necessary skills and knowledge, rather than being replaced or having their responsibilities outsourced. It also allows the organization to tailor the training to its specific needs and environment.

418. A company is developing a new mobile application that will collect and store sensitive customer data. Which of the following should be the information security manager's FIRST step in ensuring the security of this data?
a. Conduct a penetration test of the application before release
b. Implement encryption for data stored on the mobile device
c. Ensure that the application requires strong user authentication
d. Involve the information security team in the design and development process

Answer: d. Involve the information security team in the design and development process. Explanation: The most effective way to ensure the security of the application and its data is to involve the information security team from the very beginning of the design and development process. This allows security considerations to be built into the application from the ground up, rather than being added on as an afterthought. While penetration testing, encryption, and strong authentication are all important security measures, they should be part of a comprehensive security approach that begins with the design of the application.

419. An organization has experienced a significant data breach involving the personal information of its customers. Which of the following is the information security manager's BEST course of action in the immediate aftermath of the breach?
a. Conduct a thorough investigation to determine the cause of the breach
b. Notify affected customers and regulatory authorities of the breach
c. Implement new security controls to prevent future breaches
d. Terminate the employment of any staff members responsible for the breach

Answer: b. Notify affected customers and regulatory authorities of the breach. Explanation: The first priority after a data breach is to notify those who may be impacted, including affected customers and relevant regulatory authorities. This allows individuals to take steps to protect themselves (such as changing passwords or monitoring for identity theft), and is often required by data breach notification laws. The investigation, implementation of new controls, and any necessary disciplinary actions are important steps, but should come after the initial notification.

420. An organization is implementing a bring-your-own-device (BYOD) policy to allow employees to use their personal devices for work purposes. Which of the following is the MOST important consideration for the information security manager in implementing this policy?
a. Ensuring that all employee devices are from the same manufacturer
b. Requiring employees to submit their devices for regular security inspections
c. Implementing strong security controls and policies for employee devices
d. Providing employees with a stipend to purchase new devices for work use

Answer: c. Implementing strong security controls and policies for employee devices. Explanation: The most critical aspect of a BYOD policy from a security perspective is ensuring that all devices that access corporate data and networks are subject to strong security controls and policies. This may include requiring devices to be password protected, encrypting sensitive data, installing security software, and restricting the installation of unauthorized applications. The specific make and model of the devices, regular physical inspections, and providing stipends for new devices are less important than ensuring that all devices adhere to the organization's security standards.

421. An organization is evaluating its incident response capabilities and wants to ensure that its staff is prepared to handle a major security incident. Which of the following is the BEST way for the information security manager to test and improve the organization's incident response readiness?
a. Conduct regular penetration testing of the organization's systems and networks
b. Send simulated phishing emails to employees to test their awareness
c. Review and update the organization's incident response plan annually
d. Conduct regular tabletop exercises and simulations of potential incidents

Answer: d. Conduct regular tabletop exercises and simulations of potential incidents. Explanation: The most effective way to test and improve an organization's incident response capabilities is through regular practice and simulation. Tabletop exercises, which involve key personnel walking through their roles and decision-making processes in a simulated incident scenario, can help identify gaps in the incident response plan, improve coordination and communication, and give staff valuable experience in handling incidents. While penetration testing, phishing simulations, and annual plan reviews are all useful practices, they do not provide the same level of practical preparation as simulated incident exercises.

422. An organization's information security manager is developing a plan to manage third-party risks. Which of the following is the MOST important element to include in this plan?
a. A requirement for all third parties to have ISO 27001 certification
b. A process for regularly auditing third parties' security practices
c. A contractual requirement for third parties to notify the organization of any security incidents
d. A prohibition on sharing any sensitive data with third parties

Answer: b. A process for regularly auditing third parties' security practices. Explanation: The most effective way to manage third-party risks is through regular oversight and verification of their security practices. This can be achieved through a formal audit process, which may include reviewing security policies and procedures, conducting on-site assessments, and testing security controls. While ISO 27001 certification, incident notification requirements, and data sharing restrictions can all be useful components of a third-party risk management program, they do not substitute for direct verification of a third party's security posture.

423. An organization wants to improve its employees' awareness of information security risks and best practices. Which of the following is the MOST effective approach for the information security manager to take?
a. Sending regular email updates about security news and incidents
b. Requiring all employees to read and sign the organization's security policy annually
c. Implementing a mandatory annual online security training course
d. Conducting regular in-person security awareness training sessions

Answer: d. Conducting regular in-person security awareness training sessions. Explanation: While all of the listed approaches can contribute to improved security awareness, the most effective approach is typically in-person training. In-person sessions allow for interactive discussion, Q&A, and tailoring of the content to the specific audience and their roles. They also tend to be more engaging and memorable than online training or written policies. However, the best security awareness programs often combine multiple approaches, such as supplementing in-person training with regular email updates and online resources.

424. An organization is considering implementing a zero-trust security model. Which of the following is a key principle of the zero-trust approach?
a. Trusting all devices and users within the organization's network perimeter
b. Requiring multi-factor authentication only for administrators and privileged users
c. Assuming that all network traffic is untrusted and verifying every request
d. Focusing security efforts primarily on protecting the network perimeter

Answer: c. Assuming that all network traffic is untrusted and verifying every request. Explanation: The core principle of the zero-trust security model is to assume that no user, device, or network traffic should be trusted by default, regardless of whether it originates inside or outside the organization's network perimeter. Under this model, every request to access a resource must be authenticated, authorized, and encrypted. This is in contrast to traditional perimeter-based security models that assume everything inside the network can be trusted. Zero trust requires a comprehensive approach to authentication and access control, rather than just focusing on privileged users or the network perimeter.

425. An organization is implementing a data classification scheme to ensure that its information assets are properly protected. Which of the following is the MOST important factor for the information security manager to consider when defining the classification levels?
a. The size of the files or data sets
b. The format of the data (e.g., text, image, video)
c. The sensitivity and criticality of the data
d. The age of the data

Answer: c. The sensitivity and criticality of the data. Explanation: The primary purpose of a data classification scheme is to ensure that an organization's information assets are protected in accordance with their value and risk. Therefore, the most important factor in defining classification levels is the sensitivity and criticality of the data. Sensitive data, such as personal information, financial records, or intellectual property, typically requires higher levels of protection than public or non-critical data. The size, format, and age of the data are secondary considerations that may influence how the data is handled or retained, but do not determine its inherent security requirements.

426. An organization is developing a business continuity plan to ensure that it can maintain essential functions during and after a disruption. Which of the following is the information security manager's MOST important contribution to this plan?
a. Identifying critical business processes and their dependencies
b. Developing strategies to maintain customer relations during a disruption
c. Ensuring the availability and security of critical information systems and data
d. Procuring insurance to mitigate the financial impact of a disruption

Answer: c. Ensuring the availability and security of critical information systems and data. Explanation: While business continuity planning is a multidisciplinary effort that involves many aspects of an organization, the information security manager's primary role is to ensure that the organization's critical information systems and data remain available, secure, and recoverable in the event of a disruption. This may involve implementing redundant systems, backup and recovery processes, and failover mechanisms to maintain system availability. It also requires ensuring that systems and data are protected against potential security threats that may arise during a disruption. The other listed activities, while important, are typically led by other functions such as business operations, customer service, and finance.

427. An organization wants to measure the effectiveness of its security awareness training program. Which of the following metrics would be MOST useful for this purpose?
a. The number of employees who completed the training
b. The percentage reduction in security incidents caused by human error
c. The average score on the post-training quiz
d. The total time employees spent in training

Answer: b. The percentage reduction in security incidents caused by human error. Explanation: The ultimate goal of security awareness training is to change employee behavior and reduce security risks, not just to provide information. Therefore, the most meaningful measure of a training program's effectiveness is the actual reduction in security incidents that can be attributed to human error, such as falling for phishing scams or mishandling sensitive data. While the other metrics (completion rates, quiz scores, training time) may provide some insight into the reach and immediate impact of the training, they do not directly measure its effect on real-world security outcomes.

428. An information security manager is presenting the results of a recent risk assessment to the board of directors. Which of the following is the MOST important information to include to help the board understand the organization's risk posture?
a. The number of high, medium, and low risks identified
b. The potential business impact of the top risks
c. The technical details of the vulnerabilities found
d. The percentage of systems covered by the assessment

Answer: b. The potential business impact of the top risks. Explanation: When communicating with the board of directors, it's crucial to focus on the business implications of security risks, rather than just technical details. The board needs to understand how the identified risks could affect the organization's operations, finances, reputation, and strategic objectives. While the overall number and distribution of risks, technical vulnerability details, and assessment coverage may provide useful context, the potential business impact should be the key focus to drive risk-based decision making and resource allocation at the board level.

429. An organization is considering investing in a new security information and event management (SIEM) system. Which of the following metrics would be MOST useful in making a business case for this investment?
a. The number of security alerts generated by the SIEM
b. The percentage reduction in the time to detect and respond to incidents
c. The number of false positive alerts eliminated by the SIEM
d. The total data volume processed by the SIEM

Answer: b. The percentage reduction in the time to detect and respond to incidents. Explanation: The primary business value of a SIEM system lies in its ability to help the organization detect and respond to security incidents more quickly and effectively. Reducing the time to detect and respond can significantly limit the potential damage and costs associated with a breach. Therefore, this metric directly ties to risk reduction and operational efficiency. While the other metrics (alert volume, false positive reduction, data processing volume) may relate to the SIEM's technical performance and efficiency, they do not directly measure its business impact in terms of improved security outcomes.

430. An organization has implemented a new intrusion detection system (IDS) and wants to measure its effectiveness. Which of the following metrics would be LEAST useful for this purpose?
a. The number of intrusion attempts detected by the IDS
b. The percentage of false positives generated by the IDS
c. The average time to investigate and resolve IDS alerts
d. The total network bandwidth consumed by the IDS

Answer: d. The total network bandwidth consumed by the IDS. Explanation: While network bandwidth consumption may be a consideration for the overall performance and scalability of the IDS, it does not directly measure the system's effectiveness in detecting and enabling response to intrusions. The number of intrusion attempts detected, the false positive rate, and the time to investigate and resolve alerts all provide more direct insight into how well the IDS is performing its core security function. High bandwidth usage by the IDS could actually be a positive indicator if it reflects comprehensive monitoring and analysis of network traffic.

431. An information security manager wants to benchmark the organization's security program against industry standards and best practices. Which of the following frameworks would be MOST appropriate for this purpose?
a. The NIST Cybersecurity Framework
b. The ISO 27001 standard
c. The COBIT governance framework
d. The ITIL service management framework

Answer: a. The NIST Cybersecurity Framework. Explanation: The NIST Cybersecurity Framework is specifically designed to provide a common language and methodology for organizations to assess and improve their security posture based on industry standards and best practices. It provides a comprehensive set of guidelines and controls across five core functions: Identify, Protect, Detect, Respond, and Recover. While the other listed frameworks (ISO 27001, COBIT, ITIL) include some security-related components, they are not as directly focused on benchmarking an overall cybersecurity program.

432. An organization has experienced a significant increase in the number of security incidents over the past year. Which of the following metrics would be MOST useful in identifying the root cause of this trend?
a. The average time to resolve each incident
b. The distribution of incidents across different attack vectors
c. The total financial impact of the incidents
d. The number of incidents that were publicly disclosed

Answer: b. The distribution of incidents across different attack vectors. Explanation: To identify the root cause of an increase in security incidents, it's important to look for patterns or trends in how those incidents are occurring. Breaking down the incidents by attack vector (e.g., phishing, malware, insider threat, etc.) can reveal which types of attacks are becoming more frequent or successful. This insight can then guide further investigation into the specific vulnerabilities or weaknesses that are enabling those types of incidents, informing targeted improvements to security controls and processes. The other metrics, while potentially useful for assessing the overall impact and response to incidents, do not provide as much direct insight into the underlying causes.

433. An information security manager is tracking the organization's progress in remediating vulnerabilities identified through regular scans. Which of the following metrics would be MOST meaningful to report to senior leadership?
a. The total number of vulnerabilities identified in the most recent scan
b. The percentage of high-severity vulnerabilities remediated within the target timeframe
c. The average time to remediate each vulnerability
d. The number of systems scanned for vulnerabilities

Answer: b. The percentage of high-severity vulnerabilities remediated within the target timeframe. Explanation: When reporting vulnerability management progress to senior leadership, it's important to focus on metrics that demonstrate the organization's effectiveness in addressing the most significant risks in a timely manner. The percentage of high-severity vulnerabilities remediated within the defined target timeframe directly measures this outcome. It shows how well the organization is prioritizing and resolving the vulnerabilities that pose the greatest potential impact, relative to its established goals. The other metrics, while relevant for operational vulnerability management, are less direct indicators of risk reduction progress from a leadership perspective.

434. An organization wants to evaluate the cost-effectiveness of its security controls. Which of the following metrics would be MOST useful for this purpose?
a. The total cost of the security controls
b. The number of security incidents prevented by the controls
c. The return on investment (ROI) of the security controls
d. The percentage of the IT budget allocated to security

Answer: c. The return on investment (ROI) of the security controls. Explanation: To assess the cost-effectiveness of security controls, the key is to compare the benefits they provide (in terms of risk reduction or incident prevention) to the costs of implementing and maintaining them. The return on investment (ROI) metric captures this relationship by calculating the net financial benefit of the controls relative to their total cost. A positive ROI indicates that the controls are providing more value than they cost, while a negative ROI suggests that they may not be worth the investment. The other metrics, while relevant to the overall security budget and performance, do not directly measure cost-effectiveness.

435. An information security manager is preparing a report on the organization's compliance with the Payment Card Industry Data Security Standard (PCI DSS). Which of the following metrics would be MOST important to include?
a. The total number of credit card transactions processed by the organization
b. The percentage of systems that are fully compliant with PCI DSS requirements
c. The number of staff who have completed PCI DSS awareness training
d. The frequency of PCI DSS compliance audits

Answer: b. The percentage of systems that are fully compliant with PCI DSS requirements. Explanation: The core objective of PCI DSS is to ensure that all systems that process, store, or transmit credit card data are adequately protected according to a defined set of security controls and practices. Therefore, the most direct and meaningful measure of an organization's PCI DSS compliance is the proportion of relevant systems that fully meet all applicable requirements. The other metrics, while potentially relevant to the overall scope and management of the PCI DSS program, do not directly measure the actual state of compliance.

436. An organization has implemented a security orchestration, automation, and response (SOAR) platform to streamline its incident handling processes. Which of the following metrics would be MOST useful in measuring the effectiveness of this implementation?
a. The number of security playbooks automated by the SOAR platform
b. The reduction in the average time from incident detection to resolution
c. The number of security analysts using the SOAR platform
d. The percentage of incidents automatically resolved by the SOAR platform

Answer: b. The reduction in the average time from incident detection to resolution. Explanation: The primary goal of a SOAR platform is to improve the efficiency and speed of incident response by automating repetitive tasks, orchestrating workflows across multiple tools, and enabling faster decision making. Therefore, the most direct measure of a SOAR implementation's effectiveness is the actual reduction in the time it takes to resolve incidents from the point of detection. This metric captures the real-world impact of the SOAR platform in terms of faster response and risk mitigation. The other metrics, while indicative of the scale and sophistication of the SOAR implementation, do not as directly measure its impact on incident response outcomes.

437. An organization wants to measure the effectiveness of its incident response process. Which of the following metrics would be MOST appropriate as a key performance indicator (KPI)?
a. The total number of incidents handled by the incident response team
b. The percentage of incidents resolved within the defined service level agreement (SLA)
c. The average cost per incident
d. The number of incident responders on the team

Answer: b. The percentage of incidents resolved within the defined service level agreement (SLA). Explanation: A key performance indicator (KPI) should measure the organization's performance against a specific strategic goal or objective. In the context of incident response, a primary goal is typically to resolve incidents quickly and effectively to minimize impact. The percentage of incidents resolved within the agreed-upon SLA directly measures this outcome, making it an appropriate KPI. The total number of incidents, average cost, and team size, while relevant metrics, do not directly measure the timeliness or effectiveness of incident resolution.

438. An information security manager is defining KPIs for the organization's security awareness program. Which of the following would be the MOST meaningful KPI?
a. The percentage of employees who have completed the annual security awareness training
b. The number of security awareness emails sent to employees each month
c. The reduction in the number of security incidents caused by employee errors
d. The total budget allocated to security awareness activities

Answer: c. The reduction in the number of security incidents caused by employee errors. Explanation: The ultimate goal of a security awareness program is to change employee behavior and reduce security risks, not just to provide training or information. Therefore, the most meaningful KPI for a security awareness program would measure the actual impact on security outcomes, such as a reduction in incidents caused by employee errors like falling for phishing scams or mishandling sensitive data. The training completion rate, email volume, and budget are relevant program metrics but do not directly measure effectiveness in terms of risk reduction.

439. An organization is establishing KPIs for its vulnerability management program. Which of the following would be LEAST appropriate as a KPI?
a. The percentage of high-severity vulnerabilities remediated within the defined timeframe
b. The average time to patch vulnerabilities across all systems
c. The frequency of vulnerability scans conducted
d. The percentage reduction in the organization's overall vulnerability exposure score

Answer: c. The frequency of vulnerability scans conducted. Explanation: While the frequency of vulnerability scans is an important operational metric for a vulnerability management program, it does not directly measure the program's effectiveness in reducing risk. More frequent scans may identify vulnerabilities faster, but they don't necessarily translate into faster remediation or overall risk reduction. The other options - the speed of remediation for high-severity vulnerabilities, the average patching time, and the reduction in overall vulnerability exposure - are more direct measures of the program's impact on the organization's security posture, making them more appropriate as KPIs.

440. An organization wants to measure the efficiency of its security operations center (SOC). Which of the following would be the MOST relevant metric?
a. The number of security alerts generated by the SOC's monitoring tools
b. The percentage of security alerts that are false positives
c. The average time to triage and investigate each security alert
d. The total number of security incidents handled by the SOC

Answer: c. The average time to triage and investigate each security alert. Explanation: The efficiency of a security operations center (SOC) is largely determined by how quickly and effectively it can analyze and respond to security alerts. The average time to triage and investigate each alert directly measures this aspect of the SOC's performance. A lower average time indicates a more efficient process for evaluating alerts and determining the appropriate response. The number of alerts, false positive rate, and total incidents handled are relevant workload and accuracy metrics but do not directly measure the speed or efficiency of the SOC's core alert handling process.

441. An information security manager is selecting KPIs to measure the performance of the organization's security incident and event management (SIEM) system. Which of the following would be MOST appropriate?
a. The number of log sources integrated into the SIEM
b. The percentage reduction in the average time to detect security incidents
c. The total data storage capacity of the SIEM
d. The number of security analysts trained on using the SIEM

Answer: b. The percentage reduction in the average time to detect security incidents. Explanation: The primary purpose of a SIEM system is to enable faster detection of security incidents by correlating and analyzing events from multiple sources. Therefore, a key measure of a SIEM's performance is how much it reduces the organization's average time to detect incidents compared to the pre-SIEM baseline. A significant reduction in detection time indicates that the SIEM is effectively identifying and surfacing potential incidents for investigation. The number of log sources, storage capacity, and trained analysts are important factors in the SIEM's implementation and use but do not directly measure its impact on detection speed.

442. An organization is developing KPIs to track the progress of its security control implementation project. Which of the following would be the MOST meaningful KPI?
a. The percentage of planned security controls that have been fully implemented
b. The total number of security controls planned for implementation
c. The number of staff-hours spent on implementing security controls
d. The percentage of the project budget that has been spent

Answer: a. The percentage of planned security controls that have been fully implemented. Explanation: The most direct measure of progress for a security control implementation project is the proportion of planned controls that have been successfully put into place. This KPI provides a clear indication of how far along the project is toward its ultimate goal of implementing all the defined controls. The total number of planned controls, staff-hours spent, and budget utilization are relevant project management metrics but do not directly measure the actual implementation progress in terms of delivered security capabilities.

443. An organization wants to measure the effectiveness of its security policies. Which of the following would be the MOST appropriate KPI?
a. The number of security policies that have been formally approved
b. The percentage of employees who have signed the security policy acknowledgment form
c. The frequency with which the security policies are reviewed and updated
d. The reduction in security incidents related to policy violations

Answer: d. The reduction in security incidents related to policy violations. Explanation: The ultimate purpose of security policies is to define expected behaviors and controls to reduce security risks. Therefore, the most meaningful measure of security policy effectiveness is the actual reduction in incidents that occur due to policy violations. This KPI directly ties the policies to their intended outcome of preventing security breaches or issues. The number of approved policies, employee acknowledgment rate, and review frequency are important aspects of policy management but do not directly measure the policies' impact on security outcomes.

444. An organization is establishing KPIs for its third-party security risk management program. Which of the following would be MOST appropriate?
a. The number of third-party vendors in the organization's supply chain
b. The percentage of third-party vendors that have completed a security questionnaire
c. The percentage of high-risk third-party vendors with risk treatment plans in place
d. The frequency of security audits conducted on third-party vendors

Answer: c. The percentage of high-risk third-party vendors with risk treatment plans in place. Explanation: The goal of a third-party risk management program is to identify, assess, and mitigate the security risks posed by the organization's external vendors and partners. A key measure of the program's effectiveness is the extent to which identified high-risk vendors have been addressed through the implementation of risk treatment plans, such as requiring additional controls, conducting more frequent monitoring, or even terminating the relationship. This KPI focuses on the most critical risks and the program's progress in actively managing them. The total number of vendors, questionnaire completion rate, and audit frequency are relevant program metrics but do not directly measure risk mitigation outcomes.

445. An information security manager is defining KPIs for the organization's data loss prevention (DLP) program. Which of the following would be MOST meaningful?
a. The number of DLP policies configured in the system
b. The percentage reduction in incidents of sensitive data leakage
c. The volume of data traffic monitored by the DLP system
d. The number of false positive alerts generated by the DLP system

Answer: b. The percentage reduction in incidents of sensitive data leakage. Explanation: The primary objective of a data loss prevention (DLP) program is to prevent the unauthorized exfiltration of sensitive data from the organization. Therefore, the most direct measure of a DLP program's effectiveness is the reduction in actual incidents of sensitive data leakage compared to the pre-DLP baseline. This KPI ties the DLP controls directly to their intended outcome of safeguarding critical data. The number of policies, volume of monitored traffic, and false positive rate are relevant operational metrics but do not measure the DLP's impact on the ultimate goal of preventing data loss.

446. An organization wants to measure the maturity of its overall information security program. Which of the following would be the MOST appropriate KPI?
a. The number of security technologies implemented across the organization
b. The percentage of the IT budget allocated to security initiatives
c. The number of security certifications held by the information security team
d. The average maturity rating across all domains of a standardized cybersecurity framework

Answer: d. The average maturity rating across all domains of a standardized cybersecurity framework. Explanation: Measuring the overall maturity of an information security program requires a comprehensive assessment of the organization's capabilities across multiple dimensions, such as governance, risk management, controls, incident response, and more. Standardized cybersecurity frameworks, such as the NIST Cybersecurity Framework or the Cybersecurity Capability Maturity Model (C2M2), provide a structured approach to evaluating maturity across these various domains. The average maturity rating across all domains provides a high-level indicator of the program's overall state and progress. The number of technologies, budget allocation, and team certifications are important inputs to the program but do not directly measure its holistic maturity.

447. An organization is implementing a security information and event management (SIEM) system to improve its security monitoring capabilities. Which of the following data sources should be given the HIGHEST priority for integration into the SIEM?

a. Network firewall logs
b. Physical access control logs
c. Employee HR records
d. Printer usage logs

Answer: a. Network firewall logs. Explanation: When implementing a SIEM, priority should be given to data sources that are most critical for detecting and investigating security incidents. Network firewall logs, which record all traffic entering and leaving the organization's network, are one of the most valuable sources of security data. They can help identify suspicious traffic patterns, attempted intrusions, and data exfiltration. While physical access logs, HR records, and printer logs may provide useful context for certain investigations, they are generally less critical for real-time security monitoring compared to firewall logs.

448. An information security manager is investigating a potential data breach incident. Which of the following data analysis techniques would be MOST useful for identifying the source and scope of the breach?
a. Regression analysis
b. Pivot tables
c. Correlation analysis
d. Data visualization

Answer: c. Correlation analysis. Explanation: In the context of a data breach investigation, correlation analysis is a powerful technique for identifying relationships and patterns among various security events and data points. By correlating data from multiple sources, such as system logs, network traffic, and user activity records, investigators can trace the sequence of events leading to the breach, identify the systems and data affected, and potentially pinpoint the entry point and attackers. While the other techniques (regression analysis, pivot tables, data visualization) can be helpful for understanding and communicating data, they are less directly applicable to the core investigative process of connecting related events.

449. An organization is conducting a risk assessment and wants to prioritize its security investments based on the likelihood and potential impact of different threats. Which of the following data points would be MOST important to collect and analyze for this purpose?
a. Historical data on the frequency and types of security incidents experienced by the organization
b. Industry benchmarking data on the average security budget of peer organizations
c. Vendor marketing materials on the effectiveness of various security products
d. Employee survey data on perceptions of the organization's security posture

Answer: a. Historical data on the frequency and types of security incidents experienced by the organization. Explanation: When assessing risks and prioritizing security investments, the most relevant and reliable data is typically the organization's own historical experience with security incidents. By analyzing data on the types of incidents that have occurred most frequently and had the greatest impact on the organization, security leaders can identify patterns and trends indicating which threats pose the highest risk and warrant the most attention and resources. While industry benchmarks, vendor claims, and employee perceptions may provide interesting context, they are less directly indicative of the organization's specific risk profile compared to its actual incident history.

450. An organization is deploying a user and entity behavior analytics (UEBA) solution to detect insider threats. Which of the following data sources would be LEAST valuable for training the UEBA's machine learning models?
a. VPN login records
b. Email server logs
c. Database query logs
d. Building badge reader logs

Answer: d. Building badge reader logs. Explanation: User and entity behavior analytics (UEBA) solutions use machine learning to establish baseline patterns of normal user and system activity and identify anomalous behaviors that could indicate a potential insider threat. To be effective, UEBA models need to be trained on data that is directly relevant to user and system interactions with sensitive data and resources. VPN login records, email server logs, and database query logs all provide valuable insights into user activity patterns related to accessing and handling critical data. In contrast, building badge reader logs, while potentially useful for physical security monitoring, are less directly relevant to detecting insider threats in the context of data and system access.

451. An information security manager is designing a dashboard to provide real-time visibility into the organization's security posture. Which of the following metrics should be EXCLUDED from the dashboard?
a. Number of open high-severity vulnerabilities
b. Average time to patch critical systems
c. Percentage of employees who have completed security awareness training
d. Total number of security incidents in the past year

Answer: d. Total number of security incidents in the past year. Explanation: The purpose of a real-time security dashboard is to provide a current snapshot of the organization's security state and highlight any areas requiring immediate attention. Metrics included in the dashboard should be focused on present conditions and recent trends, rather than long-term historical data. The number of open high-severity vulnerabilities, average patching time for critical systems, and current employee training completion rates are all relevant indicators of the current security posture. In contrast, the total number of incidents over the past year, while potentially useful for long-term trend analysis and planning, does not provide meaningful insight into the real-time security situation and could distract from more actionable current metrics.

452. An organization is conducting a post-incident review following a major security breach. Which of the following data points would be MOST important to collect and analyze to prevent similar incidents in the future?
a. Detailed records of the incident response team's actions during the breach
b. Network traffic logs from the affected systems during the time of the breach
c. Configuration settings of the security tools that failed to detect the breach
d. Personnel records of the employees responsible for maintaining the compromised systems

Answer: b. Network traffic logs from the affected systems during the time of the breach. Explanation: To effectively learn from a security incident and prevent recurrences, it's critical to understand exactly how the breach occurred. Network traffic logs from the compromised systems during the time of the incident are one of the most valuable data sources for this analysis. They can reveal details such as how the attackers gained initial access, what systems and data they interacted with, and how they may have exfiltrated data. While incident response actions, tool configurations, and personnel records may provide useful context, the network traffic logs are most directly relevant to understanding and addressing the specific technical vulnerabilities and attack paths exploited in the breach.

453. An information security manager is tasked with creating a comprehensive inventory of the organization's sensitive data assets. Which of the following data discovery techniques would be LEAST effective for this purpose?
a. Scanning network file shares for files containing sensitive data patterns
b. Interviewing business unit managers about their data handling practices
c. Analyzing database schemas for tables likely to contain sensitive information
d. Reviewing the organization's data classification policy document

Answer: d. Reviewing the organization's data classification policy document. Explanation: Creating an accurate inventory of an organization's sensitive data requires hands-on discovery and analysis of actual data sources and storage locations. While reviewing the data classification policy is an important step for understanding the organization's data protection requirements and categories, it does not directly identify where sensitive data actually resides. Scanning network file shares, interviewing data owners, and analyzing database structures are all more proactive techniques that involve directly examining systems and engaging with stakeholders to uncover sensitive data that may be stored across the environment.

454. An organization is implementing a data loss prevention (DLP) solution and needs to establish policies for detecting and blocking unauthorized data transfers. Which of the following data classification schemes would be MOST useful for defining granular DLP rules?
a. Public, Internal, Confidential, Restricted
b. Low, Medium, High
c. Regulated, Proprietary, Third-Party Confidential, Public
d. Financial Data, PII, PHI, Intellectual Property

Answer: d. Financial Data, PII, PHI, Intellectual Property. Explanation: Effective DLP policies need to be based on a data classification scheme that is granular enough to distinguish between different types of sensitive data and their associated handling requirements. A classification scheme based on specific data categories, such as Financial Data, Personally Identifiable Information (PII), Protected Health Information (PHI), and Intellectual Property, provides the most actionable basis for DLP rules. This allows for tailored policies that can detect and block unauthorized actions relevant to each data type, such as attempts to email PII or upload intellectual property to cloud storage. More generic classification levels, while useful for overall data governance, are less directly translatable into specific DLP detection rules and actions.

455. An organization is conducting a risk assessment and needs to gather data on the potential financial impact of various threat scenarios. Which of the following data sources would be MOST relevant for quantifying the direct costs associated with a data breach?
a. Historical data on the organization's annual cybersecurity insurance premiums
b. Industry benchmark data on the average cost per compromised record in a data breach
c. Vendor estimates of the deployment and maintenance costs of breach mitigation technologies
d. Legal department estimates of potential regulatory fines and settlements resulting from a breach

Answer: d. Legal department estimates of potential regulatory fines and settlements resulting from a breach. Explanation: When assessing the financial risk of a data breach, one of the most significant direct costs to consider is the potential for regulatory fines and legal settlements. These costs can be substantial, particularly for breaches involving sensitive personal data or regulated industries. The legal department is best positioned to provide estimates of these potential costs based on the specific regulatory requirements and legal risks applicable to the organization. While insurance premiums, industry benchmarks, and mitigation costs are relevant for overall risk management planning, they are less directly indicative of the specific direct financial impact the organization could face in the event of a breach.

456. An information security manager is implementing a security orchestration, automation, and response (SOAR) solution to streamline incident handling processes. Which of the following data integration challenges is MOST important to address for effective SOAR operation?
a. Ensuring that all data is stored in a common file format
b. Maintaining a consistent naming convention for security tools and systems
c. Normalizing event data from disparate sources into a common schema
d. Securing data transmission channels between the SOAR platform and other tools

Answer: c. Normalizing event data from disparate sources into a common schema. Explanation: A key function of SOAR is to ingest and correlate security event data from multiple tools and systems to provide a unified view for analysis and automated response. However, each security tool often generates event data in its own unique format and schema. To effectively process and analyze this data, the SOAR solution needs to be able to normalize these disparate formats into a common structure. This allows the SOAR to apply consistent rules, queries, and automation workflows across the aggregated data. While common file formats, naming conventions, and secure data transmission are all important considerations, they are less directly critical to the core SOAR function of event correlation and analysis compared to data schema normalization.

457. An information security manager is preparing a presentation for the board of directors on the organization's cybersecurity posture. Which of the following topics should be given the HIGHEST priority in the presentation?
a. The technical details of recent security incidents and how they were resolved
b. The overall effectiveness of the security program in reducing risk to the organization
c. The day-to-day operational metrics of the security team's performance
d. The security team's organizational chart and reporting structure

Answer: b. The overall effectiveness of the security program in reducing risk to the organization. Explanation: When communicating with the board, the focus should be on strategic, high-level issues that are directly relevant to the organization's overall risk management and business objectives. The board is most interested in understanding how well the security program is mitigating risk and protecting the organization's critical assets, rather than technical incident details, operational metrics, or team structures. While these other topics may provide useful context, the key message for the board should be a clear assessment of the security program's effectiveness in reducing risk.

458. An organization has experienced a significant data breach, and the information security manager needs to brief senior management on the incident. Which of the following should be the FIRST priority in the initial briefing?
a. Providing a detailed timeline of the incident response team's actions
b. Identifying the individuals responsible for the security failures that led to the breach
c. Outlining the steps being taken to contain the breach and prevent further damage
d. Estimating the total financial impact of the breach on the organization

Answer: c. Outlining the steps being taken to contain the breach and prevent further damage. Explanation: In the immediate aftermath of a major security incident, senior management's primary concern is ensuring that the situation is under control and that the organization is taking all necessary steps to minimize further harm. The initial briefing should focus on providing assurance that the incident is being actively managed and that appropriate containment and mitigation measures are in place. While accountability, incident details, and impact assessment are important, they are secondary to the immediate priority of stopping the bleeding and preventing additional damage.

459. An information security manager is presenting the results of a recent risk assessment to the board of directors. Which of the following metrics would be MOST useful for communicating the organization's risk exposure in business terms?
a. The number of critical vulnerabilities identified in key systems
b. The percentage of systems that have been patched for known vulnerabilities
c. The potential financial losses associated with the top identified risks
d. The percentage of the IT budget allocated to risk mitigation efforts

Answer: c. The potential financial losses associated with the top identified risks. Explanation: To effectively communicate risk to the board, it's important to translate technical risk findings into business impact terms that align with the board's strategic and fiduciary concerns. Expressing the top risks in terms of potential financial losses, such as lost revenue, remediation costs, or regulatory fines, provides a clear and compelling picture of the risk landscape in a language that resonates with the board. While vulnerability and patching metrics, as well as budget allocations, are relevant risk management indicators, they are less directly tied to the ultimate business consequences that are most meaningful to the board.

460. An organization has recently implemented a new security awareness training program, and the information security manager needs to report on its effectiveness to senior management. Which of the following data points would be MOST compelling to include in the report?
a. The number of employees who completed the training
b. The average score achieved by employees on the post-training quiz
c. The reduction in security incidents caused by human error since the training
d. Anecdotal feedback from employees about the training content

Answer: c. The reduction in security incidents caused by human error since the training. Explanation: The ultimate goal of security awareness training is to change employee behavior and reduce risk, not just to deliver content or assess knowledge retention. When reporting on the effectiveness of a training program to senior management, the most meaningful metric is the actual impact on security outcomes, such as a measurable reduction in incidents caused by human errors like falling for phishing scams or mishandling sensitive data. While completion rates, quiz scores, and employee feedback are relevant measures of the training program's execution, they are less direct indicators of its bottom-line effectiveness compared to tangible improvements in security posture.

461. An information security manager is preparing a budget proposal for the upcoming year and needs to justify increased investment in cybersecurity to senior management. Which of the following would be the MOST effective approach to make the case for the budget increase?
a. Highlighting the growing volume and sophistication of cyber threats in the news
b. Comparing the organization's security spending to industry benchmarks
c. Quantifying the potential return on investment (ROI) of the proposed security initiatives
d. Emphasizing the reputational damage the organization could suffer from a breach

Answer: c. Quantifying the potential return on investment (ROI) of the proposed security initiatives. Explanation: To persuade senior management to approve a budget increase, it's important to demonstrate the business value of the proposed investments. The most compelling case is made by directly quantifying the expected return on investment (ROI) of the security initiatives in financial terms. This involves estimating the costs of the initiatives, the risk reduction they are expected to achieve, and the resulting savings or benefits to the organization. By presenting a clear financial justification, the information security manager can frame the budget increase as a strategic business decision rather than just a cost. While threat trends, peer comparisons, and reputational risks provide important context, they are less directly tied to the specific merits of the proposed investments.

462. An organization has recently experienced a series of minor security incidents, and the information security manager needs to keep senior management informed without causing undue alarm. Which of the following communication strategies would be MOST appropriate in this situation?
a. Providing detailed technical reports on each incident as it occurs
b. Scheduling weekly in-person meetings with senior management to discuss the incidents
c. Sending a high-priority email alert to senior management for each incident
d. Including a summary of the incidents in the regular monthly security report to management

Answer: d. Including a summary of the incidents in the regular monthly security report to management. Explanation: When communicating minor security incidents to senior management, it's important to strike a balance between keeping them informed and avoiding unnecessary escalation or panic. Including a concise summary of the incidents in the established monthly security report is often the most appropriate approach. This ensures that management is aware of the issues but in the context of regular, periodic updates rather than ad-hoc emergency communications.

Detailed technical reports, frequent meetings, and high-priority alerts are more suitable for major, high-impact incidents that require immediate management attention and decision-making. For minor incidents, maintaining a regular, measured communication cadence helps to normalize the incident management process and reinforce confidence in the security team's handling of routine issues.

463. An information security manager is presenting to the board of directors on the organization's compliance with relevant security regulations and standards. Which of the following would be MOST important to emphasize in the presentation?
a. The specific technical controls implemented to meet each compliance requirement
b. The potential penalties and legal consequences of non-compliance for the organization
c. The overall level of compliance achieved and any areas of significant risk
d. The amount of staff time and resources dedicated to compliance efforts

Answer: c. The overall level of compliance achieved and any areas of significant risk. Explanation: When reporting on compliance to the board, the key is to provide a high-level assessment of the organization's compliance posture and highlight any areas of substantial risk exposure. The board needs to understand whether the organization is generally meeting its compliance obligations and if there are any significant gaps that could result in regulatory enforcement, legal liability, or reputational harm. Specific technical controls, while important for the implementation of compliance, are too detailed for board-level discussion. Potential penalties provide useful context but should not be the primary focus. Staff resource utilization is an internal operational matter that is less relevant to the board's oversight role. The emphasis should be on summarizing the big-picture compliance status and flagging major risk areas for the board's awareness and guidance.

464. An information security manager is preparing an annual report on the state of the organization's cybersecurity program for senior management and the board. Which of the following topics would be LEAST important to include in the report?
a. Key risk indicators (KRIs) and their trends over the past year
b. Major security initiatives completed and planned for the upcoming year
c. Results of recent security audits and assessments
d. Detailed network topology diagrams and system inventories

Answer: d. Detailed network topology diagrams and system inventories. Explanation: An annual cybersecurity report to senior management and the board should provide a strategic overview of the security program's performance, priorities, and direction. It should focus on high-level indicators and initiatives that are meaningful for assessing the overall effectiveness and maturity of the program. Detailed operational artifacts like network diagrams and system inventories, while critical for the day-to-day work of the security team, are too granular and technical for an executive-level annual report. KRIs, major initiatives, and audit results, on the other hand, offer valuable insights into the program's risk management outcomes, progress against objectives, and independent validation of controls, which are more relevant for management and board oversight.

645. An organization has decided to invest in a new cybersecurity technology, and the information security manager has been asked to present the selection and implementation plan to senior management for approval. Which of the following should be the MAIN focus of the presentation?
a. The technical superiority of the chosen solution over alternative products
b. The projected timeline and resource requirements for implementation
c. The expected benefits and risk reduction outcomes of the investment
d. The competitive landscape and market share of the selected vendor

Answer: c. The expected benefits and risk reduction outcomes of the investment. Explanation: When seeking senior management approval for a cybersecurity investment, the primary focus should be on articulating the business case and expected outcomes of the initiative. Management is most interested in understanding how the investment will improve the organization's security posture, mitigate risks, and support business objectives. The presentation should clearly outline the anticipated benefits, such as reduced incident frequency, faster detection and response times, or increased compliance, and tie them to the organization's overall risk management goals. Technical product comparisons, implementation details, and vendor market positioning, while relevant factors in the selection process, are secondary to the core value proposition and risk reduction rationale for the investment.

466. An information security manager is regularly reporting to senior management on the status of the organization's security awareness training program. Which of the following metrics would be MOST meaningful to include in these reports?
a. The number of training modules developed by the security team
b. The average duration of each training session delivered to employees
c. The percentage of employees who have completed the required training
d. The pass rate for the post-training assessment quiz

Answer: c. The percentage of employees who have completed the required training. Explanation: When reporting on the status of a security awareness training program to senior management, the most relevant metric is the completion rate, i.e., the proportion of employees who have fulfilled the training requirement. This measures the program's reach and uptake across the organization, which is a key indicator of its effectiveness in educating the workforce. The number of modules and average session duration are implementation details that are less significant for management oversight. The quiz pass rate, while a useful gauge of knowledge acquisition, doesn't directly reflect the program's overall penetration and impact. Management is primarily concerned with ensuring that all employees are receiving the necessary security education, which is best captured by the completion percentage.

467. An organization has experienced a significant security incident, and the information security manager is presenting an analysis of the incident to senior management and the board. Which of the following should be the MAIN focus of the presentation?
a. The detailed timeline of the incident from initial detection to resolution
b. The technical root causes and vulnerabilities that allowed the incident to occur
c. The impact of the incident on the organization and the lessons learned
d. The performance of the incident response team in handling the incident

Answer: c. The impact of the incident on the organization and the lessons learned. Explanation: When presenting a post-incident analysis to senior leadership, the primary emphasis should be on the incident's impact on the organization and the insights gained to prevent future occurrences. Management and the board are most concerned with understanding the consequences of the incident in terms of operational disruption, financial losses, data compromise, reputational damage, or other business-relevant factors. The presentation should also highlight the key lessons learned from the incident, such as identified gaps in controls, processes, or capabilities, and the corresponding corrective actions or improvements needed. Detailed timelines, technical root cause analyses, and tactical response evaluations, while important for the internal post-mortem, are less critical for the strategic discussion with top management.

468. An organization is conducting a risk assessment for its key information assets. Which of the following approaches would provide the MOST comprehensive understanding of the risks?
a. Conducting a quantitative risk assessment only
b. Conducting a qualitative risk assessment only
c. Conducting both quantitative and qualitative risk assessments
d. Relying solely on historical incident data to assess risks

Answer: c. Conducting both quantitative and qualitative risk assessments. Explanation: A comprehensive risk assessment should include both quantitative and qualitative approaches. Quantitative assessments provide numerical estimates of risk likelihood and impact, enabling objective prioritization and cost-benefit analysis. Qualitative assessments capture contextual factors, interdependencies, and subjective perceptions that are difficult to quantify but important for understanding the full risk landscape. Using both approaches together provides a more holistic and nuanced view of risks than either method alone. Historical incident data, while useful, is backward-looking and may not reflect current or emerging risks.

469. An information security manager is presenting the results of a quantitative risk assessment to senior management. Which of the following metrics would be MOST useful for communicating the potential financial impact of the identified risks?
a. The annual rate of occurrence (ARO) of each risk scenario
b. The single loss expectancy (SLE) for each risk scenario
c. The annualized loss expectancy (ALE) for each risk scenario
d. The impact rating (e.g., high, medium, low) for each risk scenario

Answer: c. The annualized loss expectancy (ALE) for each risk scenario. Explanation: The annualized loss expectancy (ALE) is the most comprehensive and meaningful metric for conveying the potential financial impact of risks to senior management. The ALE combines the single loss expectancy (SLE), which is the estimated cost of a single occurrence of a risk, with the annual rate of occurrence (ARO), which is the expected frequency of the risk scenario in a year. By multiplying the SLE and ARO, the ALE provides a quantitative estimate of the total financial exposure from each risk on an annual basis, enabling management to prioritize risks and allocate resources accordingly. Impact ratings, while useful for high-level categorization, do not provide the same level of financial specificity as the ALE.

470. An organization is evaluating the risks associated with a critical business application. Which of the following factors would be MOST important to consider in a qualitative risk assessment of the application?
a. The exact financial cost of a potential data breach involving the application
b. The interdependencies between the application and other systems and processes
c. The historical frequency of security incidents involving the application
d. The technical vulnerabilities present in the application's codebase

Answer: b. The interdependencies between the application and other systems and processes. Explanation: In a qualitative risk assessment, the focus is on understanding the contextual and subjective factors that influence the risk landscape, rather than precise quantitative measures. One of the most critical factors to consider is the interdependencies between the application and other systems, processes, and business functions. These interdependencies can amplify the impact of a risk event beyond the immediate scope of the application itself. For example, an outage or data corruption in the application could disrupt downstream processes, cause cascading failures in integrated systems, or hinder the delivery of dependent business services. Understanding these interconnections and their potential domino effects is essential for gauging the true magnitude and organizational consequences of application risks. Financial costs, historical incident data, and technical vulnerabilities, while relevant, are more quantitative factors that would be captured separately in a quantitative assessment.

471. An information security manager is reviewing the results of a qualitative risk assessment for a cloud-based customer relationship management (CRM) system. Which of the following risk scenarios would BEST illustrate the unique risks associated with cloud computing?
a. A malware infection spreading from the CRM system to other internal systems
b. An attacker exploiting a known vulnerability in the CRM system's authentication mechanism
c. A breach of the cloud service provider's infrastructure exposing the organization's CRM data
d. A denial-of-service attack making the CRM system temporarily unavailable

Answer: c. A breach of the cloud service provider's infrastructure exposing the organization's CRM data. Explanation: One of the key risks specific to cloud computing is the reliance on the security of the cloud service provider's infrastructure and operations. When an organization uses a cloud-based system like a CRM, it entrusts the provider with storing, processing, and protecting its sensitive data and workloads. A breach of the provider's infrastructure, whether due to external attacks, insider threats, or operational failures, could potentially compromise the confidentiality, integrity, and availability of the organization's data hosted in the cloud. This is a risk that is unique to the cloud model and largely outside the direct control of the organization itself. The other scenarios, such as malware infections, authentication vulnerabilities, and denial-of-service attacks, while serious, are more general cybersecurity risks that could apply to both cloud and on-premises systems. The qualitative risk assessment for a cloud-based system should pay special attention to provider-related risks and their implications for the organization's security posture.

472. An organization has conducted both quantitative and qualitative risk assessments for its IT infrastructure. Which of the following findings would be MOST concerning from a risk management perspective?
a. A risk scenario with a high annual rate of occurrence (ARO) but low single loss expectancy (SLE)
b. A risk scenario with a high impact rating but low likelihood rating in the qualitative assessment
c. A risk scenario with a high annualized loss expectancy (ALE) in the quantitative assessment
d. A risk scenario that was identified in the qualitative assessment but not in the quantitative assessment

Answer: c. A risk scenario with a high annualized loss expectancy (ALE) in the quantitative assessment. Explanation: From a risk management perspective, the most concerning finding would be a risk scenario with a high annualized loss expectancy (ALE) in the quantitative assessment. The ALE represents the total potential financial loss from a risk on an annual basis, taking into account both the likelihood and impact of the risk. A high ALE indicates a risk that has the potential to cause significant financial harm to the organization and should be prioritized for mitigation. A risk with a high ARO but low SLE may be less concerning overall, as the total annual impact (ALE) would be relatively low. A risk with a high qualitative impact rating but low likelihood may warrant monitoring but would not necessarily be as urgent as a high ALE risk. A risk identified qualitatively but not quantitatively suggests a need to reconcile the assessments, but the mere presence of the risk in one assessment and not the other does not inherently make it more concerning than a quantitatively validated high-impact risk.

473. During a qualitative risk assessment workshop, stakeholders are debating the likelihood and impact ratings for a particular risk scenario. Which of the following techniques would be MOST effective for building consensus and resolving the disagreement?
a. Conducting a vote among the stakeholders and using the majority opinion
b. Having the information security manager make the final decision based on their expertise
c. Facilitating a structured discussion to explore the underlying reasons for the differing perspectives
d. Deferring the decision until a quantitative assessment can be conducted to provide more objective data

Answer: c. Facilitating a structured discussion to explore the underlying reasons for the differing perspectives. Explanation: Qualitative risk assessments rely heavily on the subjective judgments and perceptions of stakeholders. When there is disagreement on the likelihood or impact ratings for a risk scenario, the most effective way to build consensus is through facilitated dialogue and exploration of the underlying factors influencing each perspective. The facilitator, often the information security manager or a risk management professional, should guide a structured discussion that encourages stakeholders to articulate the reasons behind their ratings, share relevant information or experiences, and consider alternative viewpoints. This process can help surface hidden assumptions, gaps in knowledge, or differing priorities that may be contributing to the disagreement. By fostering a shared understanding of the risk context and drivers, the group can work towards a more aligned and consensual assessment. Simply voting or deferring to the manager's opinion may not address the root causes of the disagreement and could lead to a less robust assessment. Deferring to a quantitative assessment may provide additional data, but it does not replace the need for stakeholder consensus on the qualitative factors that inform the risk ratings.

474. An information security manager is reviewing the results of a quantitative risk assessment and notices that the annualized loss expectancy (ALE) for a particular risk is significantly higher than the cost of implementing a proposed mitigation control. Which of the following would be the MOST appropriate course of action based on this finding?
a. Prioritize the implementation of the mitigation control
b. Conduct a more detailed qualitative assessment of the risk
c. Accept the risk and take no further action
d. Reevaluate the likelihood and impact estimates used in the ALE calculation

Answer: a. Prioritize the implementation of the mitigation control. Explanation: If the annualized loss expectancy (ALE) for a risk is significantly higher than the cost of a proposed mitigation control, it indicates a strong business case for implementing the control. The ALE represents the total potential financial loss from the risk on an annual basis, considering both the likelihood and impact of the risk. If the cost of the control is lower than the ALE, it suggests that the control would be cost-effective in reducing the risk and preventing potential losses. In this scenario, the most appropriate action would be to prioritize the implementation of the mitigation control, as it offers a clear return on investment from a risk management perspective. Conducting a qualitative assessment may provide additional context but would not change the fundamental cost-benefit analysis. Accepting the risk without action would not be prudent given the favorable economics of the mitigation option. Reevaluating the ALE inputs could be warranted if there are doubts about the accuracy of the estimates, but assuming the assessment is sound, the high ALE relative to the control cost is a compelling rationale for action.

475. An organization is using a risk matrix to prioritize risks based on their likelihood and impact ratings. Which of the following combinations of likelihood and impact would represent the HIGHEST overall risk level?
a. Low likelihood, high impact
b. Medium likelihood, medium impact
c. High likelihood, low impact
d. High likelihood, high impact

Answer: d. High likelihood, high impact. Explanation: In a risk matrix, risks are typically prioritized based on the combination of their likelihood and impact ratings. The highest overall risk level would be assigned to risks that have both a high likelihood of occurrence and a high potential impact if they were to occur. This combination represents the most significant threats to the organization, as they are not only highly probable but also highly consequential. Risks with a low likelihood but high impact, often referred to as "black swan" events, may be catastrophic if they occur but are less likely to materialize. Risks with a medium likelihood and medium impact pose moderate threats that require attention but may not be as urgent as high likelihood, high impact risks. Risks with a high likelihood but low impact are more frequent nuisances that may require ongoing management but have limited overall consequences. The risk matrix helps organizations visualize and prioritize risks based on this two-dimensional assessment of likelihood and impact, with the top right quadrant (high likelihood, high impact) representing the highest risk level.

476. An organization has identified a critical risk during a qualitative risk assessment but lacks historical data to quantify the likelihood and impact of the risk. Which of the following would be the MOST appropriate approach for the information security manager to take?
a. Exclude the risk from the assessment until quantitative data becomes available
b. Assign arbitrary numerical values to the likelihood and impact of the risk
c. Engage subject matter experts to provide estimates based on their professional judgment
d. Assume the risk has a low likelihood and impact due to the lack of quantitative data

Answer: c. Engage subject matter experts to provide estimates based on their professional judgment. Explanation: When faced with a critical risk identified through a qualitative assessment but lacking quantitative data, the most appropriate approach is to leverage the knowledge and expertise of subject matter experts (SMEs) to provide informed estimates of the risk's likelihood and impact. SMEs, such as experienced professionals, business process owners, or industry specialists, can draw upon their domain knowledge, historical observations, and intuitive understanding of the risk context to provide reasonable approximations. While these estimates may not have the same level of precision as data-driven quantitative assessments, they can still provide valuable guidance for risk prioritization and decision-making. Excluding the risk altogether until quantitative data is available could leave the organization exposed to a significant threat in the meantime. Assigning arbitrary numerical values without any basis would be misleading and could distort the risk prioritization. Assuming a low likelihood and impact by default would be an imprudent underestimation of the risk, particularly if it has been identified as critical through the qualitative assessment. Engaging SMEs to provide their best judgments, while acknowledging the limitations and uncertainties, is a pragmatic way to incorporate critical risks into the overall risk management process.

477. An information security manager is presenting the results of a risk assessment to senior management and wants to convey the potential impact of a particular risk in business terms. Which of the following metrics would be MOST appropriate to use?
a. The risk's annual rate of occurrence (ARO)
b. The risk's single loss expectancy (SLE)
c. The risk's exposure factor (EF)
d. The risk's annualized loss expectancy (ALE)

Answer: d. The risk's annualized loss expectancy (ALE). Explanation: When communicating the potential impact of a risk to senior management, it is most effective to use a metric that expresses the risk in terms of its overall financial or business implications. The annualized loss expectancy (ALE) is the most appropriate metric for this purpose, as it combines the single loss expectancy (SLE), which is the estimated cost of a single occurrence of the risk, with the annual rate of occurrence (ARO), which is the expected frequency of the risk scenario in a year. By multiplying the SLE and ARO, the ALE provides a quantitative estimate of the total potential financial loss from the risk on an annual basis. This allows management to understand the risk's potential impact in a tangible, monetary context that aligns with their business perspective. The ARO alone only conveys the frequency of the risk, not its impact. The SLE represents a single incident's cost but doesn't account for the cumulative effect over time. The exposure factor (EF) is a percentage of asset value loss but doesn't directly translate into a financial impact figure. The ALE is the most comprehensive and business-relevant metric for expressing the risk's potential consequences to management.

478. An organization is conducting a business impact analysis (BIA) to identify its most critical processes and systems. Which of the following is the MOST important outcome of the BIA?
a. A comprehensive inventory of all the organization's assets
b. A prioritized list of critical business processes and their recovery objectives
c. A detailed technical analysis of the organization's IT infrastructure
d. A set of recommended cybersecurity controls to mitigate risks

Answer: b. A prioritized list of critical business processes and their recovery objectives. Explanation: The primary purpose of a business impact analysis (BIA) is to identify and prioritize the organization's most critical business processes, along with the resources and dependencies required to support them. The BIA assesses the potential impact of disruptions to these processes and establishes recovery time objectives (RTOs) and recovery point objectives (RPOs) for each one. This prioritized list of critical processes and their recovery objectives is the most important outcome of the BIA, as it provides a clear understanding of the organization's key operational priorities and the timeframes within which they must be restored in the event of an incident. An asset inventory, while useful, is not the main focus of the BIA. A technical infrastructure analysis is a separate exercise from the business-focused BIA. Cybersecurity control recommendations, while important, are not directly part of the BIA process.

479. During a business impact analysis (BIA) interview, a business process owner states that their process must be restored within 24 hours of a disruption to avoid significant financial losses. This statement BEST represents which of the following BIA parameters?
a. Recovery Point Objective (RPO)
b. Maximum Tolerable Downtime (MTD)
c. Recovery Time Objective (RTO)
d. Service Level Agreement (SLA)

Answer: c. Recovery Time Objective (RTO). Explanation: The business process owner's statement that their process must be restored within 24 hours of a disruption is an example of a Recovery Time Objective (RTO). The RTO is the maximum acceptable amount of time that a business process can be down before the organization suffers significant consequences, such as financial losses, customer impact, or regulatory non-compliance. It is a key parameter captured during the BIA to establish the recovery priorities and requirements for each critical process. The Recovery Point Objective (RPO) is a different metric that defines the maximum acceptable amount of data loss for a process, expressed as a time interval. The Maximum Tolerable Downtime (MTD) is the total amount of time a process can be disrupted without causing irreparable harm to the organization, which may be longer than the RTO. A Service Level Agreement (SLA) is a contractual commitment between a service provider and customer, not an inherent characteristic of a business process.

480. An information security manager is reviewing the results of a recently completed business impact analysis (BIA). Which of the following findings would be MOST concerning from a business continuity perspective?
a. A critical business process with a Recovery Time Objective (RTO) of 4 hours
b. A high-priority system with a Recovery Point Objective (RPO) of 24 hours
c. A vital record with a retention requirement of 7 years
d. A key dependency on a third-party service provider with no alternate source

Answer: d. A key dependency on a third-party service provider with no alternate source. Explanation: From a business continuity perspective, the most concerning finding from the BIA would be a critical dependency on a third-party service provider for which there is no alternate or backup source. This single point of failure poses a significant risk to the organization's ability to recover and resume operations in the event that the third-party provider experiences a disruption or outage. Without an alternative provider or contingency plan, the organization's own recovery efforts may be severely hampered or delayed. A 4-hour RTO for a critical process, while challenging, is a reasonable recovery objective that can likely be met with appropriate strategies and resources. A 24-hour RPO for a high-priority system indicates a tolerance for some data loss and is not inherently concerning if proper backup and replication mechanisms are in place. A 7-year retention requirement for vital records is a common regulatory or legal mandate and can be achieved through appropriate archival and storage processes. But a single-source third-party dependency represents a potential single point of failure that could derail the organization's continuity plans.

481. During a business impact analysis (BIA), the BIA team discovers that a critical business process relies on a legacy system that is no longer supported by the vendor. What is the MOST appropriate recommendation for the information security manager to make based on this finding?
a. Accept the risk and continue using the legacy system as-is
b. Decommission the legacy system immediately to avoid any potential disruptions
c. Develop a plan to migrate the critical process to a modern, supported system
d. Purchase an extended support contract from the vendor for the legacy system

Answer: c. Develop a plan to migrate the critical process to a modern, supported system. Explanation: The discovery that a critical business process depends on an unsupported legacy system is a significant risk that needs to be addressed proactively. Legacy systems that are no longer supported by the vendor may be vulnerable to security threats, compatibility issues, and reliability problems. If the system fails, the vendor will not provide patches, updates, or technical assistance, which could severely impact the associated business process. The most appropriate recommendation is to develop a plan to migrate the critical process to a modern, supported system. This may involve identifying a suitable replacement system, defining migration requirements, and establishing a timeline for the transition. In the interim, compensating controls and contingency plans should be put in place to mitigate the risks of the legacy system. Simply accepting the risk and continuing to use the unsupported system indefinitely is not a prudent option. Decommissioning the system without a viable alternative would disrupt the critical process. Purchasing extended support, if available, could be a short-term mitigation but does not address the underlying problem of reliance on an obsolete system.

482. An organization is conducting a business impact analysis (BIA) and has identified a critical business process with a Recovery Time Objective (RTO) of 2 hours. Which of the following strategies would be MOST appropriate to achieve this RTO?
a. Implementing a warm standby disaster recovery site
b. Performing daily incremental backups of the process data
c. Developing a manual workaround procedure for the process
d. Establishing a hot standby disaster recovery site

Answer: d. Establishing a hot standby disaster recovery site. Explanation: To achieve a Recovery Time Objective (RTO) of 2 hours for a critical business process, the most appropriate strategy would be to establish a hot standby disaster recovery site. A hot standby site is a fully equipped and operational replica of the primary production environment, with real-time data replication and failover capabilities. In the event of a disruption to the primary site, the critical process can be quickly switched over to the hot standby site, allowing operations to resume within the 2-hour RTO. A warm standby site, while better than a cold site, typically requires some level of manual configuration and data loading, which may not be achievable within the 2-hour window. Daily incremental backups, while important for data protection, do not address the need for immediate system and process availability. A manual workaround procedure may be suitable for less time-sensitive processes but is unlikely to be a reliable solution for a critical process with a 2-hour RTO. The hot standby approach, although resource-intensive, provides the highest level of readiness and the fastest recovery capability to meet the stringent RTO requirement.

483. During a business impact analysis (BIA) workshop, participants are asked to estimate the financial impact of a disruption to a particular business process. Which of the following is the MOST appropriate basis for this estimate?
a. The total revenue generated by the process over the past fiscal year
b. The direct and indirect costs associated with the process being down for a specific duration
c. The amount of insurance coverage available for business interruption losses
d. The cost of implementing disaster recovery measures for the process

Answer: b. The direct and indirect costs associated with the process being down for a specific duration. Explanation: When estimating the financial impact of a disruption to a business process during a BIA, the most appropriate basis is to consider the direct and indirect costs that would be incurred if the process were down for a specific period of time. This includes both the immediate costs, such as lost revenue, idle labor, and remediation expenses, as well as the indirect costs, such as customer dissatisfaction, regulatory penalties, and reputational damage. By analyzing these costs over a defined outage duration, participants can develop a realistic and comprehensive assessment of the financial implications of a disruption. The total revenue generated by the process in the past is not directly relevant, as it does not account for the specific impact of an outage. Insurance coverage, while important for risk transfer, does not determine the inherent financial impact of a disruption. The cost of implementing disaster recovery measures is a separate consideration from the impact assessment. The key is to focus on the direct and indirect financial consequences that would stem from the process being unavailable for a given timeframe.

484. An organization has determined through a business impact analysis (BIA) that one of its manufacturing processes has a Maximum Tolerable Downtime (MTD) of 48 hours. Which of the following is the MOST significant implication of this MTD?
a. The process must be recovered within 48 hours of a disruption to avoid irreparable harm
b. The process can be down for up to 48 hours without causing any negative impact
c. The process requires a Recovery Point Objective (RPO) of 48 hours or less
d. The process must have a Recovery Time Objective (RTO) equal to the MTD

Answer: a. The process must be recovered within 48 hours of a disruption to avoid irreparable harm. Explanation: The Maximum Tolerable Downtime (MTD) is the total amount of time that a business process can be disrupted before the organization suffers irreparable harm, such as permanent loss of customers, market share, or viability. It represents the outer limit of acceptable downtime from a business perspective. In this scenario, an MTD of 48 hours for the manufacturing process means that if the process is down for more than 48 hours, the organization is likely to experience severe and potentially unrecoverable consequences. This implies that the process must be restored within the 48-hour window to avoid such catastrophic outcomes. It does not mean that a 48-hour outage would have no negative impact at all, as there may still be significant costs and disruptions incurred within that timeframe. The MTD is different from the Recovery Point Objective (RPO), which deals with data loss rather than downtime. The Recovery Time Objective (RTO) is the target time for recovering the process, which may be shorter than the MTD to minimize impact and provide a safety buffer. The MTD serves as an upper bound for the RTO but does not necessarily dictate it.

485. During a business impact analysis (BIA), it is discovered that a critical data set used by multiple business processes has a Recovery Point Objective (RPO) of 4 hours. What does this finding indicate about the data set?
a. It must be backed up at least every 4 hours
b. It can be unavailable for up to 4 hours without causing significant impact
c. It must be replicated to an alternate site every 4 hours
d. It can tolerate data loss of up to 4 hours' worth of changes

Answer: d. It can tolerate data loss of up to 4 hours' worth of changes. Explanation: The Recovery Point Objective (RPO) is the maximum amount of data loss that a business process or system can tolerate in the event of a disruption. It is expressed in terms of time, representing how far back in time the data must be recovered to resume normal operations. An RPO of 4 hours for a critical data set means that the organization has determined that it can accept losing up to 4 hours' worth of data changes for that specific data set. In other words, if a disruption occurs, the data can be restored to a point in time no more than 4 hours prior, and the business processes that depend on that data can still function acceptably. This RPO does not necessarily dictate the frequency of backups, as more frequent backups may be taken to provide additional granularity and recovery points. It also does not imply that the data can be unavailable for 4 hours, as availability is a separate metric governed by the Recovery Time Objective (RTO). The RPO is specifically focused on the acceptable data loss threshold, not the availability or replication requirements.

486. An organization is prioritizing its business processes based on the results of a business impact analysis (BIA). Which of the following processes should be given the HIGHEST priority for recovery?
a. A process with a Recovery Time Objective (RTO) of 24 hours and a low financial impact
b. A process with a Recovery Time Objective (RTO) of 8 hours and a moderate financial impact
c. A process with a Recovery Time Objective (RTO) of 4 hours and a high financial impact
d. A process with a Recovery Time Objective (RTO) of 48 hours and a high financial impact

Answer: c. A process with a Recovery Time Objective (RTO) of 4 hours and a high financial impact. Explanation: When prioritizing business processes for recovery based on BIA results, the two primary factors to consider are the Recovery Time Objective (RTO) and the financial impact of a disruption to each process. The RTO reflects the criticality and time sensitivity of the process, while the financial impact indicates the potential monetary consequences of an outage. In this scenario, the process with the highest priority should be the one with the most stringent RTO of 4 hours coupled with a high financial impact. This combination suggests that the process is extremely time-critical and that any prolonged disruption would result in significant financial losses for the organization. The process with an 8-hour RTO and moderate financial impact would be the next highest priority, as it still has a relatively short recovery window and notable financial implications. The process with a 24-hour RTO and low financial impact, while still important, has a longer acceptable downtime and lesser monetary consequences, making it a lower priority. The process with a 48-hour RTO, even with a high financial impact, has the longest recovery timeframe and thus the lowest priority among the given options. The RTO takes precedence over the financial impact when determining recovery priorities.

487. As part of a business impact analysis (BIA), an information security manager is assessing the critical dependencies of a key business process. Which of the following dependencies would be MOST important to document in the BIA?
a. The specific software applications used by the process
b. The individual employees who are trained to perform the process
c. The network infrastructure that supports the process
d. The third-party service provider that the process relies on for a crucial input

Answer: d. The third-party service provider that the process relies on for a crucial input. Explanation: When assessing the critical dependencies of a business process during a BIA, it is most important to identify and document any external dependencies that the process relies on, particularly those involving third-party service providers. If a key process depends on a service, product, or input from an external entity, any disruption to that provider could potentially impact the process's ability to function, regardless of the organization's own recovery capabilities. Therefore, understanding and documenting these third-party dependencies is crucial for developing comprehensive continuity strategies and identifying potential single points of failure. While internal dependencies, such as software applications, trained personnel, and network infrastructure, are certainly important to capture, they are typically more within the organization's direct control and can be addressed through internal continuity planning efforts. External dependencies, on the other hand, introduce additional risks and complexities that need to be carefully assessed and managed. The BIA should prioritize documenting the most critical and impactful external dependencies, such as sole-source providers, strategic partners, or those involved in just-in-time supply chains, to ensure that appropriate contingency plans and alternative arrangements are put in place to mitigate the risks associated with third-party disruptions.

488. An information security manager is implementing a continuous improvement process for the organization's security program. Which of the following is the MOST important benefit of this approach?
a. Ensuring compliance with all relevant security regulations and standards
b. Eliminating the need for periodic security audits and assessments
c. Reducing the overall cost of security controls and technologies
d. Enabling the program to adapt and optimize based on changing risks and needs

Answer: d. Enabling the program to adapt and optimize based on changing risks and needs. Explanation: The most significant benefit of a continuous improvement process for an information security program is that it allows the program to remain agile, responsive, and effective in the face of evolving security risks, business requirements, and technological advancements. By regularly assessing performance, gathering feedback, and making data-driven adjustments, the program can proactively identify areas for optimization and implement enhancements on an ongoing basis. This iterative approach ensures that the program remains aligned with the organization's changing risk landscape and can deliver maximum value and protection over time. While compliance, audits, and cost reduction are important considerations, they are not the primary drivers or benefits of continuous improvement. Compliance is a baseline requirement, but continuous improvement goes beyond mere compliance to strive for excellence. Audits and assessments remain necessary for validation and assurance, even with continuous improvement. Cost reduction may be an outcome but is not the main goal of optimization efforts.

489. An organization has established key performance indicators (KPIs) to measure the effectiveness of its security program. Which of the following KPIs would be MOST useful for driving continuous improvement efforts?
a. The number of security incidents reported per month
b. The percentage of systems with up-to-date antivirus software
c. The average time to patch critical vulnerabilities across the environment
d. The compliance rate for annual security awareness training

Answer: c. The average time to patch critical vulnerabilities across the environment. Explanation: When selecting KPIs to drive continuous improvement in a security program, it is most effective to choose metrics that directly measure the performance of key security processes and can provide actionable insights for optimization. The average time to patch critical vulnerabilities is a strong KPI for this purpose, as it reflects the efficiency and effectiveness of the organization's vulnerability management process, which is a critical component of the overall security posture. By tracking this metric over time, the security team can identify trends, bottlenecks, and opportunities for improvement in the patching process, such as streamlining patch testing, prioritizing high-risk systems, or automating deployment. Measuring the number of incidents, while important for general awareness, does not provide clear guidance for improvement without additional context. The antivirus update rate, although a useful hygiene metric, is a narrow and reactive measure that does not encompass the full scope of vulnerability management. The compliance rate for training, while valuable for assessing awareness efforts, does not directly tie to the operational effectiveness of critical security processes like patching.

490. An information security manager wants to foster a culture of continuous improvement within the security team. Which of the following approaches would be MOST effective for achieving this goal?
a. Implementing strict performance targets and penalties for not meeting them
b. Encouraging experimentation and learning from failures without blame
c. Rotating team members through different roles and responsibilities regularly
d. Providing monetary bonuses for identifying and reporting security weaknesses

Answer: b. Encouraging experimentation and learning from failures without blame. Explanation: To cultivate a culture of continuous improvement within a security team, it is most important to create an environment that encourages experimentation, innovation, and learning, even from failures or setbacks. By fostering a blameless and supportive atmosphere, team members feel empowered to take calculated risks, try new approaches, and openly share lessons learned without fear of retribution. This psychological safety is essential for driving continuous improvement, as it allows the team to iteratively test ideas, gather feedback, and refine processes based on real-world outcomes. Punitive measures like strict targets and penalties, while intended to motivate performance, often have the opposite effect of stifling creativity and discouraging the very behaviors that lead to improvement. Role rotation, while potentially useful for cross-training and skill development, does not inherently promote a continuous improvement mindset. Monetary incentives for reporting weaknesses, although well-intentioned, can create perverse motivations and undermine the intrinsic drive for improvement. The key is to nurture a culture of psychological safety, experimentation, and learning that empowers the team to continuously evolve and optimize their practices.

491. An organization is conducting a post-incident review as part of its continuous improvement process. Which of the following is the MOST important outcome of this review?
a. Identifying and punishing the individuals responsible for the incident
b. Determining the root causes of the incident and developing corrective actions
c. Calculating the total financial impact of the incident on the organization
d. Highlighting the successful actions taken by the incident response team

Answer: b. Determining the root causes of the incident and developing corrective actions. Explanation: The primary purpose of a post-incident review in the context of continuous improvement is to thoroughly understand the underlying causes of the incident and identify actionable steps to prevent similar occurrences in the future. By conducting a systematic analysis of the incident, including the timeline of events, contributing factors, and missed opportunities for detection or prevention, the organization can pinpoint the root causes that allowed the incident to happen. These could include technical vulnerabilities, process gaps, human errors, or other weaknesses in the security posture. Once the root causes are identified, the focus should be on developing specific, measurable, and achievable corrective actions to address them, such as implementing additional controls, refining processes, or enhancing training. Assigning blame or punishment is counterproductive and hinders the open sharing of information needed for improvement. Calculating the financial impact, while important for overall risk management, is not the main objective of the post-incident review. Highlighting successes, although valuable for recognizing good work, should not overshadow the need for critical analysis and improvement based on lessons learned.

492. An information security manager is implementing a plan-do-check-act (PDCA) cycle for continuous improvement of the security program. Which of the following activities would be MOST appropriate for the "check" phase of the cycle?
a. Developing and documenting new security policies and procedures
b. Conducting security awareness training for all employees
c. Monitoring and measuring the effectiveness of implemented security controls
d. Identifying and prioritizing security risks and vulnerabilities

Answer: c. Monitoring and measuring the effectiveness of implemented security controls. Explanation: The plan-do-check-act (PDCA) cycle is a widely used framework for continuous improvement in various domains, including information security. In the context of a security program, the "check" phase of the PDCA cycle is focused on monitoring, measuring, and evaluating the performance and effectiveness of the security controls and processes that have been implemented. This involves collecting relevant data, metrics, and feedback to assess whether the controls are operating as intended, meeting their objectives, and delivering the desired outcomes. Examples could include tracking key performance indicators (KPIs), conducting security audits or penetration tests, analyzing incident trends, or gathering user feedback. The insights gained from this monitoring and measurement process provide the basis for identifying areas for further improvement and adjusting the program as needed in the subsequent "act" phase. Developing policies and procedures is typically part of the "plan" phase, where the program's goals and strategies are defined. Conducting training falls under the "do" phase, where the planned actions are executed. Identifying and prioritizing risks and vulnerabilities is also part of the "plan" phase, informing the selection and design of appropriate controls.

493. An organization is establishing a continuous improvement process for its incident response program. Which of the following metrics would be MOST useful for tracking progress and identifying areas for optimization?
a. The total number of security incidents reported per quarter
b. The average time from incident detection to containment
c. The percentage of incidents that require public disclosure
d. The number of incident responders who hold professional certifications

Answer: b. The average time from incident detection to containment. Explanation: When implementing a continuous improvement process for an incident response program, it is most effective to focus on metrics that directly measure the efficiency and effectiveness of the response process itself. The average time from incident detection to containment, often referred to as the "mean time to contain" (MTTC), is a key performance indicator that captures how quickly the organization is able to identify, investigate, and control security incidents. By tracking this metric over time and comparing it against predefined targets or benchmarks, the incident response team can identify trends, bottlenecks, and opportunities for improvement in the response process. For example, if the MTTC is consistently longer than desired, the team may need to investigate ways to streamline alert triage, accelerate decision-making, or automate containment actions. Regularly monitoring and optimizing this metric helps drive continuous improvement in the speed and effectiveness of incident response. The total number of incidents, while important for general workload and risk assessment, does not provide specific insights into the performance of the response process itself. The percentage of incidents requiring disclosure, while relevant for compliance and stakeholder management, is more of an outcome metric than a process metric. The number of certified responders, although potentially indicative of team competency, does not directly measure the actual performance and results of the response program.

494. An information security manager is conducting a benchmark analysis as part of a continuous improvement initiative. Which of the following types of benchmarking would provide the MOST relevant and actionable insights for the security program?
a. Competitive benchmarking against industry peers
b. Internal benchmarking against the organization's own historical performance
c. Generic benchmarking against organizations outside the industry
d. Functional benchmarking against similar security processes in other organizations

Answer: d. Functional benchmarking against similar security processes in other organizations. Explanation: When conducting a benchmark analysis for continuous improvement of a security program, functional benchmarking is often the most valuable approach. Functional benchmarking involves comparing specific processes, practices, or metrics against those of other organizations that excel in similar functions, regardless of their industry. For a security program, this could mean benchmarking incident response processes against those of a highly regarded computer emergency response team (CERT), or benchmarking vulnerability management practices against those of an organization known for its robust patch management. By looking beyond direct competitors and focusing on functional excellence, the security team can identify proven best practices, innovative approaches, and performance standards that can be adapted and applied to drive improvement in their own processes. Competitive benchmarking, while useful for general market positioning and strategic planning, may not provide the most relevant or granular insights for operational security processes. Internal benchmarking, although important for tracking progress over time, does not expose the team to external ideas and practices that could spur significant improvement. Generic benchmarking against unrelated organizations is less likely to yield applicable insights than targeted functional benchmarking.

495. An organization has implemented a continuous monitoring program as part of its ongoing security improvement efforts. Which of the following capabilities is MOST critical for the effectiveness of this program?
a. The ability to collect and analyze log data from all systems and applications
b. The ability to detect and alert on deviations from established baselines
c. The ability to automatically remediate identified security issues
d. The ability to generate comprehensive compliance reports on demand

Answer: b. The ability to detect and alert on deviations from established baselines. Explanation: The core objective of a continuous monitoring program is to provide ongoing visibility into the organization's security posture and enable proactive detection and response to potential issues or threats. To achieve this, the most critical capability is the ability to establish baseline configurations and activity profiles for systems, networks, and users, and to detect and alert on any deviations from these baselines in real-time. This allows the security team to quickly identify and investigate anomalous behavior, unauthorized changes, or policy violations that could indicate a security incident or increased risk. By continuously comparing actual state and activity against approved baselines, the program can surface potential problems before they escalate and provide a feedback loop for ongoing improvement. While log collection and analysis, automated remediation, and compliance reporting are all valuable capabilities that can enhance a continuous monitoring program, they are not as fundamental as the ability to detect deviations from baselines. Comprehensive log analysis, while important, is more of an enabling function for investigating and validating alerts. Automated remediation, although useful for efficiency, depends on first having reliable detection in place. Compliance reporting, while necessary for audits and oversight, is more of a byproduct than a core driver of continuous monitoring effectiveness.

496. An information security manager wants to implement a metrics-driven approach to continuous improvement of the security program. Which of the following is the MOST important consideration when selecting metrics for this purpose?
a. Choosing metrics that are easy to collect and report
b. Focusing on metrics that are specifically required by security frameworks and regulations
c. Selecting metrics that are directly aligned with the organization's key security risks and objectives
d. Prioritizing metrics that showcase the success and value of the security team

Answer: c. Selecting metrics that are directly aligned with the organization's key security risks and objectives. Explanation: When implementing a metrics-driven continuous improvement approach for a security program, the most critical factor in selecting appropriate metrics is to ensure that they are directly tied to the organization's most significant security risks and strategic objectives. The chosen metrics should provide meaningful insights into the performance and effectiveness of the security controls and processes that are most relevant to mitigating the organization's top risks and supporting its key goals. This alignment ensures that the metrics are not just vanity measures, but actionable indicators that can drive prioritized and impactful improvements. For example, if protecting customer data is a core objective, metrics related to data encryption, access controls, and breach response times would be highly relevant. By focusing on metrics that matter most to the organization's specific risk profile and priorities, the security team can optimize their efforts and demonstrate clear value to stakeholders. Ease of collection, while a practical consideration, should not override the importance of selecting meaningful and risk-aligned metrics. Compliance-mandated metrics, although necessary, may not cover the full spectrum of the organization's risks and objectives. Metrics that merely showcase team successes, without providing actionable insights for improvement, are of limited value in a continuous improvement context.

497. An organization is implementing a risk-based approach to continuous improvement of its security controls. Which of the following activities is MOST essential for the success of this approach?
a. Conducting regular vulnerability scans of all systems and applications
b. Performing annual penetration testing of the network perimeter
c. Monitoring and analyzing security events and incidents
d. Identifying and prioritizing risks based on their potential impact and likelihood

Answer: d. Identifying and prioritizing risks based on their potential impact and likelihood. Explanation: A risk-based approach to continuous improvement focuses on allocating resources and effort towards the security controls and processes that are most critical for mitigating the organization's highest priority risks. The foundational activity in this approach is to systematically identify, assess, and prioritize the various risks facing the organization based on their potential impact and likelihood of occurrence. This involves analyzing factors such as the value and sensitivity of assets, the prevalence and severity of threats, the effectiveness of existing controls, and the potential consequences of a breach or disruption. By quantifying and ranking risks in this manner, the organization can target its improvement efforts on the areas that pose the greatest danger and where enhancements will yield the most risk reduction value. Regular vulnerability scanning, while an important technical control, is more of a tactical activity that supports but does not replace strategic risk assessment and prioritization. Annual perimeter penetration testing, although useful for validating external defenses, provides only a point-in-time snapshot and does not address the full spectrum of risks. Continuous security monitoring and incident analysis, while crucial for detecting and responding to threats, are more reactive than proactive in nature. The key to a successful risk-based improvement approach is to first establish a clear understanding and prioritization of risks to guide the optimization of controls and processes.

498. An organization's incident response plan should prioritize which of the following objectives?
a. Minimizing negative publicity and reputational damage
b. Gathering evidence for potential legal proceedings
c. Containing the incident and restoring normal operations
d. Determining the root cause of the incident

Answer: c. Containing the incident and restoring normal operations. Explanation: The primary objective of an incident response plan should be to swiftly contain the incident, mitigate its impact, and restore normal business operations. While other objectives like minimizing reputational damage, preserving evidence, and identifying root causes are important, they are secondary to the immediate need to stop the incident from causing further harm and disruption. The faster the incident can be contained and systems restored, the less overall damage the organization is likely to suffer. Reputation management and legal considerations, while significant, should not override the priority of incident containment and recovery. Root cause analysis, although crucial for preventing future incidents, is typically conducted after the incident has been successfully contained and resolved.

499. During an incident response, the team discovers that the attacker has gained unauthorized access to sensitive customer data. Which of the following actions should be taken FIRST?
a. Notifying affected customers and regulatory authorities
b. Conducting a forensic analysis of the compromised systems
c. Disconnecting the compromised systems from the network
d. Activating the organization's crisis communication plan

Answer: c. Disconnecting the compromised systems from the network. Explanation: When an active security incident involves unauthorized access to sensitive data, the immediate priority should be to contain the breach and prevent further data exfiltration or damage. The first step in containment is typically to disconnect the compromised systems from the network, either by physically unplugging them or by using network segregation controls like VLANs or firewalls. This isolates the affected systems and cuts off the attacker's access, stopping the bleeding. Once containment is achieved, other important actions like forensic analysis, stakeholder notification, and crisis communication can be initiated, but they should not delay the critical first step of disconnecting the compromised systems. Forensic analysis is essential but can be performed on the isolated systems without risking further exposure. Notification and communication, while vital for compliance and transparency, are not as time-sensitive as stopping the active breach. The key is to prioritize containment actions that directly disrupt the attacker's access and ability to cause further harm.

500. Which of the following incident response team structures would be MOST effective for a large, geographically dispersed organization?
a. A centralized team located at the organization's headquarters
b. Separate, independent teams at each regional office
c. A hybrid model with a central team and smaller regional teams
d. An outsourced team managed by a third-party service provider

Answer: c. A hybrid model with a central team and smaller regional teams. Explanation: For a large organization with geographically distributed operations, a hybrid incident response team structure that combines a central team with smaller regional teams is often the most effective approach. The central team, typically located at the organization's headquarters, provides overall coordination, expertise, and support for incident response activities. They establish incident response policies, procedures, and tools, and serve as a central point of contact and escalation. The regional teams, located at key sites or offices, provide local incident response capabilities and serve as the first line of defense. They are familiar with the specific systems, applications, and business processes at their location and can respond quickly to incidents in their area. The regional teams coordinate with and escalate to the central team as needed based on the severity and scope of the incident. This hybrid model balances the need for centralized oversight and consistency with the need for local responsiveness and flexibility. A fully centralized model may struggle to address local variations and provide timely on-site response. Completely separate regional teams may lack coordination and economies of scale. Outsourcing the entire incident response function to a third party may not provide the necessary integration with internal teams and knowledge of the organization's environment.

501. An organization is conducting a lessons-learned review following a major security incident. Which of the following is the MOST important outcome of this review?
a. Assigning blame and holding individuals accountable for mistakes
b. Identifying areas for improvement in incident detection and response capabilities
c. Calculating the total financial impact of the incident
d. Updating the incident response plan with tactical steps taken during the response

Answer: b. Identifying areas for improvement in incident detection and response capabilities. Explanation: The primary purpose of a lessons-learned review following a security incident is to critically examine the organization's performance in detecting, responding to, and recovering from the incident, and to identify opportunities for improving these capabilities for future incidents. The focus should be on objectively analyzing what worked well, what didn't work, and what could be done differently or better. This may include assessing the effectiveness of technical controls, incident response procedures, communication channels, decision-making processes, and team coordination. The insights gained from this analysis should be translated into specific, actionable recommendations for enhancing the organization's incident detection and response posture. Assigning blame is counterproductive and can hinder the open sharing of information needed for improvement. Calculating financial impact, while important for overall risk management, is a separate exercise from capability improvement. Updating the tactical steps in the incident response plan, while potentially useful, should follow from the broader lessons learned, not drive them. The key is to focus on identifying systemic improvements that will better prepare the organization to handle future incidents.

502. During an incident response, the team is debating whether to shut down a compromised system or to keep it running for monitoring and evidence gathering purposes. Which of the following should be the MOST important consideration in this decision?
a. The potential for the attacker to cause additional damage or data loss
b. The importance of the system for business operations and productivity
c. The need to preserve the system in its current state for forensic analysis
d. The time and effort required to restore the system from backups

Answer: a. The potential for the attacker to cause additional damage or data loss. Explanation: When deciding whether to shut down a compromised system during an incident response, the top priority should be to minimize further harm and data loss. If keeping the system online risks allowing the attacker to continue their malicious activities, exfiltrate more data, or spread to other systems, then the prudent course of action is to shut it down or disconnect it from the network. The immediacy of stopping the attack should take precedence over other considerations. While the system may be important for business operations, the potential business impact of a more extensive breach is likely to outweigh the temporary disruption of shutting it down. The desire to preserve the system's state for forensics is understandable, but not at the expense of live data or assets. Many forensic techniques can still be applied to a shut-down system, and the team can pursue other investigative avenues. The effort to restore the system is a valid concern, but is secondary to the urgent need to contain the threat. When there is an active risk of additional damage, the incident response team should prioritize shutting down the compromised system to limit the impact, even if there are other competing interests.

503. Which of the following is the MOST important reason for involving legal counsel in incident response planning and execution?
a. To ensure that incident responders follow proper chain-of-custody procedures for evidence
b. To determine whether and when to notify law enforcement authorities about an incident
c. To advise on regulatory compliance and potential legal liabilities arising from an incident
d. To authorize the use of offensive hacking techniques against the attacker's systems

Answer: c. To advise on regulatory compliance and potential legal liabilities arising from an incident. Explanation: The most critical reason for involving legal counsel in incident response is to ensure that the organization meets its regulatory obligations and manages its legal risks in the wake of a security incident. Depending on the nature of the incident and the type of data or systems affected, there may be various breach notification laws, reporting requirements, or contractual obligations that the organization needs to comply with. Failing to do so could result in regulatory penalties, lawsuits, or other legal consequences. Legal counsel can advise the incident response team on what notifications and disclosures are legally required, to whom, and within what timeframes. They can also help assess the potential legal liabilities stemming from the incident, such as the risk of customer lawsuits or regulatory enforcement actions, and recommend strategies for mitigating these risks. While legal counsel can certainly advise on evidence handling procedures and law enforcement engagement, these are more tactical considerations that are secondary to the overarching need for regulatory and legal risk management. Authorizing offensive hacking would be highly inadvisable and is not a legitimate role for legal counsel in incident response. The key is to involve legal experts early and often to navigate the complex regulatory landscape and liability issues surrounding a significant security incident.

504. An incident response team is investigating a suspected data breach involving customer personally identifiable information (PII). Which of the following is the MOST critical information for assessing the potential impact of the breach?
a. The total number of customer records in the affected database
b. The types of PII data elements that were potentially exposed
c. The network security controls that were in place at the time of the breach
d. The identity and location of the suspected attackers

Answer: b. The types of PII data elements that were potentially exposed. Explanation: When a data breach involves customer PII, the most important factor for assessing the potential impact is the specific types of data elements that were potentially compromised. Not all PII is equally sensitive or regulated. The exposure of basic contact information like names and email addresses, while still a concern, is generally less severe than the exposure of more sensitive data like social security numbers, financial account details, or health records. The types of PII involved determine the applicable breach notification laws, the risk of identity theft or fraud for affected individuals, and the level of regulatory scrutiny and potential penalties for the organization. For example, the breach of protected health information (PHI) would trigger HIPAA obligations, while the breach of credit card data would invoke PCI DSS requirements. Understanding exactly what types of PII were at risk is crucial for accurately gauging the severity of the breach and mounting an appropriate response. The total number of records, while relevant for scoping the incident, is less critical than the data types. The security controls in place, while important for the forensic investigation and future prevention, don't change the fact that the data was exposed. The attackers' identity, while useful for law enforcement, doesn't fundamentally alter the impact to the affected individuals and the organization's responsibilities.

505. In the aftermath of a security incident, an organization is reviewing its incident response performance. Which of the following metrics would be MOST useful for measuring the effectiveness of the response?
a. The total number of staff hours spent on incident response activities
b. The percentage of incident responders who have completed relevant certifications
c. The time elapsed between initial detection and full containment of the incident
d. The number of news media inquiries received regarding the incident

Answer: c. The time elapsed between initial detection and full containment of the incident. Explanation: When assessing the effectiveness of an incident response effort, one of the most crucial metrics is the time it took from first detecting the incident to fully containing it, often referred to as the "mean time to contain" (MTTC). This metric directly measures the speed and efficiency of the organization's incident response capabilities in limiting the impact and spread of a security incident. The faster the incident can be contained, the less damage it is likely to cause in terms of data loss, system downtime, financial costs, and reputational harm. A low MTTC indicates a well-prepared and well-executed response, while a high MTTC suggests areas for improvement in detection, decision-making, and mitigation capabilities. The total staff hours spent, while reflecting the level of effort, don't necessarily correlate with the effectiveness or timeliness of the response. Responder certifications, although potentially indicating individual competencies, don't directly measure the team's actual performance under real-world conditions. The volume of media inquiries, while possibly reflecting the public visibility of the incident, is more a measure of external interest than internal response effectiveness. The MTTC stands out as the most meaningful and outcome-focused metric for gauging the success of an incident response in minimizing the incident's duration and impact.

506. An organization is setting up a security operations center (SOC) to handle incident detection and response. Which of the following capabilities should be the SOC's HIGHEST priority?
a. Conducting penetration testing and vulnerability assessments
b. Developing and delivering security awareness training for employees
c. Monitoring security events and alerts across the organization's systems and networks
d. Performing digital forensics and in-depth incident investigations

Answer: c. Monitoring security events and alerts across the organization's systems and networks. Explanation: The core mission of a security operations center (SOC) is to continuously monitor an organization's IT environment for potential security incidents and to coordinate the response to those incidents. The SOC serves as the central command center for detecting, triaging, and managing security events and alerts across the organization's various systems, applications, and networks. This real-time monitoring and alerting capability should be the SOC's highest priority, as it is essential for identifying and reacting to potential threats and anomalies in a timely manner. Without effective monitoring, the SOC would be blind to emerging incidents and unable to fulfill its primary purpose. While penetration testing and vulnerability assessments are important proactive security measures, they are typically conducted periodically and are not the SOC's core ongoing responsibility. Security awareness training, while crucial for strengthening the human element of security, is usually a function of the broader security program rather than the SOC specifically. Digital forensics and in-depth incident investigations, while certainly part of the SOC's duties, are reactive activities that come into play after an incident has been detected. The SOC's foremost priority should be the proactive and continuous monitoring that enables prompt incident detection and response in the first place.

507. An incident response team suspects that an insider threat may be responsible for a series of confidential data leaks. Which of the following actions should the team take FIRST?
a. Initiate covert surveillance of the suspected employee's activities
b. Conduct a forensic analysis of the employee's work devices and accounts
c. Interview the employee's co-workers and managers for potential leads
d. Escalate the matter to law enforcement for a formal criminal investigation

Answer: b. Conduct a forensic analysis of the employee's work devices and accounts. Explanation: When an insider threat is suspected in a data leakage incident, the incident response team's first priority should be to gather and preserve relevant digital evidence that could support or refute the suspicion. This typically involves conducting a forensic analysis of the suspect's work-issued computers, mobile devices, email accounts, network activity logs, and other IT resources to which they had access. The goal is to look for any indicators of unauthorized data access, copying, transmission, or deletion that could corroborate the insider threat hypothesis. This digital evidence is crucial for determining the scope and method of the data leaks and identifying the responsible party. Covert surveillance, while potentially useful, raises legal and ethical concerns and should not be undertaken without clear justification and authority. Interviewing co-workers, while possibly providing useful context or leads, is less directly relevant than examining the primary evidence from the suspect's own IT activities. Escalating to law enforcement, while potentially appropriate in severe cases, is premature without first conducting an internal investigation and gathering sufficient evidence to support the allegations. The key is to prioritize the forensic analysis of the suspect's devices and accounts to establish a clear evidentiary trail before taking more overt actions.

508. Which of the following BEST describes the difference between a security event and a security incident?
a. A security event is always caused by an external attacker, while a security incident is always caused by an insider threat
b. A security event is a subset of a security incident, representing a single occurrence within a larger incident
c. A security event is any observable occurrence in a system or network, while a security incident is an event that compromises security
d. A security event is a minor issue that can be automatically resolved, while a security incident requires manual intervention

Answer: c. A security event is any observable occurrence in a system or network, while a security incident is an event that compromises security. Explanation: The key distinction between a security event and a security incident lies in the impact on the organization's security posture. A security event is a generic term for any identifiable occurrence in a system or network that is relevant to security monitoring, such as a user login, a firewall alert, or a system error message. Most events are benign and do not necessarily indicate a security problem. In contrast, a security incident is a specific type of event that actually or potentially jeopardizes the confidentiality, integrity, or availability of an information asset. Incidents are events that have been determined to have a real negative consequence. The cause of an event or incident can be external, internal, malicious, or accidental. A single incident may encompass multiple related events. Some events can be resolved automatically, while others require manual intervention, but the level of response effort is a separate issue from the event/incident classification.

509. An organization is developing its incident response plan. Which of the following criteria would be MOST important for determining whether a security event should be categorized as an incident?
a. The source of the event (external/internal)
b. The duration of the event
c. The potential impact of the event on business operations
d. The type of system or device generating the event

Answer: c. The potential impact of the event on business operations. Explanation: The primary factor that distinguishes a security incident from a routine event is the actual or potential adverse impact on the organization. When developing incident categorization criteria for an incident response plan, the focus should be on assessing how an event could affect business operations, regulatory compliance, financial standing, or reputation. Events that pose a significant threat to these business priorities should be classified as incidents and trigger the appropriate response procedures. The source of an event, while potentially relevant for investigative and preventive purposes, does not inherently determine its severity or impact. The duration of an event is also not a reliable indicator, as even a brief event could have major consequences depending on its nature. The type of system or device where an event originates can influence the technical handling of the event but is less important than the business context for categorization. The key is to define incident criteria based on meaningful thresholds of operational, financial, legal, or reputational impact, aligned with the organization's risk management and business continuity objectives.

510. Which of the following security events would MOST likely warrant classification as a high-severity incident?
a. Multiple failed login attempts on a non-critical system
b. Unusual network traffic patterns between two employee workstations
c. Detection of malware on a server housing sensitive customer data
d. Automated alerts from a vulnerability scanner about outdated software versions

Answer: c. Detection of malware on a server housing sensitive customer data. Explanation: Among the given security event scenarios, the one that would most likely be considered a high-severity incident is the detection of malware on a server that contains sensitive customer data. The presence of malware on any system is concerning, but the fact that it has infected a server with highly sensitive information significantly elevates the potential impact. Malware on such a critical asset could lead to unauthorized access, data theft, or corruption, which could have severe consequences for customer privacy, regulatory compliance, and the organization's reputation. This event poses an imminent threat to the confidentiality and integrity of the organization's most valuable data assets and therefore warrants immediate, high-priority incident response. Failed login attempts, while noteworthy, are a common occurrence and do not necessarily indicate a confirmed compromise, especially if the affected system is non-critical. Unusual network traffic between employee workstations may be suspicious but requires further investigation to determine if it represents a genuine threat or just an anomaly. Alerts about outdated software, while important for vulnerability management, do not on their own constitute a live incident unless there is evidence of active exploitation.

Conclusion

As we come to the end of this CISM (Certified Information Security Manager) Exam Prep book, let's take a moment to reflect on the journey we've taken together. We've navigated through complex concepts and tackled challenging questions, all with the goal of preparing you for success on the CISM exam.

Throughout this guide, we've explored the core domains of information security management: governance, risk management, incident response, and program development. You've engaged with detailed explanations, real-world scenarios, and practice questions designed to test and expand your knowledge. Each section was crafted to build your confidence and competence, ensuring you have a solid foundation to stand on when you face the exam.

Remember, preparing for the CISM exam is more than just memorizing facts; it's about understanding principles and applying them in real-world contexts. Your dedication to studying these materials shows your commitment to becoming a proficient and effective information security manager.

As you move forward, keep in mind the importance of encouraging your own dreams and recognizing your achievements. It's easy to get caught up in the stress of preparation, but every step you take is a testament to your hard work and determination. Celebrate your progress, no matter how small it may seem.

If you encounter setbacks, don't be discouraged. Every mistake is an opportunity to learn and grow. Use them to fuel your drive, refine your strategies, and approach challenges with renewed vigor. The path to success is rarely a straight line, and your resilience is key to navigating the twists and turns.

Face your fears with confidence, knowing that you are well-prepared. The knowledge and skills you've developed will guide you through any uncertainties. Trust in your abilities and the preparation you've undertaken.

Believe in yourself and the preparation you've completed. Confirm your readiness by reviewing key concepts and practicing as much as possible. Let your intuition and understanding guide you as you approach the exam.

Lastly, find your support system—whether it's fellow colleagues, mentors, or study groups—and lean on them when needed. Share your insights, exchange ideas, and lift each other up. Together, you can overcome any obstacles that come your way.

Good luck on your CISM exam. You have the knowledge, skills, and determination to succeed. Now, go out there and show the world what you're capable of!

Printed in Great Britain
by Amazon

48161642R00282